Roy Baldwin Sterli~ ~~~

4/8/99

The three-masted schooner **Nanuk** *awaits its fate in the ice pack at North Cape, Siberia as the airmen and planes of three nations cluster about the ship in a mid-winter search for the lost Hamilton Metalplane of Carl Ben Eielson and Earl Borland during the winter of 1929-30.*

Hustvedt '72

ALASKAN
AVIATION
HISTORY

ALASKAN AVIATION HISTORY

By Robert W. Stevens

POLYNYAS PRESS

The paper in this book meets guidelines for permanence and durability of the Committee on Production Guidelines for Book Longevity of the Council on Library Resources. ∞

ISBN Number: 0-929427-01-7 (Volume I)
              0-929427-02-5 (Volume II)
              0-929427-00-9 (6 Volume Set)

Library of Congress Catalog
Card Number: 88-90907

Printed in Canada

Polynyas Press
P.O. Box 98904
Des Moines, Washington 98198

* * * * * emerging from the early era of liquid-cooled motors, whose vibrations loosened plumbing lines, with radiators that froze and burst in winter and boiled over in summer, Alaska's airmen were now being supplied with aircraft powered with reliable air-cooled engines of increasing power. Their way over this harsh environment would be eased * * *

CONTENTS

VOLUME II

ALASKAN
AVIATION
HISTORY
1929-1930

Tom Croson Collection

International Airways

Alaska-Washington Airways
Gorst Air Transport,
Incorporated

Ketchikan 1929

SOUTHEASTERN ALASKA IN 1929, was to seethe with interest in aviation, bearing some fruit as organizations expressing interest sent planes northward, triggered by a proposed inauguration of air mail service from the States into the lower region of the Territory. Much of the activity was by hopefuls trying to raise capital in the Territory to allow them to expand from the Pacific Northwest to Alaska.

Union Air Lines, parent company of West Coast Air Transport, was operating flights between Seattle and west coast cities into California. They hoped to expand into Alaska as Union Airways, Incorporated, using flying boats. Hiring F.O. Meeker of Ketchikan as their local representative, by March the company was advertising their stock in Ketchikan and Juneau. Evidently results were disappointing; the operation never developed.

Seattle Flying Service, based on Gorst field at Seattle, was another interested party, wanting to bid on the expected air mail contract between Seattle and Juneau. They spoke of using amphibian planes. Vern C. Gorst, president of the company, was acquainted with Alaska. As an old-timer of the gold rush days, he had spent six years mining in the Klondike country. The ardent flier, now fifty-seven, went ahead on his own, ordering a Keystone

*Ketchikan was visited in 1929 by both of these Lock-heed Vegas, the **Juneau**, NC 432E, in the hangar, and the **Ketchikan**, NC 657E, moored on the water. The Alaska-Washington Airways hangar was located in Kintz Boat Basin, on Lake Union in Seattle.*

Pilot Clayton L. Scott with the Keystone Loening Air Yacht, **Alaskan,** *of Gorst Air Transport, Incorporated. Scott and mechanic Gordon Graham flew the blue and yellow amphibian from Seattle to Ketchikan on April 17, 1929. The plane is shown here at the company's Seattle base on Lake Union.*

Loening Air Yacht from the factory, which could be used effectively in Southeastern Alaska. The bright yellow and blue amphibian was christened *Alaskan* on March 12, 1929, when slender, blonde Fern Naylor of Portland, Oregon broke a bottle over the bow in a Seattle ceremony held at the foot of Roanoke Street on Lake Union. Gorst planned a survey run to Alaska with the plane.

Boeing Air Transport also announced it was making a survey of the Southeast Alaska route possibilities, with the idea of using the five Boeing C-204 boats that had been built in Vancouver, British Columbia. They later dropped the idea.

Further, the Navy Department announced in Washington, D.C. on February 22, 1929, that completion of the aerial survey of Southeastern Alaska which had started in 1926 would be resumed during the coming season, with three modern Loening aircraft and the tender, *U.S.S. Gannet.*

A fourth party interested in establishing service in Southeastern Alaska was International Airways. Without a great deal of fanfare, using a six-passenger Boeing flying boat, Model B-lE, NC 115E, powered with the Pratt & Whitney Wasp C radial engine of 425 horsepower, that had just been purchased from the Boeing Company under contract to George S. Cochran and Company of Seattle (Cochran had mining interests in the Portland Canal district in Southeastern Alaska and near York, on the Bering seacoast of the Seward Peninsula) the new air service departed on a survey flight at 1:45 P.M. Thursday, March 14, 1929, for Ketchikan and Juneau. Flown by an experienced Canadian pilot, Edward Joseph Augustus

"Paddy" Burke, the mahogany flying boat carried four people in addition to the pilot: P.T. McCarthy, president of the company, and his wife; Mrs. J.W. "Jack" McCord, wife of the president of McCord-Alaska Company, who raised sheep, cattle and fox in the Aleutian Islands; and George Lortie, a mechanic.

The first stop was at Campbell River, British Columbia, where they remained overnight. Arrived at Alert Bay, British Columbia on Friday, the crew fueled the plane and the party spent the day, remaining over until Saturday afternoon. Taking off at 4:00 P.M. with inclement weather ahead, the aircraft, unheard from for the next two days, caused some concern, of which the members of the flight were unaware. They made a stop at Lowe Inlet, taking off from there Sunday to make a graceful landing on the waters of Tongass Narrows before Ketchikan, touching down at 6:30 P.M. Sunday, March 17, 1929. They were greeted by residents, including Roy Jones, who had made a similar flight from Seattle to Ketchikan in 1922. Jones was living and working in the community.

The party, after a pleasant stay in Ketchikan, boarded the Boeing B-1E on Wednesday, March 20, to be towed by a small tug out into the channel for departure to Juneau, the capital city. "Paddy" Burke took off from Tongass Narrows at 10:20 A.M. and headed north. He landed at Petersburg to refuel at 11:48 A.M., departing there at 1:25 P.M. The pilot encountered weather in the area and, in poor visibility, circled around Douglas Island, coming in from the west to land on Gastineau Channel, before the city, at 3:20 P.M. A small motorboat took the plane in tow to bring it to shore. Gerald Smith, representative for the company in Juneau the last two months, met the party and accompanied them to the Gastineau Hotel.

With business and pleasure in the city completed, "Paddy" Burke took off in the Boeing B-1E from the channel below Douglas at 11:00 A.M. Monday, March 25; Gerald Smith had joined the original five, making a full load of six persons. They stopped at Ketchikan on the way south to leave Mrs. McCord, where she boarded a steamer going north to join her husband. The International Airways pilot landed at Petersburg at 12:10 P.M., making the trip in a bit over an hour. Running into bad weather south of Petersburg, the plane returned to get more current weather reports and to permit the occupants to have lunch. The *Alaska* was in port with Mrs. McCord's sister, Mrs. McCulloch, aboard, so they all lunched on the steamer.

The flying boat left Petersburg about 3:13 P.M. on Tuesday, March 26, for Ketchikan, and almost immediately ran into rough weather. The whole southeast coast was storming. Later, Captain E.R. Smith of the Standard Oil tanker, *Richmond*, coming into Ketchikan from the south, reported one of the stormiest trips of his experience, with seas along the west coast of Vancouver Island virtually enveloping the ship. The decks were awash and one lifeboat carried away. To "Paddy" Burke and his five passengers, the wind seemed to be coming from all directions; the flying boat pitched and tossed in the turbulence, sometimes dropping several hundred feet at a time, to be thrown aloft the next instant. Burke worked his way to just about the entrance to the channel above Ketchikan but feared to proceed further with the mountains towering above. He circled, in snow, rain and gale, until low on fuel, then set down, after three hours of flying, near Guard Island, to drift helplessly for the next hour, out of fuel. An Indian fisherman picked them up, towing the plane until the Coast Guard cutter, *Cygan*, under Captain H.C. Hermann, out on a search for the overdue plane, took it in tow Wednesday morning, bringing the Boeing into Ketchikan, at 12:30. The disheveled party checked into the Ingersoll Hotel, and were invited to lunch by the Commercial Club. When the weather improved the group, except for Mrs. McCord, continued the flight to Seattle.

The Boeing, NC 115E, on its way south, left Vancouver, British Columbia on Tuesday, April 2, and entered U.S. Customs and Immigration at Port Townsend, Washington. Taking off from there, the pilot continued on to Olympia and landed in a private estuary on that same day, Tuesday, April 2, 1929. The party left the plane there and returned to Seattle by automobile.

Another company was in the running. On Monday, April 15, 1929, a sleek, stream-lined Lockheed Vega, NC 432E, on pontoons, passed over Ketchikan at 12:52 P.M. on a first nonstop flight from Seattle to Juneau. In fact, the plane had been christened *Juneau*. Flown by aviator Anscel C. Eckmann; with Jack Halloran, mechanic, and Robert E. Ellis, navigator, the blue and cream-painted monoplane made a pretty sight as it sped through the sky. Arriving over their destination at 1:48 P.M. they landed at Juneau just seven and one-half minutes before 2:00 P.M. (see Juneau—1929 Chapter 43).

Two days later, the Gorst Keystone Loening C-2-C, NC 9728, *Alaskan* was off at 7:00 A.M. Wednesday, April 17, 1929 from Lake Union on a survey flight. Flown by Clayton L. Scott, with Vern Gorst, President of Gorst Air Transport, Incorporated, as copilot, Gordon Graham, mechanic; and passengers A.C. Iverson of Cordova, and E.M. Greenwood, traffic manager for the Gorst Company; the pilot had planned stops at Alert Bay (to clear Canadian Customs), Prince Rupert, Ketchikan, Petersburg and Juneau. Gorst expected to visit his sister, Mrs. C.M. Taylor, wife of the Alaska Steamship Company agent, in Ketchikan, as well as R.H. Humber, chief of police and fellow adventurer from the days of '97. They had mushed over Chilkoot Pass together during the gold rush. Gorst, one of the organizers of Pacific Air Transport, operating planes between Seattle and Los Angeles, was a strong believer in the eventual establishment of an air mail service from Seattle to Southeastern Alaska; even traveling to Washington, D.C. to promote it. Although he had sold part of his interest in P.A.T., he still held the office of vice-president, and had other aviation interests in Seattle: Seattle Flying Service and now, Gorst Air Transport, Incorporated.

Stopping at Campbell River and Prince Rupert, British Columbia, to refuel, the bright yellow and blue Loening landed on the waters of Tongass Narrows in Ketchikan at 4:40 P.M. after seven hours and forty minutes of air time. Gorst distributed a dozen copies of that day's Seattle morning paper, renewed old acquaintances and, adding his sister to the passenger load for Juneau, was off at 10:30 the next morning, Thursday, April 18. Scott landed the *Alaskan* at Petersburg at 11:00 A.M. and, after refueling, departed at noon, to land on Gastineau Channel at Juneau at 1:24 P.M. (Juneau time). Shortly after, Scott, accompanied by his mechanic, Graham, took Governor George A. Parks and two others up for a twenty-minute flight.

For the next three days he was flying short passenger hops and scenic flights for the local residents, who were to "apply at the Gastineau Hotel or the rock dump", where the plane was kept. Eckmann was also in town during this period with the *Juneau*, the mountains reverberating with the sound of airplane engines. (see Juneau—1929, Chapter 43). On Monday, April 22, Scott took the Loening to Sitka to hop passengers, returning to Juneau the next day. That afternoon the *Alaskan* was off for Ketchikan with three passengers, making the flight in three hours, nonstop. He carried H.H. Andre of Juneau, who was hurrying to San Francisco because of the illness of his mother there. He also had sourdough Carl Berg aboard. The next day, Wednesday, April 24, the men left Ketchikan in the Loening, landing at Alert Bay, British Columbia, after four hours and forty-five minutes in the air. Continuing on to Seattle they flew another two hours and fifty minutes. The survey trip to prove the feasibility of regular passenger and air mail service to Southeastern Alaska was a success, and would strengthen Gorst's position when such contracts were offered. The following month the company made another, more extensive trip north.

Anscel Eckmann, with the Lockheed Vega NC 432E, *Juneau*, in its namesake city, left there at 4:00 P.M. Friday, April 19, accompanied by navigator Ellis and three passengers; Mrs.

C.S. Graham, Mrs. S. Stanworth, and A.H. Ziegler, for Ketchikan. Flying at 5000 feet, in sunshine, the plane was at Petersburg in one hour, from there to Wrangell in fifteen minutes, and from Wrangell to Ketchikan in forty-five minutes, landing there in the evening. The next day Eckmann flew sightseers about the area, including passengers Wendell Dawson, hydraulic survey engineer, and J.C. Shawver, vessel owner and licensed guide. Later in the day Eckmann left in the Vega for Juneau, hopping from there to Skagway early Sunday morning to pick up a $40,000 shipment of furs. The pilot returned immediately to Juneau with Charles Goldstein, owner of the furs, and flew to Ketchikan. Here the flier took Vic Lougheed, who had a broken leg, on board. It was still the morning of Sunday, April 21, and he continued to Seattle, after a stop at Port Ludlow to refuel. He arrived at his destination at 8:15 P.M. to deliver Lougheed to the specialist, and Charlie Goldstein and his furs to the market. A thirty-four pound, red king salmon placed aboard by Juneau Cold Storage was delivered to San Juan Fish Company in Seattle.

On Wednesday, April 25, the Lockheed Vega of Alaska-Washington Airways was northbound, leaving Seattle at 6:34 A.M., again piloted by Anscel Eckmann. With four passengers aboard, the plane stopped at Campbell River. Leaving there, the pilot, was again accompanied by Robert E. Ellis as mechanic-navigator; weather forced a landing at Prince Rupert, and they held for a time at the Canadian city. He arrived in Ketchikan that evening. Eckmann discharged three passengers: Roy Thornton, William Chadwick and J.M. Murphy; also Otto Jones, a Fox Newsreel cameraman, who was traveling on a complimentary ticket. The group checked in at the Gilmore Hotel to have young Pete Gilmore underfoot. Eckmann announced the impending delivery of a second Vega, to be called *Ketchikan*, with plans to station it in the city, the *Juneau* to be located at its namesake city.

Eckmann planned to fly on to Juneau on Sunday, April 28, but word came that Ben Eielson was coming in on the *Aleutian* to Ketchikan, and it was decided to fly him to Juneau where he would be honored by a resolution of the Legislature, then in session. Eckmann flew the *Juneau* out to Mary Island to meet the steamer some twenty-five miles southeast of the city, where Eielson was transferred to the plane in a small boat. The Alaska-Washington Airways plane brought him to Ketchikan three hours ahead of the arrival of the *Aleutian*. After a luncheon for the honored guest, sponsored by the American Legion in Ketchikan, the well-known aviator was flown up to Juneau in the Vega, with a stop at Craig to discharge a passenger. The plane arrived at the capital city shortly after 3:00 P.M. to land in the channel near the rock dump of the Alaska-Juneau mine, then taxied to Government Dock for ceremonies and a parade. Eckman also carried other passengers on the flight from Ketchikan: Jim Galen, Leath Russell and Otto Jones, the chief photographer for the northwest for Fox-Paramount Moving Picture Company, who took several hundred feet of film while flying north.

On April 30, 1929, Anscel Eckmann and Bob Ellis took the Vega to Ketchikan from Juneau with passengers, intending to fill their load there and proceed to Seattle the following day. After the departure, a wire was sent to Ketchikan by Larry Parks, the Alaska-Washington Airways agent in Juneau, requesting the plane return to Sitka for a charter to Seattle. Mrs. Peter Kostrometinoff, wife of a Sitka businessman who operated a theater, cannery and cold storage plant, was desperately ill with septicemia, and could be treated more successfully in Seattle. Physicians did not recommend she make the the trip by steamer. Flying her down was perhaps the only way to save her young life. The Vega left *Ketchikan* at 4:00 A.M. and reached Sitka, 170 miles away, at 5:50 A.M. of Wednesday, May 1. Knocking down the seats in the cabin, the patient was placed aboard the plane on an army cot, with her husband beside her. The pilot was off at 8:40 A.M. Staying at a low altitude so the ill woman could breathe more easily, the pilot flew the long way around Baranof Island, to arrive again in Ketchikan at 10:50 A.M. to refuel. Making the stop as brief as possible, Eckmann and Ellis were off again at 11:15 A.M. for Alert Bay, British Columbia, where they touched down at 2:55 P.M. They departed there at 3:50 P.M. to fight their way through lowering ceilings and fog in the strait between Vancouver Island and the mainland, and then on into Seattle. They arrived at the Barnes-Gorst hangar on Lake Union at 7:40 P.M. An ambulance was waiting to take the couple to Virginia Mason Hospital. The crew looked worse than the patient after the 934-mile flight; they had gone all day without food or rest. It had been the first ride in an airplane for the woman, as well as her husband, whose father, Peter Kostrometinoff, was custodian of the Russian church in Sitka. Eckmann remained in Seattle for a time, so that some needed maintenance could be made on the *Juneau*.

Gorst Air Transport, Incorporated, was coming north again. H.W. McDermott who had been named their representative in Juneau, had come up with a proposition to fly six members of the Alaska legislature from Juneau to Cordova when the session was over. (see Cordova— 1929, Chapter 45).

The Keystone Loening, NC 9728, *Alaskan*, again flown by Clayton Scott, with Gordon Graham as mechanic; landed in Tongass Narrows shortly after 11:00 A.M. on Friday, May 3, 1929. It had taken them two days to come up from their base in Seattle. They anchored at the Forestry dock for refueling.

With the Cordova charter somewhat in doubt, the two men went on that same day to Juneau, stopping at Petersburg on the way, flying in fine, calm weather. Also aboard the plane was W.W. Noyes, a boat owner and fish buyer who had had some experience with airplanes in the naval service. The *Alaskan* landed in Gastineau Channel at 4:00 P.M. to remain overnight, taking off at 10:30 A.M. Saturday, May 4 for Ketchikan. Scott was carrying two members of the House of Representatives, E.R. Tarwater and A.H. Ziegler. The pilot picked up two additional passengers at Petersburg, after a flight of an hour and fifteen minutes. Making the next leg to Ketchikan in the same flying time, Scott circled the steamer *Alaska* as she came into port. This produced some business, for he hopped passengers at Ketchikan for the rest of that day, as well as most of the next few days, many of them from the ship.

Scott departed Ketchikan on Monday, May 6 and, with the usual stop at Petersburg, arrived in Juneau at 5:30 P.M. (see Cordova—1929, Chapter 45). The following morning, May 7, 1929, the two airmen were off in the Loening for Cordova, taking three passengers. They were to be the first plane to arrive in that community.

In Ketchikan, the city council had decided to move on a project to allow better docking facilities for the increasing number of planes that were stopping at their city. The aviation committee was instructed to locate a site for the proposed float, and report to the city council. Street commissioner Tom Torry was also asked to clean the Thomas Basin tide flats of snags which might hamper planes wishing to land there. The basin, at high tide, provided a sandy-bottomed flat over which waterbased planes could taxi in; at low tide it was the town's ball field.

Anscel Eckmann and Bob Ellis, flying the Lockheed Vega, *Juneau*, left Lake Union in Seattle at 1:20 P.M. and arrived in Ketchikan at 7:00 P.M. Tuesday, May 7, the nonstop flight had taken five hours and forty minutes. A second Lockheed Vega, NC 657E, to be named *Ketchikan*, had been delivered to the company at the plant near Los Angeles, and was awaiting a new pair of Edo 4650 floats from the factory in the east, before flying north.

Eckmann took off Tongass Narrows at 12:05 P.M. the following day, carrying C.W. Cash, representative of the Northern Commercial Company, for Juneau. With a nonstop flight of one hour and forty-three minutes, at a speed of nearly 150 miles per hour, the *Juneau* was soon at its namesake city. Eckmann had brought in a large amount of movie film for Fox cameraman Otto Jones, who had come north on the previous flight. R.E. "Bob" Ellis, copilot and navigator of the *Juneau*, passed through Ketchikan on the steamer, *Admiral Evans*, enroute to Seattle to take delivery of the new Vega, *Ketchikan*. Ellis, a licensed transport pilot and ensign in the naval air reserve, had been an instructor for Aviation School, Incorporated, in Seattle. He expected to fly the new plane north in a week or ten days, and base it in Ketchikan.

Eckmann left Juneau at 7:30 A.M. Friday, May 17, going to Port Althorp to pick up August H. Buschmann, a canneryman, who had recently sold out to Alaska-Pacific Salmon Corporation. Buschmann was going to Seattle to finalize the sale. The pilot also had aboard, from Juneau, Raymond F. Haines and Larry Parks, a former boat captain who was now the Juneau representative for Alaska-Washington Airways. An unlisted passenger, a black bear cub by the name of *Skookums*, that belonged to Fred Ordway, Juneau photographer, was also making the round trip as mascot. Eckmann only stopped long enough in Ketchikan to refuel.

He was northbound in the *Juneau* on Monday, May 20, leaving Seattle at 7:15 A.M., stopping in Alert Bay, British Columbia and arriving in Ketchikan at 2:15 P.M. Passengers were Gilbert H. Skinner, president of Alaska-Pacific Salmon Corporation, August Buschmann, R.F. Haines and Larry Parks. *Skookums*, the bear cub cancelled out, he was sick from the flight to Seattle. The 1000-mile trip was made in nine hours and fifty minutes of flying time. New planes, other than the *Ketchikan*, which was expected in Seattle that day for the fitting of floats, were on order; the Vega, *Sitka*, NC 200E, was on wheels, to be presently operated around Seattle as a land plane, and a fourth Vega, which was still under construction at the factory.

The *Juneau*, after making flights out of the capital city, was on her way south again, arriving in Ketchikan at 11:30 A.M. Thursday, May 23, 1929. Through passengers were John Troy, publisher of the *Juneau Alaska Empire*, and Gill Skinner, who was picked up at Port Althorp. Mrs. S. Pedersen, wife of the chief engineer of the *Highway*, Bureau of Public Roads vessel, got off the plane in Ketchikan for a visit. The plane hopped off for Seattle about noon. The pilot was in a hurry, wanting to get John Troy to the funeral of his brother, in Olympia. They landed on Lake Union that evening. Larry Parks was also aboard.

Four Loening OL-8A seaplanes of the U.S. Naval Survey arrived in Ketchikan the evening of Wednesday, May 22, 1929. The planes, powered by 450 horsepower Pratt & Whitney Wasp engines, sported the Flying Seal emblem on the sides of the fuselage. The group, under the leadership of Lieutenant Commander A.W. Radford, would continue the aerial mapping of Southeastern Alaska which had begun in 1926. The planes were beached at the Model Dairy. (see Alaska Aerial Survey Detachment—1929, Chapter 44).

On the evening of Thursday, May 23, R.J. Sommers, Territorial highway commissioner, met with the city council, the mayor, and members of the aviation committee of the Commercial Club, to go over plans for the Ketchikan air facility. A site had been chosen to the north of the city, along the Tongass highway near the residence of Ed Elliot; the property cost approximately $12,000, and this expense was to be divided between the Territory and the city. Plans called for ways leading from the water, with a runway to lead to the machine hangars. The city and Territory would not build these hangars but airplane operators could rent the space and build hangars according to their requirements. The planes would be drawn up the sloping ramp to the level runway by a winch.

The *Juneau* left Alaska-Washington Airways base at Seattle at 9:00 A.M. Sunday, May 26, remaining at Alert Bay two hours for refueling and lunch, arriving in Ketchikan at

4:30 P.M. Eckmann took off for Juneau at 6:30 P.M. Frank Hatcher was flying with him out of Seattle as mechanic, and Larry Parks, the company's Juneau representative was also aboard with *Skookums,* the bear cub, now recovered. Passengers M.E. Stuart, of the Stuart Corporation; and George H. Wills, head of Baranof Mild Cure and Wills Navigation Company, traveled with them to Ketchikan. It was Wills' company that had brought up the Eaglerock airplane to Noyes Island the previous year, to spot fish. Peter Kostrometinoff, of Sitka, was aboard; his wife, still in Seattle, was slowly improving. Bert Green, merchandise broker, boarded the plane at Ketchikan for Juneau. Eckmann, completing his fifth trip between Seattle and Juneau, landed there that same evening, at 7:45 P.M. They had experienced perfect weather during the entire trip.

Ketchikan bid goodbye, for the time being, to the naval air mappers, and the planes took off about 1:30 P.M. for Sitka. The tender, *Gannet,* had already left at 8:00 A.M., towing the covered barge YF, used by the survey party as a portable base.

Eckmann, who had made a round trip to Sitka as well as some local flying, took off from Juneau at 6:00 A.M. Wednesday, May 29, for Seattle, with Peter Kostrometinoff as passenger. A charter at Ketchikan delayed the pilot there for a time. He took cannery representatives out of there, getting away that same morning with H.B. Friele of the Nakat Packing Company, Eigil Buschmann, general superintendent, D.F. Ryan, superintendent of Hidden Inlet cannery, and Harvey Stackpole, Ketchikan superintendent; for a flying tour of the company's canneries.

Eckmann, in the Lockheed Vega with Frank Hatcher as mechanic, was off Juneau at 1:30 A.M. Thursday, June 3 (Pacific Coast time), with Governor George A. Parks aboard, who was traveling to San Francisco to attend the graduation of his niece from Mills College in Oakland. Also aboard the plane were Joseph L. Carman, Jr., president of Alaska-Washington Airways, R.E. Robertson, Juneau attorney, and Larry Parks. The midnight start was because they planned to fly Governor Parks through to California in one day's time. When the plane arrived in Ketchikan an hour and forty-five minutes later, Larry Parks deplaned and Howard D. Stabler, United States attorney of the first division, came aboard for the trip. After an hour on the water, the *Juneau* was off again, to make one more stop for gas at Wadham, arriving over Seattle at 9:15 A.M. Eckmann had set a record for the trip from Juneau to Seattle; the actual flying time was seven hours and five minutes, or twenty-eight minutes less than any previous trip he had made. Richard F. "Dick" Gleason, of the same company, piloted the governor south. Intending originally on connecting at Portland with a West Coast Air Transport scheduled flight, Gleason was delayed with a propeller change, flying the governor all the way in his Alaska-Washington Lockheed Vega, NC 200E, on wheels. Governor Parks still made the flight from Juneau to San Francisco in less than twenty-four hours—a startling fact in those days.

Eckmann, with mechanic Frank Hatcher, was away again from Seattle in the Vega, *Juneau,* on the morning of Wednesday, June 5, 1929. The pilot stopped in Vancouver, British Columbia and picked up Owen Hill, postmaster of Hyder, Alaska. Eckmann remained in Hyder, where Hill left the plane, over Wednesday and Thursday nights, taking residents on local flights. He left there on Friday morning, stopping in Ketchikan for two hours before proceeding on to Juneau. He arrived in the capital city at 5:00 P.M. June 7, carrying C.T. McKinney, former assistant district attorney of Seattle, and Mrs. Don Bayne and A.C. Ecker, from Ketchikan. Eckmann was on his seventh round trip to Alaska.

The pilot was back in Ketchikan in a few days, to fly F.A. Metcalf and Ray McCormack to Stewart, taking Tom Davies and Edward J. Morrissey along for the round trip. On his return, the pilot carried J.B. Warrack of Seattle, from Ketchikan to Juneau, arriving there at 9:30 P.M. Wednesday, June 12, after a two-hour flight. On this leg he encountered some of the worst weather he had experienced while flying in Alaska. The Alaska-Washington Lockheed Vega was back in Ketchikan on Sunday, June 16, 1929, landing at 10:10 P.M. He left there at 8:00 A.M. the next morning, with H.P. Stackpole, local superintendent of Nakat Packing Company, to pick up cannery superintendents of the company at Hidden Inlet, Waterfall and Union Bay, for a conference to be held in Ketchikan with H.B. Friele, the general manager, who was expected to arrive from the south on the mailboat on Tuesday. The pilot arrived back with the men at 1:25 P.M. That afternoon, he made a roundtrip to Craig with passengers.

On Tuesday, June 18, the Vega was off Ketchikan at 8:30 A.M., dropping Superintendent Ryan at Hidden Inlet, Eigil Buschmann and son at Waterfall, returning to Ketchikan with C.C. Harris, superintendent at Union Bay. The plane was off Ketchikan at 1:45 P.M., stopping at Union Bay to drop Harris off. He carried N.G. Nelson, Louis Shulman and H.B. Friele on to Juneau, arriving there at 3:57 P.M., to dock at Robert Keeney's float. The pilot wanted to return soon to Seattle to have new model 4650 Edo floats, which had been ordered for the plane, installed there, as well as getting a top overhaul on the engine.

On Friday, June 21, Eckmann and Hatcher were off Juneau at 5:15 A.M., carrying N.G. Nelson and his two daughters, Grace and May, for Ketchikan. The pilot planned to pick up canneryman D. Lindenburger at Craig, as well as the superintendent of the cannery at Waterfall. He then took a doctor from Ketchikan to Hidden Inlet on an emergency trip, returning the doctor to Ketchikan before loading passengers for Seattle. Eckmann had flown over 250 hours, covering 25,000 miles since coming to Alaska in the middle of April. The company and its sleek Vega were performing well, and businessmen and officials alike, and many others, were finding it an efficient, speedy way of getting about in Southeastern Alaska, as well as to and from Seattle; the Seattle to Juneau fare was $105 one way, $70 to Ketchikan.

When Eckmann returned to Seattle, he found Alaska-Washington's new Lockheed Vega, NC 657E, Model 5 all ready to go, with *Ketchikan* painted on the forward side. The five-place float plane was wearing blue and cream paint, the same as the *Juneau*. The pilot, accompanied by his mechanic, Frank Hatcher, was off Seattle in the new plane on Wednesday afternoon, June 26, 1929. Checking in at Alert Bay, he was held overnight in Lowe Inlet, south of Prince Rupert, by foggy weather enroute. Arriving in Ketchikan at 1:45 P.M. Thursday afternoon, the pilot decided to remain overnight; there was heavy rain and fog in the area. Friday morning, June 28, the pilot took the Vega to Waterfall cannery and brought Eigil Buschmann into Ketchikan. Eckmann left for Juneau about 3:00 P.M., arriving there two hours later. Flying out of there for the next two days, he departed Juneau for Ketchikan at 3:30 P.M. Sunday, June 30. He took a load of passengers from there to Hyder, remaining there Monday and Tuesday to fly sightseers. The company was running a box ad in the *Ketchikan Alaska Chronicle*, proclaiming "Flying all Day the Fourth from the City Float"; Ralph Bartholemew, Agent, of Bartholemew & Spaeth. Eckmann did a heavy business over the holiday.

Eckmann and Hatcher were back in Juneau shortly after the holiday; leaving again for Ketchikan the evening of Sunday, July 7, with attorneys H.L. Faulkner and R.E. Robertson, John L. Larsen, a radio specialist from Seattle, and Phillip M. Elliott, as passengers. The *Ketchikan* left for Seattle at 9:00 A.M. Monday, July 8, 1929, with Doctor J.H. Mustard, Elmer Harris, and Doctor J.B. Beeson. The two doctors were on their way to Portland, Oregon to attend the American Medical Association convention.

In Ketchikan, a new aviation company was being promoted. Organized and headed by James V. Hickey, Sr., owner of Reliable Transfer and Taxi Company, it was The Northland

Jim Hickey Collection

James V. Hickey, Ketchikan businessman, left the city for Los Angeles on October 16, 1929 to enroll in a flying course. Shown here as a student in the California city, he hoped to return to Ketchikan with an airplane in two months.

Airways, Inc. and stock in the organization was available through their representative, F.O. Meeker. Hickey traveled to Petersburg and Wrangell in September to promote his company. He left with his wife and two children on the steamer, *Alaska*, on Wednesday, October 16, 1929, for Los Angeles, where he enrolled as a flying student at Aero Corporation of California. He was gone about two months. Upon completion of private and commercial pilot's courses, he expected to return to Ketchikan with an airplane, if all went well.

The Vega, *Ketchikan*, was off Seattle on Anscel Eckmann's tenth trip to Alaska, Tuesday morning, July 9. Eckmann and Hatcher overnighted in Alert Bay, British Columbia because of threatening weather, and arrived in Ketchikan the following afternoon. Continuing on to Juneau, the Vega was landed there at 3:15 P.M. Wednesday afternoon, with H.L. Faulkner and T. Carlson as passengers from Ketchikan.

The pilot did considerable flying out of Juneau before returning south. He took H.B. Friele aboard, and left at 10:00 A.M. on Wednesday, July 17; making a tour of the company's canneries before landing in Ketchikan that evening, in time for Friele to catch the steamer, *Alaska*, for the south. Eckmann wanted to meet the Vega, *Juneau*, now returning to Alaska with pilot James R. Hennessy, formerly of Maine, at the controls. Hennessy, flying for Alaska-Washington Airways out of Seattle, was making his first trip north. Accompanied by another experienced pilot, Floyd E. Keadle, he was forced down in Lowe Inlet on the evening of Wednesday, July 17, 1929. Eckmann and Frank Hatcher took the *Ketchikan* there early the next morning. After the slight damage to the pontoons of the *Juneau* had been repaired, Hennessey returned to Alert Bay and Seattle for pontoon replacement. Eckmann brought Keadle back to Juneau in the *Ketchikan*. Keadle had been flying another Vega, on wheels, NC 200E, for Alaska-Washington out of Seattle. This plane, named the *Sitka*, was a prototype model with the Wright Whirlwind J-5A powerplant. It was later sold to John Blum, a former Cordova boy who was now a Seattle pilot and airport operator. The name, *Sitka*, was given to Vega, NC 974H, which came north on floats for Alaska-Washington Airways the following year.

Eckmann and Keadle arrived in Juneau at 2:45 P.M. the same Thursday, making two trips later in the day. Keadle had flown the plane from Ketchikan to Juneau. In the following days, the two pilots alternated on the flying done out of the capital city. Eckmann made one trip to Ketchikan on Saturday, July 27, taking Fred Huffman, a cameraman, to Wrangell, and Mar Dong, a Chinese contractor, was taken aboard at Todd and flown to Ketchikan. On the return, the pilot carried O.D. Leet from Wrangell to Juneau on Sunday morning.

Floyd Keadle, accompanied by copilot Bob Ellis and mechanic Ardell Dayton, brought the Vega, *Juneau*, up from Seattle. In Ketchikan, on Tuesday, July 30, 1929, "Cowboy" Keadle put on an aerial exhibition in the plane before departure for Juneau. He carried H.B. Friele, vice-president of the Nakat Packing Company, and M.M. Houck, the company's assistant general manager, as passengers. With both the *Ketchikan* and *Juneau* in the capital city, Eckmann and Keadle did a great deal of flying that day and the next. On the evening of Wednesday, July 31, Eckmann carried O.D. Leet and Karl Thiele back to Wrangell, returning to Juneau the following morning.

Keadle and his crew, Ellis and Dayton, were off for Ketchikan the morning of Thursday, August 1, 1929; again carrying the two cannery officials. Friele deplaned in Ketchikan while Houck continued on to Seattle in the *Juneau*. A third Lockheed Vega, a six-passenger model with a longer fuselage, was reported delivered at Seattle and awaiting the fitting of pontoons.

Anscel Eckmann and Frank Hatcher left Juneau in Vega NC 657E at 5:00 A.M. Friday, August 2, 1929. Doctor Robert Simpson and son, Robert, Jr. were passengers for Seattle, Mrs. T.A. Morgan for Tenakee, and R. Pekovich for Funter Bay. The plane stopped at Tenakee to pick up another passenger for Seattle, J.T. Tenneson, superintendent of the Superior Packing Company. The flight arrived in Seattle that same evening, completing Eckmann's tenth round trip.

Eckmann, still flying the *Ketchikan*, was back, landing on Tongass Narrows at 7:00 P.M. Friday, August 9. Passengers were Foye M. Murphy, a Boston attorney, with his wife and his sister-in-law, and Robert Simpson of Juneau. The pilot had experienced heavy rain, clouds and poor visibility all the way from Seattle. The party remained overnight at Ketchikan, arriving in Juneau at 9:45 A.M. August 10. Eckmann returned to Ketchikan on Tuesday, August 20, in order to pick up August Buschmann and fly him from Waterfall to Port Althorp. They were stormbound overnight at Craig, but completed the flight the next day, with Eckmann returning to Juneau at 3:30 P.M. where he would do considerable flying in the ensuing days.

The Alaskan Aerial Survey party of the U.S. Navy, which had been in Southeastern Alaska for the summer season, had completed their work, departing Ketchikan the afternoon of Saturday, September 7, 1929. (see Alaskan Aerial Survey Detachment—1929, Chapter 44).

R.C. Mize, meteorologist in charge of the Alaska district, announced on September 15 that authority had been granted by the United States Weather Bureau for the establishment of an aircraft weather station, second class, at Ketchikan. R.J. Sommers, Territorial engineer, had arrived in the city on September 12 to confer with the city council on the proposed hydroplane landing port for Ketchikan. The land had been purchased but no further progress had been achieved in obtaining financing. Sommers' visit did the trick for, on a second council meeting on November 20, 1929, the city council awarded a bid to A.C. Kreidler in the amount of $7000 for construction of the hydroplane landing port.

While Eckmann, in Juneau, was winding up the flying for Alaska-Washington Airways for that season, Southeastern Alaska was watching with interest the halting progress of the large ANT plane, *Land of Soviets*, on its world flight through Alaska. (see *Land of Soviets*-1929-Chapter 50). While it never touched at Ketchikan, it came close, with one serious delay at Waterfall. Eckmann was planning on leaving Juneau for the season on Sunday, September 22, 1929, carrying passenger A.L. Hagar for Vancouver, British Columbia.

Major G.C. Frame, Division manager of Alaska-Washington Airways, spoke of next year's plans at a meeting of the Chamber of Commerce in Juneau on Thursday, November 21, and again in Ketchikan on Monday, December 9, 1929. He mentioned air mail contracts they were bidding on, and increased service for the coming spring. During the five months of Alaskan operations, the new company had carried more than 1500 passengers, taking in an average of $44 an hour on the Vegas. The future looked most promising.

Fisher Studio

▲ *View of Ketchikan, Alaska reflects the main resources of the region; commercial fishing, timber and water power. It also illustrates the need for aircraft which could be operated from the water. In 1973 a jet airport was dedicated on Gravina Island across from the city. A small ferry operates between the airport and Ketchikan to link the two.*

◄ *Aerial view of the city of Ketchikan. Large rafts of logs are anchored at the sawmill on the lower right.*

553

Courtesy of Robert E. Ellis

R.W. Stevens Photo

554

International Airways

Gorst Air Transport,
Incorporated
Alaska-Washington Airways,
Incorporated
Totem Air Service

Juneau 1929

THE POSSIBILITY OF AN AIR MAIL service from Seattle to Juneau created a lot of interest in aerial circles in the Pacific Northwest, as well as among enthusiasts in the Southeast Alaska cities that hoped to be served. A study by the Postmaster in Seattle, over a period of time, showed an average of 1700 pounds of first class mail going north on each steamer, with an average of 1100 pounds coming south. If as much as eight percent of this (166 pounds) could go by air mail, it would provide a payload, along with the passenger business which could be generated to pay the cost of such an operation. The postmaster, C.M. Perkins, favored three round trips weekly, with seaplanes capable of carrying passengers flying on a

▲ *Bob Ellis, left, and Anscel Eckmann, right, stand in front of the Hotel Gastineau in Juneau after the inaugural flight of Alaska-Washington Airways. Displayed on the windows are same-day copies of the morning's* **Seattle Post-Intelligencer** *along with promotional material on the aircraft.*

The **Daily Alaska Empire** *carried this box advertising a schedule which Alaska-Washington Airways tried to adhere to during the summer of 1929.*

ten-hour schedule with stops at Vancouver, British Columbia, Prince Rupert, Ketchikan and Wrangell, with Juneau as the northern terminus. One reservation Perkins had, as far as recommending the project, was the possibility of fog along the Inside passage endangering the flight schedules. The best way to counteract this was to run survey flights, and attempt to show that a schedule could be run successfully. Companies hoping for a mail contract set out to do this.

Vern C. Gorst, president of Seattle Flying Service, formed a new company, Gorst Air Transport, Incorporated, absorbing his prior firm in the process. He ordered a new Keystone C-2-C Loening Air Yacht from the factory back east, and had it shipped west. For its pilot, he chose Clayton L. Scott, a commercial pilot who had soloed first in February, 1927. Scott had flown Gorst over the Renton (Bryn Mawr) field and the newly-completed Boeing Field on March 21, 1928. The very next day, Scott made the first landing on Boeing Field, with two passengers in an OX-5 powered Travel Air biplane. When plans were completed Scott would go north with the new amphibian with Vern Gorst in the copilot seat.

March 20, 1929. Phil Jolie, Juneau auto mechanic, towed the Boeing flying boat to its mooring and posed on the hull. "Paddy" Burke, his mechanic, George Lortie, and three passengers arrived in the plane from Seattle.

Tom Croson Collection

March 20, 1929. The Boeing Model B-1E, NC 115E, flown by Edward Joseph Augustus "Paddy" Burke for International Airways arrived from Seattle to moor in the small boat harbor. The plane left March 25 for its return flight to Seattle.

Tom Croson Collection

556

Captain Edward Joseph Augustus "Paddy" Burke (on left) flew the six-passenger Boeing flying boat Model B-1E, NC 115E, from Seattle to Ketchikan and Juneau in March of 1929. He carried as passengers, Mrs. J.W. "Jack" McCord, Mr. and Mrs. P.T. McCarthy, and mechanic George Lortie (behind).

Another contender, International Airways, was first on the route. Using a six-place Boeing flying boat, Model B-1E, NC 115E, powered with a 425 horsepower Wasp engine, the survey flight departed Seattle at 1:45 P.M. Thursday, March 14, 1929, for Ketchikan and Juneau. (see Ketchikan—1929, Chapter 42). The pilot, Edward Joseph Augustus "Paddy" Burke, arrived in Juneau with his mechanic, George Lortie, and three passengers at 3:20 P.M. Wednesday, March 20. They were met by Gerald J. Smith, Juneau representative for the company, who took the party to the Gastineau Hotel. Passengers aboard the plane were P.T. McCarthy, president of International Airways, and his wife, as well as Mrs. J.W. "Jack" McCord, whose husband raised sheep, cattle and foxes in the Aleutian Islands.

After spending several days in the capital city, the plane departed for the south, taking off from the channel below Douglas at 11:00 A.M. Monday, March 25. The original five were joined by Gerald Smith, making a full load of six persons. For the story of their adventurous trip back to Seattle; (see Ketchikan—1929, Chapter 42).

Joseph L. Carman, Jr., son of a Tacoma furniture manufacturer and head of one of the

▲ *Anscel Eckmann and, presumably, his wife, stand on the float of the Vega* **Juneau**, *NC 432E. The pilot wears the Navy-type blue uniform of the company.*

April 15, 1929. Carroll Martin, left, and Anscel's brother, Ray, of the Martin & Eckmann store in Seattle hand Anscel Eckmann, pilot of the **Juneau**, *a suit of clothes for a customer in Juneau. With such a connection, the pilot was often nattily dressed.*

558

Courtesy of Jim and Bob Eckmann

▼ *Lieutenant Anscel C. Eckmann, March Field, California, 1918.*

Courtesy Jim and Bob Eckman

▲ *Following his discharge from the U.S. Army Air Service in 1918, Anscel Eckmann (standing at bow) formed Pacific Airways Company in partnership with Avery Black. They operated this former Navy flying boat HS-2L with its 450 horsepower Liberty motor on a Seattle-Vancouver and Seattle-Victoria schedule. Although a Curtiss design, Boeing Aircraft built twenty-five of the aircraft for the Navy on contract near the end of World War I. At one time there was a plan to take the* **Bluebird,** *N-CACM to Nome and operate it out of there, but nothing came of it. Now, in April of 1929, Eckmann flew the Lockheed Vega,* **Juneau,** *to Alaska on its inaugural run.*

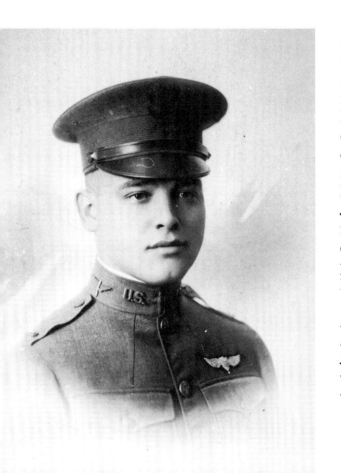

first flying schools in the Seattle area, saw the possibilities in an Alaskan route. He had organized Aviation School, Incorporated, in the spring of 1928, operating from Gorst's sandlot field, using three Waco biplanes. In the spring of 1929 a Wasp-powered Lockheed Vega on Fairchild pontoons was added to their fleet of flying equipment. It did not take the firm long to show its interest in a Seattle-Alaska run and, at 7:15 A.M. Monday, April 15, 1929, the Vega, now christened *Juneau,* was off the water at Bryn Mawr on a nonstop flight to Juneau. Alaska-Washington Airways was incorporated on the same day; with J.L. Carman, Jr. as president, W.E. Wynn as vice-president, and Don B. Bennett as secretary-treasurer.

Aboard the *Juneau,* NC 432E, as crew, were Anscel C. Eckmann, chief pilot of Alaska-Washington Airways, Incorporated, Robert E. Ellis, navigator; and Jack Halloran, chief mechanic for the Airways. There was no room for additional passengers since the cabin was filled with case gas in five-gallon cans. Ellis and

*Monday, April 15, 1929. The Lockheed Vega, NC 432E, christened the **Juneau**, lands on the waters of Gastineau Channel at the city for which it was named, following its nonstop flight from Seattle. Aboard were Anscel C. Eckmann, the pilot, Robert E. Ellis, navigator, and Jack Halloran, mechanic.*

Courtesy Jim and Bob Eckman

*The **Juneau** lies, moored to a log float near the Rock dump in Juneau during a visit in the summer of 1929. Bob Ellis is in the center of group, facing the door, with Claire Krogh at far left.*

Tom Croson Collection

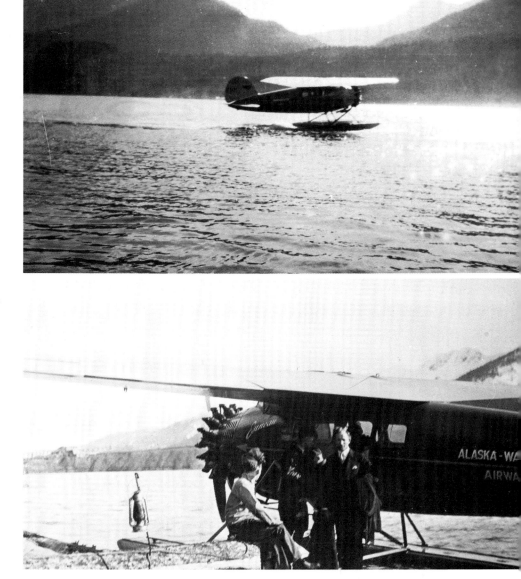

Halloran fed the additional fuel into the tanks by means of a wobble pump during the trip in order to extend the range of the aircraft, and make the long flight without landing enroute. In the end, this function irritated Ellis, sitting on some of the "leakers" and getting his pants soaked in fuel which he could do nothing about until after arrival. Ellis, a naval reserve pilot had recently taken a job as pilot for John Blum, owner of Northwest Air Service at Boeing Field, and abandoned it to join the flight north, concentrating on the navigation. The only maps available were Alaska Road Commission maps, blueprints which showed creeks, roads and rivers, but little else.

Anscel Eckmann, the pilot, was a graduate of the U.S. Air Service in 1918, too late to go overseas. He had flown an H2-SL flying boat, *Bluebird*, for Pacific Airways Company, jointly-owned by Eckmann and Avery Black, on a Seattle-Vancouver and Seattle-Victoria schedule. Continuing in flying, he was now chief pilot for the new firm. Jack Halloran was an experienced airplane mechanic.

560

GO-EAST AIR TRANSPORT PLANE TAKING OFF AT JUNEAU, ALASKA.

©29 ORDWAY, JUNEAU

Ordway Studios

*The Keystone Loening Air Yacht **Alaskan**, NC 9728, arrived in Juneau from Seattle on April 18, 1929. Pilot Clayton L. Scott made several fights about the area, leaving for Ketchikan and Seattle on April 23. The plane would return to the capital city in May.*

At 12:52 P.M., the sleek blue and cream-painted Vega was over Ketchikan, circling once before continuing on. They arrived over the capital city at twelve minutes to 2:00 P.M., circling twice before turning away to land on the water at exactly seven and one-half minutes to 2:00 P.M. They had been in the air a total of seven hours and thirty-five minutes from point to point. They had consumed 120 gallons of fuel in their flight of close to 1000 miles.

Eckmann spent the next few days in promoting the company's business about Juneau, while the crew were shown the hospitality of the city and its residents. The pilot took the plane to Sitka, hopping off at 8:45 A.M. Wednesday, April 17, to land there forty-five minutes later. He carried George Rice, Larry Parks and J.H. Walmer. Eckmann returned to Juneau at 2:25 P.M. with Rice, Parks and W.A. Eaton, who had replaced Walmer when the pilot dropped him at Chichagof; he also brought in Mrs. Theodore Kettleson, wife of the superintendent of the Pioneers Home in Sitka. The weather had been ideal during the entire flight. The pilot flew to Skagway that same afternoon, with Wallis George, Harry I. Lucas, Isadore "Ike" Goldstein and Claire Krogh.

At the luncheon of Thursday, April 18, 1929, Eckmann spoke to Chamber of Commerce members at great length on the company's future plans regarding air service in Southeastern Alaska. That afternoon, he flew two groups to Skagway and return; on the first flight

561

were H.L. Faulkner, Fred Sorri and son, Fred, Jr., Joe George and A. Hendrickson. On the second, he took Mr. and Mrs. C.J. Graham, Richard Wohr and Nick Bavard as passengers.

On Friday morning, April 19, the pilot flew flight after flight with sightseers, from the "rock dump", starting at 10:00 A.M., taking off from the water inside the breakwater. He took off down the channel toward Thane and, gaining altitude, circled back to land, giving the passengers a view of the country for miles in the clear weather, as the roar of the engine reverberated from the steep mountainsides over town. The Vega left at 4:00 P.M. that afternoon for Ketchikan, carrying three passengers: Mrs. C.J. Graham, Mrs. S. Stanworth and A.H. Ziegler. He flew sightseers out of there the following day (see Ketchikan 1929, Chapter 42) and returned to Juneau that same afternoon.

Eckmann was off Juneau for Skagway early Sunday morning, April 21, to pick up a large shipment of furs, taking the owner, Charles Goldstein along. With Ellis, Halloran and Goldstein, the pilot departed for Ketchikan, where he took a man with a broken leg on board, continuing on south to Seattle. He was there at 8:15 P.M., thus ending his first round trip to Alaska. (see Ketchikan 1929, Chapter 42). Permission to carry official air mail south from Juneau had been refused by the Post Office Department in Washington, D.C., but the plane had carried a sack of unofficial mail to Seattle.

While Eckmann was still in Juneau with the Alaska-Washington Airways Vega, a second plane arrived in the city. It had departed Seattle at 7:00 A.M. Wednesday, April 17, 1929, just two days after Eckmann's departure. The Gorst Air Transport Loening Air Yacht, NC 9728, *Alaskan*, was taxied to a berth in the basin behind the rock dump. Flown by Clayton Scott, with Vern Gorst, president of Gorst Air Transport, Incorporated, as copilot, and Gordon

The blue and yellow **Alaskan** *of Gorst Air transport, Incorporated, taxis on the water in front of Juneau in summer, 1929. Smoke rises in the air from a sawdust burner behind the amphibian.*

Following closely after the Alaska-Washington Vega flight from Seattle, the Gorst Air Transport Loening C-2-C Air Yacht, NC 9728, arrived in Juneau on April 18. The amphibian, flown up from Seattle by pilot Clayton L. Scott, with Vern Gorst as copilot and Gordon Graham, mechanic, is shown taking off the water at Juneau. It had been named the **Alaskan.**

Graham, mechanic, the bright yellow and blue Loening amphibian had overnighted in Ketchikan before proceeding north to the capital city. (see Ketchikan 1929, Chapter 42). Carrying A.C. Iverson of Cordova, E.M. Greenwood, traffic manager for the Gorst company and, picking up Gorst's sister, Mrs. C.M. Taylor, in Ketchikan, the plane touched down at 1:24 P.M. (Juneau time) on Thursday, April 18. Shortly thereafter, the pilot was aloft for a twenty-minute scenic flight of the area, taking Governor George A. Parks, Ben Mullen, grandson of B.M. Behrends, Harry Lucas, and mechanic Jack Halloran.

Gorst promptly placed an ad in the *Daily Alaska Empire*, advertising "Airplane trips—$5.00. Apply at the Rock Dump or Gastineau Hotel." At 2:30 P.M. that same afternoon the plane was off for Skagway with the three crew members aboard to scout out the area.

The following morning, Saturday, April 20, the *Alaskan* was hauling sightseers from 10:00 A.M. on, taking off from the waters inside the rock dump and heading down the channel toward Thane, climbing to gain altitude, then circling back for a landing. Scott carried well over a hundred passengers during the day, many riding in an airplane for the first time. Sunday was a repeat performance, with many more going aloft. That afternoon, Scott took the Loening to Sitka, with a full load of passengers: H.J. Hodgins, Theodore Kettelson, Oscar Shineman, Mr. and Mrs. C.L. Wortman and Lieutenant Emerson C. Itschner.

While the airplane was in the city, the schools were let out, so that teachers and students, as well as other citizens, could go up for a scenic ride. Scott returned to Juneau at 2:00 P.M. the next day, Tuesday, April 23, making the flight in fifty minutes, bringing Lieutenant Itschner. He left for Ketchikan that afternoon with two passengers, seventy-nine year-old sourdough Carl Berg and H.H. Andre, clerk of the grocery department of B.M. Behrends. Andre was hurrying to San Francisco because of his mother's illness. Scott made the flight to Ketchikan in three hours, without stopping. At 10:00 A.M. the following morning, they were off from Tongass Narrows, for Seattle, and after stopping at Alert Bay to refuel, reached there in the late afternoon to deliver his passengers.

In Juneau, Captain Larry Parks of the mail and passenger boat, *Margarita*, had resigned his post to take a position with Alaska-Washington Airways. It was their intent to operate there for the season and Parks would make flight bookings, as well as attend to other details of the company's business.

Eckmann, with the *Juneau*, was back in the city on Monday, April 29, with Carl Ben Eielson (picked up from the steamer *Aleutian* near Mary Island, Seaforth Channel in Millbank Sound) and Jim Galen, Leath Russell and Otto Jones, a photographer. The plane taxied to Government Dock for ceremonies and a parade for the famous flier; to Main Street, along Front to Seward, to Third Avenue, and to the legislative chambers where Eielson was honored by a resolution in recognition of his achievements.

On Tuesday, April 30, 1929, Anscel Eckmann, with navigator Bob Ellis and mechanic Jack Halloran, left Juneau in the afternoon for Ketchikan. He carried as passengers: J.B. Warrack, H.M. Gould and Mrs. Stoel, expecting to pick up another passenger at Wrangell. He planned to return to Juneau again before proceeding to Seattle but, upon his arrival in Ketchikan, received an urgent wire from Larry Parks, requesting he pick up Mrs. Kostrometin-off in Sitka, who was seriously ill, and fly the woman to Seattle. (see Ketchikan 1929, Chapter 42). The pilot left Ketchikan at 4:00 A.M. Wednesday, May 1, to deliver the ill woman and her husband in Seattle at 7:40 P.M. that same day.

Clayton Scott and Gordon Graham, in the Gorst Air Transport Loening, returned to Juneau from Seattle. Their agent in the capital city, H.W. McDermott, had been approached to fly six members of the Alaska legislature to Cordova when the session ended. Leaving Seattle at 4:00 P.M. Wednesday, May 1, the plane arrived in Juneau at 4:00 P.M. Friday, May 3, taking two days enroute. Scott left again for Ketchikan, taking off at 10:30 A.M. the next morning, carrying two members of the House of Representatives, E.R. Tarwater and A.H. Ziegler. With the Cordova trip in doubt, Scott remained in Ketchikan for a time, flying out of there.

Scott and Graham departed Ketchikan on Monday, May 6, and with the usual stop at Petersburg, arrived in Juneau at 5:30 P.M. The following morning the two airmen were off in the *Alaskan* for Cordova, taking three passengers. They were to be the first plane to arrive in that community. (see Cordova 1929, Chapter 45).

Alaska-Washington Airways, *Juneau*, landed in the capital city at 1:00 P.M. Wednesday, May 8, bringing C.W. Cash from Ketchikan. Eckmann, Ellis and Halloran had carried no passengers on the flight from Seattle. Alaska-Washington Airways opened an office in the old quarters of the Juneau Music House on Front Street; now Larry Parks would have a desk. This was to be their Alaskan headquarters. The evening of their arrival in Juneau, Eckmann took cameraman Otto Jones and Fred Ordway, of the Alaska Scenic Views, also a cameraman and aviation buff, on a two-hour flight to film various scenic attractions. A disinterested spectator on the flight was *Skookums*, a tiny bear cub that Ordway had been looking after. Heading over Admiralty Island, up Icy Straits and over Glacier Bay, the pilot circled Muir Glacier for the cameramen. Jones shot several hundred feet of movie film, while Ordway concentrated on stills. Returning, Eckman circled over Mendenhall Glacier and Taku Glacier, giving the film artists a tremendous opportunity in the calm, clear air.

Bob Ellis was returning to Seattle on the *Admiral Evans*, expecting to take delivery of the Vega's sister ship, *Ketchikan*, and fly it to Alaska. Eckmann and Halloran took B.F. Heintzleman, assistant district forester, and F. Gastonguay to Chichagof on the morning of

Friday, May 10, to appraise the water power development at the Chichagof Mine for the Federal Power Commission. Eckmann hoped to see more use of their mode of travel in Southeastern Alaska by Federal officials. Larry Parks accompanied the party and returned with Eckmann that afternoon. The pilot picked up the group on Sunday.

On Saturday, May 11, the seaplane, *Juneau*, was off at 9:30 A.M. for Skagway, with George B. Rice as passenger. Eckmann flew sightseers there until Rice completed some business, then returned with him. The following day the plane went to Sitka with a Chichagof passenger, Phyllis Edwards of Douglas. Eckmann made several passenger-carrying flights out of Sitka before picking up Heintzleman and Gastonguay at Chichagof and returning to Juneau. On Monday morning, May 13, 1929, Eckmann took two construction men, Alfred Anderson and V.K. Woods, to Petersburg, to inspect projects there which had been completed by the firm they represented.

Eckmann and Halloran left, in the *Juneau*, at 7:30 A.M. Friday, May 17, going to Port Althorp to pick up August H. Buschmann, proceeding to Ketchikan for a brief fuel stop before continuing on to Seattle. He also carried, from Juneau, Larry Parks, Raymond F. Haines and *Skookums*, the bear cub, for Seattle.

Juneau had an airplane. Stored in a building in Douglas for the past five or six years, there reposed a crated Curtiss JN-4D which had been purchased by a charter boat operator, Paul Kegel. Kegel, a short, stocky man with a strong German accent, was, in March of 1928, serving as mate on the Biological Survey vessel, *Seal*. Kegel had eventually sold the crated training plane to Verne Saylor, who operated a lumber mill.

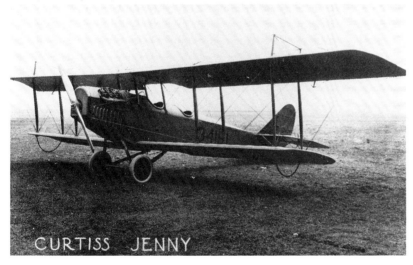

This photo of a Curtiss JN-4D "Jenny" shows the type of plane flown by Lyle C. Woods for Doctor Howe Vance's Totem Air Service in Juneau during the summer of 1929. Although the crated plane had been in a warehouse for some years, it had never been previously assembled and flown here.

On Friday, May 24, 1929, it was announced that Juneau would have a flying school in the near future. Doctor Howe Vance, a local osteopath, and some associates purchased the biplane, still in the crates, and had it moved to a warehouse on the Admiral Line dock for assembly. The former army training plane was still in fine condition, despite a layer of dust. Hundreds of the training planes were built in the Curtiss factories following a congressional appropriation of $640,000,000 on July 24, 1917, a measure intended to increase the air strength of the United States. No successful combat planes were produced; American pilots went to war in French Nieuports, Spads and other European-built fighters. When the war came to an end, there existed a multitude of the Curtiss "Jennies" at surplus prices for civilian would-be fliers to learn on.

The Curtiss JN-4D, the most popular model, was still in its war-time paint when uncrated for assembly in the Juneau warehouse, brand-new and shiny. The Hammondsport, New York Curtiss OX-5 motor of ninety horsepower, ran like a clock when tried out on Thursday, March 23, 1929.

Lyle C. Woods, a former army flier, had arrived in Juneau a short time before, to look over aviation prospects in the area. He had been associated with several flight training schools in various parts of the States, recently operating one of his own in Los Angeles. Using Woods as an instructor, Vance and his associates planned to operate such a school at Juneau, also learning to fly in the process.

Woods, with the assistance of Frank Richards, formerly with the Alexander Eaglerock Company, plane manufacturers in Colorado Springs, completed the major part of the assembly and tuned up the motor. The JN-4D, with dual controls and on wheels, was to be trucked to a flat near the Alaska Dairy, where final assembly put the airplane in flying condition. The military red, white and blue vertical bars on the tail, as well as the U.S. Air Service insignia on the wings, gave it a jaunty appearance. It was christened the *Totem*.

Alaska-Washington Airways plane, *Juneau*, flown by Anscel Eckmann, with Frank Hatcher as mechanic, landed in Gastineau Channel at 7:45 P.M. Sunday, May 26, 1929, completing its fifth trip from Seattle, with about seven hours and forty minutes flying time. They had made stops at Alert Bay and Ketchikan. On his arrival Eckmann made one sightseeing flight with passengers.

On Tuesday, May 28, the Vega left Juneau at 9:20 A.M. for Sitka; carrying M.S. Wilson, manufacturer's representative for Blake Moffit & Towne (paper manufacturers) and Arthur Van Mavern, of West Coast Grocery Company, as well as Peter Kostrometinoff, who had come up with the *Juneau* from Seattle. On the return trip, the pilot brought in Ora Kuykendall and Miss Iola B. Van Vranken, teachers from the Sheldon Jackson School at Sitka during the last year. Peter Kostrometinoff also returned to Juneau; the plane left Sitka at 6:00 P.M. for the one-hour flight. Eckmann took off the following day, at 6:00 A.M. for Seattle, with Kostrometinoff as the only passenger. He was delayed for a time in Ketchikan, flying a charter out of there, a tour of the Nakat canneries in Southeastern Alaska. Taking H.B. Friele, Eigil Buschmann, D.F. Ryan and Harvey Stockpole aboard, the Vega was off the morning of Wednesday, May 29, on the way to Waterfall, Union Bay and Port Althorp. Eckmann was in Juneau overnight, leaving there with the Vega at 11:00 A.M. Thursday, May 30, for Wrangell and Petersburg. He carried H.L. Faulkner and C.C. Mundy for Petersburg: O.D. Leet, and Leo McCormack and Nick Nussbaumer for Wrangell. He returned to Juneau in the afternoon, to pick up the Nakat cannery men, returning August Buschmann to Port Althorp; Eigil Buschmann and Mr. Friele to Union Bay. Eckmann finally got away for Seattle on Friday, May 31.

At 11:43 A.M. Friday, May 31, the city of Juneau received a visit from two planes of the Alaskan Aerial Survey Detachment of the U.S. Navy. With four Loening OL-8A amphibians, using the tender, *Gannet,* towing a covered barge, YF-88, as a floating base, the expedition, under the direction of Lieutenant Commander A.W. Radford, had been continuing the aerial mapping of Southeastern Alaska begun in 1926. The survey was presently based at Petersburg. (see Alaskan Aerial Survey Detachment—1929, Chapter 44). The visit gave Commander Radford and Mr. Sargent an opportunity to confer with Governor Parks and Commissioner Charles H. Flory regarding the season's work, as well as to look over the local harbor facilities with a view toward basing the expedition at the capital city.

On Friday, May 31, the Curtiss JN-4D, *Totem*, took to the air from a bar near the

Alaska Dairy. With Lyle C. Woods at the controls, the plane, which had received its final assembly and tuning at the site during the week, climbed to 5000 feet during the short flight. On landing, the plane overran the bar into a barbed wire fence. Only minor damage was done to the plane itself but the incident ruined the propeller. Doctor Vance had to await a new airscrew from Seattle before getting his first lesson. Two weeks passed before the biplane was ready to fly again.

A one-day flight between Juneau and San Francisco was contemplated by Governor George A. Parks, thus setting a new travel record. The governor wished to attend the graduation of his niece, Miss Mary Thompson, from Mills College in Oakland. Alaska-Washington Airways plane, *Juneau*, was on its way back from Seattle, arriving on Saturday, June 1, 1929. Never idle, Eckmann and his mechanic were up early on Sunday, trying to catch up on the business lined up by Larry Parks from his Gross Building office. The first trip, leaving at 6:30 A.M., was to the Tulsequah River with Roy O. Moore, a Los Angeles mining man. He was landed at the mouth, and after flying over the camp to signal the crew to pick up his passenger, Eckmann was back in Juneau shortly before 8:00 A.M. He left at 9:30 A.M. for Port Althorp with Territorial Health Commissioner, Doctor Harry Carlos DeVighne, returning about 2:00 P.M. Later he went to Petersburg and, shortly after midnight, was to hop off on his fourth flight of the day with Governor Parks as a passenger.

The Vega was off the water at 12:30 A.M. Thursday, June 3, with Parks, Joseph L. Carman, Jr., president of Alaska-Washington Airways, R.E. Robertson, Juneau attorney, and Larry Parks. When the plane arrived in Ketchikan, an hour and forty-five minutes later, Larry Parks deplaned and Howard D. Stabler, United States attorney of the first division, came aboard for the trip. The Vega was off an hour later, making one more gas stop at Wadham cannery, in Rivers Inlet, before arriving over Seattle at 9:15 A.M., landing at Bryn Mawr fifteen minutes later. In seven hours and five minutes of flying time, Eckmann had set a record: twenty-eight minutes under any of his previous flights from Juneau. Dick Gleason, waiting in Seattle to fly the governor south to Portland to connect with West Coast Air Transport, was delayed by an unfortunate incident. Making a turn on the south end of the field, the wheel struck a soft spot—the plane nosed up and wrecked the propeller when it struck the gravel and dirt.

Mechanics removed the propeller from the *Juneau*, installing it on Gleason's plane. He flew the governor to San Francisco, with one stop at Medford. Governor Parks had completed the entire flight in less than twenty-four hours; at least he was behind the same propeller all the way.

567

Clayton Scott and Gordon Graham, in the Keystone Loening Air Yacht of Gorst Air Transport, were on their way south after a month's successful operation out of Cordova. Leaving there on Monday, June 3, with a stop at Yakutat to refuel, the amphibian landed in Gastineau Channel at 4:35 P.M. of that same day, after flying four hours and fifteen minutes. J. Ibach, fur farmer from Middleton Island deplaned, with Charles M. Daniels, big game hunter from New York City, and H. Seidenverg, Anchorage merchant, Scott took off for Ketchikan at 7:30 P.M. and landed on Tongass Narrows at 10:00 P.M. (Juneau time). Boarding an additional passenger, Mrs. C.M. Taylor, sister of Vern Gorst, the Loening was off the next morning, Tuesday, June 4, at 4:00 A.M. From Mrs. Taylor, Scott learned that Gorst was in the east, at the Loening factory, and had also been in Washington, D.C. The Gorst company had renewed its contract for the Seattle-Victoria mail route with the government for two years.

Three hours and forty-five minutes out of Ketchikan, the *Alaskan* landed at Alert Bay to refuel. Another three hours of flying put them in Seattle, landing at home base in the afternoon of June 4, 1929. Before the month was out, Scott was flying the Seattle-Bremerton Ferry run with the colorful blue and yellow Loening; soon going east to the Loening factory to begin the flight to Seattle, on June 29, with the company's second Air Yacht, NC 9158. He arrived in Seattle on July 3, 1929.

Alaska-Washington Airways Vega, *Juneau*, was back in the capital city on his seventh round trip from Seattle, landing at 5:00 P.M. of June 7. Eckmann and Frank Hatcher were carrying C.T. McKinney, former assistant district attorney of Seattle, and Mrs. Don Bayne and A.C. Ecker, from Ketchikan. The plane departed Juneau at 9:15 A.M. the following day for Skagway; with R.R. Rudiman, R.J. Sommers and J.P. Van Orsdale as round-trip passengers; returning to Juneau, bringing Miss Vivian Talbot of Skagway. The plane arrived back at 2:30 P.M.

Eckmann made a trip to Ketchikan, returning to Juneau at 9:30 P.M. Wednesday, June 12, carrying J.B. Warrack, a Seattle construction man, on the two-hour flight. The weather was terrible.

On the following day, Thursday, June 13, a round trip to Sitka was made, leaving at 4:00 P.M. with Mr. Warrack, who was going there on business. The return was delayed by an emergency trip to Todd, in response to a wire for the plane to go there for an Indian woman, said to be dying. Doctor Hugh B. Nicholson, of Sitka, accompanied the plane, but a short time before arrival of the plane the woman had been taken aboard the *Admiral Rogers*, on which there were two physicians. Friday, June 14, 1929, Eckmann went to Sitka again, stopping on the way at Port Althorp to pick up N.E. Sagstad, the captain of the cannery tender, *Phoenix X*, bringing him to Juneau for treatment of an eye ailment. The plane returned to Juneau at noon, in one and three-quarters hours of flying time. The pilot left again for Sitka at 1:20 P.M. to bring in J.B. Warrack. Other passengers making the round trip were G.B. Rice, J.P. Van Orsdale, H.J. Gee and Miss Rae Stevens. Henry Klapisch was a passenger for Killisnoo, two miles south of Angoon. Eckmann was back at 7:00 P.M. that evening, leaving again at 8:30 P.M. The *Juneau* took prospectors Cedric Davis and William Scott, with 500 pounds of baggage, to an unnamed lake near the Canadian border in the upper Taku River district. The pilot was to return in thirty days to check on the party.

Back in Juneau, he flew sightseeing trips over Mendenhall Glacier on Saturday morning, taking Mr. and Mrs. Roy C. Lyle and Judge and Mrs. Justin W. Harding. Eckmann left, at 5:20 P.M. that afternoon, with passengers for Lake Atlin, where he enjoyed some excellent fishing with Canadian officials, catching a dozen trout. Leaving the lake at 2:20 P.M. Sunday, June 16, he returned to Juneau, landing at 3:30 P.M. His passengers on the Atlin trip were Mrs.

Saturday, June 15, 1929. The **Juneau,** *flown by Anscel Eckmann arrives at Atlin, British Columbia. He returned to Juneau the following day.*

Sightseeing boat on Lake Atlin, British Columbia. The community also boasted a fine hotel.

E.A. O'Laughlin, Miss Peggy McLeod, Doctor W.W. Council and R.B. McIvor. He left that same Sunday evening at 8:00 P.M. for Ketchikan to pick up superintendents from the company canneries for a conference with H.B. Friele, expected to arrive in Ketchikan from the south.

Eckmann brought the Vega into Juneau again, at 3:57 P.M. Tuesday, June 18, to dock at Robert Keeney's float. The uptown office in the Gross Building had been closed, and Larry Parks was moving to the Alaska-Washington Airways hangar under construction at the foot of Keeney's float. The owner was improving the float for the convenience of passengers. Eckmann brought in N.G. Nelson, Louis Shulman and H.B. Friele.

Repairs to Doctor Vance's Curtiss JN-4D plane had been completed and it made its second flight from the gravel bar near the Alaska Dairy on the evening of Friday, June 14, 1929. Lyle C. Woods, pilot of the biplane, reported the motor running smoothly during the half-hour flight. He expected to make several hops with passengers in the afternoon.

The four Loening OL-8A amphibian planes of the Alaskan Aerial Survey Detachment of the United States Navy arrived in Juneau on Monday, June 17, 1929, landing in Gastineau Channel at 9:40 A.M. The *Gannet*, with the 120-foot covered barge, YF-88, was due in at 6:45 P.M. to tie up at Government Dock during the time the air-mapping expedition was based at Juneau. They had flown in from Petersburg, which had been their base for the last three weeks. (see Alaskan Aerial Survey Detachment 1929, Chapter 44).

Eckmann wanted to return to Seattle soon to have new Model 4650 Edo floats installed on the *Juneau*; the original Fairchild floats had never quite achieved the performance he desired. Also, the engine needed a top overhaul. The pilot took a party of four: Misses Rae Stevens and Eva Tripp, Emil Gastonguay and J.P. Van Orsdale, for a round trip to Annex Creek to look over the power plant there, leaving at 11:00 A.M. Thursday, June 20, and returning to Juneau at noon, in time for the Chamber of Commerce luncheon. The plane left at 1:15 P.M. soon after lunch, for Port Althorp, to pick up August Buschmann and G.H. Skinner, president of the Alaska-Pacific Salmon Corporation, and Larry Ives, of Seattle, for a two-hour tour of their canneries in the vicinity. The party was back at 7:53 P.M. The pilot departed Juneau at 5:15 A.M. Friday, June 21, carrying N.G. Nelson and his two daughters, for Ketchikan, where he did some more flying. (see Ketchikan 1929, Chapter 42). Following this, he continued on to Seattle to complete his seventh round trip to Alaska.

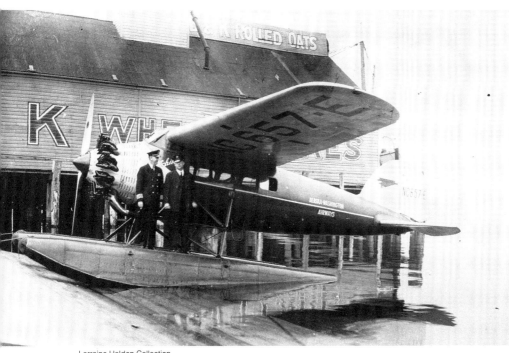

Alaska-Washington Airways second Vega to fly to Alaska was the Ketchikan, NC 657E. Shown here in Seattle with Alexander Bancroft Holden, General Operations Manager for the company, on the left, and Larry Parks, the Juneau agent, the plane left Seattle on June 26, 1929, on the company's eighth flight to the capital city.

Eckmann, with mechanic Frank Hatcher, began his eighth, and the new plane's first, trip in the company's newest Vega, NC 657E, a Model 5 named the *Ketchikan*. The men were off Seattle on Wednesday afternoon, June 26, 1929. Landing at Alert Bay, they went on north and, stopped by foggy weather, had to hold overnight at Lowe Inlet in Grenville Channel. The pilot arrived in Ketchikan at 1:45 P.M. on Thursday. They landed in Juneau at 5:00 P.M. Friday, June 28, with the new plane. It was also painted cream and blue, with the same design as the wheeled Vega, NC 200E. The *Juneau* did not have as much cream on the nose cowling as these two planes did.

▶ *In 1929 the Kintz Boat Basin, Lake Union, in Seattle, Washington, provided a base for the seaplanes of Alaska-Washington Airways. Plane in foreground is the* Ketchikan, *NC 657E, with mechanic Frank Hatcher standing on the Edo float. The planes could be brought up the sloping ramp into the shop.*

▼ *Alaska-Washington Airways Model 5 Vega, NC 657E, was named* Ketchikan. *The five-place float plane, also painted blue and cream, was the second one to be put into regular service in Alaska in 1929.*

Tom Croson Collection

Tom Croson Collection

Eckmann took a party to the Taku district below Juneau, taking off at 5:00 A.M. Saturday, June 29, with Isadore "Izzy" Goldstein, M.V. Manville, O.C. McKechnie, Lloyd E. Bowler and Dr. Robert Simpson as passengers. They looked over mining property recently discovered by Manville in the Taku River district, and returned to the capital city in the Vega, *Ketchikan*, at noon. That same afternoon, leaving at 1:15 P.M. Eckmann made a trip to Hirst-Chichagof and Port Althorp with passengers. At 5:00 A.M. Sunday, June 30, he was away again for the Taku district, taking Mrs. Belle Simpson, Miss Florence Torgerson, Victor Manville and Allen Torgerson. Leaving the men at the mining property on Big Bull Slough, above the Tulsequah River, at a ledge recently discovered by Manville, the pilot returned to Juneau with the ladies. He left immediately for Port Althorp to bring in Mrs. O.A. Larson and Mrs. August Buschmann to Juneau. The seaplanes of Alaska-Washington Airways now had use of their new hangar, recently completed by Morris Construction Company at the end of Keeney's float.

Eckmann and Frank Hatcher left Juneau at 3:30 P.M. that same afternoon of Sunday, June 30, for Ketchikan, to do some flying there, after bringing in the Manville party from the Tulsequah.

571

A party prepares to go ashore from the Alaska-Washington Airways **Ketchikan, NC 657E.** *The plane is moored tail-in on the lakeshore.*

June 29, 1929. Eckmann flies a party from Juneau into the Taku River district on a gold panning trip. Flying in the Vega **Ketchikan, NC 657E,** *the pilot returned the same day.*

June 29, 1929. Pilot Anscel Eckmann tries his hand at panning for gold in the Taku River district in Southeastern Alaska.

In Juneau, beginning about June 25, the Curtiss JN-4D, *Totem*, was busy flying off the gravel bar behind the Alaska Dairy, with pilot Lyle C. Woods. Now known as Totem Air Service, passengers who had made flights in the plane were: Miss and Mrs. Rae Stevens, Mrs. Howe Vance, Helen Whitman, Hazel Boyce, Paul Hudson, Larry Parks, Harry Murray, Roy Lund, Wayne Gerard, Buddy Martin, Ethyl Wheeler, Frank Bangart and C.K. Cummings. Those who had enrolled for a course of instruction in flying were: Miss Rae Stevens, Miss Helen Whitman, Paul Hudson, Harry Murray, Roy Lund, Wayne Gerard, Frank Bangart and C.K. Cummings.

A large, single pontoon had been included with the plane when it was shipped north to Juneau, but there were no struts to attach it to the plane. This, with two small wing floats, would make a water plane of the *Totem*. Woods sent off to Seattle for the needed parts, which were expected to arrive on the *Alameda* within a week. He hoped to be able to base the plane in the city, making flights from the water there.

Commissioner Henry O'Malley, of the United States Bureau of Fisheries, announced on Friday, July 5, 1929, that a contract had been signed with Alaska-Washington Airways for a fisheries patrol of Southeastern Alaska, using planes, to start about July 15 and continue during the spawning season. With the *Ketchikan* now in Alaska, and the *Juneau* expected soon, with James R. Hennessy as its pilot, the company expected to be able to handle the contract, along with their growing business. The Bureau wished to keep spawning grounds, streams and traps under aerial surveillance, with other government agencies cooperating later to make full-time use of a plane. A similar patrol had been in use for the past two or three years by Canadian fisheries in British Columbia waters.

Eckmann arrived back in Juneau in the Vega, *Ketchikan*, NC 657E, on Saturday, July 6; a crazed Filipino from the Peril Straits Packing Company plant at Todd was lashed in a seat. Federal authorities received him and arranged for a hearing. On Saturday afternoon, the Vega made a trip to Todd, Sitka and Port Alexander. John L. Larsen made the round trip, and Miss Harriet DeArmond returned on it to her home in Sitka. At Todd, Nick Bez, president of the Peril Straits Packing Company, and several others made a short flight in the *Ketchikan* before it continued to Sitka. Eckmann stopped on the return, to pick up the wireless man for the United States Bureau of Fisheries flagship, *Brant*, on its trip westward. Eckmann and Hatcher left for Ketchikan the evening of Sunday, July 7, with attorneys H.L. Faulkner and R.E. Robertson, John L. Larsen, a radio specialist from Seattle, and Phillip M. Elliott, as passengers. The *Juneau* was still delayed in Seattle, awaiting pontoon replacement. Eckmann left Ketchikan for Seattle on Monday morning at 9:00 A.M.

Alaska-Washington Airways Vega, *Ketchikan*, was out of Seattle on Tuesday morning, July 9, 1929, on the tenth trip north for the airway company. With stops at Alert Bay and Ketchikan, the plane arrived in Juneau at 3:15 P.M. Wednesday, bringing attorney H.L. Faulkner and T. Carlson as passengers from Ketchikan. The pilot immediately went to Crescent Lake, near the Canadian border, to bring in the two prospectors, Cedric Davis and William Scott, he had left there a month before. Larry Parks had considerable work lined up. Eckmann left on Thursday, July 11, at 8:00 A.M. with a canneryman on an inspection tour of fish traps in the Juneau area, later making a thirty-minute flight with officers from the *Admiral Evans*. The pilot was off shortly before noon for Port Althorp to take Gil Skinner on an inspection tour of the fish traps in the vicinity. He was back in Juneau at 2:20 P.M. bringing Gilbert Skinner, Mr. and Mrs. T.J. Skinner, Mr. and Mrs. August Buschmann and Mrs. Oscar T. Carlson. He took off at 3:00 P.M. for Wrangell with Mr. Moultray, of the Standard Oil Company, and O.D. Leet. He also had aboard Judge V.A. Paine and T.L. Gardner, who would be dropped at Kake on the return flight. Friday, July 11, at 10:00 A.M. he departed for Port Althorp to return the Skinner party. He was back at 2:45 P.M.

The Alaska-Washington Airways Vega was up on Sunday, July 14, making three sightseeing flights around Mendenhall Glacier and down Gastineau Channel. The pilot made a trip to Sitka, via Killisnoo, carrying Mrs. Helen di Vanzie, government nurse at Angoon, to Killisnoo, and Verne Saylor for Sitka. Mrs. Beatrice Huston, nurse at the government hospital in Juneau, and Miss Eleanor Hawver made the round trip. The plane returned from Sitka on Monday morning, also bringing in Charles Wortman, Sitka druggist, and Fred F. Schrey, mild-cure salmon packer, to land at 10:00 A.M. Eckmann was off again for Sitka at 11:45 A.M., to return in the afternoon with Mrs. Wortman, Mrs. Schrey and her two daughters, and Oscar Shineman.

Eckmann went back to Sitka on Tuesday, July 16, 1929, leaving at noon with passengers. Verne Saylor was a passenger on the return trip. As soon as he arrived, the pilot took off

◄ *Alaska-Washington Airways second Vega in Alaska, 1929, Model 5, NC 657E, Ketchikan.* Pilot Floyd Keadle stands on the float, second from left, with his mechanic, Frank Hatcher, fourth from left. Photographed at Lake Dorothy.

▼ *Alaska-Washington Airways Vega NC 200E was named* Sitka, *but never came north; instead it was operated out of Seattle on wheels. Also painted blue and cream, the prototype Vega was sold the following year to John Blum, owner of Northwest Air Service in Seattle, who flew it to victory in the Seattle-Chicago segment of the National Air Races of 1930. A later Vega, NC 974H, also named* Sitka, *a Model 5, did come north on floats in 1930.*

on an emergency trip, to bring in Henry Baumdal from the P.E. Harris cannery in Hawk Inlet. The man was suffering from acute appendicitis.

The Vega was off for Sitka at 7:30 A.M. the following morning, with Verne Saylor, Oscar Shineman, Mrs. Fred Schrey, Mrs. Charles Wortman, Peggy Schrey and John Walmer as passengers. H.B. Friele, general manager of the Nakat Packing Company, left at 10:00 A.M. that same morning, to make a tour of the company canneries, ending at Ketchikan that evening. Eckmann wanted to meet the *Juneau*, being flown up by pilots James R. Hennessy and Floyd E. Keadle, with mechanic Ardell Dayton, from Seattle.

The *Juneau* was forced down in Lowe Inlet, in Grenville Channel, by fog on the evening of Eckmann's arrival in Ketchikan. (see Ketchikan—1929, Chapter 42). Eckmann

574

July 19, 1929. Alaska-Washington Airways Vega Ketchikan, *NC 657E, on Lake Hasselborg on Admiralty Island. Sport fishing on the beautiful wilderness lake was popular with Juneau residents who could reach it easily by plane.*

and Hatcher flew there early the next morning, bringing Keadle back with them, the *Juneau* returning to Seattle.

Keadle flew the *Ketchikan* from there to Juneau on Thursday, July 18, accompanied by Eckmann and Hatcher. He was an experienced pilot on Vegas, having flown NC 200E, *Sitka*, on wheels, out of Seattle for the last two or three months. Upon arrival, the *Ketchikan* made a trip to the Tulsequah mining property, up the Taku River, taking in Pat Lynch of Lynch Brothers Diamond Drill Company of Seattle, Mrs. J.B. Stabler, Jimmy Stabler and Mrs. Charles G. Warner. In the afternoon, a passenger flight to Sitka was planned.

On the evening of Friday, July 19, the *Ketchikan* took a fishing party to Lake Hasselborg on central Admiralty Island. The lake had been named for Allen E. Hasselborg, who had for years lived a hermit existence at Mole Harbor, five miles east of the lake on Seymour Canal. The plane returned to Juneau the next morning. Over 150 cutthroat trout were taken from the lake by Doctor W.W. Council, H.I. Lucas, pilot Anscel Eckmann and Frank Hatcher, mechanic of the plane. The largest trout was nineteen inches long; several were displayed on ice at the Thomas Hardware Company. Alaska-Washington Airways continued to promote these recreational flights.

Inaugurating their new contract with the United States Bureau of Fisheries, the Alaska-Washington Vega, *Ketchikan*, flown by Floyd Keadle, was off on the afternoon of Saturday, July 20, on a four-hour trip to investigate the fisheries in the Juneau district. Taking Captain M.J. O'Connor, assistant Alaska agent of the Bureau, Winn Goddard, of the Alaska Game Commission, and M.L. Merritt, assistant district forester, the pilot covered Baranof Island, Chichagof Island, Icy and Chatham Straits districts.

While making a trip into the Taku district on Sunday, July 22, Keadle and Frank Hatcher, in the *Ketchikan*, sighted the army pursuit plane in which Captain Ross G. Hoyt was

The five-place **Ketchikan**, *back from a successful fishing charter to Lake Hasselborg, on central Admiralty Island. Word of the successful fishing soon spread and it became a popular thing to do. Seated on the engine is pilot Floyd Keadle, with agent Larry Parks and mechanic Frank Hatcher seated next to him on the wing.*

▼ *Alaska-Washington Vega NC 657E,* **Ketchikan,** *on the still waters of Lake Hasselborg, Admiralty Island, in 1929.*

Lockheed Vega, **Ketchikan,** *taking off on floats from Lake Hasselborg in July, 1929.*

attempting to make a round trip from Mitchel Field, Long Island, to Nome and return. (see Ross C. Hoyt, New York to Nome—1929, chapter 49). Two round trips with passengers for Hawk Inlet and Funter Bay were made by the *Ketchikan* that same day, one in the morning and one in the afternoon. More trips were in the offing to Hasselborg, the town's fishermen in a fever of excitement over the catches brought in. Two parties were taken in, one leaving at 3:30 P.M. and one in the evening of Monday, July 22. The latter party remained overnight at the tent camp, coming in to Juneau at 8:30 A.M. the next day. R.B. "Doc" McIvor caught the record trout to date from Hasselborg; it was twenty-one inches long.

Eckmann and Keadle, alternating with one another, flew fourteen passengers, in four flights, from the *Dorothy Alexander* on fifteen-minute sightseeing hops. The ship's captain, Graham, was a special guest. Another fishing trip to Lake Hasselborg was on, with Miss Marie Goldstein, Charles Goldstein, Doctor W.W. Council, Jack Gucker and pilot Eckmann leaving Juneau at 7:00 P.M. Wednesday, July 24, in the *Ketchikan*, flown by Floyd Keadle. After camping all night on the lake, the party returned at 9:30 A.M. with about 200 cut-throat trout.

Floyd Keadle made an

July 24, 1929. Alaska-Washington Airways floating hangar at the foot of Robert Keeney's float on Gastineau Channel with the Vega, Ketchikan, heeled in to the ramp. The plane could be towed into the hangar with a bridle fastened to the after float struts, running to a geared drum in the hangar, the plane towed in on two wheels placed on a temporary axle passing through the floats.

Navy Department Photo; in the National Archives

emergency trip to Tenakee on Thursday, July 25, 1929, bringing Anastacio Pimentel, Filipino foreman of the Superior Packing Company, to Juneau to see his seriously ill brother.

Opening of a United States Customs station at the mouth of the Taku River, to facilitate travel and freight shipments into the rapidly developing mining area across the International Boundary, was announced on July 29, 1929. It was inaugurated August 1, and located on a barge at the river mouth. T.L. Allen, appointed Deputy Collector of Customs, was in charge.

Anscel Eckmann, in the Vega, departed on Saturday, July 27, taking Fred Huffman, a cameraman, to Wrangell; and Mar Dong, a Chinese contractor, taken aboard at Todd, to Ketchikan. On the return, the pilot carried O.D. Leet from Wrangell to Ketchikan on Sunday morning. That afternoon, the *Ketchikan* went to the Taku country, to pick up Sam Feldon, John Johnson and Tom Snyder, bringing them back to Juneau.

Anscel Eckmann was back in Wrangell on Wednesday, July 31, carrying O.D. Leet and Karl Thiele as passengers. He was back at 6:30 A.M. the next morning, to begin a busy day of flying. The pilot took three men on an hour and a half trip to a lake just west of the Canadian border, returning to Juneau at 10:30 A.M., after which the seaplane went to Port Althorp, to take August Buschmann on a tour of the canneries.

Floyd Keadle, accompanied by Bob Ellis and mechanic Ardell Dayton, brought up the Vega, *Juneau*, from Seattle. He arrived in Juneau on Wednesday, July 31, carrying Haakon B. Friele and M.M. Houck, of the Nakat Packing Company. That same afternoon, Keadle piloted the *Ketchikan* to a lake beyond the Canadian border, to bring out William McKenna and W. Dickinson, who had been taken in two weeks before for a prospecting trip.

Keadle left in the *Juneau* with Ellis and Dayton and the same two cannery officials, for Ketchikan the morning of Thursday, August 1. Friele remained here, while Houck continued on to Seattle in the *Juneau*. Anscel Eckmann and Frank Hatcher left Juneau in the other Vega, NC 657E, at 5:00 A.M. Friday, August 2, with passengers. (see Ketchikan—1929, Chapter 42). The flight arrived in Seattle that same evening, completing the tenth round trip.

Lockheed Vega NC 657E, Ketchikan, at the float in Juneau, Alaska in summer, 1929.

Tom Croson Collection

The pilot was back, still flying the *Ketchikan*, to land on Gastineau Channel at the capital city, at 9:45 A.M. Saturday, August 10. Passengers were Foye M. Murphy, a Boston attorney, with his wife and his sister-in-law, and Robert Simpson, Juneau optometrist. All the way from Seattle the weather had been very poor for flying.

Sunday, August 11, was a busy day for Eckmann and Hatcher. The *Ketchikan* left Juneau at 10:40 A.M. for the United-Eastern mining camp in the Taku district, carrying W.W. Council, R.B. "Doc" McIvor and Roy Houtz. The passengers remained at the camp until afternoon, when Eckmann made another trip in to bring them out, also bringing in Joe Hill, a prospector. Shortly after noon, the pilot had flown Warren Wilson and Shelley Graves on an hour and a half flight in the vicinity of Berners Bay. After bringing back the Taku party, Eckmann went out at 5:30 P.M. with a fishing party to Lake Hasselborg, returning to Juneau about 8:30 P.M. with a good catch.

Joe Hill, prospector and fur farmer, who had made the most recent strike in the Taku district, returned to his camp at the junction of the Tulsequah and Taku rivers on Tuesday morning, August 13, expecting to remain a week. Before landing, Eckmann flew the *Ketchikan* up both rivers for a considerable distance, to allow his passengers to look over the country. For the round trip, he carried J.A. Smiley, Canadian Customs official, and H.T. Tripp. He also picked up Lawrence Carlson and C.A. Sellar from the United-Eastern property, returning to Juneau at 1:45 P.M.

The Alaskan Aerial Survey Detachment of the U.S. Navy, their mapping in the Juneau district completed for 1929, departed on the morning of Saturday, August 17, for Ketchikan. (see Alaskan Aerial Survey Detachment—1929, Chapter 44). They left Ketchikan for Seattle on September 7.

Eckmann departed for Waterfall on Tuesday, August 20, to pick up August Buschmann, but was stormbound in Craig. He expected to continue to Waterfall the next day, going from there to Kake and Port Althorp, leaving Buschmann at the latter. He was back in Juneau at 3:30 P.M. on Wednesday. Nakat Packing Company had used Alaska-Washington Airways extensively during the season.

The pilot was off at 9:00 A.M. Thursday, August 22, taking A.J. Ela, engineer in charge of hydro-electric surveys for the Chandler-Cameron pulp and paper interests, and J.A. Cameron

Tom Croson Collection

Anscel Eckmann drops an engineering party off at Lake Dorothy in Southeastern Alaska. The pilot, standing up from the cockpit of the Ketchikan, *often went flying dressed in suit and tie.*

for an inspection of timber and water power possibilities in the area of a lake recently discovered (Lake Dorothy) by the U.S. Navy survey detachment. After making a four-hour patrol for the United States Bureau of Fisheries, the pilot returned to Lake Dorothy for the men.

On Friday, August 23, the *Ketchikan* made a round trip to Sitka with passengers, leaving Juneau at 8:25 A.M. The pilot then took off on a flight for Lituya Bay, on the west coast, leaving at noon with Roy Rutherford and Bert Loomis, returning to Juneau at 5:00 P.M. The pilot had stopped on the way to pick up Nick Bez, president of Peril Straits Packing Company, as well as picking up August Buschmann at Port Althorp. He immediately left for Sitka, with passengers, on his second trip there for the day.

On Saturday, August 24, Eckmann, in the *Ketchikan*, was off for Lake Dorothy at 6:00 A.M., carrying two surveyors with several hundred pounds of equipment. Upon his return, he took Buschman back to Port Althorp, and left at 11:00 A.M. for Skagway, with Colonel and Mrs. Conrad Mann of Kansas City, Missouri. He was back in Juneau at 12:50 P.M., to take off again at 1:30 P.M. for a second round trip to Wrangell and Petersburg. He would make one more trip to drop several hundred pounds of supplies at Berners Bay for Warren Wilson and Shelley Graves.

Eckmann departed at 4:00 P.M. Sunday, August 25, with Glenn Oakes and several hundred pounds of supplies for prospectors at Lake Crescent. Before unloading of the cargo was completed the weather deteriorated to where the pilot felt it advisable to spend the night there. Eckmann and Hatcher slept in the Vega, without blankets, while Oakes joined his fellow campers at their fireside. In the morning, the pilot flew the prospectors on a trip among the many lakes in the area. The *Ketchikan* was back in Juneau at 10:00 A.M. He made a two-hour flight into the Taku River district with Joe Hill, but did not land on the river. W.L. Coates, Canadian Pacific Steamship agent in Juneau went along. Late that afternoon, A.J. Ela made a trip into Lake Dorothy. On his return, Eckmann flew Harold Galwass and friends on a half-hour trip to Taku and Mendenhall Glaciers, taking off at 6:30 P.M. He left for Wrangell at 9:00 A.M. Tuesday, August 27, 1929, on a round trip. Late that same day, the pilot flew a trip into Lake Dorothy with Emil Gastonguay and Wendell Dawson, who was in charge of stream flow investigations for Cameron-Chandler pulp and paper interests. On the next morning, Wednesday, August 28, he took off with Horace Adams and Franklin R. Pierce, a writer, on a round trip into the Taku River district, coming into Juneau by the "back door", down Gold Creek Basin. Pierce took both moving and still pictures, expressing delight over the flight.

On Friday, August 30, Eckmann was very busy, as usual, flying two trips into Lake Dorothy as well as any number of passenger hops around Juneau and the glaciers. He took up the members of the San Su Strutters band, currently playing at the Palace Theater, as well as several members of the *Daily Alaska Empire* staff. A Loening OL-8A amphibian plane, No. 2, of the U.S. Naval Survey Detachment was a visitor, flying up from their base at Ketchikan. It made a second brief visit the next day.

On Saturday, August 31, 1929, Eckmann was off at 9:00 A.M. for Lake Dorothy, with Wendell Dawson, J.A. Cameron and H.L. Faulkner. Upon his return, he left for Lake Hasselborg with Mr. and Mrs. M.V. Manville, who would remain at the lake for a week on a fishing outing. Another flight to the lake, with fishermen, would be made that afternoon.

Construction of a landing field at Skagway, for land planes, was soon started, financed by the Territory and the town of Skagway, with the Alaska Road Commission performing the work. Completion early the following year was forecast. It was located a short distance from the White Pass & Yukon Railroad roundhouse, parallel to the river.

Eckmann was off in the Alaska-Washington Airways Vega at 2:30 P.M. Wednesday,

The **Juneau**, *NC 432E, rests at the ramp in Seattle. Painted blue with a cream trim, the plane was built almost entirely of wood, the fuselage composed of plywood laminations glued together in a press. It did not have a layer of fabric over the wood, as the later models did. Wood deteriorated rapidly as used in a seaplane. When sent to the Lockheed factory for rebuild at the end of the season, the plane was junked for economic reasons.*

Author's Collection

September 4, for Funter Bay, with Frank A. Metcalf, engineer and surveyor, there for a short time. Mrs. Metcalf and Mary Case also made the trip. O.A. Nelson and Charles L. Parker were picked up at Funter Bay on the return. Late that afternoon, the pilot went to Lake Dorothy, to the camp of E.J. Ela. From here, he continued on to the boundary, to leave supplies for Joe Hill, who was prospecting in the Taku district.

The *Ketchikan* left Juneau at 1:00 P.M. Thursday, September 5, for Wrangell, to take Fred Hanford and a prospector on a trip to a mining property near the Canadian border, north of Wrangell. Eckmann expected to remain overnight at the lake, returning to Juneau in the morning.

The morning of Saturday, September 7, 1927, was a big day for the kids in town. Alaska-Washington Airways had been running a guessing contest for some time, with two prizes: for the contestants guessing closest to the number of passengers (860) carried by the seaplanes, *Juneau* and *Ketchikan*, between April 15 and August 15, and for the contestants guessing closest to the number of miles traveled by the two seaplanes during this same period.

Tom Croson Collection

Alaska-Washington Airways began flying prospectors and miners into the Tulsequah district in summer, 1929. The central point was Eaton, British Columbia, on the Taku River, where the Customs station and Taku Trading Company were located. Although Anscel Eckmann, center figure, pilot of the Vega, flew the airplane, he also liked to dress well when there was business to do.

581

Alaska-Washington Airways **Ketchikan,** *NC 657E, at the Customs station at Eaton, British Columbia in the Tulsequah district. With mining development in the upper Taku River, the planes often crossed the border here. Anscel Eckmann, the pilot, second from left.*

Five winners were taken on a fifteen minute hop to Mendenhall Glacier by Eckmann. As soon as the plane unloaded, the five winners of the second part of the contest piled in, to be taken on a forty-five minute flight to Taku Glacier. Herman R. Vanderleest, Juneau druggist, sat in the cockpit with the pilot on both flights.

On Saturday, September 7, Alaska-Washington Airways received authority to land planes in the Taku River section of northern British Columbia from the Canadian Customs Service. There were about 150 men in the mining district now, and the temporary permit would facilitate servicing these camps across the border. The United States Weather Bureau, a week later, announced the establishment of an aircraft weather station, second class, in Ketchikan. There was one first class station in Fairbanks.

The *Ketchikan* was forced to lay over for the next several days because of poor weather. On Saturday, September 14, Eckmann was off for Eaton, British Columbia, in the Taku district, with Joe Hill, Buck Sperling and Mr. Sparky. In the afternoon he would go to a Canadian lake to bring out Bill McKenna and Mr. Dickinson, who had been there since August 14. Enroute to the Manville property at Eaton, the Vega took Doctor Robert Simpson to spend a few days there. If weather permitted, Eckmann planned to land at Lake Crescent, to pick up Tom Wilson and Tom Donahue, prospectors, who would have been brought in a week ago except for the stretch of bad weather.

At 8:30 A.M. Saturday, September 21, 1929, the Alaska-Washington Airways Vega was off for the Taku district with B.M. Behrends, Ben Mullen, H.L. Faulkner, Charles Goldstein and Ike Goldstein. Returning from there about noon, the pilot was off on his second trip to Port Alexander. Doctor R.N. Rogers, who brought his patient, Chris Jarov, to Juneau in the plane the night before, was the only passenger. The pilot returned to Juneau in the afternoon, to proceed to Skagway to pick up A.L. Hagar, who had been on a hunting trip, and bring him into Juneau.

After spending the night in the capital city, Eckmann was away, on Sunday, September 22, 1929, carrying passenger A.L. Hagar for Vancouver, British Columbia.

This would end Alaska-Washington Airways' flying in Southeastern Alaska for 1929. Major G.C. Frame, Division Manager of Alaska-Washington Airways, spoke at a luncheon meeting of the Juneau Chamber of Commerce on Thursday, November 21, 1929, of expanding plans for the company in the coming year, including more airplanes, more frequent schedules, and a possibility of air mail service.

Juneau was getting ready, in its own quiet way, when Doctor W.A. Borland received his appointment by the Department of Commerce as Flight Surgeon of the Alaska District. He was now prepared to make biannual examinations of aviators; as required by the laws governing commercial aviators in the United States and its Territories.

Walter P. Miller Photo

November 23, 1929. Alaska-Washington Airways first Seattle-Vancouver, British Columbia flight leaves in the **Juneau** *from the company's terminal on Lake Union with pilot Alex Holden and four passengers. Left to Right: Alex Holden, Miss Roma E. Ray, Assistant Secretary of the Rotary Club of Seattle, with a letter to the mayor of Vancouver, and President Joseph L. Carman, Jr., of the flying concern.*

U.S. Navy photo in the National Archives

584

Alaskan Aerial
Survey Detachment

U.S. NAVY
1929

44

THE UNITED STATES NAVY ANNOUNCED in Washington, D.C. on February 22, 1929, their intention of resuming the aerial mapping survey of Southeastern Alaska. The Alaskan Aerial Survey Expedition of 1926, under the command of Lieutenant Ben H. Wyatt, had been unable to complete the work, because of inclement weather during much of the summer of 1926. With the Departments of Agriculture and Interior pressing for a resumption, the navy planned to proceed with the mapping in the coming summer. The two departments transferred to the credit of the Navy Department a sum of $15,000 to cover the cost of extraordinary expenses to the navy. The region under survey was to include Chichagof and Baranof Islands, the Alaska-Canadian border, and cover sections of the Tongass National Forest not previously photographed.

Once again, the *U.S.S. Gannet, AVP-8*, served as tender; she had the ability of craning an aircraft onto her afterdeck. The covered barge, YF-88, used by the 1926 expedition, was again towed north by the *Gannet*, to serve as a movable base for the detachment. The 110 by 40 foot barge had been stored at the Puget Sound Naval Shipyard in Bremerton, Washington. Orders were issued for rehabilitation and repair of the craft.

Alaskan Aerial Survey Detachment photographers.
Left to Right: J.M.F. Haase, in charge, with T-2, K.J.
Nevose with Akley, P.L. Hansen with T-2, C. Blattman
with Newman K-3A, in San Diego before start of
survey.

Lieutenant Commander Arthur W. Radford, USN, was assigned to duty in charge of the Alaskan Aerial Survey Detachment, to be commissioned about April 15, 1929 at San Diego, California, as a detached unit of Aircraft Squadrons, Battle Fleet. Preparations for the assembly of personnel and material were under way.

Four factory-new Loening amphibian OL-8A aircraft were used in the survey, one assigned from VJ Squadron One-B, and three from the Loening factory on the East River in New York, shipped via the *U.S.S. Langley* to San Diego. Powered by the 450 horsepower Pratt & Whitney Wasp engine, the planes would be superior in performance to the Liberty-powered Loenings of the 1926 expedition. The four planes, as follows, were named after the Alaskan cities to be used as operating bases:

A8072	No. 1	JUNEAU — factory delivery date March 20, 1929
A8078	No. 2	KETCHIKAN — factory delivery date April 2, 1929
A8079	No. 3	PETERSBURG — factory delivery date April 4, 1929
A8076	No. 4	SITKA — factory delivery date March 8, 1929

An insignia known as the "flying seal" was adopted by the detachment. It showed a winged seal rising against a background of an active volcano and the midnight sun. The logo was painted on both sides of the fuselage of each aircraft.

C.H. Flory, district forester for Alaska, returned to Juneau on the *Yukon*, early in April; he had spent most of five months in Washington, D.C. working with the Departments of Navy, Agriculture and Interior on the mapping project. R.H. Sargent, topographic engineer of the Department of Agriculture would work with the party again. The detachment was planning to arrive in Southeastern Alaska about May 25, 1929, to begin the survey. Pulp and paper interests in Los Angeles and San Francisco: both Cameron-Chandler and Crown Zellerbach indicated they would continue their private surveys also during the summer.

The aircraft tender, *U.S.S. Gannet*, departed San Diego on May 6, 1929, to pick up the barge Yoke Fox-88 in Bremerton, and tow it north. The four planes, with a total crew of twelve officers and men left North Island Naval Air Station in San Diego on May 15, arriving at the Sand Point Naval Air Station in Seattle on May 17, after stops at Fresno and Oakland in California, and Medford, Oregon. Radford had suffered a forced landing at Fresno when a fuel pump failed on his aircraft, slightly damaging the left pontoon. It was quickly repaired and a new fuel pump installed; the flight proceeded north. A dinner and reception for the members of the aerial survey was being planned at the New Washington Hotel by the Seattle Chamber of Commerce. R.H. Sargent, representing the Department of the Interior, joined the detachment in Seattle, to fly north in one of the Loenings. Members of the detachment who had previously served with the 1926 expedition were Lieutenant E.F. Burkett, executive officer, Lieutenant R.F. Whitehead, photographic officer, Lieutenant Commander A.C. Smith, medical officer, and Lieutenant E.F. Carr, paymaster, as well as several members of the enlisted personnel.

The airplane tender, *Gannet*, departed the naval shipyard with the refurbished and restocked barge in tow, on May 20, 1929, to arrive in Ketchikan on May 24. A stop of six hours at Blinkensop Bay and at Namu Harbor was made during the night. Hooked to the towing bridle of the barge was a new eight-inch manila hawser. While towing the barge, a good long scope was kept on the tow in open spaces, and was shortened when navigating in narrow spaces; the barge was taken alongside when entering harbors and while going through narrows. A sharp watch was kept for floating logs.

The four planes of the detachment departed Seattle on the morning of Tuesday, May 21,

May 1929. U.S. Navy Loening A8078, Ketchikan, No. 2, taxis on the water near Saxman. The amphibians of the Alaskan Aerial Survey Detachment remained at Ketchikan for a few days before moving north to base at Petersburg to begin their photographic mapping. They were back in Ketchikan on August 19.

1929, but were forced to return by heavy fog off Cape Flattery. They departed a few hours later, when conditions improved, making it through to Alert Bay, British Columbia, where they were able to taxi the planes up onto the beach, just above high tide level, fueling them with aviation gas delivered in drums by Union Oil Company, Limited. Lieutenant Commander Radford's Loening was equipped with an SE-1385 radio set, enabling him to communicate with ground stations. The flight was held at the port by bad weather until late the following day, Wednesday, May 22. Passing over the *Gannet* enroute, the four planes landed on the waters of Tongass Narrows, after flying in formation over the incoming *Princess Louise*. The planes were secured on a beach at the Model Dairy farm, two miles down the channel, a spot used earlier by the 1926 expedition. Those of the detachment who made the flight with Lieutenant Commander Radford (naval aviator) were Lieutenant E.F. Burkett, executive officer (naval aviator); Lieutenant Commander A.C. Smith, medical officer, Lieutenant R.F. Whitehead, photographic and aerological officer (naval aviator), Lieutenant L.P. Pawlikowski, assistant operations officer (naval aviator), Lieutenant C.F. Greber, engineering officer (naval aviator),

J.M.F. Haase, CP in charge (chief photographer), W.L. Hicks, CRM, chief radioman, H.W. Trafton, AMM1c, machinists mate, T.L. Cox, AMM, machinists mate, E.W. Read, ACMM, machinists mate in charge, and H.E. Rineau, AMM1c, machinists mate. The thirteenth member on the flight was civilian R.H. Sargent, of the Geological Survey. To break the possible jinx, a miniature of a man had been procured in Seattle to make the party up to fourteen. The group checked in at the Ingersoll Hotel in Ketchikan upon their arrival.

The *U.S.S. Gannet* arrived in the city on Friday, May 24, 1929, to tie up with the covered barge at the Lighthouse Service Dock, one mile south of the city. A Chevrolet truck, transported on the stern of the tender, provided transportation for men and supplies to and from the dock and the operations beach at the Model Dairy site.

The Commercial Club was putting on a dance at the Eagles Hall that evening for the members of the detachment and the town folk, to get them better acquainted.

Although mapping operations could have been carried out from the beach site in Ketchikan, it was decided to move nearer to the major area to be mapped. Radford, Burkett and Sargent departed in two of the Loenings for the Petersburg area on Saturday, May 25 to look for a suitable site to base the detachment, possibly Petersburg or Sitka. When the two

May 25, 1929. Loening No. 1, **Juneau,** *leaving the Ketchikan base near the Model Dairy for a flight to Petersburg to investigate facilities there prior to moving north.*

U.S. Navy photo in the National Archives

June 17, 1929. Mr. Earl N. Ohmer, Mayor of Petersburg, with Lieutenant Commander A.W. Radford, U.S. Navy Commandant of the Alaskan Aerial Survey Detachment at Petersburg. Mayor Ohmer, "Shrimp King" of Alaska, owner of Alaska Glacier Sea Food Company, was the largest shipper of shrimp in the Territory.

planes returned, it was decided to move. On Monday, Many 27, 1929, the *Gannet* pulled away from the Lighthouse Service Dock at 8:00 A.M., with Yoke Fox-88 in tow, Mr. Sargent also aboard. The tender proceeded to Petersburg. The four planes hopped off about 1:30 P.M. to land at Wrangell for an overnight stay.

At Petersburg, the planes were parked on a narrow beach directly across Wrangell Narrows from the town, while the *Gannet* and barge were secured alongside the Citizens Wharf. The base was well established, with all preparations for mapping completed when good weather arrived on May 30. From here, the Islands of Kuiu, Coronation, Warren and the southern half of Baranof were photographed.

The survey was made by drawing flight lines on a chart, showing only the coast lines, four and one-half miles apart. The plane flew these lines, using a crew consisting of a pilot, a navigator and a cameraman, shooting with the T-2 four-lens camera through an open hatch in the bottom of the Loening, from an altitude of 10,900 feet. This gave a scale at sea level of 1-20,000. Details of lakes, rivers and mountains in the interior were desired; these could not be ascertained by the surface surveys along the coastlines that had been carried out for years.

In flight, the navigator tied lines from his cockpit to the pilot's arms and by pulling on these in a fashion similar to driving a horse, he directed the pilot to the proper course to be flown. Small lights, in the pilot's and navigator's cockpits, which could be turned on by the cameraman five seconds before a photograph was to be taken, warned the crewmen to keep the aircraft steady. Since there was an interval between exposures of about fifteen seconds, the navigator could adjust the pilot back onto course between shots if it was necessary. Cold weather at the mapping altitude, along with the open hatch, caused the crews to wear heavily padded flying suits, helmets and boots. Trouble with the camera shutters, sticking from the cold, was a problem at first. But they solved most of the difficulty by operating the cameras in the cold room of the Petersburg Cold Storage on June 7, observing and adjusting them. Plungers and bushings on the shutters were rubbed with crocus cloth and thoroughly cleaned; they functioned well on the next flight. Oblique photographs of certain areas were also made for various government agencies such as the Forest Service, Geological Survey and Lighthouse Service, using a K3-A mapping camera. Three 1000-foot reels of motion picture film, recording the detachment's activities, were taken for the Bureau of Aeronautics, as well as

June 5, 1929. Alaskan Aerial Survey Detachment Loening OL-8As warming up on the beach at Petersburg.

Pilots of the Alaskan Aerial Survey Detachment. Left to Right: Lieutenant R.F. Whitehead, Lieutenant C.F. Greber, Lieutenant Commander Arthur W. Radford, and Lieutenant E.F. Burkett, on beach across from Petersburg dock.

8000 feet of negative motion picture film which was exposed (later cut to 3000 feet in San Diego), using an Akley and a DeVry.

In Petersburg, Mayor Earl N. Ohmer and other civic officials assisted whenever

June 16, 1929. Loening OL-8A **Juneau,** *No. 1, over Petersburg, Alaska. Radford and Heintzleman were returning from Bradford Canal.*

U.S. Navy photo in the National Archives

June 15, 1929. Hoisting out No. 4, **Sitka,** *onto the* **Gannet** *at Petersburg. The Chevrolet truck carried by the survey can be seen on the deck.*

U.S. Navy photo in the National Archives

possible. Aviation gasoline was delivered by the Standard Oil Company of California to the dock in fifty gallon drums, at all bases per contract. The *Gannet*'s motor sailer transported gasoline, personnel and supplies across the narrows at Petersburg, to the beach where the planes were kept. A vacant house nearby was used by the men standing guard duty on the planes at night.

Radford had been wanting to get to Juneau to confer with Governor Parks and Commis-

June 16, 1929. OL-8A No. 1, **Juneau,** *with Lieutenant Commander A.W. Radford, pilot, and B.F. Heintzleman of the Forest Service enroute to Bradford Canal, twenty miles southeast of Wrangell, for the purpose of investigating timber and water power sites.*

▼ Juneau, 1929. Standing Left to Right: Commissioner Charles H. Flory, Lieutenant Commander Arthur W. Radford, Mr. R.H. Sargent, Frank Heintzleman. Seated: R. A. Zeller, Superintendent of Tongass National Forest and Lieutenant R.F. Whitehead.

U.S. Navy photo in the National Archives

U.S. Navy photo in the National Archives

592

sioner Charles H. Flory ever since his arrival in Ketchikan, but either weather or the press of business prevented it. Lieutenant Commander Radford and Lieutenant Richard Whitehead, flying their two Loenings, *Juneau* and *Sitka*, respectively, landed in Gastineau Channel at the capital city at 11:43 A.M. Friday, May 31, 1929. R.H. Sargent, director of the topographic work being done by the mappers, was also a member of the party. Most of the afternoon was spent with the governor and Mr. Flory, as well as looking over the harbor for a base for the planes, the *Gannet* and the scow camp. The other two planes were currently at work mapping Kuiu Island; the first mapping had begun the previous day. If weather conditions remained good at Petersburg Radford hoped to be able to move to Sitka to photograph all of Baranof and Chichagof Islands; then move the detachment to Juneau and photograph the mainland shores of Icy Strait, Lynn Canal and areas immediately adjacent to Juneau, including Taku River. The two planes returned to Petersburg late in the day, to carry on their work in good weather.

After returning to Petersburg, Radford had decided to forego the Sitka move in favor of a Juneau base. He could still do the Baranof-Chichagof work from there. The four planes of the detachment landed at Juneau at 9:40 A.M. Monday, June 17, 1929, making the trip in one hour and twenty-five minutes.

The *Gannet*, 150-foot tender for the detachment, was expected in with the barge at 6:45 P.M. The YF-88 was equipped with a complete photographic laboratory, a motor overhaul shop, dispensary, quarters for the aviation personnel, galley, mess room and office. The *Gannet* and its tow would tie up at Government Dock during its stay; the planes were later secured on the wharf; hoisted on and off with the *Gannet*'s boom. While operating here, the

June 21, 1929. Alaskan Aerial Survey detachment **U.S.S. Gannet AVP-8, Barge YF-88, and Loening OL-8As on Government Dock at Juneau. The Detachment's Chevrolet truck is in the foreground, with Gastineau Channel and Douglas Island in the background.**

U.S. Navy photo in the
National Archives

Islands of Chichagof, Kruzof, Yakobi and the northern half of Baranof, as well as sections of the mainland in the vicinity of Juneau were photographed. In the summer light, the work could go on from 8:00 A.M. to 4:00 P.M. in good weather; the hours decreasing as fall approached and shadows lengthened, from 9:00 A.M. to 3:00 P.M., and finally from 11:00 A.M. to 1:00 P.M.

Personnel on the planes were:

Plane No. 1, *Juneau* (which had radio equipment); Lieutenant Commander Radford, pilot, W.L. Hicks, chief radio mechanic, Cox, aviation chief mechanics mate.

Plane No. 2, *Ketchikan*; Lieutenant E.F. Burkett, pilot, Mr. Sargent, P. Johnson, aviation mechanics mate first class.

Plane No. 3, *Petersburg*; Lieutenant R.F. Whitehead, pilot, H.E. Reneau, aviation mechanics mate first class, J.M.F. Haase, chief photographer.

Plane No. 4, *Sitka*; Lieutenant C.F. Greber, pilot, H.W. Trafton, aviation mechanics mate first class, E.W. Read, aviation chief mechanics mate.

On the *Gannet* were: Lieutenant Commander A.C. Smith, medical officer, USN, Lieutenant E.F. Carr, paymaster, and Lieutenant L.P. Pawlikowski, pilot. Personnel of the *Gannet* were: Lieutenant Thomas Macklin, Commanding Officer, Glick, chief boatswain, Dowd, boatswain, and J.O. Hoey, machinist. There were also other enlisted personnel. The detachment expected to be in Juneau about six weeks. They had done their first mapping out of Petersburg on May 30, and up to June 20 had done only four days of aerial photography related to mapping, since clear, still weather was required.

The four Loenings had been based at a beach on Douglas Island since their arrival on Monday, June 17. On Thursday, June 20, the *Juneau* and *Sitka* were brought over in the morning and hoisted onto the dock. They were followed by the *Ketchikan* and *Wrangell* that same afternoon. According to Lieutenant Whitehead, the weather looked promising for mapping the next day. *Gannet* and barge held an open house for the capital city residents and

June 22, 1929. Oblique photo of Mendenhall Glacier to the northwest of Juneau taken during the survey.

594

visitors. The detachment reported finding, in a review of the recently taken photographs, the discovery of two chains of hitherto unknown lakes in the central part of Baranof Island.

The first photography done out of Juneau was accomplished on the morning of Saturday, June 22, when Lieutenant R.F. Whitehead, pilot of No. 3, flew to Skagway and return, taking oblique photographs of intermediate glaciers and land features. He was off at 8:00 A.M., returning shortly before noon. The pilot was accompanied by chief photographer Haase and aviation mechanics mate, 1c, Homer E. Reneau. At 1:15 P.M., Lieutenant Pawlikowski was away, with Haase and aviation chief mechanics mate Reed, to take photographs in the vicinity of Speel River. Higher clouds prevented the taking of mapping photographs. The detachment in Juneau was now composed of eight commissioned officers, three non-commissioned officers and ninety-nine enlisted men.

Saturday night, June 22, a combined service team from the detachment and the cutter *Snohomish*, was battling it out with a pickup team of Juneau locals on the ball diamond at City Park. The navy came out on top in the hotly-contested game, with a score of eight to seven; everyone had a good time. Side trips and lectures were planned for the navy men, including tours through the Alaska-Juneau mine and mill, Juneau Cold Storage, as well as side trips in the *Gannet*—one to Taku Glacier and the Taku cannery, Tracy Arm, a two-day trip to Skagway, and a longer one to Sitka.

Sunday, June 23, was an excellent day for mapping, with three of the Loenings in the air: No. 2, with Radford as pilot, working Baranof and Chichagof Islands, and plane No. 3, flown by Lieutenant Greber, working the Icy Strait region. Plane No. 4, flown by Pawlikowski, made a flight around Admiralty Island, taking oblique shots for the United States Forest

June 22, 1929. An oblique aerial photo of Skagway, Alaska taken for the Forest Service during the survey. Members of the Detachment made a recreational trip to the city in the **Gannet** *during their tour of duty in Juneau.*

595

Service. Monday was not good for mapping, but Lieutenant Commander Radford, with Cox and Hicks as additional crew, went to Wrangell in Plane No. 1. Accompanying him, flying plane No. 2, was Lieutenant Burkett, with enlisted men Johnson and McGuire. Charles H. Flory was aboard, as a passenger. The commissioner had Department of Agriculture business in Wrangell.

Lieutenant Whitehead was aloft for an hour's flight in the *Sitka* on the morning of Saturday, June 29, 1929, to check on weather conditions for mapping. Oblique shots in the local area were taken, including some good views of the old Perseverance Mine, Granite Creek Basin and the Salmon Creek Dam.

Waiting for days for the proper weather for aerial mapping, all four planes were aloft on Tuesday, July 9: Loening No. 2 and No. 4 in the morning, and No. 3 and No. 1 in the afternoon. Plane No. 2, piloted by Burkett, with J.P. Williams of the Forest Service; and No. 4 flown by Greber, with Harold Smith of the same agency, made a three-hour flight over Admiralty Island to allow a close observation of timber and water power resources of the island. Flying in formation, the two planes were back about one o'clock. In the afternoon, Loening No. 1, piloted by Radford, and No. 3, piloted by Whitehead, flew over the Stikine River district. Radford, with Lieutenant W.B. Scaife of the U.S. Coast and Geodetic Survey, who was engaged in making triangulation surveys of the Stikine district, as a passenger, returned about 3:00 P.M. Lieutenant Whitehead took oblique photographs of the coast, his cameraman leaning over the side of the cockpit with the heavy K3-A, between the Stikine River and Juneau on his return trip, arriving back about 4:30 P.M.

The planes were up again, in fine weather, on the following day. The *Sitka, Juneau, Ketchikan* and *Wrangell* were away before 8:00 A.M., with Radford, Burkett, Whitehead and Greber at the controls. They intended to map the north end of Baranof Island and other districts between Juneau and Sitka. It was the second day since their arrival in Juneau on June 17, clear enough for members of the detachment to take mapping photographs from the required altitude of 10,900 feet. A second flight to photograph Chichagof Island was planned for the afternoon.

Another beautiful day followed, Thursday, July 11, with one flight made by each of the two mapping planes. They had completed Baranof Island, about one-fourth of Chichagof Island and a portion of the mainland.

Lieutenant Commander Radford, in the *Juneau*, took R.A. Kinzie of the Chandler-Cameron pulp and paper interests on an inspection trip over Admiralty Island and the Speel River district, leaving at 9:30 A.M. Wednesday, July 17, and returning shortly before noon. Planes No. 2 and 3, with Lieutenants Burkett, Greber, Whitehead and Pawlikowski, flew mapping flights during the same time period. Burkett and Greber, in plane No. 2, mapped the Icy Strait district as far as Cape Fairweather and Lituya Bay, completing approximately 700 square miles, while No. 3 mapped on Chichagof Island. No. 3 was up again in the afternoon, with Whitehead and Pawlikowski, making a photographic flight between Juneau and Skagway. The previous day, the two airmen had taken planes No. 2 and 4 to Petersburg, carrying Major Douglas Gillette, of the Alaska Road Commission, on an inspection trip of the dredge working in Wrangell Narrows. They had left Juneau at 8:00 A.M. and returned at 2:30 P.M., making in six and one-half hours a trip that would have used up several days by boat.

Thursday, July 18, was a very successful day. A four-hour mapping and photographic flight by two of the planes, over the rugged country in the vicinity of Glacier Bay, with emphasis on the glacial fronts and glacier action, for the Geological Survey and the International Boundary Commission, included fifty oblique photographs, 400 feet of motion picture film and mapping photographs showing the fronts of thirteen large glaciers in the vicinity of

Glacier Bay; with close-up photographs of Mount Fairweather, 15,300 feet high; Mount Quincy Adams, 13,560 feet high; and Lituya Mountain (Mount Crillon) 11,750 feet in height, all were circled by the planes. The 1926 expedition, with their Liberty-powered Loenings, had not been successful in topping the range, but the OL8As, with their powerful Wasp radial engines, had taken many of the photographs from 15,000 feet. The *Ketchikan*, which took the mapping photographs, was crewed by Lieutenant E.F. Burkett, pilot, Lieutenant L.P. Pawlikowski, navigator, and K.J. Moore, photographer first class. The *Petersburg*, which took the oblique photographs at 12,000 feet, and flew above the *Ketchikan*, taking moving pictures of the plane as it mapped Brady Glacier, was crewed by Lieutenant R.F. Whitehead, pilot and photographic officer for the detachment, J.M.F. Haase, chief photographer, and D.D. Lore, chief yeoman. Haase was exhausted from cold and exertion from holding the heavy seventy-five pound oblique camera, over the side of the plane, working continuously at high altitudes.

On Friday, July 26, 1929, the two Loenings: *Juneau*, piloted by Radford; and the *Sitka*, piloted by Pawlikowski; took off at 9:00 A.M. for Sitka on the official trip. Making the flight were R.H. Sargent, Geological Survey, Major Malcolm Elliott, Alaska Road Commission, Chief Radioman W.L. Hicks and Aviation Machinists Mate T.L. Cox, of the detachment.

Thursday, August 1, 1929, was a good day for mapping, motion pictures and oblique photography. Two mapping flights were made, in the morning and afternoon, over Chichagof Island. Radford piloting plane No. 2 with Pawlikowski and K.J. Moore, photographer first class, and Lieutenant Greber, piloting plane No. 4, with Burkett and B.L. Houser, photographer first class, made the flights. A three-man crew was necessary because the pilot's attention was on flying the plane; the navigation officer concentrated on directing the pilot in such a manner that the intended track, marked on the chart, was closely followed, as well as making adjustments for variation in ground speed. The photographer's whole attention was on the actual camera operation.

U.S. Navy photo inthe National Archives

July 31, 1929. Loening No. 2 Ketchikan, *returning to U.S.S.* Gannet *after mapping flight over Chichagof Island. The sixteen-foot crutches, well padded, were used to fend the plane away from the tender.*

597

Lieutenant Whitehead, accompanied by J.M.F. Haase and H.E. Reneau in plane No. 3, made a flight this same day as far west as Cape Fairweather, taking oblique pictures along the seacoast from there, eastward to Icy Strait. The plane returned to Juneau at 2:00 P.M. Following these flights, the four Loenings took off, with Radford and Doctor Philip Sidney Smith, Geological Survey, in No. 1, Burkett and Doctor A.C. Smith, detachment surgeon, in No. 2, Greber and B.D. Stewart, mining supervisor for the U.S. Bureau of Mines, in No. 4, and Whitehead, with Chief Photographer Haase, in No. 3. The amphibians flew up the Taku River and back to Juneau over the Taku Glacier, and down by way of Norris and Lemon Glaciers. Haase filmed both moving and oblique shots of the other three planes while flying in formation.

Friday, August 2, was another fine day. Burkett, with Greber and Houser, made two mapping flights over Chichagof Island in No. 4. Pawlikowski, piloting plane No. 2, with Radford as navigator and Moore as photographer, made mapping flights to the Glacier Bay area, to Johns Hopkins Glacier, and the peninsula between Glacier Bay and Lynn Canal. The work done in the plane by Lieutenant Burkett, on Friday, completed the mapping of Chichagof Island. This finished Kuiu, Baranof and Chichagof Islands, as well as practically all the work in the vicinity of Glacier Bay. Lieutenant Whitehead, flying Loening No. 3, made a flight around Chichagof and Baranof Islands, from Icy Straits to Sitka, and circled Mount Edgecumbe, taking many oblique shots. Burkett, mapping Chichagof, had also made a run across, from the side of Glacier Bay to the mouth of the Chilkat River, across the head of Adams and Davidson Glaciers. Things were going well.

On Saturday, August 3, 1929, Radford, Greber and Houser, in plane No. 4, made a mapping run up the Taku River as far as the International Boundary, leaving Juneau at 7:30 A.M. and returning four hours later. In the same plane, Greber flying and Radford navigating, with Houser still as photographer; they made a mapping flight to the Speel River district, taking off at 1:10 P.M. and returning to Juneau at 3:20 P.M. Greber, in plane No. 2, with a machinists mate and Major R.Y. Stewart of a congressional party as passengers, also made a flight over the Speel River district. On Saturday Whitehead, with navigator Pawlikowski and photographer Moore, made a trip in Loening No. 2 in the morning. They flew up the Stikine River as far as the International Boundary, later returning to Wrangell to change the

August 3, 1929. Oblique photo of the capital city of Juneau taken during the survey. Alaska-Juneau mine and mill are prominently shown to the right of the city.

U.S. Navy photo in the National Archives

film and fuel the plane. In the afternoon, Whitehead changed planes with Burkett, who flew to Wrangell to make arrangements for gassing the other plane when it returned from the Stikine trip. Lieutenant Burkett, piloting Plane No. 2, continued the mapping work in the vicinity of the Stikine River, begun by Lieutenant Whitehead that morning.

Whitehead, in plane No. 1, made a flight lasting from 12:10 P.M. until 5:40 P.M. over Baranof Island, taking oblique shots. He flew south from Sitka, taking photos of the lakes discovered in the lower end of Baranof Island during the mapping flights.

Sunday morning, August 4, Radford, piloting plane No. 1, with Haase and W.L. Musgrove, seaman first class, whose specialty was parachutes, made a mapping flight up the Taku River. In the afternoon, the pilot took Philip S. Smith, chief Alaska geologist with the Geological Survey; and Lieutenant Commander A.C. Smith, detachment surgeon, for a flight up the Whiting River, north along the International Boundary and across the head of Speel River (at the end of Snettisham), up to the headwaters of the Taku River, and back by Devils Thumb (on the Alaska-Canada boundary), and over Mount Juneau. It was a spectacular flight over some very rugged country.

Lieutenant Burkett, the same day, in Loening No. 3 with Whitehead and Moore, made morning and afternoon flights, mapping the International Boundary between Whiting and Taku Rivers. Lieutenant Pawlikowski, piloting plane No. 4, with Greber and House, also made two mapping flights in the district between Tracy Arm and Taku Inlet.

Monday, August 5, Radford, with Haase and Cox, piloting plane No. 1, was off Juneau at 10:10 A.M. to take oblique photographs of Taku Inlet and Berners Bay, to the north. They were back at 1:15 P.M. Whitehead, with Burkett and Houser, left at 9:40 A.M. in No. 3, for Berners River, on a three-hour flight, where mapping photographs were taken. Lieutenant Greber, flying plane No. 4 with Pawlikowski as navigator and Moore as photographer, was off at 9:50 A.M. for a mapping flight on the Yayik Peninsula between Chilkat and Chilkoot Inlets, up the Chilkat and Kichini Rivers to the International Boundary. They returned at 1:55 P.M.. In the afternoon, Burkett and Hicks took B.D. Stewart, in Loening No. 1, for a two-hour flight up the Whiting River to the International Boundary, north along the boundary, across the head of Speel River to Taku and Tulsequah Rivers for about ten miles, and returned to Juneau. The rapid increase of prospecting and mining in the Tulsequah and Taku Rivers district drew the interest of Mining Supervisor Stewart, of the U.S. Bureau of Mines, to the geology of the region as viewed from the air.

The Alaskan Aerial Survey Detachment had been in Juneau for about six weeks and, with the good weather in August, was rapidly winding up its work in the area. A few short runs in the Speel River and Lynn Canal sections remained. Most of Southeastern Alaska was complete, with some remaining in the Cape Fanshaw area, to be done from Ketchikan.

The *U.S.S. Gannet* left Juneau at 4:00 A.M. Monday, August 12, taking one of the Loenings on board, so that the officers and men involved in mapping could quickly return to Juneau if the current weather cleared. The barge was left at the dock. Basically a recreation trip, the *Gannet*, under Captain Thomas Macklin, would remain over in Skagway; affording the personnel a chance to visit Lake Bennett, via the White Pass and Yukon Railway. On Tuesday night, August 13, the band from the *Dorothy Alexander* gave a dance for the detachment members in Skagway. The "flying seal" insignia, designed at North Island in San Diego, was painted on the cliff, adjacent to the railway station, where the names of many of the Alaskan steamers appeared, including that of the *Gannet*, which had been placed there when she served with the 1926 expedition. The detachment members were amazed at the profusion of beautiful flowers in Skagway, returning to Juneau with armfuls when they arrived back at

▲ *August 10, 1929. Officers and men of the Alaskan Aerial Survey Detachment on the dock at Juneau, Alaska. Plane No. 1, Juneau, in the background. Mr. R.H. Sargent, Topographical engineer of the Geological Survey in center.*

▼ *August 10, 1929. Officers of the Alaskan Aerial Survey Detachment and the U.S.S. Gannet pose in front of Lieutenant Commander Radford's Loening on the dock at Juneau. Standing, Left to Right: Boatswain F.E. Dowd, Chief Boatswain J.D. Glick, Lieutenant J.G. L.P. Pawlikowski, Lieutenant C.F. Greber, Lieutenant R.F. Whitehead, Lieutenant E.F. Burkett, Machinist J.O. Hacy. Seated: Lieutenant E.F. Carr, Lieutenant Commander A.C. Smith, Lieutenant Commander A.W. Radford, Mr. R.H. Sargent, Lieutenant Thomas Macklin.*

3:00 P.M. Wednesday, August 14, 1929.

Discovery of a lake by the Alaskan Aerial Survey Detachment, capable of between 20,000 and 25,000 horsepower throughout the year, was announced on August 13 by B.F. Heitzleman, Assistant District Forester. Important to the pulp and paper industry, the lake was located on the east shore of Taku Inlet, between Greeley Point and Jaw Point, about two and one-half miles from the beach at about 2500 feet above sea level, and was about seventeen miles from Juneau. Anscel Eckmann, in the Lockheed Vega, *Ketchikan*, was to take E.J. Ela, engineer in charge of hydro-electric surveys for Chandler-Cameron pulp and paper interests, into the lake (later named Lake Dorothy by Lieutenant Commander Radford, in honor of his wife) on August 22 for an initial inspection. (see Juneau—1929, Chapter 43).

R.H. Sargent made a plea to the locals for a reduction in the amount of debris they were dumping into the waters of the Juneau harbor. Danger to the amphibian aircraft of the navy and civil companies during takeoff and landing from floating logs and other solid material was obvious, as well as to a lesser degree to boats. Boat operators had to be warned against operating in proximity to the aircraft.

Lieutenant Commander Radford came out in a Chamber of Commerce meeting with a strong recommendation for a first class airport, with facilities for both land and seaplanes; to be ready to reap rewards from the developments sure to take place in the next few years. A good site was available for both facilities on the flats near Mendenhall.

On Saturday, August 17, 1929, the *U.S.S. Gannet*, under Captain Thomas Macklin, the barge YF-88, and the four Loenings departed for Ketchikan, by way of Petersburg. The Alaskan Aerial Survey Detachment, with a complement of 110 officers and men, under the command of Lieutenant Commander Radford, had been based at the capital city since mid-June. The four planes were hoisted from Government Dock at 6:00 A.M. and the *Gannet*, with barge in tow, got underway a half hour later. Taking off for Lake Hasselborg with Governor George A. Parks, Henry O'Malley and Harry G. Watson, as guests, the flight would remain until after lunch at the lake to enjoy the trout fishing, going on to Petersburg in the afternoon.

In plane No. 1, flown by Radford, were Governor Parks and Chief Radio Mechanic Hicks; Lieutenant Burkett, flying No. 2, carried A.C. Smith, E.F. Carr and Aviation Mate Johnson. Lieutenant Whitehead, piloting plane No. 3, carried Mr. O'Malley, Haase and Aviation Mechanics Mate Reneau. No. 4, flown by Lieutenant Greber, took Mr. Watson, and Mechanics Mates Cox and Trafton. The U.S. Fisheries boat, *Brant*, Captain Earl Hunter, left for Petersburg to meet the civilians there and return them to Juneau on the next day.

The *Gannet* and barge, as well as the four planes, were in Petersburg overnight. After leaving there the morning of Monday, August 19, the flight ran into heavy weather. The planes arrived in Ketchikan in a driving rainstorm, bucking a thirty mile per hour headwind. They landed with some difficulty at the same Model Dairy beach about 11:00 A.M. after having first set down in the vicinity of Wards Cove. The *Gannet*, out of Petersburg at 6:00 A.M., was having trouble with its tow in the strong wind and waves. The heavy rains continued for some days, with roads and bridges washed out and houses undermined, bringing the detachment's work to a standstill.

To the north, there remained two important strips to be photographed south of the Taku River, which would be done from Ketchikan. By now the planes had been hoisted to the deck of the Lighthouse Service Dock. On Tuesday, August 27, three Loenings were hoisted down and put in the water. Plane No. 2, with Burkett, pilot, Pawlikowski and Moore, left shortly after 10:00 A.M. making a successful mapping flight in the area between the Chickamin River and Hyder. Plane No. 4, Greber, pilot, with Radford and Houser, flew northward to map the district in the vicinity of Unuk River and Burroughs Bay. After climbing to 10,900 feet, the mapping altitude, a minor casualty occurred to the camera and the plane returned to base. Plane No. 3, with pilot Whitehead, Haase and Watson, left shortly after the other two, flying southward, circling Revillagigedo Island, taking oblique photos of various timber projects, lighthouses and powersites.

*August 26, 1929.
Alaskan Aerial
Survey Detachment
planes on the
Lighthouse Service
Dock in Ketchikan.*

At 2:40 P.M. Thursday, August 29, 1929, Loening No. 2, with Lieutenant Burkett as pilot, and R.A. Zeller, supervisor of Tongass National Forest as a passenger, took off for Prince of Wales Island on a survey for a possible wagon road across the island. Such a road would mean that a great deal of travel to Craig and Hydaburg could be made regardless of weather conditions. For those who had ever been stormbound on the west coast of Prince of Wales, waiting for better weather until passage by boat around Cape Chacon was safe, could well understand the need. Upon reaching the island, the *Ketchikan* flew up Kasaan Bay to Karta Bay, then across to Klawok Inlet, south to Port Saint Nicholas, and back to Karta Bay in search of such a location. The plane returned to Ketchikan at 4:15 P.M. with the data.

On Friday, August 30, Radford was working in the vicinity of Unuk River in the morning, but returned to base without pictures, because of cloudy weather. Lieutenant Burkett, with navigator Pawlikowski and photographer Haase, left for Juneau in plane No. 2. They were unable to work from their mapping altitude of 10,900 feet but ran a photo mosaic from 8000 feet over Lake Dorothy and two smaller lakes, which would be satisfactory in showing their location in reference to the shoreline. Two more runs became necessary to complete the Taku district, and four runs between Juneau and Petersburg. The plane stopped in Juneau for a short period to gas at the Standard Oil dock.

The following day, Saturday, August 31, the same crew and plane made a second run at Lake Dorothy, but was again thwarted by the cloud level in attempting to map the same area from the normal mapping altitude. While over Lake Dorothy, the pilot observed the Alaska-Washington Airways Vega, piloted by Eckmann, land and later take off from the lake's surface. Again the Loening No. 2 fueled at Juneau. Climbing to altitude, the crew brought out their coffee and sandwiches, enjoying them while enroute to Ketchikan, where they landed at 5:20 P.M.

Plane No. 4 with Greber as pilot, Radford and Houser, was off that same day, about 10:50 A.M., again working the Unuk area. After two hours the plane returned to Ketchikan, with nothing accomplished, landing at 1:00 P.M. About 3:00 P.M. Radford, flying plane No. 1 with Don Meldrum, consulting engineer for the Chandler-Cameron and Crown Zellerbach paper interests, and E.B. English, pharmacists mate 1c, took off, along with No. 3, flown by Greber with F. Lofgren and D.W. Ponder, machinists mates, and with R.H. Sargent, to the north, up Behm Canal to Neets Bay, to inspect a low pass between Orchard Lake and Carroll Inlet. Continuing up Behm Canal, the flight turned eastward, passing close by Bell Island, and up the Unuk River to the vicinity of the International Boundary line. Returning to Behm Canal, they inspected some other sites, flying on to Ketchikan to land at 5:30 P.M.

Disappointing weather continued for a time. *Gannet* made a recreational trip to Prince Rupert, British Columbia, for the detachment personnel, who enjoyed it immensely. Upon the tender's return to Ketchikan the morning of Thursday, September 5, 1929, fortune smiled with a period of good weather. Two planes, No. 2 flown by Pawlikowski, with Burkett and Moore, went to the Unuk River area and completed four runs, successfully making one hundred ninety exposures (one full roll in the mapping camera). Plane No. 3, flown by Greber with Whitehead and Houser, went to the southeast about the same time, finding Boca de Quadre in the clear, completing three runs, using up their entire roll of film. Developing the film on the barge, all was found usable. Both planes arrived back about 1:30 P.M. The detachment was looking forward to a departure for home by September 14.

With the season's work so well along, and shadows lengthening in the mountains, mapping was cut to only two hours a day; suitable lighting had become so limited. Now the weather forecast on Friday, September 6, was the final straw—resulting in a decision to end the work. An immense "low" showed on the weather map, indicating the approach of one of the annual equinoctial storms which would last for days. Rather than be stormbound for an indefinite period, plans were made for an early departure.

On Saturday afternoon, September 7, the *Gannet* with barge in tow, and the four Loenings, departed Ketchikan for Seattle, taking the entire detachment. It was already raining in Wrangell, seventy-five miles to the north. The four planes made an overnight stop at Alert Bay, before proceeding down the Inside passage, between Vancouver Island and the mainland, to arrive at Sand Point Naval Air Station on Sunday, September 8. The *Gannet*, and barge YF-88, arrived in Seattle the following Thursday, September 19, with the entire detachment now gathered at Sand Point, on Lake Washington. The planes were overhauled for the flight south, and photographic work for the Departments of Interior and Agriculture was completed.

The *Gannet*, with YF-88 in tow, left for the Puget Sound Naval Shipyard in Bremerton on Monday, September 16, where the barge was turned in. The vessel left for San Diego the next day, to resume her normal duties as aircraft tender at that station.

Seattle was into the normal fall fog season caused by moist air, mixed with the smoke of burning logging slash drifting down from Vancouver Island and other Canadian mainland areas, where the rules called for such burning each fall. Forest fires in Washington and Oregon added to the problem. It wasn't until Friday, September 20, 1929, that the flight of four planes was able to leave, flying to Corning, California via Eugene, Oregon. The flight departed Corning at 10:50 A.M. the next morning and, with a stop at Long Beach airport, arrived at San Diego at 5:25 P.M. Saturday September 21, 1929. The *Gannet* arrived the following day.

The four Loenings; *Juneau, Ketchikan, Petersburg* and *Sitka* were turned over to VJ Squadron One-B, and the detachment went out of commission on October 31, 1929. The group had flown 677:40 hours during the season, using 16,887 gallons of gasoline. They had exposed forty-two rolls of "D", or fourth lens film. They had also made 692 oblique exposures, and printed approximately 5600 prints from these for government agencies. It had been an extremely successful project, with no accidents or incidents to mar it, a credit to the rugged planes and the men who flew and maintained them. It was not until 1932 that further work of this nature would be done by the navy in Alaska.

Note: Lieutenant Eugene F. Burkett, who had served with both the 1926 and the 1929 aerial surveys, was killed in an aviation accident near San Diego, California, when his Navy amphibian spun in from 1500 feet on January 7, 1930. It was announced in Washington, D.C. on May 22, 1930, that a mountain pinnacle seven miles north of Devils Thumb would be named Mount Burkett, in his memory.

September 1, 1929. Metlakatla, Alaska taken during the survey.

Gordon Graham Collection

Gorst Air Transport, Incorporated

Cordova 1929

THE RESIDENTS OF CORDOVA, Alaska were still awaiting the arrival of a first airplane in their community. A deepwater port, the city was served by the steamers that traveled between the States and the port of Seward, to the west. The Copper River and Northwestern Railroad provided transportation from dockside, through Eyak Pass, and up the Copper River valley, via Chitina, to the thriving mining community of Kennicott, also bringing back the ore from the Kennecott mines to be dumped in the holds of ships for transport to a smelter. The Kennecott Mines Company had misspelled the name.

A.A. Bennett had, on March 13, 1928, attempted to bring in Neil W. Rice, vice-president of the Fairbanks Exploration Company, to catch the steamer *Yukon* for the States. He planned to land on the ice of Eyak Lake near the city. Unable to make it through the pass in the vicinity of Mount Hayes, the pilot had returned to Fairbanks.

Owen Meals had flown over from Valdez on Wednesday, June 27, 1928, intending to land at Mile 17 along the railroad, but circled the area and returned to Valdez without landing. There was no windsock at the site to determine wind direction and he felt uneasy about setting

May 9, 1929. Keystone Loening **Alaskan** *on* **Eyak Lake**. *The amphibian, photographed by Howard W. Steward, is moored in Ecklund Slough for protection from storm and wind. The following day while aloft in the plane, the photographer was married to a local schoolteacher, Henrietta Brown.*

607

down. Meals tried again on July 3, 1928, but encountered weather enroute, and returned to Valdez.

The Chamber of Commerce in Cordova had an active airplane committee composed of F.A. Hansen, Jim Galen, Doctor Norman D. Hall and Doctor W.H. Chase. The community had under consideration four possible sites for a landing field. The Nelson townsite field was considered inaccessible because of the steeply rising terrain about it. The ball park, the best because it was close to the city, would be too expensive an undertaking to develop into an airfield. A flat area at Mile 13 (thirteen miles out of town on the railroad) was considered as another possibility but considerable runoff from glacier melt caused swampy areas, although it was clear of the mountains. (The airport in use today was eventually built on this site.)

At Mile 17, on the railroad, a large flat area could be cleared of brush and made into a field with little expense. While there was a road from town for a few miles out along Eyak Lake, the Mile 13 and Mile 17 sites were some distance from the community and communications and travel to and from would depend on the railroad.

Arriving in Cordova on Thursday, May 24, 1928, Governor Parks and Robert J. Sommers, chief Territorial highway engineer, met with the airplane committee, who recommended a site at Mile 6, located at the end of the road from town, although it was close to the mountains. Sommers inspected all the sites but the topography at its location ruled out the Mile 6 location as impractical. He considered it too confining, with insufficient room for a plane to maneuver safely in and out of the site. However, he stated he would have the proposed location further investigated by an experienced aviator as to its feasibility. Sommers made a selection of the Mile 17 site as the only practical location for an airfield. Construction was planned to begin on a Territorial airport here as soon as it could be arranged.

Gorst Air Transport, Incorporated, had a strong interest in Alaska. Vern C. Gorst, the owner, was an old-time Alaskan. He came north in the gold rush days, spending six years mining in the Klondike country. Now fifty-seven years old, he was an ardent flier, and was operating Seattle Flying Service, a flight operation and aircraft repair service in Seattle.

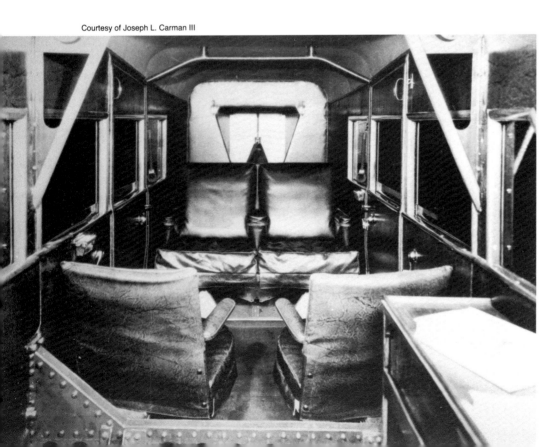

Cabin interior of the Keystone Loening Alaskan, *looking rearward. The roomy plane had six seats, with a seventh that could be made available when needed.*

Recently, in April, he had made a flight up through Southeastern Alaska, and was now prepared for more. A wire sent to the company in late April of 1929, requesting a plane to fly six members of the Alaska legislature from Juneau to Cordova as soon as the legislature adjourned, brought an immediate response.

At 4:00 P.M. Wednesday, May 1, 1929, Clayton L. Scott, a commercial pilot who had first soloed in February of 1927, left Seattle in an empty airplane, a Keystone Loening Air Yacht C-2-C, NC 9728, accompanied only by Gorst's chief mechanic, Gordon Graham. He landed at Alert Bay, British Columbia, three hours later. Remaining overnight, the fliers departed for Ketchikan in the morning. Running into poor flying weather some miles south of Bella Bella, the Loening pressed on northward until heavy rain and a dense fog forced them to land at the Canadian community, two hours and twenty minutes after their departure from Alert Bay. Later in the day they flew on to Butedale, British Columbia, a one-hour and twenty minute flight. The side-by-side cockpit, with its dual controls, gave the two airmen a chance to communicate although, being open to the slipstream and behind the 525 horsepower Wright Cyclone air-cooled engine, it was rather noisy. There was a door that led down into the empty passenger cabin, with its six seats, and a seventh which could be made available. The aircraft was painted a bright yellow, with top of fuselage and hull a contrasting blue.

Scott and Graham made the two-hour flight to Ketchikan on Friday, May 3, landing in Tongass Narrows shortly after 11:00 A.M. Fueling the Loening at the Forestry dock, the pilot waited for cabled instructions from Juneau. The Cordova trip was in doubt; apparently the legislators who were to travel were not firm in their commitment. The cost of $125 per passenger may have had something to do with their dampened enthusiasm. There were, however, passengers in Juneau for Ketchikan and, while the finances of taking the plane on to Cordova were being thrashed out, Scott took the *Alaskan*, as it was named, to Petersburg and Juneau the same day they arrived in Ketchikan; each of the two flight segments taking one hour and twenty-five, and one hour and twenty minutes, respectively. A passenger, W.W. Noyes, traveled from Ketchikan to Petersburg on the flight.

Scott landed the Loening amphibian in Gastineau Channel at four o'clock in the afternoon and, remaining overnight, departed the harbor at 10:30 A.M. Saturday, May 4, for Ketchikan. Two members of the House of Representatives, E.R. Tarwater and A.H. Ziegler were aboard. A stop at Petersburg, one hour and fifteen minutes later, was made to pick up two additional passengers before making the next hour and fifteen minute flight on to Ketchikan, where Scott circled the plane about the steamship *Alaska* as she came into port and docked. This maneuver on the part of the pilot was not without its purpose; Scott hopped passengers for the balance of that day and most of the next two days, many of them tourists from the passenger ship.

Cordova, in a fever of excitement over the intended visit of their first plane, was preparing a series of events to fill the welcoming program. Now, with cancellation of the flight certain, the residents felt let down until a wire was received from Scott, saying he would make the trip if he could book four passengers. The Chamber of Commerce immediately responded that they would supply $250 toward the expense of making the flight.

Scott departed Ketchikan on Monday, May 6 and, with a stop at Petersburg, arrived in Juneau at 5:30 P.M. In preparation for the Cordova trip, the two airmen went over the plane, taking it up for a ten-minute test hop that evening. Two reserve drums of aviation gasoline were loaded in place in the passenger cabin, where fuel could be valved from them into the main tank. Each drum held thirty gallons.

The morning of Tuesday, May 7, 1929, the two airmen were making final preparation for the flight up the Gulf of Alaska to Cordova. Three passengers were to make the trip: Paul Abbot, Alaska representative for E.I. Du Pont DeNemours & Company, State Representative Joseph H. Murray, and H.W. McDermott, Juneau representative of Gorst Air Transport, Incorporated. Scott boarded the plane a few minutes before departure to stow baggage in the rear of the already crowded cabin. Lifting up a coat before placing the bags, he was startled to see movement in the space behind the rear seats. Out scrambled two fair stowaways, Mae Pauly, leader of a local theater orchestra, and Lorraine McLeod, former resident of Ketchikan. Equipped with lunch and a bottle of water, the girls were planning a free ride on the epochal flight. The two young ladies were invited ashore and the registered passengers boarded.

Taxiing out from Robert Keeney's float, Scott warmed the 525 horsepower Cyclone engine by circling in the channel. Heading into the wind and gaining speed, the heavily-loaded *Alaskan* lifted clear of the water after a quarter-mile run. It was 10:41 A.M. A strong wind was blowing in the area, and Scott wrestled with the controls in the turbulent air as he flew down Gastineau Channel. But after about fifteen minutes of flight this condition smoothed out, and the pilot, now at 1500 feet, headed for Soapstone Point, where he crossed the wireless station at 11:17 A.M., turning to a course for Cape Spencer to continue the 460-mile flight to Cordova. While Russ Merrill, Roy J. Davis and Cyril Krugner had flown up the coast from Juneau to Seward in their Curtiss F flying boat in August of 1925, this would be the first commercial flight over the route with paying passengers.

Flying at 4000 feet, the two airmen could see the fog coming in as they crossed Cape Spencer, covering the shoreline up to about 3000 feet on the slopes. To the south lay a solid blanket of fog but the way ahead, above the cloud layer, was clear; the sharp, snow-covered peaks on their right thrusting up to 14,000 feet. Cruising at about one hundred miles per hour with their 2800 pound load, the Keystone Loening Air Yacht with its 525 horsepower Wright Cyclone, air-cooled engine performed faultlessly. Skirting along the mountains, the airmen encountered a clear stretch in the fog at Dry Bay, which continued all the way to Yakutat. Below them stretched a wide sand beach on which they could have landed in the event of trouble. An offshore landing with the amphibian was possible but it would be dangerous if the plane drifted to shore and there was any surf running at the beach line.

They crossed the fishing village northeast of Ocean Cape at 12:50 P.M., and were reported over by the wireless station there. Crossing to Icy Bay by skirting along the vast

Gorst airplane, Alaskan, arrived at City Dock, Cordova, Alaska following its flight up the Gulf of Alaska from Juneau on May 7, 1929.

Tuesday, May 7, 1929. H.W. Steward was on hand to photograph the passengers and crew of the Loening Alaskan when it arrived at Cordova from Juneau. Right to left: Abbot, mechanic Graham, pilot Scott, McDermott and Murray.

Gordon Graham Collection

moraine of Malaspina Glacier, the flight began to encounter fog again; the drifting pack ice, which had calved from the glacier face at the head of the bay, presented a beautiful sight framed in the shifting fog surrounding the scene. Harbor seals were visible on the ice below.

Crossing here, and flying in sun-filled skies, the plane passed over deepening fog that covered the shore line. Keeping at 4000 feet, Scott guided the plane inland about three miles from the shore, skirting along the mountains and across Bering Glacier to Katalla. Representative Murray, making his first flight, was enthralled by the scenery. It would have taken him thirty-eight to forty hours by boat to make the same trip.

From Katalla, they crossed the Copper River delta and, in good weather, the big blue and yellow plane came in over the city of Cordova, circling down to the bay, as steam whistles, electric sirens and horns of every description were blown by way of welcome. Half the residents of the city were down at the dock; the aviation committee had given advance warning of the expected arrival. Scott landed the plane near the government float at the City Dock at 3:01 P.M. Tuesday, May 7, 1929. The flight had been accomplished in four hours and twenty minutes and the engine had consumed 140 gallons of gasoline.

The plane was met by the Chamber of Commerce reception committee in the launch, *Kittiwake*. With the tide running strong in the bay, the pilot decided to move the Loening to Eyak Lake. Taking along five courtesy passengers: Miss Dorothy Dooley, E.W. Sandell, Doctor W.H. Chase, L.C. Pratt and Alan Craig Faith, he circled over the city to make a fine landing on the lake. The plane was safely moored.

Scott had wired ahead regarding fuel. Captain William Crooker left for the refinery at Katalla with his boat *Fidelity*, and was expected to return soon with aviation gas for the Gorst plane. In the meantime 150 gallons of fuel had been found locally. Gorst representative McDermott began lining up customers to go up on sightseeing trips; the fare was to be five dollars for local hops and ten dollars for extended trips over the mountains. Two half-hour flights around the mountains were made the same evening of their arrival at Cordova.

It stormed the following day. A banquet for 150, honoring the fliers, was set for 7:00 P.M. of Wednesday, May 8, in the Elks Hall; the regular meeting of the brotherhood had been postponed until the following week. At the banquet, Toastmaster Will Chase and other civic dignitaries welcomed the fliers, while Scott and Graham responded further, regaling the guests with stories of incidents that occurred in the plane during the flight. Scott stated he was impressed with the beauty of Alaska, and saw the country between Juneau and Cordova, not as a barrier to aviation, but ideal for air travel with an amphibian plane. He saw Cordova as a seaplane base rather than an airport site, but hoped they could have both; possibly finding a site for an airport on the other side of the mountains, in the flats along the railroad. Howard W. Steward, of Peter Pan Studios, took a flash picture of the banquet scene, following up the next afternoon by photographing the plane in Ecklund Slough on Eyak Lake.

Loading 150 gallons of Chilkat aviation gasoline, Scott flew the *Alaskan* from Cordova to Valdez, making the flight in forty-five minutes by way of Prince William Sound, landing at Valdez at 6:25 P.M. Thursday, May 9, 1929, with six passengers. He left at 7:30 P.M. that same evening, returning to Cordova with baker Pete Maas, J.W. Gilson and Mrs. W.T. Stuart, taking another forty-five minutes on this return flight. He made a thirty-minute passenger hop in Cordova on his arrival.

Scott returned to Valdez on Friday, May 10, with six Cordovans: Mr. and Mrs. Sid Stewart, Mrs. Fannie Farrell, Mrs. Oscar Olson, Ed Herman and Victor Swanberg. Landing at

May, 1929. Eyak Lake, close by Cordova, made an excellent seaplane base for the Loening amphibian. The biplane did not soak up water like many wood-structured planes that were used on floats; it had duralumin-covered hull and duralumin rib structure in wing and tail planes. The 525 horsepower Wright Cyclone engine was also a strong, reliable powerplant.

Gordon Graham Collection

hibian plane "Alaskan" on Lake Eyak near Cordova Alaska

8:05 A.M., he was away again at 10:10 A.M. with his same round-trip passengers. Again the flight consumed forty-five minutes each way, a trip that ordinarily took six hours by steamboat.

Something new in Cordova aviation occurred that same afternoon. Leaving Eyak Lake at 4:00 P.M., pilot Clayton Scott guided the *Alaskan* through the skies, while United States Commissioner E.P. Howard issued a marriage license to photographer H.W. Steward and Miss Henrietta Brown. Reverend B.J. Bingle next performed the ceremony to wed the two young people, while the deep bass notes of the Cyclone motor played an accompaniment to the singing of the wind through the struts of the biplane for a wedding march. Henrietta, of Philadelphia, had been a teacher in the Cordova schools for the past two years. Steward, who had lived in the north for many years, had moved from Latouche to Cordova three years before. The thirty-minute flight was a wedding gift from Gorst Air Transport, Incorporated and its representatives on the scene: Scott, Graham and McDermott.

On Saturday, May 11, the Seattle pilot began a full day with a thirty-minute passenger hop in the *Alaskan* over the Copper River delta. It was a courtesy flight for the staff members of the *Cordova Daily Times,* and included "Bum", F.A. "Jim" Hansen's old sled dog retired from the Interior; Wilbur Irving, circulation manager, was included, catching the aviation bug for evermore. Next was a two-hour flight over Columbia and Childs glaciers, with a stop at Latouche for lunch, before returning to Cordova. In the afternoon, he again flew sightseers for one hour and twenty minutes. Checking the plane over and refueling, Scott and Graham left their Eyak Lake moorings and were off for Anchorage at 6:30 P.M., flying over Hawkins Island and Orca Bay to cross Prince William Sound. Flying between Naked Island and Knight Island into Wells Passage to Port Wells, thence via Passage Canal and over Portage Glacier into Turnagain Arm of Cook Inlet at an elevation of 5400 feet, they came over the city to land at the Municipal Airport, ending their two-hour flight. Both Travel Air planes of Anchorage Air Transport, Incorporated, flown by Russ Merrill and Frank Dorbandt, took to the air to escort

Howard Steward Photo

◄ *Saturday, May 11, 1929. A courtesy flight for staff members of* Cordova Daily Times *included Jim Hansen's old retired sled dog,* **Bum**. *Left to right: Pilot Clayton Scott, Mr. Dalagher, Ted Tyrer, Kenneth E. Scherrer, A.C. Faith, Wilbur Irving and Leroy Foley.*

613

◄ *Saturday, May 11, 1929. Gorst Air Transport, Incorporated Loening, NC 9728, arrived on Anchorage Municipal Airport at the coastal city after a two-hour flight from Cordova. There were seven passengers plus the two-man crew aboard the aircraft. It was pilot Clayton Scott's first landing on wheels since leaving Seattle.*

the visiting plane to the airport, for its first landing on wheels since leaving Seattle. Aboard the Gorst plane were a goodwill party of seven from Cordova: Harry G. Steel, owner of the *Cordova Daily Times*, James L. Galen, president of McKinley Park Transportation Company, J.E. "Blondy" Matheson, of the Copper River and Northwestern Railroad, Fred Reed, head of the Alaska Piggly-Wiggly Company, Harold W. McDermott, of Gorst Air Transport, Incorporated, Henry Wolking, early day resident of Anchorage, and Alan Craig Faith, member of the staff of the *Cordova Daily Times*. The plane's crew of Clayton L. Scott and Gordon Graham brought the total airplane load to nine persons.

A.A. Shonbeck, president and general manager of Anchorage Air Transport hosted the visitors at a dinner at Margus Cafe that evening; the entire party attended a dance at the Pioneers Hall afterward. Frank I. Reed put the visitors up for the night at his Hotel Anchorage.

The *Alaskan* made a flight to Lake Tustumena on the Kenai Peninsula the following morning, May 12, taking off from the municipal field (park strip) on wheels and landing on the waters of the lake on its hull, retractable wheels tucked up in place. Alaska Guides, Incorporated, sponsored the trip, taking Charles M. Daniels, New York fur man, to the lake for a bear hunt. He was accompanied by Gus Gelles, secretary-treasurer of the hunting organization. Others making the flight were H.I. Staser, Russ Merrill and Frank Dorbandt. Daniels would be joined at the lake by Tom O'Dale and Al Hardy, guides, who were going in with horses for the hunt. The flight time to the lake was one hour and five minutes going down and one hour and ten minutes for the return. Loening NC 9728 left Anchorage at 2:30 P.M. that same afternoon on its return trip to Cordova, taking two hours over a more circuitous route. Rough air forced them to fly at 6000 feet through Portage Pass. Scott took his passengers around Columbia Glacier, later swooping down to within a few hundred feet of Tatitlek, then swinging over Hawkins Island to drop directly onto Eyak Lake from the west, making a smooth landing. He brought with him the first air mail to have been sent from the west to the Copper River Gateway. Scott finished up the day with an hour and thirty minutes of passenger flying after his arrival.

Clayton Scott had secured 1000 gallons of aviation fuel from the Standard Oil tanker that had recently docked in Cordova, and spent May 13 and 14 surveying the airport situation, making a trip on the Copper River and Northwestern Railroad to Mile 17 to inspect the Territorial landing field. He deemed it suitable for landings if necessary, but too remote

614

from the city for general commercial use. Believing the amphibian to be the only suitable plane for the Cordova area, he was much in favor of adequate beaching facilities at the west end of Eyak Lake, in addition to construction of a suitable float at the City Dock, which would rise and fall with the tides of the bay. The bay could be used for loading and unloading of passengers during calm weather but the lake would be the proper place to station the plane permanently; it was a protected site without tides, and in fresh water. He felt sure that the Gorst company would permanently station a plane at Cordova.

Fred Reed, head of the Alaska Piggly-Wiggly Company, had been in Cordova for the past two weeks, making arrangements to open a store. Needed in Juneau, he found the boat had already sailed. He made an agreement with Scott to try to catch the *Alaska* by using the plane. H.W. McDermott, Gorst's Juneau representative, decided to accompany him. Taking off some three hours after the steamer's departure, on May 15, the pilot caught the ship ten miles before it rounded Cape Hinchinbrook, circling the vessel to catch the attention of Captain Anderson, who brought the ship to a halt. By the time Scott landed, the captain had the sling over the side to bring the two men aboard. Others staying in the plane were Mrs. Fred Reed, Mrs. Robert Hall, wife of the local agent for Alaska Steamship Company, as well as two naval radio technicians for the wireless station at Cape Hinchinbrook. Heavy breakers made a landing there inadvisable and the two men also returned to Cordova. The flying time had been one hour and fifteen minutes.

Clayton Scott, general manager in Cordova for Gorst Air Transport, Incorporated, was running a box ad in the *Cordova Daily Times* noting his availability for flying of any kind, in and out of the area. On his return from Hinchinbrook, on Wednesday, May 15, he hosted a forty-five minute flight for circulation manager Wilbur Irving, assistant manager Dorothy Dooley, and their newsboys.

Inclement weather held the pilot on the ground until Sunday, May 19, giving Gordon Graham a chance to work on the plane. The two men ran a twenty-minute test hop on Sunday,

Gorst Air Transport Loening Alaskan, *NC 9728, at Columbia Glacier north of Cordova in the summer of 1929.*

Gordon Graham Collection

then made a flight of one hour and thirty minutes later in the afternoon to Columbia Glacier with E.W. Sandell, W.H. Chase, William Nielson, Conrad Ness and William Lubbe. He made a further thirty-minute flight with sightseers that same day.

Scott was now advertising a complete table of air fares to points throughout the area, as well as to more distant points in Alaska, and to Seattle, offering free taxi service to all passengers. Shortly after 2:00 P.M. Thursday, May 23, 1929, Scott took off Eyak Lake for an unnamed lake near Nolls Head off Gravina Bay, with his first fishing party: Paul Bloedhorn, Doctor W.A. Rystrom, George Mosser, I.D. Bogart, H.W. Steward and H.L. Reed. The round trip was made in one hour's flying time, the participants enthusiastic over the easy access to one of their favorite fishing spots. The following day he made a thirty-minute round trip to Strawberry Point, with another thirty minutes spent on passenger hops.

On Saturday, May 25, the flier hopped off Eyak Lake, shortly after 4:30 P.M. for Latouche, landing there an hour later, carrying Roy Douglas, H.L. Reed, Doctor W.H. Chase, Mr. and Mrs. Paul Graham and his mechanic, Gordon Graham. He delivered a fresh printing of the *Cordova Daily Times* to the community, and made five flights carrying local passengers aloft. One, George Karabelnikoff, liked his ride on the first trip so well, he was a repeater on the fifth trip. (Taken by the aviation bug, he was to work for many years in Alaska for the CAA and FAA, eventually retiring as Chief, Plant and Structures Branch, from this service.) After spending two hours and a half in the air with the joyriders, Scott left Latouche at 9:25 P.M. for Seward, taking as passengers: C. Rossi, George Morse, William Borg, Emil Feigner, Mike Bozich, Pete Soling and Adam Petrick. Arriving at Seward at 10:15 P.M., the two airmen put on one hundred gallons of aviation gasoline. Taking off for Latouche again with his seven passengers, at 3:50 A.M. Sunday morning, Scott landed there at 4:45 A.M. Reloading his Cordova passengers, the pilot took off for the Copper city at 5:30 A.M., planning to stop and hunt enroute. The Loening was landed at 6:15 A.M. in the sheltered harbor at Port Etches on Hinchinbrook Island, and the flier taxied to the far end, sighting a bear on the bank. Starting in pursuit of the brownie, a number of the passengers returned empty-handed, about forty-five

Sunday, May 26, 1929. Stranded temporarily by low tide, the **Alaskan** *rests on her duralumin-covered hull at the upper end of the bay at Port Etches on Hinchinbrook Island. A bad storm held Scott and Graham, with five passengers, in the bay until 6:10 P.M. on Tuesday. Doctor W.H. Chase, Mayor of Cordova in helmet and goggles, was an avid outdoorsman.*

616

minutes later, to find the tide out and the *Alaskan* lying on her duralumin-covered hull. Scott decided to wait for the tide change, digging holes in order to lower the wheels and taxi out. However, the incoming tide started to float the aircraft at 12:00 noon, Sunday, so Scott and Graham taxied the plane into deeper water, lowering the wheels so as to taxi up onto solid ground for the passengers to board.

It began to rain hard, with a rising wind. With the storm increasing in violence, the men found a more suitable beach, taxiing the *Alaskan* up onto firm ground, putting the tail to the wind and tying the Loening down. It was impossible to start a fire in the wind and rain so they all boarded the aircraft to keep dry. By 3:00 P.M. they were digging into emergency rations and passing out blankets from the roll kept aboard for such an emergency. The plane shook and quivered in the gale.

By noon on Monday, it had quieted somewhat and attempts to start the engine proved futile; the magnetos were soaked through by the wind-driven rain, shorting out all ignition. A later attempt at 5:00 P.M. convinced the airmen of the necessity of drying out the magnetos before a successful start could be made.

Monday night it was raining hard again; as the wind drove the swells ashore, waves rising up to strike against the side of the plane until it seemed they would pound their way through at any moment. It was a restless night and the men crawled out early to inspect the *Alaskan* for possible damage. Far across the bay, they discerned the outline of a boat, and at 7:30 A.M. fired distress signals, using the rifles. The *General Pershing* responded, dropping anchor in front of the party an hour later. By 9:00 A.M. the wet, exhausted group was climbing down into the hold to hot coffee, sandwiches and dry clothing; later getting some sleep in the crew's bunks. Scott and Graham went ashore in an hour to remove spark plugs and magnetos, taking them aboard the *General Pershing* to bake them dry. In three or four hours, the two airmen were once again assembling the motor. With this completed, they checked it over— turning it by hand before trying to start it. The Cyclone now started readily and the passengers once again boarded the plane. Just as they were ready to leave, the *Kittiwake* hove into sight; it had been sent by the anxious Cordova residents to look for them. A few minutes after leaving, they sighted the *Chugach*, also on the hunt for the plane; they circled it to let the crew know they were all right. They had left Port Etches at 6:10 P.M., going west out of the bay and around Johnstone Point to fly thirty miles to Cordova. Flying through two storms on the way, they arrived home at 6:55 P.M. Tuesday, May 28, 1929.

Scott flew again on Friday, May 31—a fifteen-minute flight to Shepard Point, where he did another thirty minutes of flying, hopping passengers. He then flew a roundabout way back to Cordova, taking another half hour. Here he spent forty-five minutes taking sightseers up.

On Sunday, June 2, he flew a party by Strawberry Point, taking fifteen minutes each way. The same morning he flew a round trip to Columbia Glacier, flying time one hour and thirty minutes. Taking six Cordova residents, Scott and Graham were off at 10:40 A.M. again, for Columbia Glacier and Valdez, landing at the latter at 11:45 A.M. and departing for Cordova at 5:00 P.M., arriving at Eyak Lake forty-five minutes later.

Gorst Air Transport had been contemplating a flight to Seattle for some time, merely awaiting a payload. Scott notified the Cordovans some weeks before of a willingness to carry private air mail on such a southbound flight at ten cents over the regular postage, the letters to be mailed in Seattle. Everything came together when Harry Seidenverg contacted Scott. The Anchorage merchant had received a cable telling him his daughter, Gladys, age eight years, was seriously ill in Portland, Oregon, and he was determined to rush to her bedside by the fastest available means. On the heels of this request, Charles M. Daniels, on a big game hunt

May 31, 1929. During the visit of the **Alaskan,** *H.W. Steward, official photographer for the* **Cordova Daily Times** *took this picture from the Loening while over the packing plant at Shepard Point. After landing here, Clayton Scott hopped passengers for thirty minutes before returning to Cordova.*

Monday, June 3, 1929. Southbound from Cordova, Alaska, Scott parked the Loening, NC 9728, **Alaskan** *on the beach at Yakutat to take on gasoline.*

on the Kenai Peninsula, cabled Cordova on Sunday, June 2, that business interests in New York demanded his presence. He wanted to arrange for the flight south, and would arrive in Cordova on the steamer *Alaska* on Monday. A third passenger, old-time Cordovan Joseph P. Ibach, who had a fox farm on Middleton Island, would join the flight as far as Juneau.

Scott and Graham were off Eyak Lake with their three passengers, and approximately 500 unofficial air mail letters, at 10:45 A.M. Monday, June 3, 1929, expecting to arrive in Seattle the following afternoon. They left behind a box ad, thanking the community for its interest and support, promising to return within the next two weeks, to continue their aviation activities.

Two hours and five minutes later, the *Alaskan* was pulling up on the beach at Yakutat to take on gasoline and allow the passengers to stretch their legs. Off again at 2:25 P.M. Cordova time, with perfect weather enroute, the *Alaskan* flew down the smooth-as-glass gulf, rounded Cape Spencer and continued on into Juneau. Scott landed in Gastineau channel at 4:35 P.M. Joe Ibach deplaned in the capital city; Scott and Graham took off with their remaining two passengers at 7:30 P.M., enroute to Ketchikan. Two hours and thirty minutes later, at exactly 10:00 P.M., the flier landed the plane on Tongass Narrows in front of the town.

Boarding an additional passenger, Mrs. C.M. Taylor, sister of Vern Gorst, the Loening was off the next morning, Tuesday, June 4, at 4:00 A.M. With clear weather all the way to Seattle, Scott landed at Alert Bay, British Columbia after a flight of three hours and forty-five minutes. Three hours more flying saw them in Seattle, landing at home base in the afternoon of June 4. The pilot now had a total flying time of 577:05. It had been a very successful trip, and the *Alaskan* would need some refurbishing from the month's work in the Cordova district.

Courtesy of John Selby

Gorst Air Transport AIR FERRY at the dock in Seattle with the two Loening Air Yachts, NC 9728 and NC 9158, on the ramp. When Clayton Scott returned from Cordova in 1929, both he and the* Alaskan *were kept busy here for the balance of the year.

GORST AIR TRANSPORT. INC.
SEATTLE—ELiot 0442   BREMERTON—1212

CLASS "A" CONTRACT
NAME

BREMERTON
SEATTLE

DATE APR 16 '30

This Identification Coupon to be retained by Passenger
SEE REVERSE SIDE FOR DUPLICATE COPY OF
PASSENGER'S CONTRACT WITH COMPANY
FORM 1   № 24541

Courtesy of John Selby

This orange ticket form was a receipt to the passenger for his fare on the AIR FERRY from Bremerton.

Scott left Portland, Oregon on June 24, 1929 to accept delivery of a second Loening Air Yacht, NC 9158, at the factory. He flew it from here to Roosevelt Field, New York on June 29, continuing on across the country to Seattle, to land there on July 3. The plane was put on Gorst Air Transport, Incorporated's Seattle to Bremerton AIR FERRY run, a twelve-minute hop. In two months, ending August 15, planes of the line made 834 round trips, and carried 9,458 passengers, an average of six per trip. The fare got down to $2.50 one way. The new service was so successful and so demanding that the company had little time to think of returning to Alaska then. While occasional letters or wires from the Seattle company still told of an interest in a flight operation in Cordova, there were no further flights by Gorst planes to the Prince William Sound community until July, 1930. The city carried out its Fourth of July celebration of 1929 without an airplane.

Cordova, Alaska showing Eyak Lake Beyond. The Copper River & Northwestern Railroad skirted the lake on the right side through the pass to the Copper River flats and on to the Kennecott Mines. The present-day airport is on level ground beyond the pass at Mile 13 from Cordova, with a highway passing over the old roadbed.

Percy Hubbard Collection

622

Gorst Air Transport, Incorporated

Meals Eaglerock Sales Co.

Valdez 1929

IN THE SPRING OF 1929, with snow on the Valdez airport still untrammeled throughout the winter by the track of transient or local aircraft, Owen Meals boarded the *Yukon* for the States, to buy a new aircraft. He stopped briefly in Juneau on March 21, 1929, before continuing on to Seattle. Meals was back in Valdez by Thursday, May 9, 1929, to note the arrival of Seattle pilot, Clayton L. Scott in the airport register. Scott, a pilot for Gorst Air Transport, Incorporated, accompanied by mechanic Gordon Graham, had departed Seattle on May 1, 1929, flying the company's Loening Air Yacht, *Alaskan*, up through British Columbia, Southeast Alaska and along the Gulf of Alaska to Cordova, arriving there May 7—the first plane to arrive in that community. Leaving on Thursday, May 9 for Valdez, with six passengers, Scott and Graham circled over the town, landing Loening NC 9728 on the waters of the bay and taxiing up to the float. The flight had taken forty-five minutes by way of Prince William Sound, and the landing was made at 6:25 P.M. The first air mail to Valdez was unloaded, including a letter from the *Cordova Daily Times* to the editor of the *Valdez Miner*. The plane had brought in Pete Maas, George Robbins, W.T. Stuart and three Cordova

July 9, 1929. The second **Spirit of Valdez,** *an Alexander Eaglerock Serial number 615, Registration number C 6316, is test flown, after assembly, from the Valdez airport. The biplane was powered with a 180 horsepower Hispano-Suiza "Hisso" liquid-cooled motor. Meals' first Eaglerock, purchased in 1928, had a Curtiss OX-5 ninety horsepower motor.*

623

Loening Air Yacht, Model C-2-C, with 525 horsepower Wright Cyclone engine, Registration number NC 9728, was owned by Gorst Air Transport, Incorporated, of Seattle. Pilot was Clayton L. Scott with mechanic Gordon Graham. The plane arrived in Valdez from Cordova on May 9, 1929, landing in the bay. It carried six passengers and a sack of air mail from Cordova. The plane is shown here at Cordova.

Gordon Graham Collection

Loening Air Yacht, NC 9728, dubbed **Alaskan,** *in flight near Wortmann's Roadhouse, Mile 19 of the Richardson Highway near Valdez in May, 1929.*

Clifton's Library

residents. Scott left at 7:30 P.M. that same evening, returning to Cordova with Pete Maas, J.W. Gilson and Mrs. W.T. Stuart.

Scott was back again the next day, with six Cordovans, landing at 8:05 A.M. Friday, May 10, and departing at 10:10 A.M. with his same round-trip passengers. The *Alaskan* would do some more local flying out of Cordova before leaving for Anchorage on May 12, 1929. Scott made his first ground landing in Alaska there, lowering the wheels below the hull of the amphibian, to land on the municipal airport.

Owen Meals had received his new plane, an Alexander Eaglerock, powered with a 180

624

horsepower Hispano-Suiza liquid-cooled motor. He was assembling the biplane in the hangar behind his shop. The new plane, Serial number 615, Registration number C 6316, was again dubbed *Spirit of Valdez* and lettered on the sides of the fuselage with Meals Eaglerock Sales Co., as the first one had been. He test flew the biplane on July 9, 1929, taking off alone at 3:55 P.M., to circle about the city at 2200 feet, landing again on the field at 4:30 P.M. He repeated the flight again at the same time the following day, this time climbing to 8400 feet. The pilot made two more flights on July 12 and July 22, with increasing confidence in the new plane with its more powerful motor. On Thursday, August 1, the pilot took off the field at 10:25 A.M. to shoot eleven landings before coming down on the final one at 11:50 A.M. On August 26 he flew the *Spirit of Valdez* again, from 4:00 P.M. until 4:40 P.M., making five landings. He was ready for final approval on Wednesday, August 28, when his wife, Nancy, joined him in the Eaglerock for a fifty-minute ride about the area, including two landings.

The following day he took Captain Anderson and the purser from the steamer *Alaska* aloft on a fifteen-minute local hop; the vessel was in port at the time. Meals made another local flight with three passengers on Saturday, August 31, 1929, coming down at 5:00 P.M.

On September 8, he took off with Ed Lerdahl and D.M. Thomas at 3:05 P.M. on a sightseeing flight. Lerdahl had arrived in Valdez on the *Yukon*, in mid May of 1929, to take a position as a mechanic with the Valdez Transportation Company. He must have liked the flying experience, for he was to take flying lessons later on, and became an Alaskan pilot.

The *Alaska* was again in port on Thursday, September 19, with Joe Crosson aboard as a passenger. He was returning to Alaska to aid in the search for Russ Merrill, missing out of

Owen Edison Meals, Valdez Ford dealer, branched out into the airplane business in 1928, after training as a pilot and mechanic at the Denver factory. He purchased two Eaglerock planes for his own use, one in 1928 and a second in 1929.

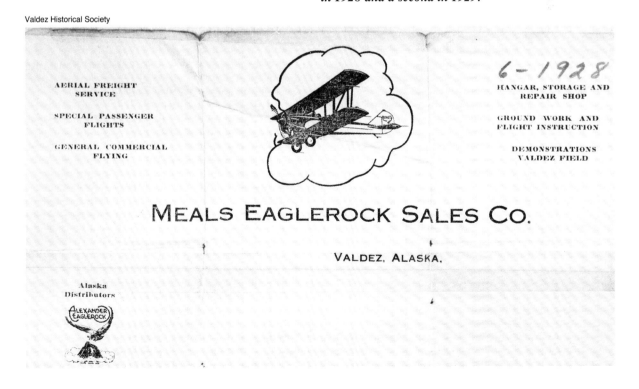

AERIAL FREIGHT SERVICE

SPECIAL PASSENGER FLIGHTS

GENERAL COMMERCIAL FLYING

6 - 1928

HANGAR, STORAGE AND REPAIR SHOP

GROUND WORK AND FLIGHT INSTRUCTION

DEMONSTRATIONS VALDEZ FIELD

MEALS EAGLEROCK SALES CO.

VALDEZ, ALASKA.

Alaska Distributors

ALEXANDER EAGLEROCK

Anchorage. Joe visited the hangar of Owen Meals, borrowing the Eaglerock to take Captain Anderson and a lady up for a forty-five minute ride. The captain was beginning to feel that a port stop in Valdez was not complete without an airplane ride.

Meals was extremely busy with his auto agency and, was flying his plane less and less. He had no cross country plans. He went aloft on Tuesday, September 24 at 2:55 P.M. for an hour's local flying with Chester A. Clifton; shooting two landings. On October 13, he was up again with Captain Anderson, the *Alaska* again in port. On October 18, Meals went aloft by himself for an hour, making seven landings; and again he was up on October 29 for an hour's flying, making eight landings on the Valdez field. When the pilot taxied in, the plane was put in the hangar for the winter, ending flying at the port city for the year, 1929.

The Richardson Highway out of Valdez provided sur-face transportation to Fairbanks and smaller enroute communities from the deep-water port. Although closed in winter with heavy snows, some freighting on sledges was done. During the World Wor II build-up in Alaska, freight was trucked over this "highway" and the Nabesna mine trail, to be flown off the Nebesna bar to Northway, and a strategic airport was built.

626

Mary Barrows Collection

Tonsina River flows along the Richardson Highway, which runs from Valdez to Fairbanks. This was an important link to the Interior.

Jack Peck Collection

628

Anchorage Air Transport, Incorporated

Alaskan Airways,
Incorporated

Anchorage 1929

Russ Merrill, the sole pilot of the Anchorage flying company, began the new year with a contract to move two trappers, Ed Holtz and John Faroe, to their winter's trapping area in the Oshetna River district. He flew the men and their outfit out of Curry, up the Alaska Railroad, starting on Thursday, January 3, 1929. The pilot took the Travel Air 7000 cabin plane to the railroad stop and checked into the Curry Hotel, a fine establishment operated by the railroad. He was still there on the fourth, awaiting better weather. Merrill thought of the new Hamilton H-45 Metalplane that had passed through Anchorage the previous week, consigned to Wien Alaska Airways. Financed with the aid of the citizens of Nome, the bright aluminum aircraft with its 400 horsepower Wasp motor had been a joy to behold. It had seats for seven passengers besides the pilot, a lavatory, a toilet and a baggage compartment in it. Russ pondered on his present situation. His company did not seem to be able to hold a second pilot and was showing no growth. Perhaps, by the time the spring business was over he could move on. He had read in *Western Flying* that Roy J. Davis, his former partner of 1926, was operating an Oriole at Beaverton, Oregon, with someone else acting as pilot. He thought it was probably the airplane he had turned over in the river there. (See Chapter 30).

1929: Pilot Russ Merrill of AAT, Incorporated, services Travel Air No. 2, plane C-193, in the Kuskokwim district.

The snow was so deep at Curry that the pilot was only able to take half a load at a time. He was still at the hotel on January 7, having moved the first half in by then. He flew in the second half later, and returned to Anchorage shortly after 11:00 A.M. Thursday, January 10.

A call for medical aid from Kenai had come over the winter trail by mail carrier to Lawing, on the railroad at Kenai Lake, to be telegraphed in from there. Merrill left that same Thursday afternoon, taking Doctor Haverstock of the Anchorage hospital to patient George Palmer. Unable to get through the fog, the two men returned. They went out again the next morning, coming back that afternoon with their patient in the cabin Travel Air. He was taken to the hospital for treatment.

At 10:30 A.M. Saturday, January 12, the pilot was away again in the plane, this time to Tyonek, across the inlet. Carrying E.J. Beck, superintendent of the Bureau of Education,

Millie Dodson

January 17, 1929. Russel Merrill flew the Anchorage Air Transport Travel Air 4000, Anchorage No. 2, to a landing on a lake in front of the P.A. Cole homestead at Kusilof, Alaska. The official name today is Kasilof. The Cole children are grouped about the open-cockpit plane.

Eddie Bowman Collection

J-4 Travel Air C-193 on skis. The plane had a side-by-side front cockpit seat for two passengers, and a rear cockpit for the pilot.

Central district, and Rudy Koch, a fisherman who was going out to make preparations for the coming season's activities at a trap site, the pilot returned with Miss Doris Robinson and her brother. On Sunday he went to Kenai for Mickey Goldstein, fur buyer, stopping at Kusilof (later Kasilof) to pick up a consignment of furs from the Williamson fox farm. He was back to Tyonek twice on Wednesday, January 16, 1929, bringing in Charles M. Robinson, principal of the Tyonek school, as well as his boss, E.J. Beck. Mrs. Robinson came over on the second trip, along with Rudolph Koch. The cabin plane was then placed in the shop for overhaul.

Taking the open-cockpit Travel Air, Anchorage No. 2, Merrill went to Kusilof on Thursday, January 17, for Perry A. Cole, a fur farmer. He set the plane back down on the Anchorage airport at 2:30 P.M.

William Gill, son of Anchorage residents, the Oscar S. Gills, had enrolled as an aviation student in a flying school at the Renton airport, near Seattle. By January 8, he had more than four hours of solo flight. Soon after enrolling at the school he had a novel experience when one of the wheels fell off the plane, following takeoff. The student and his instructor took all the arm-waving from the ground as friendly gestures until the flight school sent up a second plane, whose persistent attentions finally apprised them of the difficulty. Gill's instructor elected to land in the waters of the lake, asking the embryo pilot to climb out on the rear of the fuselage as they neared the water, to help balance the plane when it touched down. In spite of this, the plane did a nose dive, catapulting the student over the front of the ship and into the water about twenty feet distant. Picked up by a boat, unharmed, the student had a thrilling story to tell roommate Wells Ervin when he came home to their apartment in the University District.

Russ Merrill tried to take Perry A. Cole back to his fur farm at Kusilof on Sunday, January 20, but was forced to return by heavy ground fog. He was able to complete the flight on Monday. The pilot brought in Cole's son, Milton, who had become very ill during his father's absence. The young man had been loaded on a sleigh and a start made for the railroad, over the trail. When Merrill learned of this, he took off after him, picking up a Kenai resident for a guide on the way; the sled had already passed through there. After several landings along the way to reconnoiter, the sick man was overtaken and placed on board the plane for Anchorage. The pilot returned the next morning, to drop his guide at Kenai, and pick up Milton Cole's wife to bring her into Anchorage.

Merrill left for Curry on Wednesday, January 23, to take another load of supplies into the Oshetna for Ed Holz. Neither the trapper nor his partner were there. He also stopped at the camp of Blair and Ruggles, two trappers he had flown into the area earlier in the winter, and they weren't in their camp either.

Merrill took the mail to Kenai on Friday, January 25, dropping a passenger, Julius Galander, at Point Possession. Weather delayed his return. Wednesday, January 30, 1929, Mickey Goldstein, fur buyer, left with Merrill for the Kuskokwim in the morning. They had made a try for Bethel earlier in the week but had been turned back on the Kuskokwim side of the Alaska Range by a heavy fog bank; the entire valley appeared to be enveloped. Merrill returned to Anchorage from Bethel on Monday, February 4, bringing in Goldstein with a cargo of furs. The pilot was scheduled to go to the Skwentna River district the next day, to bring in the body of John Rimmer, who was found dead in his cabin on Hewitt Creek several days before. Merrill took J.H. McElroy, Rimmer's partner, in with him on Sunday, February 10, but was forced by a snowstorm to drop him at the camp of Ray Jones on the Yentna River, about forty miles beyond Susitna Station. He made two other flights to the Susitna district that same day, bringing in four passengers and a quantity of furs. Passengers brought in were Herb

J. Brown, George N. Brown, Gunnar Berget, and Fred Bayer. The furs were picked up at McDougall, east of the junction of Lake Creek and the Yentna River.

Merrill took the Anchorage Air Transport plane to the Illiamna district, 174 miles away, on Friday, February 15, 1929, with Mickey Goldstein as a passenger, enroute to the lower Cook Inlet on a fur buying expedition. The unseasonably warm winter had caused much of the fog in the region. Merrill found landing on the ice on skis dangerous, and did not do so; the lakes in that region were open or nearly so. This was particularly true in the Kuskokwim region. Merrill left in the open-cockpit Travel Air for the Kuskokwim on Tuesday, February 19, with a cargo of merchandise for Sleetmute, and returned with furs from the upper Kuskokwim. He was back with the shipment on Thursday, February 21. The following day the pilot made two flights, taking the now-recovered Milton Cole and his wife to Kusilof, stopping at Kenai on the return to bring in S. Sandstrom to Anchorage. The second flight was to welcome pilot Noel Wien and his big Hamilton H-45 monoplane to Anchorage. Three passengers Wien had brought to Fairbanks from Nome had gone on a party the night before the train left for Anchorage and Seward. They overslept, missing the train, so Noel had to fly them into Anchorage, arriving there shortly after 5:00 P.M. so the men wouldn't miss the boat for Outside. Noel was working on a contract to fly 10,000 pounds of furs from the ice-bound *Elisif,* on the Siberian coast. (see Fairbanks—1929, Chapter 51).

Russ Merrill had been writing his brother Jerry (L.J. Merrill of the Shute Savings Bank in Hillsboro, Oregon), urging him to sell out and come to Alaska to go in the aviation business with him. Citing Anchorage Air Transport, Incorporated, figures for 1928, which showed a gross revenue of $37,000 for the year, $4000 net profit after depreciation, $2000 to Wien for bringing the pilot and his airplane back from Barrow, a bill of $1800 for the overhaul of one of their motors, and only $50 per month for office rent and secretary, the prospects looked good. The outstanding stock was about $23,000. Merrill was also taking Spanish lessons; he had thoughts of lining up a job in the States, or getting on with one of the new South American lines then springing up. If the opportunity to move should arise, where to get enough money was a big worry for the pilot.

Russ Merrill mailed a financial statement on Anchorage Air Transport, Incorporated on March 7, 1929, before leaving for Bethel on March 8, taking three passengers. He dropped his three passengers enroute, picking up Mrs. Firestone, wife of the doctor in charge of the hospital at Akiak, and her baby, taking them to Bethel. He was back in Anchorage to take B.B. Mozee, head of the reindeer department of the Bureau of Education, to Akiak on Tuesday, March 13. The pilot flew Mozee on an inspection trip of the herds, then took him on to Nome. Snowbound at Bethel for a time, the Travel Air 7000 arrived in Nome to drop Mozee. Merrill was back in Anchorage late in the afternoon of Tuesday, March 26, bringing in Mr. and Mrs. Walter Andrews, who had been married in Bethel the previous fall when the pilot flew them in. They were now on their way to the States. The pilot also brought in a large consignment of furs from Nome and the upper Kuskokwim.

Anchorage Air Transport dispatched a plane to Susitna canyon with Al Blair, to pick up Blair and Ruggles' fur catch, cached near the head of the canyon when the two men had recently come out. They dragged the furs, valued at $6000, as far as they could through the deep snow, and were finally compelled to cache them when their provisions gave out, still several miles from the railroad. On his return, Merrill was scheduled for a flight down the Inlet with guide Tom O'Dale and another man. A second flight over the Inlet was scheduled for Thursday, March 27, with Bill Carlson and Gunnar Berget, who were going to work for Libby, McNeil & Libby. Later, a plane was sent into the Mount Spurr district for Valentine and

632

Nelson, who had been trapping in that section since the previous fall. All the trappers were coming in.

With the local business caught up, Merrill was away again in the Travel Air 7000, going to the Kuskokwim and Iditarod districts with two passengers for Akiak, on the lower Kuskokwim River, and one for Iditarod. Earlier in the day the pilot had made a flight to Kenai and return, taking two passengers to the Inlet town. He was now carrying Herman Oman, mining on Crooked Creek near Akiak, Mike McDermott, who would spend the summer working for the New York-Alaska (gold dredging) Company (NYAC) on Bear Creek, and E.T. Hyde, going to Iditarod to work as engineer for the Ira Wood river transportation company. The river navigation and mining teams were coming in for the season's work.

A new pilot known as Frank Dorbandt arrived in Anchorage on April Fools Day to take a flying job with Anchorage Air Transport. Merrill was held in the Iditarod by unfavorable weather. The new pilot, from Detroit, took the open-cockpit Travel Air 4000 up on a trial flight that same afternoon. The next morning, he made a flight to Susitna Station with mail, thus getting his first indoctrination in Alaska flying. He went to Kenai that same afternoon. With the season's work beginning, a second pilot had been badly needed.

Merrill was back in Anchorage No. 1, the cabin plane, the afternoon of Thursday, April 11, 1929, bringing in two passengers from Sleetmute, Tony McDonald and William Cribbie. He had made two attempts to get away from Sleetmute before he was finally able to get the plane through to Chakachamna. He had been turned back by adverse weather conditions, and finally reached the camp of George Shaben, west of Mount Spurr, but could not get through Merrill Pass. He remained at the camp overnight, coming into Anchorage early the next morning.

Merrill was off for the Kuskokwim district again on the morning of Friday, April 12, carrying three passengers: Carl Carlson and Paul Willenberg enroute to Flat, and C.O. Pearson, who would leave the flight at Berry's Landing, on the Kuskokwim River. He traveled from there to the Medfra section. The open-cockpit *Anchorage No. 2* was dispatched to the Theodore River in the Chakachmna district on the afternoon of Thursday, April 18, in search of a brother of E.G. Valentine, to notify the young man of his brother's death at Anchorage that same day. Valentine was in a trapping camp on the Theodore River.

Merrill was out of Anchorage again, on Sunday, April 21, 1929, for the Kuskokwim with three passengers, two of whom had arrived from the States on the morning train. E.W. Parks, owner of cinnabar holdings on the Kuskokwim River, A. Skidmore, traveling with him, and Mark Bates, who had been in Anchorage for some time, made the trip. On the return flight Merrill made a stop in the Lake Chakachamna district to pick up some furs cached there by Fred Nelson and Elmer Valentine, who had recently mushed in over the snow. Another flight to the Kuskokwim region from Anchorage was in the offing. Merrill made it through to Parks, a short distance below Sleetmute, but on the return was forced by bad weather in the mountains to go into Fairbanks. He landed there on Weeks Field at 3:00 P.M. Saturday, April 27, in time to meet Parker Cramer and Willard Gamble, on their way from Nome to New York. The two men in their Cessna AW had landed only four hours before Merrill. The Anchorage pilot left the next day, enroute to McGrath with Emil Anderson, intending to return to Fairbanks before going to Anchorage.

On Friday, May 3, Frank Dorbandt flew Sam Wagner and an outfit to the Fairview district early in the morning, where the prospector-miner was setting up for another season. Two trips to Lake Creek were necessary to make delivery of the entire shipment.

Ben Eielson was coming to Anchorage. The well-known Alaskan flier, formerly a

Lieutenant in the U.S. Air Service had, in April, been honored by North Dakota's Governor Shafter with a Colonel's commission in the National Guard. But, more than that, it was reputed that Eielson, leaving Seattle on the *Aleutian,* was representing eastern capital which was proposing a commercial aviation service to include all major Alaskan cities, and eventually to be extended to Siberia. Ben arrived in Anchorage on Saturday evening, May 4, 1929, and was welcomed by one of the Anchorage Air Transport planes which met the boat train some miles south of the city, circling overhead as it arrived at the depot. Recently returned from the south polar regions, Eielson had little to say about his plans for the present, although he discussed his experiences with Sir Hubert Wilkins in Antarctica. Russ Merrill and Frank Dorbandt flew him to Curry in the Travel Air 7000 to catch the train there for Fairbanks. Airmen there felt that the eastern concern would buy out the local operators. If so, Merrill was prepared to go with the new concern, whether they bought out Anchorage Air Transport or not. He was convinced that Anchorage could not compete with a company operating out of Fairbanks, as far as the interior business was concerned; the mountains, combined with the weather, caused too much delay for an Anchorage operator.

Dave Strandberg, who spent his winters in the Anchorage district and his summers in his interior Alaska mining camp on Flat Creek, left for there the afternoon of Tuesday, May 7, 1929, accompanied by his youngest son, Ted. The other two sons, William and Harold, would join him later in the season, as soon as the school term was completed. The pair left in the Travel Air 7000, now on Skeels, a new ski-wheel combination developed by Alonzo Cope, and tested by Merrill and Dorbandt. The wheels extended about five inches below the skis,

◄ *Anchorage Municipal Airport. Left to right: Mechanician Lon Cope and pilot Frank Dorbandt with* **Anchorage No. 2.** *The Travel Air is fitted with Skeels, a ski-wheel combination developed by Cope, Dorbandt and Merrill for use when both would be required on a flight.*

▲ *Left to right: Lon Cope and Rudy Gaier, the two mechanics on the staff of Anchorage Air Transport, Incorporated, in 1929 with Travel Air C-193 on Skeels.*

functioning on a dirt field; when the plane landed on snow, the wheels sank into the snow, allowing the ski to function. Testing by the pilots showed a tendency for the wheels to create drag when taking off with a heavy load on skis. This was overcome by a mechanical device, built by Cope, to allow the skis to be raised or lowered, making it possible to use the wheels when needed, or to eliminate them entirely, by dropping the skis down. There were many cases, particularly during the changing seasons, where wheels were needed at point of departure and skis at the destination, or vice versa. Cope further faired in the Skeels with sheet metal, in order to reduce the drag in flight. Today, improved versions of this ski-wheel arrangement are common in Alaska and elsewhere on light planes; the present day balloon tires causing little drag on the snow.

Merrill and Dorbandt both went on the trip to Flat with the Strandbergs, coming into Fairbanks on the way back. They were off Weeks Field the afternoon of Thursday, May 9, to land in Anchorage that same evening.

Clayton Scott and Gordon Graham had been operating the Loening Air Yacht of Gorst Air Transport, Incorporated at Cordova during the summer. (See Cordova—1929, Chapter 45). Now they were coming to Anchorage on a special flight, an invitation from the Anchorage Chamber of Commerce. Scott landed the big plane on the "park strip" municipal airport at 8:40 P.M. Saturday, May 11. A welcoming committee saw the visitors to the Anchorage Hotel. They were hosted by A.A. Shonbeck at a dinner at the Margus Cafe later in the evening. The

May 12, 1929. Pilot Clayton Scott climbs in to service Gorst Air Transport, Incorporated Loening Alaskan, *for flight to Tustumena Lake for Alaska Guides. Left to Right:* Al Hardy, guide; Harry L. Staser, unidentified, Clayton Scott and Tom O'Dale, guide.

amphibian made a flight to Tustumena Lake, on the Kenai Peninsula, the next day for Alaska Guides, Incorporated; Merrill and Dorbandt were included in the party for the flight. The Loening, NC 9728, returned to Anchorage, leaving there at 2:30 P.M. on its return trip to Cordova.

Frank Dorbandt took the open-cockpit Travel Air 4000 to Flat on Monday, May 20, making his first unescorted trip to that section of the country. He carried William and Harold Strandberg, joining their father for the season's placer mining. Dorbandt reported his arrival at McGrath that afternoon. Merrill, in Anchorage, was making an appeal to the city council to extend the present airport, or build a new, in order to retain its position as an aviation center in a growing industry.

Dorbandt took the open-cockpit *Anchorage No. 2* to Ophir on Thursday, May 30, 1929, with Mrs. Sid Paulson as a passenger. His providential arrival there gave Mrs. Louise Levenhagen, at Ophir, the opportunity to go to Anchorage and catch a southbound train to board the steamer *Alaska* for the States. Illness in her family made the trip necessary. The pilot, flying in headwinds, made the flight at night, coming into Anchorage shortly before midnight to set the Travel Air down on the field without lighting.

Frank Dorbandt took the cabin plane, now on floats, to Sleetmute and return, on Thursday, June 6. Taking off at an early hour in the morning with William Cribbie, who was traveling to his headquarters in the upper Kuskokwim, the pilot was back at his Lake Spenard base in seven and one-half hours. In good weather the pilot had crossed the mountains at an

636

altitude of 10,000 feet, flying to the left of Mount Spurr. Sighting many white objects in the Inlet on his return, he learned later they were Beluga whales, the first he had seen.

That same evening Merrill took the plane to Akiak, carrying Frank and Ed McDougall and another man, traveling to Bear Creek to work for New York-Alaska (dredging) Company. The pilot returned to Anchorage with Doctor and Mrs. Firestone at 1:30 A.M. on Saturday. Firestone was head of the government hospital at Akiak.

The City of Anchorage council, on June 5, adopted a resolution to appoint a committee to seek a site for a new municipal airport, to be jointly constructed by the City and the Territory, with the City paying out one-third the cost, not exceeding $2000. The Territory was yet to be heard from. Sealed bids for the construction of an aviation field located one and one-half miles northeast of Seward were being received by the Alaska Road Commission.

Merrill returned to Lake Spenard in the cabin plane on the morning of Wednesday, June 12. He picked up J.N. Prouty of NYAC and took him to Akiak. On the return flight, carrying Rudolph Gaier of Stony River as a passenger, the pilot made a stop at the camp of George Shaben in the Chakachamna Lake district; the pilot left there at 8:00 A.M. Wednesday, June 12, to arrive on Lake Spenard shortly before 10:00 A.M. Frank Dorbandt next took the plane to the Bristol Bay district, carrying Doctor Lawler Seeley, dentist. The Travel Air returned to Spenard on Thursday, June 13.

The two pilots of Anchorage Air Transport, taking both Travel Airs, made a flight to Kvichak on Bristol Bay on Saturday afternoon, June 22, 1929, returning to the Lake Spenard base early Sunday morning; the round trip had taken approximately twelve hours. Dave Branch, H.B. Friele and M. Tenson, cannery officials who had come north on the *Alaska*, and Howard J. Thompson, weather bureau head in Fairbanks, were passengers on the flight. Thompson made the round trip. The pilots landed the planes, both on pontoons, at Lockanok village near the head of Kvichak Bay, where the many canneries were preparing for a busy season, opening June 25.

Noel Wien came into Anchorage in his "one-winger", as the locals had dubbed the big Hamilton monoplane, on the evening of Thursday, June 27. Dropping passengers from Fairbanks, he picked up Bruce Thorne and George C. Graves, two wealthy young easterners who were going to the Arctic to hunt walrus and polar bear for a Chicago museum. They had been taken earlier to Russian Lake by Anchorage Air Transport for several days outing there. The open-cockpit Travel Air 4000 was out of service for a time. On Friday, June 28, Merrill damaged it, breaking the left wing panels when they dug into the water on a landing in good clear weather. The pilot had landed a bit fast on Lake Spenard and it got away from him. There was no other damage. Lon Cope would soon put it right.

The new Anchorage municipal airport project was moving along; with a bid on clearing brush from the two runways to be awarded by the Alaska Road Commission on Friday, July 10. When this work was completed, a further contract was let for ploughing the tract and putting it in condition for use as a landing field. The cost was shared equally between the City and the Territory, as had been done in other communities. The new airport, of approximately thirty-three acres, was standard in size, with cross runways 2000 feet in length. G.B. Barber and John Lappi were awarded the clearing contract on their bid for $30 per acre.

Merrill was off in the cabin plane, Travel Air 7000, late in the afternoon of Friday, July 12, 1929, for Bristol Bay. Stopping for fuel at the Seversen & Bailey trading post at Portage on Illiamna Lake, the pilot continued on to Kvichak Bay. He brought in H.B. Friele, general manager of A & P Products Corporation, W.E. Rooney, of American Can Company, and C.S. Daggy, of Northern Electric Company. The pilot landed in Lake Spenard on Saturday morning; his passengers left for the States that afternoon.

Merrill went to Ophir on Monday, July 15, in *Anchorage No. 1*, returning Mrs. Louise Levenhagen to her home. Earlier in the day the pilot had arrived at his Anchorage base from a flight to the Bristol Bay district, with Troy L. Carey, a sales representative for Fibreboard Products Company. On Wednesday, July 17, Anchorage Air Transport flew a load of supplies to the Oscar Vogel camp in the Nelchina district. Vogel had mushed in over the summer trail. Al Blair was brought in on the return flight, following several days stay in the area. The plane was scheduled to go to Bristol Bay that evening to bring in some cannery officials.

Ben Eielson arrived in Anchorage on the evening of Saturday, July 20, coming from the States to locate permanently in the Territory. He was representing Alaskan Airways, Incorporated, and mentioned the new company would have two planes coming up as soon as delivery could be made from the factory. Whether the new company would take over any of the present Alaskan firms had not been decided as yet. Eielson left for Fairbanks Monday afternoon.

Once again Russel Merrill was the sole pilot in the employ of Anchorage Air Transport, for Frank Dorbandt left the services of the company and took the train to Fairbanks on Tuesday, July 16, to be employed by Wien Alaska Airways, Incorporated, flying up to Nome with Ralph Wien. He would be the Nome-based pilot for the company, doing their flying out of there.

The Rainy Pass district was to be set up for extensive big game hunting for the fall; and Anchorage Air Transport would undoubtedly do the bulk of the flying. Alaska Guides, Incorporated, under field manager Andy Simons, had already booked several Outside hunters. It was planned that Simons, accompanied by Earl C. Olmstead and A.M. Crocker, would go overland with twelve head of pack and saddle horses, with a second party composed of C.W. Wagner, Tom O'Dale and Frank Revelle making the trip by boat as far as they could go. The two parties were to join there, to complete the journey together to the site selected for the base camp. Then the hunters would be brought in by airplane.

Seven of the horses belonging to the guiding company couldn't be located. Lost in the hills back of Anchorage, they had wandered off in the early part of July, probably to escape the mosquitoes by going up in the hills. Nine of the original sixteen had been recovered; two in a badly run-down condition as the insect attacks kept them constantly on the move without sufficient time to graze. Merrill went out on Tuesday, July 23, in the cabin plane for an aerial search; the pontoons had been removed in the morning for the special flight to permit emergency landings on wheels, should it become necessary. Gus Gelles, secretary-treasurer of Alaska Guides, Incorporated and Charles A. Davis, stock foreman for the company, went along as did mechanic Lon Cope. After three hours in the air, searching to the head of Eagle River, over the lakes and glaciers in that district, as well as over Indian summit almost to Turnagain Arm, the members of the search team saw no horses, except for the pack outfit which had been sent out several days before for a ground search. Merrill dropped a message with an improvised parachute to the party, made of George Belanger, Harry Sagers and George Dupre.

Merrill took an eighty-two year old tourist, Prescott Stevens, to Seward following his arrival from the Interior on Saturday, July 27, 1929. On Tuesday, July 30, the Anchorage Air Transport pilot took two newlyweds, Mr. and Mrs. C.B. Ruggles, into their winter trapping camp in a region, tributary to the upper Susitna River, on Kosina Creek. Taking the cabin plane, he loaded in five sled dogs, some groceries and the Ruggles. He had hauled their outfit in on two previous trips. Ruggles and Al Blair had spent the previous winter trapping in the district, with good results.

On Friday, August 2, 1929, it was announced in Fairbanks that Alaskan Airways, Incorporated, had taken over Bennett-Rodebaugh Company. The personnel was to remain unchanged for the present, with Charles L. Thompson continuing as manager, with pilots A.A. Bennett, Ed Young and Tom Gerard remaining on as pilots in Fairbanks. Operations were under the general direction of Carl Ben Eielson. By August 8, he had also acquired Wien Alaska Airways, Incorporated, melding it into Alaskan Airways. Eielson was acting as agent for the Aviation Corporation of America, registered in Delaware.

On August 6, Russel and Thyra Merrill took an Alaskan vacation starting in Seward where they boarded the *S.S. Yukon* for Valdez to drive with friends over the Richardson Highway to Fairbanks, and going from there by road to Circle and back. With a lot of cannery stops, it took the *Yukon* two days to reach Valdez, a normal eight-hour voyage. With a Buick and a Franklin for the party of six people, they all looked forward to an enjoyable ten-day trip, as well as a chance to see some of Alaska from the surface. Thyra had recently recovered from an operation and welcomed the travel opportunity.

Robert Gesell

Russ Merrill at Kenai in 1929. The Travel Air 7000 has been patched on the left side, obliterating a portion of its name, Anchorage No. 1. *Only two of the cabin planes were ever built by the Travel Air factory.*

Merrill was back at work on August 16, 1929, taking a load of supplies that afternoon, into the Rainy Pass district for Alaska Guides, Incorporated. He was off again, early the next morning, with a second load for the same destination, a camp the guiding company was setting up for the Stillman party of big game hunters, expected in on the afternoon train from Seward. James A. Stillman, former president of the National City Bank of New York, and James H. Durrell, vice-president of the same bank in charge of its South American interests, were off for

Russ Merrill on left, pilot of Travel Air 7000 on floats. A portion of the plane's name had been obliterated by a patch.

Larry Davis Collection

Russ Merrill in Travel Air 7000 on mud flats of Cook Inlet just before first takeoff with Durrell and Stillman, two hunters from the east, on August 19, 1929.

Anchorage Historical and Fine Arts Museum Collection

Russ Merrill taxis Anchorage No. 1 on Cook Inlet before taking off.

Bob Gesell

their base camp at the lake, with Merrill, in the cabin Travel Air, C-194, on Monday, August 19. A group of guides with a pack train were already at the site. The hunters expected to remain in the field until August 25.

Merrill was forced to return to Anchorage when he encountered heavy fog and rain up toward the pass. He set the plane down at McDougall, waiting two hours there for improvement, finally going into Anchorage. Later that afternoon he set out again for Rainy Pass with a load of Stillman baggage and Gus Gelles, of the guiding company. Leaving Gelles at the camp, he came back into Anchorage. On Thursday, August 22, 1929 he brought Gelles in when he took out the Stillman party.

Ben Eielson had arrived in Anchorage from Fairbanks on the afternoon of Saturday, August 17, piloted in by Frank Dorbandt in the Stinson Standard, NC 877, with its Wright J5-CA that Tom Gerard had brought to Alaska in 1928. Eielson was in town to discuss the acquisition of Anchorage Air Transport, Incorporated. A meeting of the company officers and shareholders was to be held in the Empress clubrooms on Monday evening to discuss the proposition. Frank G. Dorbandt took time out to wed Miss Vida Deigh, of Anchorage, a member of the clerical force at the Anchorage post office. The ceremony was performed by U.S. Commissioner Thomas C. Price at the apartments of Alonzo Cope, in the Shonbeck Building, at 1:30 P.M. An hour later the happy couple were on their way to Nome in the Stinson biplane. Mrs. Rex Swartz accompanied them; they arrived there on Tuesday at noon. Dorbandt continued flying the Stinson out of Nome for Alaskan Airways, Incorporated.

The meeting of Monday evening, August 19, resulted in the transfer of Anchorage Air Transport, Incorporated to Alaskan Airways, Incorporated. The shareholders were to receive their original investment plus some interest. The Anchorage company had not done well financially in their nearly three years of operation, and there was little objection to the sale. Transfer was made on the morning of Tuesday, August 20, giving Alaskan Airways control of all aerial companies operating in Alaska north of Juneau. Eielson declared his intention to continue to operate the two planes out of Anchorage, shifting planes and pilots to meet service requirements in the various districts. Russel H. Merrill was retained as pilot, with Lon Cope as mechanic. All the pilots who had been flying with the former companies were being retained and, in addition, Joe Crosson was scheduled to come north as soon as the Cleveland Air Races were over. His sister, Marvel, was taking part in the first women's air derby ever flown, departing from Santa Monica, California.

On Wednesday, August 21, it was announced that the work of preparing the runways of the new municipal airport in Anchorage was nearly complete, with the plowing to be completed the following day. Alaskan Airways had already made application to the council for a strip, 200 feet in length, for construction of a hangar there.

Russ Merrill took Butler F. Greer of San Francisco, to Two Lakes in the Mount Spurr district on Saturday, August 24. He had previously flown in the hunter's outfit to the camp of the Alaska Guides, Incorporated. On Sunday, he made a flight westward, bringing in Doctor Lawler Seeley from Dillingham. On Monday he went to the Iditarod district with two passengers, Joe Wills and F.E. Mathews, old-timers who were homeward bound from a trip to the States. Merrill landed at McGrath.

Fred Moller, in his Waco 9, C 2776, *Anna*, arrived at the Anchorage Airport early in the afternoon of Wednesday, August 28, 1929. A report had come in that the missing horses of Alaska Guides had been seen in the Ship Creek valley back of Anchorage. In Moller's *Anna*, Gus Gelles, Bud Whitney, with Russ Merrill as pilot, flew a search of the valley, locating the seven pack animals about twenty-five miles from town.

Father George H. Woodley, Anchorage priest and an avid hunter, was up in the Knik district in late August after Dall sheep. Securing a specimen and, after carrying it some distance, he put it down to take a rest. He was startled to see a small brown bear trying to make off with the carcass. Caching the meat, Father Woodley lay in wait for the bear, thinking it would return. Sleep came upon him on the sunny slope and he awoke to find both bear and sheep gone. In early September Father Woodley took the steamer *Alaska* for the States. His brother, Arthur, later was to become a well-known pilot in Alaska.

Russ Merrill, still on pontoons, was off for the Nelchina district with a load of supplies for a trapping outfit, on Thursday, September 6. On the return flight, he brought Mr. and Mrs. D.M. Jacobs in from Wasilla. He was in the air again the next day with a load of supplies for a hunting camp. Merrill was busy, in early September, moving San Francisco hunter Butler F. Greer and his guides, from Two Lakes, eighty miles west of Tyonek in the Mount Spurr district, to a new location on Lake Chakachamna. The Alaskan Airways manager-pilot had made two trips between the locations before returning to Anchorage late in the evening of Sunday, September 8, 1929, for another load of supplies. When he returned to Chakachamna on Monday, the pilot carried an outboard motor and lumber for a boat, which Greer and his guide used for cruising about the lake district. George Shaben, Anchorage old-timer, was still living in his little cabin on Two Lakes. He expected to come in later in the year.

F.W. Williamson, who operated a large fox-farming ranch at Kusilof was building a new fur farm about one-half mile north of Lawing, between the railroad and the lake. He came into Anchorage on the motorship *Princess Pat* on Tuesday, September 9, bringing in seven prize foxes which he exhibited at the fair during Thursday. This new form of cargo for Alaskan Airways was placed aboard the Travel Air when the foxes left for McGrath, to become the breeding stock of a new rancher. Merrill did not get away on the trip until the next day; the plane had received slight damage when changing from pontoons to wheels for the McGrath trip.

At 4:00 P.M. Sunday, September 15, Merrill made a flight in the cabin Travel Air to Tustumena Lake with three hunters who had arrived from the States on the afternoon train. He returned at 7:00 P.M., bringing in Tom O'Dale. He was up early the next morning, Monday, September 16, 1929, going back to Tustumena Lake, hopping off at 5:30 A.M. with Tom O'Dale, Gus Gelles and a load of supplies for the Alaska Guides camp there. Merrill returned to Anchorage at 9:30 A.M., bringing Gelles back. Two hours later he was enroute to the Rainy Pass district with Gelles, George Neal, and a load of supplies and horsefeed for the Alaska Guides hunting camp. Merrill returned, bringing Gus Gelles, in the early afternoon.

The pilot had a trip to Akiak planned for that afternoon, taking a piece of needed machinery for the New York-Alaska (dredging) Company (NYAC) on Bear Creek, a tributary of the Kuskokwim River. From there he went on to Bethel to pick up his shipment of live foxes and carry them on to their destination in McGrath. On his former trip he had only gotten them as far as Bethel.

The Alaskan Airways pilot, having already put in a full day, was off in the cabin Travel Air 7000, C-194, at 4:00 P.M. September 16, 1929. Carrying no passengers, he had a load consisting of one piece of mining machinery weighing about 235 pounds, and about fifty pounds of first-class mail for various points along the route of flight. The weather at the time of departure from Anchorage was calm, with a slightly overcast sky and medium visibility. At about 11:00 P.M. that evening a heavy storm arose, continuing for a number of hours; the storm was general over Cook Inlet.

Merrill had contemplated a stop at Chakachamna Lake about ninety miles from

Anchorage, or at Sleetmute, about 225 miles away. Neither the plane nor the pilot were ever reported at any known point since the departure.

Ben Eielson, general manager of Alaskan Airways, was concerned along with others about the apparent disappearance of pilot Merrill in the company's Travel Air. He arrived in Anchorage at 1:30 P.M. on Friday, September 20, flying the open-cockpit Waco 10, NC 780E. He carried two passengers, Mrs. Victor Brown and John F. Lonz. In Anchorage Eielson also met Joe Crosson who was returning to Alaska to fly for Alaskan Airways.

Using the Waco 10, and accompanied by mechanic Lon Cope, Eielson took off from the Anchorage airport shortly before noon Saturday, September 21, flying to Lake Chakachamna, the first point Merrill might have reached, as well as visiting other points along the route. The following day the two men flew to Bethel, and back to Akiak, following the line of Merrill's intended flight. Again their efforts were without success. The following day, Sunday, September 22, the two men flew to Sleetmute, making another careful search of the route. They were held here over Monday by weather but, on Tuesday, September 24, they took off from Sleetmute intending to go through to Anchorage. Weather in the mountains forced them to turn back from Chakachamna Lake and return to Sleetmute, landing again on a river bar. They did make it through to Anchorage the next day.

Joe Crosson had arrived from the States on Saturday, September 21, and proceeded to prepare the Travel Air 4000, C-193, for the search. He and Rudy Gaier, assistant mechanic at the airport, put pontoons on the ship and the two took off for Chakachamna Lake, but were forced back by weather. Gaier was well acquainted with the region where the search was being made.

On Wednesday, September 25, 1929, the search was continued with the Waco 10, NC 780E, Eielson had brought in that afternoon. With Ben piloting the ship, and Crosson and Cope acting as observers, a search of all the country between Anchorage and Chakachamna Lake was carried out, with no results.

Thursday, September 26, two aircraft were used: one of the New Standard biplanes, NC 174H, which had recently been assembled in Fairbanks and brought to Anchorage by pilot H.W. "Harvey" Barnhill, a recent addition to the flying staff of the company, and the Waco biplane, NC 780E. The Waco, piloted by Eielson, with Gus Gelles and Lon Cope as observers searched the western shore of Cook Inlet as far as Trading Bay. The New Standard, piloted by Joe Crosson, with Thyra Merrill, Barnhill and Rudy Gaier as observers, covered the same territory except they flew in the opposite direction from the path of the Waco. Thyra's boys, Bob and Dick, were in the care of friends while she was out on the search. Messages dropped to various parties on the ground brought negative signals regarding Merrill's plane, although the natives at Tyonek signalled that some wreckage had been sighted off the village the morning of September 17. A boat from Anchorage was sent to check on this.

Bankers James A. Stillman and J.H. Durrell were still waiting to be brought in from the hunting camp in the Rainy Pass area. With no float plane large enough to accommodate them and their outfit, the hunters planned to come in by boat. Arrangements were made to have Charles Smith meet them on the upper Skwentna River with his outboard dory. A note was dropped to them from the Waco informing of the change in plans. The water route was up the Susitna River to Susitna Station, thence up the Yentna River to the Skwentna and up the Skwentna to Happy River. The camp was some miles up this river.

Other flights were made on September 27, 28, 29 and 30. Also every day from October 1 through 13, resuming October 19 through 25 and October 27. Boats traveling on Cook Inlet were keeping a sharp lookout; one being dispatched to Tyonek on Thursday, September 26

Bob and Dick Merrill, taken at Anchorage with the remaining Travel Air C-193 following Russ Merrill's disappearance. Their mother, Thyra Merrill, eventually took them to the States.

with Rudy Gaier aboard, to check with the natives at the village to determine the exact meaning of the signals received from them by the men in the plane. Apparently some of them had seen some drift in the Inlet.

The Waco was out of service with engine problems but Crosson, on Friday, September 27, in the New Standard NC 174H, accompanied by Barnhill and Mrs. Merrill, went south as far as Seldovia and the Barren Islands, searching the islands and stopping at Kenai to check. They spent six hours in the air. The party returned shortly after 5:00 P.M. having thoroughly explored the east shore of the Inlet without finding a trace. Eielson went out the following day with Crosson and Thyra Merrill to Chakachamna Lake and return, searching the west shore of Cook Inlet both ways. Another flight to the lake that same day brought in the Butler Greer big game hunting party and the balance of their outfit, the New Standard landing on a bar on wheels.

Joe Crosson hopped off the morning of Monday, September 30, extending the search beyond Chakachamna to the George Shaben camp on Two Lakes, about thirty-five miles beyond. He spent five hours in the air. The pilot had been unable to reach Shaben's camp to check with him.

On Wednesday, October 2, 1929, Crosson, accompanied by Cope and Gaier, took the New Standard through to Sleetmute in the search, flying for three hours and thirty minutes. Ben Eielson and Harvey Barnhill took the Waco plane to Fairbanks; the needed engine part had come in from there on Monday. Eielson and Cope had taken the Waco to George Shaben's camp on Tuesday, October 1, dropping notes to the old-timer and receiving signals back that he had seen nothing of the missing pilot.

Crosson, Cope and Gaier left Sleetmute on Thursday, October 3, to continue the search. After some time, they returned to Sleetmute before going on to Akiak. They had been unable to reach Nyac, Merrill's destination, forced back by snow and sleet when within five miles of the place. On Friday, October 4, Crosson flew the ship to Sleetmute and on into Anchorage, taking a route which had not been searched, cutting through the mountains to the

644

Skwentna River. Merrill had been known to have followed the route on one occasion when scouting with big game hunters. The searchers were back on the Anchorage field at 6:20 P.M.

Frank Dorbandt, Alaskan Airways pilot stationed in Nome, arrived in Anchorage in the Stinson Standard, C 5652, on Friday, October 4, bringing in Doctor R.E. Smith, in charge of the government hospital in Kotzebue. Smith, accompanied by his wife, was very ill, having contracted septicemia (blood poisoning) throughout his system as a result of a scratch received during an operation on a patient in Kotzebue. The doctor and his wife left Anchorage by railway speeder, to catch the boat at Seward for the States to get medical assistance. Dorbandt's wife, the former Vida Deigh, also came in with the pilot. Dorbandt had made the flight on wheels, stopping at Takotna on the way and flying through Rainy Pass into Anchorage.

Receiving a report of rockets seen off Cape Resurrection, Dorbandt, Crosson and Cope took off for Seward at 9:00 A.M. Saturday, October 5, in the Stinson to check on that, even though it was not known if Merrill carried flares or not; they arrived at the Resurrection Bay city at 10:15 A.M. without pontoons for an overwater search and, assured the steamer *Yukon* would make a search of the coastline on the way south, the trio returned to Anchorage, coming in by way of Cook Inlet. Dorbandt returned, in the Stinson, to Nome the next day, going by way of Fairbanks.

Gus Gelles was a little concerned over the delayed return of two of the hunters, Durrell and Stillman, for whom a boat had been sent to the Rainy Pass district. Taking the New Standard, Crosson and Gelles made a flight up the Yentna River on Monday morning, October 7, locating the party at McDougall. Crosson set the plane down on a gravel bar near their camp. They were enjoying the boat trip out so much they declined the offer of a quick flight into Anchorage, continuing as they were and expecting to reach town on the next day.

Crosson, with Cope and Gaier, took off in the New Standard in the early afternoon of Tuesday, October 8, 1929, to check lower Cook Inlet to Kamishak Bay. Following the west side of the Inlet, checking the driftwood all along the beach for any signs of wreckage, the pilot continued around Augustine Island, finding a large amount of drift on all sides of the volcanic island, but no signs of plane wreckage. The lower Inlet is no place for a plane on wheels; the two observers had momentary heart failure when the engine stopped briefly as they were heading out over the water to the island. Crosson immediately switched to a reserve tank, which cured the problem. The men were in the air for five hours, returning to land in the dark, after 6:00 P.M. The following morning Crosson took Frank Lee and Russel Annabel on a scouting expedition to Eklutna and return, landing there. He was back before noon. On October 10, the men flew to Merrill Pass and return.

Suspecting that natives of the Stony River might have information on Merrill from the persistent waving of hands when the airmen flew over there during their search of the Kuskokwim basin, Crosson, with mechanics Cope and Gaier, took the New Standard of Alaskan Airways to the village. Leaving on the afternoon of Thursday, October 10, the pilot hoped to be able to land on a bar at Hungry Creek. They took a rubber boat along to use in crossing the river, if necessary. The pilot was turned back by weather at Rainy Pass, and returned to Anchorage after a flying time of two hours and forty-five minutes. They went out again the following day, landing on the bar at Hungry Creek to question the natives. They had not seen Merrill or his pontoon plane, even showing the fliers a written record kept in the village of every passing plane, and whether it had pontoons, wheels or skis. Rudolph Gaier had been left at Stony River, where a landing place was found, to check the gas cache Merrill had established nearby, to see if the pilot might have been there to replenish his fuel. Gaier would also go to the camp of George Shaben to question the old, deaf trapper to see if he might have any information on the missing flier. Crosson returned for Gaier later. The pilot and Cope went on to Two Lakes, Sleetmute and Iditarod the next day, making wheel landings enroute. The following day, Sunday, October 13, 1929, Crosson and Cope came in from Iditarod by way of Merrill Pass, bringing two of the Strandberg boys who had been spending the summer at their father's mining camp.

Allan E. Horning, son of Anchorage residents Mr. and Mrs. H.S. Horning, was now a pilot; he had ten solo hours in the air to his credit. The former *Anchorage Times* linotype operator had enrolled at the University of Washington, from which he had graduated as a mechanical engineer that spring of 1929. Enrolling at the Hancock Foundation College of Aeronautics at Santa Monica, California, he had completed his ground and air training for the license, and would now continue his training for a Transport Pilot's license. He later became a commercial pilot in Alaska.

Anchorage had a heavy snowfall and, by October 17, 1929, the New Standard was put on skis. Snow was general throughout the district. There was considerable aerial business awaiting and, as soon as the plane could get out to Stony River to pick up Rudy Gaier, three flights across the Alaska Range were made. Crosson took the train to Fairbanks on Friday, October 18; he was based out of there while Harvey Barnhill would come to Anchorage.

The mystery surrounding the disappearance of Alaskan Airways pilot Russel Hyde Merrill on Monday, September 16, 1929, was finally solved. A piece of fabric from the Travel Air 7000, C-194, flown by Merrill at the time, was found on the beach at Tyonek, on the west side of Cook Inlet. Frank Smith, owner of a fish trap site at that location found the piece of fabric on October 3. He came into Anchorage on Sunday, October 20 (he had been on a hunting trip in the interim), and brought the fabric to air company officials. Lon Cope, chief mechanic, readily identified the fabric, about a yard in length, as part of the covering used on the left horizontal stabilizer of the missing plane. Cope had placed this particular piece of fabric on the plane at the time of overhaul, about a year before. He recognized it by the manner of stitching, as well as the sage-green color of paint, not used on any other plane in Alaska, which had been renewed by Cope about a week before Merrill's final departure. The fabric, about twelve by forty inches in size, was badly torn.

William K. Leise, teacher in charge at Tyonek school, had come in with Frank Smith. His wife had observed the floating object off the village in Cook Inlet on the morning of September 17. H.W. "Harvey" Barnhill, son of an Anchorage contractor, was the Alaskan Airways pilot now based at Anchorage. He and Cope flew to Tyonek in the New Standard on skis, on Monday, October 21, 1929, hopeful of finding additional wreckage. They found nothing, but talked with Mrs. Leise and others. She informed them that when her attention was first called to the object, far out in the water, it was some distance up the Inlet in the direction of Anchorage. Not recognizing it as an airplane and, after watching it drift down with the tide for a short time, she went inside and thought no more of it. Several of the natives continued to watch it, however, following it with glasses until it had disappeared beyond the village. Comparing their memory of the drifting object with the airplane before them on the beach, they were certain it was a plane they had seen out in the Inlet several weeks before. With the tide out and their boats high up on the beach when the Merrill ship was observed, they were not sufficiently interested to launch one and investigate the floating object. It would probably have floated past in the opposite direction on the next tide but the Inlet was swept by a heavy storm before the tide turned, and nothing more was seen of the disabled craft.

It could only be concluded that Russel Merrill lost his life on or about September 16, 1929, in the waters of Cook Inlet, in the vicinity of Tyonek village, Alaska, as a result of an

On the map, handwritten annotations read:

We completely covered south of Augustine around Chugach Is.

All penned marks have been covered!

Have covered over 12,000 miles in a zigzag course over all.

Map showing the search tracks carried out by other pilots looking for Russel H. Merrill after his disappearance. Later, a piece of fabric from his missing aircraft, found near Tyonek, finally solved the mystery.

accident to the airplane C-194.

Barnhill turned to the task of taking care of the normal flying business of Alaskan Airways' Anchorage branch. He departed in the New Standard, NC 174H, at 1:00 P.M. Tuesday, October 22, for the Kuskokwim district, but was back shortly before 3:00 P.M.; he had been unable to get through the mountains. He had Elmer E. Simco and John W. Kimball aboard; they had planned to spend the winter trapping on the Tonzona River on the south fork of the Kuskokwim. The pilot was off again on Friday, October 25, taking Kimball and Lon Cope; Simco traveled on a later trip. Landing on a river bar of the Tonzona River, the pilot was held there overnight by bad weather, coming into Anchorage with Cope shortly before 3:00 P.M. Sunday. As soon as the weather cleared, the pilot expected to take Elmer Simco and the balance of the outfit in.

Barnhill hopped off in the New Standard for Fairbanks early in the afternoon of Friday, November 1. The plane was fitted with skis there and flown by the pilot into the Kuskokwim and other areas for a time. Dorbandt and Eielson were to begin moving fur in from the *Nanuk*,

New Standard D-25 on skis at Fairbanks. Alaskan Airways, Incorporated, had ordered two of the five-place planes for their initial operation in Alaska in 1929. The four passengers sat in a cockpit together, ahead of the pilot, who had the rear cockpit.

Crosson Collection

a sailing vessel icebound at North Cape, Siberia, with the Anchorage plane needed to help handle the other business out of Fairbanks for some days. The pilot returned to Anchorage with the New Standard on Thursday, November 14, 1929.

Resuming the business of flying there, Barnhill loaded Elmer E. Simco and his outfit into the New Standard, NC 174H, in preparation for a departure for the Tonzona River on Monday, November 18. Something went wrong during the takeoff, with a lower wing panel smashed in the process. Mechanician Lon Cope took the panel to the Alaska Railroad shop, hoping to have it rebuilt in a few days. Failing that, a new panel would have to be shipped from the factory.

Ben Eielson was missing in the Arctic.

Once again, Barnhill was ordered to Fairbanks. Taking the open-cockpit Travel Air 4000, C-193, he was off for the Tanana valley city the morning of Tuesday, November 19. The small plane had been idle most of the time since Alaskan Airways bought out the Anchorage firm.

Matt A. Nieminen was coming north to take a position with Alaskan Airways as a pilot. The former Anchorage flier, who had taken a relief plane to Barrow in 1928 to search for lost members of the Fox Film Expedition, had taken a job with Texas Pipeline Company when he went Outside; leaving them in August to take a rest from aviation for a time. Married in the States, the Nieminens sailed from Seattle on the *Northwestern*, at 9:00 A.M. November 16, 1929. They arrived in Anchorage on Saturday, November 23, to make it the pilot's base for the present. Matt had to wait for repairs to be completed on the New Standard before he had anything to fly. He was only in Anchorage a week before being ordered to Fairbanks to be sent on north to aid in the rapidly-growing search for Ben Eielson and Earl Borland. Matt boarded the train for Fairbanks, arriving there on Sunday, December 1. He was up early the following morning, to flight test the New Standard, NC 9190, and leave that forenoon in the plane for the Seward Peninsula. He was back in Fairbanks at 1:30 P.M., unable to get through a thick blanket of fog near Hot Springs, and flying through a heavy snowstorm on his return. The New

Standard, NC 174H, was now once again in flying condition in Anchorage. Matt came in with the open-cockpit Travel Air 4000 from Fairbanks on Saturday, December 7, to pick up the New Standard and fly it to Nome, via Rainy Pass and Ruby. He got away in the larger plane, accompanied by Lon Cope and Doctor L.J. Seeley, the dentist, at 10:30 A.M. Tuesday, December 10, 1929. Seeley disembarked at Flat, with Cope and Nieminen going on to the Seward Peninsula.

Anchorage was abandoned, as far as any service out of there by air. The small Travel Air 4000 was in the local hangar but there was no pilot to fly it. Rudy Gaier, mechanic for the company, who had been taken to Tyonek some time ago to carry on a careful search of the beaches for further wreckage of the Merrill plane, was left to his own devices; he could only return to Anchorage by following the winter trail around to Susitna Station and across to the railroad at Nancy. He crossed the Susitna River on an ice cake, using a long pole. A trapper and woodsman, he could take care of himself in the bush.

John Kimball, whom Barnhill had taken into the Tonzona River on October 25, expecting to take the trapper's partner in on the next trip, was there with insufficient supplies and no traps. Simco was still in Anchorage with the rest of the outfit. Kimball did have a gun and ammunition, and there was another trapper in the district, about ten miles from the Kimball camp. The nearest settlement, McGrath, was one hundred miles away. Al Blair, waiting for transportation to his winter camp, beyond Chickaloon, might be compelled to abandon his wintering plans. Also George Shaben was to have been brought in from his camp on Two Lakes in the Mount Spurr district. Nieminen and Cope arrived in Nome in the New Standard on Wednesday, December 11, after being overnight in Flat. They were delayed by weather in Nome for some time.

Matt brought the Stinson Standard, the old *Detroit News No. 2*, from the Seward Peninsula into Fairbanks on Saturday, December 21, 1929, accompanied by Harvey Barnhill and Fred Moller. The plane needed an overhaul. Nieminen and Barnhill returned to Anchorage on Monday, December 23, by train. Matt spent Christmas with his wife, while Barnhill, who had severed connections with Alaskan Airways, soon left for the States.

Members of the Aviation Corporation of America rescue team, enroute to the Arctic, passed through Anchorage the evening of Wednesday, December 25 on their way to Fairbanks with three Fairchild planes on board a special train. The Canadian pilots accompanying the planes, under the direction of Captain H.A. Oaks, were hosted at an informal luncheon by the Chamber of Commerce at the Anchorage Grill. The airmen were able to obtain information from Matt Nieminen, recently returned from Teller, on conditions regarding the region to which they were going.

Once again Matt was ordered to Fairbanks. He took the open-cockpit Travel Air 4000 up there for an overhaul, and expected to assist the Canadian pilots in ferrying the Fairchilds from Fairbanks to Teller. The pilot took off from the Anchorage Airport shortly before 11:00 A.M. Monday, December 30, 1929. It was twenty degrees below zero Fahrenheit, and expected to be colder north. He had tried to get through the previous day but snow and low-hanging clouds blocked passage beyond Curry. The pilot was compelled to return to Anchorage during the afternoon. Matt arrived Fairbanks on Monday afternoon, making three attempts at landing the Travel Air before he could penetrate the ice fog about Weeks Field. Nieminen relieved Canadian pilot Broatch, who had left for the States on Sunday. He wired Mrs. Nieminen in Anchorage of his safe arrival.

As of the end of 1929, no news of the Eielson and Borland Hamilton Metalplane had been received. Almost the entire aerial resources of the north were concentrating on the search;

Aerial view of Anchorage in the winter of 1929 shows the location of the first Anchorage airport on the right, and that of the new Anchorage Municipal Airport in the center, later to become Merrill Field. Both airports continued to be used by pilots for some years.

there was also Russian and Canadian assistance. Anchorage was completely without air service.

Joe Crosson and Harold Gillam would soon find the crash site, and the world would learn of the deaths of the two airmen.

▲ *Fourth Street in Anchorage, looking east, is largely deserted this winter day.*

◄ *The main street of Anchorage, looking east toward the Chugach Mountains. Few autos and pedestrians are evident in the scene.*

Parker D. Cramer

Willard S. Gamble

Chicago to Siberia 1929

I N THE SPRING OF 1929, without a lot of fanfare, two eastern fliers set out for Alaska in a relatively small airplane, planning on flying to Nome, then hopping over to Siberia before returning. Parker D. Cramer, of Chicago, and Willard S. Gamble were both fliers. Cramer had been heard of before. In August of 1928, he and another pilot, Bert R.J. "Fish" Hassell, had attempted an Atlantic flight in a Stinson Detroiter. Nearly out of fuel, they had landed the plane on the Greenland ice cap and abandoned it, making a fifteen-day trek to the camp of the University of Michigan Expedition in Greenland, whose members returned them to civilization.

The aircraft for the Siberian trip was a four-place Cessna Model AW, NC 7107,

▲ *Parker D. Cramer, accompanied by Willard S. Gamble, arrived in Fairbanks on Tuesday morning, April 23, 1929 in a Cessna, Model AW, NC 7107. The two men were on a flight from Chicago to Siberia. They left for Nome that same morning. The plane behind the Cessna is the Travel Air 7000 of Anchorage Air Transport, Incorporated. Merrill, enroute from the Kuskokwim to Anchorage, had been forced to land at Weeks Field on April 27 by bad weather in the mountains. The Cessna was in Fairbanks on the way south when this picture was taken.*

◄ *The Parker and Gamble Cessna AW, NC 7107, parked at the Wien Alaska Airways, Incorporated, hangar at Weeks Field in April, 1929.*

powered with a seven-cylinder radial engine of 110 horsepower. The Warner Scarab gave them little trouble during the flight. The airplane, though small compared to the freight haulers of the Alaskan operators, was of an efficient design and served them well. Having a forty-gallon fuel capacity, which allowed a 630-mile range. "Shorty" Cramer had to land frequently to refuel. The plane cruised at 105 miles per hour.

Leaving the Cessna Aircraft Company plant in Wichita, Kansas in early April, 1929, the two men flew to Detroit and on to Chicago, where the flight was officially to begin. They left Scobey, Montana on Sunday, April 14, to begin the Canadian portion of the flight, landing at Regina, Saskatchewan that same day. Remaining here for three hours, the pair went on to Edmonton, Alberta.

Leaving there on Tuesday afternoon, April 16, 1929, for Prince George, British Columbia, Cramer intended to follow Canadian National Railways through the Canadian Rockies at Jasper National Park.

It was here that it began to get interesting. Unreported at Prince George, fears were dispelled the following day when a message arrived from Jasper that the two airmen were safe, following a forced landing in a snowstorm at the summit, near Lucerne.

Getting away from there the following day, still following the railway along the Fraser River, the pair got as far as Goat River, before being forced to return to McBride because of a heavy rainstorm. Unable to get off again in the heavy mud, Cramer was forced to offload his companion, along with most of their tools and equipment, as well as some fuel. After a freeze during the night, which solidified the field somewhat, Cramer was able to get away, landing at Prince George at 10:45 A.M. Thursday, April 18. Gamble followed him in on the railroad, bringing the gear that had been offloaded at McBride.

Parker D. Cramer's Cessna AW, NC 7107, on Weeks Field at Fairbanks in April of 1929. Wien Alaska Airways' new Hamilton Metalplane, Model H-45, stands to left near the Wien hangar.
Hoyt Collection

Courtesy of Jesse Rust

Fairbanks airmen line up with W.S. Gamble and Parker D. "Shorty" Cramer before the Cessna AW, NC 7107, while Fairbanks citizens assemble before the Bennett-Rodebaugh Company hangers. The Service Airlines Whirlwind Swallow, C 2774, is at the right. Gamble is the third from left in the airmen group and "Shorty" Cramer is the fifth, the bareheaded man in the overcoat.

From Prince George, still following the railway line, the fliers went on to Hazelton, British Columbia. On Sunday, April 21, they flew on to Whitehorse, Yukon Territory, following a route that was to later become part of the Alcan Highway. Here they installed their skis in place of wheels, for the country to the north was still well covered with snow.

The next flight in the Cessna AW took them to Dawson, Yukon Territory. They remained overnight here, leaving early in the morning on Tuesday, April 23, 1929, for Fairbanks and Nome. The 250-mile flight to Fairbanks was accomplished in three hours. Cramer held here for two hours while the plane was refueled and weather reports obtained. Off Weeks Field at 9:40 A.M., with reports of heavy clouds at Nulato and light snow in Nome, the plane had difficulty in taking off in the wet snow on the field. The skis, which had been built Outside, were much too short for the plane to perform well on the snow.

"Shorty" Cramer landed the Cessna, NC 7107, in Nome at 2:45 P.M. Fairbanks time (1:45 Nome time) after a flight of five hours and five minutes in a strong tail wind, making well over one hundred miles per hour enroute. They had not found it necessary to stop along the way.

Cramer and Gamble expected to leave the next morning to fly to Cape Prince of Wales, then across the Bering Strait over the Diomede Islands to East Cape. Not having a permit to land in Siberia, the airmen planned to circle the cape, returning to Nome that same day. Nome was planning a reception in their honor.

▲ *Two Fairbanks ladies, Lila Rust, left, and her mother, Clara Rust, pose with the Cessna AW, NC 7107, flown in by Gamble and Cramer on their Chicago to Siberia flight in 1929. Harold Gillam loaned them a set of skis as they were having difficulty in getting off the soft snow on their return flight to Chicago.*

Cramer and Gamble, in their Cessna AW, struggle to get off Weeks Field on skis. The snow had melted and turned soft.

The two men left, as planned, on Wednesday, April 24, 1929, but found the fog so thick beyond Cape Prince of Wales, they were unable to continue. Cramer landed at York, at the mouth of Anikovik River, fourteen miles southwest of the cape, where the airmen spent the night in a cabin of tin miner, M.A. Domingos, originally from the Azores. Cramer made two

656

"Shorty" Cramer and W.S. Gamble arrived at Nome in Their Cessna Model AW, NC 7107, cabin plane on April 23, 1929. Lomen Bros. promptly photographed the two airmen with the local belles. Left to Right: unidentified, W.S. Gamble, unidentified, unidentified, Parker D. Cramer, Ida Escholtz, Gertrude Becker.

more attempts to cross the strait on the following day, Thursday, April 25, eventually deciding to return to Nome to try from there on Friday. One ski was slightly damaged in landing. They had missed the reception for them on Wednesday evening.

On Friday, April 26, Cramer took off solo for Cape Prince of Wales, Little Diomede and East Cape. He was successful, and circled, dropping packages at the cape and the island. The visibility was low and he doubted his movie shots would turn out. The flier returned to Nome to pick up his companion for the trip south.

"Shorty" Cramer and Will Gamble were off Nome at 4:55 A.M. (Fairbanks time) Saturday, April 27, 1929, landing at Weeks Field at 11:00 A.M. Takeoff had been difficult in the soft snow, and the men had encountered snow, rain and fog over the route. Wanting to continue on to Atlin that same day, they gave it up when they again encountered takeoff difficulty in the wet snow. They had hoped to get through to Chicago in five days or less. Even on a more suitable set of skis loaned by Harold Gillam, which were rigged in place by 8:00 A.M. Sunday, the plane could not gain sufficient speed to fly as melting had continued during the time they had worked at installing the skis.

At 4:05 A.M. Monday, April 29, when the snow was crusted from the night's chill, the Cessna, after two runs, got off. Cramer headed directly for Whitehorse to refuel, expecting to continue on to Atlin from there. Forced by fogbanks to deviate, and plagued by a headwind, Cramer landed at the Taylor & Drury Post on Teslin Lake to get fuel. The Cessna finally arrived in Whitehorse at 4:00 P.M., eleven hours after their departure from Fairbanks. They continued on to Atlin that same day, arriving at the lakeside settlement in the evening. They were away again the next morning, Tuesday, April 30, to follow the old trail of '98, using the government telegraph line as a marker on their way to Hazelton. They made it on through from there to Prince George and Edmonton, Alberta, gliding down through darkness onto the field to a landing at 10:00 P.M. Tuesday evening.

Parker and Gamble were off again at 6:00 A.M. Wednesday, May 1, 1929, for Regina, Saskatchewan, flying on across the continent to land at Winnipeg, Manitoba, at noon. They left almost immediately for St. Paul, enroute to LaCrosse. They spent the night in the Wisconsin city, taking off in an easterly direction early in the morning.

Cramer stopped briefly in Chicago before going on to Cleveland. The two airmen left Cleveland on May 3. Parker Cramer landed the Cessna AW late in the evening of Friday, May 4, 1929, on Roosevelt Field, New York, seven days out from Nome. The total flying time was forty-eight hours and twenty-eight minutes.

Cramer said there was no particular reason for the flight other than "to prove that it was possible to fly over the region in a stock airplane with a stock motor, and without previous arrangements for fuel, repair bases, landing fields, etc." Willard Gamble went to his home in Watertown, New York and Parker "Shorty" Cramer flew the sturdy Cessna AW, with its reliable Warner Scarab engine, back to Clyde V. Cessna's factory in Wichita, Kansas. The pilot reported by wire to the Warner Aircraft Company in Detroit that "in over ten thousand miles flying from Detroit to Nome, then Siberia, and return to New York Scarab motor functioned perfectly stop maintenance for entire trip consisted of greasing rocker arms and oiling valve stems six times, adjusting clearance on two valves and cleaning one plug stop thanks for the built-in reliability". It wasn't many years before Cessna planes began to appear in Alaska, to become a flood in later years.

Parker Cramer went on another expedition, as copilot-navigator in July of 1929, the same year; an attempt in a Sikorsky S-38, the 'untin Bowler sponsored by the Chicago Tribune. Planning on flying from Chicago, across the land and water route, by way of Canada, Greenland and Iceland to Berlin, Germany, the amphibian made the first leg of the flight to Milwaukee safely, leaving there almost immediately for Hudson Bay. The plane was completely wrecked, when beached, by an ice floe, sinking amid the ice cakes of Hudson Strait. Cramer and his fellow crew members were rescued.

In August, 1931, Cramer, with Oliver Paquette, tried again in a Bellanca seaplane, powered with a Packard Diesel engine, taking the same northern route from Detroit to Copenhagen. "Shorty" Cramer, the pilot, and his copilot-navigator did well. After leaving the Shetland Islands, their last message reported sighting the Norwegian coast. Nothing more was ever heard from them although a Danish trawler later picked up a floating bundle containing the personal papers of the two airmen. A British trawler had salvaged the wreckage of the plane some time earlier.

So vanished the pilot who believed the best route to Europe was over the northern land and water route, and the best route to Asia was through Alaska, and across Bering Strait to Siberia.

Rust Collection

A closer view of Fairbanks airmen ranked before Cramer and Gamble's Cessna AW at the Bennett-Rodebaugh Company's hanger. W.S. Gamble is third from left and "Shorty" Cramer fifth from left, in the long overcoat.

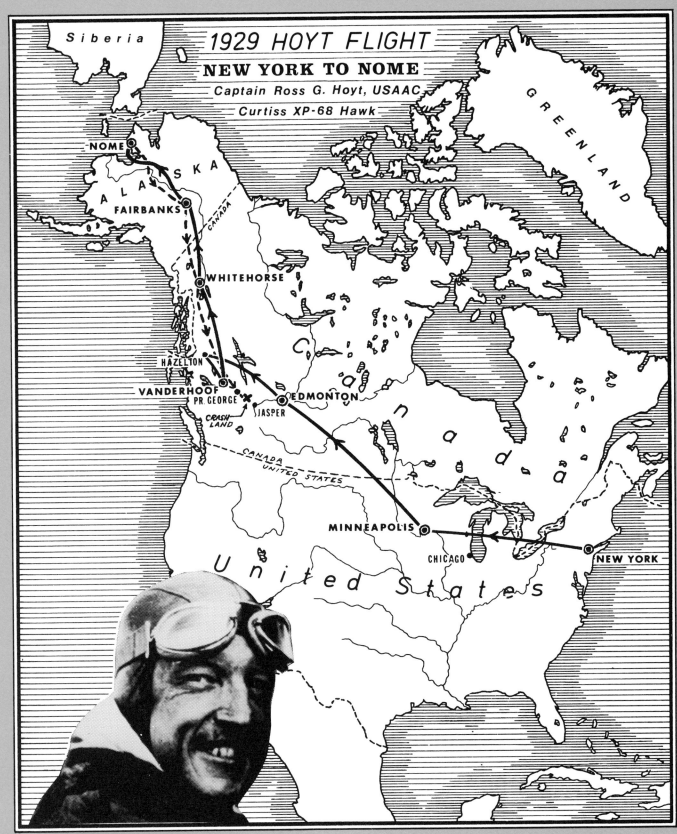

1929 HOYT FLIGHT

NEW YORK TO NOME

Captain Ross G. Hoyt, USAAC

Curtiss XP-68 Hawk

Siberia

GREENLAND

ALASKA

NOME

FAIRBANKS

WHITEHORSE

Canada

HAZELTON

VANDERHOOF

PR. GEORGE

CRASH LAND

JASPER

EDMONTON

CANADA
UNITED STATES

United States

MINNEAPOLIS

CHICAGO

NEW YORK

Artwork developed by Don "Bucky" Dawson

New York to Nome

Captain Ross G. Hoyt
 U.S. Army Air Corps
1929

On January 1, 1929, a large Fokker C2-3 army transport left the ground in Los Angeles and did not touch down again until January 7. Named *Question Mark*, the plane and its four-man crew broke all existing endurance records by remaining aloft for 150 hours fifty minutes and forty seconds. It was refueled by means of a dangling hose, in forty-three successful aerial contacts, some of them at night or in adverse weather.

While this had little to do with Alaska aviation, the pilot who flew the refueling tanker, Captain Ross G. Hoyt, was soon to be heard of in the north. Hoyt, who flew the tanker plane for the endurance flight, made twenty-seven of the refueling contacts, ten of them during the hours of darkness.

Captain Hoyt was to be the pilot of an endurance flight from New York to Nome, Alaska, by the U.S. Army Air Corps, using a Pursuit type airplane. The single-seater was the Curtiss Hawk XP-6B; developed from the P-1C, a D-12 Liberty powered biplane. The XP-6B was powered with the new Curtiss V-1570 *Conqueror* motor, a liquid-cooled V-12 of 600 horsepower. It had a fattened belly, to accommodate the additional long-range gas tanks, giving it a 258 gallon capacity. With a cruising speed of 150 miles per hour, and a top speed of 180 miles per hour, the plane was one of the fastest in the air at that time. An XP-6A and an

Map depicts route followed by Captain Ross G. Hoyt in his pioneering, long-distance flight from New York to Nome in 1929. The return flight was cut short by a crash-landing near Valemount, British Columbia.

XP-6 had taken first and second place, respectively, in the Pursuit races at the 1927 National Air Races in Spokane, well ahead of the third place Boeing FB-5.

Hoyt, a career army pilot, was stationed at the Air Corps Tactical School at Langley Field, Virginia, after completing a four-year assignment in Washington, D.C. Originally planned as a round-trip dash from Mitchel Field to San Francisco and return in forty-eight hours, the plan was scrapped when Captain Frank Hawks, a California flier in the Army Reserve, accomplished a record-breaking flight from New York to Los Angeles and return in less than thirty-six hours, flying a Lockheed Air Express model.

A new plan was adopted. The War Department in Washington announced on Monday, July 15, 1929, plans for an attempt within the next few days of a round-trip 8460-mile flight against time from Mitchel Field, Long Island to Nome, Alaska; with refueling stops planned at Minneapolis, Edmonton, Whitehorse, Fairbanks and thence to Nome. Captain Hoyt left Boling Field in the XP-6B that same day for Mitchel Field, where some final tests were run.

By Thursday, July 18, 1929, all was in readiness. Captain Hoyt, age 35, was seated on his parachute in the plane at 2:00 P.M., awaiting completion of a christening ceremony. Mrs. F. Trubee Davison, whose husband was Assistant Secretary of War for Aeronautics, arrived at the field in an auto and was driven directly to the waiting plane. Using ginger ale to christen the pursuit ship, she broke the bottle, tightly wrapped in a towel, against the side, as she announced, "I christen this ship the *Newalaska*" (a combination of New York to Alaska). Captain Hoyt shook hands with Mrs. Davison and with Captain Walter Bender, operations officer for his flight, taking off in the blue and orange biplane a few minutes later, 2:39 P.M. (EDT) July 18, 1929. He carried with him a pistol, and three one-quart thermos bottles; one filled with orange juice, one with water, and one with milk and raw eggs mixed together. There were thunderstorms ahead on the route, but spaced so that he could circle around them. While June 20-21 was the longest day of the year, his departure was timed to give him the most daylight in the northern regions for the flight.

Captain Hoyt planned on flying the 1025 miles from his takeoff point to Minneapolis in less than seven hours. Turning to a northwest heading, he flew for an hour, running through rainstorms, and later, turbulence. At 4:09 P.M. he reached Lake Erie; thunderstorms were about and it was very dark to the north. Over the lake, the pilot suffered a bad moment when his motor missed fire but, with a mixture adjustment, it resumed a steady 2000 revolutions per minute. Flying a compass course in rain, Hoyt came in sight of Long Point, Ontario at 4:25 P.M. and, flying over the land, the weather cleared. By 5:05 P.M. the pilot was enjoying perfect visibility, but the plane was bouncing about in rough air. Crossing the border in the vicinity of Port Huron, Hoyt flew on over Michigan, to cross the east shoreline of Lake Michigan at Ludington at about 7:00 P.M., following the ferry route across the lake. Ross Hoyt went on to land the *Newalaska* on Wold-Chamberlin Field in Minneapolis at 7:58 P.M. (CDT). Suffering headwinds during the flight, he had averaged 141 miles per hour and burned 219 gallons of gasoline.

▶

Saturday, July 20, 1929. Fairbanks residents gather about Captain Ross G. Hoyt's Curtiss Hawk at Weeks Field while Bennett-Rodebaugh Company employees service the fast pursuit ship. The bulbous nose allowed space for the new Curtiss V-12 Conqueror motor, as well as additional fuel tanks.

After sending telegrams from here and adding 200 gallons of fuel, Hoyt was soon away again at 9:13 P.M., for a night flight to Edmonton, Alberta, 1100 miles away. Beyond Valley City, North Dakota, the pilot found it necessary to take a path between two thunderstorms, and was soon involved in them. The next two hours were spent on instruments in the darkness, sometimes bouncing about in turbulence. Hoyt flew into clear air at 12:15 A.M., and by 2:20 A.M. was sluicing cold water from his thermos into his face to keep awake. An hour later a faint hint of dawn began to show. The tired pilot picked up a railroad, which he followed into Edmonton, Alberta. He set *Newalaska* down on the field at 3:45 A.M. (6:45 EDT). Captain Wop May drove Hoyt into town for breakfast. It was now Friday, July 19, 1929.

While Hoyt was having breakfast with the Canadian pilot, a thunderstorm passed through, leaving clear skies in its wake. But Captain Hoyt found, when he departed an hour and forty-five minutes after his arrival, that he was facing strong headwinds when he started on the 1090-mile flight to Whitehorse, Yukon Territory. He was making only one hundred miles per hour over the ground and after four hours reached Hazelton, the point at which he was to turn north for Whitehorse. He had been flying over rough terrain and the strong headwinds were making inroads on his fuel supply. He turned back to land, at 2:00 P.M., at Vanderhoof, British Columbia, along the railway west of Prince George. Captain Hoyt refueled the plane here during the afternoon, but remained overnight awaiting better weather.

After some badly needed sleep and rest, the pilot was off Vanderhoof at 4:00 A.M. Saturday, July 20. He spent a tense five and one-half hours pushing his way through low-lying clouds over the Canadian Rockies, dodging among the mountain peaks and flying up valleys, following rivers. He eventually sighted Lake Atlin, finding himself on course, and was soon landing on a surprisingly good field at Whitehorse at 7:30 A.M. local time, five and one-half hours after takeoff.

Sylvia "Tapu" Ross Collection

Two hours later, at 9:40 A.M., the *Newalaska* was away for Fairbanks, 500 miles distant, flying a direct course. Picking up the Tanana River, he arrived there to circle, and land to the east, on Weeks Field at noon (12:02 P.M.) after a flight of three hours and twenty-two minutes. Most of the population had gathered to await his arrival. While he lunched with Mayor Frank de la Vergne, C.L. Thompson, manager of Bennett-Rodebaugh Company, and reporters at a local cafe, Bill Basham, Tom Gerard and Harold Gillam serviced the Curtiss Hawk while the interested citizens

◄ *Fairbanks, Alaska, Saturday, July 20, 1929. Captain Ross G. Hoyt with mechanic Bill Basham of Bennett-Rodebaugh Company at Weeks Field. Thirty-five-year-old Hoyt had just arrived from Whitehorse, Yukon Territory.*

Mechanic positions propeller for start on the Curtiss Hawk, **Newalaska,** *at Weeks Field in Fairbanks before departure for Nome, Alaska on July 20, 1929.*

Sylvia "Tapu" Ross Collection

Saturday, July 20, 1929. Captain Ross G. Hoyt stands near his Curtiss Hawk, Newalaska, as he discusses his flight from Whitehorse to Fairbanks following his arrival there.

watched. Motion pictures of Hoyt and his plane were taken, to be sent back east with him to the newsreel services.

After talking over the route and weather condition with the locals, Hoyt was away on the last lap of his flight at 1:23 P.M. local time. He had originally intended to make a rest stop of six hours in Nome, but now would cut it to a brief refueling stop, getting some sleep in Fairbanks on his return. Hoyt flew across the Yukon flats, the river crossing and recrossing his course for the first 300 miles. Upon reaching the Koyukuk River, he turned southwest to Kaltag, the mountains on the direct course being shrouded in mist. Following the Kaltag to Norton Sound, he swung northwest to cross the sound, reaching Nome four and one-half hours after leaving Fairbanks. It was now 5:00 P.M. Nome time.

After only seventy minutes on the ground, the flier was away again, this time flying a direct compass course, on instruments, over the mountains he had previously avoided. When about 250 miles out of Nome, he dived down through a hole in the clouds, picking up the Yukon River which was easily distinguishable by its snake-like course. He landed three and one-half hours after leaving Nome. Twenty minutes to midnight by local time; it was still broad daylight in the sub-arctic summer night. Hoyt had flown 2200 miles during the day. He went to the hotel for some sleep and rest, and was back in four hours, to take off for Whitehorse at 5:10 A.M. Sunday, July 21, 1929.

The pilot reached Whitehorse, landing there at 9:15 A.M. and, after refueling, took off again at 11:00 A.M. for Edmonton, expecting to reach there early in the evening. He flew for 700 miles over broken clouds, chasing valleys through snowcapped, cloud-draped peaks, finally passing over Prince George, British Columbia. Hoyt was about half way between there and Jasper, flying at an altitude of 6000 feet along the railway, when his motor sputtered. Several times it smoothed out, as the pilot adjusted the fuel feed—the pressure was O.K. The motor continued to fail and the pilot switched to his gravity flow wing tank to no avail. Losing altitude and looking about for a possible landing spot, the pilot had about decided to jump when he spotted a clearing within gliding distance. Touching down on the field, the wheels running through soft sand among mounds about two feet high, the pilot thought he had it made when the right wheel struck a mound, throwing the left wing into the ground. The left wheel struck a second mound, throwing the nose down, and the Curtiss Hawk was thrown over on her back. The dazed pilot found himself hanging on his belt upside down with his nose a bare six inches from the sand; a longeron and several struts broken, left wing broken backward, propeller tips curled backwards, and the vertical stabilizer and rudder crushed downward. He unbuckled his safety belt, and crawled forth from the cockpit uninjured.

Mr. Cox, the postmaster of Valemount, British Columbia, a village close by, hurried to assist the pilot. Taking Hoyt home with him, Mrs. Cox fed the hungry airman while the postmaster gathered several residents together and they returned to the airplane. With the help of all, Hoyt was able to right the plane and assess the damage. It was not repairable here in any reasonable length of time. The pilot found water in the screens and gas tank sumps which, along with the way the failure had occurred, convinced him the problem had been water in the gasoline that had caused the motor to stop running. No reason for the water in the fuel could be given, unless condensation from temperature changes could have caused it; all fuel put in the airplane had been chamoised, as well as all screens and sumps checked at least every other stop.

Leaving the site, Captain Hoyt telephoned the nearest telegraph station, at Albreda ten miles away, and notified his superiors of his predicament, then set about salvaging the *Newalaska*. He was temporarily deafened by engine noise and could hardly respond to questions. He photographed the plane, and began the work of dismantling it and salvaging the instruments. By Monday, with the assistance of Harvey Brewton, a Curtiss-Wright representative at Edmonton, he had the plane disassembled and ready to load onto the automobile car placed at their disposal by Canadian National Railways. Looking back at the stripped fuselage of the Curtiss Hawk, standing forlorn in the field when he entrained for his home base on Tuesday morning, July 23, 1929, he felt remorse, but also was reminded of a kaleidoscope of memories of the fast-moving few days in Alaska and the Yukon: of the night flying between Minneapolis and Edmonton, the "valley chasing" between Edmonton and Whitehorse, the residents there presenting him with a watch chain of Yukon gold and mastodon ivory, the friendly interest of the Fairbanks and Nome residents in all things aviation, and of the newsreel footage of the Curtiss Hawk landings in Fairbanks, which he was carrying back for the New York theaters.

Captain Hoyt had set a record in flying between New York and Nome, but he had also proved the feasibility of moving squadrons of pursuit planes over long distances in case of need, especially by the use of additional tank installations to extend their range.

April, 1932. Captain Ross Hoyt in the cockpit of the latest model of the P-6 Pursuit plane, the P-6E. Passing through many model changes, the Curtiss Hawk, with its striking design lines, lent itself to the most fanciful paint jobs. The U.S. Army Air Corps was soon to change to the radial air-cooled engines in its planes.

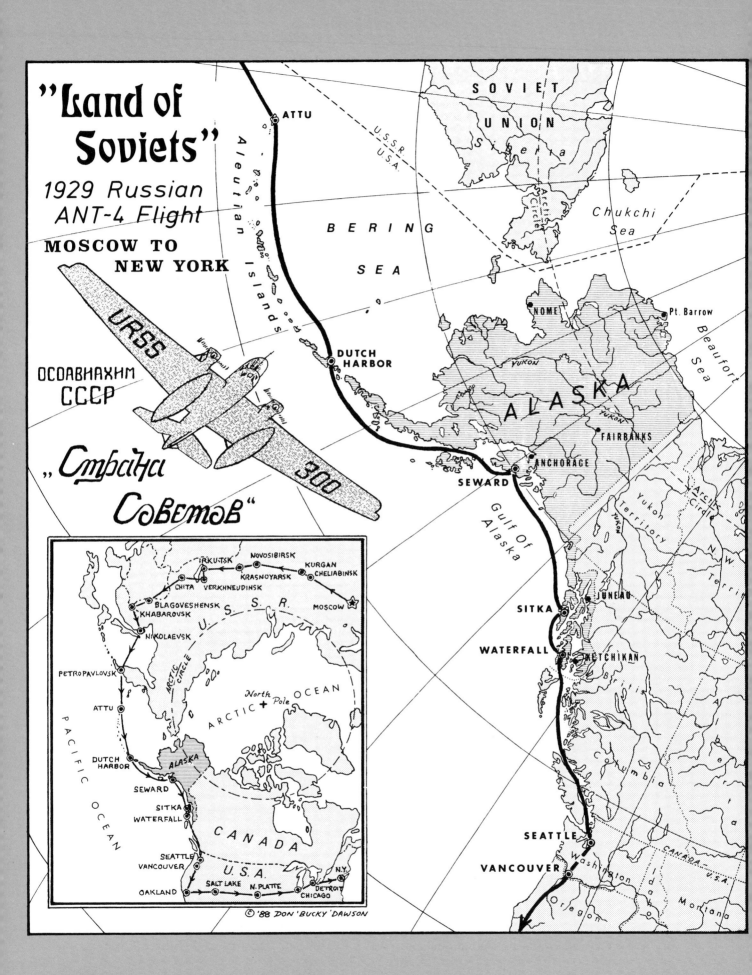

"Land of Soviets"

1929 Russian
ANT-4 Flight

MOSCOW TO
NEW YORK

URSS

ОСОАВИАХИМ
СССР

„Cmpaйa Cobemob"

300

ATTU

SOVIET UNION
Siberia

U.S.S.R.
U.S.A.

Arctic Circle

Chukchi Sea

BERING SEA

NOME

Pt. Barrow

Beaufort Sea

DUTCH HARBOR

Aleutian Islands

ALASKA

Yukon

FAIRBANKS

ANCHORAGE

SEWARD

Gulf Of Alaska

Yukon

Yukon Territory

Arctic Circle

N.W. Terri.

JUNEAU

SITKA

WATERFALL   KETCHIKAN

Columbia

SEATTLE

VANCOUVER

Washington

CANADA - U.S.A.

Idaho   Montana

Oregon

NOVOSIBIRSK

IRKUTSK

KRASNOYARSK

KURGAN
CHELIABINSK

CHITA   VERKHNEUDINSK

BLAGOVESHENSK
KHABAROVSK

U.   S.   S.   R.

MOSCOW

NIKOLAEVSK

PETROPAVLOVSK

ARCTIC CIRCLE

North Pole

ARCTIC OCEAN

ATTU

PACIFIC OCEAN

DUTCH HARBOR

ALASKA

SEWARD

SITKA
WATERFALL

CANADA

SEATTLE
VANCOUVER

U.S.A.

OAKLAND   SALT LAKE   N.PLATTE   DETROIT   N.Y.
CHICAGO

© '88 DON 'BUCKY' DAWSON

668

Land of Soviets

Moscow to New York
1929

Along with other countries of the world, the Soviets were developing their aviation capabilities. Long distance flights were in; and the Russians were planning a 12,500-mile flight in 1929, from Moscow to New York City, by way of Siberia, Alaska and the United States. A large Soviet aircraft would be used, an ANT-4, named for its designer, Andrei Nikolaevich Tupolev. The aircraft, an all-metal, silver colored, low-wing monoplane, was powered with two German BMW-VI (Bayerische Motorwerke) liquid-cooled motors of 600 horse power each. Engine design in Russian aircraft industry was lagging behind, and most of their engines came from abroad, seventy percent in 1928.

Under the direction of Osoaviakhim (Society for the Support of Defense and of Aviation and Chemical Construction) and using Amtorg, the Russian trading corporation for business with United States firms, contracts for gasoline supplies and services along the route were arranged. Spare engines and other parts were placed at strategic points along the way: Seattle, Sitka, Seward and Dutch Harbor. On July 25, 1929, Seward, one of the planned stops, received a shipment on the *Admiral Evans* of oil, gasoline, metal pontoons and anchors, for setting out a mooring buoy, as well as other equipment for the flight.

The ANT-4 carried a crew of four: Aircraft Commander Semyon A. Shestakov, pilot, age 31, Philip Bolotov, second pilot, Boris Sterligov, navigator, and Dimitri Fufaev, mechanic on board. The plane was christened *Land of Soviets* (*Strana Sovetov*). The flight was planned for early August, to start from Moscow, and making the first stop at Novosibirsk, across the low Ural Mountains to the east. The next stop, following the Siberian Railroad, would be at Khabarovsk on the Amur River, where wheels were to be removed and a large pair of floats installed. Plans were for the airmen to fly from Khabarovsk to Petropavlovsk in Kamchatka, to land on the water on their pontoons. From here, the route was to Attu and Dutch Harbor, in

669

the Aleutians, thence to Seward and Sitka, and down the coast to Seattle for a change to wheels. They would then fly south to San Francisco and eastward, across the United States to Cheyenne, Chicago and New York. It had not been decided yet whether the plane would attempt a transatlantic flight from New York to Moscow, or travel home by steamer.

The ANT-4, *Land of Soviets*, departed on the long flight from Moscow at 2:52 P.M. (Moscow time) on Thursday, August 8, 1929, making their first stop at Omsk. The plane left here the next day, landing at Novosibirsk after a three-hour flight. Flying across the steppes of Central Siberia, the plane landed on Saturday, August 10 at Krasnoyarsk, on the railroad, west of Lake Baykal.

The big monoplane left here on Sunday afternoon, August 11. It was forced down, and crashed in an uninhabited region some 170 miles from Irkutsk, near Chita; the aviators, unharmed, had completed 3726 miles of their long journey.

The crew returned to Moscow. An identical ANT-4 was made ready and marked on wings and fuselage with URSS 300, which was the registration number of the aircraft (in later years USSR) Soyuz Sovietskikh Sotsialisticheskikn Respublik, which in the Russian alphabet is CCCP. Again *Strana Sovetov, Land of Soviets*, was painted on the nose. With the same crew, the silver monoplane was off again, on Thursday, August 22, intending to make their first stop at Krasnoyarsk.

Moscow reported on September 3, 1929, their arrival at Blagovishchensk on the Amur River in Eastern Siberia, having come from Chita, on the railroad. The same day they were reported on at Khabarovsk, further down river, where the pontoons were installed in place of landing wheels for the long trip across the water. *Land of Soviets*, with its crew of four, was away again on Wednesday, September 11, flying up the river valley west of the Sikhote-alin Mountains, to land that same day at Nikolayevsk, close by the Sea of Okhotsk. Crossing this body of water put them at Petropavlovsk, on the Kamchatka Peninsula, their jumping off point for Attu. The ANT-4 had a one-quarter kilowatt radio of a special unextinguishable lamp type, with call letters ANT, and could communicate with naval radio stations in Alaska by International code, although the crew spoke no English.

The plane crossed the Bering Sea and landed at Attu at 5:00 P.M. Friday, September 21, covering the 750 miles at an average speed of 112 miles per hour, in stormy weather; the airmen ploughed their way through banks of hail, snow and fog. The Russian cutter, *Red Pennant*, had left Petropavlovsk earlier and, after fueling the ANT-4 at Attu, the boat returned to Russian waters, leaving United States Coast Guard cutters to stand by at Dutch Harbor for the next leg of the flight. The natives at Attu were startled by the arrival of the huge plane but soon gathered to place their slender resources at the visitors' disposal.

Shestakov and his crew intended to depart Attu for Dutch Harbor on September 25. However, not liking the squalls that drifted through, they left a day early, taking off Attu at 6:00 A.M. Tuesday, September 24. The plane arrived at Dutch Harbor in a driving southeast gale and rainstorm, at 2:12 P.M. Had it not been for quick action on the part of the crews from *Chelan* and *Haida*, the flight might have come to grief. Unable to pick up the buoy, and drifting down toward the rock shores, the plane was saved from disaster by the motor launches sent out from the cutters. Catching the unwieldy plane, they managed to tow it into position, mooring it to the anchored buoy that had been placed for it earlier. Taking Shestakov and his three companions aboard the *Chelan*, they were given dry clothes, hot food, and provided with staterooms in which to rest. The Coast Guard had placed a watch on the plane in case of further trouble. The "coasties" were also fueling the plane.

Delayed by the continuing gale, *Land of Soviets* did not leave Dutch Harbor until

Friday, September 27. Taking off the water at 9:30 A.M. (Pacific Standard Time) for Seward, the ANT-4 landed at 3:45 P.M. (Alaska Time). The plane first appeared high over the mountains, at the entrance to Resurrection Bay, circling down through a spectacular rainbow to land close to the buoy, which flew an American flag. They had been in the air about eight hours, making one hundred miles per hour during the flight. Rough water prevented the plane from hooking onto the buoy; it coasted up to the beach in front of San Juan Packing Company, where

Alaska State Library

September 27, 1929. Seward residents gather on the beach to greet **Land of Soviets** *and its Russian crew on its arrival at the Resurrection Bay city at 3:34 P.M.*

four heavy ropes were tied to anchors, supplied by Manager Charles Jensen of the packers, to moor the plane safely. The Stars and Stripes and the Russian flag were placed on staffs in the holder above the "greenhouse" in the nose of the strange looking craft. It was three hours before various affairs were settled, and the fliers bundled into a waiting automobile to be driven to a hotel—Mayor P.C. McMullen and President of the Chamber of Commerce Joe Urbach in the lead. Native Russians in the community came forward to serve as interpreters. Though exhausted the crew was very happy to be in Seward and out of the "cradle of storms" in the Aleutians. The fliers retired early, but were up at 6:00 A.M. to finish refueling and see to minor repairs to the ANT-4. A Chamber of Commerce luncheon and an evening dance were on the agenda for this day; it was Saturday, September 28, 1929.

Sitka, the old Russian capital, was eagerly anticipating the fliers' forthcoming visit, with entertainment and Russian delicacies planned. Sunday morning, September 10, Resurrection Bay was placid and the two-day rain was over. After circling on the water and warming the motors, Shestakov put the power to the BMW's and the plane was off at 8:11 A.M. The crew had been up since 5:30 A.M., coming aboard the plane at 6:00, stowing the canvas covering and taking down the wooden braces under it. They had topped off with an additional fifty gallons of gas before starting the motors from their compressed air tank.

The plane wheeled about and headed through Caines Head, at the entrance of the bay, at an altitude of 500 feet, then vanished around Harding Entrance. Hundreds of pictures had been taken by two motion picture photographers.

Late September is not the best weather season in Alaska. Cloud and rain are common, and the ANT-4 encountered more than their share during the flight down the Gulf of Alaska to Sitka. Shestakov was estimating about five hours for the flight. At 12:45 P.M. the Juneau radio station picked up the following: SOS Plane *Land of Soviets*, R.P.L. Latitude 48 Grad 37 Longitude 141-30 minutes, Airplane *Land of Soviets* SOS. Other stations heard the call. Considerable anxiety was expressed by listeners, and plans were made in the Governor's office, and elsewhere, to divert surface vessels to the area, as well as send out government boats; the *Cygan*, steaming on Chatham Strait, altered course for Cape Ommaney and the Pacific Ocean, to proceed to the area. The *Seal*, of the Alaska Game Commission, was being readied, to sail about 5:00 P.M. This was all made unnecessary when *Land of Soviets* slipped under the mist to land on the water before Sitka at 4:45 P.M. on Sunday. September 29, 1929, three hours over the flight plan. The crew disclaimed any knowledge of an emergency enroute, but it was later learned that the plane had been forced down when the ANT-4 blew a gasket on one motor and had to land on the water near a schooner, fishing in the vicinity. The radio operator had become excited and transmitted the SOS. Commander Shestakov jerked the antenna up, or in some way stopped communications abruptly when he became aware of it. After repairs, the plane was successful in taking off again, using full power on its one good engine, and partial power on the other.

As the residents quickly gathered on shore, the big grey-metal plane taxied to the buoy, previously placed for it, as the United States Forestry Department boat, *Ranger,* and other boats put out from shore with a reception committee. Headed by John Parramarkoff, Mayor W.R. Hanlon, Jim Roberts and John Illin, they welcomed the fliers and took them aboard the launch for the trip to shore. The Russian crew were met there by four little flower girls: Betts Hanlon, Nadja Prossof, Elaine Bolshanin and Nita Eggersgluess, who presented them with a bouquet.

Resting for a few hours, the crew was then feted at a banquet of 150 people at the Moose Hall, with Russian foods featured on the menu. Father Kashevaroff greeted Shestakov and his crew in Russian and then in English, with each of the fliers responding in Russian, telling of their trip from Moscow, and its aims of experimental long-distance flying and the promotion of goodwill. Kashevaroff translated for the other diners. A feature of the evening was the singing of *Baranof's Song*, which told of the exploits of the Baranof days in Alaska in 1808. Automobile tours for the visitors to local sites were on for the morrow, as well as a public dance in the evening at the Moose Hall.

Plans for a departure on Tuesday, October 1, were abruptly dropped that morning when Shestakov decided more work was required on the motors before taking off for Seattle. They planned to go via the outside route, west of Vancouver Island, to the Strait of Juan De Fuca, then down the strait to Puget Sound and Elliott Bay. They had no permit to travel over Canadian waters.

The entire town of Sitka visited the plane on Tuesday, with schools closing for two hours to give the children and their teachers a chance to see *Land of Soviets*, while mechanics worked all over it and supplies for the trip south were placed aboard. The fliers worked most of the day, under canvas, repairing a leaky air line and tuning up the motors; the port one had given them trouble. A delegation of Juneau Russians, headed by Sam Gazloff, had arrived by special boat and wanted to give a reception and dance for the fliers, on the *Admiral Rogers*.

672

Sitka Studio, Author's Collection

October 3, 1929. **Land of Soviets** *is readied for its departure from Sitka early in the morning. The ANT-4 was off with 5000 pounds of gasoline and its four-man Russian crew.*

The weary airmen were forced to decline. The Russian commander did later call on Captain Kolseth aboard his vessel.

Thursday, October 3, dawned partly cloudy with a southeast breeze; good weather for the departure. *Land of Soviets* was off at 5:34 A.M., planning a landing on Lake Washington in Seattle, with Port Angeles as a possible alternate. The ANT-4 dropped out of sight and sound until two of the aviators reached Craig, Alaska on Friday, October 4, on a cannery boat, to report the plane had been forced down at Waterfall, on Prince of Wales Island some 200 miles south of Sitka. Shestakov had earlier announced they would have no radio transmitter for the flight to Seattle; the generator had been removed and would be shipped to Seattle for repair.

A search had already been started; the *Unalga* had left Juneau at 12:00 o'clock, to cruise down the Alaskan coast. Commander E.S. Addison had a fair idea of the plane's intended route, through a conversation between Shestakov and Captain J.E. Kolseth of the *Admiral Rogers*. The *Haida* also came out from Seattle to join the search, and cruised the west side of Vancouver Island. With everyone notified of the plane's location, the Patrol boat, *Cygan*, searching the bays of Prince of Wales Island, at 5:25 P.M. received a message reporting the plane at Waterfall, and changed course for there.

The U.S. deputy marshal and Radio Operator Huteson at Craig were looking after the two Russians while they awaited a high tide to refloat the cannery boat, in order for them to return to Waterfall. The Lighthouse tender, *Fern*, came into Craig later on and offered to tow *Land of Soviets* to Craig, but Shestakov declined the offer. The crew was beginning to remove the offending motor which had resulted in their landing there. The motor, after leaving Sitka, had overheated, then finally froze. The flight had a large supply dump of parts in Seattle. A

673

Seattle Post-Intelligencer Library

Russian aviator on wing of **Land of Soviets** *steadies himself with a grip on the handrail along the top of the corrugated aluminum plane at Waterfall cannery, on the west coast of Prince of Wales Island, some thirteen miles southwest of Craig, Alaska. Crew members of the USCG patrol vessel,* **Cygan,** *are seen in the foreground.*

new motor would be brought by Alaska Steamship Company to Juneau, to be picked up by *Cygan* and brought to Waterfall. The BMW-VI and other supplies were placed aboard the *S.S. Alaska* in Seattle.

The *Cygan* arrived at Waterfall at 9:10 A.M. October 5, 1929, leaving twenty minutes later for Ketchikan, to tie up at the Coast Guard float at 10:20 P.M. She would intercept *S.S. Alaska* at sea, and receive the supplies for Shestakov. *Cygan* departed Ketchikan at 6:05 P.M. Monday, October 7, and at 6:40 P.M. was alongside the *Alaska*. H.C. Hermann received two crates containing motor and parts, five cases of oil and one metal tank for the plane. *Cygan* left the ship at 8:15 P.M. and at 8:35 A.M. Tuesday, October 8, was alongside the Waterfall cannery dock. The patrol boat delivered the motor and supplies to Shestakov, taking on board the damaged motor. The Russians had removed and crated it for transport to Ketchikan. The *Cygan* crew assisted in the installing of the new motor in the plane.

On Wednesday, October 9, the *Cygan* left Waterfall cannery at 10:40 A.M. for Craig, arriving there at 12:05 P.M. Shestakov, who was aboard, had a part for the motor welded, obtaining several small parts for the plane. The *Cygan* left Craig at 4:30 P.M. and returned to Waterfall at 6:05 P.M. The boat crew assisted in getting out additional moorings for the plane because of a strong lee-shore breeze. On Friday, October 12, Hermann had three men assisting in the work on the Soviet plane.

Sunday, October 13, 1929 was the big day. Overcast, rain and a moderate southeasterly breeze, and fifty-degree temperatures, greeted the men in the early morning. *Cygan* took aboard two boxes of motor parts and a metal tank, for Ketchikan. Four of Hermann's men left the vessel to handle mooring lines on *Land of Soviets*. Shestakov taxied the plane about on the water for about five minutes, warming and testing the motors, then started full speed ahead, and was off the water at 6:20 A.M. in a very pretty takeoff, disappearing into the south in a few minutes. At 6:30 A.M. the patrol boat was underway for Ketchikan to return to her regular duties. The parts from the Soviet plane were delivered to the Alaska Steamship Company dock for shipment to Seattle.

Land of Soviets arrived in Seattle at 5:27 P.M. Sunday, October 13, 1929; they had taken off at Waterfall at 7:20 A.M. (Seattle time)—a flight of ten hours and seven minutes. First appearing from the north, the plane circled several times, then glided lightly onto the waters of the lake, a navy seaplane leading the way to the landing runway. Docking at the naval air station on Lake Washington, nose into the bank with no worries of surf or rising and falling tides, the plane was soon moored safely.

The fliers were quickly engulfed by the crowd, many of Russian birth or descent wearing red ribbons. Welcomed in the gathering dusk by Doctor Charles C. Tiffin and William G. McKay on behalf of Governor Hartley, and by Mayor Edwards, the mass of people surrounding the fliers was soon encouraged to move back to permit photographers to take pictures of the event for the news services. The weary crew of the ANT-4, still in rubber hip boots and heavy flying clothes, were then motored to the Olympic Hotel where headquarters for the group was established. The plane was left in the care of Naval Captain John D. Price, commandant of Sand Point Naval Air Station, to be moved into the navy hangar for the installation of landing gear.

The following day, with no official program, the airmen, now refreshed from a night's rest in good beds following their ten-hour flight from Waterfall to Seattle, spent the forenoon in their suite. A tailor, hurriedly summoned, measured them for clothing that would make them

*Land of Soviets **arrives at the beach near Sand Point Naval Air Station on Lake Washington on October 13, 1929. As naval crews bring it ashore, the two Russian pilots stand in the open cockpit behind their windscreen on top the corrugated aluminum fuselage. A handrail, similar to that used on boat cabins, is at their right.***

October 13, 1929. Land of Soviets arrives at Sand-Point Naval Air Station in Seattle, Washington. Left to Right: Dimitri Fufaev, S.A. Shestakov, U.S. Navy Captain John D. Price, Boris Sterligov, and Philip Bolotov.

less conspicuous on Seattle's streets. They looked at scores of congratulatory telegrams and received the many visitors who came to call. A wish to see Henry Ford and Herbert Hoover, of whom they had heard much, resulted in a personal invitation from the Dearborn, Michigan industrialist to visit him. Their flight east from Oakland would include a stop there.

The fliers, driven in an army car to the new hangar at Sand Point that afternoon, spent some time inspecting the ANT-4 in the building, and discussing routes with Captain June Steadman of the United States Marine flying corps. They were to attend a banquet in their honor at the New Washington Hotel that evening, sponsored by the Chamber of Commerce. The next evening, a group known as Friends of the Soviet Union would stage a reception at the Eagles Auditorium, with delegates from Astoria, Chehalis and Portland in attendance. The Russian airmen were fitted with suits, dress shoes, white shirts and ties in time for these events. The tailors had been good to their word.

Andrew W. Petroff, vice-president of Amtorg Trading Corporation of New York, the department representing some 2000 American firms in their dealings with the Russian government, had arrived in Seattle and would return to New York on *Land of Soviets* with the airmen. With him was L.G. Gershevich of New York, representing the same company; he served as Petroff's interpreter. They wished to open an office in Seattle.

The ANT-4 was expected to leave on Wednesday, October 16, 1929. A Boeing Company crew had been brought in to make the change from floats to wheels. The complete landing gear for the plane had been shipped in earlier. Removing the wing-root fairings, Mike Pavone and the rest of the crew hoisted the huge plane from the ceiling beams of the hangar by means of cables attached to these same wing-root fittings. The floats were removed and, one at a time, the left and right landing gear assemblies were chocked up into place and bolted to their fittings. One-half inch rubber shock cords were wound on by the mechanics, to provide recoil in the gear.

Department of Commerce inspectors privately requested the mechanics go over the ANT-4 thoroughly, to be certain it was in good airworthy condition; they wanted no incidents

October, 1929. ANT-4 **Land of Soviets** *in the Sand Point Naval Air Station hangar, being readied for a change from pontoons to wheels after its flight down from Alaska to Seattle. Boeing Airplane Company mechanics would do the work. Fred Gray, foreman of the Boeing maintenance shop, stands under the right motor in grey hat and light jacket. Mike Pavone (in coveralls and cap) stands on the left float.*

or accidents in the flight across the United States. Removing inspection covers, the mechanics were startled to find several control cables in a serious condition; the cables frayed and frazzled over the pulleys. How the flight had gotten this far without a cable breaking, giving serious control problems, was a puzzle. Good fortune had smiled on the fliers. The mechanics changed eight to ten major cables, including those which controlled the stabilizer, as well as thoroughly going over everything else. The problem had been discovered shortly before the airmen arrived at the hangar for departure, causing the flight to be set up for a later day.

Shestakov and his crew, accompanied by the Amtorg men, boarded *Land of Soviets* the morning of Friday, October 18, 1929. They would be taking off the dirt runway at Sand Point in a southerly direction because of the wind, even though a bit uphill. A host of photographers rushed to the south end of the field and set up their cameras. They were doomed to disappointment as the big monoplane, free of its unwieldy floats and fueled for a relatively short flight to Oakland, was off in 900 feet, and went up like a skyrocket.

Three hours after takeoff, the plane was landing on Pearson Field in Vancouver, Washington with a faulty oil pump. Air Service mechanics there aided the Russian fliers in overhauling the pump, and departure was set up for 8:00 A.M. the following morning. They were away at 8:44 A.M. Saturday, October 19, 1929, landing at the Oakland airport at

677

Mid October, 1929, the Russian plane, Land of Soviets, URSS-300, *is shown in the new hangar at Sand Point Naval Air Station on Lake Washington, Seattle. Undergoing a change from floats to wheels for the flight across the United States, the ANT-4 is hanging suspended by cables from the steel roof trusses while a Boeing Airplane Company crew does the work.*

3:10 P.M. that same day. Dominated by scores of Russians in colorful ethnic costumes and Soviet sympathizers flaunting red shirts, skirts and even red flags, the crowd was one of the most unusual ever seen at an aviation event. While the United States did not recognize the current Russian government in those days, the flight was given every assistance, unofficially, and flown across the country with the permission of the United States government.

Heading east from Oakland, *Land of Soviets'* next destination was Salt Lake City. From here they flew on to North Platte, Nebraska, arriving there late in the day on Wednesday, October 23, 1929. Surprised airport attendants hastily organized a committee of four Junior Chamber of Commerce members who accorded them an informal reception.

Taking off on Thursday, Shestakov and his crew reached Chicago that same day,

678

spending the next four days at the lakeside city. On Monday, October 28, the ANT-4 flew on to Detroit, to land at Ford Airport in Dearborn, Michigan, site of the Ford plant. Held here by unfavorable weather, the flight finally got away at 9:10 A.M. Friday, November 1, for New York, the next stop on its world tour. Shestakov, first appearing in the west at 4:12 P.M. with an escort of local planes, landed the *Land of Soviets* at Curtiss-Wright Field, Long Island, New York, late in the afternoon of November 1, 1929, to face a crowd of thousands. Many of them were Russian sympathizers, wearing the red armbands of Friends of the Soviets and some waving red flags. The police were unable to cope with it but, with the help of airport personnel, moved the huge airplane into a hangar, shutting the crowd out. Charles Lindbergh, returning from a flight to Wilmington, Delaware, landed his blue and yellow Curtiss Falcon on the field about this time, with a large part of the crowd surging in that direction. Police placed Lindbergh on a truck, taking him to the hangar where he met the Russian fliers. Colonel Lindbergh later slipped away in a private auto.

Shestakov and his crew were taken to the roof of the hangar, to greet the crowd from an isolated point, but the din was so great that speech was useless. Smiling and waving, the fliers tossed petals from huge reception bouquets down to the crowd. Lindbergh had come out onto the roof and, removing helmet and goggles, was recognized by the crowd. Cheers from below alternated for the American and the Russian airmen.

It was now 5:00 P.M. and getting dark. The Soviet crew was taken to the Hotel Astor, where a formal dinner, hosted by the Russian American Chamber of Commerce and the Aeronautical Chamber of Commerce of America, was to be given in their honor on Wednesday evening. Shestakov, in a speech over station WJZ on November 2, hoped American fliers would visit Russia, assuring they would receive a warm welcome and every assistance in the form of weather reports and meteorological data.

The flight of *Land of Soviets* had covered a total of 13,300 miles in 141 hours and twenty-three minutes of actual flight time. Since the cruising range of the twin-engined ANT-4 was only 2500 miles, the plane was returned to Russia by steamer, rather than attempt a transatlantic flight.

Note: The flight's arrival in New York coincided with the visit of a Soviet air delegation, looking elsewhere than Germany for reliable radial engines and advanced designs in airframe construction.

Bennett-Rodebaugh Company

Wien Alaska Airways, Incorporated
Alaskan Airways, Incorporated

Fairbanks 1929

THE NEW YEAR OPENED WITH two major companies still providing air service out of Fairbanks. Bennett-Rodebaugh Company, based at Weeks Field, had continued flying through the winter, as had Wien Alaska Airways. The Wien company was based in Nome but a large part of its business was out of Fairbanks, and its new fifty by sixty foot hangar was located on Weeks Field.

On January 2, 1929, it was announced that Bennett-Rodebaugh Company had acquired the Stinson Standard SB-1, NC 877, owned by Tom Gerard, in exchange for $11,000 worth of stock in the firm. Gerard had left the biplane at Holy Cross after damaging it during takeoff from the small field in November of 1928. Tom was to be a working stockholder in the firm,

Bennett-Rodebaugh Company hangars on Weeks Field in early 1929 with the fleet lined up in front. Left to Right: Zenith, Model 6; open-cockpit Swallow, C 2774; Stinson Standard SB-1, NC 877; Gillam's OX-5 Swallow, **Arctic Prospector;** *Fred Moller's Waco 9, C 2776,* **Anna.**

Pilot A.A. Bennett with the Zenith Z-6 in Fairbanks before departing on a flight. The lady passenger (probably Fannie Quigley) sensibly wears shoepacs. Flights over the rough Alaskan terrain sometimes included having to hike out.

681

Donald E. Young Collection

serving as a pilot. Including the Stinson, Bennett-Rodebaugh Company would have four modern airplanes, all powered with air-cooled motors. Three were equipped with factory-built cabins, and the fourth, the Super Swallow, had been partially enclosed at the company's shop.

Noel Wien returned to Fairbanks in January to find his brother Ralph busily engaged in setting up the new Hamilton Metalplane H-45, NC 10002, that had been ordered in August of 1928. It had arrived by train near the end of December. Ralph, with his two helpers, moved the

Clifton's Library, Valdez

Bennett-Rodebaugh Company hangars on Weeks Field, Fairbanks, in early 1929. Airplanes Left to Right: Zenith, Model Z-6 cabin plane; open-cockpit Swallow, C 2774, with Wright J4-A Wright Whirlwind; Stinson Standard, Model SB-1, NC 877; open-cockpit Swallow with OX-5, Arctic Prospector, of Harold Gillam's; Waco, Model 9, C 2776, Anna, with OXX-6, owned by Fred Moller. Men Left to Right: Unidentified; Unidentified; Charles L. Thompson, manager; Bill Basham, mechanic; Earl Borland, mechanic; Ed Young, pilot; Tom Gerrard, pilot; Unidentified; Fred Moller, mechanic (head shows); Cecil Higgins, mechanic; Unidentified; Unidentified.

Donald E. Young Collection

crates to the new Wien hangar and already had the wings attached to the gleaming corrugated aluminum-alloy fuselage.

Noel was off Fairbanks in the Stinson "Detroiter" about noon of Friday, January 11, 1929, with a load of supplies for two trappers named Wachwitz, also carrying Ed Kammisgaard back to his home on Lake Minchumina. Noel returned to Weeks Field after dark that same day. A.A. Bennett was also away on January 11, carrying Father J.F. McElmeel, S.J., priest at the Nulato hospital, to Tanana where the cleric expected to spend a month. McElmeel had arrived in Fairbanks with Sister Mary Couer de Jesus who had suffered a broken leg when she fell on the ice at Nulato. Remaining overnight at Nenana, Bennett came into Fairbanks the following day, carrying Doctor H.W. Averill. Tom Gerard flew into Weeks Field about 1:00 P.M. of Saturday, January 12, in the Stinson SB-1, NC 877, from Holy Cross, with the motor parts damaged there in November of 1928 now replaced. He had been overnight at Tanana on the way in.

A period of heavy weather set in. Tom Gerard and A.A. Bennett were holding at McGrath on Wednesday, January 16, hoping to proceed, respectively, to Sleetmute and Bethel. Noel Wien, on that same day, was forced back to Fairbanks by a heavy snowstorm while over the Kantishna River, bound for Lake Minchumina. He was carrying Fred and Ernest Wachwitz, who were planning on trapping near the lake. Wien had already hauled the bulk of their supplies in. Flying the big new Hamilton Metalplane, NC 10002, of Wien Alaska Airways on its first cross-country trip, Wien planned to fly the H-45 to Nome later in the week,

The new Hamilton H-45 of Wien Alaska Airways, Incorporated, rests on skis before the company's new hangar on Weeks Field in January, 1929, soon after its assembly. It was the latest thing in air travel for Alaska.

683

where five passengers awaited passage. Fairbanks received its heaviest snowfall of the season that evening. For several days the planes were held on the ground.

On Wednesday, January 23, 1929, the pilots were again aloft. Tom Gerard and A.A. Bennett got away from Bethel on Tuesday afternoon for Sleetmute. They were planning on bringing in eight passengers from Bethel, Sleetmute and Ophir, most of whom were coming in connection with the murder case involving Constantine Beaver, on trial for the crime. Ed Young made a round trip to Tanana, carrying Doctor E.W. White, government physician and surgeon there, to Fairbanks. The doctor was to appear before the grand jury as a witness.

Wien Alaska Airways Hamilton Metalplane, NC 10002, on the ice near the Snake River bridge at Nome.

Noel Wien went out the same day in the Hamilton Metalplane, landing at American Creek with R.H. Ogburn, newly appointed manager of the American Creek Dredging Company, along with two other employees. He went on to Tanana to bring in 200 pounds of Nome mail which had left Nenana by stage. Noel intended to take the mail on to Nome the following day. On his return to Fairbanks, the Wien Alaska Airways pilot made a round trip to Livengood in the afternoon. The big Hamilton got off from Weeks Field for the mining camp with 1450 pounds, including six passengers and their baggage. High winds prevented the pilot from landing and he returned to Fairbanks. He went out again the next morning, Thursday, January 24, 1929, with the same load, making a successful landing at Livengood. Noel was away from Weeks Field again at 1:55 P.M. that afternoon for his first flight to Nome in the Hamilton, carrying 267 pounds of mail. Ed Young, Bennett-Rodebaugh pilot, had taken off that morning, carrying Sam Dubin for Alatna, and a load of freight and mail for Wiseman. He returned to Fairbanks Saturday afternoon from Alatna, carrying Mrs. J.J. O'Connor.

Late Saturday afternoon, Tom Gerard and A.A. Bennett came in from Bethel and the upper Kuskokwim River settlements. From Ophir, they brought in Mrs. Sid Paulson for medical attention. From Bethel and Sleetmute they brought in Deputy U.S. Marshal Frank C. Wiseman and his prisoner, Constantine Beaver, as well as Mrs. Bertha Bishop, an interpreter for the native. They also carried three native women as witnesses in the murder case.

Noel Wien, holding at Ruby for weather on his way to Nome, had returned to Fairbanks Friday for three passengers who were awaiting passage to Nome. In the meantime, he made a flight to Alatna, returning to base on Sunday morning with five passengers. All the pilots for both companies were home for Sunday. Other than flights to nearby points, Wien Alaska Airways was concentrating on the Nome business, while the Bennett-Rodebaugh Company largely took care of the Kuskokwim route.

The three passengers for Nome were James Cross and two representatives of the National Geographic Society: Horace Ashton and Earl Welch. The two were bound for Elephant Point, 175 miles northeast of Nome, to gather material on the reindeer herds in that area. Noel took off, with encouraging weather reports, in the Hamilton at 10:35 A.M. Monday, January 28, 1929. With his three passengers and the mail and freight at Ruby, he had a load of over 1500 pounds on his departure from there. Noel landed the Hamilton on the river ice at Nome at 3:45 P.M. Fairbanks time, a fast trip of five hours and ten minutes elapsed time (4:45 flight time) over a distance of 550 miles.

Bennett also left on Monday, for the Kuskokwim, carrying Mrs. Jean Grey and A.R. Eldridge for McGrath. The pilot expected to continue on to Bethel for a load of furs. Leaving Fairbanks at 9:00 A.M. he was in Bethel at 4:30 P.M. that same day, after the stop at McGrath. He started back for Fairbanks Tuesday morning.

Ed Young, Bennett-Rodebaugh pilot, was away for Fort Yukon on Thursday, January 31. He carried Herman Swendorff, radioman of the U.S. Signal Corps, for Circle City, as well as Fred Bohmer, contractor, on his way home to Fort Yukon. The man had received medical attention for a broken arm in Fairbanks. Landing at Fort Yukon, the pilot proceeded on to Circle City with Swendorff and Mrs. George Burmaster, then returned to Fort Yukon. Held there by weather, Young finally was able to return home on Sunday, February 3, bringing in George Burmaster and Harry Anthony. Anthony had owned a trading post at Old Crow on the Porcupine River for many years but had sold it to the Northern Commercial Company and was now on his way Outside.

Earl Borland, mechanic for Bennett-Rodebaugh Company, was on the southbound train from Fairbanks on Friday, February 1, 1929. He was traveling to Seattle on the *S.S. Northwestern* for a month's vacation, but stopped enroute at Juneau to visit his uncle, Doctor W.A. Borland.

Noel Wien arrived over Fairbanks at 6:45 P.M. Thursday, January 31, in darkness, landing shortly thereafter. The flight from Nome, bucking strong headwinds, had taken eight hours and fifteen minutes. Ruby to Fairbanks took three and one-half hours, an hour longer than his westbound time of two and one-half hours over the same route. He landed on Weeks Field with comparative ease, using their floodlights and his landing lights. Some of his passengers were hurrying to catch the morning train, to board the *Northwestern* at Seward for Seattle. His passengers were Grant R. Jackson, president of the Merchants and Miners Bank in Nome (and a shareholder in Wien Alaska Airways, Incorporated), Alfred Lomen, manager of the Nome Lighterage Company and Lomen Reindeer Corporation, E.F. Bauer, assistant superintendent at Nome for Alaska Road Commission, Thomas "Courageous Tom" Peterson, Teller merchant and manager of Teller Lighterage Company, and E.J. Woofter, who had been working as linotype operator for the *Nome Nugget*, and who would be a Second Division Representative at the coming legislative session. All except Bauer left the next morning on the train for the south, overnighting at the railroad hotel in Curry, as was the custom.

Harold Gillam had been practicing up his flying skills in the Swallow, *Arctic Prospector*, which he had purchased from Arctic Prospecting & Development Company in September of 1928. He made his first cross-country flight on Saturday, February 2, 1929, when he flew to Nenana. He returned to Fairbanks with Cecil L. Higgins, tractor driver for Alaska Gold Dredging company at Tofty, as a passenger, Gillam repeated the flight on Monday, February 4, taking off at 1:00 P.M., to return Higgins to Nenana. Gillam was back in Fairbanks at 2:30 P.M. He had been flying solo since the fall of 1928 but had not previously attempted a flight of any length. More would be heard of the young pilot before the year was out.

A. A. Bennett had left for the Kuskokwim on Saturday, February 2, 1929, stopping at Nenana to pick up Mr. and Mrs. J.H. Hubbard and their son, Russell. Hubbard was moving to McGrath to take over the post of deputy U.S. marshal there. He had held a similar post at Nenana for the past several months. Russell's older brother, Percy, in a short time was to become a pilot in Fairbanks. Bennett brought in T.A. Parsons, Northern Commercial Company official, on his return from McGrath, arriving in Fairbanks on Sunday, February 3, 1929.

Noel Wien flew to Fish Lake on Saturday, February 2, bringing in R.H. Ogburn, manager of American Creek Dredging. The next day he was off for Alatna, taking brother Ralph with him, as well as Wilfred J. Evans, Alatna postmaster and fur trader, who had spent a few days in Fairbanks. The Wiens flew to Walker Lake from there, to inspect, with the possibility of later purchasing, the Stearman C-2B damaged by Cecil Crawford of Arctic Prospecting & Development Company when he landed there soon after the plane was brought to Alaska. Returning to Alatna, he brought in George Webber and J.J. O'Connor, prospectors from Walker Lake in the Kobuk country, who had come that far by dog team.

Bennett left Fairbanks shortly after 8:00 A.M. Tuesday, February 5, with Deputy U.S. Marshal Frank C. Wiseman, traveling to Bethel to pick up the brother of Constantine Beaver, who would act as a defense witness in the murder trial of Beaver. The pilot expected to complete the flight to Bethel and return to Sleetmute in the same day, returning to Fairbanks on Wednesday.

Noel Wien, accompanied by brother Ralph, was away also on Tuesday morning. Flying to Livengood, the pair returned with Mrs. Frank McGarvey and Mrs. Albert Bell. In the afternoon Noel took Fred Wachwitz and a trapping outfit to the mouth of the Tolovana River for a season's trapping; the pilot returned the same day.

Ed Young came in from Fort Yukon on Friday afternoon, February 8, and was away the following morning for Circle City, Fort Yukon and Beaver, carrying Vance R. McDonald, Fairbanks merchant, who planned to return on Monday.

On Sunday, February 10, Noel Wien made thirteen local flights with sightseers in the Hamilton. The Fairbanks and Seward high school basketball team members were included as guests of the company. The pilot was away at 9:30 the next morning for Nome, carrying as a passenger nurse Emily Morgan, who was sent to assume duties at the Nome hospital. Noel had four passengers listed for the return flight to Fairbanks. The pilot was forced to land at Haycock near Norton Sound by wind and snow, to spend the night there before getting into Nome on the following day. He was held in the Seward Peninsula city for many days by high winds.

Bennett was away in the Zenith 6 on Wednesday, February 13, 1929, for Anvik with a supply of vaccine to counteract a threatened smallpox epidemic in the Yukon River village. He stopped at McGrath to offload Mrs. Peterson and infant, and was held in Anvik by weather, finally getting away on Monday, February 18. He spent that night in McGrath, returning to

Fairbanks late the following day. He brought in Frank Guskey, manager of the Northern Commercial Company store at McGrath. The Bennett-Rodebaugh pilot was off again on Wednesday morning, February 20, for Livengood. Ed Young, in the Stinson Standard, NC 877, left for Fort Yukon the morning of Wednesday, February 20, 1929, to bring in Miss Rottermount, a school teacher from the community. She had been ill for several weeks and was on her way Outside for medical treatment.

Pilot Tom Gerard of the Bennett-Rodebaugh Company was off Weeks Field on Saturday morning, February 23, for Tanana Crossing. Carrying fur buyer Barney Stejskal as passenger, the pilot was unable to land at his destination, and returned to Fairbanks. Ed Young had also departed for Alatna on Saturday, to bring in an ill woman. He had taken two passengers to Livengood the previous day.

Noel Wien had finally gotten away from Nome after flying to Candle on Wednesday, February 21, to pick up Senator Richard N. Sundquist, one of his Fairbanks passengers. The pilot left Nome at 10:30 A.M. on Thursday in Hamilton, NC 10002, with Sundquist and Representative Henry Burgh, plus another passenger, B.B. Mozee, Bureau of Education official. Jack (John) Hooper and Harry Strong, Lomen Reindeer Corporation employees from Golovin, boarded the plane when the pilot stopped at the village. Refueled at Ruby, the Hamilton arrived in Fairbanks at 6:10 P.M. that same day. The two legislators caught the train the next morning for Seward and a boat to Juneau, expecting to arrive there in time for the opening of the session. Noel flew Jack Hooper, Harry Strong and Ed Gedney to Anchorage on Friday afternoon, leaving at 2:15 P.M. The men wanted to catch the southbound train at Anchorage to board the steamer for Outside. Making the flight in three hours, Noel returned to home base the next day. That same afternoon he took R.H. Ogburn to American Creek, bringing in Leo Rogge on the return flight.

On Monday, February 25, 1929, the pilots were all busy. Bennett hopped off in the Zenith 6 for McGrath, carrying Mrs. Georgia Hagen and Miss Josie Sheehan, operators of a bathhouse in Flat, as passengers. Ed Young was away to Tanana Crossing with Barney Stejskal, on the fur buyer's second attempt. Thomas Gerard flew to Livengood in the afternoon with passenger Charles Main. Noel Wien, of the rival company, made a flight to Munson's with D.W. Flanigan, another fur buyer. On his return, the pilot took Doctor E.W. White, in charge of the Bureau of Education hospital, to Tanana.

With the trial of Constantine Beaver over, witnesses who had been called in were returning home. Ed Young, Bennett-Rodebaugh Company pilot, was away in the forenoon on Wednesday, February 27, with four passengers for Sleetmute. From there he went to Bethel to bring E.J. Cronin, manager of the Northern Commercial Company store at the river town, to Fairbanks for medical treatment. Bennett took Deputy U.S. Marshal Frank C. Wiseman and Alexi Beaver, brother of the condemned man, as well as Vance R. McDonald and Bertha Bishop, back to Bethel the following day. He was away in the forenoon on Thursday.

Fridtjof "Fritz" Wien, brother to Noel and Ralph Wien, had returned to Fairbanks on Tuesday, after spending several months Outside. He had taken a course in mechanics there in the fall, then spent the rest of the winter visiting relatives before returning to Fairbanks. A new pilot, Harry T. Davidson, arrived with Fritz, to join the staff of Wien Alaska Airways, Incorporated. Coming from Minnesota, Davidson was experienced; he had been an instructor for the Army in World War I, claiming 2000 hours in the air. He expected to bring his wife and four children to the community. He was also a musician.

In early February, Wien Alaska Airways had received a query from New York from the Swenson-Herskovits concern regarding a contract to fly several loads of valuable furs from the sailing vessel *M.S. Elisif* (a proper name in Norwegian) which was frozen fast in the ice along the Siberian coast near North Cape. If the furs were brought to Fairbanks by air they could be shipped by surface to market. The firm was anticipating a fall in price before the year was out. The vessel was owned by the Swenson Fur & Trading Company, who possessed a permit granted by the Soviet government to serve as a shipping company on the Siberian coast.

Olaf Swenson, of Swedish descent, was born in Manistee, Michigan in 1883. He was experienced in the Arctic and had traded along that coast since 1905; first with other companies dealing in "country products", and later in business for himself as Olaf Swenson and Company. He had been successful and owned a far-flung chain of trading posts in the fur-rich region until the Russian revolution had resulted in confiscation of his holdings. By 1923 the Soviets had driven out White Russian officials from Siberia and replaced them with their own. Swenson, who spoke Russian, persevered and, in 1926, still operating as Olaf Swenson and Company, obtained a five-year contract with the Soviet government to supply American merchandise, approved by the Soviets, to the Siberian settlements within the approved district, on a cost-plus basis, with an additional fee for delivery. The Soviets agreed to turn over all furs, again on a cost-plus basis, to the Swenson firm for delivery to market. It was much simpler for the Russians to handle commerce on the remote coast in this fashion than attempt to do it themselves by way of the northeast passage, or up from Vladivostok. In some years it would be impossible to get through, and the Siberian natives and Russians along that coast badly needed the essentials of life. The Soviet government also needed the hard money from the fur crop. So both sides were served.

Swenson operated with the *Nanuk* in 1926 and 1927 out of Seattle, making two seasonal runs. In 1928, together with New York associated Maurice Cantor (Cantor & Angel) and Irving W. Herskovits (Albert Herskovits & Sons), Olaf Swenson signed two more contracts with the Soviet Fur Trust, as the Swenson Fur & Trading Company. Needing an additional vessel, and unable to locate a suitable ship under American registry, Olaf went to Norway where he purchased the *Elisif*. These vessels, used much in arctic Norway, are wooden-hulled, and of heavily braced construction. The vessel wall is often one meter thick, sheathed in two-inch Australian ironbark, the hardest wood known, to resist abrasion from the ice. The *Elisif*, still under Norwegian registry, with Captain Even Larsen and a sixteen-man Norwegian crew, arrived in Seattle June 27, 1928, to take on a cargo of supplies. With Ray S. Pollister, vice-president of Swenson Fur & Trading Company as supercargo, Even Larsen of Brevik, Norway as captain, and Captain A.P. Jochimsen, ice pilot, the *Elisif* sailed from Seattle on July 10, 1928 for the Siberian Arctic, where she became icebound on August 22, approximately ten miles from North Cape. She was not to break free until July 29 the following year.

Worried about the fur market, Swenson-Herskovits paid Wien Alaska Airways $4500 for the first round trip, lowering this by $500 for subsequent trips. The Hamilton was not paid for but, if they were successful on this contract, it would be. Grant Jackson, secretary-treasurer of Wien Alaska Airways, Incorporated, was in New York on business and would attempt to obtain insurance on the plane—an effort that was doomed to failure; the insurance firms were reluctant to cover such a project. Permission for the flight into Russian territory had been secured by the Swenson-Herskovits people. The *Elisif*, with its Seattle radio operator Charles Huntley, was in contact with New York through Nome and the WAMCATS system.

With some of the details unsettled, Noel Wien took off from Weeks Field at 9:55 A.M. Wednesday, February 27, 1929, for Kotzebue, carrying C.E. Alexander and William James as passengers. Calvin "Doc" Cripe, accompanied Noel as mechanic on the flight. Arriving at Kotzebue, the pilot dropped his passengers there and flew south in the Hamilton for Nome. He and his mechanic landed there at 5:10 P.M. Wednesday. The following day, at a dinner at the Arthurs', the engagement of Ada B. Arthurs to Noel Wien was announced, with an expected wedding in May.

Ed Young, Bennett-Rodebaugh Company pilot, arrived back in Fairbanks from Akiak, a flight of 600 miles. He carried Mr. and Mrs. E.J. Cronin, the Northern Commercial Company manager at Bethel. The man suffered from an infected ear and arm, requiring treatment at a modern hospital facility. Young was off Akiak at 10:00 A.M. Friday, March 1 and, after one stop at McGrath for fuel, landed in Fairbanks at 4:35 P.M. He said that Bennett had arrived at Bethel on March 1 with his passengers and expected to go to Nelson Island for a load of furs. Young was off the following morning, with Corporal Kenneth A. Van de Water, U.S. Signal Corps, who was replacing Fred Anderson at Nulato. Anderson returned with Ed Young to Fairbanks. On the way back with Anderson on Monday, the pilot ran into strong headwinds that so depleted his fuel that he was forced to land at Tolovana, remaining there until Tom Gerard came out on Saturday morning, March 9, with a supply. Gerard returned immediately to Fairbanks, with Young to follow.

Noel Wien, in Nome, was looking at the route to North Cape and the *Elisif*. He figured it at 600 miles each way, flying from Nome to Cape Prince of Wales, thence across Bering Strait, a distance of fifty-five miles crossing over the Diomede Islands to East Cape, Siberia, then skirting the Siberian coast to North Cape. The vessel was frozen in about ten miles from there. It looked like about six hours flying time each way from Nome.

Stripping the Hamilton, NC 10002, of seats and other unneeded equipment except for emergency gear, the pilot loaded it with supplies ordered for the *Elisif*, including a whole hog and a quarter of beef from T.C. Lehman's store. The ship's company had been out of such meat for some time, although reindeer and seal were available in the area. Waterfowl had long ago flown south, not to come stringing back until May.

In Fairbanks, Ralph Wien and the new pilot, Harry T. Davidson, were carrying on the local business for Wien Alaska Airways. Using the Stinson "Detroiter" SB, Davidson was off Weeks Field at 9:45 A.M. Tuesday, March 5, 1929, for Lake Minchumina, on his first extended

March 7, 1929. Noel Wien and Calvin Cripe preparing to depart Nome for the Elisif, *a trading vessel fast in the ice about ten miles from North Cape, Siberia. The two men would bring in a valuable load of furs in the Hamilton.*

Tom Martin Collection

A whole hog and a quarter of beef are among the supplies ready for loading on Wien Alaska Airways' Hamilton Metalplane in Nome, prior to taking off for North Cape, Siberia and the Elisif at 7:20 A.M. Thursday, March 7, 1929. Fifty gallons of case gas was also included, to be used on the return flight.

flight in Alaska. Ralph Wien accompanied him, riding in a seat other than the pilot's. The plane had just been overhauled, and Ralph had test hopped it for the first time the day before. The company had also purchased, for $3500, the Stearman C-2B (NC 5415) wrecked by Crawford at Walker Lake on its first trip. They planned to make repairs at the scene and have the aircraft flown out. A new engine mount for its Wright J-4 engine had been ordered from the States. A wing panel and landing gear needed repair.

Davidson and Ralph were forced to turn back when about one hundred miles out by heavy fog. They bucked a very strong headwind on the return flight. The pair were able to go out again on Thursday, March 7, and bring in Gene Nelson and Fred Wachwitz, trappers from Lake Minchumina. The following morning, Davidson, again with Ralph Wien, was off for Hughes in the Koyukuk district, carrying C.M. Berry as a passenger. Poor weather enroute forced them to spend the night at Tolovana, where Ed Young was awaiting fuel.

On Thursday, March 7, 1929, everything was ready for the flight to Siberia. From Nome, the weather looked clear and Pollister had radioed from *Elisif* of good weather and clear to the east, which direction they could view from the ship. Noel and "Doc" Cripe were ready when word was received from the ship's supercargo. The Hamilton, on skis, broke ground at 7:20 A.M. A little over an hour later the men flew over Wales. Heading west-northwest and leaving familiar terrain, they were soon over Little Diomede Island, where the pilot turned the plane to a northwest heading for Siberia. In a little over a quarter hour they had reached East Cape, spotting a village here. The pilot turned slightly to the right to follow a mountainous coast. From Kolyuchin Bay, one hundred miles beyond East Cape, the land was difficult to separate from the sea, all under a white cover; the mountains had retreated inland forty or fifty miles. Pressure ridges and uptilted ice cakes made the difference.

Things were going well until a rise in oil pressure brought the pilot instantly alert. Frost collecting at the external exit of the vent tube of the oil tank was blocking it and causing the trouble—something the pilot had experienced before. "Doc" Cripe had to do something. Unable to get at it any other way, he opened the small, forward wing-window and, stretching his arm out into the frigid gale with a long knife in hand, was just able to reach the partially covered vent, scraping the frost away. This temporarily relieved the problem. He had to repeat this painful measure every quarter hour until they landed. It was exhausting work.

690

Calvin "Doc" Cripe astride the motor mount behind the Wright Whirlwind, 200 horsepower J4-A, while he works on a top overhaul. The Stinson Standard, C 5262, was Wilkins' Stinson **Detroiter No. 2** *before being purchased by Wien Alaska Airways. Fritz Wien facing the camera, was also a mechanic for the air service in Fairbanks. Mechanic Jim Hutchison is behind the engine and Tom Gerard at right.*

Calvin Cripe had been a stage driver on the Richardson Trail to Valdez, later driving trucks over it. He learned mechanics along the way, repairing mechanicals suffered by himself and other drivers. They nicknamed him "Doc", as he seemed to have the ability to cure any mechanical problem. He was soon a garage mechanic, and was now gaining experience in aviation. About thirty-five, he was a short fellow, agreeable and well-liked.

Watching the map closely while flying at 4000 feet, Noel spotted the cape ahead, and a black spot offshore that proved to be the *Elisif*, with its three masts. It was forty below zero. The crew had selected a landing spot on a frozen lead about two miles from the ship, and had a fire going at each end of the intended runway. They had tried to level off the hard-packed drifts but it was still a very rough landing. All the banging and pounding had not damaged the sturdy Hamilton, although the airmen were considerably shaken during the landing. Climbing from the plane they were immediately surrounded by about forty people, including about twenty Siberian Eskimos and their dog teams from a nearby village. It was two o'clock in the afternoon. With short hours of daylight still prevailing in the Arctic, the plane was to remain overnight. The pilot radioed Nome through the ship's radio operator of his arrival and intentions. The ship's crew, the two airmen and two Russian representatives from the village dined with enthusiasm on fresh pork that evening, and many were the toasts and much the gaiety.

The aviation gas stored at North Cape was old and of poor grade. Wien and Cripe mixed about seventy gallons of it with what was left in the Hamilton's tanks, plus adding fifty gallons of case gas brought from Nome. Case gas was so called since it was two five-gallon

Calvin Cripe Photo

Pilot Noel Wien and flight mechanic Calvin Cripe at the Elisif near North Cape. The representative of the Russian government has come out from North Cape to inspect the plane.

Noel Wien Photo

March 8, 1929 (Nome time). The Hamilton Metalplane, flown by Noel Wien, is loaded with sacks of valuable furs for the return to Nome. The Russian official inspects the ship's papers before departure. The two airmen were off at 12:15 P.M. (Nome time) on their return flight.

cans packed into a light wooden box, a neat way of handling it. Firepotting the engine and adding warmed oil to the tank, the engine started nicely in the forty-below weather the next day. The shock struts had also been thawed with heat. The plane had been loaded with 2000 baled fox furs, weighing 1370 pounds. Pollister, who intended to fly out on the first trip, decided to give the space over to furs.

Noel aborted the first takeoff about 11:00 A.M. when a large bump launched the plane into the air before flying speed was reached. He also realized the plane was too heavily loaded. Throttling back, the pilot stalled the Hamilton back onto the snow, lurching to a halt before running out of runway, if it could be called such. Taking 280 pounds (about 375 skins) out of the baggage compartment in the rear of the plane, the Hamilton was returned to the end of the frozen lead and repositioned. Noel and Calvin Cripe were off at 12:15 P.M. Friday, March 8, 1929 (Nome time). On the way back the motor was lagging a bit from the poor gas and the mechanic found it necessary to resume his torturous procedure with the frosting oil vent for the six-hour flight into Nome. Wien landed the plane at 6:10 P.M. to complete the first commercial flight between Nome and Siberia.

Noel used the following day, Saturday, to repair a tail skid, damaged in the takeoff at North Cape. He then picked up an injured man at Golovin, bringing him in to the Nome hospital. Carrying the load of furs, Noel took off on Sunday to complete the trip to Fairbanks, leaving Calvin Cripe in Nome. With a fuel stop at Nulato, the pilot continued on to land at Weeks Field at 6:40 P.M. The fur bales, worth an estimated $150,000, were placed in a hangar under guard overnight. A Customs inspection was performed by the U.S. marshal's office. The valuable shipment was placed aboard the train the next morning to begin the journey Outside. A wire from Khabarovsk was later received cancelling permission for any more flights to Siberia. Whether due to loose comments made in the press, or for some other reason, no one ever knew.

On Friday, March 8, 1929, A.A. Bennett was away in the Zenith 6 for McGrath, carrying Deputy U.S. Marshal Fred B. Parker and Frank Guskey, manager for the Northern Commercial Company at the river town. Stops were made at Lake Minchumina and Medfra to drop off freight. Two or three inches of water covered the river ice at Medfra and the Bennett-Rodebaugh Company pilot had a little trouble getting off.

High winds and extreme cold held the plane at McGrath until Sunday. Parker had traveled in order to pick up an insane woman there for transport to Fairbanks. Bennett was away at 1:30 P.M. Sunday, March 10, 1929, on the return trip. The patient was not violent and, although the doors of the plane were securely locked, she made no effort to leave. The pilot encountered a stiff headwind in the twenty-below-zero weather, climbing to 9000 feet in search of warmer and more stable air. They enjoyed a beautiful view of Mount McKinley and Mount Foraker as well as the entire range. The party arrived in Fairbanks at 5:30 P.M. that same day.

William Gill, Anchorage student pilot, had been in Seattle taking further flight training. It was reported that Gill spun in from 400 feet and was slightly injured but his passenger, now recovered, had been unconscious for nine hours. The accident had occurred when the motor failed shortly after takeoff.

On the afternoon of Wednesday, March 13, A.A. Bennett departed for Iditarod and Flat with John Lund and another passenger. Noel Wien also was away in the Hamilton for Nome and Elephant Point, where several passengers desired passage to Fairbanks. Ed Young was expecting to leave on Thursday in the Stinson Standard SB-1 with a load of freight for Wiseman.

Earl Rossman, explorer, author and motion picture photographer had arrived in Fairbanks on Tuesday's train, on which Earl Borland, mechanic for Bennett-Rodebaugh Company, was also a passenger. Earl had been vacationing in the States for a few weeks, his first trip Outside in a number of years. Deep snow on the route had caused trouble getting the trains through beyond Curry.

Fairbanks aviation and civic agencies had been pushing for the establishment of a U.S. Weather Bureau station in their city. Their efforts had born fruit; a wire from Washington provided the information that such an aerological station would be opened as soon as an observer could be sent from the States. Now weather reports and runway conditions from all radio stations in interior and northern Alaska would be received twice daily and also forecasts would be prepared. The service would be of great value to the aviation services as well as to other industries and individuals. Fairbanks awaited their first observer.

Pilots Harry Davidson and Ralph Wien arrived back in Fairbanks from the Kobuk in the late afternoon of Friday, March 15. Again flying the Stinson Detroiter, C 5262, they had brought in Mike Garland, C.E. Alexander and William James. The men had walked from Kotzebue to Shungnak, where they were picked up by the plane. Noel Wien had previously taken them to Kotzebue on February 27, before making the Siberian flight.

Ed Young was in from Wiseman, bringing merchant Sam Dubin, on Sunday March 17, 1929. The pilot, at a ceremony the evening before at the mining community, had been made an honorary member of Igloo No. 8, Pioneers of Alaska. It was forty-six below zero at Wiseman. Bennett had made a round trip the same day to Tanana, picking up Doctor LaRue and another passenger at Nenana on the way down. He had returned from the upper Kuskokwim on Saturday with Vance R. McDonald and Doctor C.A. Pollard, Anchorage dentist who had been working for some time in the Kuskokwim.

A.A. Bennett left on Monday, March 18 on a flight for Father Delon that was to take him to almost every community along the Kuskokwim. The plan was to fly first to Medfra, McGrath, Flat and Iditarod; then to Holy Cross where he would board Father Delon. The priest would go to every place on the Yukon River at which missions were established, also calling at Hooper Bay (Nelson Island), Akiak and Bethel, before returning to Holy Cross.

The pilot carried Mrs. Arthur Berry from Fairbanks to Medfra, and Walter Scott for McGrath. Bennett left Holy Cross for Akulurak with Father Delon on Tuesday, March 19, flying to Marshall and Mountain Village. Taking off from here, they continued down the Yukon River, taking the south fork near Frank Kern's cannery and flying to St. Mary's Mission at Akulurak. One stop was made between Akulurak and Hooper Bay. Kashunuk was the next landing point and from there they flew to Nelson Island and thence to Bethel, where Mrs. John Dull and her two children boarded the plane. They disembarked at Holy Cross, as did Father Delon. Bennett continued to Fairbanks.

On Tuesday, March 19, 1929, both remaining pilots of the Bennett-Rodebaugh Company were out; Ed Young flying to Tanana Crossing, carrying a cargo of perishables for Captain O'Flanigan's trading post and bringing in fur trader Barney Stejskal to Fairbanks. Ten miles above McCarty (now Big Delta), on the Tanana River, they sighted nine members of the buffalo herd where the animals had trampled the snow over an area of about five acres near an open creek. Ed flew to Eagle the next morning with a cargo of freight, and brought in Lee Steel, mining man, on his return. Tom Gerard, also off on Tuesday, made a round trip to Livengood, taking Frank Koda out; the balance of his load was Outside mail for the mining community. In the afternoon he was again off Fairbanks for Tanana, to bring an ill Northern Commercial Company employee to the hospital.

Noel Wien, who had gone to Nome to do some flying out of there, returned to

694

Fairbanks in the Hamilton Metalplane late in the afternoon of Thursday, March 21. He brought in Miss Eva Swenson, Earl M. Welch, Horace Ashton, D.H. Lyons, Jonas Salberg and H.L. Stokes, an old Alaskan miner on his way to San Francisco for medical attention. All except Lyons left on the morning train for the States.

Ed Young was off for Beaver on Saturday morning, March 23, carrying a load of perishables for Frank Yasuda, of the Yukon River settlement. He returned to Weeks Field early in the afternoon.

Noel Wien departed Fairbanks the morning of Saturday, March 23, for Dillingham on Bristol Bay. He was carrying A.R. Gardner, Bureau of Education official, and Mrs. Gardner. Eighty miles out of Fairbanks, at the Toklat River, the pilot encountered fog, causing him to return to Fairbanks. The flight had to be postponed. He was away again with the Gardners on Tuesday, March 26, 1929, completing the 600-mile flight in five and three-quarters hours. He returned to Fairbanks on Wednesday afternoon, after overnighting at Sleetmute.

A.A. Bennett, on a second charter with the Reverend Father Philip Delon, arrived in Bethel on Wednesday, March 27, after an inspection tour of Catholic missions along the Bering Sea coast. In seven and one-half hours of actual flight time they had completed a trip that would have taken the priest a month by dog team. Father Delon left with Bennett the next morning for Holy Cross, his headquarters.

Bennett returned to Fairbanks from Bethel, landing on Weeks Field at 12:30 P.M. of Thursday, March 28. Pilot Ed Young, who flew to Bethel the day before, carrying Mr. and Mrs. E.J. Cronin, was also expected back on Thursday. Ed had brought Cronin in from the lower Kuskokwim the last part of February for hospitalization. Tom Gerard made a flight to Livengood this same day, bringing in Nick Manich. The day before he had made a mail flight to the mining camp, bringing in Frank Koda and Fred Anderson on his return.

Noel Wien was away on a charter for Fort Yukon on Thursday morning, March 28, 1929, with Doctor J.A. Sutherland and E.B. Collins, assistant U.S. district attorney who would investigate a case in that area. After stopping at Rampart, where Doctor Sutherland examined and treated several influenza cases, the party arrived at Fort Yukon where they spent the night. The following day, Friday, word was received that the suspect, M. Lynch, was planning to cross through the pass in the Endicott Range and travel down the slope to the arctic coast. Wien departed that same day, taking Deputy U.S. Marshal William Butler of Fort Yukon, Collins and Ed Owens in the Hamilton. Wien flew over the Coleen River forty miles from the mouth, sighting Owens camp about thirty-five miles farther on. The pilot did not land but went on to Black Mountain where Lynch was reported to be living with an Eskimo group. The pilot located the camp above timber line, some sixty miles above the headwaters of the Coleen. Wien landed the Hamilton on a plateau, almost at the crest of the mountain. The pilot and Collins stayed with the plane while Deputy Butler and his guide, Owens, snowshoed the three-quarters of a mile to the Eskimo camp. Traveling about three miles farther, using the Eskimo dog teams, they located Lynch at a separate camp, where he was arrested without difficulty.

Noel Wien took off from the plateau without any problem and returned to Fort Yukon, stopping enroute to pick up Mrs. Owens and her children, needed as witnesses. Owens had filed the complaint against Lynch, of statutory rape against Owens' seventeen-year-old daughter. The pilot was carrying nine persons in the big plane when he got off for Fort Yukon. The landing lights were needed on their arrival.

With all necessary members present for a trial, an exhaustive inquiry was conducted that same Friday evening, continuing until 3:00 A.M. It was determined that Lynch had committed no more serious offense than assault; he was sentenced to six months in jail. Wien took off the next day to return Mrs. Owens and her children to their home, proceeding on to land at Black Mountain to pick up a valuable motion picture outfit belonging to Lynch. The pilot returned to Fort Yukon about 1:00 P.M., departing for Fairbanks an hour later with his party and their prisoner.

Noel Wien left Fairbanks in the Hamilton the morning of Wednesday, April 3, 1929, for Nome, carrying Shorty Barker, John Miller, and 600 pounds of supplies for Shungnak; the men intended to prospect in the Kobuk country for two years. Off Shungnak, stormy weather enroute, the pilot was forced to land at Noorvik, going on to Kotzebue and Nome later on. He arrived at Nome on Saturday. He still had not, at this time, received the notice of cancellation of further Siberian trips and, with Calvin Cripe still at Nome, there was a possibility the two would make a second such flight. Word had been received prior to leaving Fairbanks that the initial load of furs had reached the market in New York just twenty days after being shipped from North Cape.

Ed Young was away in the Stinson Standard, NC 877, for Alatna on the morning of Wednesday, April 3, 1929. He carried Henry Kruger, an employee of Sam Dubin's. The pilot stopped at Nenana, picking up a passenger for Hot Springs. Young returned to Fairbanks that same afternoon with three passengers; Henry Kruger, Mrs. Edwards and child.

A.A. Bennett left Weeks Field for Dawson the morning of Wednesday, April 3, with James Cody, agent for Northern Commercial Company of that city, and Charles O. Fowler, Fairbanks Exploration Company official who was making the round trip. Good weather was reported all along the route. The pilot arrived at the Canadian city at 2:00 P.M. after an uneventful flight. Bennett left the next day, getting as far as Eagle where he was held over until Saturday by storms. He arrived at Weeks Field Saturday afternoon, carrying Fowler and J.A. Smacker, dredgemaster for Fowler's company. The snow from Eagle to Fairbanks was re-

April 7, 1929. Leonhard Seppala, famous dog team driver, lifts his daughter, Sigrid, from the wing of Bennett-Rodebaugh Company's Stinson Standard SB-1, NC 877, in front of the Weeks Field hangar, after a flight with pilot George E. "Ed" Young, standing right.

696

Earl Rossman Photo, Donald E. Young Collection

April 7, 1929. Contrasting an earlier form of transportation with the new, Judge Cecil H.
Clegg poses with his derby-winning team of sled dogs before the Bennett-Rodebaugh Com-
pany's Stinson biplane, NC 877, with Sigrid Seppala on his basket sled. Leonhard Seppala in
parka, stands near the front of the sled. The others are, Left to Right: A.A. Bennett, Ed
Young, Charles L. Thompson, Genevieve Parker and Tom Gerard.

ported to be very deep, with mail contractors using dog teams and finding difficulty keeping to
their schedules.

Ed Young was off again on Thursday, April 4, 1929, bound for Glacier Creek with
Frank Jiles, hard-rock miner, and a load of supplies aboard. He brought in Mr. and Mrs.
Boatman, who operated a roadhouse a few miles above the mouth of the Kantishna River, on
Saturday, April 6.

Ralph Wien, pilot for Wien Alaska Airways, Incorporated, went out on Saturday, April
6, in the Stinson Detroiter, C 5262 (Wilkins former plane) for Nome Creek district. He landed
Louis Schmidt near his home, fourteen miles from the Nome Creek dredge and near the mouth
of Ophir Creek. On Sunday, April 7, the pilot went out again, making a round trip to Ruby. He
stopped at Tanana on the way out to drop off a native girl. Ralph brought in four passengers
from Ruby; Mrs. Oliver Anderson, Mrs. Hornsby and child, and Doctor Averill. Ed Young, of
the rival company, made a round-trip flight to Nenana that same day.

Bennett-Rodebaugh held a photograph party on Sunday, April 7, 1929. With long
hours of daylight and photographer Earl Rossman in town, it was a perfect opportunity. With
pilot Ed Young at the controls of Stinson Standard, NC 877, and well-known dog musher

697

Leonhard Seppala aboard, along with his daughter Sigrid, for his first flight in a plane, the party was aloft to fly over Fairbanks and vicinity. Seppala was filmed driving Judge Cecil H. Clegg's derby-winning team into the face of a temporary blizzard created by the propwash of the Stinson, then leaving the team to board the plane, thus contrasting the earlier form of Alaskan transportation with the new. Rossman intended to release the film for newsreel showing. Stills were also taken.

On Wednesday, April 10, Ralph Wien flew to Tanana but was unable to land. The next day he went to the same destination, bringing Mrs. Sam O. White and Miss Frances Steele to Fairbanks. On the way out, he had taken a Mr. Welden to American Creek. Fred Moller, Bennett-Rodebaugh mechanic, took his bright green Waco Model 9, NC 2776, *Anna*, to Nenana on Wednesday also, then flew to the Tolovana to survey a chain of lakes at the request of Nenana friends. He landed in soft snow on one lake, but took off again with no difficulty. He made the return flight from Nenana to Weeks Field in twenty minutes.

Ed Young was not so fortunate the next morning, struggling off Fairbanks in the wet snow. He was away for Nenana to pick up two passengers for Lake Minchumina and Glacier Creek. Pilot Tom Gerard also went to Livengood but was unable to find a hole in the cloud layer blanketing the area, and returned without landing. A.A. Bennett, who had departed Fairbanks on Tuesday, April 9, was at McGrath Wednesday night, on his way home from Bethel.

Ralph Wien left at 4:30 A.M. Friday, April 12, 1929, taking 800 pounds of freight to the Salcha district in the Stinson biplane. Soon after returning, he was away again for Nulato. Mr. Shaw, Mrs. Ellis and baby were passengers for American Creek. He stopped at Tanana to pick up two passengers for Nulato, reporting eighteen-above-zero there, with high clouds and excellent visibility. Tanana was the same.

With favorable weather in the area over the weekend, the pilots were in the air. Tom Gerard flew to Circle Hot Springs on Saturday, April 14, taking John Locke and Al Morency, staying there overnight and returning on Sunday. Ed Young made a round-trip flight to Wiseman on Saturday, carrying a load of freight north and bringing in Roy King on his return. A.A. Bennett was off for McGrath Sunday afternoon, with Arnold Hjelda and Milton F. Rice. The pilot had arrived from Bethel late Saturday with Mrs. N.J. Jones, accompanied by her husband and infant child. Mrs. Jones, wife of the Bureau of Education teacher at Nelson Island, had been critically ill in the hospital at Akiak but was recovering in Fairbanks.

Ralph Wien made a round trip to the Iditarod and Kuskokwim districts on Sunday, April 14, 1929, carrying three passengers from Fairbanks, Robert Lowrie for McGrath and Paul Oehme and Roger K. Nelson for Flat. The air between McGrath and Flat was turbulent and he crossed to the other side of the range for the flight back. His brother Noel was still at Nome, flying out of there. (Their new pilot, Harry T. Davidson, had apparently left as there had been no further mention of him in the airplane news.)

On Wednesday, April 17, the airmen were again busy. Of the Bennett-Rodebaugh pilots, Tom Gerard flew to Livengood with a load of mail, taking Charles L. Thompson, manager of the company along for the round trip. Ed Young had gone to Lake Minchumina on Tuesday with a load of freight for Frank Jiles. From here, he would pick up Jiles at Glacier, returning to the lake. He came into Fairbanks at 10:30 A.M. Wednesday, and was on his way to Beaver with a load of freight an hour and a half later.

A.A. Bennett had returned from McGrath about 7:00 P.M. on Monday. He also left for Tanana Crossing on Tuesday with a load of freight for John Hajdukovich, intending to cross over to Eagle to bring in Robert Gilmore and D.S. Monell on the return flight. He was back in Fairbanks the same day.

698

Wien Alaska Airways, Incorporated, had a different project in mind. They had gone ahead with the purchase of the wrecked Stearman C-2B from Arctic Prospecting & Development Company, paying $3500 for the damaged biplane. Ralph Wien was off on Tuesday, April 16, for the site at Walker Lake, taking mechanic Earl Borland in to do the repair work. As soon as it had been ascertained what additional supplies and parts Borland would need to complete the repair on the Stearman so that it could be flown in, Ralph returned to town.

A.A. Bennett had a similar chore in mind when he took off from Weeks Field Tuesday afternoon, April 16, to go to Chicken. He was carrying a mechanic to repair the company's big cabin Swallow biplane, C 3542, which had been damaged by the pilot in landing there on November 5, 1928.

Ed Young departed Fairbanks on Friday, April 19, 1929, for Nixon Fork, McGrath and Flat; Ed Whalen was a passenger for the Fork. Freight made up the load for the other two points. He was back again that same day to take a second load of freight to McGrath and bring in passengers. Tom Gerard had departed on Friday, carrying Casper Ellingen and Fay Delzene for Hot Springs, as well as freight for Circle City. He came in on Saturday from Circle City, carrying Rasmus Undahl and Mrs. Burmaster and child as passenger.

A.A. Bennett, flying the Zenith 6 as usual, also left on Friday forenoon with four passengers for Iditarod: Alex C. Matheson, Harry Steen, Edward Nightingale and Dave E. Browne, all mining men. He came in to Fairbanks on Saturday morning, April 20, bringing Father Delon from Holy Cross and Father McElmeel from Nulato. The pilot left later in the day for Kokrines with Glenn R. Day and J.C. Johnson.

Ralph Wien, flying the Stinson Detroiter, C 5262, was back from Walker Lake on Friday afternoon, April 19. Earl Borland remained there for some time, working on the wrecked Stearman C-2B. A new wing panel for the plane had to be constructed in Fairbanks from measurements and samples taken at the site. Ralph went out that afternoon to Salcha with one passenger and a load of freight. His brother, Noel, had left Nome at 11:00 A.M. (Fairbanks time), and was coming in.

Ed Young had flown to McGrath on Sunday, April 21, taking Jack McGuire and Dan McDonald to Lake Minchumina, picking up Fritz Tuttle there for the Kuskokwim destination. Bennett used Birch Lake for a landing spot for the first time when he flew a passenger onto the lake on Monday. He was also carrying Joe E. Downs on the round trip.

With Noel Wien coming to Fairbanks Saturday evening, April 20, 1929, from the Seward Peninsula, it was a chance for Wien Alaska Airways to catch up on the local business. Noel brought in A. Polet, Nome merchant, Dan Crowley, field superintendent for Lomen Reindeer Corporation, B.B. Mozee, educator, Charles Maxwell, prospector from Kotzebue, and Calvin "Doc" Cripe, who had been in Nome since the Siberian flight. The following day, Sunday, Noel flew to Shungnak; fog in the Kobuk had caused him to miss it on the trip in from Nome. He took Mozee there, as well as three prospectors: Mr. Varnell, Wileman and Carey. Returning to Fairbanks, the pilot brought Manuel Gill and Nels Giske in; they had been trapping all winter to the north.

Noel made another flight to Shungnak on Monday, April 22, 1929, with Mike Garland as a passenger, plus a heavy load of freight for the prospecting party he had taken in on Sunday. Ralph Wien flew to Ruby and Koyukuk Station on Sunday, April 21, taking Mrs. D. Vernetti home to the station. On Monday he was off again for Ruby with a half-ton of freight for Chicken Creek Mining Company.

Parker Cramer and Willard Gamble were through Fairbanks in their Cessna AW, NC 7107, on April 23, 1929, enroute to Nome. (see Chicago to Siberia—1929, Chapter 48). They were back through on April 27 on their way south.

Noel Wien made another flight on Tuesday, April 23, to Shungnak, taking William James, C.E. Alexander and another passenger. He stopped at Walker Lake on the way in to check on the progress being made on the Stearman repair. He was back in Fairbanks at 9:35 P.M. Noel made a flight to Circle City, again in the Hamilton, taking Assistant U.S. District Attorney E.B. Collins and Miss Albina Miller, secretary in the U.S. Attorney's office. Ralph Wien returned to Fairbanks on Tuesday, April 23, from a flight to Flat. He had departed on Monday from Fairbanks, flying to Flat and returning to McGrath on the same day. The pilot encountered strong headwinds coming in, and he was four and one-half hours in the air. With the trappers coming in and miners and prospectors going out, spring was always a busy season. Soon the breakup would turn many of their usual landing spots into a quagmire, or worse. It was a hard time for the pilots.

Ed Young was away in the early afternoon on Wednesday, April 24, for Fort Yukon with a load of freight, taking Manager Charles L. Thompson along. The day before he had flown to Tanana, returning with Doctors La Rue and Billingsley. Tom Gerard had gone out to Livengood with mail and freight on Wednesday. A.A. Bennett left on Thursday morning, April 25, 1929, carrying Ray Hoyt to Flat, where he spent the summer working on Alex Matheson's dredge, and Manuel Gularte, Flat merchant, who was enroute to Napaimiut. Bennett expected to go to Akiak, Holy Cross and Bethel.

Noel Wien of Wien Alaska Airways made a round-trip flight to Tanana Crossing with freight on the morning of Thursday, April 25. He was back in time to make a second trip there in the middle of the afternoon.

Lillian Osborne of Cordova, a student at the Alaska College, was starring as the Russian Princess on Saturday night in the school production at the auditorium. She would later marry pilot Joe Crosson, who was soon to return to Fairbanks.

Ed Young left Fairbanks early in the morning of Friday, April 26, 1929, for Wiseman, to pick up Mrs. John E. Woll. Mrs. A.A. Bennett accompanied him as a round-trip passenger. They were holding for weather at Bettles or Beaver on their return. Young finally came into Fairbanks with Mrs. Bennett, Mrs. Woll and her two children at 3:40 P.M. on Monday, April 29. A.A. Bennett had also left on Friday for Bethel, expecting to return the following day.

On Friday, April 26, Noel Wien was off at 6:00 A.M. for a mining district about forty miles north of Tetlin, carrying Abe McCord and Gus Buhmann, prospectors. Additionally, over 1100 pounds of supplies were carried in the sturdy Hamilton H-45. The pilot saw long stretches of open water, some nearly thirty miles in length, along the upper Tanana River.

C.H. Gillam, in his Swallow, *Arctic Prospector*, had started out on a short flight on Thursday, April 25, and had not returned. Anxiety over his absence was relieved when Tom Gerard reported finding him near Chena. While landing, with Charles Showers aboard, the aircraft had nosed over in soft snow, breaking the propeller. Gillam remained with Showers while Tom Gerard brought him another propeller. Gillam flew the plane in to Fairbanks on Saturday.

A surprise visit to Fairbanks by Russel H. Merrill occurred when he landed at Weeks Field at 3:00 P.M. Saturday, April 27. The Anchorage pilot had flown from there to Parks, a short distance below Sleetmute, then, forced by weather in the mountains, had come in to Fairbanks. He was away Tuesday morning with Emil Anderson, enroute to McGrath.

Monday morning, April 29, Noel Wien departed Weeks Field carrying Captain Alfred H. Williams for Kokrines, and Mrs. May Hornsby and child, and Mrs. Alex Brown and child for Ruby. The pilot was back at home base that same day, landing about 3:30 P.M. He brought

Hamilton H-45 Metalplane of Wien Alaska Airways on Weeks Field during spring breakup, always a problem time for Alaskan pilots during that time of year.

Cann Studio Donald E. Young Collection

in two passengers from Tanana and five from Fish Lake. The capacity of the Hamilton for either passengers or freight was a big asset.

The open-cockpit Swallow, C 1713, flown by Tom Gerard, nosed completely over in making a landing at the Livengood field on Monday, April 29. The plane, fitted with skis, ran into mud; the rapid stop caused the incident. Bennett flew over to pick Gerard up. They planned to bring the damaged plane in to Fairbanks by boat, if it could not be repaired at the site and flown out.

Noel Wien departed Weeks Field on Tuesday, April 30, 1929, enroute to Fort Yukon. He landed at Circle to drop off Warren S. Harding, federal prohibition officer, then taking aboard E. Simon, an Indian under sentence to six months in the federal jail at Fairbanks, on the technical charge of "pointing firearms". The pilot returned to Weeks Field about 3:00 P.M. bringing Assistant U.S. District Attorney E.B. Collins and Miss Albina Miller, secretary, picked up at Circle Hot Springs, as well as the prisoner.

Ed Young was away in the Stinson SB-1, NC 877, on the morning of Tuesday, April 30. He was bound for Alatna and Wiseman, carrying Mrs. Edwards, her child and her brother for Alatna, and E.C. Workman for Wiseman. A.A. Bennett was also away, in his Zenith 6, for Lake Minchumina, Medfra and McGrath, carrying Captain George Green, Kuskokwim River skipper; and J.P. Taylor, Takotna dredgeman, as passengers for McGrath. He picked up Miss Bertha Albi at Lake Minchumina, who was also going to McGrath.

Earl Borland had been at Walker Lake since April 16, working on the wrecked Stearman C-2B, NC 5415, which Wien Alaska Airways had purchased. Taking Hamilton, NC 10002, Noel Wien with his brothers, Ralph and Fritz, took off from Fairbanks on Wednesday, May 1, 1929, enroute to the lake. Fritz, now working for the company as a mechanic, had taken welding tanks along so that certain parts on the plane could be welded. They also carried a prefabricated wing panel for the Stearman that could be assembled and covered at the site.

After considerable work, the plane once again was whole, sitting on skis in the snow. Ralph was to fly it into Fairbanks but Noel decided to test hop it first. He took off, the plane turning to the left as the skis lifted off. Sensing something wrong, the pilot quickly cut the power and was able to land the plane. In replacing the wing panel, the cables controlling the

Fairbanks mechanicians in 1929. Left to Right: Harold Gillam, Bill Basham, Cecil Higgins and Herb Larison.

ailerons had been crossed, resulting in the controls being reversed from their normal movement. With this problem corrected, Ralph flew the Stearman in to Fairbanks, with Noel, Fritz and Earl Borland coming in with the Hamilton, also bringing the tools, equipment and other gear from the salvage job.

A.A. Bennett and Ed Young both returned to Fairbanks on Tuesday, April 30, from flights to McGrath and Wiseman. Bennett brought in Dan McDonald from Lake Minchumina. Tom Gerard and Bennett went to Chicken the following day to bring the red cabin Swallow, C 3542, in to Fairbanks. It had been badly damaged there in a landing November 5, 1928. The plane had now been repaired by mechanic Ed Moore, formerly with the Kinner Airplane and Motor Corporation of Glendale, California, who had been flown to Chicken by Bennett on April 16. The mechanic had been assisted in the repair job by an experienced cabinetmaker, Gordon Springbett, who was living at Chicken. The woodworker later took a job in Fairbanks in aircraft repair, eventually becoming a mechanic for Pan American Airways at Fairbanks.

Ben Eielson returned to Fairbanks in style. After visiting in Anchorage, he had been flown to Curry by Russ Merrill and Frank Dorbandt, to catch the train there. As the train pulled into the station at Fairbanks on Monday evening, May 6, 1929, three airplanes piloted by Noel Wien, Ralph Wien and Fred Moller circled overhead. The airmen had met the train several miles out and followed it in. In addition to being greeted with a band and by most of the townsfolk, the famous flier was honored that evening at a banquet, held at the Model Cafe. Eielson spoke briefly concerning his Antarctic experiences with Sir Hubert Wilkins, Joe Crosson, Orval Porter and a radio operator during their six months in the south polar regions. Eielson had been presented with the Harmon Trophy by President Hoover, made a colonel in the North Dakota National Guard, and raised from the rank of lieutenant to captain in the Army Air Corps Reserves. The trophy, given annually, is presented to the aviator considered to have made the greatest contribution to aviation in the United States. The flier was also presented with a watch fob in the shape of a golden heart at the banquet as a token of appreciation by the people of Fairbanks.

In addition to the genuine welcome accorded Eielson, there was a strong interest in his future plans, for rumors had circulated that Ben Eielson was representing eastern capital interested in establishing a commercial aviation service that would include all major Alaskan cities.

The morning following the banquet, Tuesday, May 7, 1929, both Wien brothers were off on flights, Noel going to Nome in the Hamilton with R.S. Stewart and Barney Bellview as passengers. The plane was also carrying 351 pounds of first class mail for Nome, as well as 221 pounds for Ruby. All the snow was gone from Weeks Field and skis had been replaced by wheels. Ralph Wien left for Wiseman in the recently acquired Stearman biplane (NC 5415), carrying 200 pounds of mail for Wiseman, sixty-seven pounds for Bettles and eighty-four pounds for Alatna. He brought in Martin Christensen from Wiseman.

Russ Merrill and Frank Dorbandt had arrived in Fairbanks, after taking the Strandbergs from Anchorage to Flat in the Travel Air 7000 of Anchorage Air Transport, Incorporated. Taking off from the interior city the afternoon of Thursday, May 9, they struck directly across country for Anchorage.

This same day a message had been received from Wiseman; Ralph Wien had not arrived there in the Stearman. He could be holding enroute at Alatna or Bettles due to weather. If his brother did not turn up by Saturday, Noel, who was returning from Nome, would make a search.

Noel fueled the Hamilton at Golovin and struck out for the Koyukuk, making a fruitless search of the upper river. He saw where Ralph had made a landing on the ice at Alatna. Ralph had also made a stop at Bettles, where the snow-covered ice on the river appeared as solid as it had at Alatna. But such was not the case; two feet of overflow slush was under the snow. Running into this on wheels resulted in a turnover, bending the propeller of the Stearman. Aided by two white men and two natives, Ralph had turned the plane upright and straightened the metal propeller, a slow task. He had a pair of skis made to put on in place of wheels as there was considerable snow yet to the north. The plane was ready on Thursday morning and, checking the fuel for water and warming up the motor, the pilot began to taxi into position when the axle broke. It was not repaired until 2:00 P.M., with Ralph taking off for Wiseman at 2:30 P.M. Friday, May 10. In the meantime, Ralph's wife, Julia, her children and his mother arrived in Fairbanks from the States on Sunday, May 12, 1929.

Noel landed the Hamilton at Weeks Field at 12:30 A.M. on Monday, May 13; he had been in the air over ten hours, including his search time, since leaving Nome. He got some sleep, and was away again at 1:00 P.M. that same day, accompanied by Harold Gillam and Sam White. They covered the north fork of the Koyukuk River, where Wiseman residents had reported hearing the sound of a motor, three times without result. They refueled at Wiseman and returned to Fairbanks at 11:00 P.M. that same evening. Sam White had left the Hamilton at Wiseman, planning to cover the stretch between Wiseman and Bettles by land. Tom Gerard would go out with Noel the next day, and Bennett-Rodebaugh Company had offered the use of planes and personnel for the search. It ended on Tuesday, May 14, when the missing pilot trudged wearily into Bettles, following the winter trail. He told of leaving Bettles for Wiseman on May 10, with a strong tail wind speeding the Stearman along. In fifteen minutes he had covered thirty-three miles, passing the north fork of the Koyukuk and heading directly for his destination. The weather ahead looked poor, and he decided to pick up the winter mail trail and follow it back to Bettles. At 300 feet over the hills, the engine quit. Suspecting water in the gas, the pilot switched from the top tank to the bottom one, getting another fifteen seconds of running time out of the Whirlwind before it ceased again. Too low to even turn into the wind, Ralph landed the Stearman on the brush and moss of a long slope, with considerable speed. Skidding along on the nose through the brush, the plane turned turtle and came to a stop. It was 2:45 P.M. on Thursday, May 10. The rocker arm stands of the Wright Whirlwind radial engine were broken and the wings badly damaged. The pilot was not injured.

Storing the mail in the cockpit and covering it against the weather, Ralph gathered his few supplies and was on the trail at 3:00 P.M. He had a little food, his parka and plenty of matches. Walking in two and one-half feet of snow, without snowshoes, he covered the quarter mile to the winter trail, but found it was impossible to travel on the trail because the packed snow was too soft. He walked in the snow alongside the trail. By 11:00 P.M. the flier had covered about thirteen miles before stopping and sleeping in his parka on a river bank. Awakened by the strong light at 3:00 A.M. he walked for the next nineteen hours, with occasional rest periods, making slow progress. The following evening, Saturday, Ralph bedded down on top of a hill in sight of a river. Sleeping until noon to allow the snow crust to melt for easier walking, he rose on stiffened tendons and sore muscles, to trek onward. He crossed the stream, which later proved to be Wild River, continuing on for several hours. Following the dog team trail, he eventually arrived at Bettles. He had seen Noel fly over several times during the trek but had been unable to attract his attention. The outline of the wrecked plane, a mile and half from the Koyukuk River, was obscured by the willows and the dull colors of spring, hiding it from the searching pilot. Ralph was picked up at Bettles by Noel Wien, Tom Gerard and Sam White, and returned to Fairbanks on Tuesday, May 14, 1929. The wrecked plane was expected to be brought in to Fairbanks by boat later in the season.

Bennett had left Weeks Field at noon on Monday, May 13, taking four passengers for Flat: Harry Donelley, Harvey A. LaZelle, Arnold Kobler and Joe Linke. Ed Young had flown to Ruby the day before, on a round trip with Joe Freeman as passenger. He was off again the next morning with D.B. Scringeour, insurance adjuster, who was going to Ruby as a passenger. A recent fire had practically destroyed the town's business district. The pilot and his passenger were back in Fairbanks on Wednesday morning. Bennett was expected back Tuesday to aid in the Ralph Wien search.

Noel Wien was back to commercial flying, going out with the Hamilton on the morning of Wednesday, May 15. Taking commercial travelers Lyle F. Hebert, H.C. Dunlap and A.W. Weaver, he was off for Fort Yukon. From there, the three men would come down the river by small boat to Tanana, where they had a motorboat stored. They expected to travel until July, calling on customers along the way.

A.A. Bennett had returned on Tuesday from Flat, and was once again away on Wednesday morning, carrying Doctors Bart C. LaRue and F.A. Billingsley.

Ben Eielson had been having discussions in Fairbanks with the air service operators regarding the possibility of an expanded air service in Alaska, possibly into Asia. There was a chance of combining the present services into the new company if negotiations went well. After completing his business affairs and visiting with old friends, Ben left Fairbanks on the morning train Thursday, May 16, 1929. He went directly to New York to meet with the eastern backers. Eielson indicated the likelihood of his return to the interior city in approximately two months.

Noel Wien was away for Nome on Thursday morning, May 16, taking his brother Fritz, and his mother, Mrs. J.B. Wien, along, as well as Senator R.N. Sundquist and Representative Henry Burgh. That Sunday, May 19, Noel Wien, president and chief pilot of Wien Alaska Airways, was married to Ada Bering Arthurs at a public wedding in the Federated Church in Nome. A reception was held at the Odd Fellows Hall following the ceremony. The couple planned to make their home in Fairbanks. They boarded the Hamilton that evening, taking only one passenger, H.L. Stull, mining man from Deering. The rest of the plane was filled to capacity with furs, mail and baggage. The couple was away for Fairbanks at 10:15 P.M. and, with a fuel stop at Ruby, landed on Weeks Field at 5:00 A.M. (Fairbanks time) Monday, May 20, 1929. In a few days Noel left again for the Seward Peninsula. He always carried a full load, and passengers were waiting at the other end, sometimes holding a lottery to see who would go. Business was good and the Hamilton was proving its worth.

A.A. Bennett had flown to Wiseman on Sunday, May 19, with a full load of freight, returning on Monday evening. The pilot was scheduled to take George Burmaster to Fort Yukon that same afternoon at 3:00 P.M. He was away again in the Zenith 6 on Wednesday, May 22, 1929, taking Harold Strandberg to Flat. Harold, who had been attending Alaska College, was joining his father, Dave Strandberg, for the mining season on Flat Creek.

Noel Wien was also off in the Hamilton the same morning. The heavily-loaded plane bounced twice before struggling off the ground just short of the end of the runway. There were six passengers in the plane with all their baggage, one hundred pounds of mail and 140 gallons of gasoline. The passengers: H.C. Kelling, W.C. Chesney, F. Nordstrom, Tom Peterson and Mr. and Mrs. C.B. White, of Spokane, were all bound for Nome. Noel arrived there at 2:55 P.M. on his second subsidy air mail trip of a new contract with the postal service. He returned to Fairbanks about 11:15 P.M. Sunday, May 26, 1929.

Grant Pearson, student flier from McKinley Park, was heard from when it was noticed in a news release from Chehalis, Washington on May 23, that he had crashed on sandy ground on a solo flight when the control stick came out of its socket and he was unable to get it back in place. The uncontrolled plane struck the ground and turned bottom side up. Residents near the airport extracted the dazed pilot from the wreckage. He was suffering from slight cuts about the face, bruises and possible broken ribs, but able to walk.

A.A. Bennett was off for Livengood the morning of Monday, May 27, 1929, with Joe Haley as a passenger. He brought in C.H. LaBoyteaux, U.S. commissioner in the mining community, to Fairbanks.

Harold Woodward, driver of the Fairbanks Exploration Company's messenger car, had purchased a Waco Model 9 (No. 1) with OX-5 liquid-cooled motor from James S. Rodebaugh. With the aid of Freddie Moller, the damaged plane had been rebuilt and the motor overhauled during the past winter. Noel Wien had the plane up about June 1 for a test hop, and was now instructing Woodward in the art of flying it.

Pilot Ed Young of the Bennett-Rodebaugh Company made a round trip to Wiseman on Tuesday, June 4. He was off again for the mining camp on Wednesday morning, June 5, with a load of supplies and one passenger, Captain E.G. Rowden, owner of the Detroit Gold Mining Company. A.A. Bennett had flown to McGrath on Monday, June 3, 1929, with Gus Rosen and Mr. Scribner, employees of the Flume Dredging Company, and John Strand, mining operator. He went again the next evening, taking G.N. Russell, manager of Flume at Takotna, to McGrath.

Adolph Muller, Kaltag trader, was once again in the news. He had purchased a second airplane, and had arranged for an experienced pilot, Charles A. Rector, to fly the trader to Fairbanks in the plane, planning to leave on Monday, June 10, 1929. The day before the two were to start, the plane caught fire in the air while Rector was aloft over Seattle with three passengers. Fighting the fire with a hand extinguisher, the pilot sideslipped the plane in to Boeing Field where all evacuated the plane safely. A broken fuel line was found to have caused the fire, which badly damaged the left wing panel. Muller had lost his first plane, a four-place Stinson, in a crash during a flight to Tacoma in October of 1928.

On Saturday, June 8, 1929, Ed Young flew to Livengood with Ole Niemi as a passenger for the mining camp, returning with Henry Struck. Bennett was off at 5:00 A.M. the following day for American Creek, carrying Luther C. Hess. The pilot remained there most of the day while Hess was transacting his business, then bringing his passenger in to Livengood. Bennett landed back at Fairbanks at midnight.

The Bennett-Rodebaugh Company pilot was away again the night of Tuesday, June 11, bound for Eagle and Chicken. Passenger Frank Barrett offloaded at the latter point. Ed Young was also away about the same time, carrying a load of freight for McGrath. A new plane, a Waco 10, two-passenger craft, had been ordered by the company and was expected in two weeks. It would be used for short hauls. Bennett, on his return from Chicken, had a difficult time, flying most of the way through a rainstorm at low altitude in poor visibility. There were two passengers at Chicken for Fairbanks but the field was in such bad shape he was barely able to get off alone. He took an employee of the Alaska Road Commission from Eagle to Chicken, to work on the field and improve it.

Noel Wien had been holding his departure for Nome because of weather in the Fairbanks area. The U.S. Signal Corps station at Fairbanks was now receiving twice-daily weather reports from Cordova, to the south, and Point Barrow, to the north, for use by the air services. They were awaiting the arrival of Howard J. Thompson to inaugurate the Fairbanks Aerological Station where such reports would be used in forecasting weather.

Noel was away in the Hamilton on Friday, June 14, 1929, to land at Nome at 7:30 P.M., six and one-half hours after his departure from Weeks Field. His wife, Ada, and Charles Maxwell went as passengers on the flight. The *Victoria* had docked in Nome on its first trip of the season, with Grant R. Jackson, who was president of the Miners and Merchants Bank at Nome, as well as secretary of Wien Alaska Airways, Incorporated, aboard. He expected to fly to Fairbanks with Noel on his return.

Fred Moller, Bennett-Rodebaugh Company mechanic, was away in his Waco Model 9, C 2776, on a prospecting trip that was intended to take him to Nenana, thence to American Creek, Fort Yukon, the Koyukuk and Chandalar. He was off Weeks Field in *Anna* on Saturday night, June 15, for Nenana. "Freddie", a former miner, had learned to fly at the local field, claiming nearly 200 hours of flying time. He delayed in Nenana to assist in an aerial search for the bodies of three men who had been drowned in the collapse of the bridge across the Nenana River at Healy Fork on Tuesday afternoon. Moller made flights on Thursday and Friday of June 20 and 21, taking A.A. Johnson, Alaska Railroad freight and passenger agent and wartime aviator on the second flight, searching the river bars without result.

A.A. Bennett was off Fairbanks at 5:30 A.M. on Wednesday, June 19, for Nome, carrying Ernest W. Sawyer, executive assistant to the Secretary of the Interior, who was making a tour of Alaska, and Major Malcolm Elliott, president of the Alaska Road Commission, making a landing at McGrath at 10:20 A.M. After conducting their business there, the party was off at 4:30 P.M. to arrive in Unalakleet two and one-half hours later, where Sawyer inspected the Bureau of Education facilities and discussed the reindeer industry with residents. The Zenith 6 was away again at 10:45 P.M. in the long hours of daylight, to land at Nome at 1:00 A.M. of June 20, 1929. After inspecting governmental facilities (including making an allotment for the purpose of extending the runway at the Nome airport) the party departed this same field at 7:00 P.M. Friday, June 21, in the Zenith 6, making a stop at Ruby where Bennett's plane suffered a blown tire on the rough field. The party went on to Tanana, arriving there at 2:15 A.M. Saturday, June 22, and leaving at 2:20 A.M. Sunday morning, enroute to Fairbanks, stopping at Nenana for forty minutes to refuel, and arriving in Fairbanks at 5:30 A.M. There had been good weather all the way and the officials were well pleased with the trip.

Ed Young had returned from Flat the night of Wednesday, June 19, and left for Nome the next evening for a charter. Passengers were backlogged at Nome and wanted out. Young dropped Vance R. McDonald at Ruby when he refueled, and went on to Nome. Fog conditions on Norton Sound made this second leg of the trip difficult for the pilot. He arrived at 9:30 A.M. in the Stinson SB-1 biplane, NC 877.

Carrying commercial travelers Joe Meherin and Oscar Hart, who had chartered the plane, Ed was off Nome at 10:30 A.M. on Saturday, June 22. Held at Ruby that night by steady rain, he came in to Fairbanks Sunday afternoon, also bringing McDonald back from Ruby.

Noel Wien, with his brother Fritz, departed Nome at 7:30 P.M. Friday, June 21; the rest of the plane was filled with U.S. mail. Making a nonstop flight in five hours and thirty-five minutes, he arrived at Weeks Field at 2:30 A.M. Saturday. Noel had sighted Bennett's plane, with the Sawyer party, and had flown alongside for some time.

On Wednesday, June 26, 1929, an extensive flight was made by Noel Wien over the Fairbanks mining district. Carrying G.A. Bigelow, Fairbanks Exploration Company official; James E. Barrack, Samson Hardware head; and Sam L. Godfrey, manager of Nome Creek Dredging Company, the pilot flew the Hamilton over the F.E. Company ditch line, in addition to side trips to Tolovana valley and the Beaver country, including Nome Creek. On his return, Noel flew a dozen tourists on sightseeing tours that evening.

The Hamilton, with Noel at the controls as usual, was off for Anchorage at 6:20 P.M. Thursday, June 27, carrying as round-trip passengers M.J. Anderson and Arthur Frodenburg. The pilot landed at Anchorage at 9:40 P.M. He was back in Fairbanks at 6:00 P.M. on Friday, also bringing Bruce Thorne and George Graves, scientists from the Field Museum of Chicago, who had chartered a schooner at Nome to seek scientific specimens in the Arctic. On the return the pilot flew close to Mount McKinley at 9000 feet and his passengers got some excellent photos in the clear air. Over one hundred Dall sheep were sighted in McKinley Park, scurrying for cover when the plane flew by.

Taking Thorne and Graves, as well as Roy C. Lyle, federal prohibition administrator for the Twentieth District, Noel was off for Nome at 6:00 A.M. Saturday June 29, He also picked up Father Delon at Ruby, and arrived at their destination at 2:30 P.M. that afternoon. Coming in for their Nome landing, the party sighted a herd of about 10,000 reindeer that had been rounded up on the beach by their herders, an impressive scene.

A.A. Bennett was scheduled to fly to Livengood the evening of Friday, June 28, to bring in Jack Gucker, commercial traveler, and another passenger. Ed Young, also of the Bennett-Rodebaugh Company, flew to the Kuskokwim the same evening, stopping to pick up Miss Bertha Albi and another passenger at Lake Minchumina.

Fred Moller, aviator-prospector, came in from Nenana by train, to get a magneto from his plane repaired. He had left Nenana in the plane on Sunday, June 23, for American Creek, and was well on his way until, in checking his magnetos in flight, discovered one not working. He returned to Nenana and removed the malfunctioning part for repair. Noel Wien took Freddie back to Nenana Thursday evening, June 27. Besides the two search flights along the river, the pilot had flown several joyriders aloft at the rail terminal in his Waco 9.

Tom Gerard was off for Chicken on Tuesday, July 2, 1929, bringing Mrs. Gordon Springbett and Miss Freda Traub to Fairbanks. He made a round trip to Livengood that evening, and on Wednesday would make the first flight of the season to Palmer Creek on the upper Chena, a placer mining site. Ed Young was off for the Kuskokwim on Tuesday evening, taking Ora Barnhardt to McGrath, then picking up Mrs. Georgia Hagen and Ivar Chilson at Takotna for Fairbanks.

A.A. "Benny" Bennett was away for Nome on Monday evening, July 1. He returned on Saturday, July 6, with Otto F. Ohlson, general manager of the Alaska Railroad, and L.J. Palmer, in charge of the reindeer experimental station at Alaska College. Ed Young brought in Robert Frothingham, a member of Ohlson's party, from Ruby, arriving fifteen minutes after the train had departed. Frothingham was taken back to Nenana to get aboard there, joining Ohlson.

Noel Wien, of Wien Alaska Airways, departed for Nome at 1:00 P.M. Sunday, July 7, making a nonstop flight of five and three-quarters hours, to arrive at his destination at 4:45 P.M. (Bering Sea time). He carried Julius H. Hart, new U.S. attorney for the second division, who would be making his headquarters at Nome.

A.A. Bennett, chief pilot and shareholder of Bennett-Rodebaugh Company, departed Fairbanks in the Zenith 6 for Nome on Monday morning, July 8. His wife accompanied him. The pilot remained at Nome for the next ten days or more, working out of there on surveys for the Lomen Reindeer Corporation.

Frank Dorbandt, pilot for Anchorage Air Transport, Incorporated, in Anchorage, had left his position there and arrived in Fairbanks to accept a similar position with Wien Alaska Airways. He arrived by train on Tuesday, July 16, 1929. He was to be the Nome-based pilot for the company, flying out of there. Noel Wien came in from Nome at 3:00 A.M. the next day, after a six-hour flight. He brought his mother, Earl Borland, and passenger C.S. Blair with him in the plane. Borland, mechanic for the company, was learning to fly and he piloted the Hamilton during the greater part of the flight to Fairbanks. Noel's father, J.B. Wien of Cook, Minnesota, had also arrived in Fairbanks for a visit, coming in on the train on July 9.

Frank Dorbandt and Ralph Wien took off for Nome on Thursday afternoon, July 18, in the Stinson Standard, C 5262. Dorbandt was stationed there with the Stinson, while Ralph returned with the Waco 9, C 2775 (No. 3) which had been at Nome since June 28, 1928. Noel had, earlier in the year, hired pilot Harry T. Davidson from Outside, intending for him to staff the Nome base but the man had left the company prior to the stationing. Beside the two pilots, the Stinson carried two passengers for Holy Cross: E.J. Beck, Bureau of Education official, and Miss Marjorie Major, bureau nurse.

In Fairbanks, Captain Ross G. Hoyt landed his Curtiss Hawk pursuit plane at 12:02 P.M. Saturday, July 20, 1929, on his record breaking New York to Nome flight. He was away again at 1:23 P.M. The army flier was back the next day, to take off from Weeks Field at 5:10 A.M. for Whitehorse, southbound. (See Captain Ross G. Hoyt—New York to Nome—1929, Chapter 49).

Ed Young, Bennett-Rodebaugh Company pilot, returned from the Kuskokwim on Monday night, July 22. He had been holding there for the last four days on account of poor weather conditions. Young expected to leave the next evening, carrying Irving McKenny Reed, mining consultant, to Wiseman, and W.H. Merrin, mineral examiner for the land office, to Chandalar.

Ben Eielson was returning to Fairbanks as promised, as general manager and vice-president of the newly-formed Alaskan Airways, Incorporated. The former Fairbanks flier left the northbound train at Nenana, coming in with Noel Wien in the Hamilton on Tuesday, July 23, 1929. Organized in New York during the summer, with the backing of eastern capital, the new company had ordered two New Standard biplanes, powered with Wright Whirlwind motors to be shipped north in August and operated from the Fairbanks municipal field (Weeks). Alaskan Airways, Incorporated, was a division of a holding company, The Aviation Corporation (AVCO) registered in Delaware. The corporation held an interest in many aviation enterprises, including American Airways, Incorporated (later American Airlines).

A.A. Bennett returned to Fairbanks at 9:40 P.M. Friday, July 26, after an extended stay at Nome. He brought his wife with him. Forced down by bad weather on a flight to Kotzebue on July 21, he had experienced a difficult time before finally completing the flight.

Tom Gerard, Bennett-Rodebaugh pilot, flew a round trip to Livengood on Friday evening, July 26, carrying Miss Ella Hansen. Tom McKinnon was a passenger on the return flight. On Saturday evening, the pilot repeated the trip, with a load of mail.

July 29, 1929, Carl Ben Eielson announced the purchase of all Bennett-Rodebaugh Company stock by Alaskan Airways, Incorporated. Left to Right: Tom Gerard, pilot-mechanic; A.A. Bennett, pilot and shareholder; Carl Ben Eielson, pilot and general manager; G.E. "Ed" Young, pilot; and Charles L. Thompson, manager.

Ben Eielson, on the afternoon of Monday, July 29, 1929, announced the purchase of the entire outstanding shares of stock in the Bennett-Rodebaugh Company, Incorporated, the oldest operating aviation company in Alaska. Concluding negotiations begun in May, the sales price was rumored to be $65,000 for the company which had been organized by James S. Rodebaugh in May of 1926. The new company was acquiring a fleet consisting of three cabin biplanes, one open-cockpit Waco 10, NC 780E, and well-equipped hangars located on Weeks Field. No changes in personnel were planned.

Ed Young came in from the north, with W.H. Merrin, of the general land office, who had been making mineral examinations in the Chandalar for several days. Young had also freighted two tons of supplies for Wiseman merchant Sam Dubin, between Bettles and Wiseman. The pilot reported Fred Moller, aviator-prospector, as having reached Wiseman safely and that he was then prospecting on Minnie Creek. The Stearman C-2B, NC 5415, which Ralph Wien had wrecked enroute to Wiseman on Friday, May 10, 1929, was now at Bettles, and planned to reach Fairbanks within the next two weeks. The pilot also reported the early signs of winter in the north: six inches of new snow on the Beaver hills.

Alaskan Airways, Incorporated, officially began operations on Thursday, August 1, 1929, waiting until the July business was completed by Bennett-Rodebaugh Company. Charles L. Thompson continued as manager, reporting to Eielson. For its first operating day, the company sent out two flights: Ed Young was off at 9:00 A.M. for Takotna, bringing in H.W. Terhune, executive officer of the Alaska Game Commission. A.A. Bennett went to Tanana with Doctor John Cooper, United States Commissioner of Education. Ben Eielson was off in the afternoon, the same day, August 1, flying with Noel Wien in the Hamilton H-45, NC 10002, of Wien Alaska Airways, Incorporated. Noel had ordered a Pratt & Whitney Hornet of 525 horsepower for the plane, to replace the 425 horsepower Wasp engine with which the plane had been originally equipped. The engine had already left the factory by July 25, and would soon be available in Fairbanks. Flying the plane with Ben and Noel were Ralph Wien and his father, J.B. Wien, plus a load of mail. Noel's student pilot, Harold Woodward, had soloed in his own plane, a Waco 9 (No. 1), on Wednesday evening, July 31, 1929. He and Freddie Moller had rebuilt the plane over the winter while Harold studied his ground school courses.

The flight to Nome by Ben Eielson had startling results. Eielson inspected the field and facilities there, and further discussions with Noel, Ralph and Grant Jackson, who were respectively, president, manager and secretary-treasurer of Wien Alaska Airways, Incorporated, resulted in an announcement in Nome of the purchase of the stock of the Wien company by Alaskan Airways, Incorporated. The sale included the fleet, consisting of the Hamilton Metalplane, NC 10002; Stinson Standard, C 5262; Waco 9, C 2775; and the damaged Stearman C-2B, NC 5415; as well as the hangar in Fairbanks. Noel was to remain on as pilot for the company, and Ralph was also offered a position as mechanic and backup pilot. The contract stipulated neither would fly for a competing company, nor organize a competing service of their own until a time period of three years had elapsed. The two brothers and Grant Jackson received $25,000 each for the purchase of their stock. Frank Dorbandt remained as resident pilot in Nome.

Noel Wien, accompanied by his father, Ben Eielson and E.J. Mathews, mining engineer and investor from Seattle, was aboard the Hamilton when it landed in Fairbanks shortly after 9:00 P.M. on Friday, August 9, 1929. The plane also carried 450 pounds of gold from Nome.

A.A. Bennett, now a pilot for Alaskan Airways, was off Weeks Field for Wiseman the morning of Friday, August 9, 1929, after holding several days because of rainy weather. He picked up Judge Clegg and Miss Louise Parcher, court reporter, and flew them to Ruby, where a short session of the district court was being held. Alaskan Airways pilot Ed Young was

The Wien Alaska Airways hangar on Weeks Field in 1929 before the air service was sold to Alaskan Airways, Incorporated, in August, 1929. Two of the company planes, Stinson Standard, C 5262, and the Hamilton Metalplane, NC 10002, stand to the left of the hangar.

leaving also for the Kuskokwim and Takotna. He was taking Miss Ruth Secor to the latter, where she was to take charge of the school. Miss Anna Morris was also a passenger for Flat.

Freddie Moller was back in Fairbanks by August 15, 1929, after a summer of flying to various prospecting locations in his Waco 9, C 2776. After leaving Nenana, he had spent time at Tanana. Here he flew an unsuccessful search for a missing prospector by the name of Rhoads. Later, the man's bones were found, with indications he had been killed by a bear. Moller left Tanana on July 6, 1929, landing at Alatna on a river bar. After holding here for two days because of rain, he continued on to Bettles, again landing on a bar of the John River. Dropping mail here, he went on to Wiseman the same day, landing on their field. Leaving his *Anna* here, he went to the hills with Mike Angel, prospecting on Marion, Moore and Minnie Creeks.

On August 2, Moller took off from Wiseman for Twin Lakes, near the headwaters of the Bettles River. Encountering fog and strong headwinds, he flew for five hours and fifteen minutes, landing on a bar when nearly out of fuel. Building a raft, the aviator-prospector floated down to Alatna. Here he secured fuel and was brought upstream in a canoe that had to be lined upriver. Fueling the plane, he continued on to Alatna. From here he flew one prospector out, but was unable to effect a landing due to high water.

Enroute from Alatna to Tanana, Freddie stopped once on Leo's bar, where he met some prospectors traveling with a horse and a mule, an unusual sight in contrast to his plane.

Russel H. Merrill, Anchorage Air Transport pilot, arrived in Fairbanks on Saturday, August 10, 1929, traveling over the Richardson highway from Valdez by auto with his wife,

711

Thyra, and Doctor and Mrs. Haverstock; he was on a vacation from his flying job. The Merrills returned home to Anchorage on the Alaska Railroad Brill car the morning of Thursday, August 15. The pilot was to make a flight the following day.

Mechanics were working full time at installing the new Pratt & Whitney 525 horse-power Hornet motor in the Hamilton Metalplane, NC 10002, with Noel Wien standing by to test fly the plane. With a new cowling, engine mount, exhaust manifold, starter, propeller and other changes, it was a lot of work, but the plane's performance would improve with the additional power available. The engine itself cost the company $8500.

Frank Dorbandt, Alaskan Airways pilot based in Nome, arrived in Fairbanks about 11:00 A.M. Friday, August 15, in the Stinson biplane, C 5262. He had departed Nome on Wednesday with two passengers, Mrs. A.W. Newhall and Ted Scroggins, plus the mail. The pilot had been delayed at Unalakleet by bad weather, and held overnight at Tanana by rain. Ralph Wien, bringing in the Waco 9, C 2775, was off Nome on Thursday, at noon. He was also held overnight at Unalakleet by weather, coming in to Fairbanks at 1:45 P.M. on Friday.

Ed Young, Fairbanks pilot, flew to Livengood on Thursday afternoon, taking Miss Kay O'Brien as passenger. Noel Wien left Saturday, August 17, for Ruby, to bring in Judge Clegg and Louis Parcher. They had expected to come in from there on the Alaska Railroad steamer *Alice*, but the boat was tied up near Nulato with a broken crankshaft.

Ben Eielson, general manager for Alaskan Airways, Incorporated, was away at 10:00 A.M. Saturday, August 17, 1929, for Anchorage, flying with Frank Dorbandt in the Stinson Standard, NC 877, brought to Alaska by Tom Gerard. With clear weather on the coast, and a good tailwind from the north, Dorbandt landed the Stinson in the port city early in the afternoon. Eielson was in town to discuss the acquisition of Anchorage Air Transport, Incorporated, by Alaskan Airways, Incorporated. Transfer was made on the morning of Tuesday, August 20, 1929.

Dorbandt also had business in the city of another kind: at 1:30 P.M. on Monday he wed Miss Vida Deigh, a member of the clerical force at the Anchorage post office. The couple was off an hour later in the Stinson, NC 877, for Nome, where the pilot continued to fly for the new company. In Anchorage, the two Travel Air planes, C-193 and C-194, joined the fleet of Alaskan Airways, Incorporated, together with pilot Russel H. Merrill and mechanic Lon Cope.

Ben Eielson had announced in Fairbanks that former Fairbanks pilot Joe Crosson was returning to join the staff of Alaskan Airways as soon as the Cleveland Air Races were over. Marvel Crosson, Joe's twenty-seven year-old sister, was scheduled as a participant in the first women's air derby. Miss Crosson, who had spent considerable time in Fairbanks the previous year, left on September 2, 1928, to return to San Diego to continue her flying there. Marvel set a new altitude record on May 28, 1929, reaching 23,996 feet in a Ryan Brougham over Los Angeles. An accomplished pilot, she was on the second leg of the race from Santa Monica to Cleveland when an incident occurred on Monday, August 19, 1929, that resulted in her death. There were indications in the cockpit of her wrecked plane that she had become so airsick in turbulent air and desert heat that she had been unable to control the plane, bailing out moments before the crash. Although Marvel had experienced a problem with the engine on the first leg of the race, Department of Commerce Inspector J.W. Noel, on the scene, found nothing to indicate that either the motor or the plane had failed prior to the crash. Her body was found in a mountainous region six miles north of Welton, Arizona, her parachute released, but unopened. An insurance firm, offering to insure one plane in the women's race, had selected Marvel's. Her winning smile and enthusiasm for Alaska would be remembered.

With the consolidation of Bennett-Rodebaugh Company, Anchorage Air Transport and

Wien Alaska Airways into the new concern, Alaskan Airways, Incorporated, the company now had a total of ten airplanes, with two more to be added when the New Standard biplanes arrived from the factory. The Travel Air 4000, C-193; and 7000, C-194, were to remain in Anchorage. The Stinson Standard SB-1, NC 877, was now based at Nome. Stinson Standard, C 5262, Wilkins old Stinson "Detroiter", was in the hangar in Fairbanks undergoing overhaul. The remaining six airplanes in Fairbanks were the Hamilton Metalplane, NC 10002; a Zenith 6 biplane; a cabin Swallow, C 3542; a Waco Model 9, C 2775; a Waco 10, NC 780E; and a Stearman C-2B, NC 5415. The Swallow, Hamilton and Zenith were cabin airplanes. When the two New Standard biplanes, NC 174H and NC 9190 arrived, it would give the company a total of twelve planes, all but the Waco 9 having efficient air-cooled motors. The Stinson, C 5262, and the Stearman were in the process of being rebuilt; new wings had been ordered for the latter. Pilots for Alaskan Airways, not counting Ben Eielson, the general manager, were Ed Young, Noel Wien, Tom Gerard, A.A. Bennett, Ralph Wien, Russ Merrill and Frank Dorbandt. Gerard was also chief mechanic, with a crew of six mechanics at Fairbanks: C.H. Gillam, Earl E. Borland, Fritz Wien, Bill Basham, Ed Moore and J.T. Hutchison, and Lon Cope in Anchorage. Gillam was also about ready for his transport license, and Fritz Wien and Earl Borland had time in the air.

The Graf Zeppelin was coming to Fairbanks. On Thursday, May 9, 1929, an announcement had been made in Washington, D.C. by the Arctic International Society for Exploration of Arctic Regions that a contract had been signed for the use of the Graf Zeppelin for a flight to either Nome or Fairbanks, to be made in April or May of 1930. The route, as outlined, would be from Friedrichshafen to a northern mooring mast at Vadso, Norway, thence over Greenland and Canada to Fairbanks. Doctor Fridtjof Nansen would head the scientific group, and Doctor Hugo Eckener was to command the silver airship. It was expected that a mooring mast would be borrowed from the United States government for use in Fairbanks. The Commercial Club of Fairbanks wired an offer of assistance to the Society in early August, receiving a reply that Fairbanks was to be a stopping point.

By August 20, 1929, use of a plot of land adjacent to Weeks Field had been secured from Paul J. Rickert, and a survey was in progress. It was intended to use the land later as an extension of Weeks Field, to meet a growing demand. Wilkins had used this extension during the 1925 expedition when a longer runway was needed for the large Fokkers. Sealed bids for the clearing of brush from the land, to be in by August 31, 1929, were called for.

Saturday, August 24, 1929, saw three departures of Alaskan Airways planes from Weeks Field for various points. Ed Young was first off, heading for Chicken to bring in the Misses Traub. A few minutes later, the Hamilton, piloted by Noel Wien and Earl Borland was away at 10:30 A.M. From now on the large plane carried a flight mechanic on every flight. Noel carried Ada Wien, G.W. Rathjens, who was now interested in a mining deal in the Kobuk, Irving McKenny Reed, Territorial mining engineer, and H.J. Thompson, in charge of the airway weather service station in Fairbanks. Thompson was to organize the weather service in the Nome district. The pilot landed there at 1:30 P.M. (Nome time). A.A. Bennett was off Weeks Field shortly, in the Zenith 6, with Ike P. Taylor, assistant chief engineer of the Alaska Road Commission, and Roy King, mining man from the Koyukuk. Bennett was back, to depart again on Monday, August 26, 1929 for McGrath, Flat and Holy Cross, to bring in Major Douglas H. Gillette, engineer officer of the Alaska Road Commission, and Mrs. Gillette to Fairbanks.

Ed Young was off Fairbanks again on the morning of Tuesday, August 27, for Fort Yukon, with Paul Simonson in the passenger seat, and went on from there to Chicken, to bring in Gordon Springbett. Noel Wien was holding at Nome because of unfavorable weather. He came in to land at Weeks Field early in the afternoon on Friday, August 30, flying under a low ceiling from the Seward Peninsula. Noel brought his wife, Ada, Alvin Polet, who was coming in from Nome to attend the Alaska College, flight mechanic Earl Borland and Howard J. Thompson.

Alaskan Airways had now received the new Wright Whirlwind motor, to be installed in Waco 10, NC 780E, which would give it a speed of 136 miles per hour, making it the firm's fastest plane. The Waco, with the new motor installed, was test flown on Sunday, September 1, 1929, by pilots Ed Young and Noel Wien, who were enthused over its performance. Besides the pilot, it could carry two passengers in the front cockpit. It did not have the "elephant ears" on the ailerons like the earlier Waco Model 9. On September 4, 1929, Charles L. Thompson announced that Harvey W. "Barney" Barnhill was joining the company as a pilot. Claiming over 2500 hours in the air, Barnhill had arrived in Fairbanks with his wife about a month before; he had come to the Territory from Montana. The pilot had moved to Havre in 1927 from Iowa, where he had barnstormed and instructed in flying. Barnhill made a familiarization flight with A.A. Bennett to Livengood and Wiseman on September 4. The two men brought in U.S. Marshal V.O. Green, from the latter stop, for medical attention at Fairbanks, landing at 7:00 P.M. the same day.

Ben Eielson also hopped off for Nome at 11:30 A.M. Wednesday, taking Alaska authoress Barrett Willoughby with him in the new Waco 10, NC 780E, planning on a nonstop flight. They were successful, landing at Nome five and one-half hours after departing.

Frank Dorbandt, making one stop at Ruby for fuel, came in to Fairbanks from Nome on Thursday evening, September 6, 1929, in the Stinson Standard, NC 877. He brought Ray S. Pollister, vice-president of the Swenson Fur & trading Company, and A.P. Jochimsen, ice pilot, both from the schooner, *Elisif*. The ship had remained locked in the ice over the winter near North Cape, finally breaking free on July 29, 1929. Traveling in company with the *Nanuk*, another sailing vessel of Olaf Swenson's company, the *Elisif* was badly holed by the ice west of Cape Billings, Siberia, on August 11. Beached by her crew, the schooner was a total loss. Leaving two volunteer crew members to salvage cargo from the *Elisif*, the rest of the crew left, on August 18, in two small barges and two launches for North Cape. Arriving there on the fifth day, the crew rested overnight before setting out for East Cape, Siberia in the small craft, reaching the village of Uelen, at the cape, August 27. They were forced to leave early on the morning of the following day; there was a possibility that a rising wind would cause ice to move onshore. Unable to reach shelter, the men set out in the small boats for Big Diomede Island, twenty miles away. The voyage was accomplished under severe hardships, losing one barge and then the other, but the men finally fought their way to Little Diomede Island, where they were able to get all safely ashore through the surf to shelter at the village there. The cutter *Northland* later picked up the men, including Pollister and Jochimsen, bringing them in to Nome. (See *Icebound in the Siberian Arctic* by Bob Gleason). Traveling to Fairbanks by plane, the two men took the train on Saturday, September 7, for Seward and a boat for the States, going on to New York. Dorbandt left for Nome at 5:00 A.M. on September 7, but was forced to land at Nenana to wait for the fog to lift. He was finally able to continue but ran into such heavy weather he was forced to land at Nulato.

Fairbanks received an addition to its aerial fleet when Territorial Game Warden Samuel O. White received a crated Golden Eagle Chief, NC 569K. Uncrated at the hangar of Alaskan Airways on Thursday, September 5, 1929, the parasol type monoplane was assembled during that same night. Manufactured by Golden Eagle Aircraft Corporation of Inglewood, Cali-

714

fornia, the small plane was powered with a ninety horsepower, seven-cylinder radial LeBlond 7-D motor. It was fitted with an N.A.C.A. cowling to reduce drag, thus giving it a faster speed—108 miles per hour in cruise. Front and rear open cockpits held one person each. Sam paid $3500 for the plane but it was never satisfactory for what he wanted it for.

Warden Sam White, who had pounded the trails and waterways for years by dog team and boat, had visions of tracking down game violators in short order with his plane. Sam had married the former Mary Burgess, then a nurse at the Fort Yukon hospital, in 1928. The plane was privately owned by Sam and his wife. The Golden Eagle was test flown by Noel Wien, and Sam later made arrangements to take dual instruction from Ralph Wien. With his training spread out over a long period of time, Sam took fifteen or sixteen hours to solo, almost a year later, on August 1, 1930.

Alaskan Airways was busy. Pilot Tom Gerard brought Mrs. Paul Glasgow and her two children in from Chicken on Saturday, September 7, 1929, to winter in Fairbanks. Bennett had gone out on Friday for Nulato, taking Bevan Presley, superintendent of Kennecott Copper Corporation at Latouche, a Mr. Richardson and John Barrett to Hot Springs. He brought in a sick passenger, Mrs. Wilfred Evans, from Nulato on Saturday. A.A. Bennett was off for Nome at 5:00 A.M. on Saturday, but was forced to hold at Nenana on account of fog. Leaving there, he encountered heavy weather along the river, coming down at Nulato. Ben Eielson was away from Nome in the Waco 10, NC 780E, on Friday morning, September 6, with Miss Barrett Willoughby and a small amount of first class letter mail, headed for Fairbanks. The pilot arrived there late Saturday afternoon after holding at Unalakleet on Friday night for weather.

Harvey Barnhill, the new pilot, was away for Wiseman on Monday morning, September 9, to bring two passengers in to Fairbanks.

The Fairbanks Commercial Club was still going ahead with plans for a landing site for the Graf Zeppelin. They had decided to purchase sixty and one-half acres of land, adjacent to Weeks Field, from Paul J. Rickert for approximately $1500. Captain Austin E. Lathrop volunteered to pay the sum immediately, to be reimbursed by the Commercial Club later. By owning the land, and treating it as an expansion of the adjacent municipal airport, participation by the Territory and the Alaska Road Commission was assured. An option was taken on an additional nine and one-half acres. Blueprints and specifications for the dirigible project had been received from Washington. The eight concrete anchors for the mast would have to be set before freezeup. The work of clearing the site of brush was begun on Thursday, September 12, 1929, on a bid of $28.50 per acre.

A.A. Bennett was off Weeks Field the morning of Tuesday, September 17, for the Fortymile district, carrying Anchorage residents Tom Morgan and Steve Thornton, who planned to prospect in the area. The pilot had made an earlier round trip to Hot Springs, bringing in Jay Busby, manager of the Northern Commercial Company store there.

Ed Young was away for Nome on Thursday forenoon, taking the Stinson Standard, C 5262, company No. 8, back to Dorbandt. Wings and fuselage of the damaged plane had been recovered with new fabric and a new motor was installed. Alaskan Airways was now painting its fleet all one color and putting a company number on each plane, including the repaired Stinson. The pilot arrived in Nome the same day. Young would bring in the Stinson Standard, NC 877, currently in Nome.

Noel Wien, newly married, had not taken a vacation since his return to Alaska on March 19, 1927. He and Ada had not even had a honeymoon. The Wiens departed Fairbanks by train on Thursday, September 19, 1929, not knowing if they would ever return. The pilot's logbook showed 2440 hours of flying; a little over 1785 hours of it was Alaskan time. Taking the steamer *Alaska* at Seward, they visited with Doctor W.A. Borland in Juneau on Tuesday, September 24, 1929, on their way south.

The two New Standard biplanes, NC 174H and NC 9190, arrived in Fairbanks by train on Wednesday, September 18, 1929. The 20,000 pound shipment, in boxes, was transported to the Alaskan Airways, Incorporated, hangars the following day. The planes, manufactured by the Standard Aircraft Company of Patterson, New Jersey, were arranged with the usual pilot cockpit to the rear and, forward of this, a large open cockpit seating four passengers, two by two in tandem. A canopy could be placed over this space if desired. Powered with the Wright Whirlwind J-5 motor, the plane cruised at one hundred miles per hour with a fuel range of eight hours when the tanks were filled.

Joe Crosson was returning to Fairbanks to fly for Alaskan Airways. The former Fairbanks Airplane Corporation pilot had left in November of 1927. At this time, Ben Eielson, Joe Crosson and George King had formed a paper corporation called Alaska Consolidated Airways of Fairbanks, Alaska, with a dream of consolidating the air services there and raising capital for new equipment. Crosson and King had searched far and wide in the States for support, finding little. Finally, early in 1928, Joe Crosson had taken a flying job with Western Canada Airways, Limited, doing essentially the same type of work as he did in Alaska. George E. King was with him for a time. Sought by Wilkins in the fall of 1928 to join his Wilkins-Hearst Antarctic Expedition as second pilot under Ben Eielson, Crosson left Canada at the end of August, 1928, proceeding to the Lockheed factory and ferrying a second Vega to New York for Wilkins. The first use of an airplane in Antarctic exploration took place when Wilkins, Eielson, Crosson and mechanic Orval Porter went by ship with the two Lockheeds to set up a base at Deception Island, where they were to remain for six months. George King remained behind in New York, where he parlayed his limited flying experience into a good job as Company Sales Pilot for the Junkers Corporation of America at Roosevelt Field, demonstrating and delivering the Company's all-metal planes. George remained with Junkers from October, 1928 until 1931, returning to the Pacific Northwest and to Alaska in 1932, where he went back into mining.

When Ben Eielson and Joe Crosson returned from Antarctica, Alaska Consolidated Airways had been largely forgotten. But not by Eielson. With the additional stature gained as a Wilkins pilot on the 1928 polar flight, plus serving as pilot on the Wilkins-Hearst Antarctic Expedition, he now had the ear of the aviation community in the east, and its investors. When he returned to Alaska he was not representing his own company, but something much larger, with more financial clout. Now he wanted Joe Crosson on the team. The pilot had been doing odd flying jobs for Lockheed, and delivering new planes to Detroit and New York through the summer. The new company in Alaska would be getting an experienced pilot, seasoned in Canada and Alaska in the type of work needed.

Crosson sailed from Seattle on Saturday, September 1, 1929. Ben Eielson met him in Anchorage. The general manager of Alaskan Airways, Incorporated, left Fairbanks at 10:20 A.M. Friday, September 20, in the Waco 10, NC 780E, an airplane that was to become a favorite of Crosson's. Taking Mrs. Victor Brown and John F. Lonz as passengers, Eielson landed at the Anchorage airport at 1:30 P.M. after a flight of three hours and ten minutes.

Russ Merrill, Anchorage based pilot for the company, had departed on a flight for a mining company (that later became a town of NYAC) on September 16, 1929, and was unreported. Eielson, accompanied by Lon Cope, went out on Saturday, September 21, in the Waco 10 to search the route, without result. Crosson arrived in Anchorage the same day, to join the search. (See Anchorage—1929, chapter 47, for details). Merrill was never found.

In Fairbanks, one of the New Standards, NC 174H, was test flown the afternoon of Saturday, September 21, 1929, by A.A. Bennett. Other than a few minor adjustments, the plane was ready for service. Ed Young left Nome on Sunday afternoon, September 22, with the Stinson Standard, NC 877, to return it to Fairbanks. He brought in Jack Morton and Irving M. Reed. On Monday, September 23, Mr. and Mrs. Harvey Barnhill presented the aviation community with a daughter, born at St. Josephs Hospital in Fairbanks. On the same day, Earl Borland, mechanic for Alaskan Airways and student aviator, made his first solo flight, making three landings. Ralph Wien was his instructor.

Sir Hubert Wilkins announced on September 25, 1929, that he would sail again for Antarctica in a few days on his second Wilkins-Hearst Antarctic Expedition. Parker Cramer was going with him as a pilot, as was Al Cheesman. Orval Porter was along again as expedition mechanic.

Local businessmen in Fairbanks had raised $3000 for the Zeppelin airport fund, half of that required locally to finance the project. Depositing of the check by the Zeppelin finance committee on Saturday, September 8, 1929 would enable the Alaska Road Commission to proceed with work on mast and anchor foundations. Thursday, October 3, was declared a half-holiday, with cooperating businesses to close at noon, and all able-bodied citizens were asked to lend a hand in preparation of the landing site. The volunteer workers cleared off an immense amount of moss and other growth to be placed in piles and burned. A work crew was digging seven by seven by nine foot holes for the anchor and mooring mast foundations which were to be of poured concrete.

A.A. Bennett was off for Livengood and Tanana the morning of Wednesday, October 2, 1929. For Livengood, he carried G.E. Bigelow, Fairbanks Exploration Company engineer, and John Radak, Livengood miner. From Tanana, he brought Andy Vachon to Fairbanks. The next day the flier, accompanied by Harold Gillam, flew to the headwaters of the Tanana River to pick up Jack Carroll, an injured miner. Landing first at McCarthy, the pilot planned to fly to Chisana (pronounced Shushana) to pick up the man, bringing him to McCarthy where he could be transferred to the Kennicott hospital by rail.

Bennett and Gillam arrived at McCarthy on Thursday, October 3, to find they would have to wait there for gasoline to arrive from Cordova on the Copper River and Northwestern Railroad. The next day the pilot, accompanied by Billie James as guide, tried to cross the mountains, climbing to 12,000 feet, but was unable to get through. They tried again the following day and succeeded, crossing the Wrangell Mountains and reaching Chisana in forty minutes. The miner, Jack Carroll, had been hurt in a cave-in, suffering two crushed legs and head injuries. He could never have been transported over the two glaciers to McCarthy except by air. He was placed in the Waco 10, NC 780E. Snow was falling and Bennett, unable to recross the mountains, went around them on the west side by following the divide at the headwaters of the Nabesna and Copper Rivers, then flying down the Copper River to Copper Center, and from there to McCarthy. He landed late in the evening, after more than three hours flying compared to the forty minutes going over.

Bennett and Gillam were held at McCarthy until Friday, October 11, by fog. Encountering snow between Summit Lake and Donnelly, they still made a fast trip over the Richardson highway route, two hours and twenty minutes, landing in Fairbanks at 12:45 P.M. on Friday. By then Carroll was recovering in the Kennicott hospital.

Ben Eielson and Harvey Barnhill, who had gone to Anchorage earlier with the New Standard, NC 174H, to assist in the search for Merrill, came into Fairbanks in the Waco 10, NC 780E, on Wednesday, October 2, 1929. The men were accompanied by Butler Greer, big game hunter. Crosson was still on the search in Anchorage.

Ed Young was off for the Koyukuk again on Thursday morning. He planned stops at Alatna, Bettles and Wiseman, using the New Standard, NC 9190. Frank G. Dorbandt had made a flight from Nome to Anchorage, stopping at Takotna on the way, coming in through Rainy Pass. He returned to Nome, via Fairbanks, in Stinson, C 5262, landing on Weeks Field on Sunday, October 6. Mrs. Dorbandt and her mother, Mrs. Edward Mable of Anchorage, accompanied the pilot to the interior city.

Young came in Sunday, October 6, from a special mail flight to the Koyukuk, bringing Steve Spicer, engineer on Sam Dubin's riverboat, to Fairbanks. Barnhill brought in Miss Louise Holland and Mrs. John Raap from Livengood the same day.

Ben Eielson was off for Takotna on Thursday morning, October 10, 1929, to bring in four passengers who wanted to come to Fairbanks. It was reported to be snowing heavily at his destination shortly after the pilot had departed. Ben was back at Fairbanks, landing shortly after 3:00 P.M. the next day, bringing in Gilbert H. Russell, Gus Rosen, Hans Ericksen and T.E. Scribner, all of the Flume Dredging Company.

Harvey Barnhill had made two trips to Livengood on Wednesday, October 9, bringing Mr. and Mrs. Michael Beegler, George Gadoff and Tony Ban to Fairbanks. The pilot was away again for Livengood in the New Standard, NC 9190, the next day, to pick up Mrs. Blanche Cascaden, Tony Silva and Jack Esorde and bring them to Fairbanks. On Friday, he brought Luther C. Hess and G.A. Bigelow from Livengood. Soon after, Barnhill was transferred to Anchorage to fly out of there, while Crosson came to Fairbanks.

Percy Hubbard, of the Service Motor Company in Fairbanks, accompanied by Doctor J.A. Sutherland, flew to McGrath with A.A. Bennett on Sunday, October 13, 1929. Percy's mother, wife of the U.S. deputy marshal at McGrath, was ill and needed medical attention. Ed Young had come in from Akiak with Deputy Marshal Pat O'Connor, who was accompanying a prisoner and an insane Indian from there. Bennett took Young's passengers into Fairbanks while Ed remained overnight, bringing Percy, his mother and Doctor Sutherland to Fairbanks on Monday, October 14, where the ill woman was taken to the hospital.

Ben Eielson flew to Hot Springs on Thursday, October 17, bringing in Mike Kelly and D.J. McDougall. Tom Gerard came in from Livengood the same day; he had been marooned there for a time with a broken rocker arm until Bennett brought him repair parts on Wednesday. Eielson, accompanied by Borland, took the Hamilton, NC 10002, on the forenoon of Friday, October 18, and headed for Nome, where four passengers awaited him. Carrying mail, the plane arrived at the destination that evening. Ben was back in Fairbanks at 3:00 P.M. Wednesday, October 23, 1929.

Friday had been a busy day at Weeks Field. Joe Crosson arrived by train from Anchorage on Thursday, October 17, after a long absence. He had been taking part in the search for Russ Merrill at the port city. Going immediately to work, he flew two round trips to Livengood on Friday, October 18, in Waco NC 780E, taking Miss Evelyn Greenway, Miss Grace Lowe, Chub Douglas and August Alm as passengers. Eielson had left that morning for Nome, and two planes came in from the Kuskokwim in the afternoon within minutes of each other: A.A. Bennett, carrying Mrs. Carl F. Lottsfledt and Mrs. Frank Guskey and child, all of McGrath, and Ed Young, with Mrs. Georgia Hagen and Miss Josie Sheehan, both of Takotna and Flat.

Joe Crosson made a second pair of trips to Livengood on Sunday, October 20, 1929, taking over Mrs. Raap, Carl Olander and Tony Ban, and bringing in U.S. Commissioner C.H. LaBoyteaux. Ed Young also got away on Sunday for Beaver and Fort Yukon, carrying mail and freight. Bennett started in the forenoon for McGrath and Flat.

718

A new innovation for the safety of pilots flying into Fairbanks after dark went into effect the evening of Tuesday, October 22, 1929, when anti-collision lights were installed and turned on. With a red light on top of the wireless tower, another a third of the way down and another two-thirds of the way to the ground, the warning lights were kept burning from sunset to sunrise to warn pilots of the obstruction.

Joe Crosson was off for Nulato in the Waco 10, NC 780E, on Monday, October 21, 1929, arriving there two hours and twenty-five minutes later. The following day he continued on to Tanana and Wiseman, and was in the air for five hours and fifteen minutes. He flew two round trips on Wednesday between Wiseman and Bettles, coming in to Fairbanks that same evening; he had flown five hours of air time. Ed Young flew to Hot Springs to pick up baggage left there from a former trip.

Carl Ben Eielson, arriving from Nome in the Hamilton on Wednesday, October 23, 1929, announced in Fairbanks on the following day that a contract had been signed between Alaskan Airways, Incorporated, and the Swenson Fur & Trading Company for up to fifteen trips to North Cape, Siberia, where the Swenson schooner, *Nanuk*, was fast in the ice. It was to be an operation similar to the one Noel Wien and Calvin Cripe had performed in March, 1929, when the two men had reached the *Elisif*, another Swenson vessel, and returned with a valuable load of furs. This time Alaskan Airways was to bring in a great amount of Siberian furs plus all the excess personnel on the vessel, which would undoubtedly remain fast in the ice until the following summer.

With the *Elisif* frozen in the previous winter, Olaf Swenson, then at North Cape, Siberia, had left there prior to the arrival of Noel Wien, making a grueling journey through Siberia. Leaving the cape on October 19, 1928, in company with the local representative of Gostorg (Russian government trade organization in Siberia), a half-breed boy and two Chukchi natives driving dog teams, Swenson reached Yakutsk on January 16, 1929. Dog teams had given way to reindeer sledges, and eventually horses. He reached Irkutsk and the Siberian railway in the middle of February, taking the train on to Moscow. (See *Northwest of the World* by Olaf Swenson.)

Swenson continued on to Seattle to prepare a second vessel, *Nanuk*, for the trip to Siberia to carry a load of supplies for the arctic coast. He also installed a radio station aboard, contracting with Radiomarine Corporation of America for the installation of the long-wave transmitter and receiver, and its twenty-two-year-old operator, Bob Gleason. The vessel, under the command of Captain R.H. Weeding, with Swenson and his seventeen-year-old daughter, Marion, aboard, sailed from Seattle the evening of June 15, 1929, and cleared from Cape Flattery the following day. The story of its epic journey to rendezvous with *Elisif* in the ice near North Cape, today renamed Cape Schmidt (Mys Schmita), and with a Russian steamer, *Stavropol*, the loss of the *Elisif* in the ice near Cape Billings, to the final freezing in of the *Nanuk* and the *Stavropol* at North Cape on October 4, 1929, is best told in Robert J. Gleason's book, *Icebound in the Siberian Arctic*. At one point in their journey, when first making contact with *Elisif* at North Cape and unloading yearly supplies at the settlement there, the *Nanuk* was visited in July by a Russian Junkers W-33, a single-engined plane on floats. Flown by Russian airmen Krassinski, Valvitca and Leongard, the plane had arrived by ship at Saint Lawrence Bay, from where they had flown to Wrangel Island to check on a Russian colony there, returning to North Cape before taking off up the coast for the Kolyma River, New Siberian Islands, the mouth of the Lena River, Yakutsk and Irkutsk, on the Siberian railroad.

For Alaskan Airways, Incorporated, the route from Fairbanks to North Cape, Siberia encompassed about 1100 miles. The pilots were familiar with it as far as the jumping-off point on the coast at Cape Prince of Wales, where they had to cross the Bering Strait to East Cape as Noel Wien had done, before following the coastline on the Siberian side to North Cape and the *Nanuk*. There was a village, Uelen, at East Cape, and a Chukchi village near North Cape, with a Russian representative in each. Between these were occasional small Chukchi family groups at odd spots on the coast. It was the largest contract yet for an Alaskan flying company, and Eielson intended to be a part of it. He flew the large Hamilton Metalplane, NC 10002, taking Frank Dorbandt with him from Nome; Dorbandt flew the Stinson Standard, C 5262, that was currently based there. Beside the added safety factor in using two planes, it would cut the number of crossings in half, as well as expedite the transfer of furs and personnel.

In Fairbanks, the pouring of concrete for the mast and anchors of the Zeppelin field was begun on Thursday, October 24, 1929. The field, including the roundway on which it was intended for the Graf Zeppelin to weathervane about the mast, had been cleared and leveled, the surface in good condition. Steel fittings to mount the mast and the anchoring cables were cast into the large concrete bases. By Saturday noon, the concrete had been poured in five of the eight anchor foundations and the mast foundation, leaving three unfinished. Six and a half yards of concrete were needed for the anchor foundations, and eight for the mast. Five Alaska Road Commission trucks and a tractor were removing moss from the runway. A canister containing records of the project was to be buried in concrete at the base of the mast. In New York, the stock market was crumbling, a collapse soon to be felt across the nation. It was another urgent reason to get the Siberian furs to market, before the price fell.

Ed Young was off Weeks Field for Shungnak in the Kobuk country on Thursday, October 24, 1929, to bring Colonel G. W. Rathjens, now head of a Kobuk mining company, to Fairbanks. A.A. Bennett was off that same morning for McGrath and Flat, to pick up passengers for Fairbanks at both stops. Crosson had come in the previous afternoon in Waco, NC 780E, and was away again Friday, October 25, this time flying the Stinson Standard, NC 877. He flew to Medfra and McGrath. Crosson also flew a round trip from McGrath to Takotna before stopping for the night. He left McGrath the following day, Saturday, for Fairbanks but returned after an hour and a half, forced back by weather. The pilot was away again the next day, making it in to Nenana in heavy weather, and overnighted there. Crosson came in to Fairbanks the next day, Tuesday, October 29, in the Stinson, landing about noon. Bennett was also at Nenana on the way in. The two pilots brought in four passengers between them: Mrs. Louise Levenhagen, John Collins, and Frank Meir, all of Ophir, and Walter Jewell, a local carpenter who had completed a contract at Iditarod. Ed Young had also gotten away for the upper Kuskokwim in the New Standard biplane, NC 9190, on Monday morning, October 29, 1929. Crosson flight tested Stinson Standard, NC 877, on Wednesday, October 30, and attempted to go to Wiseman but had to return. The aircraft had now been put on skis for the winter. In the afternoon of the same day he took the New Standard, NC 9190, to Livengood and return.

Ed Young left Fairbanks the morning of Thursday, October 31, for Chisana, to bring C.A. Simons, trading post operator and postmaster, in for treatment at the Fairbanks hospital. Running into fog and snow, the pilot was forced to land at Teslin Lake, unable to get away again until Tuesday, November 5. Upon reaching Chisana, he learned the man had died on October 30, before the pilot left Fairbanks; the funeral was held the following day. The telegraph station was so far from Chisana the flight could not have been cancelled in time to save Young from making the trip. Young returned to Fairbanks on the night of Tuesday, November 5, bringing in Chisana resident B.J. Davis.

Harvey Barnhill, Anchorage pilot for Alaskan Airways, brought the New Standard, NC 174H, to Fairbanks on Friday, November 1, where the plane would be fitted with skis. Barnhill

▲   *Alaskan Airways, Incorporated, planes at Weeks Field in 1929; a New Standard D-25 to the left and the Stinson Standard SB-1, NC 877, to the right.*

▼   *The New Standard biplanes, NC 174H and NC 9190, arrived in Fairbanks by train on September 18, 1929. Bennett test flew the first one on September 21. The two planes were a welcome addition to Alaskan Airways' fleet.*

New Standard D-25 with its Wright Whirlwind J-5 motor of 220 horsepower is shown in flight. The company had installed a long range fuel tank above the center section of the upper wing to extend the range of the aircraft. The plane is easily identified by its graceful upswept wings.

flew out of Fairbanks for a time to help handle the business out of there.

Ben Eielson and Earl Borland were off for Nome in the Hamilton Metalplane, NC 10002, to begin the flights to Siberia. Ben was, by now, an experienced pilot in many types of planes. He had returned to the U.S. Air Service as a lieutenant following the airmail contract of 1924, and had not only accumulated service time but had flown for Model Airways out of Langley Field for a short time, and for Florida Airways for a longer period. By September 6, 1927, his logbook totalled 2392:02 hours of flying time. He had added to this with the Detroit News-Wilkins Expedition of 1928, and followed that with the Wilkins-Hearst Antarctic Expedition. He had been flying the Hamilton out of Fairbanks in the meantime. Eielson and Borland, with a load of mail from Fairbanks, arrived in Nome at 3:00 P.M. (Bering Sea time) of Tuesday, October 29, 1929. He was delayed here for a time so that a gear strut, damaged in the landing, could be repaired. Frank Dorbandt, flying the Stinson Standard, C 5262, had gone on ahead to Teller. Here he changed wheels for skis, thinking he would need them for the landing at North Cape.

Dorbandt took off from Teller at 8:15 A.M. Tuesday, October 29, 1929. He arrived at North Cape, Siberia at 2:30 P.M., to land neatly and taxi up to the *Nanuk* on the skis. The big pilot brought mail, cigarettes, and a case of coffee; the rest of the load was all case gas for the return journey.

With good radio communication from the *Nanuk*, Dorbandt advised Eielson to remain

722

Pilot Frank Dorbandt dressed for the Arctic. The Stinson Standard he flew for Alaskan Airways in 1929 forms a background.

on wheels as there were good landing places with little snow along the coast. The pilot decided to wait for the Hamilton so they could return to Nome together. Eielson and Borland came in the next day, Wednesday, October 30, with the Hamilton, flying from Nome in four hours and twenty minutes. The furs to be taken on the first trip were loaded that afternoon and the aircraft serviced. The quiet aboard the *Nanuk* was disrupted that evening when Eielson's quiet, friendly manner contrasted with Dorbandt's loud voice. On his arrival Dorbandt had dispatched a radio message to a New York newspaper, calling attention to his flight from Teller to Siberia.

Dorbandt took four passengers in addition to a small amount of furs in the Stinson, while Eielson and Borland carried the weightiest passengers. George Hunter, assistant engineer, Clarke Crichton, cook and steward, Clarke Crichton, Jr., age 16, and G.V. Johansen, seaman, boarded the Stinson Standard. O. Holmstrom, first mate, and M. "Paddy" Foley, seaman, boarded the Hamilton. Dorbandt was off at 9:30 A.M. Thursday, October 31, with Eielson following soon after. Eielson returned shortly, to shut off the cabin heat, fearing it would affect the furs. He was away again at 10:10 A.M. With the new 525 horsepower Hornet engine, there was plenty of power.

Weather conditions at Teller and the Bering Strait were unfavorable, with neither plane reaching Teller that night. Due to snow squalls, Dorbandt landed about ninety miles west of East Cape, Siberia, at an Eskimo settlement near Cape Serdtse-Kamen. Eielson was overhead shortly thereafter, landing alongside. Realizing they would be remaining overnight, Hunter and Crichton decided to walk toward the shore, reaching it after traveling about a mile and one-half over the ice. Walking another mile along the beach in a stiff wind, with temperatures below freezing, they reached the Eskimo camp. The natives, hearing the planes, were already going out to bring the visitors in. The passengers and crew took refuge here for the next four days while the storm blew itself out.

Life in a Chukchi yarang (skin hut) was not of the best. Built of skins on a pole frame of driftwood, the hut resembled half an orange, with a hole at the top to evacuate the smoke, and was about nine by twelve feet. A partitioned room was within; the spaces along the outer walls of the yarang were left for storage of meat, gear, dogs or whatever. The inner room, made of skins stretched over sealskin lines, was heated with seal oil lamps with moss wicks, upon

Frank Dorbandt reached the Nanuk *at North Cape, Siberia on October 29, 1929, on the first trip, with Eielson and Borland, in the Hamilton, coming in the next day from Nome.*

Eddie Bowman Collection

Bob Gleason Photo

Alaskan Airways, Incorporated, Stinson Standard, Model SB-1, No. 8, C 5262, flown by Frank Dorbandt, arrived at the Nanuk *on October 30, 1929 (Siberian date).*

*Eielson arrived at the **Nanuk** on October 30, 1929, with the Hamilton. He was able to land on the ice on wheels. Leaving here with a good load the next day, Eielson went in to Nome, with a delay enroute at a Chukchi village. It was on the second trip on November 9, 1929, that the two airmen came to disaster.*

which the natives also cooked. It was so warm within this cubicle the tenants must remove the greater part of their clothing. While the native hospitality was the greatest, so was the stench. While the *Nanuk* people had experienced this before, it was new to the airmen. Making the best of it, the visitors joined the crowd, except Eielson and Borland who slept in the plane the first night.

When the storm was over, the men shoveled out the drifted-in planes and warmed the engines. The skis of the Stinson were frozen in and it took some work to break them free. The *Nanuk* people were afraid they had missed the *Sierra*, the last boat of the season out of Nome. The small motor vessel, operated by the Lomens, had loaded a full cargo of reindeer carcasses and hides at Golovin. She was due to arrive in Nome on November 3, to sail for Seattle about November 5, with the meat, furs, mail and a few passengers.

Firepotting and warming the lubricating oil with the plumber's blowpots was completed by 9:30 A.M. Dorbandt was away for Teller, where he changed to wheels. Eielson and Borland followed a half hour later. They overtook the slower Stinson as they were crossing Bering Strait. Much open water was seen between the Diomede Islands. Frank Dorbandt arrived in Nome from Teller at 2:45 P.M. Monday, November 4, 1929. Eielson had come in earlier, without stopping, landing at 12:30 P.M. Their passengers were in time to catch the *M.V. Sierra*. The two planes left Nome the same evening, to return to Teller to gas up for their next trip to North Cape. They were to remain at Teller for some time because of poor weather. North Cape was wrapped in snow and fog.

Back in Fairbanks the remaining pilots were carrying on the other business for Alaskan Airways. Joe Crosson, in the other Stinson Standard, NC 877, left for Wiseman. With 1086 flying hours under his belt, he was a seasoned flier. Harvey Barnhill accompanied Crosson, flying a second plane load. They were carrying Doctor L.W. Fromm, dentist, and his father, C.F. Fromm, laboratory technician. The two men were establishing a temporary dental office at Wiseman. A.A. Bennett followed the two planes off a short time later, bound for Chandalar with Charles Mayben, who was inspecting roads for the Alaska Road Commission. Freezeup of the Yukon River was imminent, with ice running bank full at Circle. Crosson came in to Fairbanks from Wiseman the following day, having flown fifty minutes each way. Harvey Barnhill also returned.

Crosson started out for McGrath in Stinson, NC 877, on Wednesday, November 6, 1929, but was forced back to Weeks Field by weather. He left again the next day, with Bennett and Barnhill in their planes, to bring in New York-Alaska (Gold Dredging) Company personnel. With the season ending, the miners and boatmen were coming in; most would go Outside for the winter. Many of the dredgemen worked on gold dredges in California during Alaska's off season. Crosson made it to McGrath on Thursday, going to Whitefish Lake the next day. From here he flew in to Akiak, where they were assembling their load, arriving on Friday, November 9, 1929, flying a round trip from there to Foothill Lake and a second round trip to Bethel. On Monday, November 11, he flew from Akiak to McGrath. Overnighting there, he continued on the next day, flying to Minchumina to hold an hour and a half before going on to Fairbanks, where he landed at 4:30 P.M.; Bennett, with Barnhill accompanying him in his plane, had taken off shortly after Crosson. Bennett passed the other two planes soon after leaving McGrath, and they lost sight of him; he was not visible when they landed at Lake Minchumina, where snow cut the visibility. The two planes brought seven passengers: Frank Lott, Jerry Franki, R.T. Hirsch, Tom Lent, Chris Asmussen, R.A. Johnson and H. Ford.

Bennett, cut off by weather, had landed at Hot Springs. He came in to Fairbanks the next morning, Wednesday, November 13, bringing J.K. Crowdy and Frank and Ed McDougall from the lower Kuskokwim. It was his last flight for Alaskan Airways; he and Mrs. Bennett left on the train for Outside on Thursday, November 14, 1929. As passengers on the *Yukon*, the Bennetts passed through Ketchikan on Tuesday, November 19, bound for San Diego, where he had been located before coming to Alaska. The raspy-voiced pilot spoke of buying a new plane there and touring the States. He could very well do it, having in his poke a share of the proceeds from the sale of Bennett-Rodebaugh Company to Alaskan Airways, Incorporated.

Ed Young had taken off Weeks Field at noon on Saturday, November 9, for Tanana and Ruby. He was taking Mrs. Brown to Ruby, and intended to pick up Edgar Kalland at Tanana on his return flight. The man had been shot in the leg and needed medical attention. The pilot was back, to make a round-trip flight to Fort Yukon the following day, returning two natives who had served out their federal jail sentences to repay their debt to the community. He was off again on Monday, November 11, to Tanana and Ruby. He took Mrs. H. Sagers to Tanana, where she had a position as staff nurse at the Bureau of Education hospital there. He took his previous passenger, Mrs. Brown, from Tanana to Ruby. Young had been unable to complete the flight to Ruby on the previous Saturday. On his return flight, he stopped at Hot Springs with an adverse wind making it difficult to land on the field, but finally got down on the river ice.

Fred Moller, mechanic at Alaskan Airways, and sometimes aviator, was off on Monday morning, November 11, in his Waco 9, *Anna*, for Circle Hot Springs. The plane was loaded with spare parts in case trouble developed. He was back on Weeks Field early in the afternoon of Wednesday, November 13, bringing in Mrs. Alexandria Smith. Although twenty-five below at the Springs, Moller reported a brisk business at the pioneer resort, with many interior Alaskans soaking out their aches and pains in the curative waters.

Joe Crosson was away in the Stinson Standard, NC 877, on the morning of Wednesday, November 13, 1929, for Bettles and Wiseman. He carried merchant Sam Dubin for Bettles and J.E. Woll for the latter stop. Returning to Bettles the same day, he flew a second round trip to Wiseman the next day, continuing on to stop at Alatna and Fairbanks, and landed on Weeks Field late in the afternoon.

Harvey Barnhill was away Wednesday morning, November 13, for Hot Springs, carrying Mrs. Windish and her two-week-old daughter, joining Mr. Windish at the Springs. The third passenger in the plane was Sidney Ridge. Barnhill left the next day in the New Standard, NC 174H, for Anchorage where he resumed flying out of there for Alaskan Airways. The pilot arrived at the port city the same day. Ed Young was also off Weeks Field on the morning of Thursday, November 14, bound for Bethel. Two passengers were picked up at the river community, and Father Concannon joined the flight at Holy Cross, coming in to Fairbanks for medical attention. A shipment of live mink was to be loaded on the plane at McGrath. Five days later Young was still held at McGrath by weather. On Monday, November 18, he made a round trip to Flat, bringing three passengers to McGrath. Six others were waiting at Flat for transportation to Fairbanks. On the following day the pilot flew to Iditarod, to bring in more passengers to McGrath but, held by weather, did not return that day. He came in to Fairbanks early in the afternoon of Thursday, November 21, with a load of passengers. On this trip the pilot had been away from home for a week.

Crosson took a new plane aloft on the morning of Friday, November 15, 1929, for Livengood. He flew the Zenith 6 which had been Bennett's pet. Carrying Miss Evelyn Greenway as passenger, he returned to Fairbanks without reaching his intended destination. Crosson repeated the flight the next day in the Stinson Standard, NC 877, making two round trips to Livengood, taking mining man Chub Douglas out on one of the flights.

Early November, 1929. On the ice at Grantley Harbor, before Teller, Alaska, the Hamilton Metalplane, NC 10002, flown by Carl Ben Eielson and Earl Borland; and the Stinson SB-1, C 5652, flown by Frank Dorbandt and Clark Bassett, await better weather before taking off for Siberia. The Stinson is pushed into a nose hangar on the ice, erected to give shelter when the mechanics serviced the engine.

In Teller, Alaska, Ben Eielson and his flight mechanic, Earl Borland, with Frank Dorbandt and Clark Bassett, his Alaskan Airways mechanic from Nome, were waiting to continue the flights across to Siberia. The weather continued bad, with snow and fog at North Cape frequently reported by the *Nanuk* radio operator. Holding since November 4, living in the roadhouse at Teller in close quarters, cabin fever developed. Dorbandt, who also had his wife with him, began to get on everyone's nerves, with his loud, overbearing personality. On Saturday, November 9, 1929, the weather at Teller was good, but only possible at North Cape. Urged by Dorbandt, Eielson decided to make the attempt. The two planes were off the snow at 10:45 A.M. (Bering Sea time) for Siberia. Dorbandt was back in an hour and a half; he had run into weather. Eielson did not return. Dorbandt, flying the Stinson Standard, C 5262, went on in to Nome that same afternoon. With him in the plane were his wife, Vida, Mrs. Jack Warren, wife of the roadhouse operator, and James H. Anderson, radio operator at Teller. The party returned to Teller that afternoon.

No concern was felt for the first few days over the missing pilot and mechanic, knowing there were Chukchi villages as well as many landing places along the Siberian coast where the airmen could wait out the weather. The Hamilton carried 160 gallons of gasoline in the tanks and Eielson had taken 180 gallons of case gas with him, stowed in the cabin, to use on his return flight. Dorbandt, in Teller, was preparing to go again but the weather had deteriorated. When the pilot was finally able to depart on Saturday, November 16, the Stinson Standard, heavily loaded with gasoline, was brought to a halt by the pilot during the takeoff, sustaining landing gear and wing tip damage. The craft could not withstand the pounding over the rough surface with such a load. Dorbandt and his mechanic, Clark Bassett, attempted to make repairs at Teller, but the two men ended up flying the Stinson in to Nome on Wednesday, November 20, arriving at 3:15 P.M. It was necessary to get a cracked axle properly welded, as well as make minor repairs to wing tips, damaged in the unsuccessful takeoff. Mechanics worked all night on the repairs. Bassett and Dorbandt returned to Teller on Tuesday, November 26, 1929.

There had been two flyable days reported at North Cape, but the Hamilton had not appeared. Now the people involved were becoming concerned. The *Nanuk* had word that the plane had been sighted in the fog, flying sixty miles from the ship about the same date as their departure from Teller. A second report from a Russian trapper told of his hearing the plane in the fog about fifty miles from the *Nanuk*. Olaf Swenson sent out the ship's dog team in the direction of the reported location to check on it, as well as contact any villages for news of any kind about the plane. A dog team arrived at the *Nanuk* on Saturday, November 23, from Kolyuchin Bay, some 150 miles southeast in the direction of East Cape, reporting no signs of a plane along the coast in that direction.

In Fairbanks, Alaskan Airways pilots were continuing to handle the business out of there. Joe Crosson was off in the open-cockpit Waco 10, NC 780E, on Sunday, November 17, for Circle Hot Springs and return. He dropped Joe Quigley, Kantishna miner, at the Springs. Charles L. Thompson, manager of Alaskan Airways in Fairbanks, was rearranging his personnel and equipment, with Bennett leaving and two planes and crews on the *Nanuk* contract. Planning on sending Crosson and Harvey Barnhill to the Seward Peninsula, he was again forestalled when, during a takeoff at Anchorage on Monday, November 18, 1929, Barnhill smashed a lower wing panel on the New Standard, NC 174H. Taking the open-cockpit Travel Air 4000, C-193. the pilot was off for Fairbanks the next morning, arriving there about noon. Matt Nieminen, former Anchorage Air Transport, Incorporated, pilot, was on his way north to a flying job with Alaskan Airways at Anchorage. He arrived there on Saturday,

November 23, 1929, to be ordered a week later to Fairbanks, to aid in the rapidly widening search for Ben Eielson and Earl Borland.

Joe Crosson was off in the Stinson Standard, NC 877, the morning of Tuesday, November 19, for Medfra, McGrath and Iditarod. He took Mrs. M.A. Berry, her daughter, and eight live mink in the plane. The mink were breeding stock for the Berry fur farm, near Medfra. The pilot also carried mail and freight for Flat and McGrath. Crosson returned the following day, from Iditarod to McGrath, coming in from the Kuskokwim river town, with Ed Young, on Thursday, November 21, to land at Weeks Field. The two pilots had seven passengers between them.

Fred Moller was away in his Waco 9, C 2776, on the morning of Tuesday, November 19, seeking to land two prospectors at Caribou Creek, in the Salchaket country. Finding the surface there swept clean of snow by wind, and the river bars covered with boulders and the rivers open, he returned to Fairbanks. With a stiff headwind going, it took him an hour and a half to fly the sixty miles, and only thirty minutes for the return flight.

Barnhill made a round trip to Livengood on Tuesday afternoon, November 19, carrying mail both ways, flying in strong winds and twelve-degrees-below-zero temperatures on the return. The pilot was off again in the Waco 10, NC 780E, the morning of Thursday, November 21, for Chicken. Carrying Bill Williams and Paul Glasgow, he delivered the two men and returned to Fairbanks the same day.

Crosson was away for McGrath in the Stinson Standard, NC 877, on the morning of Friday, November 22, taking three hours and thirty minutes enroute. The following day he attempted a flight downriver to Bethel, but was rebuffed by weather, landing back at McGrath after flying for one hour and twenty minutes. The next day, Sunday, November 24, 1929, he flew from McGrath to Iditarod, and from there to Cripple Creek the following day, making two landings on the three-hour flight. On Thursday, November 26, he flew the Stinson from Cripple Creek to Minchumina to Fairbanks. The day after his arrival, he took the Stinson to Livengood and return, with Don Adler, aviation editor of the News-Miner along for the round trip. He was away in the Stinson again on Thursday, November 28, to Medfra and return. This ended his flying out of Fairbanks for a time as he was sent to Nome to take part in the Eielson-Borland search.

On Friday, November 15, 1929, a shipment of four cases of Veedol lubricating oil was received at the Alaskan Airways hangar with a request that it be stored awaiting the arrival of George E. King. Recuperating from his accident near Atlantic City, New Jersey, the former Fairbanks Airplane Corporation mechanic and student pilot, who was now a sales pilot for the Junkers company, had written in July from Dessau, Germany, that his company was interested in expanding its commercial routes across Bering Strait from Siberia to Alaska and beyond. The Junkers company was already operating a commercial service from Berlin to Irkutsk, Siberia. By October 24, 1929, the pilot was planning a flight, expecting to leave Berlin for Moscow on November 20, 1929, and to reach Fairbanks on December 14. A Junkers W-34, fitted with a Pratt & Whitney Wasp motor of 420 horsepower was used on the flight. At 7:15 A.M. on November 18, 1929, George King, with Flugkapitan Schnebele and his mechanic (both from Lufthansa) were off Templehof Field in Berlin, bound for Koenigsburg and Moscow, a distance of 1000 miles. They arrived at their destination after a flight of eight and one-half hours, escorted to a landing by a Russian pilot.

While they had permission to fly over Russian territory, the permit for the trip through Siberia was yet undecided. King met with various officials concerned, but was unsuccessful. It was during this period of time that Eielson disappeared, and Russian aid was sought in the search. The decision against granting King a permit was based on the premise that any fuel and supplies on the route would be used by search parties. Pressing for permission to join the search for Eielson and Borland, King was finally permitted to go as an observer. The Junkers crew had now returned the plane to Germany from Moscow. George King left the city by train with a search party headed by Ivan Tchuknovsky, a well-known Russian flier, at 7:00 P.M. on New Year's night. Semyon Shestakov, who had been originally selected for the position, was worn out; he had just returned from the *Land of Soviets* world flight, and had entered a hospital for rest.

The party reached Krasnoyarsk on January 3, 1930, where planes were to be ready for them. The group was all ready to go in late January when a radio message from the *Nanuk* announced the finding of the wrecked Hamilton. George King took a train from Krasnoyarsk to Vladivostok, a northern seaport, on the evening of January 28, 1930, arriving in Moscow three days later. His attempted Siberian flight, as well as his attempt to aid in the Eielson-Borland search was over.

Ed Young, flying the New Standard, NC 9190, and Harvey Barnhill with the Zenith 6, left Fairbanks on Sunday, November 25, 1929, for the Seward Peninsula. Reaching Ruby that afternoon, the fliers were held there by heavy fog for the next few days. Meanwhile, Dorbandt had arrived back in Teller on November 26 from Nome. Unable to wait longer for the planes held at Ruby to reach him, he took off in the Stinson Standard, C 5262, for North Cape on the morning of Wednesday, November 27, 1929. The weather was very cold, thirty-four degrees below zero at 2000 feet, and the engine did not turn up enough revolutions in the air to continue. Dorbandt turned back and landed again at Teller. He worked on the plane, trying to cowl the engine tighter, to get it to run at a higher heat. He took off the following day, getting as far as Cape Prince of Wales, encountering fog and snow, and he had to return again to Teller.

In Ruby, clearing weather along the lower Yukon on Friday, November 29, 1929, sent the pilots to their planes. Ed Young had taken off for Nome the previous day, but was forced back to Ruby by weather. The landing gear on NC 9190 was damaged somewhat when he landed. Joe Crosson left Fairbanks for Ruby on November 29, in Waco 10, NC 780E. On arrival, he sent Harvey Barnhill back to Fairbanks with the New Standard. It had originally been intended that Barnhill return with Dorbandt's Stinson Standard, C 5262, so that further repairs could be done in Fairbanks. Crosson continued on to Nome, shortly after his arrival at Ruby, unloading a big load of mail there before going on to Teller that same day. He had been in the air, all told, five hours and thirty-five minutes. The pilot could get together with Dorbandt and work out a plan for getting to North Cape and the *Nanuk*. Eielson and Borland had now been missing for three weeks. If they were down somewhere they were not short of food, for they had a primus stove, a case of eggs, hams and bacon in the plane for the trading schooner.

In Fairbanks, chief mechanic and pilot for Alaskan Airways, Tom Gerard, was off in the forenoon of Friday, November 29, 1929. Taking a load of freight and express to Fort Yukon, he came back to land at Weeks Field about 2:30 P.M. with Deputy U.S. Marshal Bill Butler of Fort Yukon as a passenger. Harvey Barnhill came in that same afternoon from Ruby with the New Standard, NC 9190, carrying William Midgely as a passenger. Freddie Moller received from the Department of Commerce a permit entitling him to operate as a transport pilot, pending the next visit of a departmental inspector. Moller had an Industrial Pilot license in addition to mechanic and rigger licenses from the department.

Barnhill, wanting to return to Anchorage, left on the morning of Saturday, November

30, 1929, in New Standard, NC 9190, but ran into a snowstorm and was forced to return to Fairbanks. He was still there on Monday, December 2, Matt Nieminen, new pilot for Alaskan Airways, Incorporated, arrived in Fairbanks by train from Anchorage on Sunday, December 1. Up early the next morning, to flight test the New Standard, NC 9190, he left early in the afternoon of that same Monday for the Seward Peninsula. He ran into a heavy blanket of fog near Hot Springs and returned to Fairbanks, to land about 1:30 P.M. That same afternoon Charles Harold Gillam was testing his Swallow biplane, *Arctic Prospector*, purchased from Arctic Prospecting & Development Company in September, 1928. He had installed a new Warner Scarab 110 horsepower, air-cooled motor and it performed well. The young pilot had plans for locating soon at Copper Center or McCarthy. Ed Young left Ruby on Tuesday, December 3, at 10:30 A.M. and, encountering fog and snow on the flight, was having to "feel" his way through along the route.

Frank Dorbandt Photo, Mary Barrows Collection

Cape Prince of Wales, the westernmost tip of North America. It is from here the pilots jumped off to cross the strait to Siberia.

Alaskan Airways, Incorporated, Stinson Standard flown by Frank Dorbandt. Residents of Teller, Alaska are grouped in front.

Eddie Bowman Collection

731

Back in Teller, Crosson and Dorbandt were trying to get across Bering Strait to East Cape. On Saturday, November 30, the two pilots took off from Teller, with Crosson in Waco, NC 780E, and Dorbandt in Stinson, C 5262. Weather conditions at the *Nanuk* were reported as thirty-five degrees below zero with a forty mile wind and no visibility. The two planes got as far as Cape Prince of Wales before returning to Teller; they were in the air for an hour and a half. On December 3 they made another attempt, returning to Teller after being in the air one hour and forty-five minutes. With no fuel on the Siberian coast, the pilots had to overload with case gas for the return flight. The Hamilton was a long-range aircraft, and had worked well on the first flight. The planes they were now using were of a shorter range and load capacity. There was talk of federal aid with military aircraft, but the wheels of government turn slowly. With the short hours of daylight in midwinter, they were limited; there was an even shorter span of daylight on the Siberian coast to the north. Gasoline for the engine that powered the electric generator at the *Nanuk* was in short supply. To conserve it, Radio Operator Gleason had to reduce the number of transmission schedules per day from the ship although he could run his receiver most of the time; it used little power from the batteries.

Back at Fairbanks, there was minimal aviation activity. Fritz Wien, who had been working as a mechanic for Alaskan Airways, left there for Minnesota on Friday, December 6. He departed from Seward on the steamer *Yukon* on Saturday. Arthur F. Hines, partner in the Service Motor Company, also was aboard the ship for Seattle, on his way to Kansas City. Hines, and his partner, Percy Hubbard, had just received a Wright Whirlwind 225 horsepower motor, which they intended to install in their Swallow biplane. Both men had been receiving flight instruction in C 2774.

December 1929. The open-cockpit Swallow belonging to Art Hines and his partner, Percy Hubbard, sits on skis at Weeks Field. Now powered with a Wright Whirlwind motor of 225 horsepower, the Swallow, NC 2774, is being used as a trainer. Ralph Wien, Percy's flying instructor, stands on the left, with Hubbard on the right.

Fairbanks Studio   Percy Hubbard Collection

December 1929. Percy Hubbard, left, and Ralph Wien, right, in front of the Swallow, NC 2774, in which Ralph was giving Percy flight instruction.

Ed Young was away for Fort Yukon and Beaver on Saturday morning, December 7, 1929. He was returning Bill Butler to Fort Yukon, and carried Frank Yasuda, Beaver merchant, and his wife, for the latter stop. C.H. Gillam was also away for Fort Yukon, a load of freight in his Swallow, *Arctic Prospector*. The pilot had recently received notice of his appointment as agent for Swallow airplanes in the Territory of Alaska, and had already sold a Swallow trainer to Percy Hubbard and Art Hines. Delivery was expected in February, 1930.

The New Standard, NC 174H, was once more in flying condition in Anchorage. Matt Nieminen came in with Travel Air 4000, C-193, on Saturday, December 7, 1929, to pick up NC 174H and fly it to Nome, via Rainy Pass and Ruby.

Crosson and Dorbandt had again attempted a takeoff from Teller on December 6, 1929, but the battering the aircraft received forced them to discontinue before getting airborne. Sastrugi (hard-packed wavelets of wind-driven snow) coupled with the heavy loads, caused some damage to the landing gear. A runway was now being built on snow-covered ice at Grantley Point, a more sheltered area where the surface was smoother. Teller residents gave them all the help they could.

Barnhill, accompanied by mechanic Fred Moller, in NC 9190, left Fairbanks on Saturday morning, December 7, to join the pilots at Teller, reaching Nome on Sunday. They brought in Miss Robbins, a nurse at Ruby, as well as the mail from the damaged plane at that stop, which had now been returned to Fairbanks. They also carried supplies and repair materials for Dorbandt's Stinson, C 5262, which was rather badly damaged in the attempted takeoff on December 6. Crosson's Waco, NC 780E, had received minor damage and was quickly repaired. Barnhill and Moller joined the pilots at Teller early on Tuesday, December 10, 1929, landing there at 11:30 A.M. Crosson had gone aloft the day before to take weather observations in the area, remaining up for thirty minutes.

Help was on the way. Advised by the army and the navy that they had no planes suitable for a rescue operation, the Aviation Corporation (AVCO) had moved ahead on their own. With substantial funds and political clout, they made arrangements for three Fairchild 71 cargo planes to be shipped by boat and rail to Fairbanks. Arctic-wise Canadian pilots and mechanics, under the leadership of H.A. "Doc" Oaks of Montreal, accompanied them north. The husky load carriers were powered with the powerful Pratt & Whitney Wasp motor of 420 horsepower, a powerplant similar to that of the Hamilton when received by Noel Wien. The wings could be manually folded back for storage.

The Russian icebreaker *Litke*, coming from a trip to Wrangel Island to check on a Russian colony at the remote bit of land, had returned to Vladivostok. The icebreaker, with two Junkers F-13 monoplanes and crews, had left the northern port on November 1 to return to the area. The Russians had their own problems. The *Litke* was anxious to leave Providence Bay, where it had been since November 23, 1929, but a small steamer of theirs, *Stavropol*, was also frozen in at North Cape, only three miles northwest of the cape. Aboard the steamer, in addition to the regular crew, were thirty-two civilians, nine of whom were members of the Academy of Science at Leningrad, a scientific expedition that had traveled down the Kolyma River to Nizhne Kolymsk. Sixteen of these passengers, who had left the *Stavropol* on October

The small Russian steamer Stavropol, *normally with a crew of thirty-five, was frozen into the ice about three miles from the* Nanuk.

27, reached Providence Bay and the *Litke* on the evening of November 24, 1929, by traveling the 350 miles down the coast by dog team. The *Litke*, already in ice of one foot in thickness, eventually offloaded the two Junkers F-13's and they were flown to North Cape by Russian crews on January 29, 1930, to assist at the wreck site.

Two more planes of Alaskan Airways, Incorporated, left Fairbanks on Monday, December 9, 1929, to join the search. Ed Young, flying the Stinson Standard, NC 877, and young Harold Gillam in the open-cockpit Stearman, NC 5415, now powered with the J4-B motor, reached Nulato that day. Both arrived at Nome at 12:10 P.M. on the following day. Leaving there shortly before 2:00 P.M. they flew on to Teller on Wednesday, December 11. Crosson had been out in Waco, NC 780E, for an hour and one-half, but returned about the time the two Fairbanks fliers came in.

Matt Nieminen and pilot-mechanic Lon Cope had left Anchorage at 10:30 A.M. on Tuesday, December 10. Doctor L.J. Seeley, Anchorage dentist, accompanied them as far as Flat. Stopping overnight there, Nieminen and Cope arrived in Nome in the New Standard, NC 174H, at 2:10 P.M. Wednesday, December 11. Teller was getting fog, and their departure was delayed for some days. The men made an attempt to reach Teller on Tuesday, December 17, but had to return to Nome after encountering a severe storm. The airmen made it to Teller the following day, leaving Nome at 10:00 A.M. Joe Crosson, flying Waco, NC 780E, had left Teller on Friday, December 13, 1929, in an attempt to join them in Nome but had been unsuccessful and returned to Teller after flying for one hour.

On December 16, 1929, the New York office of The Aviation Corporation appointed businessman Alfred J. Lomen, at that time in Teller, to take charge of the Eielson-Borland relief operation, relieving Frank Dorbandt of that responsibility. Lomen promptly named Joe Crosson to the position of chief pilot. While Lon Cope remained in Teller, Matt Nieminen left there for Nome, flying the New Standard, NC 174H, on the same day of his arrival, Wednesday, December 18, 1929, bringing in Ben Mozee, a native girl by the name of Tate, and Fred Moller, who was returning to Fairbanks. Matt was to bring the Stinson "Detroiter", C 5262, in

Alaskan Airways planes await flying weather at Teller, Alaska during the search for Eielson and Borland.
Crosson Collection

Big and Little Diomede Islands in the Bering Strait between Alaska and Siberia. The 180th Meridian passes between these two, with Big Diomede being Russian territory and Little Diomede being United States territory. When it is today on the Alaskan side of the meridian, it is tomorrow on the Russian side.

Broken ice of the Arctic Ocean crossed over by the pilots in 1929 on their way to Siberia. The ice, cracked by wind and tide, is never a solid mass offshore.

Frank Dorbandt Photo, Mary Barrows Collection

Crosson Collection

to Fairbanks for overhaul. It had sustained a considerable beating and needed much work. Matt Nieminen landed in Nome at 12:30 P.M. The following day, Thursday, December 19, Frank Dorbandt brought the Stinson, C 5262, to Nome in the afternoon. He carried Mrs. Dorbandt, Fred Moller, Harvey Barnhill and Alf Lomen as passengers. Dorbandt was expected to return to Teller on Friday with the New Standard, NC 174H. Frank, accompanied by Vic Ross, Northern Air Transport, Incorporated, pilot in Nome, finally got away for Teller Saturday morning, December 21, to land there about noon.

New planning for the relief expedition resulted in a decision to use the Stearman, NC 5415, and the Waco 10, NC 780E, as search planes on the Siberian coast, with the heavier planes used for hauling fuel from Teller to a point midway between East Cape and North Cape, at Kolyuchin Bay. The two open-cockpit planes were the fastest, with the least fuel consumption. They could cover more ground in the search. While there was some Russian gasoline at North Cape, it was known to be of poor quality because of its age, and permission had not been received for its use. On the morning of Wednesday, December 18, 1929, an assault on the crossing was mounted by all four pilots: Crosson, Gillam, Young and Barnhill. Two of the pilots, Barnhill and Gillam, returned to Teller just as Matt Nieminen was taking off for Nome. The other two returned later, two hours in the air. There were severe snowstorms over Bering

736

East Cape, Siberia, was the point the pilots reached after crossing Bering Strait, before turning down the Siberian coast to head for North Cape.

Frank Dorbandt Photo, Mary Barrows Collection

Strait. This narrow strait between the headlands of Alaska and Siberia forms a double funnel, one on the Bering Sea and one on the Arctic Ocean. In November, December and March, the winds sweep off the arctic coast into the funnel, and nothing flows back. The strait is not always frozen in, because of the ocean current, and open leads are the cause of intense fogs as the cold air passes over the less-cold water and on to the ice again. It could be clear at both Teller and at North Cape, but impossible to cross the strait.

At 10:00 A.M. Thursday, December 19, 1929, Crosson and Gillam left Teller to cross the Bering Strait to Siberia. Each of the open-cockpit planes carried a sleeping bag, primus stove and enough rations to last for a thirty-day period. Into each plane the pilots had carefully stacked thirteen five-gallon cans of gasoline.

At this time of the year the flying light was limited to four hours on clear days and much less on cloudy days, so the pilots elected the village on the Siberian coast near Cape Serdtse-Kamen as a destination for the day's flight; Eielson had stopped there on his first flight from North Cape. The two airmen were anxious to get in touch with anyone on the other side who spoke English, to get the Siberians interested in the search.

Harold Gillam's report, made in Fairbanks on March 13, 1930, describes the flight across as follows: "We started to climb immediately after taking off and had reached 6,000 feet when we started across Bering Strait. We could see the islands plainly, also the tops of mountains in Siberia. Our flying time from Teller to the Diomedes was just one hour—we were making excellent time. From the Diomedes on, we ran into a haze which we could see through by looking straight down but could see nothing looking ahead. The visibility changed depending on the nature of the floor. Over water, which showed black, everything was fine, while over white ice, we could see nothing. We came down to within 200 feet of the ice opposite Whalen (Uelen, just beyond East Cape). From Whelan to Cape Serdze (Serdtse-Kamen) precipitous bluffs form the shore line and, as they showed black, served as a real good mark to fly by. At Serdze, the fog opened out a little and we climbed up on top. We stayed on top for forty-five minutes before finding a hole large enough to go through. We had seen nothing of the beach for forty-five minutes and we did not know what our ceiling would be, but fortunately we went through over an open lead, the water giving us a chance to judge our distance accurately. Flying now at one hundred feet, we started looking for a place to land. The villages along here are only about ten miles apart. The Chukchi houses (yarangs) showed dark, and gave us a chance to check our altitude visually. We were flying close together and were out of sight of each other most of the time. It was getting thicker with the fading of daylight so we landed at Pelikii (a Chukchi village) without locating our original objective. Joe and I congratu-

737

Chukchi skin hut, or yarang, at North Cape, Siberia. Snow igloos were only built by the Eskimos of arctic eastern Canada and Greenland. The hut in the right background was the headquarters of the representative for the Russian government at the settlement. The masts of the Nanuk *show from behind the yarang at the left.*

lated each other several times that night on getting through and we both vowed we would wait for better weather before continuing."

The following day, December 21 (Siberian date and time since the pilots had crossed the International Date Line), Gillam and Crosson emerged from the yarang in which they had spent the night, to find the thermometer lashed to their interplane struts showing thirty-six below zero, and a wind from the north at twenty miles per hour. By 10:00 A.M. it was light enough to take off and, having firepotted and warmed their engines, the pair departed. Visibility was somewhat improved over the previous day, with a streak of light showing to the east.

Reporting on the flight, Gillam related: "We climbed to 2,000 feet and started across Kolyuchin Bay. That slender streak of light was all we had to fly by and we had to get about 2,500 feet to clear the hills on the west side of Kolyuchin Bay. After crossing the bay, the hills under us would be visible for a few seconds at a time and the light in the east was gradually fading. After a few minutes at 2,500 feet, we swung north, trying to locate the shore line so we could get down out of that fog. It was while flying north that I missed Joe. He was slightly higher and a little behind me. I turned south and caught a glimpse of him—he seemed to be going down. I returned to the place where I thought he had gone through but I could not see down so decided I would look for a better place before descending as I knew we were still over the hills. I flew around in circles until I finally sighted a frozen stream directly under me—so I went down. No sign of Joe but, believing he would proceed on to North Cape, I climbed back out of this valley and headed north. I believed it impossible to return the way we had come. In about ten minutes I sighted an open lead and knew I was away from the hills so went down to within 200 feet of the ice. I was between Capes Vankarem and Onman. These two capes are about twenty miles apart and between the two is a stretch of smooth ice running along the shore. I flew to Vankarem, then returned to Onman, thinking Joe might have flown out to the shore line and landed. Not seeing him, I turned around and proceeded to North Cape, arriving at 1:45 P.M. (Siberian time)." It was the shortest day of the year, with only a few hours of twilight at midday. Gillam had completed his almost 600-mile trip from Teller safely. It was twenty-three degrees below zero at the *Nanuk*.

Arrangements had been made to use five or six hundred gallons of the Soviet gas there, to be replaced when the heavier planes arrived. Gillam was preparing his Stearman, NC 5415, for flight the following day, Saturday, December 21, 1929, when Crosson landed at the *Nanuk*. Relieved at finding his fellow pilot at the ship, Crosson explained that he had lost sight

Harold Gillam, coming from Teller, Alaska, arrived at the Nanuk at 1:45 P.M. December 21, 1929 (Siberian date and time). He and Joe Crosson, who was flying the Waco 10, overnighted at Pelikii, a Chukchi village, the previous night, and had gotten separated after leaving there. Crosson came in the following day.

▼ Harold Gillam and Stearman C-2B, NC 5415, at North Cape, Siberia. Gillam had only been flying a short time.

Bob Gleason photo

Crosson Collection

of him in the fog, and returned to the Chukchi village, where he spent a second night.

Crosson needed rest, and went aboard the *Nanuk*. He had removed his goggles for a period during the flight in order to see better, and had frosted his eyes. Gillam, taking Olaf Swenson with him, flew along the foothills to the southeast where a smoke had been reported a month previously. They sighted a camp of the reindeer people but nothing else. That evening, for the first time, the rescuers were able to bring all their sources of information together, other than sparse radio accounts which had flowed back and forth. Ed Young, who had expected to follow Crosson and Gillam with a load of gasoline and dogfish, had departed Teller on Friday, December 20, 1929 (Nome date), but could not find a suitable place to land at East Cape, and had returned. The "fishburners" at North Cape were out so much, helping with a ground search, that the community was running low on dog feed to give the teams on the trail.

▲ *Alaskan Airways pilot Ed Young with the New Standard D-25 at Teller, Alaska.*

▼ *New Standard D-25 on skis at Teller, Alaska in 1929.*

One of the hangars acquired by Alaskan Airways, Incorporated, in the purchase of existing companies, goes up in flames on the evening of December 22, 1929. The Zenith Z-6, a Swallow and a Waco were pushed clear, although the Zenith's wing tip bows and horizontal stabilizer ends were somewhat damaged when the cabin plane was run out.

On Friday, December 20, Matt Nieminen left Nome in the Stinson Standard, C 52562, for Fairbanks, taking Harvey Barnhill

The Alaskan Airways fire, which burned the former Bennett-Rodebaugh hangar, started when mechanic Ed Moore was washing down the motor on the historic Stinson Standard, C 5262, Detroit News No. 2, with gasoline while it was in the hangar. The Stinson burned. The company still retained the former Wien hangar and its tools, and would continue to assemble the Fairchild 71s in it.

and Fred Moller along, plus some first class letter mail. The three men spent the night at Nulato, coming in to Fairbanks the next afternoon. It was the last flight of the venerable plane, for Ed Moore, an Alaskan Airways mechanic, was washing the engine down with gasoline on December 22 in the company hangar, when an electric spark from a short circuit in a defective light socket set it afire. The conflagration spread rapidly, the mechanic unable to stop it with hand extinguisher, and forced to flee. The Alaskan Airways hangars at Weeks Field were burned to the ground, including the plane and a large amount of supplies and parts. Fast work on the part of firemen and others saved the other three planes in the hangars: the Zenith 6, the cabin Swallow, C 3542, and the Waco Model 9, C 2775.

The Stinson Standard, C 5262, had an interesting history; it had come to Fairbanks as Stinson *Detroiter No. 2* with the Wilkins 1927 expedition, been sold to Wien Alaska Airways and absorbed into Alaskan Airways, Incorporated. While the blaze did between $35,000 and $40,000 worth of damage, the company still had the former Wien Alaska Airways hangar which was equipped with tools. The wing and horizontal stabilizer tips on the Zenith 6 had been damaged in rushing it from the hangar.

Matt Nieminen and Barnhill caught the train out of Fairbanks of Sunday, December 22, for Anchorage; Matt to spend Christmas with his wife and Harvey Barnhill, who was leaving Alaskan Airways, Incorporated, would soon leave for the States.

On Monday, December 23, 1929, a news dispatch from the Berlin offices of the Zeppelin company announced cancellation of the proposed arctic flight of the *Graf Zeppelin*. Other than a difference of opinion between Doctor Hugo Eckener, commander of the dirigible, and Captain Walter Bruns, secretary of the Aero-Arctic Society, as to the feasibility of the flight, neither had been able to obtain insurance for the journey. A few die-hards in Fairbanks remained optimistic for a time but the project soon sank into anonymity. The city gained an extension on Weeks Field and years later, when a contractor excavated the huge concrete base and anchors during another construction project, there was considerable speculation as to their purpose.

In Teller, Frank Dorbandt, who had brought in the New Standard, NC 174H, from Nome on December 21, 1929, was standing by, along with mechanics Lon Cope and Clark Bassett. Dorbandt and Cope went out in NC 174H on Monday, December 23, to look for Bill Graham, who had started out for the Elephant Point in the Stinson of Northern Air Transport, Incorporated, on Tuesday, December 17, and was reported not to have arrived there. Checking over the Elephant Point route, thence to Candle, the airmen learned that Graham was at Deering, awaiting better weather. Dorbandt returned to Teller. A message was received there on Friday, December 27, telling of the loss by fire of the Nome radio station on Christmas Eve; the operator was requesting replacement forms and supplies from the Teller operator. Taking Vic Ross and Lon Cope with him, along with the requested supplies, Frank Dorbandt flew the New Standard to Nome the same day, Friday. Alf Lomen decided to hold the plane there, awaiting the arrival of the Fairchild 71s that were joining the search. Alaska Road Commission and Hammon company tractors were engaged in cutting down and leveling snow on the municipal field in expectation of their arrival, so they would not have to seek a landing on the ice in front of town, or at Safety Lagoon.

On Friday, December 23, 1929, Crosson and Gillam got away from *Nanuk* to search, flying in the arctic twilight in good visibility. Crosson had Olaf Swenson with him as observer; while Gillam took Demetri Miroshnishenko, the young Russian government agent at North Cape. Both men knew the coast and the location of native yarangs. Searching east of North Cape for two hours and fifteen minutes, they saw nothing unusual. A severe storm moved in and the pilots were held at the ship for several days. The Chukchi men, at Crosson's request, built a nose-hangar out of blocks of snow to shelter the front end of the plane when warming the engine, but it was not very successful. While it stormed, snow blew in every crevice despite the wrapping of canvas about the engines. In very low temperatures they could not satisfactorily warm the engines by allowing them to run on the ground; they simply cooled down and stopped. Consequently the pilots taxied out and took off as soon as they got the motor running; the higher power used in the air kept them warm despite the slipstream of frigid air.

Christmas was spent on the *Nanuk*, with a large reindeer roast for dinner. When the

742

Chukchi children and adults from the native village at North Cape took great interest in the unusual activity about the Nanuk.

Charles Bisel Collection

Siberian Eskimos at North Cape in 1929. A cheerful lot, they were a great help with visitors to their rugged land.

Eddie Bowman Collection

wooden vessel first froze in for the winter, Swenson had sent dog teams inland to a native village of reindeer people, bringing back several loads of whole carcasses for a fresh meat supply. The crew was also able to shoot about 153 ducks on one of the last ponds of open water near the ship, to augment the larder.

On December 31, 1929 (Siberian time) the two pilots prepared their planes. Crosson and Swenson were able to search again for an hour and a half east of North Cape, again without result. Gillam was less fortunate for, after having difficulty in starting, his engine failed on takeoff and the Stearman, NC 5415, was damaged in landing on rough ice and snow aft of the *Nanuk*. The left ski was torn off, dragging the left, lower wing tip. The right landing gear was also damaged, as well as the cabane struts that supported the upper wing. Neither the pilot nor

Twenty-three year-old Robert J. Gleason served as the Radio Operator aboard Nanuk during the adventurous winter of 1929-30, handling all radio communications to and from the schooner. He also kept the radios and other electrical equipment in working order. Bill Bissner, the vessel's engineer, signed Bob on as assistant engineer in the spring.

Bob Gleason Photo

On the afterdeck of the Nanuk. Left to Right: Willie Williams, seaman; James Hearn, seaman; Jimmie Crooks, who worked for Olaf Swenson on the Siberian coast; R.H. Weeding, Captain; Bill Bissner, Chief Engineer.

▲ *To these two Chukchis fell the daily task of cutting and sieving out the ice about the rudder of the* Nanuk, *in case either the ship or the ice should move, damaging this very important part of the ship.*

▼ *November, 1929. Three forms of transportation at North Cape, Siberia: the ship, the search planes, and Olaf Swenson with the* Nanuk's *dog team. The team was part of their salvage from the* Elisif.

Bob Gleason photo

▲ *North Cape, Siberia, December 30, 1929. Engine failure on takeoff near the Nanuk resulted in damage to Harold Gillam's Stearman C-2B. Neither the pilot or his passenger, Demetri Miroshnishenko were injured and the biplane was repaired and flown three weeks later.*

▼ *North Cape, Siberia, December 30, 1929. Demetri Miroshnishenko, standing with back to camera in foreground, surveys the damage to Alaskan Airways Stearman, NC 5415. Gillam was forced to land on rough ice aft of the Nanuk when his engine quit on takeoff with Demetri. They were going out to search for Ben Eielson's lost Hamilton Metalplane.*

Bob Gleason photo

Miroshnishenko suffered any injury. The two pilots, with the aid of Russian engineers from the *Stavropol*, went to work on repairs and the plane was to fly again about three weeks later.

The Eielson-Borland relief expedition of The Aviation Corporation rolled into Fairbanks on a special Alaska Railroad train at 2:10 A.M. Thursday, December 26, 1929. The U.S. Coast Guard cutter *Chelan* had been moved to Smith Cove in Seattle on December 18, to receive the planes as they arrived: one coming from Los Angeles on December 16, and another by rail from Chicago the following day. The third was expected from Winnipeg on Wednesday, December 18. The first Fairchild 71 was being partly crated for loading; the stripped-down fuselage with landing gear and motor intact was deck loaded within a crate. A fast trip north, leaving Seattle on December 21, by the *Chelan* put the Coast Guard cutter in Seward shortly before noon on Wednesday, December 25, the ship entering Resurrection Bay in a blinding snowstorm. The planes with their crated components and accompanying airmen were quickly transferred to the waiting railway cars. With a farewell blast of the *Chelan*'s whistle, the train steamed away at 5:20 P.M. on their twenty-one-hour run.

Horsedrawn sleds had already been placed along the tracks, and unloading of the planes began within fifteen minutes of the train's arrival. They were taken to the former Wien Alaska Airways hangar on Weeks Field to be assembled by the Alaskan Airways mechanics and the three mechanics accompanying the relief expedition. With the assistance of Major H.C. Deckard, production manager of Fairchild Airplane Manufacturing Corporation, work was to continue day and night.

The expedition was made up of eight members, with H.A. "Doc" Oaks, winner of the McKee Trophy in Canada for 1927, coming from Northern Aerial Minerals Exploration, Limited, (N.A.M.E.). He was a bush pilot and a founder of Western Canada Airways, Limited. T.M. "Pat" Reid, chief pilot, was also from N.A.M.E. In September he had completed a six-months expedition of three planes that were flown all through the Hudson Bay district and on to Coronation Gulf in arctic Canada. B.W. "Bill" Broatch was a pilot for Dominion Explorers, and G. Swartman was a pilot from the forestry patrol of the Province of Ontario. Mechanics Sam Macauley and W.I. Hughes were also from the forestry patrol. C.F.K. Mews, another mechanic, was from Northern Aerial Minerals Exploration, Limited. All were experienced in winter operation of aircraft in the Arctic and sub-Arctic.

The three Fairchild 71 aircraft were single-motored monoplanes, powered with Pratt & Whitney Wasp engines of 425 horsepower. With a cruising radius of 800 miles at an average airspeed of one hundred miles per hour, and a hefty cargo capacity, the seven-place (including pilot) planes were suited to the job ahead. They would be assembled and tested at the remaining Alaskan Airways, Incorporated, hangar (Wien's) and flown on skis to North Cape. The trim-looking Fairchilds, painted in red and cream, were practically new; one had been flown about one hundred hours as a demonstrator, and the others so slightly used they could be considered new. Alaskan Airways planned to keep two of them in Alaska after the relief expedition was ended, returning the third one to Winnipeg.

A winter kit, weighing between three and four hundred pounds, including provisions for two men for a month, was carried in the planes. Although the airmen brought along Russian and marine charts of the Siberian coast, Charles L. Thompson, manager of Alaskan Airways, supplied them with maps giving more detailed information. At Nome the fliers reported to Alf Lomen, manager of the Lomen Reindeer Corporation, to operate under plans outlined by him.

Assembly of the first of the three Fairchilds was completed the morning of Saturday, December 28, 1929. Pilots Reid and Swartman test flew it shortly thereafter and found it to be ready except for minor adjustments. Mechanics were working on the second ship, but the third

Bennett-Rodebaugh Company planes in winter, the Stinson Standard SB-1, NC 877, on the left and the Zenith 6 on the right.

Jack Peck Collection

one was still uncrated because the hangar could hold only one at a time. The planes were fitted with exceptionally wide skis and tail skis.

A new report had come in on December 28, of Russian hunters sighting an airplane a few miles west of Kolyuchin Bay, the plane supposedly circling twice over the camp before disappearing toward the west. A renewed interest was felt by everyone. Alaskan Airways called in Matt Nieminen from Anchorage. Flying the open-cockpit Travel Air, C-193, he arrived in Fairbanks on Monday afternoon, making three attempts at landing before he could penetrate the ice fog about Weeks Field. Matt replaced Canadian pilot Bill Broatch, who left for Outside by train on Sunday, December 29, 1929. Two of the Fairchild 71s were scheduled to leave soon. The second one was out of the hangar on Monday, December 30, to have its motor started up and checked. It would be test flown next. The chairs were removed from the

cabins on the Fairchilds to make room for storage of supplies and case gas. The light wooden boxes held two five-gallon cans each, and were easily stacked.

The year ended with Carl Ben Eielson and Earl Borland in the Hamilton Metalplane, NC 10002, still missing since November 9, 1929. Joe Crosson and Harold Gillam were at the *Nanuk* with the Waco 10, NC 780E, and a damaged Stearman C-2B, NC 5415. Ed Young was in Teller with Stinson Standard B-1, NC 877, and New Standard, NC 9190; Dorbandt in Nome with New Standard, NC 174H. In Fairbanks, a damaged Zenith 6 and the cabin Swallow, both earlier favorites of A.A. Bennett, made up the fleet of Alaskan Airways, Incorporated, along with the Travel Air 4000, C-193, and the three Fairchild 71s of the relief expedition.

The suspense was soon to end, the wrecked Hamilton was discovered by Crosson and Gillam on January 26, 1930, (See *Icebound in the Siberian Arctic* by Bob Gleason).

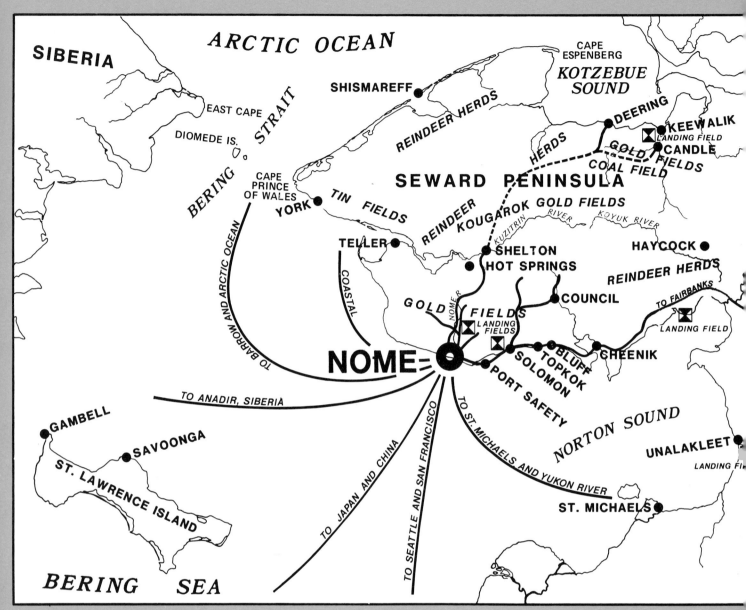

ARCTIC OCEAN

SIBERIA

CAPE
ESPENBERG

KOTZEBUE
SOUND

SHISMAREFF

EAST CAPE

DIOMEDE IS.

DEERING

KEEWALIK
LANDING FIELD

REINDEER HERDS

HERDS

GOLD
FIELDS

CANDLE

COAL FIELD

CAPE
PRINCE
OF WALES

SEWARD PENINSULA

YORK

TIN FIELDS

REINDEER

KOUGAROK GOLD FIELDS

RIVER

KOYUK RIVER

KUZITRIN

TELLER

SHELTON

HAYCOCK

HOT SPRINGS

REINDEER HERDS

GOLD FIELDS

NOME

LANDING
FIELDS

COUNCIL

TO FAIRBANKS

LANDING FIELD

NOME

BLUFF

CHEENIK

TOPKOK

PORT SAFETY

SOLOMON

TO ANADIR, SIBERIA

NORTON SOUND

UNALAKLEET

GAMBELL

LANDING FI

SAVOONGA

ST. LAWRENCE ISLAND

ST. MICHAELS

BERING   SEA

750

Bennett-
Rodebaugh
Company

Wien Alaska Airways,
   Incorporated
Northern Air Transport,
   Incorporated

Nome 1929

WIEN ALASKA AIRWAYS, INCORPORATED, the company which provided most of the service to and from Nome, was set up to enter 1929 in a positive fashion. With their big, new hangar on Weeks Field at Fairbanks, and the new Hamilton Metalplane H-45 now being assembled there, air service for Nome and other Seward Peninsula communities would take a step forward. The company still had the Stinson Standard, C 5262, which Noel eventually planned to base at Nome, the Waco Model 9, C 2775, (now at Nome), and they would later purchase the Stearman C-2B, NC 5415, now in a damaged condition at Walker Lake.

Noel Wien, in the Hamilton Metalplane, NC 10002, arrived at Nome for the first time on Monday, January 28, carrying three passengers from Fairbanks: James Cross, Horace Ashton and Earl Welch. The pilot landed on the river ice at Nome, making the 550-mile journey with an air time of four hours and forty-five minutes. Noel was away on Wednesday, January 30, 1929, taking Welch and Ashton on to Elephant Point, and his other passenger, Jim Cross, to Candle. He brought in Mr. Miller, of the Biological Survey, from Elephant Point, as well as Tom Peterson from Teller. He was off a second time, the same day, flying eastward to Golovin with William Oliver as a passenger. The pilot went on to White Mountain, to pick up a woman passenger and returned to Nome at dusk.

Noel was away at 9:00 A.M. Thursday, January 31, 1929, to land on Weeks Field at 6:15 P.M. in almost total darkness, using his landing lights and the field floodlights. With

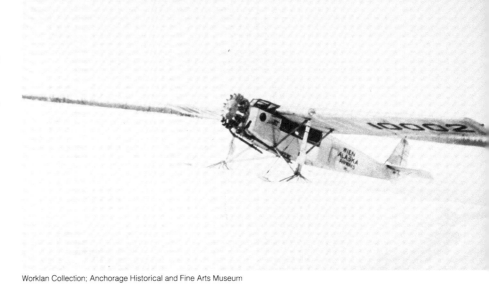

Wien Alaska Airways' Hamilton Metalplane H-45, NC 10002, was an immediate success. Flown by Noel Wien, the powerful load carrier first arrived in Nome on Monday, January 28, 1929. Powered with a Wasp Model B of 425 horsepower when received from the factory, the performance was improved by the installation of a new Hornet motor of 525 horsepower in mid August of 1929, following the purchase of the Wien company by Alaskan Airways, Incorporated, on August 1, 1929.

Worklan Collection; Anchorage Historical and Fine Arts Museum

strong headwinds, and a fuel stop at Ruby, the trip had taken eight hours and fifteen minutes of flying time. He had brought in five passengers and the mail.

The Wien Alaska Airways pilot made his second trip from Fairbanks to Nome on Monday, February 11, leaving Weeks Field at 9:30 A.M. in the Hamilton. He was carrying nurse Emily Morgan, who was to assume duties at the Maynard-Columbus Hospital in Nome. Noel was forced to land at Haycock, near Norton Sound, by wind and snow; he spent the night there before getting in to Nome on the following day. He was held at the Seward Peninsula city for many days by high winds.

On Wednesday, February 21, Noel Wien was away for Candle, carrying William Arthurs and his daughter, Ada, on a round trip. Arthurs had just been nominated as postmaster at Nome. The pilot also carried L.E. Robinson, of the Bureau of Education, who was also enroute to the Koyuk, as well as a woman passenger for White Mountain. The Hamilton was back at 3:15 P.M. with the Arthurs and Senator Richard Sundquist of Candle.

Noel was off in the Hamilton at 10:30 A.M. Thursday, February 22, with Sundquist and Representative Henry Burgh, and Ben Mozee. He stopped at Golovin for Jack Hooper and Harry Strong, Lomen Reindeer Corporation employees on their way to New York, and refueled at Ruby. The pilot arrived in Fairbanks at 6:10 P.M. that same day.

Noel arrived back in Nome at 5:10 P.M. on Wednesday, February 27, 1929, after dropping two passengers: C.E. Alexander and William James, at Kotzebue. With him in the Hamilton Metalplane was Calvin "Doc" Cripe, as flight mechanic. Cripe, a garage mechanic, had worked for Owen Meals at his Ford agency in Valdez; he had also received some exposure to aviation mechanical work on Meals' airplanes. He gravitated to Fairbanks, and the hangar shops there, continuing his education in aviation. A versatile individual, he had been nicknamed "Doc" because of a reputation of being able to repair anything of a mechanical nature.

There was a contract being negotiated between Wien Alaska Airways and the Swenson-Herskovits people in New York to fly a valuable cargo of furs, as well as some of the crew, from the icebound trading vessel, *Elisif*, to Fairbanks; where connection could be made for surface travel to the States. (see Fairbanks—1929, Chapter 51). The vessel had been fast in the ice since August, at a point on the Siberian coast near North Cape. There was also a possibility of a trip for the Soviet government from North Cape to Wrangel Island, to bring needed supplies to a Russian colony there. Grant Jackson, currently in New York, was working with Swenson-Herskovits to secure insurance for the flight but his efforts were in vain. The aviation firm finally decided to take the risk; the contract price of $4500 for the first flight was deemed worth it.

Noel Wien pondered the 600-mile route between Nome and the *Elisif*, some ten miles from North Cape. It would be best to cross the fifty-five miles over the Bering Strait from Cape Prince of Wales, via the Diomede Islands to East Cape, then proceed up the Siberian coast to North Cape, now Mys Shmidta (Cape Schmidt). Not only did ocean currents flow through the strait, keeping the ice open in long leads, but the air currents, driven by storm, funneled between the headlands of the two capes, sometimes creating violent weather systems. Picking up moisture from the open leads, then passing over the colder ice fields, air masses in the region were fertile breeders of snowstorms and fog at certain times of the year. It appeared to be about a six-hour flight each way in the Hamilton.

Stripping seats and unneeded equipment from the plane, Cripe and Wien loaded the Hamilton with supplies ordered by radio from the *Elisif*. This included a whole hog and a quarter of beef from T.C. Lehman's store. Fifty gallons of case gas, two five-gallon cans in each light wooden case, was also stored in the cabin for use on the return journey.

Ray Pollister, supercargo on the *Elisif*, radioed of good weather at the ship and clear to the east. With clear weather at Nome, Noel Wien and Calvin Cripe boarded the Metalplane and were off on skis at 7:20 A.M. Thursday, March 7, 1929, for the flight to Siberia. (see Fairbanks—1929, Chapter 51). Passing over Cape Prince of Wales an hour later, the pilot headed west-northwest across the Bering Strait. Passing near Little Diomede Island (on the American side of the International Date Line dividing the two countries at this point) Noel turned to a northwest heading for Siberia. In another quarter hour the Hamilton was over East Cape, a rocky headland; the airmen spotting a Chukchi village below. Turning slightly to the right to follow a mountainous coast, they passed by Kolyuchin Bay, one hundred miles beyond East Cape. The mountains retreated inland, leaving a flat coastline that blended into the sea ice. A frosted-over vent pipe from the oil tank gave the pilot some anxious moments until "Doc" Cripe, stretching to his maximum into the frigid slipstream with a hunting knife in hand, was able to scrape the vent clear, thus allowing the rising oil pressure to subside. He had to repeat the tortuous process about every fifteen minutes until they landed.

Flying at 4000 feet, Noel spotted the conspicuous North Cape ahead; a black spot offshore proved to be the three-masted schooner, *Elisif*. The crew of the ship had tried to level a landing spot on a frozen lead, and had a fire going at each end. With the shocks frozen, it was a very rough landing; the banging and pounding over the rough surface shook the airmen up but caused no damage to the sturdy Hamilton. Immediately surrounded by about forty whites, Russians and Eskimos, with their dog teams, they were welcomed. Nome was advised of their arrival and intentions via the *Elisif* radio. A portion of the hog carcass graced the table that evening.

The following day, the case gas was added to the Hamilton's tanks, plus about seventy gallons of poor quality fuel that had been in storage at North Cape. With engine warmed and the shock struts thawed by heat, the plane, now fully loaded with baled fox pelts, was ready for departure. Noel aborted the first takeoff, removing about 280 pounds of furs from the rear baggage compartment. They were off the ice at 12:15 P.M. Friday, March 18, 1929 (Nome time) to land at Nome at 6:10 P.M., completing the flight. The return had been much the same as their trip over, with Calvin Cripe again scraping the frost intermittently from the vent pipe. The following day, Saturday, was spent in repairing a tail skid, damaged in the takeoff at the

Hamilton Metalplane H-45, flown by Noel Wien, rests on its eighteen-inch-wide skis with villagers grouped about. If left for any time in cold temperatures, the skis would freeze to the ice. Pilots often ran the skis up on poles or other solid objects when leaving the plane overnight, in order to prevent this.

Elisif. Noel also flew to Golovin, bringing an injured man to the Nome hospital. Leaving Calvin Cripe in Nome, Noel departed there on Sunday, March 10, with the furs. Fueling at Nulato, he arrived in Fairbanks at 6:40 P.M. with the $150,000 shipment. The total flying time from Nome to North Cape to Nome to Fairbanks was eighteen hours.

Noel was off again for the Seward Peninsula on Wednesday morning, March 13, 1929, intending to stop at Golovin. He landed at Nome at 4:20 P.M., bringing Al Bigger from Fairbanks, as well as Dan Crowley, Mrs. Henry Burgh and baby from Golovin. He also had a good-sized load of first class mail.

On Thursday morning, March 14, the pilot was off in the Hamilton H-45 for Teller, Candle, Kotzebue and Elephant Point to pick up passengers. He took Frank Miller and Billy Guisler to Teller, expecting to pick up Earl Welch at Kotzebue as well as five other passenger at Elephant Point. The pilot carried mail for all stops. He planned to leave for Fairbanks after flying to Point Barrow to bring in Doctor Newhall, who was ill there with pneumonia, and Mrs. Newhall. However, the doctor passed away on Sunday and the trip became unnecessary.

The pilot was away Monday morning, March 18, taking Marshal Charles D. Jones as a passenger for Candle. Unable to reach the destination due to weather, Noel Wien circled around by way of Teller, bringing Miss Eva Swenson from there back to Nome, as well as the marshal. He would try for Candle on the morrow. Taking Marshal Jones, Tom Roust, and Horace Ashton who was making the round trip, his Tuesday, March 19, flight to Candle was successful. The pilot returned to Nome at 3:15 P.M., after also picking up Joe Dexter at Golovin.

Mrs. Ben Mozee, wife of the reindeer supervisor of the Bureau of Education for Alaska, had been expecting her husband in, flying up from Bethel with Anchorage Air Transport pilot, Russ Merrill. Held there for some time by snow, the Travel Air 7000, C-194, arrived in Nome at 1:30 P.M. Thursday, March 20, 1929, bringing Mozee and a native girl named Olive, originally from Wales. The pilot was glad to see his Nome friends again. He was back in Anchorage on March 26, 1929.

Noel Wien had departed Nome for Fairbanks at 9:00 A.M. Thursday, March 20, with a full load. Taking Mrs. C.P. Boyne to her home in Unalakleet, and Fairbanks passengers Dave Lyons, Harold L. Stokes, Eva Swenson, Horace Ashton, and Earl Welch, the pilot filled in the load with mail, baggage, express and furs. He made the trip to Fairbanks in six and one-half hours of flying time, despite foggy weather at Golovin and stops at Unalakleet and Ruby. It was fifty degrees above zero on his arrival at Weeks Field.

Still flying the Hamilton, NC 10002, Noel Wien left Fairbanks on the morning of Wednesday, April 3, 1929, intending to drop a load at Shungnak before going on to Kotzebue and Nome. Leaving Shungnak, he was forced to land at Noorvik by stormy weather, remaining there until 10:00 A.M. (Bering Sea time) Saturday, April 6. He flew to Kotzebue to check on the Nome weather. The radio station there had not been able to transmit since April 1, but was able to receive transmissions from other stations. The weather was fine so, taking Charlie Maxwell and Gene Comer from Kotzebue, he arrived in Nome at 1:46 P.M. that same day. He had also brought in one hundred pounds of first class mail and about 400 pounds of express.

Noel was to be held in Nome for a week by storm and poor visibility, finally getting away on the morning of Saturday, April 13, 1929, for Saint Michael. Taking Marshal Jones, who was traveling to bring in an insane person from the Norton Sound community, and also Ada Arthurs, L.E. Rynning and Art Harris, the pilot only got as far as the Golovin vicinity before setting down on the snow because of poor visibility. He taxied the Hamilton the remaining ten miles to Golovin to let passenger Rynning off. The weather did not clear and, after a time, the pilot returned to Nome.

Taking off on the morning of Wednesday, April 17, Noel was away in the Hamilton for Teller, Shishmaref and Candle. Running into fog, he was only able to reach Teller by flying low over the surface and following the coastline. Leaving Bill Guisler there, he returned to Nome with his passengers for the other two stops. He would try again on the morrow, weather permitting. Flying in the other direction, Noel Wien was away at noon of the same day, for Saint Michael, taxiing to a spot in front of the government wharf. The villagers all turned out for the plane's arrival. With the marshal and his charge aboard, the Wien Alaska Airways pilot took off the ice at 3:30 P.M., arriving over Unalakleet some forty-five miles distant. Noel landed there to refuel before going on to Nome.

The Hamilton of Wien Alaska Airways, Incorporated, was away from Nome the morning of Saturday, April 20, 1929, for Fairbanks by way of Shungnak. Noel carried L.E. Robinson for Shishmaref, Ben Mozee for Shungnak, Anton Polet, D.E. Crowley and Charles Maxwell for Fairbanks. In addition, Calvin "Doc" Cripe, who had been in Nome since the Siberian flight, was returning to Fairbanks, and his job at the Wien hangar. The Soviet government had cancelled permission for further flights to North Cape. The pilot wanted to stop at Deering to pick up H.L. Stull for Fairbanks, as well as a passenger at Kotzebue. In addition to the passengers, Noel carried a load of furs and mail.

Due to heavy fog banks, the pilot was unable to land at his planned stops, leaving Robinson at Igloo instead of Shishmaref. From here, Noel flew to Ruby, on the Yukon River, where he fueled the plane. He arrived in Fairbanks that same evening, Saturday, with his passengers. He took Ben Mozee to Shungnak the following day.

Parker Cramer and Willard Gamble were through Fairbanks in their Cessna AW, NC 7107, on Tuesday, April 23, 1929, enroute to Nome. (see Chicago to Siberia—1929, Chapter 48). The plane was first sighted by J.D. Harlan, manager of the Hammon Consolidated Gold Fields, landing in Nome at 1:45 P.M. The men wanted to continue to Siberia but, not having a permit to land, they expected to fly to East Cape, circle and return. The two men departed in the Cessna on Wednesday, April 24, but found the fog so thick beyond Cape Prince of Wales they were unable to continue; they landed at York, fourteen miles southwest of the cape, where they spent the night in the cabin of a tin miner. Making two more attempts to cross the Bering Strait on the following day, Thursday, April 25, they eventually decided to return to Nome. One ski was slightly damaged in the landing. The fliers missed the reception and dance planned for them at the Log Cabin home of the Chamber of Commerce on Wednesday.

On Friday, April 26, Cramer took off solo for Cape Prince of Wales, Little Diomede and East Cape. He was successful; and circled, dropping packages at the cape and the island. The flier returned to Nome to pick up his companion for the trip south. The airmen were presented that evening with honorary memberships in the Nome Kennel Club. They took four hours off for rest, followed by a light breakfast at 3:00 A.M. of Saturday, April 27, 1929. Taking off in the Cessna AW at 3:55 A.M., the pair landed on Weeks Field in Fairbanks at 11:00 A.M. (Fairbanks time). Takeoff had been difficult in the soft snow, the pilot making two runs; but leaving Nome at an early hour before temperatures had warmed, resulted in a firmer surface for the skis.

Noel Wien had been busy in Fairbanks for some time, but was now again on his way to Nome. He left Weeks Field in the Hamilton Metalplane, on wheels, taking off on Tuesday, May 7, 1929. The pilot arrived that same day, about 5:00 P.M. Bringing as passengers from Fairbanks, R.S. Stewart and Barney Bellview, as well as 351 pounds of first class letter mail for Nome, he had also dropped off an additional 221 pounds at Ruby. The passengers reported that twenty-two buildings had burned there on Sunday morning; the only places saved were the Northern Commercial Company store and the radio station.

In Nome, the snow was gone in town; the fire department changed from the winter bobsled runners and was once again on wheels, the fire mains were also filled with water.

Noel had bid on a Territorial air mail subsidy contract for three trips between Fairbanks and Nome. The aeronautical committee of the Nome Chamber of Commerce received a wire from Governor Parks on May 13 that Wien Alaska Airways had been awarded the contract: three trips to originate in Fairbanks May 15, 21 and 28, at 8:00 A.M., weather permitting. The pilot was in Golovin on Monday, May 13, when he received word that his brother, Ralph, was unreported at Wiseman. Fueling the Hamilton, Noel headed straight for the Koyukuk, making a fruitless search of the upper river before going on into Fairbanks. (see Fairbanks—1929, Chapter 51). The pilot landed the Hamilton at 12:30 A.M. Monday, May 13, after over ten hours in the air since leaving Nome. Ralph was picked up by Noel at Bettles on Tuesday, May 14; he had trekked in along the dog team trail after cracking up the Stearman in a forced landing short of Wiseman.

Noel arrived back in Nome on his first mail subsidy flight with the Hamilton about 4:00 P.M. Thursday, May 16, bringing his brother, Fritz, and his mother, Mrs. J.B. Wien, and also Senator R.N. Sundquist and Representative Henry Burgh. He took off about noon of the following day, taking Sundquist to Candle, continuing on to Kotzebue with mail. On his return, the pilot picked up H.L. Stull at Deering, also George McKay and Ben Mozee, bringing them all in to Nome about 6:15 P.M. He had been unable to land at Candle, dropping Sundquist at Keewalik instead.

That Sunday, at 3:00 P.M. May 19, 1929, the pilot was married to Ada Bering Arthurs, at a public wedding in the Federated Church. A reception followed at the Odd Fellows Hall. The couple planned to make their home in Fairbanks. Taking only one passenger, the pair were off for there at 10:15 P.M. Fueling at Ruby, the Hamilton was on Weeks Field at 5:00 A.M. Monday.

Noel was off Weeks Field, on the second air mail subsidy flight, the morning of Wednesday, May 22, 1929, carrying six passengers and their baggage, one hundred pounds of mail and 140 gallons of gasoline. The pilot arrived in Nome at 2:55 P.M., to unload Mr. and Mrs. C.B. White, of Spokane, Harry C. Kelling, who was setting up a new dredge on the Solomon River for the Goldsmith Dredging Company, and T.A. "Tom" Peterson. Noel was away at 7:00 P.M. that same evening, carrying "Courageous Tom" Peterson on to his home in Teller. He attempted to go on to Deering with a passenger but was forced back to Nome by heavy fog banks. Noel was back in Fairbanks to land at Weeks Field about 11:15 P.M. on Sunday, May 26, 1929. He still had his third air mail subsidy flight to make.

Representative Alfred J. Lomen and Grant R. Jackson had been working with the Seattle office of the U.S. Signal Corps to improve radio communications on the Seward Peninsula, with a new station to be erected at Teller. Lomen arranged free transportation for the radio equipment on his company's motorship *Sierra*, and a building in Teller for the station, as well as the two masts now at Teller, owned by the Lomen Reindeer Corporation, which were to be turned over to the government. Jackson, secretary-treasurer of Wien Alaska Airways, also arranged free transportation on the company airplanes for James H. Anderson, authorized by the U.S. Signal Corps to travel for the purpose of selecting sites for radio stations at Candle and Teller. The new facilities, when completed, would be a boon to any aviation concern in the area, as well as other parties. Anderson was soon to become the operator at the new station in Teller.

Poor weather in the Fairbanks area held the Wien Alaska Airways Hamilton H-45 there for some time. Finally, away on Friday, June 14, 1929, the pilot landed Nome at 7:30 P.M., six and one-half hours after departure from Weeks Field. Noel's wife, Ada, and Charles Maxwell were passengers on the nonstop flight. Noel was away on Sunday evening, June 16, for Deering and Candle, carrying Maxwell for Kotzebue, and Mr. and Mrs. Sam Magids, Boris Magids, Al Bigger and Lucky Peterson for Deering. The following afternoon the pilot took off with Frank Redwood and George Laiblin for Deering, and Leo Loners and James H. Anderson for Candle.

A.A. Bennett, of the Bennett-Rodebaugh Company, arrived in Nome, landing at 1:00 A.M. of June 20, 1929. Long hours of summer daylight resulted in pilots putting in more hours. The pilot carried Ernest W. Sawyer, executive assistant to the Secretary of the Interior, and Major Malcolm Elliott, president of the Alaska Road Commission, on an inspection tour of Alaska. The party departed at 7:00 P.M. Friday, June 21, for Fairbanks in the Zenith 6, flown by Bennett. Noel Wien, accompanied by his brother, Fritz, departed Nome for Fairbanks a half-hour later, carrying mail but no passengers. The Hamilton arrived on Weeks Field after a nonstop trip of five hours and thirty-five minutes.

A third flight, with Ed Young piloting the Stinson Standard SB-1, NC 877, arrived in Nome at 9:30 A.M. Friday, June 21, 1929. Fog conditions over Norton Sound had caused some delay. The Bennett-Rodebaugh pilot was carrying two commercial travelers, Joe Meherin and Oscar Hart, on charter. The men, having completed their business in Nome, were away with Young at 10:30 A.M. Saturday, June 22. Picking up Vance McDonald at Ruby, where steady rain had held the plane overnight, Ed Young arrived back in Fairbanks on Sunday afternoon.

Noel Wien, flying the Hamilton H-45, NC 10002, from Fairbanks, arrived in Nome at 2:30 P.M. Saturday, June 29. He had brought in Bruce Thorne and George Graves, from the Field Museum of Chicago, also Father Delon, coming from Ruby. The fourth passenger was Roy C. Lyle, Prohibition Director of the 20th District, which included Washington, Oregon and Alaska. Thorne and Graves had chartered the trading vessel *Dorothy* for a voyage into the Arctic in the direction of Wrangel Island, for the purpose of taking walrus and other arctic specimens for the Chicago museum.

A.A. Bennett left Fairbanks for Nome on Monday evening, July 1. The tired pilot, who had done some flying out of Fairbanks before leaving there, was met on his arrival at the Nome field, about midnight, by Alfred J. Lomen. When it was explained to him that an injured man, Fred Mebes, a miner, was expected to arrive at Golovin aboard a boat from Council, and needed to be brought to Nome for removal of a piece of steel from his eye, the pilot agreed to go. Accompanied by Lomen, he was away in the Zenith 6 within the hour. The boat with Mebes did not arrive in Golovin until 6:00 A.M. Bennett came in to Nome with the man at 9:00 A.M. and, upon being taken to the hospital, the steel was successfully removed from the man's eye. The following day, the pilot flew to Golovin and Council, returning Mebes to Council, and taking L.E. Robinson, of the Bureau of Education, and E.F. Bauer, of the Alaska Road Commission, on an inspection trip.

On Thursday evening, Bennett flew A.V. Cordovado and Charles Milot to Deering, bringing the latter back on the return journey. He departed for Fairbanks at 11:00 A.M. Friday, July 5, 1929, with Colonel Ohlson, general manager of the Alaska Railroad, Robert Frothingham, a writer from New York, and L.J. Palmer, of the Biological Survey, as passengers.

Noel Wien, taking Roy C. Lyle and former District Attorney Fred Harrison as passengers, had left Nome about 10:00 P.M. Sunday, June 30, 1929, for Fairbanks. Flying nonstop in the Hamilton, the pilot landed there at 8:00 A.M. on Monday. Ada Wien accompanied her husband on the flight in. Air time was six hours and fifteen minutes. The pilot was back in Nome on Sunday, July 7, landing at 4:45 P.M. (Bering Sea time) after a nonstop flight of five and three-quarters hours. He brought in Julius H. Hart, new U.S. attorney for the Second division, who was making Nome his headquarters.

A.A. Bennett, accompanied by his wife, arrived back in Nome on Monday morning, July 8, flying in the Zenith 6. The Bennett-Rodebaugh Company pilot would be working out of there for the next ten days or more, on surveys for the Lomen Reindeer Corporation. The pilot took Mr. and Mrs. Carl Lomen and R.B. Julian to Elephant Point on Tuesday, returning about midnight. While there, he had made several hops with passengers to other points, including Deering and Kotzebue.

Noel Wien was off for Council the morning of Wednesday, July 10, on an important mission. Carrying Commissioner C.W. Thornton, the pair returned that afternoon with the office equipment and records of the Council Recording District; now annexed to the Nome Mining and Recording District. On Saturday afternoon, about 3:30 P.M., the Wien Air Alaska pilot was away for Teller, Deering, Candle and Kotzebue, with Mr. and Mrs. Grant Jackson and U.S. Marshal Jones as passengers. The party returned to Nome on Sunday afternoon.

Bennett, accompanied by his wife, had taken Mr. and Mrs. Dan E. Crowley to Golovin on the evening of Thursday, July 11. The Bennetts returned to Nome on Friday morning. Road commission crews were at work enlarging the municipal field and improving it. Bennett left again on Monday afternoon of July 15, for Deering, Candle and Elephant Point with four

Pilot Noel Wien, right, with a group of his customers in front of the Hamilton Metalplane H-45.

Noel Wien Photo

passengers: H.L. Stull for Deering, Alf Lomen, Andy Bahr, reindeer foreman, and Mike Nukkla for Elephant Point. Noel Wien had left that same evening for Teller and Wales, with two women passengers. Unable to land at Wales due to fog, the pilot returned to Nome. Tuesday morning he was away again with six passengers, taking E.J. Mathews and a school teacher to Candle, and Doctor and Mrs. D.H. King, Reverend Newton and another school teacher to Kotzebue. He had only a short rest before leaving for Fairbanks.

Noel Wien came in to Fairbanks from Nome at 3:00 A.M. on Wednesday, July 17, 1929, following a six-hour flight. He brought in his mother, Earl Borland, and a passenger, C.S. Blair.

Frank Dorbandt, pilot for Anchorage Air Transport, Incorporated, had left his position there for a flying job with Wien Air Alaska. He was to be the Nome-based pilot for the company. Dorbandt and Ralph Wien planned to take off from Fairbanks for Nome on Thursday afternoon, July 18, in the Stinson Standard, C 5262. Dorbandt was to be stationed there with the Stinson, while Ralph planned to return to Fairbanks with the Waco 9, C 2775, which had been at Nome since June 28, 1928. The pilot did not get away until a few days later, arriving in Nome early in the morning of Tuesday, July 23, 1929, after spending the night on the beach between Solomon and Safety, because of heavy fog banks over Cape Nome. Ralph Wien had remained at Fairbanks.

Captain Ross G. Hoyt had landed his Curtiss Hawk pursuit plane in Fairbanks at 12:02 P.M. Saturday, July 20, 1929, on his record-breaking New York to Nome flight. He was away again at 1:23 P.M. The army flier reached Nome in four and one-half hours of flying time, arriving at 5:00 P.M. (Nome time). After only seventy minutes on the ground, the flier was away again for Fairbanks, landing on Weeks Field three and one-half hours after leaving Nome. (see Captain Ross G. Hoyt—New York to Nome—1929, Chapter 49).

Wien Alaska Airways no longer had the Nome business to themselves, for Bennett-Rodebaugh Company came out with a large box ad in the Nome Nugget on Saturday, July 20, quoting passenger and express rates to all Seward Peninsula points. Nome to Fairbanks passenger fare was quoted at $600 for one, reduced by one-half for two or three passengers. Express was quoted over the route at seventy-five cents a pound.

Frank Dorbandt, Wien's new pilot in Nome with the Stinson Standard, C 5262, was soon busy. Taking a couple of thrill seekers up on the afternoon of Thursday, July 25, the pilot gave the town an exciting buzz job, zooming over flagpoles and church steeples. He was away at 1:45 P.M. Friday, July 26, 1929, for an inspection tour of landing fields to the north of Nome, carrying E.F. Bauer of the Alaska Road Commission. Flying first to Pilgrim Hot Springs, to land on the field built the previous summer, the pilot found the landing strip rough; Mission folks there promised to make the changes he suggested immediately. Taking a large sack of fresh vegetables from the Mission gardens, the two men left for Candle, where the fresh produce was eagerly received. Taking aboard E.J. Mathews, president of the Keewalik Mining Company as a passenger for Nome, the party went on to Keewalik (later Kiwalik) to inspect the field there, where Bauer conferred with foreman Frank Redwood of the Alaska Road Commission. Dorbandt landed back in Nome at 11:00 P.M. after a flight of one hour and forty minutes. It was reported that the equipment for the new radio station at Teller had gone north on the motorship *Silver Wave*, and communications should be established in a few days. The poles and antenna were already in place.

A.A. Bennett was back from Kotzebue at noon on Thursday, July 25, 1929. He had taken Nome's lady dentist, Doctor L. von M-Zesch to Kotzebue on July 21, to make connections there with the cutter *Northland*, for Barrow. The Bennett-Rodebaugh Company pilot became trapped on Shore's Peninsula in a pass surrounded by mountains in thick fog. Unable to see ahead, he landed the Zenith 6, surviving the unexpected incident without damage to the plane or its occupants. Bennett and Doctor von M-Zesch struck out on foot for Kotzebue, forty-five miles away, and arrived there twenty-seven hours later. It was an arduous trip but they had stood it well.

The cutter *Northland* was at Kotzebue as reported. Captain Jones promised help in getting the plane out. The pilot crossed by boat, along with three natives, to the Kobuk Lake side of the peninsula, then walked the mile and a half to the plane. Captain Jones moved the *Northland* to the other side, sending fourteen sailors to help the pilot get the plane out of the swamp. Skids were built to assist the plane over the rough spots and, with combined man and motor power, the Zenith was moved to the Kobuk Lake beach. When a swamp had been crossed, the skids were removed and the pilot was able to drive the plane ahead over the tussocks with motor power alone. The skids would be replaced at the next swamp, and manpower added to engine power.

Bennett took off from the beach with no difficulty, continuing north to Kotzebue. Doctor L. von M-Zesch boarded the *Northland* for the trip to Barrow, and the Bennett-Rodebaugh Company pilot returned to Nome with the Reverend R.Z. Newton, who had flown to Kotzebue earlier with Noel Wien. Bennett was off in the Zenith 6 that same evening for White Mountain, carrying Reindeer Supervisor Ben Mozee on a round trip. The two men returned to Nome at 2:30 A.M. Friday, July 26, 1929.

Ben Eielson was in Fairbanks awaiting Bennett's return. Eielson wanted to discuss the purchase of the Bennett-Rodebaugh Company by the newly-formed Alaskan Airways, Incorporated, a subsidiary of The Aviation Corporation (AVCO), a New York based holding company registered in Delaware. Bennett, taking his wife along, was off Nome at 1:45 P.M. Friday, July 26, for Fairbanks, carrying U.S. mail. The pilot landed at Weeks Field at 9:40 P.M. that same day; he had been away since July 8. On Monday, July 29, 1929, Eielson announced the purchase of all the outstanding shares of stock in the Bennett-Rodebaugh Company. The new company, Alaskan Airways, Incorporated, officially began business on August 1, 1929.

Carl Ben Eielson, traveling with Noel Wien in the Hamilton Metalplane H-45, was off Weeks Field in the afternoon of August 1, 1929, for Nome. In the plane with Ben and Noel were Ralph Wien and his father, J.B. Wien, plus a load of mail. The group arrived in Nome about 2:00 P.M. on Friday, August 2. Other than meeting with old friends, Eielson inspected the field and facilities there, while further discussions with Noel, Ralph and Grant Jackson, president, manager and secretary-treasurer of Wien Alaska Airways, Incorporated, respectively, resulted in an announcement in Nome of the purchase of the stock of the Wien company by Alaskan Airways, Incorporated.

Frank Dorbandt, in the Stinson Standard, C 5262, was off on Monday afternoon, July 29, 1929, with Reindeer Supervisor Ben B. Mozee, on an aerial inspection of grazing tracts to the east of Nome. Making a three-hour stop at Council, the party went on to Golovin. A landing at Moses Point, the next stop, was made on the beach to allow Mozee to go to Elim in a skiff. Back at the plane, the two men flew to the mouth of the Koyuk River, then on to Egavik, landing on the beach and remaining for a few hours before taking off for Unalakleet. Flying a distance of 550 miles in the thirty-two hours they were gone, Mozee felt it would have taken him six weeks of surface travel to accomplish what had been done.

Frank Dorbandt and Noel Wien went out on Saturday, August 3, at 10:00 A.M. in the Stinson Standard, C 5262, to pick up Ed C. Bradley at Unalakleet. The roadhouse man had injured his arm badly in a power saw. The two pilots were back in the afternoon, sending Bradley to the Nome hospital for treatment.

Noel Wien, accompanied by his father, Ben Eielson and E.J. Mathews, left Nome at 11:00 A.M. Friday, August 9, 1929, in the Hamilton, NC 10002, for Fairbanks. Also carrying 450 pounds of gold, the pilot landed at Weeks Field at 9:00 P.M. that same day. Ralph remained behind to bring in the Waco 9 from Nome.

The new company, formed by the consolidation of Wien Alaska Airways and Bennett-Rodebaugh Company with Alaskan Airways, Incorporated, was represented in Nome by the Lomen Reindeer Corporation, with Frank Dorbandt as Nome-based pilot for the company. Dorbandt, flying the Alaskan Airways, Stinson Standard, C 5262, took off at 10:30 A.M. Friday, August 9, for Kotzebue and Candle. Carrying Deputy Marshal W.E.H. Cremer, who was traveling north to bring in a prisoner, as well as mail, the pilot was over Kotzebue in fifty minutes. The flight returned to Nome the same day. Dorbandt was out again for Teller Sunday, August 11, 1929, returning to Nome with Mr. and Mrs. Carl Lomen and Mrs. Gillis and child, who were enroute to Nome on the *Silver Wave*, which was stormbound at that port.

Frank Dorbandt went to Golovin on Sunday morning, August 11, to bring in L.E. Robinson of the Bureau of Education. The passenger wished to contact the motorship *Boxer*, due to arrive in Nome that day. Following his return, the pilot went out to make landings on various gravel bars up the Nome River at summer fish camps. The Alaskan Airways pilot departed in the Stinson Standard for Fairbanks on Wednesday, carrying Mrs. A.W. Newhall

Clark Bassett, Alaskan Airways, Incorporated, mechanic stationed in Nome in 1929, with Stinson SB-1, C 5262, flown out of there by Frank Dorbandt in the fall of 1929.

Art McLain Collection

and Ted Scroggins as passengers; and the U.S. mail. Dorbandt, delayed at Unalakleet by bad weather, and held overnight at Tanana by rain, arrived in Fairbanks about 11:00 P.M. Friday, August 16, 1929. Ralph Wien, bringing in the Waco 9, C 2775, landed behind him at 1:45 P.M. Ralph had left Nome at noon on Thursday. He was also held overnight at Unalakleet, coming in to Weeks Field the next day. All the planes of Alaskan Airways were now in Fairbanks, although it was expected to send one to Nome in the near future. The new company was advertising their services in the Nome and Fairbanks papers.

Ben Eielson, general manager for Alaskan Airways, flew to Anchorage with Frank Dorbandt on Saturday, August 17, 1929, taking the Stinson Standard, NC 877, which had been acquired from Bennett-Rodebaugh Company. Eielson was in the port city to discuss the acquisition by Alaskan Airways of Anchorage Air Transport, Incorporated. Transfer was made on the morning of Tuesday, August 20, 1929.

Dorbandt had other business in mind for, at 1:30 P.M. on Monday, he wed Miss Vida Deigh. The pair was off an hour later in the Stinson, NC 877, for Nome, where the pilot was to operate the airplane for the new company. Accompanied by Mrs. Rex Swartz, the pair arrived at Nome on Tuesday, August 20, at noon. The following day the pilot flew Alfred J. Lomen and Charles H. Milot to Pilgrim Hot Springs, returning the same afternoon.

On Thursday, August 22, Dorbandt went to Teller with August Homberger and Alf Lomen as passengers, making connections with the *Sierra*, to allow Homberger to be taken north to Elephant Point, to work as a carpenter for Lomen Reindeer Corporation. Dorbandt made a scenic flight over the Nome area on Friday, carrying Judge G.J. Lomen, his wife and Master Jerry Lomen.

Noel Wien was off from Weeks Field for Nome at 10:30 A.M. Saturday, August 24, 1929, in the Hamilton. A new 525 horsepower Pratt & Whitney Hornet engine had been installed in the plane in place of the original Wasp of 425 horsepower. Noel was accompanied by his wife, and company mechanic and student pilot Earl Borland. He carried three additional passengers: G.W. Rathjens, Irving McKenny Reed and H.J. Thompson, plus 101 pounds of first class letter mail. Flying nonstop in four hours and twenty-five minutes, Noel landed at the Nome airfield, two miles out of town, at 1:30 P.M. (Nome time). The new motor had shortened the usual enroute time.

Noel took off at 1:30 P.M. Thursday, August 29, for Fairbanks. Ross J. Kinney, superintendent of the Alaska Road Commission, was a passenger for Unalakleet, together with Alvin Polet, who was going to Fairbanks to enroll as a student in the School of Mines. Ada Wien, Earl Borland, and weather observer H.J. Thompson, along with seventy-five pounds of first class letter mail, made up the rest of the load. The pilot, flying under a low ceiling from the Seward Peninsula, landed the Hamilton on Weeks Field early in the afternoon of Friday, August 30, 1929.

Frank Dorbandt, Alaskan Airways pilot in Nome, made a flight to Council on the morning of Friday, August 30, in Stinson Standard, NC 877. Leaving Irving Reed there, he returned with Miss Amelia Brunnell, local telephone operator, as a passenger; and also picked up Wallace Porter at Golovin. The pilot was off again, shortly after his arrival, taking Doctor F.J. O'Hara with him, to bring in Doctor Smith at Kotzebue for medical treatment; Smith was reported dangerously ill. Dorbandt returned to Candle and Deering on Tuesday, September 3, with mail for both stops. He picked up Irving McKenny Reed at Deering, taking him to Teller. The pilot took O.S. Weaver, manager of the Alaska Telephone and Telegraph Company, along on the day's flight.

Carl Ben Eielson was off Fairbanks in the Waco Model 10, NC 780E, (Alaskan

Airways No. 4) at 11:30 A.M. Wednesday, on a nonstop flight to Nome. Carrying authoress Barrett Willoughby and a small amount of letter mail, weather forced the pilot to hold at Unalakleet, and he arrived on the Nome field late Saturday afternoon.

Frank Dorbandt was off from Nome on Thursday, September 6, 1929, for Fairbanks in the Stinson Standard biplane, NC 877. Carrying R.S. Pollister, supercargo, and ice pilot (ishavskipper) Jochimsen, both from the wrecked trading vessel *Elisif*, the pilot made it through to Weeks Field in seven hours, with a fuel stop at Ruby. He landed in Fairbanks at 6:15 P.M. Dorbandt was back in Nome with the Stinson on Monday, September 9. He had left Fairbanks on Saturday, at 5:00 A.M. but was forced to hold at Nenana because of fog. Leaving there, he encountered heavy weather along the Yukon, coming down at Nulato for a second delay. He brought Jack Morton, a Fairbanks college student who was studying airplane mechanics, for the round trip, and also picked up R.J. Kinney at Unalakleet. The day following his arrival in Nome, Tuesday, the Alaskan Airways pilot was away on a mercy mission for Kotzebue. Taking Mrs. Rex Swartz as nurse, he went to pick up Mrs. Minnie Calhoun, a severe appendicitis case. Placing the sick lady in the plane, he also boarded Mrs. Swartz and Miss Vera Wheeler, taking off on the return flight. Impeded by fog and darkness, the pilot landed at Candle, coming in to Nome the following day about nine o'clock in the morning.

Frank Dorbandt, taking Jack Morton with him, was away on Monday, September 16, 1929, landing the Morlander family at Kotzebue, before going on to Elephant Point. Circling here, they dropped the mail from the air, before proceeding on to Candle to deliver their mail. Remaining overnight, they discovered the next morning that the river had risen during the night, with water nearly up to the axles of the Stinson Standard. Only a portion of the river bar used for landing was visible. Lightly loaded, the plane was successfully flown out. Dorbandt and his helper were back in Nome that afternoon after an hour and a half flight. The Alaskan Airways pilot was away again the following day, Thursday, taking Irving McKenny Reed to Solomon, Peter Lee to Council, and Mrs. B.M. Buckley and two children to Golovin, planning on going out to White Mountain. However, engine trouble about ten minutes out forced Frank to return for adjustments on the Wright Whirlwind before going out again. He was off again on Saturday, September 21, 1929, for Kotzebue, carrying Mrs. Grant, a nurse, and Mr. Mock, to be associated with Tom Berryman's six trading stations in the Kotzebue district. Berryman's Kotzebue Fur & Trading Company had posts at Kotzebue, Selawik, Okok Point, Long Beach, Kobuk, Noorvik and Kivalina. Tom and his wife came to Nome on the return flight.

Ed Young left Fairbanks on Thursday, September 19, for Nome, taking the Stinson Standard SB-1, C 5262, company No. 8, back to Dorbandt in Nome. Wings and fuselage had been recovered with fabric and a new motor installed in the plane. The company was now painting all their planes, during overhaul, in standard company colors, as well as putting on the Alaskan Airways logo and a company number on each. The pilot brought in Outside letter mail and a quantity of express. Leaving the newly refurbished plane for Dorbandt, he was off for Fairbanks on Sunday afternoon, September 22, in the somewhat battered Stinson Standard, NC 877, to return it to Weeks Field for repair. Jack Morton, now returning to school, accompanied him, along with Irving McKenny Reed, whom Dorbandt had just brought in from Solomon.

Noel Wien, with his wife, departed Fairbanks by train on September 19, 1929, for the States. The pair caught the steamer *Alaska* at Seward. They planned to take an extended vacation, the Alaska pilot seeking employment Outside.

Dorbandt, in the Stinson Standard, C 5262, was off Nome on Wednesday, September 25, for Golovin, to answer a call for help. Mrs. Mathias Petersen, of the Council area, had been operating a boat with a mast on the Fish River, near White Mountain, when the mast fell suddenly on her, breaking both legs below the knee. Brought down to Golovin in a small boat, she was placed aboard the plane there, arriving in Nome about noon to be taken to the hospital. The flight was made in rain and foggy weather. The Alaskan Airways pilot was off the next day for Kotzebue, with twenty-seven passengers in the Stinson: Hugo Eckhardt and twenty-six foxes, sixteen of which were blues, and ten silvers. The man had purchased the breeding stock from a fur farm in Wisconsin, and accompanied the animals north. The miner was establishing a fur farm in a timbered section a short distance up from the mouth of the Kobuk River. He also picked up some white fox at the Teller farm. On the return flight, Dorbandt picked up Frank R. Redwood, foreman for the Alaska Road Commission at Deering and Candle, taking the man from Deering to Candle where they remained overnight. Leaving the next morning, the men encountered such heavy rain and fog in the mountains that, upon reaching the Nome River divide, they were forced to return and land at Pilgrim Hot Springs. The field had recently been ploughed crosswise, and was so rough that it was necessary to use up the day, dragging the field with a team of mules. A group of children also helped.

Dorbandt was off Nome on Friday, September 27, 1929, to pick up Tom Berryman at Kotzebue to bring him in to Nome. It was Tom's second trip by airplane from there. The pilot was off again the same afternoon for Bluff, taking Mr. and Mrs. James Keenan and A.G. Blake, a surveyor. He returned before dark with Mrs. Keenan.

Dorbandt, in Alaskan Airways, Incorporated, Stinson SB-1, C 5262, was off Nome on the morning of Tuesday, October 1, 1929, on a flight to Kotzebue, carrying Alfred Lomen, Mr. and Mrs. A.E. Porsild and Tom Berryman. Landing was made without incident and the plane fueled for a flight to Elephant Point. The Lomen Reindeer Corporation was under contract to the Canadian government to deliver 3000 head of deer on the hoof, a drive that might take a year and a half. Porsild represented the Canadians. Gassing at Elephant Point, Dorbandt took Porsild, Lomen and Andrew Bahr, who was in charge of the drive for Lomen, on a flight to the head of the Colville River, over the route of the intended drive. After flying for some hours, the pilot encountered snow and rain in the Waring Mountains beyond the Selawik River, and was forced to return to Elephant Point. Porsild and Bahr remained there to complete arrangements for the start of the drive while Dorbandt and Alf Lomen took off for Candle, to remain overnight there.

Leaving the following morning for Nome, they encountered snowstorms from Imuruk Lake to Mount Bendeleben, forcing the pilot to reroute to the opposite side of the mountain, reaching the coast at Point Isaacs, then following the coastline to Nome.

Doctor R.E. Smith, brought in from Kotzebue by Dorbandt on August 30, 1929, was still in the Maynard-Columbus Hospital at Nome. Smith's condition was so serious it was decided the pilot would fly him and his wife to Anchorage, to catch the next boat at Seward for the States, in the hope of saving his life. The pilot was away in the Stinson, C 5262, at 10:00 A.M. Friday, October 4, with the patient and his wife aboard. Dorbandt's wife, Vida, also made the trip. Stopping at Takotna, then coming in through Rainy Pass, the pilot landed at the Anchorage Municipal Airport. Doctor Smith had contracted septicemia (blood poisoning) throughout his system as a result of a scratch received during an operation on a patient at Kotzebue, where he was in charge of the government hospital. He stood the trip to Anchorage well. He and his wife were put on a railroad speeder and sent to Seward, where connections were made with the *Yukon*. Dorbandt returned to Nome, via Fairbanks, landing on Weeks Field on Sunday, October 6, 1929. The pilot, accompanied by his wife, arrived back in Nome on the evening of Wednesday, October 9, with a big load of mail. He reported on the loss of Russ

Merrill in Anchorage, who had now been missing for over three weeks.

Shortly after noon the following day, the Alaskan Airways pilot was away in the Stinson Standard, C 5262, for Council, bringing in Frank Brunnell from there, to land in Nome at 4:15 P.M. Dorbandt was out again on Monday, October 14, coming back from Kotzebue and Candle with Alf Lomen, Leo Loners and Hilkey Robinson.

Ben Eielson was coming to Nome in the Hamilton Metalplane to take a load of passengers to Fairbanks. Leaving Weeks Field in the forenoon of Friday, October 18, accompanied by flight mechanic Earl Borland and, with a load of mail, the plane came in to Nome that same evening. Dorbandt, in the Stinson Standard, C 5262, returned to Nome on Saturday morning, with E.H. Gagen, Lars Rynning and Charlie Traeger, from Unalakleet. He was off again that same afternoon for Candle and Deering, to bring a number of passengers to Nome.

The steamer *Victoria*, of the Alaska Line, arrived in the roadstead at an early hour on Monday, October 21, making its last trip of the season to Nome. Aboard the ship was a four-place Stinson "Junior" SM-2AA, NC 475H, monoplane, which was to become the nucleus of Northern Air Transport, Incorporated. President Victor Branson Ross was also aboard with his wife. Vic had arrived in Nome in 1926 from California. By 1929 he was a

Mechanic Clark Bassett with Stinson Standard C 5262 of Alaskan Airways. Frank Dorbandt flew the plane across Bering Strait to North Cape, Siberia on October 29, with Carl Ben Eielson following in the Hamilton Metalplane. Both planes arrived back in Nome on November 4, with furs and passengers from the Nanuk.

Crosson Collection

master mechanic for the Alaska Road Commission in Nome. Becoming interested in flying during the past two years, he had taken a few lessons from Noel Wien before going Outside in the spring to Portland, Oregon, for flight instruction toward a license. With the help of backers in Nome, Ross had purchased the plane and was accompanying the cabin monoplane to Nome. Vic had acquired his license, which permitted him to haul freight, but not paying passengers. Consequently, he had engaged a pilot, W.R. "Bill" Graham, who had been his instructor in Portland. Graham, also on the *Victoria*, was experienced; he had been an army flier in 1918-19, with the St. Louis Aircraft Corporation in 1920, barnstorming in 1921-22-23, with the Texas Rangers in 1924-25, privately employed in 1926-27, and an instructor at Rankin's school and with the Forestry Patrol in the State of Oregon during the years 1928-29. Bill Graham claimed 5000 hours of flying time.

Graham and Ross completed assembly, at the airport, of the Stinson Junior on Tuesday morning, October 22, 1929, making a test flight over town that same day. Besides Graham and Ross, Frank Dorbandt and Julius Silverman went on the flight. It was an unqualified success. Northern Air Transport, Incorporated, plane No. 1, departed on its first commercial flight in Alaska at 1:15 that afternoon, taking Mr. and Mrs. Ray Monroe who had just arrived on the

Northern Air Transport, Incorporated, in Nome. Left to Right: Vic Ross, pilot W.R. "Bill" Graham and mechanic George Laiblin.

Sylvia Ross Collection

Victoria from Hyder, Alaska, to Shishmaref; they were associated with George H. Goshaw's fur farm there. The new air service in Nome was in business. The fleet eventually grew to ten planes.

Passengers were coming in to catch the last southbound trip of the season of the *Victoria*, as well as flying out to Fairbanks. Dorbandt made two trips in the Stinson Standard from Candle and Deering on Sunday, October 20, bringing in four passengers, including Mrs. Tom Roust and Mr. and Mrs. Sam Magids. Monday he was out again to Council and, after returning home, went out to Golovin to bring in Wallace Porter and Mr. Rylander. Ben Eielson and Earl Borland left for Fairbanks the morning of Tuesday, October 22, taking Attorney R.L. McWilliams, enroute to his home in San Francisco.

On Wednesday, October 23, 1929, Bill Graham and Vic Ross, flying together on these early flights, flew to Teller with three silver fox for George McClean, returning in the afternoon. Dorbandt was off that same morning in the Stinson Standard, C 5262, with a full load of mail for northern communities. The pilot was back at 1:00 P.M. on Thursday, coming from Kotzebue. He brought in a Mr. Simmons as a passenger, as well as taking Dan E. Crowley from Candle to Elephant Point, and two other passengers from Kotzebue back to Elephant Point.

Pilots Graham and Ross, flying the Northern Air Transport, Incorporated, Stinson SM-2AA, NC 475H, No. 1, were away on the morning of Thursday, October 24, for the north, bringing in A.V. Cordovado and another passenger from Deering. They were off again on the same afternoon for Council, to bring in William A. Oliver, a mining operator, to Nome.

Following Eielson's recent visit to Nome, it was announced in Fairbanks on October 26, 1929, that a contract had been signed between Alaskan Airways, Incorporated, and the Swenson Fur & Trading Company for up to fifteen trips to North Cape, Siberia, where the Swenson schooner, *Nanuk*, was fast in the ice. Alaskan Airways was to bring in a large amount of Siberian furs, along with all the excess personnel on the vessel, which would undoubtedly remain frozen in the ice until the following summer. (see Fairbanks—1929, Chapter 51). While Olaf Swenson, head of the trading company, and his seventeen year old daughter Marion, along with other crew members, were still on the *Nanuk* at North Cape, Siberia, members of another company vessel, *Elisif*, had recently come in to Nome from Little Diomede Island on the cutter *Northland*, to depart by ship for the States and home. The *Elisif*

Bob Gleason Photo

August 1, 1929. North Cape, Siberia. Russian Junkers W-33, on floats, landed near the **Nanuk** *and* **Elisif.** *The Russian crew had flown the plane from the Cape to Wrangel Island and return, to check on Russian colonists there. Both schooners were in trouble before the year was out.*

769

had been crushed in the ice, beached at Cape Billings, and was a total loss. radio contact with *Nanuk* was being carried on through the shipboard station on the vessel and its twenty-three year-old radio operator, Bob Gleason. (see *Icebound in the Siberian Arctic* by Robert J. Gleason).

Eielson wanted to be a part of the operation. It was decided by the company to use the Hamilton Metalplane, NC 10002, flown by Ben Eielson, and the Stinson Standard, C 5262, flown by Dorbandt, to make the flights, with Teller as a jumping off point. There was a possibility of having Joe Crosson, who had arrived back in Fairbanks on October 17 to fly for Alaskan Airways, Incorporated, come to Nome for stationing. He was to do the flying out of there while Dorbandt was on the Siberian contract. Eielson and Dorbandt planned to follow the same route Noel Wien and Calvin Cripe had taken on the single flight they had made to the *Elisif* from Nome on March 7, 1929.

Ben Eielson and Earl Borland, in the Hamilton Metalplane, NC 10002, left Fairbanks, arriving in Nome at 3:00 P.M. Tuesday, October 29, 1929. Delayed here for a time in order to repair a gear strut damaged in the landing, the airmen loaded the plane for the trip to Siberia. Dorbandt, in the Stinson Standard SB-1, C 5262, had gone ahead to Teller, to change from wheels to skis there, before crossing Bering Strait. Eielson was on wheels.

Frank Dorbandt was away from Teller at 8:15 A.M. Tuesday, October 29, arriving at North Cape and the *Nanuk* at 2:30 P.M. From Teller, he had flown to Cape Prince of Wales, across Bering Straits via Little Diomede Island to East Cape, and down the coast to North Cape. The flight from Teller had taken six hours and twenty minutes, bucking headwinds and fog. He advised Eielson, using the schooner's radio, to remain on wheels as there were frequent landing places enroute. The pilot decided to await Eielson's arrival in order that they could depart in company with each other. Eielson came in the next day, Wednesday, October 30 (Nome time), flying from Nome with the faster plane in four hours and twenty minutes. Both planes were carrying case gas to be used on the return journey. The two planes were loaded and serviced for the departure on the following day.

Dorbandt took four passengers in addition to a small amount of furs in the Stinson; while Eielson and Borland carried the weightiest passengers. (see Fairbanks—1929, Chapter

Northern Air Transport, Incorporated, Stinson Junior, NC 475H, was received by the company in Nome on October 21, 1929. A landing at an Eskimo village always drew a crowd.

51). Dorbandt was off at 9:30 A.M. Thursday, October 31, (Nome time) with Eielson finally getting away at 10:10 A.M. He had returned briefly to shut off the cabin heater to protect the furs with which he was loaded.

Neither plane reached Teller that night; Dorbandt landed about ninety miles west of East Cape, Siberia, at a Chukchi Eskimo settlement near Cape Serdtse-Kamen, due to snow squalls. Eielson landed alongside shortly thereafter. The passengers and crew took shelter with the natives for the next four days while the storm blew itself out. (see Fairbanks—1929, Chapter 51, for details).

The two planes, after much work on the part of the men in heating and starting the engines, were finally able to get away. Dorbandt was off at 9:30 A.M. for Teller, where he changed to wheels again. Eielson and Borland followed a half hour later. They overtook the slower Stinson as they were crossing Bering Strait. Eielson and Borland landed in Nome at 12:30 P.M. Monday, November 4, 1929, with the Stinson arriving from Teller at 2:45 P.M. Their six passengers, worried about catching the last boat of the season for Outside, the *Sierra*, were in time. The two planes left Nome that same evening to return to Teller and prepare for their second flight to Siberia. They landed at Teller in the dusk.

While this was going on, Nome's second air service, Northern Air Transport, Incorporated, was carrying on with the local business. Bill Graham, with the Stinson Junior SM-2AA, NC 475H, returned to the Nome airport about 12:30 P.M. Tuesday, October 29, from Kotzebue, where he had been stormbound for two days. Off at noon the next day for Candle and Kotzebue with a full load of freight and express, the cabin monoplane was back at Nome on Thursday, October 31, again carrying freight and express. The pilot had encountered snowstorms most of the day. Winter was on the land, and on Saturday, November 2, 1929, Graham and Vic Ross were busy installing skis in place of the wheels. Pilot Graham took off for the north on Monday, November 4, and arrived at Kotzebue.

Graham brought in Alfred Bigger to Nome from Candle on Saturday, November 9. The pilot had been at Elephant Point helping in a reindeer roundup that brought together approximately 12,000 animals. He also took Deputy U.S. Marshal George Wagner from Candle to Kotzebue. The Northern Air Transport pilot was scheduled to take off on Sunday, November 10, for Golovin and Haycock, with Wallace Porter for the first point, and Frank McCoy for the second. The Stinson Junior and its knock-down hangar was moved about the middle of the month from the Municipal Airport to the winter landing area on the Snake River at Belmont Point. The skis were not working out as there was insufficient snow on the ice to steer the plane with a ski on the tail skid. In fact, there was not a great deal of snow anywhere so far this winter, where the wind could get a sweep at it. The plane was refitted with wheels.

Eielson and Dorbandt, waiting out a long period of stormy weather at Teller, had finally gotten off for Siberia on Saturday, November 9, 1929, taking off the snow at 10:45 A.M. for Cape Prince of Wales and East Cape. Dorbandt and his mechanic, Clark Bassett, ran into heavy weather and were back in an hour and a half. The other plane did not return.

Dorbandt, taking his wife, Mrs. Jack Warren, wife of the roadhouse operator at Teller, and James H. Anderson, the U.S. Signal Corps operator at Teller, came in to Nome the same day, landing there shortly before noon. The party, with the Stinson Standard, returned to Teller that same afternoon.

Bill Graham was off Nome in the Northern Air Transport monoplane, NC 475H, No. 1, on Sunday, November 17, 1929, for Egavik with Mrs. George Lomen as a passenger, and Marshal Jones, returning a prisoner to Marshall. The pilot was held at Egavik the eighteenth

Victor Branson Ross, Northern Air Transport, Incorporated. 1929.

Alaskan Airways, Incorporated, Stinson Standard and Hamilton at Teller, Alaska, before Eielson and Borland were lost on November 9, 1929.

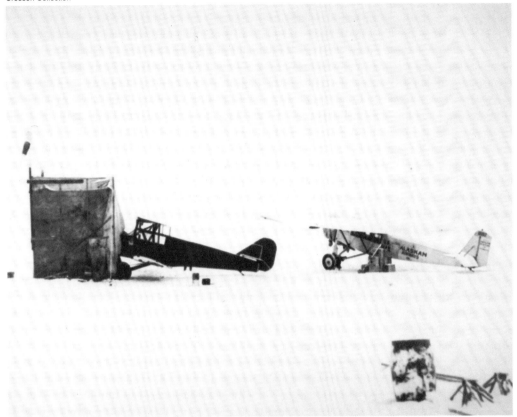

Alaskan Airways flight mechanics, Earl Borland (on left) and Clark Bassett, taken at Teller, Alaska. Borland flew with Eielson in the Hamilton and Bassett with Dorbandt in the Stinson Standard shown behind the two men.

and nineteenth, going to Unalakleet on Wednesday, November 20, and was stormbound again at that point.

Dorbandt, in Teller, attempted a takeoff for Siberia on Saturday, November 16, but the heavily-loaded plane was unable to stand the pounding over the rough snow surface, and was brought to a halt by the pilot, sustaining landing gear and wing tip damage. Dorbandt and his mechanic, Clark Bassett, attempted to make repairs at Teller but the two men ended up flying Stinson C 5262 in to Nome on Wednesday, November 20, arriving there at 3:15 P.M. The axle was welded and several minor repairs made to the wing, mechanics working most of the night. Bassett and Dorbandt returned to Teller on Tuesday, November 26, 1929.

Joe Crosson, flying the Waco 10, NC 780E, arrived in Nome on Friday, November 29, landing on the Snake River ice shortly after Bill Graham, who had been gone for several days, arrived. Unloading the plane of its cargo of mail, Crosson was off for Teller. Graham had come in from Saint Michael with Marshal Charles Jones and two prisoners, one from Marshall and the other from Saint Michael. While stormbound at Mountain Village, the pilot had found it

Jack Warren and his wife operated the roadhouse at Teller in 1929, where Jack was also commissioner. Much of the brunt of the comings and goings during the Eielson-Borland search fell on them, upsetting normal winter routine. They gave every assistance possible.

Crosson Collection

Crosson Collection

The roadhouse at Teller, Alaska, in 1929, where the searchers stayed when they were on the American side of Bering Strait.

necessary to construct a pair of skis in order to get off for Saint Michael. Putting his wheels back on there, he had come in to Nome.

In Teller, Crosson and Dorbandt had been trying to get across Bering Strait but were rebuffed by weather each time. Eielson and Borland had now been missing for three weeks. (see Fairbanks—1929, Chapter 51). Crosson and Dorbandt, with the Waco 10, NC 780E and Stinson C 5262, respectively, made another attempt to take off on the rough surface at Teller on Friday, December 6, 1929, but the battering the heavily-loaded aircraft received forced them to discontinue the takeoff; the planes had suffered damage to the landing gear. It was necessary to carry case gas for the return journey, yet the planes could not stand the pounding over the rough surface. A runway was now being built on the ice at Grantley Point, a more sheltered area where the ice was smoother. Crosson's Waco was quickly repaired but Dorbandt's Stinson was rather badly damaged.

Bill Graham, in Northern Air Transport's Stinson Junior, left Nome for Teller at 1:15 P.M. Saturday, December 7, 1929. He had changed to skis again. Alf Lomen, Ben Mozee and Martin Corliss flew to Teller in the plane. Unable to proceed to Shishmaref, Corliss and Lomen continued by dog team, expecting to be gone about ten days. Graham left for Nome at

Arrival of a plane at any Alaskan village was an occasion, with residents flocking to greet the pilot and his passengers. Here the Eskimos are grouped about the Stinson Junior SM-2AA, NC 475H, of Northern Air Transport, Incorporated. They quickly learned to stay clear of the whirling propeller. The air service, based in Nome, began operating out of there with the one plane on October 22, 1929.

Sylvia Ross Collection

2:15 P.M. but fog and snowstorms on the route back forced him to land ten miles west of the Sinrock River, near the coast. The pilot remained with the ship through the uncomfortable night, having no bedroll or food with him. Taking off about 12:40 P.M. the following day, he landed on the river at Nome about 1:00 P.M. Sunday. He was off again in a short time for Pilgrim Hot Springs, taking M.J. Walsh as a passenger, along with his son, Joe Walsh, a round tripper.

Alaskan Airways, Incorporated, pilot Harvey Barnhill, accompanied by mechanic Fred Moller, arrived in Nome on Sunday with the New Standard, NC 9190. They brought in Miss Robbins, a nurse from Ruby, as well as a load of mail from the disabled plane at that stop. Carrying supplies and repair materials for Dorbandt's Stinson Standard, the two airmen delayed long enough to be fitted with fur clothing at Nome, before joining the pilots already at Teller on Tuesday, December 10, 1929, landing there at 11:30 P.M.

Northern Air Transport pilot Bill Graham was off in the Stinson Junior at 9:30 A.M. Monday, December 9, on his first trip from Nome to Fairbanks. Carrying passengers J.D. Harlan and C.K. Sears, both enroute to the States, the pilot also had mail and express aboard. Graham returned to Nome from Fairbanks, landing about 2:00 P.M. Friday, December 13. He had left in poor visibility, landing at Ruby to refuel. He brought in packages and a sack of first class mail from there, as well as a load of parcel post from Fairbanks. Leaving Ruby, the pilot had overnighted at Nulato. Departing there at 10:30 A.M. Graham, also an excellent navigator, set up a course for Moses Point, later sighting the oil tank at Solomon, the bridge at Nome River, and then the city of Nome. His plane was hardly visible as he droned over town in the fog to a landing. He expected to leave the next day for Elephant Point with R.B. Julian and W.B. Miller. From here, he would fly out over the route to connect with the reindeer drive of 3000 animals which the Lomen Reindeer Corporation had underway from Elephant Point to northern Canada.

Two additional Alaskan Airways planes left Fairbanks on Monday, December 9, 1929, to join the search for the missing airmen, Eielson and Borland. Ed Young, flying the Stinson Standard, NC 877, and Harold Gillam, in the open-cockpit Stearman, NC 5415, arrived in Nome at 12:10 P.M. on Tuesday, December 10, leaving at 2:00 P.M. the next afternoon to proceed to Teller. Coming from Anchorage in the New Standard, NC 174H, Matt Nieminen and mechanic Lon Cope arrived at Nome at 2:10 P.M. Wednesday, December 11. Wanting to go on to Teller the following day, they were to be held in Nome for some time. They tried to reach there on Tuesday, December 17, but had to return, after encountering a severe storm. They made it to Teller the following day, leaving Nome at 10:00 A.M.

One of the two New Standard biplanes waits for better weather at Teller, Alaska, during the 1929 search for the lost Hamilton Metalplane in Siberia.

Stinson Standard SB-1, NC 877, of Alaskan Airways, Incorporated, at Nome, Alaska in 1929. This plane, originally brought to Alaska by Tom Gerard, was flown to Nome on December 10, 1929 as a replacement for C 5262. Matt Nieminen flew the Stinson Standard SB-1, C 5262, Wilkins' **Detroiter No. 2,** *to Fairbanks on December 20 for overhaul. The plane was consumed by fire in the hangar at Weeks Field.*

Nome businessman Alfred J. Lomen, at this time in Teller, was appointed on December 16, 1929, to take charge of the Eielson-Borland relief operation by the New York office of The Aviation Corporation. Lomen promptly named Joe Crosson as chief pilot. Plans were laid to use the small, fast, open-cockpit Waco and Stearman for search planes on the Siberian coast, with the larger planes hauling gasoline and supplies to a point near East Cape. Three Canadian Fairchild 71s, along with experienced Canadian pilots and mechanics were on the way north to bolster up the search efforts.

With Lon Cope remaining at Teller, Matt Nieminen, flying the New Standard, NC 174H, returned to Nome the same day he arrived at Teller, Wednesday, December 18, 1929. He took in Ben Mozee, a native girl and Fred Moller, who was returning to Fairbanks. Matt was to bring the Stinson *Detroiter No. 2,* C 5262, to Fairbanks for overhaul. Matt landed in Nome at 12:30 P.M.

The following afternoon, Thursday, December 19, Frank Dorbandt brought in the Stinson Standard, C 5262, from Teller. Bringing his wife, Vida, Harvey Barnhill and Alfred Lomen; he was expecting to return to Teller on Friday with New Standard, NC 174H. Frank, accompanied by Vic Ross, finally got away for Teller on Saturday morning, December 21. He had made an emergency trip to Golovin on Friday in the New Standard, returning with a passenger.

The Northern Air Transport Stinson Junior, NC 475H, had departed Nome at 11:00 A.M. Tuesday, December 17, 1929, with pilot Bill Graham at the controls. He carried passengers W.B. Miller of the Biological Survey, and R.B. Julian, agent for the Lomen Reindeer Corporation, as well as baggage and express, and was off for Elephant Point. Graham was held by weather at Deering for some days in the bitter cold.

On Wednesday, December 18, 1929, an assault on the crossing of the Bering Strait was mounted by all four pilots: Crosson, Gillam, Young and Barnhill. Two of the men, Barnhill and Gillam, returned to Teller just as Matt Nieminen was taking off for Nome. The other two returned later, after two hours in the air. On December 19, Crosson and Gillam were off again from Teller, making it across to land near Kolyuchin Bay that afternoon. Staying in a Chukchi yarang (skin hut) that night, at Pelikii, Gillam reached the *Nanuk* at dusk the following day, landing at 1:45 P.M. (Siberian time). Losing sight of Gillam's Stearman in the fog, Crosson had returned to the Chukchi village to spend a second night, frosting his eyes when he removed his goggles for better vision during the landing. Gillam was readying his plane for flight when Crosson landed near the *Nanuk* on Saturday, December 21. He needed rest, and went aboard the *Nanuk* while Gillam, taking shipowner Olaf Swenson, flew to the southeast, finding no sign of the lost plane.

On Friday, December 20, Matt Nieminen left Nome in the Stinson Standard, C 5262, for Fairbanks, taking Harvey Barnhill and Fred Moller along. It was the last flight of Wilkins' Stinson *Detroiter No. 2*; it was consumed by fire at Weeks Field, taking the hangar with it.

The loss of the radio station at Nome by fire on Christmas Eve was a blow. Frank Dorbandt, flying NC 174H to Nome on Friday, December 27, 1929, taking spare U.S. Signal Corps forms and supplies from the Teller station that had been requested by the Nome operator, arrived in Nome that same day. He was accompanied by Lon Cope and Vic Ross. Alf Lomen decided to hold the plane there, awaiting the arrival of the Fairchild 71s from Fairbanks. Using tractors, the snow was being removed and leveled on the Municipal Airport in anticipation of their arrival. The local planes had all been using landing spots on the ice in front of town, on the Snake River, or at Safety Lagoon, usually swept clear of snow by the wind.

On Friday, December 23, Gillam and Crosson had both gotten away from *Nanuk* to search for the missing plane, without result. They were held at the ship by storm until December 30; Crosson went out again and found nothing. Gilliam was less fortunate; his motor failed after takeoff and he came down on a rough surface, which resulted in considerable damage to Stearman C-2B, NC 5415. Repairs to the plane would consume the following three weeks. (see Fairbanks—1929, Chapter 51).

The year would end with Carl Ben Eielson and Earl Borland still missing, since November 9, in the Hamilton Metalplane, NC 10002. The wreckage would be discovered on January 26, 1930.

Stinson Junior SM-2AA, NC 475H, at an arctic village in the winter of 1929. It was the first of the Stinsons received by Northern Air Transport, Incorporated.

Fisher Studio

Fisher Studio

780

Alaska-Washington Airways, Consolidated

Gorst Air Transport,
Incorporated
Pioneer Airways, Incorporated

Ketchikan 1930

SOUTHEASTERN ALASKA HAD BEEN WITHOUT air service since the
Alaska-Washington Airways Lockheed Vega *Ketchikan* departed Juneau for Seattle on September 22, 1929, with pilot Anscel C. Eckmann at the controls. During the winter months the company had been concentrating on their Seattle to Victoria, Seattle to Vancouver, and Seattle to Wenatchee, Ellensburg and Yakima schedules, the latter operated with wheeled planes.

Structural changes were taking place within the aviation concern. Alaska-Washington Airways, Consolidated, was organized and incorporated at Olympia, Washington in the first week of January, 1930, with 100,000 shares of common stock valued at $10 per share. The new holding company was formed to finance and control the operations of the three existing units of Alaska-Washington Airways: the Alaska-Washington Airways, Limited, of British

Ketchikan, Alaska taken from a Pioneer Airways Stinson in 1930.

Salmon cannery near Ketchikan showing the floating fish traps in storage without their netting. Unable to drive piling in the rocky bottom, the traps were anchored in favored locations with the netting suspended from the floating log frame. Photo taken from a Pioneer Airways Stinson in 1930.

Alaska-Washington Consolidated Airways

Operating

ALASKA WASHINGTON AIRWAYS OF PUGET SOUND.
ALASKA WASHINGTON AIRWAYS OF B. C. LTD.,
ALASKA WASHINGTON AIRWAYS OF ALASKA.

Spring Fares & Schedules
Puget Sound & British Columbia Division

Seattle to Vancouver, B. C.	$12.75	Round Trip	$25.00
Seattle to Victoria	7.65	"	15.00
Victoria to Vancouver	7.65	"	15.00
*Seattle to Vancouver via Victoria	15.00	"	29.00
*Seattle to Victoria via Vancouver	20.00	"	39.00
*Triangular Tour-Seattle-Victoria-Vancouver-Seattle			27.00
*Stop-over privilege allowed.

SEATTLE TO VICTORIA. SCHEDULE

Leave Seattle	9:10 A. M.	Leave Victoria	10:10 A. M.
Arrive Victoria	9:55 A. M.	Arrive Seattle	10:55 A. M.
Leave Seattle	3:00 P. M.	Leave Victoria	4:05 P. M.
Arrive Victoria	3:45 P. M.	Arrive Seattle	4:50 P. M.

VICTORIA TO VANCOUVER

Leave Vancouver	10:30 A. M.	Leave Victoria	11:30 A. M.
Arrive Victoria	11:15 A. M.	Arrive Vancouver	12:15 P. M.
Leave Vancouver	1:45 P. M.	Leave Victoria	2:45 P. M.
Arrive Victoria	2:30 P. M.	Arrive Vancouver	3:30 P. M.

SEATTLE TO VANCOUVER

Leave Seattle	9:00 A. M.	Leave Vancouver	1:20 P. M.
Arrive Vancouver	10:15 A. M.	Arrive Seattle	2:35 P. M.
Leave Seattle	11:25 A. M.	Leave Vancouver	3:45 P. M.
Arrive Vancouver	12:40 P. M.	Arrive Seattle	5:00 P. M.

On Seattle-Victoria Division, planes will stop at Port Angeles on advance bookings. 30 Pounds baggage carried free. Freight and Express carried.

CHARTER TRIPS MADE

Announcement of the extension of the service to include Tacoma, Olympia and Nanaimo B. C. will be made with summer schedules and fares.

Alaska Service will be resumed April 1st between Seattle, Ketchikan, Petersburg, Wrangel, Sitka, Juneau and Skagway. Also trips made in to Atlin and other lakes and rivers in the interior.

TICKETS ON SALE AT ALL LEADING TRAVEL AGENCIES AND AIR TRANSPORT OFFICES

The Alaska Washington Airways (Main Office).
Phone Main 2840   414 University Street.   Seattle, Washington.
Hangar—Phone Capitol 1474

The Alaska Washington Airways of B. C. Ltd.,
Phone 2900   756 Yates Street   Victoria, B. C.

The Alaska Washington Airways of Alaska
Phone Main 2840   414 University Street.   Seattle, Wash.
Alaskan Headquarters, Juneau, Alaska.
Agents in various Alaska Cities.

Schedule and Fares subject to change without notice.
Schedule 5-B
Printed in U. S. A.

Author's Collection

Schedule card naming the three companies that made up Alaska-Washington Consolidated Airways (the holding company). The Alaska schedule is not shown as it may have been in the planning stage at this time.

Reverse side of the small blue schedule of the Eastern Washington route gives the locations where information was available and tickets could be obtained.

Main Office at Seattle, 414 University Street.   MAin 2840

DISTRICT TRAFFIC AGENTS

At Wenatchee...Doris Morrison
c/o Auto Club...............Columbia Hotel...............Phone 984 Blue

* * *

At Ellensburg...E. E. Munday
Chamber of Commerce...Phone Main 134

* * *

At Yakima...Musa Brodie
c/o Auto Club...............Commercial Hotel...............Phone 1579
Tickets at all leading travel agencies, hotels,
and Auto Club Offices

STOP OVERS. One way ticket good for continuous passage only. All stop overs subject to local rates and must be arranged prior to commencement of trip.

**LOCKHEED AND STINSON PLANES
ENCLOSED AND HEATED**

Our traffic department will make bookings on all major air transport lines

Author's Collection

Columbia, the Alaska-Washington Airways of Puget Sound, and the Alaska-Washington Airways of Alaska. The Alaska unit had been the first established, after its organization in April of 1929, inaugurating service with a nonstop flight to Juneau on April 15 of that year. The British Columbia unit had been organized in September to operate the seaplane service between Victoria, Vancouver and Nanaimo; Canadian laws did not permit an American

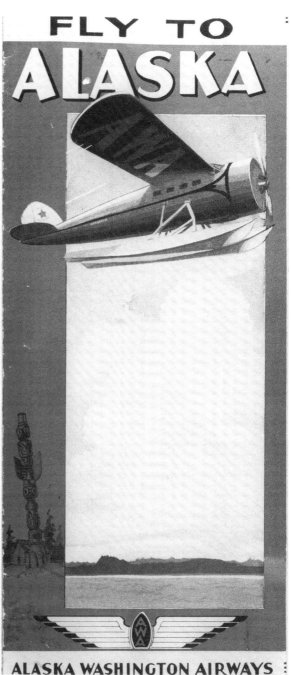

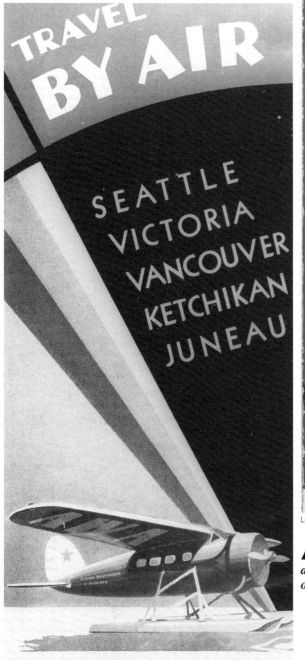

▲ ◄ *Alaska-Washington Airways colorful brochures advertising their services depicted an artist's rendering of their Lockheed Vegas in the air and on the water.*

ALASKA WASHINGTON AIRWAYS
Eastern Washington Schedule and Fares

FROM SEATTLE		ONE WAY	ROUND TRIP
To Wenatchee		$12.00	$23.00
To Ellensburg		12.00	23.00
To Yakima		12.00	23.00
FROM WENATCHEE			
To Ellensburg		$5.00	$9.50
To Yakima		7.50	14.25
FROM ELLENSBURG			
To Yakima		$5.00	$9.50

30 lbs. of baggage free.
Cab furnished to and from Seattle terminal.

SCHEDULE

EAST BOUND		WEST BOUND	
LEAVE SEATTLE	10:45 A.M.	LEAVE YAKIMA	2:00 P.M.
ARRIVE WENATCHEE	12:00 A.M.	ARRIVE ELLENSBURG	2:20 P.M.
LEAVE WENATCHEE	12:10 A.M.	LEAVE ELLENSBURG	2:35 P.M.
ARRIVE ELLENSBURG	12:30 A.M.	ARRIVE WENATCHEE	2:55 P.M.
LEAVE ELLENSBURG	12:35 A.M.	LEAVE WENATCHEE	3:10 P.M.
ARRIVE YAKIMA	12:55 P.M.	ARRIVE SEATTLE	4:25 P.M.

Express carried at rate of 15c per pound or 200 cubic inches by bulk with a minimum of 50c per package. Parcels must be left and picked up at company's offices.

Schedules and fares subject to change without notice.

Schedule 6-C.

Alaska-Washington Airways of Puget Sound, one of the three branches of the holding company, offered handy cards printed with their land plane schedule.

company to operate between Canadian points. H.B. Olson, president of Gray Line Tours in Vancouver was principal stockholder and president of the company.

The Puget Sound unit began operation between Seattle and Victoria on August 19, 1929, later extending service to Tacoma and Olympia. A direct service between Seattle and Vancouver was also opened, and would be under Alaska-Washington of Puget Sound. The board of directors of the new holding company was to consist of twenty-one influential businessmen of both Canada and the United States. (This was later reduced to eleven).

With an infusion of capital from additional stock sales, the company was ordering additional equipment and planning an operating schedule to Juneau and Ketchikan during the summer, coordinating the first arrival in time to take advantage of the increase in aerial traffic created by the beginning of Alaska's tourist season.

The logo of Alaska-Washington Airways was printed in color on baggage stickers to promote the air service.

784

egular Air Service Between
eattle - Victoria - Vancouver
Luxurious New Seaplanes...

L Alaska - Washington Airways cabin seaplanes
regular service daily between Seattle, Victoria and
A cruise of just forty minutes, soaring gracefully
land waters, carries you between Seattle and Vic-
n Victoria and Vancouver is a matter of only 45

or pleasure travel between these cities, this is the
speedy, delightful, conserving of your time, con-

laska leave Seattle at 8:00 a.m. on Tuesday and
ch week, arriving in Ketchikan and Juneau the
n. Seattle-Victoria-Vancouver planes operate sev-
ly on convenient schedule.

/AY AND ROUND TRIP FARES
(SUBJECT TO CHANGE WITHOUT NOTICE)

AND		Seattle	Victoria	Vancouver	Ketchikan	Wrangell	Petersburg	Juneau
O.W.			$ 7.65	$14.75	$75.00	$90.00	$90.00	$105.00
R.T.			15.00	28.00	142.50	171.50	171.50	199.50
O.W.		$ 7.65		7.65				
R.T.		15.00		15.00				
O.W.		14.75	7.65					
R.T.		28.00	15.00					
O.W.		75.00				20.00	22.50	35.00
R.T.		142.50				35.00	40.00	65.00
O.W.		90.00			20.00		7.50	20.00
R.T.		171.50			35.00		12.00	35.00
O.W.		90.00			22.50	7.50		20.00
R.T.		171.50			40.00	12.00		35.00
O.W.		105.00			35.00	20.00	20.00	
R.T.		199.50			65.00	35.00	35.00	

ormation inquire at any leading hotel or travel agency

LOS ANGELES   SEATTLE
707 So. Hill St.   418 University Street   VICTORIA
  MAin 2840   756 Yates Street
                                 Victoria 2900
et

BOEING FIELD
TICKET OFFICE

Lon Brennan Collection

▲ *1930. Schedule advertising the fares and flights of Alaska-Washington Airways reflects the business-like manner in which the company carried out its effort to establish a scheduled air service.*

▶ *Gordon K. McKenzie went to work for Alaska-Washington Airways in July of 1929. He was soon flying a Fairchild 71, NC 115H, that was transferred to Canadian registration, CF-AJP, under Alaska-Washington Airways of British Columbia, Limited, and named* Victorian. *He flew it daily between Victoria and Vancouver, British Columbia in his navy-type uniform. Some years later he would be well-known in Alaska as a bush pilot.*

Tom Croson Collection

    Pilot R.E. "Bob" Ellis and flight mechanic Frank A. Hatcher departed Seattle at 8:13 A.M. Friday, April 25, 1930, in the new seven-place Lockheed Vega *Taku*, NC 102W. The pilot, flying in beautiful weather, landed the float plane at Ketchikan after a five hour and thirty-two minute nonstop flight. Accompanying the pilot was his bride of a few weeks, the former Margaret Roehr whom he had married on March 8. W.E. Wynn, general operations manager for the company was also a passenger from Seattle, as was Lyle C. Woods, coming to Ketchikan to serve as local manager for Alaska-Washington Airways, and A.B. "Cot" Hayes who was to be in charge of the Alaska division of the company and would have an office in Juneau.

    The *Taku* was away for Juneau at 3:00 P.M., following an hour's halt for lunch.

In Seattle, use of the hand starter on the Wasp engine of an Alaska-Washington Vega is demonstrated. A forceful winding of the two-handed crank brought a small steel wheel up to high speed. When the crank was removed and the engaging lever pulled, the inertia contained in the spinning wheel turned the engine over two or three times to start it running.

Juneau 1930. Alaska-Washington Airways flight mechanic Frank Hatcher with seaplane **Taku** *in Juneau, Alaska.*

1930. Pilot Robert E. Ellis and his flight mechanic, Frank Hatcher, stand on the 4650 Edo float of the **Taku.**

Stopping at Petersburg to drop off a passenger, salesman Albert Brown, the pilot landed on the waters of Gastineau Channel at the capital city at 6:05 P.M. and with Bob Ellis and his wife, mechanic Frank Hatcher, Operations manager Wynn and Division manager Hayes, debarked from the plane. The Vega had been delivered from the factory to Seattle on April 19 and made a pretty sight with its color design of dark blue with cream-colored trim. The upper surface of the wing was trimmed in red. (see Juneau—1930, Chapter 54).

Lyle Woods set about establishing a headquarters for Alaska-Washington Airways in Ketchikan, for a second Lockheed Vega to be based at the city was expected shortly. The new hydroport, recently built on the Tongass Highway north of town, would be an asset for it had a ramp that sloped down to the water where planes could be parked, or brought ashore if necessary. The *Taku*, NC 102W, was back in Ketchikan on the afternoon of Monday, April 28, 1930, landing at 3:40 P.M. after making an hour's stop at Petersburg and also one at Wrangell. Along with the company employees W.E. Wynn and Juneau agent Larry Parks, the *Taku* carried R.H. Stock and C.R. Wright from the capital city. The two men, contractors from Aberdeen, Washington, were bidding on an additional road construction project at Ketchikan. The *Taku* took off at 9:30 A.M. of the following day to return to Juneau.

Anscel Eckmann made his first trip of the season to Alaska in the Lockheed Vega *Juneau*, NC 432E, leaving Seattle at 7:00 A.M. Saturday, May 17, 1930, under charter to Gilbert Skinner, president of the Alaska-Pacific Salmon Corporation, who was making a round of the company's canneries in Southeastern Alaska. Mrs. Skinner, Mr. and Mrs. Larry Ives and Marion Cummings were also aboard the blue and cream-painted float plane. Bad weather enroute had forced two lengthy stops, with the plane arriving late Saturday night.

Taking off from the Sunny Point cannery at 10:00 A.M. Sunday, Eckmann planned on stops at Chomly, Rose Inlet and Kake, before reaching Juneau to overnight. Eckmann returned with Skinner and his party to the Ketchikan area at 6:55 P.M. Monday, May 19, to remain overnight. Taking the party aboard the following day, the pilot departed the Sunny Point cannery on the southeast coast of Prince of Wales Island at 12:35 P.M. on Tuesday, for a nonstop flight to Seattle. He covered over 2000 miles in a period of four days.

Gorst Air Transport, Incorporated, was again planning a summer's flying in Alaska. Pilot Clayton Scott, with flight mechanic Frank Wadman, was away from Seattle at 7:15 A.M. May 19, 1930, with Mrs. C.M. Taylor, sister of Vern Gorst, as the only passenger. She was returning to her home in Ketchikan from a Hawaiian vacation. Piloting Gorst's Boeing B-1E, NC 115E, flying boat, Scott landed three hours later at Alert Bay, British Columbia, to refuel. With servicing completed, the pilot took off again and landed at Ketchikan after flying for an additional four hours. Scott reached the City float at 3:20 P.M. They had flown in rainy weather all the way, but found it sunny at their destination. Scott immediately placed a box ad in the *Ketchikan Alaska Chronicle* advertising "Fishing Parties, Charter Trips and Passenger Flights." The pilot could be contacted at the Ingersoll Hotel, which boasted thirty-two rooms with bath at rates from $1.50 to $4.00.

The pilot got instant results for he was away the next day, Tuesday, May 20, 1930, on a forty-five minute flight to Craig, soon returning, with an equal amount of air time on the way back. He was away again that same day for Prince Rupert, landing at the Canadian coastal city one hour and ten minutes later. Remaining overnight, Scott returned to Ketchikan the next morning, shaving five minutes from his outbound time. He made a ten-minute local hop on his return.

Pilot Bob Ellis and his flight mechanic, Frank Hatcher, had been doing considerable flying out of Juneau with the Vega *Taku*, NC 102W. An emergency flight from the capital city to Victoria, British Columbia, departed at 3:00 A.M. Wednesday, May 21, carrying William Strong to the bedside of his critically-ill wife, stopping at Ketchikan to refuel. General Manager A.B. "Cot" Hayes left the plane there to await its return northbound. Ellis and Hatcher landed in Victoria at 2:15 P.M. that afternoon (Ketchikan time), going on to Seattle after dropping their passenger. The pair were back in Ketchikan with the *Taku* the following day at 4:30 P.M., continuing on to Juneau at 6:15 P.M. Passengers from Seattle were Mrs. Hatcher and her daughter, the mother and sister of the flight mechanic, who were on their way to Juneau for a visit. "Cot" Hayes boarded at Ketchikan to return to the capital city.

On Friday, May 23, the *Taku* was back in Ketchikan at 5:00 P.M. bringing Doctor Harry Carlos DeVighne. Following a two-hour visit with Doctor S.C. Shurick, the Juneau physician returned home on the plane. Ellis and Hatcher had picked up three passengers at Wrangell on the southbound flight and expected to stop at Petersburg and Wrangell on their return flight to Juneau, picking up passengers.

1930. Gorst Air Transport Boeing B-1E, NC 115E, takes Ketchikan resident Stanley Adams and some friends in to Ella Lake to set up camp for a fishing holiday.

Stuart Adams Collection

The Gorst Air Transport Boeing, NC 115E, crewed by Clayton Scott and Frank Wadman, was hard at work. On Saturday, May 24, 1930, the pair began a series of round trips from Ketchikan to Prince Rupert, British Columbia, making four that day, taking an hour and five minutes each way. They flew a trip out of their base to Lake Ella to drop some sport fishermen who would camp there. The lake was a thirty-minute flight out of Ketchikan each way. Returning from there, Scott took off for Prince Rupert again, to remain overnight. He now had an agent, Stanley Adams, in the J.R. Heckman & Company store, where all the fishermen bought their lines and lures. He advertised "Not Flying Fish, but Flying Fishermen!"

788

◄ Stanley Adams, the Gorst agent in Ketchikan, seated on the lower wing panel of NC 115E at a favorite fishing spot in 1930.

▼ 1930. With the tide out, Gorst Air Transport Boeing B-1E flying boat rests on its mahogany hull on the new hydroport ramp a bit north of the city proper in Ketchikan, Alaska.

Gorst Plane. At. New Air Port.

Ketchikan's New Air Port.

Completed in the spring of 1930, the new Ketchikan hydroport, built with matching funds from the Territory and the community, made it easy for Clayton Scott and Frank Wadman, his mechanic, to get the Boeing flying boat out of the water.

789

The following morning Scott returned to Ketchikan to fly another round trip to Prince Rupert, going again to Ella Lake in the Boeing B-1E, and returning to his base. He made one more round trip to the Canadian city that day. On Monday, May 26, the Gorst pilot made a twenty-minute local hop before taking off the bay again and flying to a landing near the new $12,000 city hydroport, with its ramp sloping to the water. The plane was positioned on the ramp, tail toward the land, and blocks placed beneath the hull to hold the plane level. When the tide went out the plane was poised, high and dry on the new airport for a photograph, and inspection of the hull. The next morning, Sunday, when the tide refloated the Boeing, Scott flew it back to the City float from which he made two fifteen-minute passenger hops. At both Wrangell and Petersburg work was underway on a new hydroport for airplanes. The Wrangell port was half-finished. They were being built under contract, to be paid for by the municipalities and the Territory, on a fifty-fifty basis.

Clayton Scott and Frank Wadman were off for Mirror Lake on Revillagigedo Island on Wednesday, May 28, 1930. One of the sport fishermen carried in, Steve Selig, slipped on a sunken log when pushing the plane off and fell backward into the lake, getting a good wetting. His companions thought it hilarious. They all made a good catch and returned in the plane the same day, Scott flying for one hour on the round trip.

On a fishing trip to one of the lakes near Ketchikan in Gorst's flying boat, Clayton Scott sits above the cockpit while Stanley Adams, left, and two friends stand before the wing. Adams, employed at Heckman Hardware, was also the Gorst agent in the community.

Stuart Adams Collection

Clayton Scott, the pilot of the Boeing flying boat, sits on edge of hatch while Stanley Adams (on the right of the group) and two fellow fishermen help in getting the boat moored in one of the nearby lakes that teemed with eager trout.

Stuart Adams Collection

On Friday, May 30, 1930, the Boeing was again away on a sport fishing trip, this time to Karta River. They returned to Ketchikan the same day with a nice catch. The Boeing was a good piece of equipment for this kind of work. On the return, the pilot was away for Bell Island, to remain overnight. The Alaska-Washington Airways *Taku* had come down from Wrangell to Ketchikan that same afternoon, with Bob Ellis and Frank Hatcher, returning to Juneau by way of Petersburg.

Scott left Bell Island Saturday morning, May 31, and flew back to Ketchikan, taking forty minutes, equal to his down time. He took the Boeing B-1E to Prince Rupert later in the day, flying it in one hour. They remained overnight, and it was here that they met Edward Joseph Augustus "Paddy" Burke, who was headed for Atlin in the Cassiar, with a Junkers F-13, CF-AMX, with an L-5 motor. The plane, on floats, was owned by Air Land Manufacturing Company of Vancouver, British Columbia. It had been delivered there, on wheels, on Wednesday, April 24, 1929, by George E. King and Charles A. Anderson, sales pilots for the Junkers Company in New York. (Ironically, Charles Anderson, later in the flying business in Ketchikan, was to die in a fiery crash on April 9, 1936, near the city).

Burke was a thirty-nine-year-old pilot with many years of experience in the Royal Flying Corps, beginning his training in 1915 and serving through the balance of World War I as well as later. He had flown the same Boeing boat, NC 115E, that Scott was flying, to Juneau and back in March of 1929. At that time it was named *Thunderbird*. Scott was intrigued by a small sign posted in the Junkers by Burke that read, "When I lands, I sleeps; when I sleeps, I eat my breakfast—maybe." This was to prove somewhat prophetic for the Canadian pilot later.

Burke was heavily loaded with a total of two persons, freight and camping gear aboard, and was unable to take off for Ketchikan. Scott circled around overhead while the Canadian pilot tried several times to get off the glassy water on his wide floats without success. Scott landed and took the other pilot's flight mechanic, a German named Emil Kading, aboard the Boeing B-1E on Sunday, June 1, when he made the one-hour flight back to Ketchikan from Prince Rupert. Burke followed in the Junkers, CF-AMX, going on to Juneau that same day. (see Juneau—1930, Chapter 54). Scott made a thirty-minute round trip to White River on Revillagigedo Island that same day, making seven passenger hops in the two hours following his return from there. He made a one-hour round-trip flight to "Gill Lake" (Colloquial), ending the flying for the day.

Clayton Scott was away from Ketchikan at 9:15 A.M. Monday, June 2, 1930, on a round trip to Hyder, Alaska in the Gorst plane. Taking Attorney A.H. Ziegler of Ketchikan, Donald E. Martin, deputy United States marshal at Hyder, and Mrs. Martin and Mrs. Alex Frazier of Hyder, the pilot found the weather fine both ways, and landed back at Ketchikan at 4:45 P.M. Attorney Ziegler returned on the plane.

Scott flew a round trip to Bell Island on Wednesday, June 4, taking thirty-five minutes each way. On his return he took off for a second trip to the same destination, but after flying for twenty minutes, he was back on the water at Ketchikan. The weather was terrible and he could not get through. He completed the aborted trip the following day, June 5, also making a round trip to Petersburg in the afternoon, flying one hour and twenty minutes on the way north and taking an additional ten minutes over that on his return to Ketchikan.

A charter over Revillagigedo Island was on, for the Zellerbach corporation, for the purpose of determining a possible route for an electrical transmission line from Manzanita Bay to Ketchikan. Taking off on the evening of June 6 with Wendell Dawson and William Fromholz, employees of the paper company, Clayton Scott accomplished in one hour's flying time what would have taken the two men five or six days by any other means of travel. The

791

1930. Gorst Air Transport, Incorporated Boeing B-1E, NC 115E, at the Public Dock in Petersburg, Alaska. The local boys found pilot Clayton Scott and his flying boat a never-ending source of interest.

pilot was back at 6:15 P.M. Other passengers aboard were Mrs. Wendell Dawson and Stanley Adams.

Alaska-Washington Airways Vega, *Taku*, had left Juneau on June 5, stopping at Tulsequah on the Taku River to pick up Bill Strong and fly him to Victoria, British Columbia again; his wife was reportedly dying. Ellis and Hatcher went on to Seattle from there with the plane. They departed Lake Union the next day at 1:30 P.M. Friday, June 6, 1930, to arrive at Ketchikan five hours later, at 6:30 P.M. (Ketchikan times). Carrying no passengers, it had been a speedy trip. An hour later, still without passengers, they were away for Juneau.

Scott flew the Boeing B-1E to Reflection Lake on Revillagigedo Island on June 7, with the Cunningham-Waltz party. Cunningham was with the Pacific Marine Supply Co. of Seattle. He returned the same day, taking forty-five minutes of flying each way. The pilot made a thirty-minute passenger hop before flying a round trip to take a fishing party out to Gill Lake. He returned for the party the following day, Sunday, June 6, and was able to bring them in. It was his worst trip of the summer, raining and storming, and on his return flight the Boeing heaved its way through the turbulent skies in poor visibility. He was glad to get down at Ketchikan.

Waiting through the next day for the storm to blow itself out, Scott made a twenty-minute round trip to Metlakatla on Annette Island on Tuesday, June 10, 1930. On the following day he made a round trip from Ketchikan to Prince Rupert, taking two hours in the air. That afternoon he flew the Boeing B-1E to Wrangell and back, with two hours and fifteen minutes of air time. On Thursday he was away again, going to Hyder and returning, to go out again on a flight to Dall Bay, Loring and back to his base at Ketchikan.

On Friday, June 13, Scott took the flying boat to Dawson Lake and return, an hour and one-half trip. He went out again that day to take an advance party for RKO Studios on a flight about the area, flying for two hours and twenty minutes. The company was preparing to film *The Silver Horde* based on Rex Beach's novel, and much of the movie was to be shot at Loring. Clayton Scott returned to Ketchikan, also making a fifteen-minute passenger hop that afternoon.

Scott and his flight mechanic, Frank Wadman, departed Ketchikan in the Boeing, NC 115E, on Friday, June 13, going to Hyder to remain overnight. Returning to Ketchikan on Saturday, they completed a round trip to Bell Island before taking off for Manzanita Lake with a fishing party. Staying overnight at the lake, they flew to Dawson Lake and back to Ketchikan, making another round trip to Manzanita Lake before ending the day's flying.

On Monday, June 16, 1930, Scott was out early, cleaning out the Boeing and polishing it where needed, for the pilot's girl friend was coming in on the steamer *S.S. Yukon*, and he planned to go out in the plane to meet her. It had all been previously arranged with Captain Anderson, a flying enthusiast who often took a ride with Owen Meals in Valdez whenever his vessel arrived there. Anderson brought the *Yukon* to a stop somewhat south of Ketchikan when he sighted the plane approaching. Scott landed the Boeing and taxied up to the ship. Myrtle E. Smith, a Seattle schoolteacher, was placed in a cargo sling and hoisted over the side where Wadman and Scott, frantically fending the plane away from the vessel's hull near the bow, awaited. Myrt was carefully lowered to the Boeing's hull and entered the cabin through the hatch; her baggage passed after her. Scott, trying to push the plane away from the ship's hull against the wind and tide, was unsuccessful, only getting a cracked windshield in the process. Captain Anderson, seeing the difficulty, carefully backed the large steamer away from the plane, setting it free for the pilot to start the engine and take off. Scott returned to Ketchikan where some of Myrt's schoolteacher friends awaited. The girls were traveling together in Alaska that summer.

Clayton Scott made a quick trip to Seattle, leaving on the same day Myrtle Smith arrived in Ketchikan, Monday, June 16, 1930. He was under charter to two men traveling from there to the Puget Sound city. Stopping at Alert Bay on the way down, he made it in seven hours of flying time. Scott returned the next day, again stopping at Alert Bay for fuel, but flying for eight hours and forty-five minutes to a landing at Ketchikan. The tired pilot was out the next day, Thursday, June 19, on his way to Juneau, with a stop at Wrangell, flying for two hours and thirty-five minutes. He left the capital city that same day with Governor Parks, again fueling at Wrangell on his way to Ketchikan. He went on to Prince Rupert, British Columbia before overnighting, making it in one hour additional flying time.

Scott returned to Ketchikan the next morning, Friday, June 20, 1930. He made two passenger hops about the city on his return. The weekend fishermen were ready to go out to the lakes for trout, and Scott went out with a party on Saturday morning to Lake Manzanita, one of the favorites, returning later in the day. On Sunday, June 22, he took a party to Mirror Lake, returning to Ketchikan to go once again to Manzanita. With his fisherman all home, he took the Boeing B-1E to Wrangell, overnighting there.

Monday morning, the pilot left there on a roundabout flight, stopping at Petersburg, Sitka, Windom Bay and then in to Juneau. He left there that afternoon, to stop at Petersburg, Pybus Bay and back again to Petersburg to overnight at the fishing center. He had been in the

A Ketchikan resident grins in appreciation of a successful fishing expedition to one of the land-locked lakes in the vicinity in the Boeing flying boat with Clayton Scott. Before the airplane came into use, many of these lakes were unknown and unreachable.

air for four hours and fifteen minutes that day, making seven stops. Scott returned to Ketchikan the following day, Tuesday, June 24. He made a ten-minute trip from the Ketchikan hydroport, taking off later in the day to fly to Prince Rupert where he overnighted. He was on his way to Seattle to pick up Starr Calvert, president of the Peril Strait Packing Company and treasurer of the San Juan Fishing and Packing Company, to make a survey of his fishing interests in Alaska. Scott left Prince Rupert on Wednesday morning, to complete his trip, refueling at Alert Bay before continuing on to Seattle. The entire flight from Ketchikan took eight hours and forty minutes of flying time. It was a busy season for the pilot and plane. He now had a total flying time of 1247:55 hours.

A new aviation service for Ketchikan and Southeastern Alaska had been announced on June 18, 1930 in Seattle. Pioneer Airways, Incorporated, organized by Aberdeen, Washington contractor C.R. Wright, Vern C.Gorst and Roy F.Jones, had ordered two factory-new Stinson SM-8A four-place monoplanes through Washington Aircraft and Transport Corporation in Seattle, and the first was ready to fly north. Wright expected to get the contract to build an additional length of road from Ketchikan, while Gorst had always been interested in aerial transportation as well as Alaska. He currently had a flying boat working out of Ketchikan under his own company. Roy Jones was no stranger to Ketchikan, having in 1922 brought the first airplane north to work out of the city. He had subsequently lived and worked in Ketchikan until the previous fall, at which time he had taken his family to Seattle. Jones expected to bring them north again in the near future.

Pioneer Airways SM-8A Stinson Sea Pigeon, *NC 935W.*

The first Stinson, *Sea Pigeon*, NC 935W, arrived at Ketchikan on the evening of Saturday, June 21, 1930, with company pilot Loren H. McHenry, former West Coast Air Transport Company pilot, landing the float-equipped plane on Tongass Narrows to taxi in to the City float. C.R.Wright and Roy Jones were passengers on the flight up, which had taken eight hours of flying time in beautiful visibility, although plagued by headwinds. A stop of two hours had been made at Alert Bay. The following afternoon, Sunday, the pilot had taken C.R. Wright, president of Wright Construction Company (also president of Pioneer Airways and its largest investor); R.H. Stock, construction superintendent for Wright on the Tongass Highway project; and Charles W. Wilson, resident engineer for the Bureau of Public Roads, on an aerial inspection of the Ward Cove to Mud Bay road, a distance of 2.97 miles in length. Bids on the project were to be opened on July 16, with work estimated to begin about the middle of August. (Who could foresee then that there would one day be a multi-million dollar pulp mill in Mud Bay, at the end of this road?)

Roy Jones had placed a box ad in the *Ketchikan Alaska Chronicle* advertising "Sea-plane for Charter—$40 per hour. Student Instruction—$35 per hour." Roy Jones was the local manager for the new company and handled the general business affairs in Ketchikan, working out of the Ingersoll Hotel. He was once again back in the aviation business.

Pioneer Airways *Sea Pigeon* was not long idle. Loren McHenry departed Ketchikan at noon on Tuesday, June 24, taking Assistant District Forester B.F. Heintzleman to Juneau, and Jack Otness to Petersburg. Roy Jones was also aboard. The plane arrived in Juneau at 4:30 P.M. the same day. McHenry and Jones left the next morning in the *Sea Pigeon* to return to Ketchikan.

795

McHenry was busy on Thursday, June 26, 1930, flying *Sea Pigeon* to Noyes Island on a trip for the New England Fish Company, departing Ketchikan at 11:00 A.M. Returning from there, the pilot took off at 2:00 P.M. for Mirror Lake, taking C.R. Wright and W.A. Bates for a fishing trip. While the two men did their best to outwit the finny residents, McHenry and Roy Jones took the plane on a survey expedition into and around the Unuk River country, cruising for an hour at about 10,000 feet. They were principally interested in the location of lakes on which to establish prospectors' bases; there had been an interest in this area. One was located on the Blue River with good approaches, and a number of small emergency lakes were located. The pair returned in the Stinson to Mirror Lake to pick up Wright and Bates for Ketchikan, both having big catches of fine trout.

The *Sea Pigeon* made a flight to Klawock Lake on Prince of Wales Island the next day, taking Arthur Skelhorne and Arthur Watson as passengers. Skelhorne, a mining engineer, was to inspect mining properties there owned by Watson, as well as other of Maxfield Dalton's properties. Pioneer Airways services were temporarily suspended when, on the morning of Sunday, June 29, 1930, McHenry overshot a landing on Reflection Lake, running into a log jam at the end of the lake. One pontoon was badly broken and the other one damaged, and the plane came to rest with its tail high in the air. McHenry was

Courtesy of Gwen Jones Whyte

▲ *Pioneer Airways* Sea Pigeon *on Mirror Lake in 1930. Roy Jones, company manager is to the right.*

◄ *June 26, 1930. Piloted by Loren McHenry. Claude R. Wright and Bill Bates exhibit a fine catch of trout before Pioneer Airways Stinson SM-8A,* Sea Pigeon, *at Mirror Lake near Ketchikan. Wright, who headed a construction company building an extension of the Tongass Highway out of the city, was the heavy shareholder in Pioneer Airways.*

Jim Hickey

June 1930. Pioneer Airways Stinson SM-8A **Sea Pigeon** *on Mirror Lake out of Ketchikan. Left to Right: William A. Bates; Loren H. McHenry, pilot; and Roy Jones.*

Courtesy of Gwen Jones Whyte

Pioneer Airways Stinson SM-8A **Northbird,** *NC 991W, on Edo 3300 floats. The Stinsons were black with orange wing and striping and upholstered in gray. They were powered with Lycoming engines of 210 horse-power.*

Stuart Adams Collection

alone in the plane, returning to the lake after taking one fishing party back to Ketchikan and now returning for a second party. He was uninjured.

When the *Sea Pigeon* failed to return, Roy Jones had contacted Clayton Scott and the two men flew to the lake that same Sunday in the Gorst Boeing, where they picked up McHenry and the fishermen.

Pioneer Airways was awaiting a decision by insurance adjusters before repairing the Stinson SM-8A. It was relatively undamaged except for the floats and one wingtip.

797

On June 29, 1930, pilot Loren McHenry overshot a landing at Reflection Lake in the Sea Pigeon, *wiping out the floats. The plane was later repaired by a ground party and flown out on Friday, August 1, 1930 by pilot Jim Dodson.*

Courtesy of Lloyd Jarman

Clayton Scott had picked up Starr Calvert in Seattle for the charter to Alaska, departing there on June 26, 1930. He also picked up a new flight mechanic from the Gorst shops, John Selby. Frank Wadman was no longer with him. Scott landed at Campbell River on the east side of Vancouver Island after two hours of flight. The next stop, after an hour's flying, was Alert Bay. The ceiling was coming down and they were having trouble with fog. They went on to Bull Harbor, on the north tip of Vancouver Island at Hope Island. Taking off from here they continued on to Namu. Landing on the water because of fog, they taxied on the step for a time as the water was still and smooth. One hour and one-half after departure, they arrived at Namu to tie up and spend the first night. The following morning, Friday, June 27, 1930, Scott made a thirty-minute flight in the Boeing B-1E to Bella Bella, followed by a longer flight of three hours to Ketchikan. That afternoon the pilot took Starr Calvert from there to Peril Strait, between Chichagof and Baranof Islands. They returned to Ketchikan that same day—a flying time of two hours and thirty minutes each way. Scott was still in Ketchikan on Sunday, June 29, luckily, when Jones contacted him regarding the missing *Sea Pigeon*. In bringing McHenry and his fishing party back to Ketchikan, Scott had additionally flown two shuttles between Reflection Lake and Bell Island, to get all the party to some place where he could get a takeoff area long enough to haul them all in to Ketchikan in one load.

Scott was away in the Boeing B-1E, NC 115E, on Monday, June 30, 1930, flying from Ketchikan to George Inlet, to Dall Bay and back to Ketchikan, taking thirty minutes on the short hops. That same day he flew to Reflection Lake and Bell Island, before returning to base. This gave him another hour and twenty minutes for the day, finishing up the month of June. It had been a full one.

Alaska-Washington Airways had been doing a lot of work out of Juneau with the Lockheed Vega *Taku*, NC 102W, flown by Bob Ellis and flight mechanic Frank Hatcher. The company was now sending up their Vega, Model 5B, a seven-place, blue and cream-painted monoplane named *Skagway*, NC 103W. Mounted on Edo 4650 floats, it arrived at Ketchikan at 4:45 P.M. on Saturday, June 28, 1930, enroute to Juneau. Flown by Anscel Eckmann, with flight mechanic Brian Harland, the plane carried J.L. Carman, Jr., president of the company; passenger Watkin Davies of Stockton, California; E.B. Kellens of Topeka, Kansas; and Max Smith of Skagway. The plane departed at 6:00 P.M., taking two additional passengers aboard for the capital city, Mr. and Mrs. Ralph Bartholomew. Bartholomew was the new agent for the airways in Ketchikan.

Eckmann was back Monday, June 30, on his way to Seattle, landing at Ketchikan at 9:30 A.M. to refuel. Mr. and Mrs. Bartholomew, who had made the round trip to Juneau, got off the *Skagway*. Gilbert Skinner, who had returned to the city on Saturday from an inspection tour of the Alaska-Pacific Salmon Corporation canneries in Southeastern Alaska, joined Joe Carman, Jr. in the cabin of the *Skagway* for the trip to Seattle. Others aboard were Davies and Kellens, making the round trip out of Seattle, and Larry Parks who had boarded at Juneau. Rain and bad weather had plagued the pilot on the flight from Juneau. Carman was promising a Ketchikan-based plane by July 2, in time for the Fourth of July.

The filming of *The Silver Horde* by RKO was now underway, with the studio troupe on location at Loring the first week of July, 1930. Fifty tons of equipment, including the RCA sound recording truck were on location with eleven boats, three scows and the Alaska-Washington Airways plane, *Skagway*, under charter to the movie company. Bright weather prevailed throughout the area.

Clayton Scott was out in the Boeing B-1E on Wednesday, July 2, for a full day of flying. Making a round trip from Ketchikan to Reflection Lake, he was off again on a brief flight to the *S.S. Explorer* and return. He next flew a round trip to Sulzer, a mining location on Prince of Wales Island at the head of Hetta Inlet. The pilot's next flight was again to the *S.S. Explorer*, going on from there to Wrangell and Petersburg. From the latter stop, he returned to Ketchikan by way of Craig and Waterfall, ending the day with a total flying time of six hours and fifteen minutes.

The following day, he was away to the north, bound for Cordova, taking schoolteacher Myrtle Smith as his only passenger. She was on a visit to her sister, Mrs. Roy Douglas, who lived there. Scott's flight mechanic, John Selby, was also aboard. Flying from Ketchikan to Petersburg to Port Althorp, on the north coast of Chichagof Island, took three hours and thirty minutes of flying time. Departing there in the flying boat, the trio flew up the Gulf of Alaska to Yakutat, and then to Cordova, taking another four hours and fifteen minutes in the air. Landing on Eyak Lake near the city, where he had based the Gorst Keystone Loening Air Yacht, *Alaskan*, the previous year, Scott had made the flight in one day and was in time for the Fourth of July. He flew out of there for a week, not knowing then that he was to lose the B-1E following a forced landing on the way south on July 10. (see Cordova—1930, Chapter 55). The Boeing, NC 115E, was officially christened *Nugget* in Cordova on July 6, 1930.

In Ketchikan, a brief visit by the Alaska-Washington Airways *Taku*, flown by Bob Ellis and Frank Hatcher, brought Division Captain M.J. O'Connor, assistant agent of the U.S. Bureau of Fisheries, and H.W. Terhune, executive officer of the Alaska Game Commission, from Juneau on an inspection trip through the district. They all returned to the capital city at 7:00 P.M. Saturday, July 5, 1930. Cannery operators had reported the fish as "hitting good."

The *Skagway*, NC 103W, had returned to Ketchikan as promised. Now flown by pilot Robin "Pat" Renehan, with flight mechanic Frank J. Wadman, the plane made a charter flight from Ketchikan to Juneau for Gilbert Skinner on Monday, July 7. Wadman, who had previously served as flight mechanic with Clayton Scott in the Gorst Boeing, had left the company, only recently returning to Alaska to take a similar position with Alaska-Washington Airways.

The *Skagway* was back in Ketchikan to take Gilbert Skinner to Manzanita Bay, and from there across Revillagigedo and north along the Cleveland Peninsula. Accompanied by Attorney Lester O. Gore, Skinner had departed Ketchikan the afternoon of Friday, July 11. The fish packer's family, Mrs. Skinner and her two children, Sally and Ned, arrived from Seattle on the *S.S. Alaska* early the following morning. The family left with Gilbert Skinner at 3:15 P.M. Monday, July 14, in the *Skagway*, NC 103W, for a tour of the company's canneries in Southeastern Alaska. Renehan and Wadman returned with the plane at 10:00 A.M. Wednesday, bringing in mechanic John Selby from Juneau.

A group of four New England Fish Company officials flying to Ketchikan to meet a second plane, the *Taku* of Alaska-Washington Airways, to travel to Yakutat and Cordova as part of their inspection trip of company properties, was involved in a bad crash at Butedale, British Columbia, on Thursday, July 17, 1930. A.L. Hager, western manager of the New England Fish Company, R.R. Payne, production manager of canneries, William J. Rich and Louis B. Goodspeed, Boston directors of the company, had departed Vancouver, British Columbia on Monday, July 14, in a Dominion Airways, Limited, seaplane flown by pilot G.S. Jones-Evans with a flight mechanic. New England Fish Company and its subsidiaries controlled eighteen canneries and three cold storage plants in British Columbia, and six cold storage plants and three canneries in Alaska. It was while circling down to land at the lake, just above the plant of the Canadian Fishing Company, Limited (a subsidiary) at Butedale, that the plane, caught in a downdraft, struck the side of the mountain among the trees. Hager and Rich suffered cuts and bruises; Goodspeed a fractured thigh. The pilot, catapulted through the windshield, was uninjured but his mechanic sustained fractured ribs and a broken breastbone in the 1:00 P.M. crash. The plane was a total loss.

Hager was brought to Prince Rupert in a Canadian Fisheries Patrol flying boat, which returned to Butedale with Doctor W.T. Kergin, who attended the injured. They were all brought in to the General Hospital at Prince Rupert the following day on the oil tanker *Gardena*.

Hager, Rich and Payne, with only minor injuries, arrived in Ketchikan on Saturday night, July 19, 1930. After inspecting the local New England Fish Company plant, Hager and Rich returned to Prince Rupert on Sunday night, while production manager Payne, who was uninjured, continued on to Juneau on the steamer *Aleutian* on Monday, to complete the inspection trip of the Alaska canneries.

Alaska-Washington Airways Lockheed Vega *Ketchikan*, NC 657E, an earlier five-place model, had been returned to the factory for rebuild, as well as conversion to a Model 5B seven-place float plane. Now painted a deep-orange, and renamed *Wrangell*, it was expected in Seattle from California on Monday, July 21. With Robin "Pat" Renehan as pilot, and Frank Wadman as flight mechanic, the new-looking plane was away from Seattle at 8:20 A.M.

◄ July 18, 1930. Robin "Pat" Renehan, seated on wing above cockpit, picks up part of RKO movie troupe at Loring with NC 657E, to bring them to Ketchikan. They had been filming The Silver Horde.

▼ July 18, 1930. Robin "Pat" Renehan, wearing his beret, stands on the wing of the Lockheed Vega, Ketchikan, *with members of the RKO movie troupe about the Alaska-Washington Airways plane. The pilot had made three flights, bringing in the movie people from Loring to Ketchikan.*

Alaska Historical Library

Alaska Historical Library

Friday, July 18, 1930, with Larry Parks,the company's Juneau agent, and two passengers for Juneau: Mrs. Clara D. Poitras and W.H. Gannett, a newspaper man from Maine. Stopping at Vancouver and Nanaimo, British Columbia, the *Wrangell*, NC 657E, arrived at Ketchikan at 6:00 P.M. that same evening. The Vega, a sister ship of the *Taku* and *Skagway*, was the third of five such Lockheeds to be delivered to Alaska-Washington Airways during the year. The fourth plane, which would probably be named *Sitka*, was scheduled for delivery on July 22.

On his arrival, the pilot made three flights to Loring to bring the RKO movie troupe in from location. The following day, Saturday, the *Wrangell* flew a round trip to Prince Rupert, returning to Ketchikan at 1:00 P.M. before departing for Juneau to pick up Mr. and Mrs. Gilbert Skinner, who had gone north the first of the week on the *Skagway*, NC 103W.

Renehan and Wadman picked up Gilbert Skinner, Juneau attorney R.E. Robertson, and H.Y. Baird, Seattle representative of the Burroughs Adding Machine Company, at Kake, Alaska on Saturday, where they had been left by the *Taku*, and returned with them to Ketchikan. Baird continued to Seattle by steamer, while Skinner spent some time in the Ketchikan area. Sixty-three members of the RKO movie troupe embarked on the *S.S. Yukon* for Seattle the evening of Tuesday, July 22, to trans-ship for California to shoot the interior scenes for *The Silver Horde*. Cameraman John W. Boyle, his assistant William Clothier and Charles Kerr, the company business manager, remained in the city until some final "shots" were taken. The project had brought a lot of business to the air services and more would be forthcoming when the troupe returned later in the fall to film another of the Rex Beach stories, *The Iron Trail*. Meanwhile, the *Wrangell* was fogbound at Ketchikan, with a period of poor weather prevailing.

A new pilot for Pioneer Airways, James M. Dodson, arrived in Ketchikan about July 22, 1930. With his wife and company manager Roy Jones, the pilot had traveled from Seattle by steamer. His first task was to salvage the *Sea Pigeon* from its precarious position on

Pilot James M. "Jim" Dodson arrived in Ketchikan about July 22, 1930, to fly for Pioneer Airways. A former Naval Reserve pilot, he was accustomed to flying off the water. His first task was to salvage the **Sea Pigeon** *from its precarious position at Reflection Lake.*

Reflection Lake, where it had been wrecked shortly before the Fourth of July. Dodson had graduated from the University of Washington in education, teaching mathematics and science at Franklin High School in Seattle for a time. He had learned to fly in the Naval Reserve. In 1929-30 he was on active duty, flying from the carrier U.S.S. Lexington, among other activities. Operating from the water was something he was familiar with.

John Selby, Clayton Scott's flight mechanic, had left Cordova July 16, flying with Bob Ellis to Juneau, and going on to Ketchikan in a second Alaska-Washington Vega. With the loss of Gorst's Boeing B-1E, NC 115E, at Icy Bay, (see Cordova—1930, Chapter 55), he was no longer needed as a flight mechanic and was on his way to Ketchikan to work as a mechanic for Pioneer Airways. New Edo 3300 pontoons had arrived for the damaged *Sea Pigeon*. Roy Jones, manager of Pioneer Airways, pilot Jim Dodson and their new mechanic soon left by a chartered fishing boat, taking the floats with them. There was a swampy trail from salt water to the lake where the *Sea Pigeon* awaited them. Dodson, Jones, Selby and the skipper from the fishing boat lugged one of the floats about three miles uphill to the site at the lake, struggling through the swamp and climbing through devil's club and over slippery rocks. The other float on the Stinson was serviceable, but it would take them some days to effect repairs. The men set to work, rigging a hoist to lift the plane in order to replace the damaged float and the supporting struts. When this was accomplished and the plane once more sat erect, it was necessary to repair the damaged wing tip and dope some new fabric over it. Fortunately a period of sunny weather facilitated the repair; it would have been difficult to get the patch to adhere in the usual rainy spells.

Alaska-Washington Airways was now advertising the seven-place *Skagway*, NC 103W, for charter out of Ketchikan, with Ralph Bartholomew as their agent. He was on hand to greet the company's newest seven-place Lockheed Vega, *Sitka*, NC 974H, on its arrival from Seattle at 7:00 P.M. Friday, July 25, 1930. Manufactured in August, 1929, the *Sitka* was the most beautiful of the fleet, with a rich, red fuselage, cream-colored wing and trim and black and gold license numbers and striping. It was the first of the Vegas with a full NACA speed cowling, streamlining the previous lumpy look of the engine and giving it a sleek appearance, as well as adding to the plane's cruising speed by an additional fifteen miles per hour. The company had previously owned a Lockheed Vega named *Sitka*, NC 200E, which had been operated on wheels out of Seattle, but it had been sold to John Blum. The new *Sitka* had a 425 horsepower Pratt & Whitney engine and it cruised at 150 miles per hour. The plane had left Seattle at 11:30 A.M. on Friday, making two stops enroute, completing the flight up in five hours and fifteen minutes of flying time. Passengers aboard were Haakon B. Friele, M.M. Houck, and Leif C. Buschmann. Flown by Anscel Eckmann, who had recently been made chief pilot for the company, the plane also carried pilot Eugene A. "Gene" Meyring and mechanic Chandler Hicks. Meyring, a former naval pilot and an officer in the Naval Reserve, had been flying Alaska-Washington's triangle run out of Seattle, but was now being transferred to Alaska. The *Sitka* would be based out of Juneau and, upon arrival there, the pilot would take command of the new plane.

The *Sitka* took off for Juneau at 11:30 A.M. the following day, Saturday, July 26, carrying Mr. and Mrs. Gilbert Skinner, Leif Buschmann and Larry Parks. Additional crew members, Meyring and Hicks, were also aboard. Pat Renehan, flying the *Wrangell*, arrived back at his Ketchikan base from Juneau on Friday evening, bringing Mr. and Mrs. Gilbert Skinner and their friends, Mr. and Mrs. Arthur McCann. The McCanns continued to Seattle by steamer.

Pat Renehan, flying the *Wrangell*, NC 657E, took off from Ketchikan at 7:15 A.M.

803

Sunday, July 27, 1930, on a fish trap inspection tour. Carrying F.W. Hynes, Bureau of Fisheries agent, W.C. Arnold, United States commissioner, and Lester O. Gore, local attorney, the pilot was gone for fifteen hours on a lengthy cruise throughout the southern area of Southeastern Alaska, covering in excess of 1400 miles. From Ketchikan, the pilot flew to the Portland Canal district, then to Chacon, where all the traps in Cordova Bay were visited; from there to Waterfall and out around Baker and Hecate islands; then around the north part of Prince of Wales Island and to Wrangell; from there to Anan Creek where bears fished the tumbling waters. Hynes and one of the wardens remained here while the plane made a flight to Craig, returning from there to pick up the officials for the return trip to Wrangell and on in to Ketchikan. Between 450 and 500 traps had been inspected from the air, a simple process to the knowledgeable in trap construction. Two traps appeared to be open in the closed period but upon closer inspection, they were found to be closed.

Pat Renehan left Ketchikan again in the *Wrangell* at 9:20 A.M. Monday, July 28, 1930, to make a tour of the Nakat Packing Company holdings in Southeastern Alaska, taking general manager Haakon B. Friele and M.M. Houck, assistant general manager, as well as Territorial Senator J.R. Heckman of Ketchikan. Renehan expected to fly to Union Bay, going from there to Waterfall cannery and, in the late afternoon, overtake the cannery tender *Petrel*, transferring his passengers from the plane to the boat which was enroute to Hidden Inlet to spend the night, returning on the cannery tender the next day. Renehan returned from the *Petrel* to Ketchikan and picked up Charles Daggy, taking him to Kake to repair the radio on the Alaska-Pacific Salmon Corporation cannery tender *Virginia*.

Once again the airplane was called in to provide transportation in an emergency. Peter Johnson, a Ketchikan troller, was working the fishing season at Port Alexander on the southeast coast of Baranof Island. On Monday, July 28, 1930, the man had arisen about six o'clock to build a fire in his stove with what he thought was kerosene, but which proved to be gasoline. In the explosion that followed, his face and hands were badly burned and his clothes set afire. Jumping overboard to extinguish the flames, he was rescued by other trollers nearby and the fire on his boat extinguished. Pilot Gene Meyring, in the *Sitka*, NC 974H, responded to the call, rushing the badly-burned Johnson from Port Alexander to the Ketchikan hospital, landing at 11:00 P.M. that evening.

Pat Renehan, flying the *Wrangell*, left Ketchikan at 7:30 A.M. the next day, Tuesday, with Mrs. Walter Anderson for Bell Island Hot Springs. From there he went to *Wrangell* to pick up the RKO film party, returning them to the city.

Gene Meyring and flight mechanic Frank Hatcher came in to Ketchikan from *Skagway* and Juneau at 1:00 P.M. Thursday, July 31, 1930. They were flying the Vega *Sitka*, NC 974H. The *Taku*, NC 102W, with pilots Anscel Eckmann and Pat Renehan at the controls, had departed for Seattle at 10:30 A.M. the previous day. The plane was due for an overhaul. Bob Ellis, who had brought the plane from the capital city to Ketchikan, returned to Juneau with the *Wrangell*, accompanied by Mrs. Ellis. Pat Renehan was expected to return from Seattle with a new Lockheed Vega *Petersburg*, NC 336H. Bob Ellis, with mechanic Chandler Hicks, returned to Ketchikan in the *Wrangell* on Friday, August 2, dropping and picking up passengers enroute.

By the end of July, Roy Jones and pilot Jim Dodson had returned from Reflection Lake, where they had gone with a new pontoon and other repair materials for the recently-damaged Stinson SM-8A *Sea Pigeon*, NC 935W. A new magneto for the plane had arrived from the south on July 31, and the men were leaving again with it. They expected to fly the plane to Ketchikan in a few days.

Ketchikan 1930. Mechanic Bert Seaton stands looking out of the cockpit hatch of the **Wrangell,** *NC 657E, at the Southeastern Alaska city.*

Alaska-Washington Airways' new plane, *Petersburg*, NC 336H, left Seattle for Southeastern Alaska at 8:40 A.M. Friday, August 1, 1930. Painted a deep orange with black trim, the former Lockheed demonstrator had been rigged on Edo 4650 floats, the number indicating the displacement of the float in cubic inches, as were the other Vegas. The plane was a seven-place (six passengers plus the pilot) Model 5. Flown by Pat Renehan, the seaplane arrived at Ketchikan at 4:30 P.M. that same day, making one fuel stop at Namu, British Columbia. Passengers aboard were D.H. Freeman, Jr., vice-president and treasurer of United States-Alaska Packing Company, who was enroute to Port Herbert, and Mrs. Gene Meyring, wife of the Alaska-Washington Airways pilot. J. Clark Wing, relief pilot for the company was also aboard. Shortly after its arrival, the *Petersburg* was on its way to Hidden Inlet with Clark Wing at the controls. Carrying Haakon B. Friele and M.M. Houck, officials of the Nakat Packing Company, the pilot returned with his passengers from the cannery at 9:00 P.M. that same evening.

Gene Meyring and Frank Hatcher, who had been registered at the Ingersoll Hotel, had departed for Juneau in the *Sitka* at 5:30 P.M. August 1, an hour after the arrival of the *Petersburg* from Seattle. The pilot made three stops enroute to the capital city: the first at Port Alexander where logger J. Burdette disembarked; the next, Port Herbert, where D.H. Freeman, Jr. left the plane; and the third at Funter Bay. Mrs. Gilbert Skinner and her guest, Mrs. F.J. Clancy disembarked there. Mrs. Meyring was accompanying her husband to Juneau on the flight.

Frank Dorbandt, flying a Fairchild 51, NC 5364, on floats, had departed Seattle at 11:15 A.M. Friday, August 1, 1930, for Anchorage. Accompanied by Mrs. Dorbandt and mechanic Lon Cope, the flier stopped at Alert Bay, British Columbia and arrived at Ketchikan at 7:45 P.M. that same evening. The plane departed for Juneau the following morning.

Pioneer Airways *Sea Pigeon*, NC 935W, arrived at Ketchikan at 5:00 P.M. on Friday, August 1, 1930. Flown out of Reflection Lake by pilot Jim Dodson, accompanied by mechanic John Selby and Roy Jones, the recently-repaired Stinson SM-8A was flown to Seattle by the three men, who departed at 6:00 A.M. The aircraft required inspection and relicensing. Word had been received by Jones that the second Stinson SM-8A, NC 991W, *Northbird*, was ready

August 1, 1930. Pilot Jim Dodson brings the Pioneer Airways SM-8A **Sea Pigeon** *in to the float at Ketchikan after it had been repaired at Reflection Lake. The plane had been damaged in an overshoot on June 29. Mechanic John Selby, who did most of the repair work, stands on the float of the Stinson.*

for delivery in Seattle. Dodson flew the new plane back the first of the week, to be based in Ketchikan, while the *Sea Pigeon* remained in Seattle for an overhaul.

The *Wrangell* was busy on Tuesday, August 5, flying cannery officials over the fishing area, taking C.J. Alexander and Lester O. Gore out, followed by a flight with manager Friele of the Nakat Packing Company. The following day, Wednesday, the *Wrangell* went out with J.R. Heckman, William A. Bates and Alfred M. Howe on a trout-fishing expedition. Hydroplane mooring ports at Wrangell and Petersburg had now been completed and approved, with a third underway at Sitka, as well as a landing field at Skagway. Construction of a hangar by Pioneer Airways was underway at Ketchikan in preparation for the return of the *Sea Pigeon* and the arrival of their second Stinson, the *Northbird*.

The Alaska-Washington Airways Vega, *Taku*, NC 102W, which had served Southeastern Alaska so well, was no more. While on a flight for the company, on Monday, August 4, 1930, the pilot, W.A. "Bill" Williams, landed the plane on the water at the entrance of Hood Canal near Kingston, Washington, because of engine troubles. Along with the intermittent firing of the engine he had other troubles for, after getting on the water, he noticed smoke in the cabin. Pulling up a floor board, he was greeted with a burst of flame; the plane was on fire. Ordering his five passengers out on to the pontoons, he tried to fight the fire with an extinguisher but was unable to contain it. A Coast Guard boat and fishermen picked up the pilot and his passengers but the Vega, of wooden construction, was burned; only the Wasp engine and the pontoons were saved. It was an $8000 loss and the end of a good plane.

The Vega *Petersburg* was winging its way south to replace the fire-destroyed *Taku*, NC 102W. With Robert E. Ellis as pilot, and accompanied by Mrs. Ellis and manager A.B. "Cot" Hayes, the plane was away from Ketchikan at 5:00 A.M. Wednesday, August 6, 1930.

The *Skagway*, NC 103W, departed Seattle at 8:30 A.M. Saturday, August 9, 1930, for Juneau, with pilot Bob Ellis at the controls. Carrying as passengers the pilot's wife, Margaret, Mrs. John W. Gilbert, Cot Hayes and Barbara Wing, the plane lifted off Lake Union and headed north. Mrs. Wing, wife of the company's relief pilot in Alaska had just bid her mother, Mrs. G.H. Dowling, a fond goodbye in Seattle; she was on her way to Vancouver to board the steamship *Princess Alice* for a voyage to Skagway. Little did Barbara know she would be greeting her surprised mother at the pier in Juneau upon her arrival there. When the girl heard about the flight north of the *Skagway*, she decided to join her husband in Juneau and packed a bag, and that gave her the chance to meet her mother.

Ellis landed at Namu, British Columbia, to refuel, and arrived at Ketchikan that same afternoon. Mr. Gilbert boarded the plane here to join his wife for the flight to Juneau, with the pilot landing in Gastineau Channel at the capital city at 7:00 P.M. The *Skagway* was to be based here, to replace the *Petersburg* which had recently flown south.

The second Stinson SM-8A *Northbird*, NC 991W, of Pioneer Airways had now arrived in Ketchikan. Flown up by pilot Jim Dodson, the aircraft was powered with a 210 horsepower Lycoming, as was the *Sea Pigeon*. Roy Jones, company manager, was running a box ad in the *Ketchikan Alaska Chronicle*, advising prospective customers to contact him at the Ingersoll Hotel. They would have two planes in service when the *Sea Pigeon* returned from Seattle.

Pat Renehan left Kake in the *Sitka*, NC 974H, late in the afternoon of Wednesday, August 14, 1930. Taking Mr. and Mrs. Gilbert Skinner, Mr. and Mrs. John Gilbert, and company pilot E.A. "Gene" Meyring with his wife, the pilot landed at Ketchikan late in the

A Canadian Boeing B-1E, CF-ABB, Pintail, carried two officials of New England Fish Company from Ketchikan to Prince Rupert, British Columbia on August 16, 1930. The plane, owned by Western Canada Airways, Ltd., is shown here in Vancouver, British Columbia. Major D. R. MacLaren was the pilot on the trip.

day. It was intended to base the *Sitka* with Gene Meyring as its pilot here now. Renehan intended to continue to Seattle by ship, to pilot seaplanes for the company on the Seattle-Victoria-Vancouver, British Columbia triangular run.

Friday, August 15, Meyring was out with the *Sitka* on a flight to Noyes Island and return, bringing in New England Fish Company's production manager R.R. Payne and engineer G. Benners, to Ketchikan. The two men left the next morning for Prince Rupert, British Columbia, on the Canadian Boeing B-1E, *Pintail*, CF-ABB, owned by Western Canada Airways, Limited of Vancouver, and piloted by Major D.R. MacLaren, DSOMC. Meyring was out again on Saturday morning in the *Sitka*, going to Hyder to pick up some prospectors for a reconnaissance trip to the Unuk River section where a strong interest had developed in gold mining possibilities. As passengers on the flight from Ketchikan to Hyder, the pilot carried Nowell Traversy and Miss Sanford, a resident of Hyder.

An injured man, Joe Fenbly, was brought in to Ketchikan at 8:00 A.M. Monday, August 18, 1930, to be placed under the care of Doctor J.B. Beeson at the Ketchikan General Hospital. Prospecting some thirteen miles from Hyder, his right leg was fractured when a large rock rolled on it. Carried in relays by twenty-two men, he was brought in to Hyder to be picked up by the plane for Ketchikan.

Alaska-Washington Airways planes *Wrangell* and *Skagway* had been in Juneau for some time and kept very busy. Clark Wing, flying the *Wrangell*, left the capital city for Ketchikan on Sunday morning, August 17, carrying J. DeCano as a passenger for the south. The pilot expected to return to Juneau the following day, but remained in Ketchikan to do some flying out of there. On Tuesday morning, August 19, pilot Wing brought Sam Bartholomew, superintendent of the Alaska-Pacific Salmon Corporation, in to the city from Rose Reef. He immediately left on another flight, taking Harvey Stackpole of Nakat Packing Company, J.R. Heckman and Lester O. Gore to Waterfall. In the afternoon he left for the west coast with F.W. Hynes, local agent of the Bureau of Fisheries, who was directing stream operations there during the fishing season. The weather was fairly good in the Ketchikan area; partly cloudy at 3000 feet, unlimited visibility with a three-mile southeast wind.

Courtesy of Millie Dodson

Pioneer Airways Stinson SM-8A, **Northbird,** *moored at Ketchikan.*

808

Pilot Jim Dodson, in the *Northbird*, NC 991W, flew to Juneau on Tuesday, August 19, taking Mr. and Mrs. Gilbert Skinner and a guest of theirs to the capital city. The pilot returned to his base that same evening.

Thursday morning, August 21, 1930, newspapers from Seattle arrived in Ketchikan aboard the rebuilt Stinson SM-8A *Sea Pigeon* at 6:30 P.M., the same day they had come from the press. Piloted by Gerald Joyce "Jerry" Smith, the Pioneer Airways plane had departed Seattle at 9:00 A.M. Roy Jones and two company mechanics, John Selby and Tom Johnson, were also aboard the Stinson. Jerry Smith, who had accompanied Roy Jones on his initial flight to Ketchikan in the original *Northbird* flying boat in July of 1922, had recently been involved in an impending Seattle to Tokyo aerial attempt with Jack Allen, when Jones persuaded him to take a job in Ketchikan with Pioneer Airways. A mechanic on Jones' early flight, Jerry Smith was now an experienced pilot; he had made trips to South America and flown over the Andes in a Bellanca, as well as having flown about the United States and Canada and even in Europe. It was intended to have Selby serve as a mechanic for the *Northbird* and Johnson as a mechanic for the *Sea Pigeon,* and Smith and Jim Dodson were the pilots for the company. There were now four planes at one time at the City float on Friday, August 22: the two Stinsons of Pioneer Airways and the two Vegas, *Wrangell* and *Sitka.*

Clark Wing, flying the *Wrangell,* departed that same day for Seattle, taking Mr. and Mrs. Gilbert Skinner, Mr. Shannon and Pedro Santos of Ketchikan, as well as two Juneau passengers—a full load. The attractive wife of the pilot, Barbara Wing, was now "manning" the Juneau office of Alaska-Washington Airways in the Valentine Building.

Pioneer Airways Photo

Kake, Alaska. August, 1930. Pioneer Airways pilot Gerald J. Smith with a local resident, holds a bag of mail, carried from Petersburg to Kake. Stinson Sea Pigeon, *NC 935W, was used on the flight.*

With two planes available, Pioneer Airways was actively promoting business in the area; Roy Jones declaring the planes available to the fishing industry, government agencies, sport fishing enthusiasts, tourists and travelers. The *Northbird*, NC 991W, flown by Jim Dodson, made a trip to the west coast with Mr. Van Mavern and Herbert Coleman. In each village visited the natives were eager customers to be taken up for rides. A blind native wanted to be taken up. "But you can't see," protested the tired Dodson. "Me fly anyway!" said the native, and he was taken up. Dodson, flying the *Sea Pigeon*, left Ketchikan again on Friday morning, August 29, 1930, for Klawock, Kake, Petersburg and Wrangell, carrying passengers outbound. He returned in the afternoon to make a round trip to Hyder, with a second one scheduled for the morrow. A convention of the Moose Legion was in progress there, with many other members going up by boat.

Shortly before noon on Saturday, August 30, 1920, an unfamiliar airplane on floats was sighted approaching from the south. Circling the city to a smooth landing on the channel, the plane taxied in to the City float. Two young men from Boston, Laurence M. "Laurie" Lombard and Frederick N. "Pete" Blodgett, climbed from their De Havilland Gipsy Moth 60-GM biplane *Flit*. The two were on their annual summer vacation and wanted to see as much of Alaska as possible in their four weeks of free time, as well as hunt for a trophy bear while they were at it. Lombard, thirty-five, was an attorney with a law firm in Boston, while Blodgett, twenty-eight, worked for a banking firm in the same city. The two-place plane was not federally-registered and therefore had no NC in front of the tail number 137M. It was registered with the State of Massachusetts as number 36. The same was true of Lombard, its owner, for he carried a Massachusetts pilot license in his pocket and was licensed to fly within his own State. He had a visual problem and could not meet the federal requirements for a medical certificate that existed at that time.

Powered with a Gipsy 1, four-cylinder, air-cooled engine of ninety-eight horsepower, the open-cockpit plane had been built by the Moth Aircraft Company of Lowell, Massachusetts under a license agreement with De Havilland Aircraft Company, Limited, of Great Britain. A safety plane of excellent design, it was practically spin-proof and stall-proof, having automatic "wing slots". It was also fitted with folding wings for easy storage. Lombard had logged 150

L.M. Lombard Photo

Boston, Massachusetts. Left to Right: Laurence M. Lombard and his companion on the 1930 flight, Frederick N. Blodgett, ready to depart in the Gipsy Moth for Alaska on Sunday, August 17, 1930.

◀ *Route of the Gipsy Moth, 137M, on Lombard and Blodgett's 1930 flight across the United States to Alaska, and return.*

L.M. Lombard Photo

▼ *The Gipsy Moth,* **Flit,** *powered with a Gipsy 1, four-cylinder air-cooled engine of ninety-eight horsepower, is shown on wheels in the States.*

L.M. Lombard Photo

hours of flying time while his companion, Pete Blodgett, had only five hours in the air when they had departed East Boston airport on Sunday, August 17, 1930. The plane had a twenty-three gallon fuel tank in the upper wing center section and the pilot had a reserve tank installed in the front cockpit above where his companion's knees would be. Their combined fuel capacity gave the plane a range of 400 miles at a cruising speed of eighty miles per hour, but they were to have trouble with leaks in both tanks.

Flying across country and over mountain ranges, by way of Cleveland, Chicago, Des Moines and Cheyenne to Salt Lake City, they turned northwest to Boise, and a forced landing in an Idaho farm field near Mountain Home. The oil was low and the motor had overheated. An obliging farmer drove Lombard the eight miles in to town to obtain the needed oil. A crowd of locals had gathered and all helped the two airmen move the plane to the main road, using a horse hitched to a drag sled placed under the tail skid. A cowboy went down the road to stop any traffic that might appear and the pair took off the crowned surface while going around a gradual bend. It was an interesting experience for the airmen and an entertaining day for the citizens. *Flit* soon arrived at Mountain Home where they landed at the Varney Air Lines emergency field and tied down for the night.

Lombard and Blodgett reached Boise on Sunday morning, gassing the plane here before going on west over Baker to land again, at Pendleton, Oregon. Flying through the Columbia River Gorge to Portland, they turned north for Seattle. Prior to leaving Boston, Lombard had purchased a pair of second-hand floats for the De Havilland. He had installed them on the plane to make several landings and takeoffs on the water so he could become accustomed to flying the plane on floats. They were then removed and shipped to Alaska-Washington Airways in Seattle to await his arrival, since he would need them on the journey north. While "Jump" Goodwin saw to the installation of the floats and serviced the plane, Anscel Eckmann spent some time with the two airmen, going over the route from Seattle to Skagway with the aid of charts. He pointed out the salmon canneries where they could get gas, and the settlements where there were floats or slips where they could tie up for the night. Goodwin, a former navy mechanic, removed the troublesome gas tank from the upper wing center section and soldered it up, replacing the fabric over it.

Departing from Seattle on Wednesday, August 27, 1930, the two tourists idled their way north on a wandering route that permitted stops at Alert Bay, where they cleared Canadian Customs with the aid of a letter from Eckmann, and Prince Rupert, before arriving at Ketchikan on Saturday morning. *Flit* left Ketchikan the same day, for Mole Harbor in Seymour Canal on Admiralty Island, where they got in touch with Allen E. Hasselborg who lived there in isolation in a cabin on the bay, and who sometimes guided parties about the area and to Hasselborg Lake, an 8.5 mile-long body of water on Admiralty, about seventeen miles northeast of Angoon.

The guide took the enthusiastic pair in hand and they spent the next two days hunting the area with still and movie cameras, and in observing the large bear that frequented the area. They were surprised to learn that bears do not bat the fish from the water, a popular misconcep-

L.M. Lombard Photo

Two young men from Boston brought the De Havilland Gipsy Moth, **Flit,** *to Southeastern Alaska in early fall, first landing at Ketchikan on August 30, 1930. They had flown it across country on wheels, had floats installed at Seattle, and came north to see the country.*

tion, but seize them in their jaws or bring one or both paws down on the fish in a lightning-like move before picking it up by mouth or dining on the fish while they stand on it.

The pair made a two-day flight in *Flit* to Juneau for groceries and other supplies on Tuesday, September 2, 1930, returning on the second day to the Mole Harbor cabin, where Hasselborg, his summer guest and his nephew, waited. (see Juneau—1930, Chapter 54). Guided by Hasselborg, the two young men each killed a large brown bear on September 4, one at Mole Harbor and the other at Pleasant Bay—trophies of their adventurous trip to Alaska.

The airmen returned from Mole Harbor to Ketchikan in their plane on Friday, September 5, where they were dinner guests of Mr. and Mrs. Jim Dodson at the Revilla Apartments. They left Ketchikan in the Gipsy Moth the following morning to return to Seattle, have the floats replaced by wheels, and return to Boston. They took the southern route, down the coast through California and east through Arizona, New Mexico and Texas before turning northeast for home.

(In the summer of 1972, Laurence M. Lombard, then a partner of a prestigious law firm in Boston, Hemenway & Barnes, made a nostalgic visit to Alaska with his wife and son. They visited Hasselborg Lake among other spots and served as host at a dinner for Warren "Ace" Dodson, Jim's son, who was also now a pilot. Lombard had, in later years, published a book on the adventurous summer in the Gipsy Moth, 136M: *"Flight to Alaska—1930"* by Laurence M. Lombard).

Meanwhile the planes of Alaska-Washington Airways and Pioneer Airways had been doing some flying. Gene Meyring, in the *Sitka*, NC 974H, took a fishing party from Ketchikan to Mirror Lake on Sunday, August 31, 1930. The next day the plane was away to the westward, flying F.W. Hynes, local agent for the U.S. Bureau of Fisheries, and Harvey Stackpole, of the Nakat Packing Company, to check on the run of salmon for spawning purposes. The run on the north end of Prince of Wales Island looked very good but the salmon were apparently not running as heavily on the southern end as yet. Opening and closing of fishing periods depended heavily on escapement into the spawning streams for future use of the stocks.

Pioneer Airways, with the Stinson SM-8A *Northbird*, NC 991W, arrived in Juneau on Tuesday, September 2, 1930. Accompanied by manager Roy Jones, pilot Jim Dodson had left Ketchikan on Monday morning, going to Wrangell where a number of passengers were taken up in the four-place monoplane. After flying a trip up the Stikine River, the pilot went on to Tenakee where he hoped to meet the other company plane, *Sea Pigeon*. Jerry Smith had already left there on a flight to Sitka. Overnighting in Tenakee, Dodson and Jones hopped off the next morning for Juneau. The manager spoke of the hangar under construction at Ketchikan and of the possibility of basing the *Sea Pigeon* in Juneau. The *Northbird* returned to Ketchikan late that afternoon. The other Stinson was still in Sitka. Pioneer Airways was now running a box ad in the *Daily Alaska Empire* in Juneau.

The Alaska-Washington Airways Vega *Skagway* with pilot Bob Ellis and flight mechanic Chandler Hicks was still operating out of Juneau, with the *Wrangell*, crewed by J. Clark Wing and Frank Hatcher, also operating out of the capital city. While the company intended to station certain planes in certain bases, they soon found that demand for their services and the very nature of air commerce did not conform to their plans, and the planes were often far from the intended base. The fishing business was a heavy user of their services but this largely disappeared when the season was over. They were looking for support in getting an air mail

The **Northbird**, *NC 991W, rests on its beaching wheels after a successful flight to one of the nearby lakes in the Ketchikan area where trout abound.*

contract, the real answer to a year-round air service in Southeastern Alaska as well as elsewhere.

In Ketchikan, Jim Dodson made a flight to Windham Bay with the *Northbird* on Sunday, September 7, 1930, taking Pete Hanson and E. Anderes, of the Ketchikan Dairy, who would spend a week in prospecting the area. While in Wrangell the pilot also flew two prospectors over Groundhog Basin, twelve miles east of Wrangell, and made a flight up the Stikine River with two more prospectors. Coming in to Ketchikan on Sunday, Dodson made a trip to Mirror Lake to pick up W.A. Bates and C.R. Wright, who were sport fishing there. Monday morning the pilot was out with Wright and L.T. Watson, for Boca de Quadra estuary (Quadra Bay) where the men were landed to get samples of ore. Jerry Smith arrived from Juneau in the *Sea Pigeon* to take passengers on a return flight.

Both Lockheed Vegas from Juneau, the *Skagway* with Bob Ellis and Chandler Hicks, and the *Wrangell* with Clark Wing and Frank Hatcher, made a fuel stop at Ketchikan on Tuesday, September 9, on their way to Seattle with passengers from the capital city. The *Skagway* came in at noon and the *Wrangell* two hours later, carrying General R.E. Wood and company employees Barbara Wing and Brian Harland.

The *Sitka*, NC 974H, based at Ketchikan, made an out-of-the-ordinary flight on Tuesday, September 9, 1930. Taking Deputy United States Marshal Ernest Jones, game warden Frank Dufresne, and prohibition officer F.L. Chidester, pilot Gene Meyring and mechanic Frank Wadman flew to Heceta Island off the west coast of Prince of Wales Island, where the federal officials served a warrant on A. Owens, arrested their man, returned him to Ketchikan and haled him in to court where he was fined $500 for violation of game laws.

Chidester had been dropped off at Craig to conduct his business, and picked up on their return flight. Leaving at 12:00 o'clock, the plane was back in Ketchikan in two hours. The former means of accomplishing the task by chartered boat would have consumed three days at a far greater cost.

The *Skagway*, returning to Juneau, left Seattle at noon of Thursday, September 11, and arrived in Ketchikan at 7:30 P.M. Carrying authoress Elizabeth Lippincott McQueen of California, and mechanic Brian Harland as passengers for Juneau, Bob Ellis and Chandler Hicks overnighted at Ketchikan. Leaving at 8:00 A.M. the next morning with their passengers for Juneau they added Robert E. Proctor who was going to Douglas. The *Wrangell* and *Petersburg* were in Seattle and the company's fourth Vega, the *Sitka*, was in port in Ketchikan. The *Petersburg*, NC 336H, was to be out of service for some time; an accident near Mercer Island, Washington on September 12, 1930, had resulted in the Vega being sent to the Lockheed factory for replacement of the fuselage and elevators. The fleet had dwindled from six to four.

The *Wrangell* was also being returned to Juneau. Piloted by Anscel Eckmann, operations manager of Alaska-Washington Airways, the plane left Seattle Sunday morning, September 14, making stops at Vancouver, British Columbia, Alert Bay, and Prince Rupert. Flying from Prince Rupert, the pilot overheaded Ketchikan to go directly on to Juneau, arriving there on Tuesday, September 16. Don B. Bennett, business manager of Alaska-Washington Airways, was also aboard. The *Sea Pigeon* of Pioneer Airways was still flying out of Juneau.

Anscel Eckmann was back in Ketchikan on Thursday, September 18, 1930, on his way to Seattle with a full load of passengers. Due to adverse weather, the plane was unable to leave until Saturday morning, September 20. A diverse load of passengers was aboard: W.M. Fraser, real estate dealer of Tacoma, R.O. Reekie, medical student of Seattle, O.W. Wiley, real estate man of Seattle, Don B. Bennett, business manager and secretary-treasurer of Alaska-Washington Airways, John W. Troy, owner and publisher of the *Daily Alaska Empire*, and Frank Barnes, boat owner of Wrangell. John Troy took the steamer, *S.S. Queen* from Ketchikan back to Juneau, and his place on the flight south was filled by Charles Conover of Ketchikan. While holding at Ketchikan, Bennett spoke of his company's plans, which were to arrange for a two-plane floating hangar at Ketchikan and at Juneau, probably a sixty by sixty or eighty by eighty foot structure with a ramp to draw the planes out of the water, and a machine shop within. They were also expecting delivery of a seven-plane floating hangar to serve as the company's base in Seattle: a two-story structure of one hundred by fifty-seven feet, with storage space, radio room, machine shop and a waiting room on the upper floor. They planned a radio shop and Customs office, as well as the plane storage on the lower floor, and fantail ramp to assist the planes in taxiing up in varying wind directions. The company was still pressing, in Washington, D.C. for a mail contract and, if successful, they planned on maintaining a schedule of three round trips a week between Seattle and Ketchikan and Juneau, calling at Wrangell and Petersburg. They wanted to start the service on April 1 of the coming year, while still basing planes at Ketchikan and Juneau.

Pioneer Airways Stinson, *Northbird*, was a casualty of the storm that had been sweeping through Ketchikan. Moored at the city float, with its tail to the wind, in the early morning hours of Friday, September 19, it began to take on water in the pontoons and the tail from the rising swell off the ocean. As the water filled the ship, she became less buoyant, finally taking a tail dive into the briny deep off the float. Kept by tie-down ropes from completely submerging until the *Elsinore* and *Confidence* could get their winches into play, the partly-submerged ship was hoisted on to the float to drain out. Some repairs, particularly to the fabric on wings and fuselage were necessary before the plane could be put in to service again. The Alaska-Washington Airways *Sitka*, NC 974H, was the only plane currently operating out of Ketchikan, although the *Sea Pigeon* of Pioneer Airways was to come in briefly on September 22, from Juneau. The Vega, with Gene Meyring and Frank Wadman as usual, made a flight on Tuesday, September 23, 1930, to Klawock, Hydaburg and Waterfall. J.S. Whitney was a passenger for Waterfall, H.A. Berry, Ed L. Norland and Captain Ahues for Klawock, and Robert Lee of Carnation Milk Company, a round-trip passenger. The following day the pilot made a trip to Metlakatla with R. Booth, West Coast Grocery Company salesman, then going to Craig to pick up three passengers for Ketchikan. Pioneer Airways was down to one plane again on September 24 when news came of the swamping of the *Sea Pigeon* in an emergency landing on the water at Juneau that afternoon. The plane was dismantled by its pilot, Jerry Smith, and his mechanic, Thomas Johnson, to be hauled to a warehouse to dry it out and determine the extent of the damage. (see Juneau - 1930, Chapter 54).

On Sunday, September 28, 1930, Gene Meyring answered an emergency call in the *Sitka*, flying to Port Alexander on the southwest coast of Baranof Island. He brought in E. Hansen who was taken to the Ketchikan General Hospital to be placed in the care of Doctor R.V. Ellis. Hansen had caught his hand in a fish wheel, badly mangling it; amputation was necessary.

A second emergency call was received from Benchen & Heinen's herring plant in Port Armstrong the following day. Despite very poor weather, Meyring elected to take the risk and took off in the *Sitka*. The pilot and his mechanic, Frank Wadman, were having a tough time. Flying at one hundred feet over the white-crested waves, sometimes in a down-pouring rain and fog that severely limited visibility, they managed to reach a point near Cape Decision on their way to Port Armstrong on Baranof Island. To cross Chatham Strait, they faced a very cauldron of foaming waves, lashed by a southeast gale off the open Pacific. Considering the risk too great, the pilot sought shelter in a harbor on Kuiu Island. Flushed out of there by rising wind, the pilot took off for home. On the way down Clarence Strait, the weather improved somewhat and, thinking he might have a chance later, he turned aside and flew to Wrangell. During the night the weather became even worse and manager Larry Parks wired him to return to Ketchikan. Ordinarily a forty-five minute flight, an hour's flying time was necessary because of the half-gale from the southeast, the pilot reaching his home port Tuesday morning. The trip was a fitting requiem for the summer's frantic flying business, for Alaska-Washington Airways was again cutting business in Southeastern Alaska for the winter season. The *Sitka* had departed early in October for Seattle, carrying as passengers a group of big game hunters. The plane would remain there for the winter. The *Skagway* with Ellis and Hatcher, had arrived from Juneau on October 3 with passengers, and now made a flight to the south of Ketchikan on Monday, October 6, 1930, with passengers Steve Selig and R. Parks, who were checking on a boom of logs being towed south by the *Akutan*. Before turning back Ellis stopped at Prince Rupert where Hatcher put on fifty-eight gallons of Union aviation gasoline at thirty cents a gallon at the marine dock. After their return on the same day, the plane continued on to Juneau, with Larry Parks, company agent there, aboard.

Ellis and Hatcher departed the capital city with the plane on Tuesday, October 7, for Seattle where the *Skagway* would undergo a thorough overhaul, and probably be used on the company's other runs during the winter. Accompanying the airmen were the pilot's wife, Margaret Ellis, as well as Frank Dorbandt and Alonzo Cope of Anchorage. The two men were on their way south to secure a second plane for the air service in Anchorage. Mrs. Charles Burns was also a passenger when the *Skagway* left Ketchikan on the morning of Tuesday, October 8, 1930.

The *Sea Pigeon* of Pioneer Airways, still in Juneau, had been moved to Thane from the warehouse on Willoughby Avenue. If all went well Jerry Smith planned to test fly the assembled plane on the afternoon of Saturday, October 4. The plane would then be flown to Seattle for an inspection by a Department of Commerce aeronautics inspector; there was no inspector available in Southeastern Alaska at that time. The *Sea Pigeon* arrived in Ketchikan from the capital city on Wednesday, October 8, with pilot Jerry Smith, mechanic Tom Johnson, special mechanic Burras Smith, and manager Roy Jones aboard. It was decided to keep the *Sea Pigeon* here. Burras Smith could do what was needed on the Stinson. A hangar had been constructed at the airport on the Tongass Highway where it was planned to keep the two planes when the weather was too rough for them to remain at the city float. The two Stinsons would now be based at Ketchikan and put in good shape before the spring business began.

On Sunday, October 12, 1930, Pioneer Airways pilot Jim Dodson took the *Northbird* to Juneau, carrying C.R. Wright and Alfred N. Howe of Ketchikan as passengers. Dodson took his passengers to Pybus Bay the next morning for a bear hunt. Following this, the two men were to return to Petersburg to join friends for a duck hunt before returning to Ketchikan.

Doctor W.E. Peterson, Ketchikan dentist, was on a hunting trip to Duncan Canal on Wednesday, October 15, 1930, when his wife received word of the death of her husband's father in Spokane. With no other rapid means of reaching the dentist, Jerry Smith took the Stinson, *Sea Pigeon*, out and located the man, bringing him in to Ketchikan that same day. The pilot flew the dentist to Prince Rupert, British Columbia, where he could catch a steamer to Victoria, and a plane from there, in order to arrive in time for the funeral.

With Alaska-Washington Airways temporarily out of the picture, the two Pioneer Airways planes were busy, and the weather was favorable. On Monday, October 13, the *Sea Pigeon*, piloted by Jerry Smith, had taken Milton and Eldon Daly of the Ketchikan Spruce Mills, and Charles MacDonald of the MacDonald Logging Company, on a timber cruise. The following day the pilot flew James Freeburn to Petersburg to catch the *S.S. Northwestern* on which Nick Bez was traveling. The two were associated in mining properties. From Juneau, the pair planned a flight to Chichagof on the *Northbird* with Dodson.

On his return to Ketchikan, Smith flew Paul Abbott of the Dupont Powder Company, and J.A. Talbot, to View Cove, Dall Island, and from there to Hyder. Smith returned in the *Sea Pigeon* Thursday morning with Talbot and two other passengers while Abbott remained in Hyder. On Sunday, October 19, 1930, Jerry Smith brought in Deputy U.S. Marshal J.A. Nielson from Craig, along with a witness. He left for a second trip to the community but was forced back by low ceilings over Prince of Wales Island. He went out again on Monday to complete the flight. The *Northbird* also came in, bringing Alfred Howe and C.R. Wright, who were returning from their hunt at Pybus Bay.

Paddy Burke, Air Land Manufacturing Company, Limited, pilot was missing for a second time in the Laird country with the Junkers F-13, CF-AMX. (see Juneau - 1983, Chapter 54). Alaska-Washington Airways in Seattle dispatched Robin "Pat" Renehan at his own request, along with flight mechanic Frank Hatcher in the Vega *Skagway*, NC 103W, to go to Atlin, British Columbia and begin a search for the missing plane. They picked up Sam Clerf in Vancouver, British Columbia on their way north; the prospector-rancher from Washington was on his way south after spending a summer with Burke in the Laird. Clerf had crossed over on the White Pass and Yukon Railroad to Skagway, catching a steamer there, and was due in Vancouver when the flight was being arranged. Renehan was an old friend of Burke's; they had flown together in England. Renehan and Hatcher met at the Alaska-Washington Airways floating hangar on Lake Union, taking little with them, but loading in a set of wheels to be installed on the plane at Atlin in place of the floats, as they were going inland. Leaving Seattle at noon on Tuesday, October 28, in the Vega, for Vancouver, British Columbia, they flew to the Canadian city and picked up Clerf. They went on north to land at Butedale, British Columbia, a coastal stop on Princess Royal Island, south of Prince Rupert. With an hour's daylight remaining, the *Skagway* departed there at 4:15 P.M. to fly to Prince Rupert. Other than a reported sighting by a British Columbia fisherman, in Grenville Channel, nothing more was heard of the plane.

When Renehan did not appear at Prince Rupert or Ketchikan, it was first thought that he may have landed and sought shelter among the many islands and inlets that made up the coastline. The U.S. Coast Guard cutter *Cygan* left Ketchikan on November 5. Other vessels, both American and Canadian, put out to search the coast.

Anscel Eckmann, chief pilot for Alaska-Washington Airways, departed Lake Union in Seattle at 3:30 P.M. Monday, November 3, 1930. Accompanied by Larry Parks and flight mechanic Frank Wadman, he searched the Canadian coastline south of Prince Rupert. Dense fogs over the northern coast delayed the start for thirty hours. Eckmann got as far as Nanaimo that day, remaining overnight at the Vancouver Island city. He was away again at 11:00 A.M. on November 5 and, after making a preliminary search along the coast, reached Prince Rupert where he remained overnight with the Vega *Wrangell*, NC 657E. Eckmann, Wadman and Parks reached Ketchikan at noon, November 6, 1930.

Eckmann continued his search out of Ketchikan. He cabled the commandant of the Sand Point Naval Air Station in Seattle, urging that U.S. Navy planes be brought into the search. The weather along the coast continued to be bad and there was new snow on the shore, possibly covering any wreckage that might otherwise be seen. The pilot, with Wadman and Parks, was in Ketchikan again on Tuesday, November 11, 1930, returning to Prince Rupert that afternoon. The following day the three men returned in the *Wrangell*, searching enroute. The *Cygan* came in to the city Tuesday night from covering the waters where Renehan was believed to have gone down, reporting no results. The Coast Guard vessel left again on Wednesday to continue their efforts.

Two Canadian Fairchild photographic-type float planes, manned by pilots of the Royal Canadian Flying Corps, were sent from Vancouver Island to join the search but had been storm-bound at Alert Bay for two days, leaving for Prince Rupert on Tuesday morning, November 11, where they met Eckmann in the *Wrangell*, conferring with him that evening. Flown by Lieutenant L.E. Phinney and Flying Officer C.R. Dunlap, accompanied by Sergeant A.H. Warner and Corporals W.C. Atwood and M. Squires, the Fairchilds searched Portland Canal the following day in response to a report that some wreckage had been seen there. Eckmann, Parks and Wadham, returning from Prince Rupert on November 12, made a flight to Cape Chacon on the west coast of Prince of Wales Island when they found a blanket of fog over Ketchikan. They returned in the *Wrangell* to the city later in the day.

On Tuesday, November 11, Jim Dodson, in the *Northbird*, had also gone out to the westward to bring in Mr. and Mrs. Frank Louth and their small son from Craig. The boy was very ill and was taken to the Ketchikan General Hospital. The pilot had brought in Mrs. Frederick George from Hydaburg the day before. She was also hospitalized. Gerald J. "Jerry" Smith, the other Pioneer Airways pilot had caught the steamer *Northwestern* for Juneau on the night of November 3, 1930.

A request from Senator Wesley L. Jones of the State of Washington to the Navy Department in Washington, asking for U.S. Navy planes to aid in the search, had been referred back to Captain Zeno Briggs, Acting Commandant of the Bremerton Navy Yard. Without suitable planes for a search mission, at his request two Loening amphibians were dispatched to Seattle from San Diego. The two planes, which departed San Diego Naval Air Station on November 14, 1930, were under the command of Lieutenant C.F. Greber, who was piloting one plane, with Chief Electrician Claude G. Alexander piloting the second plane. "Dutch" Greber was no stranger to Southeastern Alaska; he had piloted a Loening on the 1929 Alaskan Aerial Survey Detachment under Lieutenant-Commander Radford. Alexander had served as radio officer with the 1926 Alaskan Aerial Survey Expedition under Lieutenant Ben H. Wyatt. Alaska-Washington Airways offered to furnish guide pilots for the flight north from Seattle and Bremerton, if the Navy so desired.

Alaska-Washington Airways pilot Anscel Eckmann, accompanied by his flight mechanic Frank Wadman and observer Larry Parks, had gone out from Ketchikan again at 9:00 A.M. Thursday, November 13, with relatively good flying conditions prevailing although there were scattered areas of fog. In response to a report from Stewart that a floating body had been seen, they searched Portland Canal to Hyder and Stewart, British Columbia, but without result. Sergeant Potterton of the Provincial Police at Stewart informed the pilot on his arrival at Hyder (just across the border from Stewart) that the body was that of a local man who had drowned. Landing at Hyder was extremely dangerous because of the ice floating in the bay. Ice on the wings of the Vega also caused a reduction in load carrying capability and made flying difficult. They made a second flight the same day to search to the northeast of Lucy Island lighthouse, returning to Ketchikan about 5:00 P.M. Lighthouse keepers at Lucy Island, about eighty-four miles south of Ketchikan, had reported that Renehan's ship had passed over the station about seven o'clock the night he had disappeared, flying low before a thirty-mile-an-hour southwest wind in rain and darkness.

The *Wrangell* was held at Ketchikan over November 14 and 15 by an unexpected turn in the weather, unsuitable for flying. The Vega got away on Monday, November 17, unsuccessfully searching for three hours along the shores of Behm Canal as far as the Unuk River. Along with Wadman and Parks, Eckmann carried Captain Barney Smith, an old-time Alaskan gas boat man, as navigator. Forced to land twice because of ignition trouble, they ran into snow just south of Ketchikan, again landing six miles out of their base in a blinding snowstorm, to taxi the rest of the way in.

The two U.S. Navy planes, Loening OL-8As, that were struggling up the coast from San Diego in rain and fog had left Red Bluff, California on Sunday, November 16, and landed at Medford, Oregon three hours later, and were held there by storm. They reached Seattle on Tuesday, November 18. The mine sweeper *Swallow* was being fitted with cranes and was to be sent north from Bremerton to serve as a mother ship to the two Loenings. The aircraft carrier *Lexington* had left San Pedro for Bremerton with supplies and parts for the Navy planes.

An Indian had reached Prince Rupert on Sunday, November 16, to report sighting the missing plane in the gathering dusk of October 28, somewhat south of the north entrance to Grenville Channel. In halting English he stated, "It was near dark. The plane seemed to be touching the tops of the trees. I said to my friends that it would hit the mountain in front of it." It was agreed likely that the plane did not crash at that spot since it had been reported farther north, but as in other reports, the plane was said to be flying very low. The area was only a half-hour's flying time from Ketchikan. The Coast Guard cutter *Cygan* left Ketchikan on Sunday to cover the shore of Behm Canal for some sign of the lost plane. The Royal Canadian Air Force planes had made short, unsuccessful flights from Prince Rupert on Saturday, seeking

Renehan and his companions. They were also searching the area between Lewis Island, at the entrance to Grenville Channel, and Lucy Island lighthouse because of the report.

The Wasp motor in Eckmann's *Wrangell*, NC 657E, was becoming unreliable and the pilot would have to return to Seattle for an engine change. He was able to get away from Ketchikan at 9:30 A.M. Wednesday, November 19, 1930, and made it as far as Prince Rupert, British Columbia, before being forced to hold by a snowstorm. Eckmann went on to Alert Bay the next day, landing there in the afternoon. Still with Wadman and Parks, he flew in to Seattle on Friday, November 21, landing on Lake Union about noon. Conferring with naval officials in Bremerton, including pilot Greber, he learned that the tender, *Swallow*, had left Bremerton at 3:00 P.M. that same day, Friday, for Alert Bay. The two Loening amphibians were to depart in the morning to join the tender, which would then move to Grenville Channel, thirty miles south of Prince Rupert, to establish a base. After one false start the Navy planes departed as planned, reaching Alert Bay on Saturday at 3:00 P.M. Leaving there at 10:40 A.M. Sunday, November 23, they were forced by poor visibility to land at the northern entrance of Grenville Channel, taxiing for more than a half-hour before taking to the air again. They landed at Ketchikan at 3:34 P.M.

The Loenings were taken to the Ketchikan hydroport on the Tongass Highway where they were quartered. The tender, *Swallow* was enroute to join them, to provide base support in Ketchikan. Lieutenant Greber's crew in Loening F-J-4 consisted of Pilot I.P. Moragne and radioman L.E. Geselle. Alexander carried as crew in Loening F-J-5, Pilot S.T. Pigott and radioman R.J. Scott.

The two Loening OL-8As were off Tongass Narrows at 12:45 P.M. Wednesday, November 25, 1930, on a search to the southeast of Ketchikan. Greber and Alexander were piloting the two amphibians. The U.S. Coast Guard cutter *Cygan* also left for Nakat Inlet, to interview cannery watchmen and others living along the route, in a search for new clues to the lost airmen. The *Swallow* was due to dock in Ketchikan at 7:00 P.M. She was moored at the Sunny Point cannery dock while the planes were kept at the hydroport.

The Junkers, CF-AMX, piloted by Paddy Burke and missing since October 11, 1930, was found on Tuesday, November 24, frozen in the ice at the headwaters of the Laird River in Yukon Territory. Everett Wasson, who made the find, was unable to land because of his gasoline supply and had returned to Whitehorse to make his report. He had seen no one about the plane. (see Juneau -1930, Chapter 54). But the search for Pat Renehan and his companions must go on. It had been a month since their disappearance.

On Thursday, November 27, the two Loening OL-8As went aloft on test flights; the weather was unfavorable for a search. The following day, Friday, the two planes left again about 10:30 A.M. Alexander was forced to return but left again about noon for Cholmondeley Sound to search it while Greber was combing Twelvemile Arm off Kasaan Bay on Prince of Wales Island. The navy planes were equipped with radio and maintained contact with the *Swallow*'s radio room.

In Prince Rupert, British Columbia the two Canadian Fairchild planes searching out of there concluded that there was no further use in continuing, and departed for Vancouver, British Columbia on Friday, November 28, 1930. They arrived there on Saturday, after stopping overnight at Comox, British Columbia, landing on Comox Lake. Eckmann was still in Seattle, for mechanics had stated that they would need at least a week to put his plane in top condition. Larry Parks was returning to Ketchikan by steamer.

With a final search of the Vallemar Bay on the northwest side of Gravina Island, where a sixty-nine-year-old homesteader by the name of Bill Folkes had reported hearing a crash, the navy concluded their part of the search. The two U.S. Navy Loenings departed Ketchikan shortly after 10:00 A.M. Thursday, December 4, 1930 and, after circling the city, proceeded to the northwest end of Gravina Island where for more than an hour they flew back and forth over the section where Folkes had heard the crash, until clouds and rain forced them to turn southward, hoping to comb Annette and Duke Islands enroute. The *Cygan* sent a shore party up the mountain back of Folke's homestead for a closer inspection of the area.

The tender *Swallow* departed the Sunny Point cannery dock the same morning, to proceed to Fort Simpson and anchor overnight. The amphibians joined her there, refueling the next morning for their flight to Alert Bay. As an added safety precaution the *Swallow*'s radio station could monitor the two planes, which usually maintained visual contact with each other. The Navy Loenings reached Alert Bay, later going on to Seattle's Sand Point Naval Air Station. They reached there late on Saturday, December 6, 1930. They would continue on to their base in San Diego by easy stages.

Alaska-Washington Airways pilot Anscel Eckmann and flight mechanic Frank Wadman departed Lake Union in the re-engined *Wrangell*, NC 657E, on January 2, 1931, arriving at Victoria, British Columbia to have wireless radio equipment installed in the plane there by Provincial Police. Eckmann went on to Vancouver, British Columbia to meet with Harry Blunt, a Pacific International Airways pilot who was returning to the States by steamer. He wanted to interview the other pilot regarding the report of an unidentified plane that was seen by a telegraph lineman 180 miles north of Hazelton, hoping it might provide a clue to Renehan's disappearance. Continuing on to land at Alert Bay the following day, Sunday, January 4, 1931, Eckmann and Hatcher planned on another search out of the Prince Rupert area, supported by the Dominion and Provincial governments of Canada and British Columbia.

Associated Screen News, Ltd.

Alaska-Washington Airways Vega, NC 657E, **Ketchikan,** *arrived at Victoria, British Columbia on January 2, 1931, to have radio put in by the Provincial Police. Left to Right: Frank Wadman, mechanic; Anscel Eckmann, pilot; Sergeant Owen, British Columbia Provincial Police, Victoria.*

821

The real clue to the disappearance of the Renehan plane on October 28, 1930, lay closer to home than that, as it had for some time. Reverend Marsden, pastor of the Presbyterian Church in the Tsimshian village of Metlakatla on the west coast of Annette Island, only fifteen miles south of Ketchikan, had, on about November 7, 1930, picked up from the shore near Point Davidson an inflated tire affixed to a wheel. He was out alone in his outboard motorboat at the time, hunting and fishing. At the head of a small bay he noticed the wheel and on his return, picked it up. He placed it on the porch of his house in the village, where it remained until early January when little Jimmie Leask, with an interest in such things, cried "That's an airplane wheel!" The Reverend Marsden gave the wheel to Ted Benson and Frank Williams, who brought it to Ketchikan on the *Theodora* on Tuesday evening, January 6, 1931, delivering it to the office of the *Ketchikan Alaska Chronicle*. The paper sent out a representative at daybreak, chartering the Pioneer Airways Stinson *Northbird*, stopping first at Metlakatla to interview Reverend Marsden before flying down the coast to find the second red-painted wheel two miles farther south of the location at which the first had been recovered.

Anscel Eckmann, then at Prince Rupert preparing to proceed to the Interior to search for Renehan, was notified of the find and left for Ketchikan, landing there at 2:30 P.M.

Mechanic Gordon Graham stands near the red-painted wheels from the lost **Skagway** *that were found on the shore of Annette Island, one on November 7, 1930 and one on January 7, 1931. The wheels provided the first real clue to the mystery surrounding the disappearance of the Alaska-Washington Airways plane. The photo was taken at the Alaska Southern Airways hangar in Juneau at a later date. The propeller blades have no relation to the incident.*

Lloyd Jarman Photo

Wednesday, January 7, 1931. He recognized the wheels as the pair Renehan had placed in the cabin of the *Skagway* before departing Seattle. It was doubtful they had been thrown from the plane in flight as fliers are extremely cautious about throwing heavy objects from a plane; they might strike tail surfaces or pontoons, inflicting serious damage. The feeling was that the Alaska-Washington Airways Vega may have plunged into the waters of Dixon Entrance, or waters adjacent thereto, and the wheels, being buoyant, had drifted to their point of discovery. A Metlakatla resident reported seeing a blanket on the shoreline of Duke Island, a bit south of Metlakatla, early in November but did not pick it up. There were blankets in Renehan's plane.

A new report surfaced: a low-flying plane over Duke Island the night of October 28, had been heard by a Metlakatla citizen. A half-dozen search parties went out by boat to comb the shores of Duke, Percy, Hotspur and adjacent islands, led by the *Cygan*. Eckmann left for Prince Rupert on Thursday, January 8, 1931, to confer with Provincial officials. Hoping to search the shoreline of Annette Island on his way south, he would return to Ketchikan later.

The search was to continue all through January. An expedition financed by the *Ketchikan Alaskan Chronicle* and the *Seattle Daily Times* resulted in the finding of a piece of drift about two feet long; pieces of blue airplane fabric and one tie rod were attached to it. Found by Clarence N. Myers, of the trolling boat *Lois*, and Bob Miller, on the shore of the northeast island of the Percy group southwest of Ketchikan, the piece tapering from a width of about one foot was identified by Anscel Eckmann and Frank Wadman as a part of the right side of the fuselage of the missing *Skagway*, housing the cockpit. It was apparent that the airplane had struck with some force, breaking up its wooden structure in the crash.

Eckmann and Wadman left Ketchikan, Alaska in the *Wrangell*, NC 657E, on Thursday, January 29, 1931, for Seattle, temporarily leaving the field to Jim Dodson and Pioneer Airways *Northbird* and *Sea Pigeon*. Manager Roy Jones had left the local company in November of 1930 for Seattle, where he had taken a position as pilot with the U.S. Customs Service, flying a Waco they had confiscated from a rumrunner and put to their own use.

Jones struck the mast of a steamship, *Curacao*, of the Admiral Line, which was moored in Lake Union on Thursday, January 15, 1931. A blanket he was using for protection blew up over his face, temporarily blinding him. Falling to the surface of the water, he was rescued and the plane towed ashore. With appropriations drying up, the Customs Service gave up its plane and Jones remained on as a Customs inspector.

Courtesy of Jim and Bob Eckmann

Ordway Studio

824

Alaska-Washington Airways

Pioneer Airways
Air Land Manufacturing
Company (Burke)

Juneau 1930

T HE NEWLY-CONSOLIDATED ALASKA-WASHINGTON AIRWAYS was
forming plans for a scheduled service between Seattle and Juneau with the opening of the
flying season in Southeastern Alaska. The company's floating hangar was towed from its
winter moorings near the greenhouse on Glacier Highway about April 10, 1930, and was back
in its former location near the Femmer Dock off Willoughby Avenue. Workmen were making
minor repairs to put it in shape for the arrival of the first plane, a new seven-place Lockheed
Vega, which had arrived in Seattle from the factory on Saturday, April 19. The plane, to be
flown north by Robert E. Ellis, had been christened *Taku*.

▲ *1930. Alaska-Washington Airways* **Skagway,** *NC*
*103W, near Juneau. The plane was painted blue with
cream-colored trim and had an international orange
panel painted on top of the wing.*

◄ *1930. Alaska-Washington Airways* **Taku,** *NC*
*102W, in Juneau. Fred Ordway, a commercial photog-
rapher in Juneau, was intensely interested in aviation
and later became a flying student. He died in a plane
crash on February 17, 1938 on a cross-country photo
trip in a rented plane while flying from Seattle to
Salem, Oregon. He took many of the aviation pictures
in Juneau in the '30s.*

Ellis, along with flight mechanic Frank Hatcher, departed Seattle at 8:13 A.M. Friday, April 25 in the *Taku*, NC 102W. Stopping at Ketchikan and Petersburg, the plane landed on the waters of Gastineau Channel at 6:05 P.M. that same day. Ellis was wearing the company's blue navy-type uniform with gold trimmings when he debarked from the inaugural flight. With him, in addition to his mechanic, were his wife, Margaret, W.E. Wynn, operations manager for Alaska-Washington Airways, and A.B. "Cot" Hayes, who remained in Juneau as manager of the Alaska division of the company. Hayes, a former naval air service mechanic in World War I had decided to stay in aviation after returning from Europe. He took a job as sales manager of Joe Carman's Aviation School, Incorporated, and was now coming to Alaska in a new position. The flight from Seattle had taken seven hours and thirty minutes of air time, flying in excellent weather at elevations between 2000 and 3000 feet all the way. The Vega was winched up the ramp into the company hangar, tailfirst, on a set of wheels placed beneath the pontoons.

Ellis and Hatcher flew a round trip to Sitka on Sunday, April 27, 1930, taking Eddie Ryan and his wife, Cliff Graham, Cot Hayes and W.E. Wynn, all round-trippers. On their return, the pilot made several flights with sightseers. He left Juneau at 12:40 P.M. on Monday, April 28, for Ketchikan, going by way of Petersburg and Wrangell, and carrying C.R. Wright, R.H. Stock, W.E. Wynn and Larry Parks, the company's Juneau agent. Ellis took off in the *Taku* the following day at 9:30 A.M. to return to Juneau. The pilot brought in Fred G. Hanford, Union Oil Company representative at Wrangell. He flew a round trip to Sitka on May 1 with Juneau traveling salesmen M.S. Wilson and A.S. Brown.

That afternoon at Sitka Frank Hatcher received a bad cut on his forehead from the propeller as the engine was turned over. On the front end of a pontoon with a paddle in hand, he was struck a glancing blow, receiving a deep cut on his forehead and over one eye. It had resulted from a misunderstanding in signals between mechanic and pilot. A number of stitches in the wound were taken at Sitka. The twenty-four-year-old mechanic was in his regular place the next morning, when Ellis flew Governor George A. Parks, Highway Engineer Robert J. Sommers of the Territorial Road Commission, Major Malcolm Elliott, President of the Road Commission, and Ike P. Taylor, Assistant Engineer of the Alaska Road Commission, on an

Lon Brennan Collection

1930. Alaska-Washington Airways published a number of brochures, schedules and timetables advertising their services.

inspection trip of the proposed site for the Skagway airport.

Larry Parks, the Juneau agent, was running a box ad in the *Alaska Daily Empire*, "Travel by Air, Seaplane *Taku*, Flights to any Point Desired!" It was to be a busy summer for Alaska-Washington Airways.

Floyd Keadle, Alaska-Washington Airways pilot in Juneau the previous summer, was very ill in a Portland hospital on May 1. Since leaving Juneau, the pilot had been flying for Varney Air Lines. The company was installing radios in their planes and it was necessary for the pilots to be fitted with individual earpieces. During the molding of the piece, plaster of Paris was accidently pushed in to his ear drums. An operation to remove it was necessary and, during the process nerves were mistakenly cut leaving the pilot with loss of hearing and partially–paralyzed. Another operation followed but did not improve his condition. The pilot never flew again, and the $10,000 settlement did little to compensate for that. (Keadle later got a job running a "cat" on the Bonneville Dam project in summer. Catching a bad cold on the job, he passed away from complications).

Ellis and Hatcher were away in the *Taku*, NC 102W, at 11:00 A.M. Wednesday, May 7, 1930, on a round trip to Hoonah and Tenakee, intending an hour's stop at each point to allow traveling men A.S. Brown and Mr. Brennan an opportunity to call on customers there before returning to Juneau. Steve Kane, Hoonah merchant, also went out and Larry Parks was along both ways. On Friday morning, May 9, Ellis brought Highway Engineer Sommers in from Sitka where he had surveyed a site for a municipal hydroport for planes, soon to be built with City and Territorial matching funds. Bids were also to be opened for the construction of similar hydroports at Wrangell and Petersburg.

Despite low ceilings, Ellis made a two-hour round trip from Juneau to Tulsequah, leaving the capital city at 11:00 A.M. Saturday, May 10, with Elliott Fremming and James D. Smith, miners, for Tulsequah, and Guy McNaughton and William C. Freeman for the round trip. He also brought in Ward McAllister, Ray Race and Ray Walker to Juneau.

Ellis had a busy day with the *Taku* on Sunday, May 11, 1930. Going to the Pacific American Fisheries plant on Excursion Inlet in the morning, the pilot carried forty passengers aloft on sightseeing trips. For a round trip out of Juneau he had carried Miss Anne LeRoy, Miss Hedvig Samuelson, Margaret "Peg" Ellis, Larry Parks and A.B. "Cot" Hayes. About 2:00 P.M.

Alaska-Washington Airways floating hangar at the foot of Willoughby Avenue in Juneau, Alaska.

Alaska-Washington Airways **Ketchikan**, *NC 657E, showing the beaching wheels placed under the floats to roll the planes up the sloping ramp from the water and into the hangar.*

he returned to the capital city to bring in his round-trippers and gas up. Going out shortly after, with Parks and Brian Harland in the cabin, he flew to the Astoria-Puget Sound cannery at Excursion Inlet, where he took up another forty-five sightseers. On Monday morning the pilot took the *Taku* on a sightseeing trip with Roberta Watson, C.J. Graham and Art Beaudin, before leaving for the Taku River at 1:00 P.M.

Departing at 9:30 A.M. Wednesday, May 14, for Tulsequah, Ellis and Hatcher took Joe Hill, Sr. and Joe Hill, Jr., George Bacon and J.A. Russell as passengers on the flight. Returning at 11:00 A.M., the pilot was away again at 1:30 P.M. for Sitka and Chichagof, carrying Fred Magill to the first point and Al Wick, Dupont Powder man, to the second. Late in the day they both returned with the pilot. The *Taku* was out again on Friday, May 16, going to Skagway and return. Doctor R.E. Southwell, Juneau optometrist and optician, made the one-way trip, with A.E. Wick, A.J. Nelson, E.E. Fitzwater and H.Y. Baird making the round trip.

The four-place Vega, *Juneau*, NC 432E, left Seattle at 7:00 A.M. Saturday, May 17, for Juneau and Port Althorp, under charter to Gilbert Skinner of the Alaska-Pacific Salmon Corporation. Anscel Eckmann brought the blue and cream Vega in to Juneau from Funter Bay

828

*The second Lockheed Vega to be christened with the name, **Juneau**, crashed in California on the day of delivery from the factory and was "washed out". The original **Juneau**, NC 432E, made its last trip to Alaska on May 17, 1930, before being returned to the factory for rebuild. The plane was scrapped because the plywood skin, which was not covered with fabric as the others were, had separated through the intrusion of moisture. The name, **Juneau**, was not seen on the Vegas again. This second **Juneau**, NC 102N, was being tested by Lockheed pilot Marshall Headle, with Alaska-Washington Airways mechanic Frank Hatcher riding in the cabin, when they struck a wire and crashed. Neither was injured, but the plane was a loss.*

at 5:15 P.M. on Sunday, her first visit since the previous fall. Eckmann, with his usual diving, zooming, circling arrival left no doubt in anyone's mind as to who was flying the airplane. The *Juneau* carried Mr. and Mrs. Skinner, Mr. and Mrs. Larry Ives and Marion Cummings to Funter Bay, and the party remained there while Eckmann came in to Juneau to refuel. The pilot left at 8:30 A.M. the next morning, to pick up his passengers and take them on to Port Althorp. Skinner was on a tour of the company's canneries. Ellis had left in the *Taku* on Sunday for a tour of the Mendenhall Glacier with a party, going the next day, at 10:00 A.M. Monday, May 19, to Sitka with Mrs. Snyder and Mrs. Burdich as one-way passengers, and Mrs. B. Zynda and Mrs. Sandborn for the round trip. Bob Ellis returned to Skagway on Tuesday, May 20, leaving at 11:00 A.M. to pick up Doctor Southwell and return him to Juneau. He also took Lew J. Walker to Skagway, and carried Tom Smith, H.P. Smith, H.B. Paulson and Larry Parks on the round trip. As their Juneau agent, Larry was always eager to fly when there was an empty seat.

William Strong, whose critically-ill wife had suffered a relapse in a Victoria, British Columbia, hospital, wanted to get there in a hurry. Bob Ellis, in the *Taku*, left with him at 3:00 A.M. Wednesday, May 21, 1930. Cot Hayes, company manager in the capital city, flew as far as Ketchikan, disembarking there to await the return of Ellis and Hatcher. The *Taku* arrived in Victoria at 2:15 P.M. the same day, then went on to Seattle. The plane was back in Ketchikan at 4:30 P.M. the following day, and continued on to Juneau to arrive there at 6:15 P.M. Frank Hatcher brought his mother and sister, Mrs. Myrtle Hatcher and Mrs. E.J. McGinty, up from Seattle for a visit. Cot Hayes boarded at Ketchikan to return to Juneau.

829

A.A. Bennett, former pilot from Fairbanks who had sold the Bennett-Rodebaugh Company to Alaskan Airways in 1929, was a speaker at the Chamber of Commerce luncheon in Juneau that day. He spoke glowingly of plans to establish a new air service in the capital city with two float-equipped Zenith cabin planes, the first one to arrive early the next month and the second to arrive in mid-July. Evidently he was unable to generate financing, for nothing ever came of it.

Shortly after the arrival of the *Taku* on May 22, Ellis was off for the Alaska-Pacific Salmon Corporation plant at Funter Bay, bringing Pedro Damocles, who was suffering from rheumatism, in to Juneau. The *Taku* left for Ketchikan on Friday morning, May 23, taking Doctor Harry C. DeVighne for a two-hour visit with Doctor S.C. Shurick. Dr. DeVighne returned to Juneau on the plane, landing at 8:00 P.M. Ellis had also taken two round-trip passengers from the capital city to Petersburg on the flight: Miss Mae McGuire and Miss Catherine McLaughlin, plus picking up three passengers at Wrangell for Ketchikan. On his return to Juneau the pilot had a flight booked for Sitka and Goddard, Alaska, a hot-spring resort on the west coast of Baranof Island about fifteen miles south of Sitka, for the following day. Leaving on the trip at 8:00 A.M. Saturday, May 24, he dropped Henry Sully, local traveling man, at Sitka and went on to the resort with Doctor F.L. Goddard, his grandson Jack Goddard who was to spend the summer at his grandfather's resort, and Doctor R.E. Southwell who was making a business trip to both Goddard and Sitka. Ellis returned to Juneau at 1:00 P.M. the same day, with Eiler Hansen, Lon Garrison, May Sarvela and W.B. Taylor as passengers. The same afternoon he flew a round trip to Tulsequah, with Charles Goldstein making the round trip while Fred Brentlinger, Clement Gilbert and Ray Race were one-way passengers.

Alaska-Washington Airways *Taku*, flown by Bob Ellis and Frank Hatcher, left shortly after 1:00 P.M. Wednesday, May 28, 1930, for Haines with Mrs. E.F. Graves and A.B. Hayes as round-trip passengers. Doctor Graves also made the return trip from Haines. He and Paul Kegel were leaving on a prospecting trip, their destination a closely-held secret. Ellis left in the *Taku* for Wrangell, taking off at 7:25 A.M. Friday, May 30, with Cot Hayes, R.J. Sommers and Cash Cole. Jim and Tom Cole, the Territorial Auditor's sons, went as round-trip passengers. Sommers visited both Wrangell and Petersburg, checking on the two hydroport projects. The one at Wrangell was being built by Anderson & Hatton, who expected it to be ready for service in about two weeks. The Petersburg hydroport construction was just beginning, with the contract awarded to Henry Hasbrouck. Each represented an investment of approximately $8000, shared equally by the community and the Territory. Sommers, Territorial Highway Engineer, and Cash Cole, Auditor, went on to Ketchikan with Ellis in the *Taku* to wind up the details of the contract on the Ketchikan hydroport and make arrangements for final payment. It had just been completed at a cost of about $11,000. Cash Cole was to return by steamer later on, while Sommers went back on the plane to Wrangell where the rest of the party boarded the Vega and returned to Juneau Friday evening.

Plans for a flight to Whitehorse, Yukon Territory, had been in the making. Bob Ellis left the capital city in the *Taku* at 9:00 A.M. Saturday, May 31, 1930, with James Carlson, D.S. Weyand, Mary Young, C.J. Graham and Larry Parks. The passengers were to join an excursion party going in by train but the *Taku* arrived after the other party. Ellis remained in the Interior overnight, returning to Juneau at 1:00 P.M. on Sunday.

E.J.A. "Paddy" Burke, flying the Canadian-registered Junkers, CF-AMX, belonging to Air Land Manufacturing Company of Vancouver, British Columbia, left Vancouver at 8:00 A.M. Friday morning and arrived in Juneau from Ketchikan at 8:00 P.M. Sunday, June 1,

Whitehorse, Yukon Territory in 1930 when visited by an Alaska-Washington Airways Vega, Taku, flown by Bob Ellis and Frank Hatcher.

Tom Crosson Collection

Alaska-Washington Airways Vega, Taku, at Whitehorse, Yukon Territory. Some of the old sternwheelers that plied the river can be seen in the background.

Tom Crosson Collection

1930. Burke and his flight mechanic, Emil Kading, had a full load and were headed for the Laird country with the two airmen and three passengers. Fueling and servicing the all-metal float plane, Burke was away shortly after noon. Flying by way of the Taku River to Atlin, where it was intended to base the plane for commercial and charter work, the F-13 with its L-5 motor had its work cut out for it in crossing over the mountains. The community would hear more of Burke later in the season.

A one-hour trip to the head of Chatham Straits was made by Ellis and Hatcher in the *Taku* on Tuesday afternoon, June 3, taking Mr. and Mrs. H.S. Graves and James Carlson. The next day the pilot left at 11:00 A.M. for Tulsequah, with William Spiller, Inspector of the Provincial Police of British Columbia, E. Martin, Canadian gamewarden, and E.M. "Win" Goddard, acting executive officer of the Alaska Game Commission. The Canadians, headquartered in Prince Rupert, had arrived that day on the Canadian government boat, P.M. L. No. 8 (Provincial Motor Launch No. 8). The airplane party visited the new Taku River mining camp, and returned to Juneau the same day.

▲ *Juneau, Alaska. June 1, 1930. Paddy Burke's F-13 Junkers monoplane, CF-AMX, enroute from Vancouver, British Columbia to the Laird country.*

▶ *Captain Edward Joseph Augustus "Paddy" Burke at Wolf Lake, Canada with the Canadian-registered Junkers F-13, CF-AMX, which he was flying when forced down in the upper Laird River country in the fall of 1930.*

Monday night, June 2, 1930, mechanics worked from sundown to sunrise at the Alaska-Washington Airways hangar to install a new pair of Edo 4650 pontoons on the *Taku*, NC 102W. Pontoons did not as yet have water rudders that could be lowered to give the pilot better directional control on the water. It would be at least another year before this improvement in design appeared in Alaska. However, the *Taku* did have the first vertical stabilizer under the fuselage, which gave the Alaska-Washington Airways fleet better directional stability.

Bob Ellis and Frank Hatcher, along with assistant flight mechanic John Stewart, who remained Outside, were off in the newly-floated *Taku* at 2:40 A.M. Thursday, June 5, 1930. Going to Tulsequah, British Columbia to pick up mining operator Bill Strong before going on to Victoria, British Columbia with the man, Ellis flew in calm

Juneau, Alaska 1930. Mechanic Brian Harland (on the left) and Bob Ellis on the Edo float of an Alaska-Washington Vega.

Lloyd Jarman Photo

air under lowering skies. Strong's wife, still in the hospital in the Canadian city, was reportedly dying. Strong disembarked there at 2:00 P.M. and the three-man crew went on to Seattle in the *Taku*. They departed the following day, Friday, at 1:30 P.M. and arrived at Ketchikan a few hours later. With no passengers, the Vega had made good time. An hour later, still without passengers, Ellis and Hatcher were off for Juneau, landing there at 8:36 P.M. that evening.

Bob Ellis took a party, made up of A.E. Wick, H.J. Eberhardt, Beatrice Hancock and Anna May Folta, for a round trip to Funter Bay, leaving Juneau at 4:15 P.M. Thursday, June 12, 1930. He left again in the *Taku* for an all-day flight to Sitka on the following morning, carrying B.F. Heintzleman, Wellman Holbrook and B.M. Behrends. Also aboard was Mrs. D.J. Williams for Hirst-Chichagof. Under charter to the U.S. Forest Service, the pilot picked up Mr. Charles G. Burdick at Sitka to fly to the lower end of Baranof Island on an inspection tour.

Back in Juneau, Ellis departed at 4:00 A.M. Sunday, June 15, for Lake Hasselborg, with sport fisherman Doctor W.W. Council, Mrs. O'Loughlin, Adrian "Casey" Roff, Phil Jolie and Ed Swenson. Fishing both ends of the lake, they caught one basketful at the outlet. Ellis had some difficulty during landing and takeoff with the slush ice on the lake, which also gave the fishermen some trouble. Returning to the capital city at 9:30 A.M. the pilot next flew a party of tourists over *Taku* Glacier, the Vega's namesake. Later in the day he flew Mr. and Mrs. A.T. Koski and Julia McCann on a similar flight over Mendenhall Glacier. Ellis made another Mendenhall flight the next morning, on Monday, with a party from the steamer *Queen*, captained by Olaf Hansen.

Tuesday morning, June 17, the pilot was away on a round-trip flight to the Alaska-Pacific Salmon Corporation plant at Funter Bay. Carrying Mrs. Clarence Withrow, wife of the superintendent, Mrs. Beatrice Bird, a friend of hers, and Miss Donna G. Alexander, daughter of C.J. Alexander, general manager of Alaska-Pacific, he delivered his passengers and returned to Juneau. Mrs. O.E. Schombel made the round trip with him. That same evening, at 6:30 P.M., Ellis and Hatcher left for Yakutat, carrying R.R. Payne, production manager of the New England Fish Company, and H.L. Faulkner, Juneau attorney, on a business trip. Remaining overnight, the pilot took off from Yakutat Bay at noon of the following day, to arrive on Eyak Lake at Cordova before 5:00 P.M. that afternoon. Attorney Faulkner remained at Cordova while the Vega went on to Driver Bay on Knight Island, where the rest of the party remained overnight. Ellis was back in Cordova at 5:00 A.M. Thursday, June 19, to pick up Haakon B. Friele who had arrived a half-hour earlier on the steamer *Yukon* from Ketchikan. Ellis and Hatcher were off again at 9:00 A.M. for Kvichak Station in Bristol Bay with the fish packer. Delivering their passenger, the two airmen were back in Cordova that evening. Taking attorney Faulkner and R.R. Payne, Ellis took off at 4:00 A.M. Friday, to return to Juneau. Stopping briefly at Chatham, they arrived back in the capital city at 8:30 A.M. The airmen had been in the air a total of eighteen hours on the two and one-half day trip, flying 2,160 miles.

Ellis and Hatcher were away again in the *Taku* early in the morning of Saturday, June 21, 1930, going to Tulsequah and the Taku mineral area. Carrying Warren H. Wilson and W.E. Butts outbound, the pair returned to go out on an extended trip to the westward. Carrying Mrs. Lloyd Minard for Port Althorp, Mr. and Mrs. Lee Atkinson and children for Chichagof, and Mrs. Julia McCann for Sitka, the pilot was back at his base that evening.

Sunday, June 22, Ellis flew four sightseeing trips with passengers from the steamer *Dorothy Alexander*. Three were made over Taku and one over Mendenhall Glacier. On Monday he made four more, with tourists from the *Admiral Rogers* on three of them, and with a party from the yacht *Wajola* going on the fourth flight. Tuesday morning the pilot went to Funter Bay, taking aboard Gilbert Skinner, Mrs. Clarence Withrow, and Mrs. Beatrice Bird before going on to Tenakee to pick up Miss Alexander. He had brought the ladies out to the Funter Bay cannery on June 17 and was now returning them to Juneau. The pilot left for Sitka in the afternoon to bring in five passengers.

Ernest Gilligan, a Juneau youth employed at the Annex powerhouse, departed June 24 on the *Princess Charlotte*, enroute to St. Louis to take up the study of aviation at Parks Air College. On that same day a new seaplane came to town, flown by pilot Loren H. McHenry, who was accompanied by Manager Roy Jones and a passenger from Ketchikan, Regional Forester B.F. "Frank" Heintzleman. The *Sea Pigeon*, a black and orange Stinson SM-8A, NC 935W, was the first of the new company's two planes to come north. It had arrived at Pioneer Airways' Ketchikan base four days ago. (see Ketchikan—1930, Chapter 53). Arriving in Juneau at 4:30 P.M. on Tuesday, the plane returned south to Ketchikan the following morning, Wednesday, June 25, 1930, with McHenry and Jones aboard.

The Alaska-Washington Airways Vega, *Taku*, with Ellis and Hatcher, left Juneau shortly before 1:00 P.M. on Wednesday, making a quick round trip to Ketchikan. With Willis R. Lebo as a one-way passenger, and C.J. Graham, Roberta Watson, Art Beaudin and C.J. Krogh as round-trippers, the pilot remained in Ketchikan one hour in order to give his passengers an opportunity to walk about town. They returned to Juneau early in the evening.

The Vega, *Taku*, flown as usual by Bob Ellis and Frank Hatcher, was off early in the morning of Friday, June 27, 1930, to drop Frank Heintzleman and Wellman Holbrook at Thayer Lake. Miss Pearl Peterson went along for the round trip. Returning at 7:30 A.M., the float plane was away almost immediately for Tulsequah with Doctor F.A. Kerr, P.R. Bradley and J. Williams as passengers. Coming back to Juneau, the pilot returned that afternoon to Thayer Lake to return Frank Heintzleman and Holbrook to the capital city. Ray Taylor of the U.S. Forest Service and Mrs. E.W. Loveridge of Washington, D.C. went along as round-trippers. That same evening the pilot flew to Turner Lake with a fishing party composed of Doctor W.W. Council, Mr. O'Neil and Bob Murphy. He went out early the next morning to return the party, but was balked by low fog at the lake entrance. A second attempt later in the morning was successful, the *Taku* returning with the fishing party to Juneau about noon. Ellis was expecting a new Vega, *Skagway*, which had just been delivered to Alaska-Washington Airways

*June 27, 1930 at Thayer Lake, with **Taku**, NC 102W. Left to Right: Wellman Holbrook, U.S.F.S.; B. Frank Heintzleman, U.S.F.S.; Robert E. Ellis, pilot, and Frank Hatcher, flight mechanic.*

in Seattle, and would come north soon.

Flown by Anscel Eckmann, the chief pilot for the company, the *Skagway*, NC 103W, a seven-place (six passengers plus a pilot) Model MB-5, also painted blue and cream similar to the *Taku*, arrived in Juneau from Seattle at 7:00 P.M. Saturday, June 28, 1930, eleven hours after taking off from the Puget Sound city. Brian Harland was accompanying the pilot as flight mechanic. Brian, a Juneau youth, had been named to an alternate appointment to West Point early in the year. On February 22 he traveled to Haines to take the entrance examinations to the academy at Chilkoot Barracks. He was now going into aviation. The plane also carried J.L. Carman, Jr., company president, Watkin Davies of Stockton, California, E.B. Kellens of Topeka, Kansas and Max Smith, of Skagway. After a short stop at the capital city, Eckmann went on to deliver Smith at Skagway. Kellens went along on the round trip, returning to Juneau late in the evening with the two airmen.

Sunday afternoon, June 29, both the *Skagway* and the *Taku* were aloft, with Fred Ordway, local photographer who had first opened his Juneau studios on April 30, 1928, going along to photograph the planes in flight against the scenic background of the Gastineau Channel area. Changing from one airplane to the other, he was able to get memorable scenes of both for Alaska-Washington Airways. Sightseers who accompanied the flights were Carman, Kellens, Davies and Larry Parks in the *Taku*, while Harry Lucas, Ralph Bartholomew and John Johnson flew in the *Skagway*. That evening Eckmann flew a party, composed of Doctor Council, Mr. O'Neil, Mr. Kellens and Mr. Carman to Hasselborg Lake, while Bob Ellis took John Worcester and Pio DeCano to Funter Bay, and Mrs. Metcalf and Mary Metcalf to Excursion Inlet.

Early in the morning of Monday, June 30, 1930, the *Skagway* left for Seattle with her

835

◄ *Joseph L. Carman, Jr., President of Alaska-Washington Airways which he organized in 1929. The photo was taken in 1936.*

▼ *Alaska-Washington Airways Vega* **Skagway**, *NC 103W, in flight near Juneau, Alaska in Sheep Creek Basin, 1930.*

Ordway Studio

incoming group, and Larry Parks as an additional passenger for the flight south. (see Ketchikan—1930, Chapter 53). The *Taku*, flown by Ellis and Hatcher, and accompanied by mechanic Brian Harland, left for Killisnoo at 1:30 P.M. Monday, taking Mrs. Vincent Soboleff to the community. Margaret Ellis and Miss Ann LeRoy joined the crew for the round trip.

Ellis and Hatcher were out in the *Taku* in the first week of July, taking M.J. O'Connor of the U.S. Bureau of Fisheries and H.W. Terhune, executive officer of the Alaska Game Commission, on an inspection trip through the district. Visiting Ketchikan, Behm Canal, Olive Cove and Wrangell, the party returned to Juneau at 7:00 P.M. Saturday, July 5, 1930. With several hours in the air they had covered an area that would have taken several days by boat.

The *Skagway* was back in Alaska. Now flown by pilot Robin "Pat" Renehan, with flight mechanic Frank J. Wadman, the Vega arrived in Juneau from Ketchikan on Monday evening, July 7. Coming up from Seattle, the plane brought Gilbert Skinner, head of the Alaska-Pacific Salmon Corporation, to Juneau. After gassing up, the plane continued on to Funter Bay to remain overnight, returning to the capital city in the morning. Ellis then took Skinner in the *Taku* to Port Althorp, expecting to return that afternoon. Pat Renehan went out at

836

Gordon Graham

Flight mechanic Chandler Hicks standing up through hatch in Alaska-Washington Airways **Skagway** *at Juneau, Alaska.*

1:00 P.M. that same day to Tulsequah, to deliver Elliott Fremming and Homer Ficken to the mining camp. Miss Nell McCloskey and Mr. and Mrs. Charles O. Sabin were round-trippers on the flight.

Bob Ellis, in the *Taku*, took a charter for the Alaska-Juneau Gold Mining Company to Skagway on Friday, June 11. P.R. Bradley, consulting engineer for the company, was enroute to the Treadwell-Yukon Company, Limited, camp at Wernecke in the Mayo district of Yukon Territory. His purpose was to survey conditions there, returning in a few weeks. Three additional passengers, Miss Virginia Metzgar, Mrs. Florence Oakes, and Mrs. W.S. George were round-trippers.

The Gorst Air Transport, Incorporated, Boeing flying boat, NC 115E, had been working out of Ketchikan earlier in the season. Pilot Clayton Scott and his flight mechanic, John Selby, had left there on July 3, 1930, enroute to Cordova by way of Port Althorp, bypassing Juneau on the way north. (see Cordova and Ketchikan—1930, Chapters 53, 55). The plane which had left July 10 from Cordova for Ketchikan carried no passengers, and was reported on July 12 to be missing. When contacted by Vern Gorst in Seattle, Alaska-Washington Airways promised immediate assistance. The *Taku*, flown by Ellis and Frank Hatcher, left Juneau at 5:30 A.M. Sunday, July 13, 1930, to search the coastline along the Gulf of Alaska for the missing plane. They landed twice, at Lituya Bay and at Yakutat, seeking any information on the plane. At Icy Bay, Ellis spotted a cabin through a hole in the fogbank he was flying over. Making it down underneath, he saw a message written deeply in the beach sand, and spotted the two missing men on the roof of the cabin. They had heard the plane in the distance and went up to get a better view. Ellis managed to get the *Taku* down in a narrow, ice-choked lagoon near the cabin and taxied it to a sand beach cluttered with large chunks of ice. He learned the Gorst plane had been forced down on July 10 by a failing engine. Scott landed the flying boat at the entrance of Icy Bay between Katalla and Yakutat, soon losing the left, lower wing tip to the pounding waves. (see Cordova—1930, Chapter 55). Working their way through the ice cakes, the airmen finally beached the plane on an unprotected shore, where the waves further damaged the plane. Seeking shelter the next day in a cabin across the lagoon, they remained there until the welcome sound of the Alaska-Washington Vega brought them from the cabin.

Making a difficult takeoff from the lagoon, Ellis brought the two grounded airmen in to Cordova, landing in Eyak Lake shortly before noon.

Ellis and Hatcher had a charter to Bristol Bay to make before returning to Juneau. Scott and his girl friend, schoolteacher Myrtle Smith, who was then visiting her sister in Cordova,

837

traveled by steamer to Juneau. John Selby, the flight mechanic, awaited the return of Ellis in order to return in the *Taku*. The Gorst flying boat, *Nugget*, was a loss, although a Ketchikan canneryman, J. Iverson, salvaged the remains in August and had them shipped from the vicinity of Yakutat, south to Seattle aboard the Admiral Watson.

Bob Ellis and Frank Hatcher returned to Cordova on Wednesday, July 16. (see Cordova—1930, Chapter 55). Leaving shortly after arrival, with Haakon B. Friele and John Selby aboard, Ellis arrived in Juneau late that same afternoon. Clayton Scott and Myrtle Smith did not arrive in Juneau until Monday, July 21, 1930, coming by passenger vessel from Cordova.

The *Skagway*, NC 103W, with Pat Renehan as pilot and Frank Wadman as flight mechanic, was in Juneau taking up the slack while Ellis was up north. Coming from Seattle, Renehan brought Gilbert Skinner from Ketchikan, dropping his passenger at Funter Bay on the way. Arriving in Juneau at 6:00 P.M. Monday, July 14, the pilot was away the next morning at 9:30 A.M., taking Doctor Council to Warm Springs Bay to render first aid to Oliver Anderson before bringing the patient in for medical treatment. Renehan picked up Gilbert Skinner at Funter Bay on the way in. At 3:00 P.M. the pilot took off again, returning Skinner to Funter Bay before coming in to place the *Skagway* in the Alaska-Washington floating hangar for the night.

Renehan and Wadman, in the *Skagway*, proceeded to Ketchikan late in the day of Wednesday, July 16, 1930, bringing John Selby to a new job with Pioneer Airways. The pilot also had a charter out of there for the following day. With Ellis and Hatcher coming in to the capital city on Wednesday, July 16, they were dispatched in the *Taku* to Funter Bay at 2:00 P.M. the next afternoon to pick up Gil Skinner and take him to Port Althorp. Ellis and Hatcher then went on to Point Retreat, where the *Fairweather*, a fishing boat out of the Hawk Inlet cannery had foundered, leaving a man there to refloat the craft. The pilot returned to Funter Bay, picking up four passengers from the steamer *Queen*, landing at Juneau with them in the evening.

Early the next morning, Friday, July 18, 1930, Ellis was out on two flights over Mendenhall Glacier, taking tourists from the steamers then in port. Eleven, in all, made the sightseeing trips. At 11:00 A.M. the *Taku* again flew to Funter Bay to take Gil Skinner to Port Althorp, where he remained a short time before being returned. Back in Juneau at noon, the pilot received an emergency call and left immediately for Excursion Inlet to bring in an injured man from a cannery there. In two hours he was back with Nick Branavich, one of the crew of the seine boat *Florida* of the Peril Straits Packing Company. The man was taken to the hospital for treatment.

Ellis left soon after his arrival, for Tenakee, with Mrs. Frank Reeder, Mr. and Mrs. H.S. Sully, J.B. Burford and Mr. H.Y. Baird, who represented the Burroughs Adding Machine Company in Seattle, as passengers. On his return the pilot went to Haines, returning from there to go to Hawk Inlet before coming back to Juneau in the evening.

The Alaska-Washington Vega, with Ellis and Hatcher, went out the next morning, Saturday, to Hawk Inlet where they picked up Hans Floe of the P.E. Harris Packing Company there, bringing him in to Juneau. The pilot was off soon after, taking attorney R.E. Robinson and Mr. Baird to Funter Bay, where he picked up Gilbert Skinner and took the three men to Kake. The *Wrangell*, NC 657E, flown by Pat Renehan and Frank Wadman, came up from Ketchikan that afternoon, picking up the three passengers at Kake and flying them to Ketchikan. Ellis left Juneau Saturday afternoon for Waterfall, with W.E. Rooney and C.M. Witt, representatives of American Can Company. They spent Saturday night at Todd, and got as far as Petersburg on Sunday; the weather was too unfavorable to fly. They were still there at noon the next day. Intending to pick up attorney Robinson in Ketchikan, Ellis was unable to do so and returned to Juneau from Petersburg. The *Wrangell* was also being held in Ketchikan by the same low ceilings and fog. Cot Hayes was expecting a new Vega, *Sitka*, NC 974H, in the coming week. It was to have arrived from the factory in California on Monday.

Ellis and Hatcher flew the *Taku* to Atlin on Monday, July 21, 1930, taking Joseph L. Hill, a mining man, and Doctor Forrest A. Kerr as passengers. Intending to bring in Ernest W. Sawyer, assistant to the Secretary of the Interior, Mrs. Sawyer and their son, so as to enable them to catch the steamship *Aleutian* for Seward, the pilot was unable to cross the mountains because of dense clouds, and the Sawyers missed their connections. The party came in on Tuesday by way of the Taku River canyon, arriving at 4:30 P.M. Ellis took the Sawyers out to Port Althorp early in the evening to catch the *Aleutian* there, also dropping R.R. Payne at Chatham, Starr Calvert at Todd and Ross Smith at Funter Bay. Sawyer was on his way to Fairbanks and the Seward Peninsula. Ellis remained overnight at Port Althorp, coming back in to Juneau Wednesday morning, where he made five sightseeing flights over the Mendenhall Glacier with tourists from the *Dorothy Alexander*. He left that afternoon to take Juneau attorney H.L. Faulkner to Ruins Point on Kosciusko Island in the Alexander Archipelago, picking up Harold Walker at Tenakee and Captain M. O'Connor, fisheries agent, at Sitka on the way. They visited the cannery of the Petersburg Packing Company at Ruins Point and stayed overnight at Shakan before flying the same courses on the return flight. The pilot and his mechanic made a flight to Chatham and Todd to bring in R.R. Payne, of New England Fish Company, attorney H.L. Faulkner and his daughter, Jean, before shutting down for the night next to the *Wrangell*. Ellis was scheduled for a flight to Sitka the next afternoon with a group promoting farm extension work in Southeastern Alaska.

The *Wrangell*, flown by Pat Renehan and flight mechanic Brian Harland, had been used by Gil Skinner to visit his fish packing interests in the Juneau area. Accompanied on these flights by Mrs. Skinner and Mr. and Mrs. Arthur McCann of New York, Skinner had returned to Juneau on Thursday evening, July 24, 1930. Renehan took up a party of sightseers from the steamship *Prince George* late that evening for a half-hour flight. He left the next morning with Skinner and his party for a round trip to Skagway. On his return he flew the party to Ketchikan, by way of the Alaska-Pacific cannery at Kake, where the McCanns could board a southbound steamer. It was not unusual at this time of the year to catch a steamship at one of the canneries for they often stopped to load canned salmon for shipment south.

The newest Vega of Alaska-Washington Airways arrived in Juneau from Seattle and Ketchikan on the afternoon of Saturday, July 26, 1930. A beautiful sight, the *Sitka*, NC 974H, Model 5, whose body was painted a rich red color instead of the blue and cream of the *Taku*, with other parts cream-colored with gold and black stripes and lettering, was the first with a full NACA speed cowling over the engine, giving it a racy, streamlined look. With less wind resistance, it also added fifteen miles per hour to the plane's speed. Along with Chief Pilot Anscel Eckmann and flight mechanic Chandler Hicks was a new pilot for the Alaska division, Eugene A. "Gene" Meyring. A former naval officer, he had been flying for Alaska-Washington Airways on their triangle run out of Seattle. The *Sitka* would be based in Juneau, with Meyring as pilot, while Eckmann returned to his duties in Seattle. Passengers arriving on the *Sitka* were Mr. and Mrs. Gilbert Skinner, Leif Buschmann and Larry Parks. The seven-place (six passengers plus the pilot) Vega had made a record run of five hours and fifteen minutes air time from Seattle to Ketchikan the previous day, making two stops enroute. They had departed Ketchikan at 11:30 A.M. Immediately after its arrival in the capital city, the *Sitka* went to Funter Bay and Port Althorp.

Bob Ellis and Frank Hatcher had returned from Sitka with the *Taku*, NC 102W, on Friday afternoon, July 25, 1930. Going to Skagway with Richard Gross, general manager of the B.C. Packers, they left their passenger there and returned by way of Funter Bay, bringing in three cannery workers. Going out the next morning, July 26, the *Taku* went to Hood Bay, then to Sitka, returning to Juneau later in the afternoon.

Eckmann and Chandler Hicks, accompanied by Clayton Scott, who had arrived by steamer from Cordova on July 21, and Miss Anita Banta of New Orleans, had flown in the *Taku* to Port Althorp on Sunday afternoon, July 27, to pick up Mr. and Mrs. Gilbert Skinner and take them to Funter Bay. Scott and Miss Banta returned in the plane to Juneau. At 5:00 P.M. that evening, the *Taku* was off again for Funter Bay, with Doctor Council, John H. Mulkey and Miss Winifred Carlson as passengers. Mrs. Skinner and John Gilbert of the Alaska-Pacific Salmon Corporation boarded the plane there and the entire party flew to Lake Kathleen on the west coast of Admiralty Island where they enjoyed excellent trout fishing. Returning Mrs. Skinner and John Gilbert to Funter Bay, the pilot brought his other three passengers back to Juneau.

The *Sitka*, NC 974H, flown by Gene Meyring with flight mechanic Frank Hatcher, went out to Lake Hasselborg at 4:00 A.M. Sunday, July 27, with a sport-fishing party. Those who went were Mr. and Mrs. Harry Sperling, Mr. and Mrs. Keith Wildes and Wellman Holbrook. The *Sitka* returned at 10:00 A.M., its passengers having made a good catch. Later in the morning the crew were off in the *Sitka*, taking Captain M.J. O'Connor of the Federal Bureau of Fisheries on a patrol. They returned late in the afternoon, then going out to Funter Bay to pick up Gilbert Skinner and his party for a flight to Ketchikan, by way of Waterfall. Anscel Eckmann was also aboard, intending to catch the steamship *Prince Henry* at Ketchikan to travel to Vancouver, British Columbia, then fly to Seattle on one of his company's planes. Bringing Mrs. Gilbert Skinner, Miss Banta and Eckmann, the *Sitka* landed at Ketchikan on Monday, July 28, about 5:00 P.M. (see Ketchikan—1930, Chapter 53).

In Juneau, the *Taku*, with pilot Bob Ellis and flight mechanic Frank Hatcher, was away for Cordova on the morning of Monday, July 28. Carrying W.H. Gannett, a newspaper man from Maine, Mrs. Ellis and Larry Parks, the plane was forced by foggy weather to return to Juneau when some distance out. The flight was not repeated and the *Taku*, flown by Eckmann and Renehan left for Seattle for an overhaul. Bob Ellis, accompanied by his wife, flew it to Ketchikan where Eckmann and Renehan went on with it. Eckmann had been named Chief of Operations for Alaska-Washington Airways to succeed Commander W.E. Wynn. The Ellises returned to Juneau on the *Wrangell*, with Bob as its pilot.

Gorst Air Transport pilot Clayton Scott had been in Juneau since July 21; he had arrived from Cordova by ship following the loss of the Boeing flying boat *Nugget* at Icy Bay. He planned to fly an American plane from Whitehorse to Seattle for its owner. The Travel Air 6000B, NC 377M, had been impounded several weeks before by Canadian Customs authorities when flown from California through British Columbia and to Whitehorse, Yukon Territory without obtaining the necessary permits and authorizations from the Canadian government. The eight-place monoplane with a 425 horsepower Wright Whirlwind motor was owned by a man from San Francisco by the name of Edmonds. The plane had been flown north along the highway to Hazelton, staying inside the coastal mountains. Scott planned to take it back over the same route since it was on wheels. Myrtle Smith would accompany him on the trip to Seattle.

Taking a steamer to Skagway, and the White Pass & Yukon Railway to Whitehorse, the pair arrived at the interior city at the end of July to inspect the plane and get it ready for the

Clayton Scott Photo

August 9, 1930. Telegraph Creek, British Columbia from the cockpit of the Travel Air 6000B, NC 377M, that Clayton Scott flew from Whitehorse to Seattle on his return from Alaska. He was accompanied by Myrtle Smith, who later became his wife.

August 9, 1930. Hazelton, British Columbia. Travel Air 6000B, NC 377M, flown by Clayton Scott from White-horse, Yukon Territory to Seattle. Myrtle Smith, who accompanied the pilot on the flight, relaxes near the right front wheel while Scott makes further repairs to the deteriorated fabric on the belly of the plane.

Clayton Scott Photo

flight. The battery had been left in the plane for weeks and the acid fumes had deteriorated the belly fabric in its vicinity. The pilot screwed a piece of sheet metal over the area beneath the plane to cover it temporarily, and made some other minor adjustments.

Sunday, August 3, 1930, the pilot went aloft for a one-hour test hop in the Travel Air, shooting some circuits to get used to landing on wheels again. Myrt went along. On August 6, the couple were away for Atlin, landing there an hour later. Traveling in a leisurely fashion, Scott flew the next leg to Telegraph Creek on August 9, with an air time of one hour and forty-five minutes. They went on to Hazelton the same day, taking another two hours and forty-five minutes of air time. A stop was made here while the pilot made further repairs to the deteriorated fabric on the belly of the plane. With pleasant weather, Myrt made a picnic of it at the hayfield airport.

The pair departed Hazelton for Prince George on Sunday, August 10, landing there after a flight of two hours and fifteen minutes. The following day they made their longest flight, landing at Vancouver, British Columbia in the Travel Air 6000B after flying three hours and thirty minutes. Remaining overnight in the coastal city, Scott flew the plane on to Seattle the next day, a one hour and twenty-minute leg. (The route he flew over from Whitehorse has been used much in ensuing years by pilots ferrying planes to and from Alaska.)

Scott went back to work flying the Loenings for Gorst on the Bremerton Air Ferry and other places. He was to return to Alaska in the summer of 1932 in a Loening Commuter. Myrtle Smith resumed her teaching duties in the Lafayette school in Seattle. Scott and Miss Smith were married Saturday evening, October 27, 1934. Scott was by then employed as personal pilot for W.E. Boeing of Boeing Aircraft Company.

Alaska-Washington Airways officials were preparing to send their newest Vega, the *Petersburg*, NC 336H, north in late July. Inclement weather in southeast Alaska, particularly in the Ketchikan area, was causing a delay. The *Wrangell* was in the hangar in Juneau, after going out to Funter Bay on Thursday, July 31, to pick up Gilbert Skinner and take him to Kake. Remaining overnight, the pilot flew Skinner from there on an inspection flight to various fish traps belonging to Alaska-Pacific Salmon Corporation before returning him to Funter Bay. The pilot, Bob Ellis, then returned to Juneau. Gene Meyring and Frank Hatcher were in Ketchikan with the *Sitka*, and the *Taku* had gone to Seattle for an overhaul.

The new seaplane for Alaska-Washington Airways, the *Petersburg*, left Seattle at 8:40 A.M. Friday, August 1, 1930. The seven-place Model 5, NC 336H, was painted a deep orange with black striping and, like the *Taku*, had the additional vertical fin below the empennage for better directional stability. It also had the NACA cowling over the motor. Pat Renehan and Frank Hatcher were crewing the ship. A new Alaska-Washington Airways pilot, Clark Wing, and Gene Meyring's wife were also aboard the plane, as well as D.H. Freeman, Jr., the treasurer of the United States and Alaska Packing Company. The two airmen transferred from the *Petersburg* to the *Sitka* at Ketchikan, coming in to Juneau the evening of Friday, August 1. Enroute from Ketchikan, the *Sitka* landed J. Burdette at Port Alexander and D.H. Freeman, Jr. at Port Herbert. At Funter Bay, Mrs. Gilbert Skinner and her houseguest, Mrs. F.J. Clancy, disembarked. The plane had been out on fish trap and cannery patrol duty that morning. It had been a long day.

*Pilot Bob Ellis stands on the float at left in his plus-4s while passengers load into the Vega **Petersburg**, NC 366H, in Kimshan Cove on the west coast of Chichagof Island. Brian Harland is at right.*

Bob Ellis and Chandler Hicks left Juneau for Ketchikan in the *Wrangell* on Saturday, August 2, 1930. They would leave the plane there and fly the *Petersburg* up to Juneau, where it was intended to base the new Vega. From Juneau, the *Wrangell*'s passengers were Karl Thiele, Secretary for Alaska, on his way to Wrangell, and attorney Grover Winn for Kake. The pilot picked up Gilbert Skinner and John Gilbert at Funter Bay, taking them to Ketchikan. The plane would remain at the city. (see Ketchikan—1930, Chapter 53).

Highway Engineer R.J. Sommers returned to Juneau from an inspection trip covering the southern end of the Division to announce on August 4, 1930, the completion of the two hydroports at Wrangell and Petersburg. They were now available for any seaplanes landing at the two ports. In 1930 two other landing ports were under construction in Southeastern Alaska: a hydroplane port at Sitka and a land field at Skagway.

Frank Dorbandt and Lon Cope, flying a Fairchild 51, NC 5364, on floats, from Seattle to Anchorage to use for their air service in that city, arrived in Juneau from Ketchikan late in the afternoon of Saturday, August 2. Departing the next day, shortly after 9:00 A.M., the plane reached Anchorage that afternoon. Dorbandt's wife, Vida, accompanied the two airmen. (see Anchorage—1930, Chapter 57).

The *Petersburg* had flown to Juneau from Ketchikan on August 3, to be put in service there. The *Sitka* with Gene Meyring, pilot, and Frank Hatcher, mechanic, had flown to Ketchikan on Monday, August 4, 1930, returning to the capital city that same evening with John Gilbert and two tourists from New York. Canneries were visited on the way up and a

Alaska-Washington Airways Vega, **Petersburg,**
moored at a beautiful pristine shore at Tulsequah on
the Taku River.

sightseeing flight was made over Glacier Bay. Following its arrival, the plane flew a trip to Tulsequah with passengers. The next day both planes were busy, making cannery service and forestry inspection flights, also sightseeing flights over Taku and Mendenhall glaciers. That afternoon the *Sitka*, with Ellis and Hatcher as crew, took three officers of the British cruiser *Dauntless*, and Mrs. R.H. Moore, wife of the commander of the vessel, on a flight over Atlin Lake, British Columbia, returning that same afternoon. The *Sitka* then took James Spencer, an official of the Astoria and Puget Sound Canning Company to their plant at Excursion Inlet, leaving him there. The pilot also dropped James V. Davis and his daughter Grace at Funter Bay, returning to Juneau in the evening.

The *Petersburg* was not long in Juneau; that same Tuesday it departed for Ketchikan on its way to Seattle. Pilot Bob Ellis, with Chandler Hicks, was carrying Mrs. Ellis and Cot Hayes. Stopping at Hood Bay to drop a welding outfit needed for repairing a boiler at the Hood Bay Packing Company plant, Ellis continued south from Ketchikan on Wednesday. The plane arrived in time to fill in for the *Taku*, NC 102W, which had burned after a forced landing on August 4 at the entrance to Hood Canal. (see Ketchikan—1930, Chapter 53). The plane was being operated on the Seattle-Victoria-Vancouver, British Columbia route at the time. It had just come out of overhaul No one had been injured but only the motor and the pontoons were saved. The propeller, stopped in a horizontal position, had caught across the top of the floats when the motor dropped from the burning plane, or it would have fallen into deep water.

In Juneau, the *Sitka*, crewed by Gene Meyring and Brian Harland, was off on Wednesday morning, August 6, to pick up Gilbert Skinner at Funter Bay and fly a patrol of the company's fish traps. The use of airplanes had practically killed the fish piracy of the traps that commonly existed prior to its use. The fish pirates, brailing company traps, never knew when a plane would swoop out of the sky and identify their boats for prosecution. The trap robbers would sell the fish to a competitor's plant, claiming they had been caught at sea, although net marks on fish were distinctive from trap marks. That same afternoon the plane went to Todd, to fly patrol service for the Peril Straits Packing Company, going up again late in the evening with a party of four from Juneau, to fly up the Taku River.

Early morning of Thursday, August 7, 1930, saw the *Sitka* aloft, flying three round trips between Juneau and Funter Bay, taking workers from there to the Funter cannery. With Gilbert Skinner aboard, they spent the next three hours on trap patrol. Late in the forenoon the *Sitka* left the capital city, carrying Dave Housel, owner of the Alaska Hotel, and Commissioner C.H. Flory of the Department of Agriculture, to Kuiu Bay and Sitka. Flory wanted to visit the Agricultural Experiment Station at Sitka and Housel got off at Security Bay where he had a fox farm. Meyring made a three-hour patrol of fish traps for Peril Straits Packing Company that afternoon, going out to pick up Housel and Flory in the evening to return them to Juneau. Larry Parks, the Juneau agent for Alaska-Washington Airways, served as flight mechanic on the day's flying. The battered Gorst flying boat, which had been salvaged from Icy Bay, passed through Juneau on Friday, August 8, deck-loaded on the *Admiral Watson*. It was on its way to Seattle. The vessel also had 29,000 cases of canned salmon aboard, picked up at various stops, with more coming aboard before she left Alaska.

Bob Wark and Eddie Brown, off Tacoma on August 10, 1930, in the *Pacific Era*, enroute to Whitehorse on their way to Tokyo, were forced to land at Vancouver, British Columbia, less than three hours after their departure. They had intended to fly the North Pacific by way of Whitehorse, Fairbanks, Nome and Petropavlovsk. After cleaning clogged gas lines on the plane at the Lulu Island airport, Wark attempted to fly the *Pacific Era* back to Ladner Field to resume the flight to Whitehorse but overshot the runway, wrecking the plane and injuring himself. This finished their Pacific attempt via Alaska.

The Alaska-Washington Vega, *Skagway*, NC 103W, was being ordered back to Juneau. Departing Seattle at 8:30 A.M. Saturday, August 9, 1930, piloted by Robert E. Ellis with flight mechanic Frank Hatcher, the Vega carried relief pilot Clark Wing, his wife Barbara Wing, Margaret Ellis, Mrs. John W. Gilbert and Alaska manager A.B. "Cot" Hayes. Stopping at Namu, British Columbia to refuel, Ellis landed the plane at Ketchikan that same afternoon, where John W. Gilbert boarded the plane to join his wife for the flight to Juneau. Ellis arrived in the capital city at 7:00 P.M. that evening. The *Skagway* was to take the place of the *Petersburg*, which was now in Seattle. With unfavorable flying weather, the *Skagway* remained in the company hangar all day Sunday. Using the *Sitka*, Clark Wing and Frank Hatcher made a round trip to Funter Bay to deliver Mr. and Mrs. Gilbert to the cannery there. Mrs. Wing and Miss Madge Hildinger made the round trip.

Pat Renehan, flying the *Wrangell*, NC 657E, arrived at Juneau Tuesday evening, August 12, and departed immediately for Funter Bay, where he spent the night. He left the next morning with Gilbert Skinner and Mrs. Skinner, taking them to Kake. Here the Skinners boarded the *Sitka*, the controls of which were taken over by Renehan, who flew it on to Ketchikan that same day. He carried the Skinners, Mr. and Mrs. Gilbert, pilot Gene Meyring and his wife to Ketchikan, arriving there late in the day. Renehan continued to Seattle by steamer, to fly company planes out of there, with the *Sitka* now based at Ketchikan, Gene Meyring as its pilot.

Clark Wing, Alaska-Washington Airways relief pilot, returned the *Wrangell* to Juneau on Wednesday, where the plane spent the night in the hangar. It was now based at the capital city. A flight to Anchorage to bring down William Howard Gannett of Augusta, Maine, publisher of *Comfort Magazine*, was cancelled, with the man now planning to take the steamer *Alaska* to Juneau. The weather on the route was poor for such a flight. Alaska-Washington Airways was promising complimentary scenic rides to Misses Muriel Jarman, Grace Naghel and two friends of each of them as soon as more pleasant weather appeared. The young ladies had recently been cast in the Elks Show and, as a result, had been awarded the free rides.

Bad weather kept the *Wrangell* and the *Skagway* in the hangar on Thursday and Friday forenoon. Pilot Clark Wing and mechanic Chandler Hicks flew the *Wrangell* to Hoonah in the afternoon, flying a cannery and fish trap patrol out of there. On Sunday morning, August 17, the *Wrangell* was out again, going to Ketchikan with J. DeCano as a passenger. Clark Wing remained at the city with the plane, to do some flying out of there. (see Ketchikan—1930, Chapter 53).

Pilot Robert E. Ellis and flight mechanic Chandler Hicks were manning the *Skagway* at Juneau. Sunday, August 17, they were out on cannery and trap inspection for several hours, taking Doctor Willis H. Rich, a scientist for the U.S. Bureau of Fisheries, and Captain M.J. O'Connor, assistant agent of the Bureau of Fisheries, to the southern end of the district. The pilot stopped at Craig, Olive Cove and other points. In the late afternoon and evening the Vega made short sightseeing flights with tourists from the steamship *Prince Henry*. Monday morning, August 18, 1930, the pilot was out again in the plane, going to Port Herbert to pick up D.H. Freeman, Jr., vice-president and treasurer of the United States and Alaska Packing Company, bringing him in to Juneau.

By Wednesday, August 20, Alaska-Washington Airways had established new offices for the company at the store of J.B. Burford and Company in the Valentine Building in Juneau. The aerial headquarters was manned by comely Barbara Wing, wife of Clark Wing. Pilot Bob Ellis and Chandler Hicks were off in the *Skagway* at noon, carrying fishing men Lyle Davis and

George Franklin to Wrangell. The Stinson SM-8A *Northbird*, NC 991W, had flown in from the Ketchikan base of Pioneer Airways on Wednesday, August 20, with pilot Jim Dodson at the controls. He brought Mr. and Mrs. Gilbert Skinner, with their guest, from Ketchikan, returning there in the evening with the seaplane. The company's second Stinson, *Sea Pigeon*, NC 935W, arrived in Ketchikan from Seattle the next evening. It had been rebuilt at the Puget Sound city, and was now flown by a new pilot for Pioneer Airways, Gerald J. "Jerry" Smith. Jerry had made the initial flight with Roy Jones in the Curtiss MF *Northbird* in July of 1922 from Seattle to Ketchikan.

Ellis and Hicks, in the *Skagway*, returned from Wrangell the forenoon of Thursday, August 21, after overnighting there. They made a round trip to Funter Bay shortly after their arrival. The two airmen had taken Ike Goldstein, Juneau merchant, Vic Manville, Taku mining man, and D.C. McKecknie, of the Canadian Consolidated Mining Company, to the Taku district on Wednesday, before making their flight to Wrangell. They went out now and brought the men in to Juneau that evening. The *Wrangell* and *Sitka* were still at Ketchikan.

There was trouble in the Laird district of British Columbia. The Junkers seaplane CF-AMX, flown by Paddy Burke, that had stopped in Juneau to refuel on June 1, 1930, leaving shortly thereafter for Atlin, was missing. The pilot had left his base at Atlin on Sunday, August 17, for the Laird River district to the northeast. His young German-born flight

The Air Land Manufacturing Company's Junkers, CF-AMX, flown by Paddy Burke in the Laird country during the summer of 1930.

mechanic, Emil Kading, had remained behind but the pilot was accompanied by Washington State prospector-rancher Sam J. Clerf. Unreported for a week, Air Land Manufacturing Company of Vancouver, British Columbia was sending up a second float-equipped Junkers F-13 to make a search. The all-metal monoplane, flown by W.A. Joerss, a German pilot in the World War and who was now employed with the Canadian company, arrived at Juneau the afternoon of Tuesday, August 26, 1930. Servicing the plane and refilling fuel and oil tanks, Joerss was soon away for Atlin, going by way of the Taku River.

The search plane left there the next morning to look for the missing Junkers. Carrying some local men as observers, the pilot began a search of an area in which Burke was most likely to be found. For four hours he flew over the wild area, a land of many small lakes, until one of his outlook observers called attention to a fire on the shore of a small lake. Circling over the spot, Burke and Clerf were sighted on the shore near a tent, their plane riding nearby on the waters of the lake. They were about 125 miles northeast of Teslin.

It was late in the afternoon and the lake, lying between high cliffs, was barely 1500 feet in length, too small to risk a landing with their present load. Joerss dropped cigarettes, matches and a note saying the pilot would return alone the following day, Thursday. He was as good as his word; he came in to the tiny lake in an empty plane, carrying gasoline for Paddy Burke's CF-AMX. The pilot had originally landed on the small lake when his fuel had become exhausted by strong headwinds. Both planes took off successfully later in the day, arriving at Atlin, British Columbia that evening. Burke was to visit Juneau briefly in September to meet his wife, Muriel, and their two children, Brian and Margaret, who had arrived by steamer from Vancouver. He took them back to Atlin in CF-AMX.

With good flying weather in the Juneau area on Tuesday, August 26, 1930, Bob Ellis and Frank Hatcher were away that morning in the *Skagway*, for Pybus Bay, fifty-three miles east of Sitka, to pick up James Davis and his daughter, and bring them to the capital city. Lyle Davis and Hans Floe were the passengers outbound. Later in the day the plane went to Funter Bay on the west coast of nearby Mansfield Peninsula, nineteen miles southwest of Juneau, on a charter for Admiralty Gold Mining Company. On his return, Ellis took Nick Bez, A.F. Knight, Martin Thompson and Lou Garrison to Sitka. He and Hatcher returned later in the evening with F.P. Ulrich, government employee, and Mrs. Ulrich and their children, who had cabled from Sitka requesting passage to Juneau. The seaplane *Wrangell*, flown by pilot J. Clark Wing, was expected up from Ketchikan where it had been operating. Joseph L. Carman, Jr., President of Alaska-Washington Airways, was in Washington, D.C. at the end of August, attempting to convince postal authorities of the need of a scheduled Air Mail service to Southeastern Alaska and to secure a contract for it. It would mean a consistent schedule through the winter to the communities served.

A group of Indians, who had often observed Mendenhall Glacier from below, chartered the *Skagway* for a flight over the glacier on Friday, August 29, 1930. They were amazed at the extent of the icefield back of the glacier and enjoyed the ride. On Saturday morning, Bob Ellis and Chandler Hicks flew the *Skagway* to Tenakee with Mrs. Bessie E. Rowe of Newport, Oregon as a passenger. From there the two airmen flew a few hours of patrol work for the Superior Packing Company, then returned to Juneau. The pilot had a round trip to Sitka scheduled before ending his day.

The seaplane *Wrangell* with pilot Clark Wing and flight mechanic Frank Hatcher came in to Juneau the morning of Saturday, August 30, from Ketchikan. Larry Parks was aboard. After servicing the plane, the airmen departed, carrying H.S. Graves, his wife, and daughter Alice, for an inspection of the man's mining properties. Pilot Wing expected to return that afternoon.

Two aerial tourists arrived in Juneau on Tuesday, September 2, 1930, in a float-equipped De Havilland Gipsy Moth biplane 60-GM named *Flit*. Two young Boston men, Laurence Lombard and Frederick "Pete" Blodgett, had flown the open-cockpit plane across the United States from Boston to Seattle. Alaska-Washington Airways had installed their previously-shipped floats here and briefed them on their route north. Arriving in Ketchikan on Saturday, August 30, they went on that same day to Mole Harbor on Admiralty Island, to seek out the recluse, and sometimes-guide, Al Hasselborg. He took the pair in hand and guided them about the area for two days, during which they photographed bear and fished. Blodgett wanted to take an Alaska brown bear for a trophy but regulations required a licensed guide for an Outside hunter; Hasselborg's guide license had expired and needed to be renewed. The two flew in to

Hasselborg Lake, foreground, located on Admiralty Island, became one of the prime fishing lakes when the airplane made it more accessible to anglers. This photo, taken for the Forest Service in 1929 by the Alaskan Aerial Survey Detachment, reveals other unnamed lakes in the unspoiled environment beyond Hasselborg.

FS.T18B 4/22/29

Juneau to purchase proper boots, plus other supplies. Hasselborg would have none of the airplane, which threatened to be a problem because it was required that he be present to obtain his license renewal, but Win Goddard, Game Commissioner, knew Al and gave the men the license renewal to take back to their guide.

The weather at Juneau on their arrival had given them considerable difficulty with low cloud, mist and rain prevailing. Flying in wretched visibility just over the water, Lombard landed the De Havilland a short distance past the coal docks and, with the help of Cot Hayes and Larry Parks, of Alaska-Washington Airways, they had moored the plane for the night. Leaving that day was out of the question. Checking into the Gastineau Hotel, they made a social evening of it and were soon on good terms with most of the dancing population of the city.

The following morning was not conducive to their returning to Admiralty Island, with alternating mist and rain, but they had an opportunity to complete the errands they had come for. By noon the sky was brighter, with a promise of clearer weather a few miles south of the harbor entrance. The pair took off after lunch, heading south down Gastineau Channel, and were soon clear of the low-hanging clouds. Back at Mole Harbor, they circled Hasselborg's cabin and he and his nephew, Raymond, who was staying with him for the summer, came running down to help beach the plane.

In the ensuing days, both visitors were to acquire a "Brownie" along the creeks that led up from tidewater. Anxious to return to Boston in their allotted vacation time, the two airmen were off the waters of Mole Harbor at 2:40 P.M. Friday, September 5, 1930, arriving back at Ketchikan after a two hour and twenty-minute flight, where they spent the night before continuing south the following day. (see Ketchikan—1930, Chapter 53).

Pioneer Airways Stinson SM-8A, *Northbird*, had arrived in Juneau on Tuesday, September 2, making several stops on the way up from Ketchikan. (see Ketchikan—1930, Chapter 53). Pilot Jim Dodson brought Roy Jones, general manager of the company, with him.

Pioneer Airways Stinson **Sea Pigeon**, *NC 935W, at the dock in Hoonah, Alaska on September 2, 1930. An identical Stinson SM-8A, the* **Northbird**, *was the company's second plane.*

Jones spoke of basing the *Sea Pigeon*, flown by Jerry Smith, in Juneau, and having their second Stinson, *Northbird*, flown by Dodson, stationed at Ketchikan. The four-place Stinsons, painted in black, with orange trim, were offered at forty dollars per hour, a lower charter rate than the seven-place Vegas of Alaska-Washington Airways. The *Northbird* returned to Ketchikan later that same day while the *Sea Pigeon* came in to the capital city from Sitka the following day. Pioneer Airways was running a box ad in the local paper, inviting interested customers to contact Jerry Smith at the Gastineau Hotel. The *Sea Pigeon* departed Juneau on Thursday, September 4, with passengers for Sitka, scheduled to return that evening.

Sitka, Alaska, in 1930. Pilot Jim Dodson behind the Lycoming engine, walking on the float of the Sea Pigeon.

Courtesy of Warren "Ace" Dodson

Pilot Gerald Joyce "Jerry" Smith in Sitka Bay with the Sea Pigeon *in 1930.*

Gerald Smith Collection

The Alaska-Washington Airways *Wrangell*, NC 657E, crewed by Clark Wing and Frank Hatcher, went out on a round trip to Warm Springs Bay on the east coast of Baranof Island the evening of Tuesday, September 3, 1930, while the *Skagway*, NC 103W, with Bob Ellis and Chandler Hicks made a similar trip to Sitka. Clark Wing was out the next day, in *Wrangell*, to Funter Bay to bring in miner Lazo Bazovich who had broken an arm while out on a hunting trip. The man was taken to St. Ann's Hospital to have it set. The two airmen were out on a round trip to Haines the next day, returning late in the forenoon. Ellis and Hatcher also went out that afternoon in the *Skagway*, making a trip to Funter Bay and return, before flying a similar trip to Lake Dorothy before nightfall.

The steamer *Alameda* was in the capital city the morning of Saturday, September 6, with Clark Wing and Frank Hatcher taking up a group of the passengers on a brief pleasure flight in the *Wrangell* before leaving for Tenakee. There the pair picked up J.T. Tenneson of the Superior Packing Company, and his family, bringing them to Juneau. The other Alaska-Washington crew, Ellis and Hicks, went out for fish patrol duty in the *Skagway*, under charter to Dennis Winn and N.O. Hardy of the Federal Bureau of Fisheries.

The *Skagway* made two round trips between Juneau and Warm Springs Bay on Sunday, September 7, bringing in Mr. and Mrs. H.C. Davis and George Franklin on the last flight. The *Wrangell* was out to Haines and Skagway on pleasure flights the same day. On Monday, Ellis and Hicks took the *Skagway* out for a brief flight, while Clark Wing and Frank Hatcher took the *Wrangell* to Lake Optimo to pick up H.S. Graves and his mining partner, bringing them in to Juneau. Jerry Smith, Pioneer Airways pilot, made a flight to Ketchikan in the *Sea Pigeon* on Monday, September 8, to bring passengers up to Juneau from there.

Both Lockheed Vegas of Alaska-Washington Airways departed Juneau for Seattle on Tuesday, September 9, 1930. The *Skagway*, with Bob Ellis and Chandler Hicks, was off at 8:00 A.M. with Mr. and Mrs. Lyle Davis, her sister Esther Hayland and John Franklin as passengers. The plane arrived at Ketchikan at noon to refuel. Clark Wing and Frank Hatcher took the *Wrangell* to Point Retreat to meet the steamer *Aleutian* and take off General R.E. Wood, a well-known businessman of Chicago and New York. With Wood, Barbara Wing and Brian Harland as passengers, the plane again departed Juneau at 10:30 A.M. Picking up Mrs. J.W. Prichard, whose husband, the editor of the *Wrangell Sentinel*, had died in Vancouver, British Columbia, the plane arrived at Ketchikan at 2:00 P.M. to take on fuel. The *Skagway* was expected to reach Seattle at 6:00 P.M. and the *Wrangell* at 8:00 P.M.

The Alaska-Washington Airways Vega, *Skagway*, NC 103W, was back in Juneau the morning of Friday, September 12, 1930, having left Seattle shortly before noon on Thursday, remaining overnight at Ketchikan. Ellis and Hatcher brought in, as passengers from Seattle, Mrs. Ulysses Grant McQueen of California, Director of the Women's National Aeronautical Association, and company mechanic Brian Harland; they also picked up Robert E. Proctor of Indiana in Ketchikan, the Grand Worthy President of the Fraternal Order of Eagles. The *Wrangell* and *Petersburg* were still in Seattle, the *Sitka* in Ketchikan.

Alaska-Washington Airways operations manager, Anscel Eckmann, brought the *Wrangell* north to Juneau on Tuesday, September 16, after a leisurely flight from Seattle. Don B. Bennett, business manager for the company, was aboard, as well as O.W. Wiley, W.M. Frazer, R.O. Reekie and Mr. and Mrs. James Carlson. Without a flight mechanic, the plane was filled on its arrival. Stopping at Vancouver to pick up Mr. and Mrs. Carlson, as well as at Alert Bay and Prince Rupert, the plane overheaded Ketchikan, coming directly to the capital city. The Pioneer Airways *Sea Pigeon*, still flying out of Juneau, also arrived there from Sitka on Tuesday morning. Jerry Smith, the pilot, was to take Mrs. G.R. Shotter to Hoonah, and

J.C. Coleman to Kake that afternoon, and was scheduled to go to Sitka on its return; but the flight was delayed until the following morning. Off at 9:00 A.M. Wednesday, September 17, Smith took Mrs. Shotter to Hoonah and J.B. Hottel, an insurance man, to Sitka. That afternoon the *Sea Pigeon* was off again, taking Frank Chestic, a fur farmer, to Skagway and Frank Preuschoff to Haines, before returning late in the afternoon.

Eckmann and Hatcher were out that afternoon in the *Wrangell*, taking Doctor Council, R.O. Reekie, O.W. Wiley and W.M. Frazer to Lake Hasselborg on a fishing expedition. It was Eckmann's second trip to the lake and he was eager to try his luck again with the cutthroat trout. They were back in the evening with a great catch.

The Alaska-Washington Vega, *Skagway*, with a crew of Ellis and Harland, went to Lake Dorothy that same morning, carrying William Fromholz, an engineer for the Cameron pulp and paper interests. Returning that afternoon, he brought out a transit and other surveying equipment left at the company's camp near the lake by engineers engaged in surveying the water power site there.

Eckmann left Juneau for Seattle in the *Wrangell* on Thursday, September 18, 1930. A favorable weather condition on the route was the determining factor. With Reekie, Wiley, Frazer and Don B. Bennett aboard for Seattle, and John W. Troy, publisher of the *Alaska Daily Empire*, for Ketchikan, the pilot had a good load. The weather at their first stop caused a delay, with the flight finally departing on Saturday morning, September 20. (see Ketchikan—1930, Chapter 53).

Pioneer Airways pilot Jerry Smith went out from Juneau in the *Sea Pigeon*, making a round trip to Sitka on Thursday, September 18, taking Cash Cole, Territorial Auditor; Robert J. Sommers, Territorial Highway Commissioner, and B.N. Barnes. The new landing field at Skagway for wheeled planes was now completed and in service, lying adjacent to the town and close to the Skagway River. A dike was being constructed between the river and the field to protect the latter from high water. The *Sea Pigeon* returned with Cole, Sommers and Sitka businessman W.P. Mills that afternoon.

Smith went out to Sitka in the Stinson SM-8A the following day, carrying Charles Raatikainen, a fisherman, and Miss Nancy Burke, a Juneau visitor. The flight over took an hour but the return flight was held overnight because of stormy weather. The *Sea Pigeon* came in to Juneau early the next afternoon, Saturday, September 20, 1930, bringing Doctor R.E. Southwell and B.N. Barnes as passengers. Pilot Jerry Smith and his mechanic, Thomas Johnson, went out to Sitka the afternoon of Tuesday, September 23, with Thomas Berkland as a passenger. They also dropped off Herbert L. Coleman at Angoon on their way. The pilot had been to Ketchikan the previous day.

The *Northbird* of Pioneer Airways had been swamped at the Ketchikan float by high waves during the early hours on September 19, and would not be flyable for some time. (see Ketchikan—1930, Chapter 53). Jerry Smith brought Sam Collins to Petersburg and Arthur Van Mavern to Juneau in the *Sea Pigeon*. The Ketchikan incident was not the end of the bad news for Pioneer Airways for, after returning from a flight to Haines in the *Sea Pigeon* on Wednesday, September 24, with Robert E. Coughlin as a passenger, Jerry Smith set out for Skagway shortly after 2:30 P.M. on a second flight. Again carrying Coughlin, as well as Vernon Nelson and his wife, the pilot was scarcely in the air before he noticed a supporting strut connected with a pontoon was broken. Smith circled in the air, indicating a problem, and a small power boat came out from the shore. The pilot landed nearby and, without the support of the strut, the *Sea Pigeon* ended up on its nose in the water.

The passengers opened the cabin door and scrambled into the boat which had immediately approached the plane, hardly getting their feet wet. The pilot followed without delay. The harbor was now filled with small boats swarming to their assistance but they were not needed. The unbalanced plane slowly turned over from the weight of the engine and came to rest upside down with just the bottoms of the floats above the water. It was towed to the Alaska-Juneau Mining Company dock and deposited on the pier by hoisting it out of Gastineau Channel with a crane. Jerry Smith and mechanic Thomas Johnson dismantled the Stinson the following day, hauling its components to the Cash Cole warehouse on Willoughby Avenue, where the pair would ascertain the damage to the plane and dry it out after washing out all the salt water with fresh, to prevent corrosion. It would not fly again until October 4, when it was moved to Ketchikan.

Bob Ellis and Frank Hatcher took the *Skagway* to Sitka on Saturday, September 27, 1930. Four passengers from Juneau; Joseph H. Meherin, J.B. Hottel, Oscar Shineman and meteorologist Ralph C. Mize were aboard. The plane was to return late in the afternoon with a stop at Hoonah on the way. The *Skagway*, with Ellis and Hatcher as crew, had gone with passengers to Ketchikan on Friday, October 3. They did not return to Juneau until October 6, bringing Larry Parks up from Ketchikan. Cot Hayes, the Alaska-Washington Airways general manager for Alaska, announced that the company was suspending aerial service until at least December. The *Skagway* was in need of an overhaul and would be sent to Seattle. The floating hangar was to be dragged from its present location at the foot of Willoughby Avenue for storage at a beach location above the high water mark.

Bob Ellis and Frank Hatcher departed Juneau with the *Skagway* on Tuesday, October 7, 1930, carrying the pilot's wife, Margaret, as well as Frank Dorbandt and Alonzo Cope, two Anchorage airmen on their way south to bring up a second plane for their air service at the Cook Inlet city. Mrs. Charles Burns was an additional passenger for Seattle when the *Skagway* left Ketchikan on the morning of Wednesday, October 8, 1930.

The Pioneer Airways Stinson *Sea Pigeon*, NC 935W, had been moved from the Cash Cole warehouse to Thane, a bit south of Juneau proper. She was once again assembled, ready for a test flight. Following this, it was intended to take the plane to Seattle for further work, as well as a Department of Commerce re-license. The *Sea Pigeon* was in Ketchikan on Wednesday, October 8, with pilot Jerry Smith, mechanic Tom Johnson, special mechanic Burras Smith and Manager Roy Jones aboard. The Company now had a hangar on Tongass Highway at the hydroport and it was decided to keep the *Sea Pigeon* here, doing a general overhaul before the spring business began.

With the *Northbird*, NC 991W, back in service again, the company decided to continue in business with it at both Ketchikan and Juneau. On Sunday, October 12, Pioneer Airways pilot Jim Dodson took the plane to Juneau, carrying the company's main stockholder, C.R. Wright, and Alfred M. Howe of Ketchikan, as passengers. They arrived there that afternoon. Dodson took his passengers to Pybus Bay the following morning for a bear hunt. Following this, the two men planned to go to Petersburg to join friends in a duck hunt, before returning to Ketchikan.

Canadian pilot E.J.A. "Paddy" Burke was again missing in the Laird region of British Columbia in the Junkers F-13, CF-AMX. Burke had left his base at Atlin, British Columbia on October 10, 1930, flying to Laird Post with "Three-fingers" Bob Martin, a prospector and trapper from Wrangell, Alaska, and Emil Kading, his young German-born air engineer (flight mechanic). Martin wanted to consult with his partner, Oscar Anderson, concerning a quartz property in the Atlin district, and had chartered the plane. Nothing more had been heard from or about the party. Burke's wife at Atlin, following the pilot's instructions, had notified the authorities.

1930. Whitehorse, Yukon Territory. Emil Forrest, on the left, was Everett Wasson's French-Canadian aviation mechanic in Whitehorse while he was on the Burke search. Wasson, on the right, was originally from San Diego and had been in Canada for about two years.

Frank Dorbandt and Lon Cope left Seattle in the new Pacific International Airways Bellanca Pacemaker, NC 259M, on Tuesday, October 21, on their way to Anchorage by way of the Interior route. They had been authorized by Air Land Manufacturing Company, the missing airmen's employer, to search for Captain Burke on their way north. Dorbandt arrived at Prince George, British Columbia, to overnight there before proceeding on the following day. The airmen arrived at Hazelton, British Columbia that same day, Wednesday, October 22. Dorbandt and Cope arrived at Atlin in the Bellanca on October 26, 1930.

With a full load of fuel,

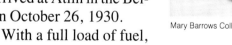

Mary Barrows Collection

the pair departed from there the next day, Monday, flying a search along a chain of lakes between Laird Post and Atlin, feeling Burke would surely be down on one of them. They found nothing. Going out again the following day, Tuesday, October 28, they landed at Laird Post to find that Burke had been there on October 10, and had left for Atlin the following day, flying in balmy weather and intending to go by way of Teslin, Gladys and Surprise lakes to Atlin. There was little telegraph and radio in the Laird district and most communications went by surface travel, in winter usually by dog team.

The Pacific International Airways airmen left Laird Post to continue the search, finally having to set down on Paddy Lake that evening, some fifty miles south of Atlin, with fuel running low. They were still there on October 29, but the needed fuel was being started to them that night by dog team from Atlin. When the fuel arrived, Dorbandt and Cope flew the Bellanca, NC 259M, in to Atlin on Friday, October 31. The two airmen flew to Whitehorse, Yukon Territory on Sunday, November 2, accompanied by Gold Commissioner Frank Wright,

854

to make arrangements with Livingston Wernecke for the use of the company's Fairchild in the search. Dorbandt and Cope joined forces with Treadwell-Yukon Company, Limited, pilot Everett L. Wasson, who was preparing to enter the search in the Fairchild *Claire*, GC-ARM.

From Seattle, Alaska-Washington Airways was sending the Lockheed Vega *Skagway*, NC 103W, to join the search, flown by Robin "Pat" Renehan and flight mechanic Frank Hatcher, and accompanied by rancher-prospector Sam Clerf, who had been with Burke in the Laird country during the past summer while on a prospecting trip. He knew the country and he knew Burke's habits, and he was concerned about him. They planned on going to Atlin, British Columbia where they could operate from Atlin Lake on floats, at least until freeze-up. There were plenty of other lakes in the region where they would be searching. Renehan and Hatcher were off Lake Union, to land at Vancouver, British Columbia to pick up Sam Clerf who had just come south on the steamer, on his way to join his wife and child. The three men departed the Canadian city at noon on Tuesday, October 28, 1930, flying north to land again at Butedale, British Columbia. They departed there at 4:15 P.M. for Prince Rupert, with an hour's daylight remaining. Nothing more was heard from the plane. (see Ketchikan—1930, Chapter 53, for details on the search and the finding of final fragments).

The search for Captain Burke would now depend on the two planes at Whitehorse. Wasson, a twenty-four-year-old flier who had come to Canada from San Diego, California two years before, taking out citizenship papers, was employed by Treadwell-Yukon Company, Limited, at Mayo as a pilot on their Fairchild FC-2W2, GC-ARM. With Alex Crone, Vancouver air engineer, Wasson departed Whitehorse on Monday, November 3, accompanied by Dorbandt and Cope in the Pacific International Airways Bellanca Pacemaker. They reached Atlin that same day. When Wasson and Dorbandt reached Laird Post, finding they were unable to make a landing there in the heavy snow, they dropped notes attached to small parachutes asking the post manager if Burke had been there. Osborne snowshoed a message in the snow in the affirmative: "Yes, Burke left here October 11 for Teslin, Teslin", the last word stamped out twice. Wasson knew Burke had a cache of food and supplies there, but he had already checked that and found that no one had been there.

Wasson and Dorbandt flew off to search the district, scanning the country as far as Teslin and spending four and one-half hours in the air that day, returning to Atlin at 3:30 P.M. In clear weather, the visibility had been over a hundred miles but they saw no sign of the missing plane. With a change in the weather the following day the planes were held at Atlin. They would fly another search on November 5 in the direction of the Laird on a more northerly route when it cleared.

Believing that other planes were on the way and wanting to get on with the business at Anchorage, Dorbandt and Cope left Atlin for home base on Thursday, November 6, spending that night at Tanana Crossing and arriving at Anchorage at 1:30 P.M. Friday, November 7, 1930 with the Bellanca, NC 259M. Wasson left Atlin for Mayo on that same day, November 7. Winter was well on the way in the Interior and he wanted to put skis on his plane and fly a mail run out of Mayo, some 200 miles north of Whitehorse, before returning to continue the search.

Pacific International Airways of Anchorage was bringing two additional planes north from San Francisco. A Fairchild 71 flown by Harry Blunt, and a Consolidated Fleetster flown by Joe Barrows, departed Vancouver, British Columbia on Monday, November 10, 1930. They interrupted their northward journey to lend aid in the search for the missing Burke plane. At Smithers, British Columbia they removed the wheels from the two planes, installing the skis they had carried with them. Delayed by stormy weather, they were at Telegraph Creek on Wednesday, November 26, where they were preparing to take off Sawmill Lake, on skis, to continue their journey. Harry Blunt crashed after taking off, demolishing the Fairchild. Barrows gunned the Fleetster over the ice to get to the other side of the lake and assist his companion but the heavier plane sank through the ice and a drenched pilot scrambled forth onto the frozen surface. This ended their part in the search. (for details of their journey to this point and the eventual salvage of the Fleetster, see Anchorage—1930, Chapter 57).

Air Land Manufacturing Company of Vancouver, British Columbia was sending a second Junkers F-13 on floats to Atlin, to join the search for Burke and his companions. Pilot R.I. Van der Byl, with second pilot W.A. Joerss and air engineer T.H. Cressy left Vancouver on Sunday, November 9, for Atlin, planning on reaching Prince George by nightfall. Van der Byl had been a pilot in the British air services during the war, and his companion, Joerss, had been an ace in the German flying corps at the same time. Van der Byl and air engineer Cressy had worked for Alaska-Washington Airways prior to going to work for Air Land Manufacturing Company, Van der Byl as traffic manager in Seattle and Cressy as a mechanic. The trio reached Prince George as planned, taking off the water the following day, Monday, November 10, 1930, to reach Dease Lake where they spent the night. They departed in the Junkers seaplane on Tuesday, heading north for Atlin. The farther they flew, the more rugged the terrain and the worse the weather. Forced by wing icing and a snow squall to land that day at Thutade Lake some three hundred miles northeast of Hazelton, British Columbia, they found the bulk of the lake frozen over with thin ice except for an area about 1500 feet long. Normally, the lake is twenty-four miles in length and one and one-half miles in width.

The following day the men attempted to take the plane off. Running out of the open area of the water into the thin ice resulted in sheets of it being thrown up into the propeller and engine, and piling up on the floats. Even after draining off excess fuel, the loaded plane was too heavy for the takeoff area. Van der Byl, in charge of the expedition, ordered Joerss to take the plane back alone; he was "the only one of the two pilots who knew the country well enough to get the plane out", as explained later by Van der Byl. There was an Indian trapper at the site, with a cabin and a food supply, so the two remaining men made out well enough. They came out later by dog team.

Joerss got away on Wednesday, November 12, in the lightly-loaded plane, flying to Takla Lake where he was able to arrange with H. McCorkell, a trader, to send in two Indians with dog teams to bring Van der Byl and Cressy out from where they waited at Thutade Lake.

Joerss arrived in the Junkers F-13 at Burns Lake on the Canadian National Railways in a thick snowstorm on Friday, November 14, 1930; there was a telegraph at Burns Lake. He waited here for a time for the arrival of his two companions who were traveling by dogsled from Thutade Lake out of the mountains along a chain of lakes.

Unreported since leaving Dease Lake on November 11, the news of the German pilot's arrival at Burns Lake without his two fellow airmen was distorted all out of proportion, fueled by undercurrents of resentment left over from the war. Joerss left Burns Lake at 2:55 P.M. Flying the float-equipped Junkers, he arrived at Vancouver, British Columbia alone, on Monday, November 17, to be met by an official of the Civil Aviation Department, A.T. Crowley, who announced that "he had permanently cancelled the pilot license of W.A. Joerss for all time, for infractions of air regulations." Joerss hotly demanded a Board of Inquiry on the matter. When pilot R.I. Van der Byl and air engineer Cressy returned to Vancouver some time later, they confirmed Joerss' statements and the pilot was fully exonerated and appropriate apologies extended.

Everett Wasson felt it unsafe to search with a single plane but he was willing to try. He returned to Whitehorse, Yukon Territory with the four-seated Fairchild FC-2W2, GC-ARM,

Fueling the Fairchild FC-2W2, G-CARM, Claire. This photo was taken at another time as the hyphen in the registration number has been moved to its proper position. The Claire was named for Livingston Wernecke's daughter, who soloed the following year.

Claire. The plane was now fitted with skis. He would use Whitehorse as a base, going out when weather permitted. The two Pacific International Airways planes were still held at Smithers, British Columbia. The Alaska-Washington Airways plane flown by Pat Renehan had disappeared on the west coast, and the Air Land Manufacturing Company Junkers was being returned to Vancouver. It was too late in the year for the float plane to be operated in the Laird country. Wasson was a knowledgeable north-country pilot, having flown for the past two years out of Mayo, Yukon Territory, some 200 miles north of Whitehorse. Livingston Wernecke, his boss, had mining operations out of Mayo and other places. He had used planes in the company business, and commercially, for some years.

Everett Wasson was out on search on Friday, November 14, 1930, but was forced back to Whitehorse by a heavy snowstorm. Wasson prepared to go out again. Taking an experienced prospector and woodsman, Joe Walsh, who was from Mayo and had accompanied the pilot from there, the men loaded the ski-equipped Fairchild FC-2W2 with extra gasoline, a Yukon stove, tent, snowshoes, sleeping bags, food and other camping equipment. Their fourth flight in the past two weeks, they would go to Laird Post via the Francis Lake district, searching, then land on some small lake and camp overnight before continuing. Leaving on Friday morning, November 21, the pair were eventually obliged to land on a small lake about forty miles from Laird Post. In attempting to take off the following morning, they found the lake too small and surrounded by trees.

One thing they did learn from a party of Indians camped near the lake was that Burke had flown over the camp, and the direction he had taken. They hired the Indians to swamp out 300 feet of timber, giving them room to take off on Sunday in the Fairchild, flying in the direction the natives had indicated.

Running into a snowstorm, Wasson could not land on the Laird River, so he cut over the Pelly Mountains and landed a second time on a small lake. Again the men camped overnight, having difficulty in getting off the next morning, Monday, November 24, 1930. They made several attempts, finally tramping down a pathway on the snow for the skis. Once free of the lake, Wasson flew back to the river where they found a second Indian camp, the residents confirming the earlier report that the Burke Junkers was last seen heading up stream, flying at a low altitude.

Going on upstream another camp was sighted. The two women who were its sole occupants fled into the woods at sight of the plane. Wasson continued on up river, both men keeping a sharp lookout. About forty miles north of the last Indian camp, in a narrow gorge, the two men spotted the Burke plane. Covered with snow, its pontoons fast-frozen into the river ice, it was a forlorn sight. Circling the site at about 800 feet, the plane appeared undamaged. There was no sign of life about it. Unable to land in the rocky country, or on the river ice filled with hummocks, Wasson climbed to 7000 feet to look the country over for a landing spot. They selected a small lake about fifteen miles away before turning back to return to base. The Fairchild was low on fuel by then, only ten gallons remaining on their arrival in Whitehorse.

The two men, impatient to get on with the next step, were held on the ground here by unfavorable weather conditions for several days. It was hoped that the Burke party had fallen in with Indians and were in good shape. On Thanksgiving Day, Thursday, November 27, Wasson and Walsh were away in the Fairchild, landing on the lake they had previously selected. Putting on snowshoes and shrugging into packs, the men struck off across country for the downed plane. The country was rough and uneven and the snow deep. The men reached the ice-locked Junkers and found only a note left by the three lost men, carved on a tree at their camp some fifty yards from the plane, saying they had gone upstream on October 17, 1930, headed for Wolf Lake which was located about fifty miles northeast of Teslin. Also that they needed food badly. The plane appeared undamaged but the searchers could not see the damage to the bottoms of the floats as they were frozen in the ice. Four feet of snow covered the vicinity of the plane.

Wasson and Walsh returned to the Fairchild and took off from the lake, searching thoroughly between there and Wolf Lake without finding any trace of the missing men. They also landed at an Indian camp fifty miles down the Laird River from the deserted Junkers, where the natives reported Burke had flown over their camp looking for a place to land on the lake, but it was frozen at the time. Things looked bad for Burke and his party as Wasson and Dorbandt had earlier seen no sign of life at Wolf Lake when they were there. Burke and his party had evidently remained at their plane for six days before setting out on their own. Wasson and Walsh returned to Whitehorse at 12:30 P.M. Thursday, December 4, 1930, after an absence of several days.

There was some conjecture the missing men might have traveled toward Pelly Post on the Upper Pelly River, or fallen in with Indians. Pilot Everett Wasson and guide Joe Walsh departed Whitehorse at 10:00 A.M. Saturday, December 5, flying the Fairchild GC-ARM for Pelly banks at the head of the Pelly River, to check out this possibility. Taylor and Drury had a trading post in that district where Campbell Creek joined the river. The two airmen intended to make a low-level search over the district as well as land at any Indian camp sighted. Word from the natives had proved their best leads so far. When Wasson reached the Pelly banks on December 6, clouds were covering the peaks of the Pelly Range. While the pilot circled about, looking for a low spot to get across the range the guide, Joe Walsh, saw a puff of white smoke and called the pilot's attention to it. Circling over, both men saw the camp with two men weakly waving from the ground. Had they not been forced to circle by weather, they would have gone over the range, missing the men they were seeking.

Walsh kicked out a box of food over the camp. Afraid the men might miss it, a second box containing the balance of their own food supply was dropped, containing a note saying the rescuers would be coming upstream to them. Wasson landed the plane on a lake about ten miles from Kading and Martin's camp. The pilot and guide spent most of the following hours building up logs under the skis to keep the plane from freezing in. They started upstream that

The gaunt, starved face of Emil Kading, air engineer for Paddy Burke, when found with Martin in the Pelly banks country on December 7, 1930.

Mary Barrows Collection

Mary Barrows Collection

Wrangell, Alaska prospector Bob Martin shows the effects of starvation and frostbite when found by Everett Wasson and Joe Walsh near the Pelly banks on December 7, 1930.

Left to Right. Emil Kading, holding the make-shift skis axed out of a spruce tree by Joe Walsh for his own use; Bob Martin with the extra pair of snowshoes the rescuers had brought; and Joe Walsh, with the snow-shoes he would soon give to Kading for the trip out from the final camp to the plane. The four men reached the **Claire** *on December 9, 1930, and camped for the night.*

Mary Barrows Collection

Four-seated Fairchild FC-2W2, GC-ARM, **Claire** *of the Treadwell-Yukon Mining Company which Everett Wasson was flying when he and Joe Walsh found and rescued the Burke survivors.*

Mary Barrows Collection

Whitehorse, Yukon Territory, December 10, 1930. The rescued and the rescuers stand near the hangar after their arrival. Left to Right: Emil Kading, Bob Martin, Joe Walsh and pilot Everett Wasson.

Mary Barrows Collection

night but were forced to camp in a snowstorm. Picking up their landmarks the next morning, they figured they had passed the two men in the storm and were some distance upstream of them. Returning toward the plane and having difficulty finding the location they sought, the two men shouted and fired off a rifle when they decided the lost men were nearby. Too weak to answer, Kading fired off an answering shot, using their last cartridge which they had been saving for such a need. Everett Wasson and Joe Walsh found Kading and Martin at the camp at 4:00 P.M. Paddy Burke, starving and ill, had passed away earlier.

The two rescuers cooked some food for the gaunt, starved men from the two boxes of food they had dropped. The pair had found both boxes. The two rescuers were also hungry for they had dropped all their food the day before. They had brought one extra pair of snowshoes with them and Joe Walsh axed out a pair of makeshift skis from a nearby spruce tree for his own use, giving his snowshoes to Kading. It was slow going back to the plane, with Wasson and Walsh helping the other two along. Slush built up on the snowshoes and skis, and had to be cleaned off periodically. They finally made it back to the plane where they camped for the night of Tuesday, December 9, 1930.

Wasson left everything on the lake but guns and sleeping bags to lighten the load. Carefully cleaning wing and tail surfaces of snow and ice, they prepared for flight. The party arrived in Whitehorse in the Fairchild at noon on Monday, December 10, 1930. Air engineer Kading suffered a frost-bitten hand and passenger Bob Martin, two slightly-frozen toes. They were both weak from lack of food.

The story of their ill-fated trip could now be told. Burke, in the Junkers, CF-AMX, had left Laird Post on October 11 for Atlin. After encountering a snowstorm, he doubled back hoping to reach Wolf Lake but was forced by poor visibility to land. Taking off again the same day, he could not make it through and returned to land again in the narrow, rocky reaches of the upper Laird River. This time he tore the bottoms of the floats on the rocks although the plane itself was undamaged. The cabin of the Junkers was filled with a load of knocked-down sluice boxes belonging to Martin. He had left the skis for the plane and most of their emergency gear behind. They did have their sleeping bags but no snowshoes.

Burke and his two companions camped near the plane for six days, attempting to shoot game with a rifle and the twelve rounds of ammunition they had, but with little success. Now weak from lack of food, they started for Wolf Lake on October 17, leaving the message carved in a tree at their campsite. It was slow going in the deep snow and cold weather. Burke lost strength rapidly; he was not a well man. He had suffered from colitis in India during his army career and, of slight build, he was not as strong as an ordinary healthy man. On November 15, Kading shot a caribou that wandered near. Cooking bits of liver on a stick and boiling some of the meat for a broth, they attempted to feed Paddy Burke. He was unable even to swallow the soup. The pilot died five days later, after writing a letter to his wife, Muriel, then in Atlin.

Covering the body with logs and marking the spot, the two remaining men continued on toward Wolf Lake, reaching a point some forty miles from Burke's plane before they became too weak to proceed. They first sighted Wasson's plane on November 25, and again five days later, but were unable to signal. Without even a decent camp, lying in the snow in their sleeping bags, the men awaited. They did prepare a pile of wood for a signal fire to attract attention from the air if the opportunity again arose. They kindled the blaze on Saturday, December 6 upon hearing the sound of the motor of the low-flying Fairchild approaching, throwing everything they had that was combustible on the blaze. Fortune smiled, and Walsh saw the tendril of smoke rising from the spot.

With Kading and Martin in good hands, Wasson took off the next day for Mayo, to

December 16, 1930. Sergeant Leopold of the Royal Canadian Mounted Police, with Everett Wasson, right, leave in the **Claire** *to recover the body of Paddy Burke. They returned to Whitehorse on December 18, their task accomplished.*

report to his employers. He returned soon to Whitehorse to go out and recover Paddy Burke's body. Taking a toboggan to transport the pilot's remains to their plane, Wasson and Walsh, accompanied by Sergeant Leopold of the Royal Canadian Mounted Police, were away from Whitehorse on Tuesday, December 16, 1930. They returned on December 18 with the body of the Canadian airman, which weighed less than ninety pounds. Following the inquest in Whitehorse on December 20-22, the body of Edward Joseph Augustus Burke was taken to Atlin to be buried with appropriate ceremony on Monday, December 29, 1930.

The Federal and Dominion governments awarded $1500 to Everett Wasson and $500 to Joe Walsh in recognition of their outstanding achievement. The time Wasson spent in Whitehorse was not wasted for, on Saturday, January 17, 1931, he and a nurse from the Whitehorse hospital, Miss Florence Jones, arrived in Vancouver, British Columbia on the *Princess Norah* from Skagway. They were married the next day at the home of the bride's parents in West Vancouver. Bob Martin, Wrangell trapper, and his wife, who boarded the boat at Wrangell, had also come south on the steamer. Wasson and his bride would go to San Francisco to sail by way of the Panama Canal for New York, where he would purchase a new plane for his employers and fly it back.

As a result of the inquest in Whitehorse a ruling was put in effect that all aircraft flying in the Yukon Territory between October 1 and April 1 would be required to carry adequate emergency supplies for all on board. It is still in force today.

Emil Kading, who had been employed by Air Land Manufacturing Company for the past year, returned to service with them. Desirous of salvaging the Junkers, CF-AMX, from the headwaters of the upper Laird River, the insurance underwriters, in an arrangement with the flying concern, sent W.A. Joerss and R.I. Van der Byl to Skagway on Thursday, January 22, 1931, on the *Princess Norah*, where they would travel on the White Pass and Yukon Railway to Whitehorse. Joined by air engineer Emil Kading, the three men were flown in to the upper Laird by Stan McMillan in a Bellanca that had been flown by the pilot up to Whitehorse from Vancouver. The five-man party landed on the lake and set up a camp. Jacking up the Junkers, CF-AMX, after freeing the plane from its floats, they installed a set of skis brought

Two members of the salvage party from Vancouver, British Columbia at the Air Land Manufacturing Company Junkers F-13 flown by Paddy Burke. The plane was placed on skis and flown out in February, 1931. Canadian pilot Stan McMillon at right.

In late January of 1931, pilot Stan McMillan flew four others including Joerss, Van der Byl and Emil Kading in to the lake near where Burke's Junkers rested in the ice. Placed on skis, it was flown out. McMillan took the men in to the site in this Bellanca which had been flown up from Vancouver, British Columbia for the purpose.

for the purpose. It was reported by Atlin on February 11, 1931, that the plane, flown out by Joerss and Van der Byl, had arrived there. The two pilots left Atlin in the Junkers, intending to return to Vancouver, British Columbia by way of Telegraph Creek and Prince George, changing over to wheels at Hazelton since there was no snow in Vancouver.

*February, 1931. The Air
Land Manufacturing
Company Junkers F-13,
CF-AMX, after skis had
been fitted to it in place
of the floats.*

*Paddy Burke's Junkers F-13
after being salvaged from the
upper Laird River country by the
four men. Stan McMillan second
from left.*

Coming out with the plane, Joerss, Van der Byl and Emil Kading left Atlin for Telegraph Creek, next leaving there on Saturday, February 31, 1931. Nothing more was heard from the trio until they mushed in to Fort St. James from Buckley House on the north end of Takla Lake. The Junkers had a damaged engine. The airmen caught the train at Vanderhoof on March 7 for Vancouver.

The plane was later repaired and flown out by a pilot named McClusky. Suffering a forced landing on the way to Vancouver, the Junkers was put down on the railway line at Boston Bar, British Columbia, finishing its trip by rail. It was eventually rebuilt.

The total score in the Burke matter was horrendous. Burke dead and his two companions nearly so; Renehan, Hatcher and Sam Clerf gone in the Alaska-Washington Airways

Vega; Joerss barely able to return to Vancouver with the second Junkers of Air Land Manufacturing Company, his two companions to follow by surface means; the Pacific International Airways Fairchild 71 demolished, its pilot, Harry Blunt, injured, and their second plane, the Consolidated Fleetster, water-logged but repairable, its pilot, Joe Barrows, also water-logged and sick with rheumatic fever.

But the willingness to try, so prevalent among airmen, was still intact.

By November there was little happening in aviation in Juneau. The Alaska-Washington Airways floating hangar, stored for the winter in front of the Bethel House, broke loose from its moorings the night of Saturday, November 1, 1930, and drifted up Gastineau Channel to ground on the Mendenhall bar opposite Alaska Dairy, where it sat neglected.

A Juneau youth, Ernest M. Gilligan, returned for the winter. He had completed a flying course at Parks Air College in St. Louis, with fifty-three flying hours in his logbook and a Limited Commercial License in his pocket. Gilligan, who had left in June, returned to his old job at the Annex Creek power station for the winter.

It would be April before the mountains around Juneau would again reverberate with the sound of airplane engines, signifying their return, like the swallows of Capistrano, for another busy season in Southeast Alaska.

Paddy Burke's Junkers, CF-AMX, and the Bellanca that brought in the salvage party, is parked on the shore of a lake.

John Selby Photo

Courtesy of Clayton Scott

866

Gillam Airways

Gorst Air Transport,
Incorporated

Cordova 1930

CORDOVA HAD PASSED THROUGH THE winter and spring of 1930 without any airplane activity. The first event of the season occurred when Harold Gillam arrived in the city in mid-April on the Copper River & Northwestern Railroad, to take care of some business in the city. Gillam, now owner of two Swallow biplanes, had established headquarters at Chitina and was intending to operate out of Copper Center when he got things going. He had recently completed his first contract; hauling a ton of cargo and two passengers into Snag River for Chisana Mines, Incorporated. He mentioned it as his largest contract of the season and, in truth, it was—being his first.

Along with explaining business plans for expanding his service, the pilot urged the city fathers to do everything possible to provide a suitable landing field in their community. The Alaska Road Commission had been building airstrips as rapidly as possible throughout the Territory and he felt that a request from the City of Cordova would expedite matters. There

▲ *Gorst Air Transport, Boeing B-1E flying boat, taking off the water at Cordova, Alaska in the summer of 1930.*

◄ *Mechanic John Selby checks the engine of the Boeing B-1E after it was beached and damaged following a forced landing at Icy Bay on July 10, 1930. Bob Ellis picked up Scott and Selby. The remains of NC 115E were later salvaged by a Ketchikan canneryman, J. Iverson.*

were two or three possible sites that had been considered. Gillam returned to the interior by rail on Saturday morning, April 19, 1930.

The Alaska Road Commission was publishing a book, listing and describing all sixty-one landing fields currently available for use in Alaska. Along with descriptions, the book contained two blueprints of each, showing its relative location to the community or camp, and a detailed diagram of the field itself; with length, width and obstructions plainly marked. Availability of gas and oil, spare parts, mechanics, and the type of accommodations were listed along with other pertinent information. Ordered from the Juneau office, it was of great value to a traveling aviator.

The Chamber of Commerce, meeting on Wednesday, May 28, 1930, to go over the proposed Old Town loop road, also took up the airport project. While Gillam had favored the ball park site, because it was closer to town, the cost of clearing and filling in gravel was estimated at about $25,000. The present law provided for twenty percent to be contributed by the community, with the Territory of Alaska bearing the balance of the cost. The site would

With cowling removed from the Pratt & Whitney Wasp engine for servicing, the Lockheed Vega, Taku, rests on the water of Eyak Lake at Cordova in 1930.

Courtesy of Bob Ellis

Pilot Robert E. Ellis and his flight mechanic, Frank Hatcher, with Alaska-Washington Airways Vega, Taku, *NC 102W, in which they made two flights in 1930 to Bristol Bay from their base in Juneau, stopping over in Cordova. Ellis was twenty-seven years old and Hatcher, twenty-two, in 1930.*

provide an airstrip of 800 feet in length, suitable only for small planes, while the Department of Commerce regulations called for a minimum runway length of 1320 feet. It was decided that the site at Mile 17 (seventeen miles out of town on the railroad) would be the best, all things considered.

June 13, 1930, a party consisting of Territorial Highway Engineer Robert J. Sommers, Auditor Cash Cole, along with Cordova Chamber of Commerce members F.A. Hansen and J.L. Galen, went to inspect the Mile 17 site. They traveled on a railway speeder. Finding the recent heavy overflows had cut channels through the field, they arranged for immediate temporary repairs to the strip, using a tractor and grader from Alaska Transfer Company. Any real improvements to the field would have to await some means of water protection and drainage, for it would be subject to continuous washouts. The field could be put into usable condition for the summer but a more permanent solution must await the following year, if the site was confirmed for a municipal airport.

The first plane of the season into Cordova did not land on the newly-scraped landing strip, but landed on its pontoons on Eyak Lake. Pilot Robert E. Ellis and mechanic Frank Hatcher arrived in the Alaska-Washington Airways Lockheed Vega, *Taku*, NC 102W, carrying Attorney H.L. Faulkner of Juneau and R.R. Payne of Vancouver, production manager of the New England Fish Company.

Ellis had left Juneau at 6:30 P.M. June 17, 1930 in the twin-float seaplane for Yakutat, remaining overnight there. The two airmen and their passengers continued the flight the following day, taking off at noon from Yakutat Bay to reach Cordova before 5:00 P.M. that afternoon. Flying up the coast in the 120-mile-per-hour seaplane was very pleasant. Faulkner disembarked and Ellis continued on with Mr. Payne to Driver Bay on Knight Island in Prince William Sound, where they remained overnight.

The *Taku* returned to Cordova at 5:00 A.M. Haakon B. Friele of Seattle, vice-president and general manager of Nakat Packing Company, came in on the steamer *Yukon* from Ketchikan at 4:30 A.M. that same day, and at 9:00 A.M. he left aboard the Lockheed Vega for Kvichak station in Bristol Bay, where the company's Kvichak River cannery, Nakeen, was located. Ellis and Hatcher delivered their passenger and were back in Cordova that same Thursday evening.

Shortly after 4:00 A.M. Friday, June 20, 1930, Ellis and Hatcher took off from Eyak

Lake with Faulkner and Payne on their return to Juneau. Three and a half hours later the pilot landed the Vega at Chatham, in the northern part of Chatham Strait and, after a short stop, came on to Juneau, arriving there about 8:30 A.M. They had been gone two and a half days and put eighteen hours in the air. It had been a fast, efficient operation in a good piece of equipment; the two airmen had covered 2160 miles on the flight.

The newly-scraped field on the flats at Mile 17 was soon put to use. Harold Gillam, flying his Swallow, NC 430N, landed there on the evening of Tuesday, June 24, 1930, coming from Copper Center in one hour and thirty minutes of flying. He ran into a fogbank shortly before reaching the field, and circled for a few minutes before landing. The pilot carefully loaded 200 feet of cable and some marlin pins for the Nabesna Mining Company and was away again, using only 350 feet of the strip on the takeoff.

Gorst Air Transport was returning to Cordova with an airplane, planning to be in the city over the Fourth of July. Clayton Scott, the pilot who had brought the Keystone Loening Air Yacht, NC 9728, to Cordova in May of the previous year, was in Ketchikan with a Boeing B-1E flying boat, NC 115E, later named the *Nugget*. Scott, with his mechanic, John Selby, left Ketchikan on Thursday, July 3, 1930, making it through to land on Eyak Lake in one full day. The Boeing carried one passenger, Scott's girl friend Myrtle Smith. The school teacher from Seattle had been visiting in Ketchikan when the opportunity to fly to Cordova had arisen,

Harold Gillam, in the cockpit of Swallow, NC 430N, warms his engine at the Copper Center field he began operating from in 1930 with the two Swallow biplanes.

Pilot Clayton Scott arrived in Cordova on July 3, 1930 in the Boeing B-1E flying boat, NC 115E, to land on Eyak Lake. Accompanied by his flight mechanic, John Selby, and his one passenger, Myrtle Smith, he was in time for the Fourth of July celebration.

allowing her to visit her sister, Mrs. Roy Douglas, in Cordova.

On the way up, the pilot had landed at Petersburg and at Port Althorp, on the north coast of Chichagof Island; flying time was three hours and thirty minutes. Leaving there in the flying boat, Scott flew on up the coast of the Gulf of Alaska to Yakutat, and then to Cordova, using another four hours and fifteen minutes of flying time. The route was not strange to Scott; he had flown it both ways in 1929 with Gordon Graham in the Loening *Alaskan*. It had been a long day but it was pleasant to see all his friends again in the Prince William Sound community. He had arrived in time for the Fourth.

Scott was busy the following day flying sightseers from Eyak Lake in the Boeing boat. He was in the air for three hours, taking a number of people up to see the area from the air. The plane's activities added to the excitement of the many events put on in the community. On July 5 the pilot made a flight to Cottonwood Point at the mouth of the Copper River, returning the same day with a round-trip air time of an hour and a half. He also made a fifteen minute passenger hop on his return.

On Sunday, July 6, the flying boat was officially christened *Nugget* and the pilot flew an extended sightseeing trip over Miles and Childs glaciers, northeast of Cordova, spending one hour and fifteen minutes in the air. That same morning he took a party of four passengers from Cordova to Valdez, landing NC 115E on the bay near the city at 10:00 A.M. Scott departed with the party at 12:30 P.M. the same day. The pilot landed on Eyak Lake in the summer's daylight with a flying time of two hours for the round trip, giving Scott a total flying time of 1288:30 hours. He was away again that afternoon for a round-trip flight to Hinchinbrook Island, taking an air time of one hour. Not yet through for the day, he made six passenger hops before tying the Boeing up for the night. He added another two hours and forty-five minutes of flying to his total with these. It had been a full Sunday.

Scott was finishing up the flying in Cordova as fast as he could, for the Gorst Air Transport had a lucrative contract coming up soon in Ketchikan. Radio Pictures Corporation was filming a movie based on the Rex Beach novel, *The Silver Horde*, out of Ketchikan. They were making a second film, based on the same author's novel, *The Iron Trail*, most of which would be shot out of Cordova using the Copper River & Northwestern Railroad. Scott intended to use the Boeing to do some movie flying out of Ketchikan before returning to Cordova to fly aerial cameramen out of there. The pilot invited residents to send air mail with him at no charge when he returned to Ketchikan in the near future.

On Monday, July 7, 1930, the pilot was away from Cordova for a round trip to Latouche, taking two hours of air time. He did another one and a half hours of flying on his return, hopping passengers. With bad weather on the following day, the pilot and his mechanic, John Selby, spent a good part of the afternoon servicing the plane in preparation for the flight down the gulf to Ketchikan. Scott made a flight out to a nearby cannery and back the next day, taking only ten minutes each way. *The Cordova Times* was running a large box ad for Gorst Air Transport, advertising for passengers for Juneau and Ketchikan on the flight south. The fee was $100 to Juneau and $130 to Ketchikan. But there were no takers. Most Alaskans, unless there was an emergency or business reason, enjoyed the social trip south on the steamer, meeting friends from all over the Territory. If they weren't acquainted at the time of boarding, they were well-acquainted by the time the ship docked in Seattle.

Scott and Selby were off in the Boeing *Nugget*, NC 115E, at 3:00 A.M. Thursday, July 10, 1930, for Ketchikan. They were back on Eyak Lake two and a half hours later. Bad weather and very strong headwinds down the Gulf of Alaska had eaten into their fuel supply so that the pilot deemed it advisable to return to Cordova. An impenetrable fog on the coast had been the deciding factor; he climbed to 5000 feet but had been unable to top the thick layer.

Delaying until 2:20 P.M., the two airmen were off a second time, hoping for improvement although radio reports indicated rain all the way down the coast. Clayton Scott estimated their arrival in Ketchikan at 11:00 P.M. that same evening.

The Gorst Air Transport plane was still unreported two days later. While some concern was felt, it was thought that Scott was probably in some isolated, sheltered bay, waiting out the weather. There were several along the coast and among the islands below Cape Spencer. Queries to all radio stations between Cordova and Ketchikan brought no reports of anyone sighting the plane.

While the governor's office in Juneau had been contacted by the U.S. Commissioner in Cordova, more positive relief was provided by Vern C. Gorst in Seattle, upon learning the *Nugget* was missing. Contacting Alaska-Washington Airways, it was arranged to send out their Lockheed Vega *Taku*, with pilot Robert E. Ellis and mechanic Frank Hatcher. Loading the plane with relief supplies, including extra gasoline and oil, the pair departed Juneau at 5:30 A.M. Sunday, July 13, 1930, planning on searching every inlet along the coast between Juneau and Cordova. They had only recently been over the same route.

Clayton Scott and Selby, following their departure from Cordova on July 10, were making good time. Flying at 1200 feet, somewhat offshore along the Gulf of Alaska, they had reached a point between Katalla and Yakutat, opposite Icy Bay, when suddenly the radial engine became very rough, backfiring through the exhaust stack and losing much of its power. Turning toward the shore and losing altitude, with the Wasp B engine barely turning over, the pilot guided the plane down to a landing on the crest of a large wave, about 500 feet out from the entrance to Icy Bay. As soon as the *Nugget* settled in the water, a following wave broke six feet off of the lower left wing tip, in addition to the wing float.

Riding the swells and the waves through the entrance, working their way through the loose ice that calves from the glacier, and for which the bay is rightly named, the fliers found a clear spot on the beach and worked the plane up as far as possible.

Finding the trouble to be in the number seven cylinder, Scott and Selby attempted to remove it but it was impossible under the conditions. (It was later discovered the head of the exhaust valve had broken off and gone through the top of the piston; the metal fragments had gone into the crankcase section).

The tide was on the rise, with wind and waves increasing in violence. Attempting to save the *Nugget* from further damage, the men unloaded the plane and, with each surge of the water, pulled it further up on the beach. The lower left wing panel, which was damaged and without its float, was down in the water and the waves took their toll; the rest of the wing gave way to the battering. The two men unloaded the plane completely, carrying the material up the beach to the shore. The surging of the waves finally broke the upper left wing panel loose; it had been weakened by loss of support from the lower panel. Continuing their efforts to save the plane, the men swung the ship around, putting the good right panels toward the gulf, but their efforts were unsuccessful, and the remaining wing panels gave way under the pounding of the waves. Feeling their only hope of rescuing themselves was to save the hull and use it as a boat, they gave up on this when the tail succumbed to the pounding force of the water. They turned the plane with the bow toward the waves and it rode easier until a large wave rolled in and tossed the remains of the *Nugget* high up on the beach on its side, where it rested out of reach of any more pounding. Scott and Selby, after their five-hour fight to save the *Nugget*, prepared for a night on the barren sandspit. A spot less than ten by twenty feet in size remained above high tide. Massing all their equipment at this haven, the airmen built a fire of driftwood and made themselves as comfortable as possible.

The following morning, Friday, July 11, 1930, Scott sighted a cabin across the bay from their camp and he decided to move. Not having proper camp equipment, and concerned over the many bear tracks observed on the sandspit, the pair began to walk around the beach at low tide, taking an axe and a thirty-eight caliber revolver for moral support. Reaching the deserted cabin some three hours later, they found food, and prepared a breakfast of rice and beans—their first real meal since departing Eyak Lake at Cordova.

Locating an old skiff near the cabin, they tipped it over to drain the accumulated rainwater, and rowed it across the bay to retrieve their equipment from their former camp. One or the other kept a lookout from the roof of the cabin, occasionally firing a flare at night to attract the attention of possible relief parties. Their hopes were rewarded when Ellis and Hatcher sighted the cabin, zooming overhead at 9:30 on Sunday morning.

The Alaska-Washington Airways airmen had searched every inlet, lake and creek from Cape Spencer to Icy Bay. They landed twice, at Lituya Bay where they learned that the Gorst plane had not been seen, and again at Yakutat, where the missing plane had planned to refuel. No such landing had been made there. Whenever a cabin was sighted, Ellis circled it to bring the occupants outdoors. Encountering two fogbanks on the way, they ran into a third approaching Icy Bay. Looking down through a hole in it, Ellis spotted the cabin, and written deeply in the sand on the beach the words, "Drop Food" and "Send Boat From Yakutat". The two missing men had heard the sound of the approaching plane before it was visible to them and were on the roof of the cabin. Ellis recognized them at once.

There was a lagoon about a mile long in front of the cabin, containing a great deal of floating ice. Circling for twenty minutes, Ellis searched it for a lane of clear water in which to set the *Taku* down. Then he turned out over Icy Bay, thinking to land there and taxi into the

July 13, 1930. The rustic cabin at Icy Bay where Bob Ellis and Frank Hatcher found Clayton Scott and John Selby following the loss of the Gorst Air Transport, Incorporated, Boeing B-1E, NC 115E. Left to Right: Alaska-Washington Airways pilot Bob Ellis, Clayton Scott (in plus-fours) and John Selby. Ellis took the two men back to Cordova where their flight had originated.

Courtesy of Clayton Scott

July 13, 1930. Icy Bay, Alaska. The Lockheed Vega Taku, NC 102W, is dwarfed by grounded ice chunks as it sits, nosed-in to the sand, in the narrow lagoon Bob Ellis landed the plane in to pick up Scott and Selby after their enforced landing off Icy Bay with the Boeing boat Nugget, NC 115E, on July 10, 1930.

Courtesy of Clayton Scott

lagoon but it turned out to be even more cluttered with ice. The pilot finally landed in the lagoon and taxied to shore before the cabin, just four hours after leaving Juneau.

In haste, the men removed the fifty gallons of gasoline and the oil from the cabin of the Vega, brought along in case it was needed by Scott, and placed it in a cache at the cabin for some future need. With everyone aboard, Ellis pointed the nose of the plane toward the approaching fogbank and, delaying ten minutes for the fog to thin, took off from the surface of the lagoon. With only fifty feet of water, clear of ice, ahead of him when his pontoons left the surface, the pilot zoomed up through the fog.

Bringing the Gorst Air Transport airmen back to Cordova, the Alaska-Washington Airways pilot landed on Eyak Lake shortly after noon with a flying time of one and a half hours enroute. Other than exhaustion and suffering from a lack of sleep, Scott and Selby were in good shape. A searching party, leaving to search the shoreline aboard the launch *W.J. Crooker*, was cancelled before its departure from Katalla. It had been organized by U.S. Commissioner Robinson from Cordova. It was Sunday, July 13, 1930.

Clayton Scott, and Myrtle Smith who had been awaiting the next steamer for the south, returned to Juneau by ship; Ellis and Hatcher were going on to Bristol Bay with the Vega. John Selby remained in Cordova awaiting its return; he would fly to Juneau with the Alaska-Washington Airways plane. (see Juneau—1930, Chapter 54). The Boeing B-1E *Nugget*, almost totally insured for its $15,000 to $20,000 value, was considered a loss. However, a Ketchikan canneryman, J. Iverson, acquired the rights to the wreckage from the insurance company and retrieved the plane from the beach at Icy Bay. Although the wings were smashed and the tail broken, the hull and engine were in relatively good shape. Towing the badly-damaged *Nugget* to Yakutat Bay, a distance of about sixty-five miles, the new owner had it hoisted to the deck of the *Admiral Watson* for the remainder of its journey. The steamer arrived in Juneau on Friday, August 8, on her way from Seward to Seattle. Iverson intended to have the plane rebuilt.

Robert E. Ellis and twenty-two-year-old Frank Hatcher had a further task to perform before heading south from Cordova. A trip to Bristol Bay was in order. Taking local photographer Howard W. Steward along, they were away from Cordova at 1:00 P.M. Monday, July 14, 1930, in the Vega *Taku*, NC 102W. The pilot intended to land on one of the westward lakes near the Valley of Ten Thousand Smokes for the night, going on to Illiamna Bay the following morning to pick up Henry O'Malley, U.S. Commissioner of Fisheries, before proceeding to Nakeen. Foiled by fog conditions, Ellis was unable to land in the Katmai or proceed to Bristol Bay; finally he flew on over Illiamna Bay to Illiamna Lake. The party spent Monday night on the Illiamna River. Again thwarted by fog at Illiamna, they were unable to pick up the O'Malley party. The fisheries men would travel over the portage and by lake boat to Bristol Bay, the normal surface route from Cook Inlet.

The pilot landed the Lockheed Vega at Nakeen at 8:30 A.M. Tuesday, July 15, 1930, and was awaiting favorable weather before finally departing for Cordova at 6:00 A.M. on Wednesday morning. Ellis and Hatcher, with charter passenger H.B. Friele and Cordova photographer Howard Steward landed in Seward at 9:00 A.M. to check the Cordova and Yakutat weather reports. They were away from the Resurrection Bay city before noon, arriving at Cordova soon after. Taking Gorst Air Transport mechanic John Selby and H.B. Friele, Ellis and Hatcher were off Eyak Lake shortly after noon on that same day, Wednesday July 16. Arriving in Juneau late in the afternoon, their two passengers continued south in a second Alaska-Washington Airways plane. (see Juneau—1930, Chapter 54). Encouraged by the amount of business being done through Cordova, company officials spoke of plans for basing a Lockheed Vega at Cordova in the near future; however this did not occur in 1930.

Harold Gillam was leaning more toward Cordova than Valdez as a coastal base for his operations. The seaport and the railroad provided more economic incentive for him and much of his flying was along the Copper River corridor and the railbelt. Gillam was in Cordova for a few days during the last week of July. The pilot had been busy flying to the more remote mining sections, making several trips to the head of the Chitina River, with two more to make for Martin Harrais and William Sippert, who were developing gold properties in that part of the country. Gillam had flown William Sulzer in to Fairbanks a few weeks before, and had made three flights into the Nabesna for Carl Whitham, with supplies for his Nabesna Mining Company. The miner had installed a tram and started work on the foundations for a mill, with eight men now working. The pilot was looking forward to flying milling samples and concentrates out later for the operation.

Gillam had also hauled perishables and a U.S. mining inspector into the Chisana country. Further, he had made two flights to Chicken Creek, carrying a cargo of eggs, oranges and apples in, the same day they had arrived by boat in Cordova, and were brought up to Gillam at McCarthy by train and flown in that night by the pilot. Gillam had also made a flight in to Eagle with a dentist, as well as one with supplies and perishables to Tanana Crossing. He was looking forward to flying a special international highway commission to make a reconnaissance survey of the route between McCarthy and the boundary, and to the head of the White River country in August. By now the pilot was under a sub-contract to make a monthly trip there with the mail.

Cordova residents were able to read fresh news—only two days old—when Frank Dorbandt arrived in Cordova with copies of the *Seattle Post-Intelligencer* of Friday, August 1, 1930. Dorbandt, bringing up a float-equipped Fairchild 51, NC 5364, had left Seattle on that date, accompanied by his mechanic, Lon Cope, and Mrs. Dorbandt. (see Anchorage—1930, Chapter 57). Headed for Anchorage to open a new flying business with the four-passenger plane, Dorbandt landed on Eyak Lake on Fairchild P-4 floats late in the afternoon of Sunday, August 3, 1930, where the two airmen hurried to refuel the plane, soon departing. The weather ahead was not good.

Unable to cross the Chugach Mountains by way of Portage Pass because of fog, the pilot landed in the fjord and taxied up it, before turning to taxi out of the fog and make a new start. Dorbandt took off again, setting a course for Seward, flying from there to Skilak Lake and on in to land on Lake Spenard at Anchorage.

In Cordova, Harold Gillam was off the Mile 17 airport on Sunday, August 3, 1930, in his Swallow, NC 430N, carrying Miss Virginia DeHart and Gus Gelles, of the Alaska Guides Association. The business manager was arranging for a hunting party to go into the White River country in August. Gillam was looking forward to flying in similar hunting parties. Wilbur Irving, circulation manager for the *Cordova Times*, and an aviation booster, married Miss Dorothy Dooley on Thursday morning, August 7, 1930. Later Irving was to own his own plane and be involved in an air service.

In September, Gillam was still operating his two Swallows from Copper Center, with his headquarters at Chitina. Up to the twentieth of September he had, in that month, flown two flights to Chisana, two to Nabesna, two to the head of the Chitina River, one trip to McCarthy and two to Hudson Lake, which lay fifty-seven miles northeast of Valdez in the Chugach Mountains. On one of these trips he brought out 300 pounds of ore from the Nabesna Mine for a mill test. Carrying the mail, he was making a trip on the first of each month on the route from Gulkana to Chisana. With the White River Recording Precinct made a part of the Chitina Recording Precinct, Gillam had been authorized to bring the records in to Chitina by plane.

Gillam had flown Asa Baldwin, U.S. mining surveyor, to the head of the Chitina River to make a survey for Martin Harrais. He went after him in a few days, moving him to Nabesna to make a mineral examination of the property of the Nabesna Mining Company.

In August, Major Malcolm Elliott and Superintendent R.J. Shepherd, of the Alaska Road Commission, had flown about 600 miles with Gilliam, making a reconnaissance survey of the route for a road into the Nabesna and White River country. The Alaska Road Commission was also about to survey the ground along the Richardson Highway, five miles north of Chitina, intending to construct a landing field there, possibly early in 1931. A field was to be constructed at Chistochina near Earl Hirst's place the same fall. Using that field, Gillam planned on serving the territory north and east from there.

On Thursday, October 16, Gillam came in to the Mile 17 airport at Cordova with his Swallow, NC 430 N, carrying Deputy Marshal S.J. Nichols as a passenger from Valdez. Joe Crosson and his wife, Lillian, arrived there by steamer after an extended vacation in the States. Gillam flew his two friends from the Mile 17 airport at 10:55 A.M. on Friday, taking them to Copper Center to remain overnight. He flew them on to their home in Fairbanks the following morning, arriving at Weeks Field in mid-afternoon.

Harold Gillam flew in to Valdez on November 6, 1930, to stake down his Swallow and depart on the *Alameda* for the States. He was going to seek out an additional plane and pilot for his growing business, and return early in January.

The Copper River valley now had its own thriving air service.

Bob Ellis and Frank Hatcher picked up Clayton Scott and John Selby at this cabin at Icy Bay on July 13, 1930, following the loss of their Boeing flying boat. The large, roomy cabin had been brought in and used by an oil exploration party. This picture was taken at a later date when much of the ice surrounding it was gone.
Courtesy of John Selby

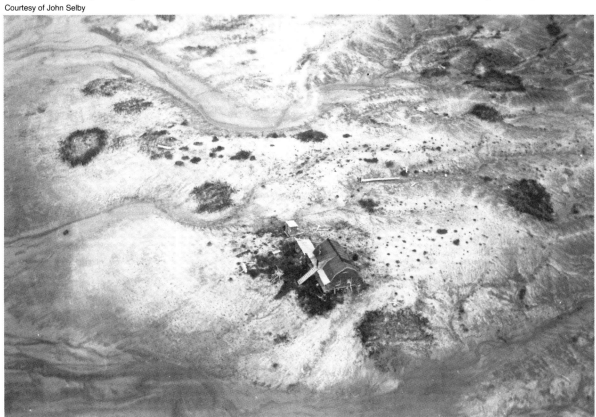

878

Gillam Airways

Meals Eaglerock Sales Co.

Valdez 1930

WITH THE STORING OF Owen Meals' Alexander Eaglerock, C 6316, *Spirit of Valdez*, at the end of October, 1929, aviation in the community had been at a standstill over the winter. On Friday, February 21, 1930, the steamer *Alaska* docked in Seward after a stormy trip across the Gulf of Alaska. Aboard the ship were two Swallow biplanes. One, NC 430N, consigned to Charles Harold Gillam, was offloaded at Valdez when the ship stopped there on the southbound trip. The other, a two-place Swallow TP (Training Plane), C 688H, also consigned to pilot Gillam, traveled by rail to Fairbanks for assembly there. (ownership was transferred to Percy Hubbard and Art Hines of Service Airlines before assembly).

Gillam, recently returned from Siberia, left Fairbanks in his open-cockpit Swallow biplane, *Arctic Prospector*, on March 18, 1930, with the intention of starting a flying service at McCarthy to serve the Copper River valley and other points. He had been planning this before going to Siberia with Crosson, and had ordered the second plane. Gillam had also obtained the

▲ *Valdez, Alaska. April 1, 1930. Residents of the community clustered about Harold Gillam's new Swallow, NC 430N, prior to his departure for Chitina and McCarthy. He had test flown the three-place biplane on March 28, following its arrival on the steamer* Alaska. *Gillam is on far right. Nancy Meals (Owen's wife) is the very short lady in front center.*

◄ *April 1, 1930. Harold Gillam with his new Swallow biplane in Valdez. The plane was powered with a Wright Whirlwind J6-7 of 225 horsepower.*

879

Swallow agency for Alaska.

Gillam flew the *Arctic Prospector* on skis to Lower Tonsina, a roadhouse in the Copper basin some sixty-four miles northeast of Valdez. Prevented from continuing by weather, he traveled by dog team to Chitina, then took the Copper River & Northwestern Railroad to Cordova, thence to Valdez on the steamer *Yukon*, arriving there on March 22, 1930. The citizens put on a reception and dance in his honor that evening, at which he told of his experiences in Siberia and of his plans for an air service.

Gillam was soon at work in the shop at the Meals Garage, assisting in the assembly and rigging of his new plane. Owen Meals, a licensed pilot, also was a Department of Commerce licensed mechanic and, along with running his Ford agency, assembled most of the planes that were shipped into Valdez in the coming years, to be flown out of the seaport to their respective bases. By Friday, March 28, 1930, the work on the plane was completed and Gillam made two test flights that morning, taking off on the first one at 10:32 A.M. and returning at 11:00 A.M. He was off on the second at 11:25 A.M., returning to land at 11:55 A.M. The plane, powered with a 225 horsepower Wright Whirlwind J6-7, performed well. He was now awaiting favorable weather before flying the new biplane out to Chitina. Meals had ordered a set of skis for his own Alexander Eaglerock, still in storage.

Valdez residents gathered at the airfield on Tuesday, April 1, 1930, to cluster about the new plane for a photograph session. With bright, clear skies, Harold Gillam prepared for takeoff. He was away in the mild breeze from the light snow surface at 1:15 P.M. spiraling up for altitude to almost 10,000 feet before taking up an easterly course for Chitina and McCarthy. Circling over the first point for twenty minutes to show off the new plane, he continued on to land at the second point at 3:00 P.M., his first flight from Valdez to McCarthy for the new independent airplane company.

Gillam had a contract with William Sulzer, former governor of New York and head of Chisana Mines, Incorporated, which was operating in the White River country. Making landings on a temporary field between McCarthy and Chitina, the pilot hauled in William J. McCauley and Dan Segrue to Snag River; then began freighting in a ton of supplies. The pilot flew in via the head of the Copper River, making four trips. Gillam had never been in that section of Alaska before and, following maps, he landed on a small lake, right where they wanted to go. Returning to McCarthy, he flew direct, crossing Chisana Pass (pronounced Shushana), flying at 13,000 feet and crossing over the Wrangell Mountains in clear weather. The *Arctic Prospector*, which he had left at Lower Tonsina, must remain there until all the snow disappeared and the field enlarged sufficiently for him to get the Warner Scarab-powered plane out on wheels. Gillam had now established his headquarters in Chitina. He expected to bring in a second pilot.

Gillam spent a few days at Copper Center, leaving on Thursday, April 24, 1930, for Lower Tonsina. He put wheels on the Swallow in preparation for removing it. Owen Meals had installed his new skis on his Alexander Eaglerock, C 6316, and tuned up the 180 horsepower Hispano-Suiza motor in preparation for a test flight on the skis.

Gillam made two more flights from McCarthy on Thursday, April 24, 1930, flying south into the Coast Range to the head of the Bremner River, carrying a prospector and part of his supplies. Leaving the man there, Gillam was back in an hour with the balance of the outfit. Stringing a cable between two trees and caching the outfit on it out of reach of bears and wolverines, the pilot and his customer returned to McCarthy. The man and his partner, both then working at the Kennecott Mines Company, would prospect the area the coming summer, going in to their cache when the snow was gone.

880

Gillam came in to Valdez from Copper Center, arriving at 3:57 P.M., May 4, 1930, in Swallow, NC 430N. He was bringing Mr. and Mrs. C.C. Williams, summoned to appear as witnesses before the grand jury at the court city. The one hour and twenty minute flight was without incident. The pilot was away again at 4:25 P.M., May 6, for Copper Center, taking Deputy Marshal Stanley Nichols with him. Delayed by stormy weather, they had landed on the beach enroute. Gillam brought the deputy in to Valdez at 2:35 P.M. Saturday, May 10, also carrying A. Smith of Chistochina, who had been indicted by the grand jury.

The next day, Sunday, May 11, Gillam was busy taking local residents aloft in his Swallow, NC 430N. On the first aerial sightseeing hop at 2:45 P.M., he carried Miss Anna May Dolan and Mrs. Thomas about the city for fifteen minutes before landing. Mrs. Clarita Wheeler and Mr. H.G. Cloes were next, away at 3:05 P.M. and back at 3:30 P.M. Next he took up H.P. Sullivan and Fred Alderson, followed by Billy Egan and Chester A. Clifton. The last flight of the day, carrying Anna May Dolan for a second time, with George Ashby, the pilot was away at 4:25 P.M. and landed at 4:35 P.M. In the fine weather, with the sound of the motor reverberating among the shining peaks, the flights were a joy to all, both on the ground and in the air. Gillam was away in the Swallow at 10:50 A.M. the next morning, Monday, May 12, 1930, for Copper Center. He was alone in the plane.

May 1930. Parked on skis, Gillam's Swallow, NC 430N, on the left and Owen Meals' Alexander Eaglerock Spirit of Valdez (No. 2), C 6316, on the right await the coming of summer and a change to wheels. Meals had the Eaglerock agency for Alaska and Gillam had the Swallow agency for the Territory.

Owen E. Meals now had his Eaglerock, *Spirit of Valdez* (No. 2), tuned up and ready to fly, with the new skis installed. He was away at 11:00 A.M. for an hour's test flight on May 23, 1930, making seven landings. Satisfied with the way the biplane performed, the Valdez pilot went up again at 5:15 P.M. that afternoon, carrying three passengers during his five consecutive flights: Bill Egan, Chester Clifton and Dwight Thomas. The boys had a fine time. Meals repeated the performance on Monday morning, May 26, taking Ed Lerdahl and Billy Egan; making two landings and returning from the last flight at 12:10 P.M. The following day, Tuesday, May 27, he was off at 1:15 P.M. in the Alexander Eaglerock, making six landings with Bill Egan and one of the Clifton boys as willing passengers. He was back at 3:18 P.M. to park the plane on its skis at the edge of the field.

Harold Gillam took Mrs. Martin Harrais from McCarthy to the head of the Chitina River on Monday, May 26, 1930, landing on a gravel bar which turned out to be pretty rough. The woman's husband, who was doing patent work on a group of mining claims in that section, left at the same time as his wife, going overland, but did not arrive until some days later. After landing, the pilot spent some time clearing rocks and driftwood from the bar to make a better landing spot; but more work was needed to make it safe for an airstrip. The upper Chitina valley was about five miles wide with numerous high gravel bars. There was a second one about twenty-five miles from the one Gillam had picked; it would also make a landing field with some improvement.

Flying the Swallow, NC 430N, the pilot had taken forty-five minutes enroute on the way in, returning to McCarthy in forty minutes. Shortly after Gillam had taken off from the bar, a large grizzly had appeared at the miner's cabin and stayed around most of the day. Mrs. Harrais, alone at the site, locked her door and stayed inside. The following day two more of the bears appeared and hung around for two days. It was a worrisome time for the lone woman, and she was happy and relieved when her husband finally appeared.

Harold Gillam's Swallow biplane, NC 430N, on Valdez Airport.

Gillam came in to Valdez from Upper Tonsina the next day, Tuesday, at 6:18 A.M., bringing A.M. Dieringer and Mike J. Knowles. The pilot was off at 8:12 A.M. that same morning, May 27, for Copper Center, carrying Miss Anna May Dolan and Miss Virginia DeHart. He returned at 5:00 P.M. that afternoon with Miss Dolan, coming from Tonsina. Owen Meals went aloft in his Eaglerock, C 6316, that evening; taking Marie Whelan, Dwight Thomas and Henry Swinquist up on a series of flights that included nine landings. Taking off at 6:30 P.M. on his final flight for the day, the pilot taxied in at 7:50 P.M.

Harold Gillam was away for Cordova in his Swallow at 7:28 A.M. Wednesday, May 28, 1930, carrying Ernest Michaelson. Landing on the field below Eyak Lake at Mile 7 to deliver his passenger, he returned alone to Valdez, landing at 9:00 A.M. that same morning.

The pilot departed in the Swallow for Fairbanks, taking off alone on the morning of Thursday, May 29, 1930. He landed on Weeks Field at 2:15 P.M. the following day. Wylie R. Wright, Department of Commerce inspector, was giving airmen examinations there and Gillam's was successful; he received the coveted Air Transport Pilot License while in the Interior city. He went back to doing what he had been doing, but now he was legal.

Harold Gillam taking off the Valdez mudflats with his Swallow, NC 430N.

A new airplane visited Valdez on Monday, June 2, 1930, when Alaskan Airways, Incorporated, pilot Matt Nieminen came in from Anchorage in the Travel Air 4000, C-193. The pilot landed the open-cockpit wheel plane on the Valdez field with Anchorage attorney Harry F. Morton and canneryman A.I. Ellsworth, who was operating the Magill cannery at the port city, as passengers. The pair were in Valdez on court business. Nieminen took off with the two men several hours later, returning to Anchorage on a direct course over the Valdez Glacier. The city council, in a meeting that evening, decided on field improvements to the Valdez airport, including extending it several hundred feet to the westward to tidewater. This allowed amphibian planes, landing on the waters of the bay, to be brought easily up onto the field. Construction of a city hangar capable of housing two planes was also planned for the field, with Gillam agreeing to build, at his expense, an adjoining machine shop to repair planes. Gillam and A.A. Bennett, former Fairbanks flier, had been discussing a partnership, with Bennett bringing up a Zenith cabin plane on floats for service in the district. While this never came to be, Gillam later acquired a wheel-equipped Zenith of his own, and an amphibian plane. Nevertheless, the city of Valdez, with its deep-water seaport, a highway to Fairbanks and an airport, was making a bid to become a center of air transportation between the coast and the Interior. Standard Oil Company was also putting in a bulk plant for their products in Valdez, making aviation fuel more accessible as well as their other fuel and oil products for marine and land use.

Wednesday, June 4, 1930, dawned clear and bright in Valdez, the mountains shining in the sun. Owen Meals went aloft in his Alexander Eaglerock, *Spirit of Valdez*. With the 180 horsepower Hispano-Suiza running well, the pilot decided to make an altitude test of the plane and its powerplant. Eventually reaching 15,000 feet, Meals saw a fantastic panorama spread about him, extending to Cape St. Elias on the east, Seward and Anchorage to the west, and the many miles of the Copper River valley extending into the Interior. He came down awed and exhilarated by it all. Such a sight would become commonplace to travelers in the more powerful planes of later years.

The steamer *Aleutian* was in port on June 5, 1930, with Mrs. S.E. Robbins and Miss Barbara Nudd aboard, traveling to Fairbanks. The ship's Captain Anderson, with Mrs. Robbins, went aloft in the Eaglerock with Owen Meals for a sightseeing flight. The pilot made two flights that same day, carrying two other passengers from the steamship on the first one.

Matt Nieminen was back in Valdez at 3:50 P.M. Tuesday, June 10, 1930, bringing a Third Division court party made up of Harry Morton, A.I. Ellsworth and two witnesses. He was flying a Fairchild 71, NC 153H. The pilot departed alone at 4:50 P.M. to fly back to Anchorage. His passengers returned later by steamer.

Owen Meals was up in his Eaglerock, C 6316, Serial No. 615, at 2:38 P.M. Friday, June 13, on a local flight, to practice maneuvers by himself. He landed at 3:50 P.M. The pilot took off again at 4:20 P.M. with a passenger by the name of Armstrong, on a local flight, landing at 5:10 P.M. He was away in the plane for Copper Center at 6:00 P.M. Sunday, June 15, 1930, to meet Department of Commerce Inspector Wylie R. Wright. The man was to arrive there the next day to give Meals his written examination and flight test for an Air Transport Pilot License. The Alexander Eaglerock was also to be relicensed. On Tuesday afternoon, Meals and Harold Gillam left Copper Center for McCarthy in Swallow, NC 430N, where they worked on Gillams' first Swallow, *Arctic Prospector*, with its Warner Scarab engine, getting it to readiness for relicense. Flying the airplane back to Copper Center, Gillam was successful in the inspection. On Tuesday evening, with his new Air Transport Pilot License in his pocket and a current license certificate in the celluloid pocket of the Eaglerock, Meals left Copper Center for Valdez. Passing through a heavy cloud bank to the east of the city, he made a good landing at 10:00 P.M. on his home field.

Copper Center, where Gillam operated from, with his actual headquarters in Chitina. Copper Center, having large, grassy open spaces was a much better area for an airport. Gillam's Swallow, NC 430N, on right.

Owen Meals took Lee Albin up in the *Spirit of Valdez* on Thursday, June 19, taking off at 2:55 P.M. and arriving back on the field at 3:10 P.M. The man wanted to meet the inbound steamer *S.S. Yukon*. That afternoon he took the ship's master, Captain Anderson, aloft in the Eaglerock, climbing to 9500 feet; they were back from the hour's flight at 5:45 P.M. It was becoming a regular thing for the seafarer to go for an airplane ride during his stop in Valdez. The Alaska Road Commission crews that had been ploughing out last winter's snow on the Richardson Highway over Thompson Pass for the past weeks announced the road open for the summer on Friday, June 20, 1930, the earliest the summit had been opened in some years.

Flying at Valdez languished for a few days until Gillam came in from Copper Center on Wednesday, June 25, 1930, landing his Swallow, NC 430N, on the field at 9:05 A.M. He had brought it in for a top-overhaul on the Whirlwind J6-7 radial engine. The pilot departed in the ship for Copper Center at 10:00 A.M. June 29, the work completed. Meals made one local flight to 6200 feet on Sunday, June 30, carrying Mr. and Mrs. Wooden on a fifty-minute sightseeing trip.

Meals took the Eaglerock, C 6316, up at 8:00 A.M., July 1, 1930, for a half-hour local flight, landing at 8:30 A.M. He was up again at 9:35 A.M. on July 4, taking Alaska Road Commission mechanics Lee Albin and Raymond Huddlestone for a ride, landing at 10:18 A.M. He went up again at 12:25 P.M. with Dwight M. Thomas, another Alaska Road Commission mechanic, for a twenty-five minute ride.

Harold Gillam, flying his Swallow, NC 430N, arrived at McCarthy the evening of July

4, 1930, capping the festivities at the rail town. Coming from Copper Center with two passengers: R.J. Shepherd, superintendent of the Alaska Road Commission, and O.A. Nelson, U.S. Commissioner at Chitina; the flight had taken one hour and ten minutes. Following the plane's arrival, with ideal flying weather prevailing, the pilot made several short flights about the area with sightseers. Flying over the Kennicott Glacier and the well-known Kennecott Mines, his passengers had an exciting view of their surroundings.

Leaving McCarthy at 5:00 A.M. Monday, July 7, 1930, with Mr. Truitt, a Territorial engineer, and a gravel scraper, the pilot flew to the head of the Chitina River in his Swallow, landing on the bar. Leaving the scraper there for the use of prospectors William Sippert and Martin Harrais to use in smoothing a runway on the bar, the two men left again.

Clayton Scott, with mechanic John Selby, came in to Valdez from Cordova at 10:00 A.M. on July 6, 1930. The Gorst Air Transport, Incorporated, B-1E flying boat, NC 115E, landed in the bay with a full load—four passengers—aboard. Scott was off again, shortly after noon (12:30 P.M.) on his return to Cordova with the same party. The passengers had an excellent view of the glaciers and mountains enroute. Scott had flown two hours on the round trip. (see Cordova—1930, Chapter 55, on Gorst).

Meals made two local flights, alone in the *Spirit of Valdez*, on the morning of July 14; coming in at 8:12 A.M. He was to pick up Percy Hubbard for a third flight that evening at 8:10 P.M. It turned out to be a demonstration flight, for the Service Airlines pilot was so enthusiastic about the plane that he ordered an Eaglerock, powered with the Wright J-5 motor of 225 horsepower. It was delivered in Fairbanks on October 15, 1930.

Meals flew the Alexander Eaglerock, C 6316, on August 3, 1930, taking off solo for a forty-minute local flight. He went up again at 11:35 A.M. on Friday, August 14, flying about locally for two hours and thirty minutes, carrying four sightseers and making four landings to change passengers. On August 18, 1930, he took game warden Sam White and his wife aloft in the Eaglerock, flying for fifty minutes. They had motored over the Richardson Highway to Valdez. Sam owned a Golden Eagle plane in Fairbanks. He ordered a Swallow later through Gillam's agency.

Harold Gillam came in on Thursday, August 19, flying his Swallow, NC 430N, bringing two passengers, Earl F. Woods and Mrs. J. Baker from Copper Center. Landing on the Valdez field at 5:00 P.M., he was away for Copper Center again at 2:15 P.M. on August 21, taking Mrs. C.C. Williams and her sister, Miss Sammie Gallaher, who had arrived on the *Aleutian* from California. The pilot returned to Valdez at 11:35 A.M. on August 27, bringing one passenger from Copper Center in his Swallow, NC 430N. Gillam departed that same day, at 2:20 P.M., returning to Copper Center with a passenger.

The new municipal hangar on the Valdez airport was nearing completion, with Joe Walters and William Jackson doing the work.

Owen Meals, again taking time off from his Ford agency and garage, was up in the *Spirit of Valdez* (No. 2) on Thursday, September 11, taking off at 5:25 P.M. with Raymond Huddlestone to meet the *S.S. Alaska*. Returning at 6:05 P.M. he parked the Eaglerock for another ten days. It was announced that John Blum, son of the late Sam Blum of Valdez, was the winning pilot of the men's Class A aerial derby from Seattle to Chicago; collecting nearly $11,000 in prize money. Blum was owner and operator of Northwest Air Service with an airfield near Bryn Mawr, close to Renton, Washington.

Meals took his Eaglerock biplane aloft at 5:15 P.M., September 22, 1930, for a thirty-minute ride by himself about the area. He was practicing airwork. He did not fly again until Saturday, October 4, 1930, going up at 3:40 P.M. to test a pair of airwheels he had just

Earl F. Woods, Gillam's mechanic, in Copper Center
with Gillam's 1928 model Swallow biplane.

installed on the plane. The low-pressure tires smoothed out a lot of the bumpiness of the three landings he made in the plane. His usual fans, including Billy Egan, Sam Bakshus, Robert Dixon and Billy Zharoff, occupied the passenger seat.

(Bill Egan loved flying, and his parents' house was close to where Meals parked his plane. He was later to take flying lessons in May of 1932 in a Monocoupe; in 1937 acquiring his own Aeronca light plane. Bill Egan went on to other things ''higher than the sky'' as the State of Alaska's first governor, serving a total of three terms. William Allen Egan never lost interest in aviation and its people.)

Ed Lerdahl, mechanic for the Valdez Transportation Company, another fan, was leaving on the *S.S. Alaska* for the States, intending to take up flying, acquire a license and return in the spring with an airplane. Thirteen inches of snow were reported in the first week of October on the summit of Thompson Pass on the Richardson Highway, making travel difficult. High winds soon drifted the snow, making auto travel between Valdez and Fairbanks impossible.

Harold Gillam arrived in Valdez at 10:10 A.M. Monday, October 13, 1930, in his Swallow, NC 430N, coming from Copper Center to pick up some parts and to overhaul his motor. He had flown in a strong southeast wind most of the way. The pilot remained on the field until Thursday, taking off in the Swallow for Cordova at 12:30 P.M. with Deputy Marshal A.J. Nichols as a passenger. Joe Crosson, Chief Pilot for Alaskan Airways, Incorporated, and his wife Lillian arrived in Cordova by steamer from a vacation in the States. Gillam departed Mile 17 airport at 10:55 A.M. Friday, October 17, 1930, with the couple in the passenger seat of his Swallow. He arrived at Copper Center in the early afternoon, to remain overnight.

887

Taking off the following day, Saturday, the pilot landed the Crossons on Weeks Field in the mid-afternoon that same day.

Gillam returned to Valdez in the Swallow biplane, NC 430N, arriving at 5:00 P.M. November 6, 1930. Coming from Copper Center, where winter had set in with eight inches of snow on the field, his plane was to remain at the port city into January of 1931, while the pilot left on the *Alameda* for the States, to locate another plane for Gillam Airways. Once more Owen Meals had stored his Eaglerock, *Spirit of Valdez*, for the winter. A.A. Bennett had given up his intentions of relocating in Alaska; he had set up Bennett Air Transport in Oregon, using a Zenith 6 and a couple of other airplanes. He expected to use Elbert E. Parmenter and Hap Roundtree as additional pilots in his airway service. He later relocated in Boise, Idaho.

Courtesy of Frank and Marian Thomas

While Harold Gillam had, during the summer, discussed a possible partnership with A.A. Bennett, early Fairbanks flier, it never came about. Bennett eventually settled in Idaho and, in 1932, was working on a contract hauling oil in to Yellow Pine Mine in the Primitive Area of Idaho, using the Zenith Z6-B, NC 134W, shown here in front of the factory in Midway City, California, plus one other Zenith. Gillam later acquired a Zenith Z6-B, NC 977Y, for his own work in the Copper River country.

On the River of No Return

Frank and Marian Thomas

A.A. Bennett established and operated the Flying B Ranch in the Primitive Area of Idaho, flying in sportsmen for the superlative hunting and fishing experience.

PACIFIC INTERNATIONAL
AIRWAYS OF ALASKA
DORBANDT & COPE
"ALASKANS SERVING ALASKA"

Fly in comfort to all points in Alaska in our four-passenger cabin plane. Large baggage compartment separate from the cabin. Equipment for water landings.

Sightseeing Trips, Any Time $5.00 Per Passenger

For Rates to Alaska Points——See

ROBERT H. ROMIG   Phone 285-R

SEPTEMBER 15, 1930

Eddie Bowman Collection

890

Alaskan Airways, Incorporated

Dorbandt & Cope Commercial
Flying Service
Pacific International
Airways, Incorporated

Anchorage 1930

THE CITY OF ANCHORAGE BEGAN THE NEW year without airplane service, for Matt Nieminen, the sole pilot based there, had taken the Travel Air 4000, C-193, to Fairbanks on Monday, December 30, 1929, for an overhaul. Matt was also to relieve Canadian pilot Broatch on the Eielson-Borland Relief Expedition. Suspension of air service from Anchorage created problems for trappers who had been flown out by plane. One man, Andrew Kvale, came in to Anchorage by railroad on Friday evening, January 3, 1930, after hiking more than eighty miles from a trapping camp to Chickaloon, where he boarded the train. He and two companions were flown by Russ Merrill into the site with a part of their outfit early in September. They had been living on a straight meat diet for some time; the last contribution to the stew pot was a small brown bear the men had shot. Kvale, in a somewhat better condition than his companions, had volunteered to walk out. With no plane available, a letter explaining

▲ *From* **Anchorage Daily Times**

◄ *Five-place Fairchild F-51, NC 5364, at the hoist at the Lake Spenard base near Anchorage. The plane, powered with the J6-9 of 300 horsepower, was fitted with Fairchild P-4 floats. It was an efficient workhorse and was particularly suited to Alaskan flying.*

the situation, as well as enough supplies to last the other two men until they could mush out, was taken in by H.H. Gubser, a predatory animal hunter who was traveling in that direction. There were other similar cases in the district.

Matt A. Nieminen and Alonzo Cope returned to Anchorage early in the afternoon of Thursday, January 16, flying the New Standard biplane, NC 174H. Coming from the Seward Peninsula, by way of Fairbanks, the pilot and mechanic immediately resumed commercial air service for Alaskan Airways, Incorporated, out of Anchorage; particular attention was devoted to rounding up those trappers who had been taken to various locations during the early winter, and who were now on short rations.

Nieminen made a flight to Seward in the New Standard on Saturday, January 18, 1930. Taking Doctor Rex Swartz, chief surgeon of the Alaska Railroad, the pilot was off at 8:00 A.M. to answer a call to attend a Mrs. Weybrecht, who was very ill. Swartz remained in Seward for an hour; Matt waited to return the doctor to Anchorage.

The New Standard was grounded at Anchorage for a time, awaiting repair parts for the motor. They finally arrived from Fairbanks on the afternoon of Friday, January 24, and Lon Cope quickly repaired the Wright J-5, 220 horsepower engine. Matt Nieminen, accompanied by Lon Cope, landed Waino Puntilla and his trapping outfit on Stillman Lake at Rainy Pass that same day, where the man would trap for the remainder of the season. The pair went on to Tonzona River, some 200 miles beyond, to locate trapper Jack Kimball, who had been landed there by Harvey Barnhill, without a full outfit, early in the winter. Kimball's partner and the rest of his equipment had not been delivered when air service was discontinued. With little food and no traps, it was believed that Kimball had probably abandoned the camp long ago. Circling the site, the airmen could see no signs of recent use, and flew on to another camp six miles away. Here they could see several dogs, but no people, indicating the camp was in use but the men probably out on their trapline. The pilot visited the district again later in the week. Kimball had probably joined his neighbor or gone downstream to an Indian village when he decided the plane was not coming back with the rest of his outfit. Nieminen and Cope brought in a load of trophies left last fall at the Stillman party camp.

On Sunday, January 26, 1930, Nieminen and Cope made a flight in the New Standard, NC 174H, down the Inlet to Nikolai, returning to Anchorage with oldtimer Henry Gottberg, who was in need of medical treatment. Matt had been able to land the plane on the flats about three-quarters of a mile from the cabin. Some native boys had reported the man's difficulty at Tyonek.

Matt took a load of supplies to a trapping camp on Stephan Lake, north of Anchorage, on Thursday, January 30, 1930. Nieminen left for McGrath on Saturday morning, February 1, in the New Standard. Accompanied by his wife, he also carried Mr. and Mrs. Oliver Anderson to the river community, where Anderson took over management of the Northern Commercial Company station.

The pilot took the Rainy Pass route to Tonzona, again looking for Kimball in that area. Going on to Berry's Landing, some distance down the south fork of the Kuskokwim River from where Tonzona River enters, and not far from the Kimball camp, Matt made inquiries there. He learned from Jack Nixon, a mining partner of Clinton Winans, that Kimball had been trapping with Winans, and the pair was doing well. Nieminen went on to McGrath with the Andersons, where the community put on a dance for them Saturday evening. Matt and his wife also enjoyed the festivities.

Returning to Anchorage on Sunday, Matt followed the Mount Spurr route to pick up George G. Shaben at his cabin camp near Twin Lakes. The previous fall the elderly trapper had indicated that he wanted to come out about the first of the year. Instead, the pilot found three notes from Shaben addressed to the "air pilot": the first written on January 10, 1930, mentioning that the man had frosted his feet and was suffering considerable pain; the second on January 26, told how Shaben had returned to his camp after having set out for Lake Clark to make a new start; the third note written on January 27 advising he was starting again at 7:00 A.M. He requested that nothing be left at the camp for him.

Thinking that he might see the old trapper along the trail, Matt flew in the direction of Lake Clark. He landed at the old Valentine camp some fifteen miles down the trail, finding the cabin had been used the previous night. The stove was still warm. It later proved to have been occupied by another trapper by the name of Barnhart. The pilot took off again, flying in the direction of Lake Clark for twenty minutes, about two days travel on foot, without seeing anything of Shaben. Matt went on in to Anchorage, needing fuel and engine oil, landing there shortly before 5:00 P.M. on Sunday, February 2, 1930.

There was talk of stationing one of the Fairchild 71 planes at Anchorage when no longer needed on the Eielson-Borland Relief Expedition. Major H.C. Deckard, who had accompanied the planes north, passed through Anchorage on his way Outside. He left Seward on the *Alameda* for Seattle on February 3, 1930. The ship had unloaded a fourth Fairchild on the dock, to replace the one that had crashed in Fairbanks.

With concern being expressed by friends of Shaben, as well as a feeling of responsibility for the man, arrangements were made by U.S. Commissioner Thomas C. Price for the plane to return for a thorough search, the expense to be borne by the Territory of Alaska. The oldtimer had been provided Territorial aid under the provisions of the prospector aid act, in getting into the Mount Spurr district. Matt A. Nieminen and mechanician Alonzo Cope left the Anchorage Municipal Airport on Tuesday, November 11, in the New Standard, NC 174H. The pilot had made an attempt to reach the search area the previous day, on his return from Trading Bay, but was prevented from reaching it by weather.

Nieminen and Cope landed first at the Shaben cabin at Twin Lakes, finding Barnhart there, but he had seen nothing of Shaben recently. He told the searchers of a trail leading to the headwaters of the Telaquana River, where there was an Indian village at the lake, no more than five miles from Shaben's cabin. There were no Indians there but the two airmen were able to pick up the old trapper's trail, leading across the plateau in the direction of Lake Clark. Finding an Indian camp at the lake, they learned that Shaben had arrived there eleven days before in company with some natives he met on the trail. He had remained overnight, setting out the following morning for the lower end of Lake Clark, in company with an Indian with a dog team.

The airmen resumed their flight, stopping at the Seversen & Bailey camp at Lake Illiamna to find that Shaben had been taken to Illiamna village five days before. While landing on the lake, headed offshore, Nieminen felt the ice giving way underneath the plane, and immediately put on the power, to take off again and land toward the shore, where the ice was firmer.

Feeling sure that Shaben was safe and would be able to cross the portage to Illiamna Bay, and reach Seward aboard Captain Heinie Berger's mailboat, *Discoverer*, the two fliers returned to Anchorage to report. But Shaben was to wait a long time at Illiamna Bay because of ice conditions on Cook Inlet. He finally arrived in Seward four months later, on Sunday, April 13, 1930.

Nieminen, in the New Standard, made a flight to Hope in the afternoon of Thursday, February 20, taking Charles Mathison, oldtimer of the Hope mining district. Mathison had

Friday, March 14, 1930. Lon Cope, left, and Frank Dorbandt at the Eielson funeral train in Anchorage. Carl Ben Eielson and his flight mechanic, Earl Borland, flying two planes, were lost after taking off from Teller, Alaska.

arrived in Anchorage several days before from the Yentna River, where he had spent the greater part of the winter trapping. Matt expected to fly to Sleetmute on Saturday, February 29, to deliver Jack Smeaton to his home. The trader had just returned from the States.

Pilot W.H. "Barney" Barnhill was returning to Alaska, passing through Anchorage on Saturday, March 1, 1930, enroute to Fairbanks. He was to fly for Service Airlines at the Interior city. Percy Hubbard was the principal owner of the independent air service.

Frank Dorbandt, Alaskan Airways pilot from Fairbanks, arrived in Anchorage with the Travel Air 4000, C-193, on March 9, after a strenuous trip. The flier, accompanied by his wife, Vida, was taking a Deering trader, Boris Magids, to Seward to catch the steamer *Northwestern*. Dorbandt ran into a storm in Broad Pass on the way down and had been forced to land in deep snow when his motor conked out from fouled spark plugs. He and Magids turned the plane around to shelter the engine from the wind, spending three and a half hours making the repair. Firepotting the engine for starting, they were finally able to continue the trip, arriving at Seward in time for Magids to catch the 6:30 P.M. sailing. The trader was hurrying to the States because of the sudden death of his brother and partner, Sam Magids, in Miami. Lon Cope accompanied Dorbandt from Anchorage to Seward while Mrs. Dorbandt remained to visit.

Matt Nieminen left at noon on Monday, March 10, 1930, for Fairbanks, to attend the funeral services on Wednesday in honor of the late Carl Ben Eielson and Earl Borland. The pilot's wife, Mrs. Hupprich and Robert Watson accompanied him. The bodies of the former airmen were being taken Outside on the steamer *Alaska* for burial, with memorial services to be held in communities along the route. The train bearing the funeral party reached Anchorage on the afternoon of Friday, March 14, with the Canadian and Russian airmen hosted at a well attended luncheon at the Anchorage Grill. Ole Eielson, father of the pioneer pilot, and Mrs. Borland and her children, were members of the party; they visited with friends instead of attending the luncheon. The guard of honor of the American Legion, as well as officers and members of the Chamber of Commerce met the train. Frank Dorbandt, returning from Seward,

894

C.A. Davis Collection

▲ *March 14, 1930. Among those gathered to pay their respects when the Eielson funeral train arrived at the Anchorage depot were the American Legion color guard and the school children of Anchorage, who had been let out for the day.*

▼ *The American Legion pays last respects to Carl Ben Eielson aboard the steamer* **Alaska** *at Seward. The body was taken to Seattle.*

Hewitt's Photo Shop

Crosson Collection

▲   *In mid-March of 1930, airmen who had taken part in the search for Carl Ben Eielson and Earl Borland in Siberia accompanied the caskets of the two Americans to Seattle, departing Seward on the steamer* Alaska. *Left to Right: Fabio Fahrig, Russian flight mechanic; Bill Hughes, Canadian mechanic; Sam Macauley, Canadian mechanic; Mavriki Slepnyov, Russian pilot; and T.M. "Pat" Reid, Canadian pilot. The Canadians were returning home and the Russians would return to Fairbanks soon and dismantle their Junkers F-13 for shipment back to Russia.*

▶   *March 15, 1930. On board ship at Seward. Fabio Fahrig, left and Mavriki Slepnyov, Russian flight mechanic and pilot who took part in the Eielson-Borland search at North Cape, Siberia, in 1930.*

Crosson Collection

896

met the train some miles north of Anchorage, convoying it to the station as he slowly circled above. He was again in the air, to fly above the train when it departed for Seward. Pupils of the Anchorage school marched to the depot in a body, to assemble on the station platform as a tribute when the train departed.

Anchorage was now to have two planes, with an additional seaplane plan-

► *Alaskan Airways, Incorporated, operated two of the New Standard D-25 biplanes in Anchorage in 1930; NC 174H and NC 9190, both powered with the Wright Whirlwind J-5 motor of 225 horsepower. NC 9190, No. 2, is shown here on skis. The extra-long upper wing with its graceful upsweep gave the aircraft good performance characteristics and a pleasing appearance. A third New Standard Model D-25, NC 9193, had been ordered and was being shipped.*

▼ *The Travel Air 4000, C-193, the former Anchorage Air Transport, Incorporated plane, now owned by Alaskan Airways, Incorporated, was returned to Anchorage in March, 1930, following an overhaul in Fairbanks. Matt Nieminen, who had flown the plane for the former owners, would operate it again.*

ned for later in the season. The Travel Air 4000, C-193, following its overhaul in Fairbanks had been returned by Frank Dorbandt following his flight from Seward. In addition, Matt Nieminen returned to base on Tuesday afternoon, March 18, 1930, with the New Standard, NC 174H, bringing his wife with him from Fairbanks. He was soon at work, taking off for a flight to Kenai the following morning. Art Ellsworth and Captain H.A. Faroe made the trip, with two additional passengers, George Palmer and a man named Weaver coming in, both for medical treatment. He was away again that same afternoon, in the Travel Air 4000, for Stillman Lake, intending to bring in Waino Puntilla, who had been trapping the area for the last several weeks. On his return from there, he took Doctor A.D. Haverstock to Kenai to attend Mrs. Charles Watson, wife of the deputy U.S. marshal at the Inlet community.

Matt Nieminen left in the New Standard on the morning of Friday, March 21, 1930, for Dillingham on Bristol Bay. He brought in a sick man from there, plus a second passenger, stopping at Illiamna to board a third. The pilot expected to be in on the morrow, going next to the Chickaloon district for Mr. and Mrs. C.B. Ruggles who were awaiting transportation in from their trapline. Anchorage was twelve-below-zero and clear.

It was announced on Tuesday, March 25, that Matt A. Nieminen would be in general charge of all local flying operations for Alaskan Airways at the Anchorage base. A cabin for passengers was provided on the New Standard in the form of a removable canopy over the four-place passenger cockpit. The airplanes had originally been designed for this. In addition to providing a seaplane, the company planned to erect a suitable hangar, with shop facilities, on the new Municipal Airport (later Merrill Field), and install radios in the company planes. Most of the pilots knew Morse code, which was the means of communications in these early sets. Considerable use of the new field had been made during the winter but it was a sea of mud during the breakup, necessitating continued use of the "golf course" strip between Ninth and Tenth. Pioneers of Alaska were laying plans to pay tribute to the service given the community by the late airman, Russ Merrill, by naming the Municipal Airport in his honor; as well as erecting a suitable memorial at the field. The offices of Alaskan Airways, Incorporated, which had remained in the Shonbeck Building after the acquisition of Anchorage Air Transport, were moved the first of April to the R.M. Courtnay offices at 340 Fourth Street. (Fourth Street later became Fourth Avenue).

Major Wylie R. Wright, aeronautical inspector for the Department of Commerce, who had been in charge of the Portland, Oregon area, was being assigned to duties in Alaska. He was coming north to make an inspection of aircraft, as well as examine pilots and mechanics working in the Territory.

Matt Nieminen made a flight to Kenai for Farwest Fisheries on Monday, April 2, 1930, taking two passengers south and returning with one. He was up the following day on a local flight.

Frank Dorbandt, former Alaskan Airways pilot, who had now left the company, passed through Anchorage the afternoon of Friday, April 11, on his way Outside. He spoke of extensive plans for an airline from the States to Alaska, intending to search for capital for the project while in the States. His efforts bore some fruit, for they resulted in a new air service in Alaska later in the year, Pacific International Airways, Incorporated.

Dorbandt, looking at airplanes and searching for a backer, moved down the coast to Oakland, meeting a pilot there by the name of Joe Barrows. Barrows, along with another pilot, Harry L. Blunt, whom he had recently taught to fly, were doing forestry patrol in California on a contract Barrows had bid in. Joe had been offered a Fairchild dealership at the Los Angeles Air Show. To finance the deal, he had acquired a partner, Edward A. "Ted" Lowe, Jr., who operated Edward Lowe Motors Co. at Van Ness and Jackson in San Francisco, just across the bay. With Lincoln motor cars, Ted added Fairchild airplanes to his business card, along with Joe Barrows, salesman.

Barrows took the Alaska pilot to the Lowes' apartment above San Francisco, for an evening; Dorbandt regaled them with stories of Alaska and its natural beauty, as well as many adventures in flying in the Territory. He also talked about the Yukon and Kuskokwim mail routes that were coming up for bid, and competition for the contracts that was expected between air or surface bidders. Frank thought this a real opportunity for an air service, but did not have the financing to bid on it himself. Dorbandt, Cope, Joe Barrows and Lowe formed a partnership, laying plans for the establishment of an air service in Anchorage. Lowe would supply most of the financing and a Fairchild 51 that Barrows had flown on a six-weeks Fairchild Aerial Surveys mapping contract, as an FC2. Barrows, taking his wife, Mary, with him, had flown the plane, NC 5364, back to the factory on Long Island, New York, in the spring of 1929, converting the plane to a Fairchild 51 by changing its motor. It was to be the first airplane to go north for the company.

Joe Crosson arrived in Anchorage from Fairbanks, flying an Alaskan Airways Fairchild 71, NC 9153, on Saturday, April 12, 1930. Accompanied by General Manager Arthur W. Johnson, the pilot came to meet his mother, Mrs. E. Crosson, as well as two new pilots, Grant N. Elliott and Sanis E. Robbins, arriving from the south on the steamer *Yukon*. Robbins was from San Diego and Elliott from Seattle. With Dorbandt leaving, and a backlog of work in hand, Alaskan Airways, Incorporated, had need of the additional flying personnel. Crosson had known them both in San Diego. Joe returned to Fairbanks with his passengers that same evening; he had been in the air a total of six hours and fifteen minutes for the round trip.

Pilot Matt Nieminen was off Anchorage on Sunday, April 13, 1930, for the Kuskokwim, taking three passengers: C.O. Pearson for Berry's Landing, and Charles Mathison and Harry Steen, recently up from the States, to Iditarod. Mrs. Frank Guskey was a passenger between McGrath and Takotna. The pilot spent the night at Sleetmute, leaving there at 6:00 A.M. on Monday, stopping at Valentine's camp to pick up a rubber boat left there the previous fall during the search for Russ Merrill. Matt was back in Anchorage before noon the same day.

Walter Brewington Photo

Friday, April 11, 1930. Junkers F-13, CCCP-177, of Slepnyov and Fahrig passes through Anchorage on the way to Seward. The plane played a part in the Eielson-Borland search at North Cape, Siberia, before coming into Fairbanks.

Friday, April 11, 1930. Anchorage residents and crew of the Russian F-13 Junkers gather before the dismantled plane when it arrived in Anchorage. Left to Right: unidentified man, George Mumford, Mavriki Slepnyov, Myrtle Morton, Ione Morton, Harry Morton, Jeanette Nieminen, Matt Nieminen, Mrs. Nieminen, Fabio Fahrig (flight mechanic).

Walter Brewington Photo

The two Russian airmen, Mavriki T. Slepnyov and Fabio B. Fahrig, who had accompanied the bodies of Eielson and Borland to Seattle, returned to Fairbanks to arrange for shipment of their Junkers F-13 monoplane, CCCP-177, to Seattle, where it was transported on an American vessel to Japan, to then cross Japan by rail and board a Russian steamer at Matsura for the balance of the journey. Leaving the ship at the northern port of Vladivostok, the plane then proceeded by rail to Moscow. Leaving Fairbanks on Thursday, April 10, 1930, with the dismantled airplane on two flat cars, the party was in Anchorage the following day, to be met by residents of the city. Going on to Seward, the plane was put aboard the *Yukon*, which sailed on Sunday, April 13. The ship arrived there on Friday. There was a possibility the Russian airmen might return home by way of New York.

Matt Nieminen, Alaskan Airways pilot, was off from Anchorage at an early hour on Tuesday, April 22, 1930, for the Iditarod district. Carrying Dave Strandberg to Flat, where the mining man resumed his summer operation on Flat Creek, the pilot returned in the Travel Air 4000, C-193, the same afternoon. The company was sending the Waco 10, NC 780E, to Anchorage, where it would be equipped with a new set of pontoons that were to arrive from the States within another week. The plane would then operate out of Anchorage. The New Standard, NC 174H, was test flown by Matt in Anchorage on Thursday, April 24, with its new cabin canopy installed. It could be flown with it or without it. A veteran Alaskan, Doctor J.H. Romig, coming from Fairbanks, assumed his new duties on May 1, as chief of the Alaska Railroad surgical staff in Anchorage. Doctor L.J. Seeley, Anchorage dentist, returned from Seattle about May 10, where he had accumulated five hours of flight instruction at Boeing Field. He wanted to go further in the flying game.

Lon Cope, mechanician for Alaskan Airways at Anchorage, went Outside on Friday, May 16, 1930, on vacation. Cecil Higgins, transferred down from the Fairbanks shop of the company, now looked after the mechanical work. Higgins had been an Alaskan resident since 1923, working with Harold Gillam until joining Alaskan Airways the previous year. He had

Alaskan Airways New Standard D-25, C 174H, company No. 3, with factory-made canopy installed over the front cockpit was test flown with the new installation by Matt Nieminen in Anchorage on April 24, 1930. This created a cabin for the four passengers in the front cockpit, protecting them from weather and wind. Mechanician Lon Cope stands before the plane with the pilot, probably Matt Nieminen, in the rear cockpit.

recently been with Joe Crosson and Ed Young in Teller on the fur haul. On May 20, it was announced that A.H. McDonald, agent of the Alaska Steamship Company, had been appointed local agent for Alaskan Airways, with the office of the air service established temporarily at the Anchorage Drug Store, where the office of the steamship company was located.

Matt Nieminen received a request from Manager Arthur W. Johnson to proceed to Takotna to pick up a sick man awaiting transportation to the Anchorage hospital. He was taken up the Kuskokwim River from McGrath on Thursday, May 22. There was no landing field there but pilots used the river ice in winter. Matt left for Takotna on Friday, May 22.

Nieminen was off again on Sunday, May 25, in the New Standard, NC 174H. He was taking three passengers, recently arrived from the States: Archie Higgins, dredgeman, and Gus Rader for Takotna, and Tony Lindstrom for Flat. The pilot picked up Carl Lottsfeldt, Kuskokwim superintendent for the Alaska Road Commission, at Takotna on the way over, landing him at Flat. Nieminen was off in the Travel Air 4000, C-193, early on Monday, June 2, taking canneryman Ellsworth and Attorney Morton to Valdez. The flight, by way of Chickaloon and the glacier, posed no problem, consuming two and one-quarter hours each way. The trio returned to Anchorage at about 6:00 P.M. the same day. Ellsworth had transacted some court business in one day that would have meant several days travel by boat, otherwise.

The newly-overhauled Waco 10, NC 780E, promised for Anchorage, arrived the morning of Tuesday, June 3, 1930, flown in by S.E. Robbins. He brought Lyle F. Hebert as a passenger. Hebert's wife was critically ill in the Anchorage hospital. Pontoons were installed on the plane immediately. It would be the only water based plane currently operated by Alaskan Airways. Matt flew the plane, on pontoons, the next morning, Wednesday, June 4, making several landings and takeoffs from Cook Inlet. Robbins returned to Fairbanks on Saturday, June 7, with the New Standard, NC 174H, taking with him his wife and Miss Barbara Nudd, of Seattle; both had come north on the steamer *Aleutian*. Arriving in Fairbanks that afternoon, Miss Nudd became the bride of Alaskan Airways pilot Grant Elliott in a midnight ceremony the same day.

Matt Nieminen was holding the fort at Anchorage, having two planes: the Waco 10, NC 780E, on floats, as well as the Travel Air 4000, C-193, on wheels. Both were open-cockpit planes. During the two weeks previous to June 9, 1930, he had carried thirty-three passengers, flying a total of fifty hours and forty-five minutes, using the Waco 10, the Travel Air 4000, and the New Standard prior to its departure for Fairbanks. One flight could not be completed because of weather conditions and another was not finished because of mechanical problems.

Matt went to McGrath with the float-equipped Waco on Saturday, June 7, bringing in Mr. and Mrs. Charles Mespelt, who operated the only gold quartz mine in the Kuskokwim district. The couple were enroute to the States for a vacation. The pilot went again to McGrath on Sunday, to bring in Percy Hubbard, Service Airlines pilot, who had wrecked his J-5

Newly-overhauled Waco Model 10, NC 780E, was brought to Anchorage on Tuesday, June 3, 1930, to be operated out of there by Alaskan Airways, Incorporated. Put on floats at the Lake Spenard base, and test flown the next day, the plane would be flown by Matt Nieminen. It is shown here at Hope, Alaska, a small mining community up Turnagain Arm from Anchorage. The plane served the company well until a motor failure put the Waco on Kashwitna Lake on September 17, where it spent a large part of the next two months awaiting a new motor, returning to Anchorage again on November 14, 1930. Joe Crosson had flown the plane when he found the wreckage of the Eielson-Borland Hamilton near North Cape.

Harry L. Millar Photo

Eddie Bowman Collection

Joe Crosson, flying the Fairchild 71, NC 153H, arrived in Anchorage June 9, 1930, to land on the "golf course" Municipal field at Anchorage, between Ninth and Tenth Streets.

Swallow, C 2774, at McGrath on Friday, June 6, while making a landing there. The field was soft, and the plane had turned over, causing considerable damage to it, but Percy Hubbard and Ernie Gunther, his brother-in-law, were unhurt. Neiminen also brought in Gunther.

Chief Pilot Joe Crosson, of Alaskan Airways, Incorporated, flew the Fairchild 71, NC 153H, to Anchorage on Monday, June 9, leaving Weeks Field at 11:15 A.M. He arrived at the port city after a flight of two hours and thirty minutes, carrying Arthur W. Johnson, Carl J. Lomen and mechanician Bill Basham. Plans to return the following day were cancelled, poor weather held him at Anchorage. Matt Nieminen took the Fairchild 71 to Valdez on Tuesday, June 10, with four passengers, arriving there at 3:50 P.M. and leaving an hour later without his four passengers. He reported Valdez to be planning the construction of a municipal hangar, capable of housing two planes. It was also intended that the present field be extended to tidewater, so that amphibian planes, landing on the water of the bay, could easily be brought up to the field. Crosson took the Fairchild 71, along with his same three passengers from the Interior city, back to Fairbanks, departing from Anchorage at 10:50 A.M. Sunday, June 15, 1930.

Matt Nieminen, Alaskan Airways pilot, was off for McGrath again on Tuesday, June 17, 1930. The float-equipped Waco 10 was much in demand at the Kuskokwim River town, as they were without an airport and the plane could land on the river. Leaving to pick up passengers there, the plane was held at its Lake Spenard base for a time in order for auto parts, urgently needed in McGrath, to be rushed to the lake. The parts arrived in the river community that afternoon.

A Canadian pilot, Captain L.S. Punnett, arrived in Anchorage on Friday, June 27, from Victoria, British Columbia. He came to look over the remains of the Roy J. Davis and Russ Merrill Curtiss F flying boat, No. 475-U, that had reposed in the Brown & Hawkins warehouse since the fall of 1925. The plane had been wrecked on the beach at the Chugach Islands, some twenty-three miles south of Seldovia, by a storm on the night of September 4, 1925. Whether or not Punnett did ship the plane parts out is not known.

Matt flew to Bristol Bay in Waco, NC 780E, on June 30, 1930, taking Mrs. J.C. Lowe, widow of the late postmaster and trader of the Dillingham area, and her brother, Charles Griffin, back to her home. Landing on the water at Snag Point in Nushagak Bay, Nieminen spent the night at the Wood River cannery of Alaska Salmon Corporation. On his return flight he stopped at Libby's, at Seversen's on Lake Illiamna, at O.H. Dutton's and I.E. Kashley's on Lake Clark. He was back in Anchorage on Tuesday, July 1, 1930. He left for Fairbanks the same day, accompanied by Cecil Higgins, taking the Travel Air 4000, C-193, to the shop there for its annual rebuilding. The pilot was back the next day with a Fairchild 71, NC 9153, to be based in Anchorage. Higgins returned with him.

The Fairchild 71 gave Matt a sizeable land plane with which to hop passengers over the Fourth of July. The pilot also carried a number of handbills granting free entrance to the Empress Theater for the movie *Flight*, a special attraction to be shown over the holiday. Matt scattered these ducats over town for the lucky finders. The Waco 10, NC 780E, was also temporarily put on wheels for the Fourth of July, and the pilot put on an airshow for the crowd, including a "dead stick" landing to the new Municipal Airport at the end of Fifth Street (later changed to Avenue), with the pilot attempting to land the plane with the motor shut off, to a predetermined mark.

Lon Cope, former mechanician for Alaskan Airways in Anchorage, notified Matt Nieminen on July 8 that he did not plan to return to his position with the company. Cope, in Oklahoma, wired that he was joining interests with Frank Dorbandt, who had found backing for an airplane they intended to bring north.

The army radio station on government hill at Anchorage resumed business on Tuesday, July 15, 1930; it had been closed for upwards of two years. Now it was available for civilian usage for emergency messages, and the transfer of money to any point in the United States and Canada.

Matt Nieminen took Governor George A. Parks aloft on July 16, in the Fairchild 71, for a pleasure flight over Anchorage and down Cook Inlet. Others aboard the flight were the pilot's wife, Deputy Marshal Harry Staser, Attorney Harry F. Morton and Reverend E.L. Winterberger.

Matt was away again in the Waco 10, NC 780E on floats, the morning of Tuesday, July 22, 1930. He carried a shipment of perishable freight, including strawberries from the first picking of the season from Anchorage gardens, destined for the Kuskokwim side of the Alaska Range and Iditarod areas, as well as some mail. The pilot ran into a heavy "blow" on the Kuskokwim side of the Alaska Range, causing him to remain over at McGrath. Stops were made at Berry's Landing, McGrath, Iditarod and Sleetmute, the pilot experiencing no difficulty in setting the float plane down on the interior rivers. He was back to land on Lake Spenard at 9:30 P.M. of Thursday, July 25. The pilot brought in Einar Carlsen, a trapper, picked up at McGrath.

Thyra Merrill, widow of the former Anchorage pilot, Russ Merrill, was now living in Palo Alto, California, with her two boys. She had enrolled as a flying student with Curtiss-Wright Flying School in San Mateo, taking ground school and flying courses toward a private and a commercial license.

Mrs. Dorbandt, the former Vida Deigh of Anchorage, wired her mother, Mrs. Ed Mahle of that city, on Saturday, July 26, that she and her husband, Frank, as well as mechanic Lon Cope, planned to return shortly to Anchorage, bringing a Fairchild 51 on floats, to be based there. It was a seaplane so they would follow the coast up from the States.

Nieminen was away from Lake Spenard in the pontoon-equipped Waco 10 at 1:00 P.M. Thursday, July 31, 1930, carrying Charles Mespelt and his brother Fred, taking them to Medfra on the upper Kuskokwim River. The pilot went on to McGrath, from where he telephoned the Takotna radio operator, asking him to listen for a 5:30 P.M. weather report from Anchorage. The pilot had prearranged this with Sergeant Frawley at the army radio station on government hill. The Anchorage report came through as arranged, and Matt set out on his return flight, leaving McGrath at 6:00 P.M., to arrive back in Anchorage at 8:45 P.M. The radio

Pilot Frank Dorbandt left Alaskan Airways, Incorporated, in the spring of 1930, going Outside to seek backing for an aviation venture of his own. Shown here in California, he teamed up with Lon Cope, returning to Anchorage with the Fairchild 51, NC 5364, in August of 1930. The two men began operating the float-equipped plane that was the beginning of Pacific International Airways, Incorporated.

Alex Holden Collection

station was a help in expediting his return.

Frank Dorbandt, flying a Fairchild 51, NC 5364, powered by a Wright R-975 of 300 horsepower, left Seattle at 11:15 A.M. Friday, August 1, 1930, for Anchorage. Mrs. Dorbandt and Lon Cope accompanied the former Alaskan Airways pilot in the float-equipped plane for the 1650-mile journey. Refueling at Alert Bay, British Columbia, the trio proceeded to Ketchikan, arriving there at 7:45 P.M. Friday evening.

Starting for Port Althorp the following morning, Frank ran into heavy fog, and after flying low over the water for some time, decided to land and check their surroundings. The pilot took off again and altered course for Juneau, remaining overnight there and setting out in better weather for Port Althorp the next morning, departing shortly after 9:00 A.M. on Sunday. A fuel stop was made at Cordova before going on to cross Prince William Sound. Unable to cross the mountains at Portage, because of fog, the pilot landed in the fjord, taxiing up it before turning to taxi out of the fog to make a new start. They took off, setting a course for Seward, flying from there to Skilak Lake and on in to land on Lake Spenard at Anchorage. The total flying time was less than nineteen hours from Seattle.

The five-place plane, equipped with Fairchild P-4 floats and powered with the J6-9 (R-975) of 300 horsepower, had a cruising speed of one hundred miles per hour. It carried four passengers, the pilot, and 300 pounds of baggage. The tanks held gasoline sufficient for six and one-half hours of flying. It was particularly suited to Alaskan flying. Having been so successful on the northbound flight from Seattle, Dorbandt talked of running flights to the States with it. The four-passenger plane, previously used in aerial photography, had an aperture in the floor for taking vertical pictures, as well as a special window in the back of the cabin for oblique photography.

Alonzo Cope, partner and chief mechanic in Pacific International Airways at Anchorage, was later to become a pilot for the concern.

The three travelers had covered a lot of ground since leaving Anchorage. The Dorbandts flew to San Francisco from Seattle, buying an auto there and driving it over 3500 miles before starting for Seattle again. Frank flew Lon Cope to Denver in the Fairchild, to speed him on his journey east. He also flew some for the Gorst company in Seattle, while Lon repaired a plane used on the Seattle-Bremerton route for them. The Dorbandts took an apartment in the Shonbeck building, intending to make a permanent home in Anchorage. A large box ad appeared in the *Anchorage Daily Times* of Tuesday, August 5, 1930, advertising the services of the Frank Dorbandt & Alonzo Cope Commercial Flying Service. Robert A. Romig represented them at the Alaska Transfer Company office.

Alaskan Airways, Incorporated, was planning a regular service to lower Cook Inlet points. Jack Bailey, from the Bailey & Seversen trading post on Lake Illiamna, had just arrived from the States, and made arrangements for service into that point. The flying company planned on initiating flights as soon as water navigation closed for the season. The communities would now be less isolated during the winter months.

Frank Dorbandt took local photographer Denny Hewitt, of Hewitt's Photo Shop, aloft in the Fairchild 51 on Wednesday, August 7, 1930, for a tour of the Anchorage area. At 7000 feet, sometimes above and sometimes below the clouds, the photographer was so thrilled he neglected to use his camera. Hewitt was a confirmed airplane buff from then on, often seen about the airport taking pictures of the airmen and their planes. Attorney Harry F. Morton also made the flight.

Frank Dorbandt, of Dorbandt & Cope, was off for the Kuskokwim and Nome in the Fairchild 51, NC 5364, carrying Leo W. Brewer, Territorial commissioner of education, who

906

was making a general survey of the schools, and E.J. Beck, who had accepted a position as superintendent of the Nome school. The pilot departed Anchorage on Saturday afternoon, August 9, 1930 also taking his partner and mechanic, Lon Cope, in the pontoon-equipped plane. Flying through Rainy Pass to the upper Kuskokwim, numerous stops were made along the river, including a side trip to Iditarod. On floats, they were able to visit communities without landing strips. An attempt to fly directly across from Bethel to the Yukon River was thwarted by heavy fog; the pilot circled about to come into the Yukon far above the mouth, then followed the river course.

The party overnighted on Sunday at a fishing village near New Hamilton on the Yukon-Kuskokwim delta, the two airmen sleeping in the plane while their two passengers spent the night in their sleeping bags in a village cabin. Brewer and Beck were taken on to Saint Michael, arriving at the Norton Sound community in time to connect with the motorship *Donaldson* for Nome. Returning to the lower Kuskokwim, the two fliers boarded Mr. and Mrs. Benson, government school teachers, at Bethel. They were on their way to Afognak, a picturesque island just north of Kodiak.

This gave Dorbandt and his companions an opportunity to view the Valley of Ten Thousand Smokes, as it lay on their route. The spectacular region, created by volcanic eruption in 1912, had been seen by few people. The pilot made a stop at Snag Point, near Dillingham, before entering the Katmai reservation at its northwest corner. Frank circled the valley, close to the many fumaroles which were sending up smoke at every point. The valley was overhung by fog that obscured the upper levels of Katmai and the surrounding peaks.

Dorbandt and Cope returned to Anchorage to land on Lake Spenard at 9:20 P.M. Tuesday, August 12, 1930. They had covered about 2000 miles in twenty-two hours and forty minutes of flying time. The pilot's enthusiasm for flying tourists to the Katmai region on sightseeing trips later resulted in his being contacted by Father Bernard R. Hubbard, head of the geology department of Santa Clara University, who had just completed a three-month expedition exploring the Alaska Peninsula; his trip had included climbing Mount Veniaminof and Aniakchak Crater. In the following years Hubbard used a plane in his explorations on the Alaska Peninsula.

Pilot Matt Nieminen of Alaskan Airways, Incorporated, left Anchorage with mechanic Cecil Higgins in the Fairchild 71, NC 9153, at 10:45 A.M. Wednesday, August 13, 1930, in an attempt to fly over the top of Mount McKinley. A few days before the two men had tried it but, upon reaching the top, they found it obscured by clouds. Matt had attempted the climb in the Travel Air 4000 on Friday, April 13, 1928, taking photographer Earl Rossman with him. The men had climbed above 19,000 feet at that time but had been unable to reach the top. The mountain has an elevation of 20,320 feet.

Flying directly to the mountain, a distance of 150 air miles, the two airmen climbed steadily up to 18,000 feet. After that, the climbing rate was reduced by the loss of power with altitude, although the Pratt & Whitney Wasp motor of 425 horsepower performed well. Reaching 24,000 feet, the pilot circled about the peak while Higgins shot still and motion picture photos of the peak and the slopes below them. The men stood the high altitude well. It was twenty degrees below zero on the cabin thermometer inside the plane. Some mist was forming as they left the mountain to head back to Anchorage, landing there at 3:00 P.M. Flying tourists to Mount McKinley was big business out of Fairbanks; the pilot thought that perhaps more of it could be done out of Anchorage.

The Anchorage Woman's Club was now sponsoring a movement to erect a memorial to Russ Merrill, in the form of a beacon light mounted on a steel tower at the Municipal Airport, to serve also as a guiding light to airmen. Charlie Bisel prepared a model, complete in detail, of the tower design. Built on a concrete base, six feet square and six feet high, resting on a sub-base twelve feet square, the revolving beacon rested on a steel tower that reached forty-six feet six inches above the ground level. A bronze tablet, suitably inscribed, was mounted on the face of the concrete base. The project, estimated to cost under $2000, was to be financed by donations: money, labor and materials.

Matt Nieminen made a flight to McGrath the afternoon of Saturday, August 16, in the pontoon-equipped Waco 10, NC 780E. He took Miss I.E. Chenowith, Territorial school teacher of the upper Kuskokwim, who had arrived in Anchorage from the south a few days before. Matt returned with two passengers, making a stop at Medfra enroute.

On Tuesday, August 19, 1930, a new name for the Dorbandt & Cope company surfaced. The firm was now known as Pacific International Airways, Incorporated. Dorbandt was off Cook Inlet the same morning in the Fairchild 51, carrying as a passenger Territorial Highway Engineer Robert J. Sommers. The pilot made a landing on the Kuskokwim River at Takotna, going by way of Rainy Pass. Sommers, on a general inspection of Territorial road projects and landing field requirements in the Kuskokwim district, was joined at Takotna by Carl Lottsfeldt, Alaska Road Commission superintendent in the district. The men flew down-river to determine the feasibility of building a landing field at Bethel. They believed it doubtful because of the low and swampy ground, although float planes could land on the river in summer, and ski equipped planes could land there on the ice in winter. Lottsfeldt returned to Takotna in the plane. On the return flight Dorbandt followed a route through the mountains up Ptarmigan valley to the Styx River; it was somewhat longer but it could be flown in almost any weather conditions. The pilot also brought in Mrs. Mabel Ranum from the upper Kuskokwim; she had been teaching school at McGrath for the past two years; they arrived in Anchorage on the evening of Wednesday, August 20, 1930.

Alaskan Airways pilot Matt Nieminen was off Lake Spenard in the Waco Model 10 on Tuesday, August 19, bound for Unalakleet with two passengers: Major E.L. Atkins, engineering officer of the Alaska Road Commission, and Ernest Walker Sawyer, special representative of the general manager of the Alaska Railroad. Encountering unfavorable weather conditions enroute, the pilot found it necessary to stop at Kalskag, on the lower Yukon. He was further delayed upon reaching Unalakleet, with poor flying conditions on the return journey, especially in the mountains. The pilot took the long route through, going by way of the south fork of the Kuskokwim and Happy River. Making stops at McGrath and Takotna on the return flight, Matt returned to base at Lake Spenard with his two passengers the afternoon of Thursday, August 21, 1930. Atkins had been recently assigned to the road commission, taking over from Major Douglas Gillette. As a federal body, its head talent came from the military.

Frank Dorbandt, in the Pacific International Airways Fairchild 51, NC 5364, was off for lower Cook Inlet and Kodiak on a survey flight of conditions on the route. Taking Lon Cope and Jack Morton, lawyer Morton's son, he was away the morning of Monday, August 25, arriving in Kodiak that same day. Here the pilot hopped passengers, many of whom had never ridden in a plane. A Doctor Griggs and his son were awaiting passage on the steamer *Redondo* for Seward. Two of his first passengers, they had just returned from the doctor's second visit to the Valley of Ten Thousand Smokes—his first visit had been in 1919.

On the return flight to Anchorage, the pilot stopped at Afognak and at Seldovia, later seeing a large school of Beluga whales sporting in the Inlet off Tyonek. Dorbandt, Cope and Morton were back on Lake Spenard on Wednesday morning, August 27, 1930.

An emergency call from Flat to Alaskan Airways, Incorporated, in Fairbanks, resulted

August, 1930. Fairchild F-51, NC 5364, at the Lake Spenard base in August, 1930. Left to Right: mechanic's helper Jack Morton, Attorney Morton's son, and Chief mechanic Lon Cope.

in three of the company's planes being dispatched to the Iditarod district. Young Odin Strandberg, son of mining operator Dave Strandberg, had lost four fingers in a sheave block at the mine. Of the three planes: Ed Young, going from Fairbanks, "Robbie" Robbins, flying from Mount McKinley Park, and Matt Nieminen, going from Anchorage, only one was able to get through; the weather was such that the others were compelled to abandon the flight. Blocked by weather in Rainy Pass, Matt went on down the Inlet to Kustatan, then crossing over to the upper Kuskokwim by way of Twin Lakes. He pushed on to Iditarod to pick up Strandberg and his son, and went on to McGrath, stopping at Takotna to pick up Carl Lottsfeldt enroute. The boy's hand was dressed that night, Wednesday, August 27, at McGrath by Mrs. Oliver Anderson, where the party remained overnight. Despite a leaking pontoon and bad weather, the pilot took off the next morning, landing in Anchorage shortly after noon on Thursday. The pilot had bucked rain and wind throughout the flight. Dave Strandberg placed his fourteen-year-old son in the government hospital for treatment.

Frank Dorbandt was off in the Pacific International Airways Fairchild 51 early in the morning of Friday, August 29, 1930, having been thwarted from taking off the Inlet the previous day when strong winds created waves high enough to prevent the plane from gaining enough speed to lift off. Taking Doctor Lawler Seeley of the Dental Clinic, the pilot was away for McGrath. The same day Matt Nieminen flew an aerial survey from Anchorage to Kenai,

Ninilchik and other points along the Inlet south of Anchorage, carrying Commissioner Charles H. Flory, of the Department of Commerce, and R.C. Ingraham, resident engineer of the Bureau of Public Roads. He used the Waco 10, on floats.

On Saturday, August 30, 1930, Nieminen took the Fairchild 71, NC 9153, taking Senators Kendrick of Wyoming and Thomas of Idaho, on a sightseeing trip around the Anchorage district. The senators had made similar flights at Fairbanks and at Mount McKinley.

The City of Anchorage aldermen, in regular meeting on the evening of Wednesday, September 3, 1930, authorized the special aviation committee, of which Oscar S. Gill was the chairman, to lease areas on the airport for hangar use. Alaskan Airways, Incorporated, had applied for an area with 200 feet of frontage on the field, wanting to move its hangar from the "golf course" airfield between Ninth and Tenth to the new site on the Municipal Airport, already being called Merrill Field. Pacific International Airways had applied for an area having a 300-foot frontage on the field. The leases were to extend over a period of five years, at a rental charge of five dollars for each one hundred feet of frontage.

Matt Nieminen, accompanied by his brother-in-law, George Mumford, flying Fairchild 71, NC 9153, was away for Fairbanks the morning of Thursday, September 4, to pick up Charles P. Sisson, assistant U.S. Attorney General, of Washington, D.C., and Arthur W. Johnson, general manager of Alaskan Airways. The pilot returned with the two men, plus mechanic Cecil Higgins, the same evening. He was away the next morning for the Iditarod in the Waco 10, taking Dave Strandberg back to Flat Creek to his mining operation, his son Odin now out of danger from his recent accident. The following day, Saturday, the Alaskan Airways pilot took Mr. and Mrs. Chester V. Brink from McGrath to Takotna, and Superintendent Carl Lottsfeldt from Iditarod to Takotna. He was back in Anchorage to take Gus Gelles to Kusilof (later Kasilof) on Sunday, September 8, 1930; later he went on to Tustumena Lake, where Alaska Guides had a number of big game hunters in the field.

Frank Dorbandt was away in the Fairchild 51, flying a honeymoon couple, Mr. and Mrs. John Balios, to La Touche and Seward on the morning of Friday, September 5. The Pacific International Airways pilot went on to Tustumena Lake to bring in Mr. Gray, a big game hunter, his eighteen-year-old daughter and young son. The young lady had taken a very large moose. Dorbandt went out again to Illiamna, bringing in a Bureau of Fisheries man, plus carrying teacher William K. Leise from Illiamna to Nondalton. He was off again for Snag Point, making a stop on the way to visit his wife's brother, Elmo Deigh. His next flight took him to Bristol Bay. He returned to Anchorage the evening of Monday, September 9, 1930, with three passengers: Mrs. Marguerite Lowe, trading post operator to the westward region, and Gerald Fitzgerald and Robert W. Acherson, of the U.S. Geological Survey.

Matt Nieminen, Alaskan Airways pilot, was away on Monday, September 8, in the pontoon-equipped Waco 10, NC 780E; on a survey flight with Charles H. Flory, commissioner of agriculture for Alaska, and Ernest Walker Sawyer, reindeer investigator for the Alaska Railroad, as passengers. Going first to McGrath, on the Kuskokwim River, thence to Takotna, Iditarod, Flat and across to the Yukon River, the pilot then made stops at Anvik and Holy Cross. Returning to the Kuskokwim by way of the Portage, a stop was made for the night at Bogus Creek, forty-two miles northeast of Bethel. The next day a stop was made at Tuluksak River, spending that night at Akiak, on the lower Kuskokwim. Hopping off for Bethel the following day, flying downriver, the trio spent several hours there before following the river down to its mouth on Kuskokwim Bay. Visiting Goodnews Bay next, the pilot flew from there across the peninsula to the Togiak River, a center of considerable reindeer activity. After McGrath, their flight had largely been through reindeer country.

From Togiak, Nieminen flew to Nushagak Bay, with stops at Dilliingham, Naknek, Koggiung and up the Kvichak River to Illiamna Lake, where there was a herd of about 600 deer. The pilot made a stop at Seversen's trading post, and a second one at the Dutton camp on Lake Clark, before flying the party through scenic Lake Clark pass on a direct course for Anchorage, landing there at noon on Friday, September 12, completing the extensive flight of over 1600 miles. Government officials, as well as the private sector, were finding the airplane a most efficient way of getting a prodigious amount of work done in a very short time.

A wireless message from Seldovia arrived at the office of Pacific International Airways at 8:45 A.M. Thursday, September 11, 1930, and sent Frank Dorbandt and Lon Cope off Lake Spenard in the pontoon-equipped Fairchild 51, NC 5364, at 9:30 A.M. Flying to Seldovia, they had returned four hours later with J.C. Waller. Landing first, to pick up a Mrs. Young, they went on to an isolated cove where Waller's fox farm was located, to pick up the ill man, who needed an operation. The two airmen had to walk in some distance and carry Waller out to the plane. Mrs. Young, who had come to aid the man, was let off at Seldovia before the plane, with its patient, went north to Anchorage. Waller was suffering from acute appendicitis and, as soon as his condition stabilized, could be operated on. He was the brother of Anchorage attorney, J.L. Waller.

Pacific International Airways announced plans for a flight from Anchorage to Seattle within a few weeks, using the Fairchild 51. They were planning on going Outside to see about getting some additional flying equipment for the air service. Some mail contracts were in the offing and the company wanted to be prepared to bid on them. Cope was building a set of ski-equipped landing gear for the plane, in anticipation of winter flying; there was already some snow showing on the hills.

Dorbandt, still on pontoons, made a flight to Gravel Lake, about twelve miles beyond Chickaloon, on Tuesday, September 16, to deliver a load of supplies to trappers J.R. Lowden and his partner. The two had traveled to Chickaloon a week before by train, establishing a camp near the lake in preparation for the trapping season. The pilot had no difficulty in landing and taking off empty from the lake. Dorbandt made a flight to Seward on the morning of Thursday, September 18, to return Seward residents Elwyn Swetman, P.C. McMullen and Doctor A.R. Roberts (dentist) to their homes. (Doctor Roberts' son, Gerald, would one day be a pilot in Anchorage for Pacific Northern Airlines).

Matt Nieminen was off in the Alaskan Airways Waco 10, NC 780E, on Wednesday, September 17, 1930, for the Kosina River district, carrying Elmer Simco and a load of supplies. He was to have returned to town for Dick Tousley and the balance of the outfit but, developing engine trouble, was forced to land on a lake near Kashwitna. The motor was smoking badly before the pilot landed on the lake a short distance from the railroad. Examination revealed the damage to the Wright Whirlwind was so extensive it required a new motor be brought in by rail and dragged from the railroad to the lake through brush and tussocks. Simco cached his outfit at the lake and returned to Anchorage by rail on Friday afternoon.

Dorbandt and Cope went out in the Fairchild 51, still on pontoons, on the afternoon of Thursday, September 18, intending to take Dick Tousley and his load of trapping supplies to Clarence Lake. Pushing through a storm, the pilot found it impossible to land on the two-mile-long lake in the rising snowstorm. With some difficulty he set Tousley down on a lake some sixteen miles away, barely able to see in the snow and fog. Unloading the plane, the Pacific International Airways pilot took off in the semi-darkness. He fought his way to the lake near Kashwitna, wanting to ascertain the location and intending to bring the balance of the outfit from Anchorage to Clarence Lake, before picking up Tousley and Simco at their two locations.

The pair intended to trap together at Clarence Lake. Dorbandt reached Anchorage in the dark at 8:00 P.M. Unable to see Lake Spenard, he would have to land in Cook Inlet and spend the night. Looking to the rear, Cope saw the street lights snap on suddenly and shouted to the pilot. Wheeling about, the men were able to make out the location of the lake and landed safely.

Captain A.P. Jochimsen, ice pilot, was once again on the Siberian coast. He had served on the *Elisif* when she foundered near Cape Billings, Siberia, the previous year, and he was now in command of the *Karise*, a third Swenson Fur & Trading Company vessel. The *Karise*, now near Cape Serdtse-Kamen, had radioed for a plane; Jochimsen was seriously ill and needed hospitalization in Nome.

Frank Dorbandt responded to the call. Bringing the float-equipped Fairchild 51, NC 5364, from Lake Spenard to Cook Inlet, as all pilots did when they were heavily loaded and need a longer takeoff run; he and Cope fueled it to capacity with gasoline. The two men intended to fly straight through to the *Karise*. Dorbandt, accompanied by Cope, was off the Inlet late in the afternoon of Saturday, September 20, 1930, having received favorable weather reports from the Seward Peninsula. Compelled to overnight at Unalakleet, the two airmen were off again the following morning, landing in Nome at 10:00 A.M. Sunday to refuel before taking off again, reaching the *Karise* without delay and setting the plane down in slushy open water near the vessel, where crewmen in a small boat had kept it free of ice.

Placing the sick man on board, after refueling the Fairchild, Dorbandt and Cope returned to the American side to land at Teller at 6:00 P.M. Sunday, and spent the night there. They came in to Nome with Captain Jochimsen on Monday morning, September 22, 1930, where the sick man, suffering from kidney trouble and unable to speak, was taken to the Maynard-Columbus Hospital. Dorbandt wired the *Karise* of ice conditions he had observed in their vicinity as an aid to the vessel in navigating free of the threatening ice pack. The pilot also thanked Captain Jones of the cutter *Northland* for standing by in Bering Strait when the plane had made its crossing. The Fairchild 51 was the only float plane available in Anchorage, as Alaskan Airways Waco 10 was still tied up with a damaged engine on a lake near Kashwitna.

Dorbandt, still in Nome on September 24, received another call for help; a request to fly a supply of anti-toxin to Dillingham to use in counteracting an epidemic of diphtheria. There was also a call from Holy Cross; a sick man was awaiting transportation to the hospital at Anchorage.

Dorbandt and Cope reached Holy Cross on Wednesday, September 24, to find Matt Nieminen had already picked up the patient a short time before. Going on to Bethel, they took aboard Mrs. John B. Hall and her small son as passengers for Anchorage. Delivering the anti-toxin at Dillingham, he picked up another passenger, Fred Frederikson, at Snag Point, one mile northeast. The two airmen with their three passengers arrived in Anchorage, by way of Illiamna, on the evening of Thursday, July 26, 1930.

Matt Nieminen, Alaskan Airways pilot, was away for Holy Cross at 11:00 A.M. Wednesday, September 24, to pick up Matt Vaughn and bring him to the hospital. Flying the Fairchild 71, NC 9153, the pilot returned to Anchorage late that same night with the elderly man.

Vaughn had broken a shoulder bone some time previously, and had been treated at a hospital on the lower Kuskokwim River. The break continued to bother him and, in addition, he had developed what he thought was a severe attack of sciatica in his leg. He was in great pain when lifted to the Loudermilch & Kitzmiller ambulance at the Anchorage Municipal field. When examined at the hospital, the supposed sciatica turned out to be a broken thigh bone; the oldtimer had fallen from his bed a day or two previous to Nieminen's arrival. The old shoulder break, badly set, was beyond further repair, leaving Vaughn permanently disabled to some extent.

Frank Dorbandt, with the only float plane available, was completing delivery of Elmer Simco and Dick Tousley to Clarence Lake. Simco, with the remainder of their outfit, left in the Fairchild 51 on Friday, December 26, for Kashwitna, to pick up the trapper's gear there before going on to Clarence Lake. Dorbandt would then pick up Tousley and his outfit at a lake sixteen miles from Clarence, where he had dropped him on September 18, then bring him back to Clarence, where the two partners would base their trapping operation.

Upon arriving at Clarence Lake, finding no timber about the two-mile body of water, Elmer Simco decided to go on to where Dick Tousley was located. The trapper had found a cabin to serve as a base camp and the pair decided to locate there for the season. Tousley had already taken a big grizzly bear close to the camp. Dorbandt returned to his Lake Spenard base at 7:00 P.M. that same evening, flying the 185 miles in an hour and a half.

On Monday, September 29, 1930, Dorbandt flew the Fairchild to Tustumena Lake, bringing in two brothers, Wilton Lloyd-Smith and Van S. Merle-Smith, big game hunters; from New York. Andy Simons, field manager for Alaska Guides, Incorporated, came in with the men. Finding, upon arrival in Anchorage, that one of the hunters had left his ammunition in camp, Dorbandt returned to the lake to obtain the forgotten cartridges. They were for an English-made double rifle; that particular caliber was not obtainable elsewhere. The hunting party went on to Carlo by railroad speeder to hunt caribou.

Dorbandt and Cope had been planning on flying the Fairchild 51 to the States, going by way of the Interior, along the route of the proposed international highway through Canada. The airmen expected to return with a new seven-place Fairchild 71, leaving the Fairchild 51 Outside to be overhauled. In preparation, NC 5364 was flown from the Lake Spenard base on Monday afternoon, September 29, to Cook Inlet, where it was taxied beneath the railroad bridge over Ship Creek. Lifted from the water by a railroad steam crane and placed on a truck, the wings were folded back and the plane hauled to the "golf course" airfield to have the pontoons replaced by wheels for the flight south.

Dorbandt, flying the Fairchild 51 on wheels, and accompanied by Lon Cope and Attorney Harry F. Morton, began his takeoff from the airstrip between Ninth and Tenth streets on the morning of Thursday, October 2, 1930, for the flight to the States. It was not to be; vision obscured by frost on the windshield and the sun shining into his eyes, Dorbandt ran the plane the full length of the field into the brush, before coming to rest against a large stump about one hundred feet beyond the limits of the field. Undoubtedly some frost on the wings contributed to the loss of lift. The men were unhurt but the plane was considerably damaged, including a broken landing gear.

The gear was temporarily repaired at the site, the wings were removed and the plane hauled to a small building at the rear of the Alaska Commercial Company. In this temporary hangar, repairs were made under the supervision of Fred Bowman, of the same company. Damage was estimated in the vicinity of $500; the main troubles were ripped fabric, a bent propeller and a broken landing gear. The plane was eventually stripped of fabric, and sufficient material ordered from the States to recover it. Fred Bowman, with his considerable experience in repairing planes, would do the work.

Dorbandt and Cope left Anchorage by rail for Seward on Friday, October 3, 1930, to connect with the steamer *Alaska* for Seattle, to pick up the new plane and fly it north. The two men left the steamer at Juneau, flying the rest of the way with Alaska-Washington Airways in the Lockheed Vega, *Skagway*, piloted by Bob Ellis.

Pacific International Airways Fairchild 51, NC 5364, with J6-9 engine of 300 horsepower, after cracking up on takeoff at the Anchorage "park strip" airport October 2, 1930, caused by frost on wings and windshield. Pilot Dorbandt, mechanician Cope and Attorney Morton were uninjured although their flight to the States in the plane was terminated. Dorbandt stands with back to camera looking at the engine.

Courtesy of Cecil Higgins

A strange piece of drift, with the appearance of a part of an airplane rudder or aileron, was picked up at Anchor Point, near Homer, and sent over to Seldovia. Thinking it might have some relation to Russ Merrill's Travel Air 7000, C-194, the piece was sent in to Anchorage on the motorship *Princess Pat*. The find arrived in the city on Sunday, October 5, to be examined by local airmen. The fabric, covered with aluminum paint, bore the markings: ND4, AND4, 10-3-28, with small letters imprinted with a stencil, in blue paint, on the fabric. Matt Nieminen, who had flown the Merrill ship many times, declared it had not come from there. Remaining a mystery, the piece was placed on display in one of the large windows of the Alaska Commercial Company. It was surmised it may have come from one of the ill-fated planes engaged in the search for the lost Dole fliers in the Pacific.

The Aviation Corporation (AVCO) in New York announced plans on October 1 for the expansion of the Anchorage base by sending two new planes, including an amphibian with wheel or pontoon capabilities, by use of a single control from the cockpit. Shipment had already been made of a set of floats for the Fairchild 71 already on station, having left the factory on September 26. It was intended to send in a New Standard biplane as well as additional pilots, as needed. Instead of moving the original hangar to the new Municipal Airport, the company planned to build a new one of larger dimensions on the leased site in the spring. The hangar at the "golf course" field could be used as in the past but, with the structure lined and made more comfortable for winter use.

Mail for the Kuskokwim and Iditarod districts would be routed through the Anchorage post office henceforth, so that Alaskan Airways planes could carry mail when the ships flew to those points from the port city.

Even radio communications played a part. With the new station functioning, Fairbanks no longer had the advantage. Previously it had been possible to send messages to Fairbanks from the Kuskokwim for seventy cents, and get an answer the same day, while the rate to Anchorage was one dollar and ninety cents—and two days were required for an answer. This

914

resulted in most of the air business from there being diverted to Fairbanks. Frank Reed, proprietor of the Hotel Anchorage, was awarded the contract to connect the power line to the new U.S. Army radio station; the transmitter site was located two miles out on the Loop road, and the receiving station was on government hill above the city. Reed, also president of the Anchorage Light & Power Company, started work on the project the morning of Monday, October 6, 1930.

Frank Dorbandt and Lon Cope wired from San Francisco that they had reached there on Thursday, October 9, at 3:00 P.M. to take delivery of the new Fairchild 71 for Pacific International Airways. The pair had flown from Juneau with Alaska-Washington Airways to Seattle, and had continued down the Pacific Coast by air.

In Anchorage, Matt A. Nieminen, Alaskan Airways pilot, was off in the company's Fairchild 71, NC 9153, for Takotna. He could use the wheel plane since an airstrip had now been constructed there. The pilot learned on arrival that the Alaska Road Commission intended to spend another $1500 in enlarging the field in the very near future. Matt doubted whether he could have gotten off with the big Fairchild from the short field if there hadn't been a strong wind blowing. He was off Anchorage the afternoon of Thursday, October 9, and was back at 5:30 P.M., bringing in Gus Rosen and Emil Anderson, who were on their way to the States for the winter. He also had a consignment of gold and a quantity of mail aboard.

Winter had come to the Kuskokwim; the pilot saw snow all the way from Knik Arm to Takotna. Frozen lakes in the Rainy Pass district and much snow in the mountains was observed. Considerable game was on the move in the flat country; the pilot noticed up to a thousand caribou and a large number of moose. Checking trapping cabins on the way, as the pilots usually did, he noticed many of the trappers near their cabins, making preparations for the season. A friendly wave for the pilot gave assurance that everything was normal. Later in the season they were seldom seen for they were usually out on their traplines. The pilot expected to leave soon for Takotna again, to bring in Archie Higgins, dredgeman.

Frank Dorbandt and Lon Cope departed Oakland on Wednesday, October 15, 1930, with a new airplane for the Anchorage firm. The Bellanca CH-300 "Pacemaker", NC 259M, was powered with a Wright J6-9 of 300 horsepower. The six-place monoplane was painted a deep orange, almost red, color. Purchased in Los Angeles, the plane was not only a good load carrier but would cruise at 125 miles per hour. The two airmen spent the night in Chehalis, Washington, coming in to Seattle the following day.

Awaiting favorable weather reports before continuing on to Anchorage, with intentions of stopping at Wenatchee and Whitehorse, Yukon Territory, on the way, Dorbandt learned that Joe Barrows had departed for the east coast to pick up a new Consolidated Fleetster. He planned to follow Dorbandt and Cope to Anchorage, accompanied by Harry Blunt, piloting a Fairchild 71. This would bring the Pacific International Airways fleet up to four aircraft. The company had acquired its name when Ted Lowe and Alex Holden had attempted to inaugurate a triangular air service between Seattle, Victoria and Vancouver, with a base at Victoria. The plans had come to nothing but the name stuck.

Meanwhile, in Seattle, a New Standard Model D-25 open-cockpit, NC 9193, biplane built at the factory in New Jersey, was shipped north to Alaskan Airways. The amphibian plane, a Keystone Commuter planned for Anchorage, had also arrived at Seattle about mid-October. The pontoons for the Fairchild 71 had already arrived in Anchorage but, because it was too late in the season, weren't installed. Business had slowed for the Anchorage firm, awaiting the freezing of lakes and the coming of snow in the localities where flights were to be made. The fall freezeup and the spring breakup were always bad times for the operators and their pilots. The company had contracts to fulfill as soon as conditions improved. Matt Nieminen was taking the Fairchild 71, NC 9153, to Fairbanks on the afternoon of Tuesday, October 21, 1930, landing at Weeks Field about 4:00 P.M. to confer with Alaskan Airways, Incorporated, General Manager Arthur W. Johnson. He expected to return to Anchorage by way of Takotna and McGrath.

Frank Dorbandt and Lon Cope left Seattle for Wenatchee on Tuesday, October 21, with the Bellanca, NC 259M. Landing there, they took off again at noon of the same day for Prince George, British Columbia, arriving at the Canadian city that afternoon, having to deviate from their route somewhat due to low cloud conditions. They averaged a speed of 130 miles per hour. The two Pacific International Airways airmen went on the following day to arrive at Hazelton, British Columbia that same day, Wednesday, October 22. Frank wired Robert H. Romig, their company agent in Anchorage of their arrival, adding that they had been commissioned to search for Canadian pilot Captain E.J.A. Burke, by the Air Land Manufacturing Company of Vancouver, British Columbia, owners of Burke's plane. The pilot was missing in the Laird region with two companions in a Junkers F-13, CF-AMX. Dorbandt and Cope reached Atlin on October 26, 1930.

Fueling the Bellanca to capacity, the two airmen departed Atlin on Monday, October 27, arriving at Laird post, to discover that the Burke plane had been there on October 10, starting back the following day. The Pacific International Airways fliers flew a search of the chain of lakes between Laird and Atlin, without finding the missing Junkers, CF-AMX. Running short of fuel, Dorbandt was forced to land the Bellanca on Paddy's Lake, some fifty miles south of Atlin. Stranded here for four days, the two fliers returned to Atlin on Friday, October 31, after fuel for the Bellanca had been delivered to them.

Dorbandt, making a second search with Everett Wasson, had little confidence in the Burke party being found alive. He also wanted to get on with the business at Anchorage. Flying to Whitehorse, Yukon Territory, from Atlin on Sunday, November 2, he was assured that two planes from there would take over, one from the Treadwell-Yukon Company, Limited and the other from Klondike Airways, both commissioned by Air Land Manufacturing Company. It was Everett L. Wasson, pilot for the mining company, that eventually found the missing plane on November 24, 1930.

Dorbandt and Cope left Atlin for Anchorage on Thursday, November 6, 1930, spending the night at Tanana Crossing and arriving over the city about 1:30 P.M., November 7, to circle several times to show off the new plane before landing at the "golf course" airport between Ninth and Tenth streets. The six-place Bellanca CH-300, NC 259M, manufactured by the Bellanca Aircraft Corporation of New Castle, Delaware, was a Pacemaker model that had taken first, second and third prizes at the Chicago Air Show for general efficiency. The plane could carry a payload of about 1250 pounds, and land and take off from a short field.

The fliers had spent Thursday night at Tanana Crossing, coming on from there on Friday. The flight from Chickaloon to Anchorage had taken only a half hour. Joe Barrows and Harry Blunt, flying up the Consolidated Fleetster and the Fairchild 71 to add to the Pacific International Airways fleet, would also be involved in the Burke search, getting into considerable trouble with their planes at Telegraph Creek, British Columbia. They were not to arrive in Anchorage until months later, early in 1931.

By Tuesday, October 28, in Anchorage, the contractor, Dahl & Wanstad, had nearly completed the task of lining the small hangar on the "golf course" airport, with only the sliding doors left to install. Mechanic Cecil Higgins had devised a new heating system to keep the building comfortable. Orval H. Porter, mechanic, who had been with Wilkins, Eielson and

916

Crosson in the Antarctic, arrived in Seward on Saturday, November 1, to take a position with Alaskan Airways, Incorporated, in Fairbanks. His wife, the former Orpha Boreen of Anchorage, accompanied him.

The Keystone Commuter and the New Standard D-25 biplane were expected in soon at Seward. A banking level attached to a piece of wood had been brought in by Art Coates; it had been found on the beach about a mile below the J.R. Campbell cannery on the east shore of Cook Inlet. The instrument, previously loaned to Russel Merrill by John Cook, of the Anchorage post office, was positively identified by the owner. This further confirmed the loss of the Travel Air 7000 and its pilot, Russel Merrill, in the Inlet.

Beginning November 10, Alaskan Airways inaugurated bi-weekly plane service between Anchorage and Flat, with stops enroute at Medfra, McGrath and Takotna. They planned a similar schedule, beginning November 17, 1930, between Fairbanks and Nome. Insurance coverage on the company's passengers at $10,000 per seat had been in effect for some time. It had now been raised to $15,000 per seat, without additional cost to the passenger.

Matt Nieminen, Alaskan Airways pilot, was off for Takotna in the Fairchild 71, NC 9153, on Friday, November 7, to bring in a sick man, August Hellberg. He was back that afternoon, sending the man in to the hospital, where he was operated on immediately and soon recovered. The pilot was away again on Sunday, November 9, making another flight to Takotna and return.

Fairchild 71, NC 9153, was based in Anchorage for part of 1930. Flown by Matt Nieminen, the plane gave good service. It was later named the **Yukon.**

Crosson Collection

Joe Crosson came in the same day from McGrath in Fairchild 71, NC 153H, *Yukon*, returning to Medfra to spend the night. Crosson had brought in Joe Linke, Bernard H. Ivey, and two Strandberg boys from Flat, while Nieminen carried as passengers Doctor L. von M-Zesch, Oscar Keturi and his son, Elmer Keturi, from Flat. The new Keystone Commuter, aboard the steamer *Northwestern*, was delayed when the vessel dropped its rudder near Port Althorp after leaving Juneau. The plane was expected to be transferred to the *Alameda* and sent north. In the absence of Cecil Higgins, Orval Porter had been held over in Anchorage to see to the assembly of the plane. Higgins was at Kashwitna installing a new motor in Waco NC 780E.

Dorbandt, Pacific International Airways pilot, was away for Flat in the Bellanca, NC 259M, on Sunday, November 9, 1930. He returned shortly after noon of the following day, bringing in two passengers, miners Carl and Paul Wabnig, father and son, flying the 310 miles in two hours and ten minutes in the new plane. A friendly race with Matt Nieminen on the way out had resulted in a win for the Pacific International Airways pilot by six minutes. Dorbandt left the next morning with a load of supplies for Flat, Iditarod and McGrath, returning that Tuesday evening at 5:10 P.M. with Harry Steen as a passenger. Nieminen came in at noon the

November 1930. Consolidated Fleetster Model 17-2C, NC 750V, of Pacific International Airways, Incorporated, shown here in the States, was taken north by Pilot Joe Barrows in November of 1930 as an addition to the company's fleet. Misfortune on the way prevented it from arriving in Anchorage until early the following year.

Gordon S. Williams Collection

same day, carrying passengers, express and mail, and completing the first scheduled run over the route.

Additional planes and pilots were on the way for Pacific International Airways, Incorporated. Joe Barrows had gone east to take deliver of a dark blue Consolidated Fleetster, NC 750V. Barrows wrote to his wife, Mary, who was then living with their two children in Victoria, British Columbia, that they would soon be going to Alaska with Mr. and Mrs. Lowe in the new all-metal plane. Flying it across Canada, the pilot landed in Vancouver to show it off, then coming on to Victoria to visit his family. The children remained in Victoria with a competent lady and Mary's sister, Edith. Barrows went on to California to pick up the Lowes, dropping them in Vancouver, British Columbia on Tuesday, November 4, before returning to Seattle. He was joined there by Harry Blunt, who brought up a Fairchild 71; he would fly it north with the Fleetster.

Late Sunday afternoon, November 9, 1930, the two planes were away from Boeing Field in Seattle for Vancouver, British Columbia. Joe landed at Lulu Island airport there but Harry Blunt, in the Fairchild, had to return to Boeing because of weather. He came in the next morning to join the rest of the party, who had spent the night at the Vancouver Hotel. The Lowes also had a friend, Miss Jean Boyd, along for the trip. The amount of clothing and equipment the Lowes had brought along was huge. In addition, there were two bulky sets of skis for the planes, then on wheels. After stuffing the two planes and leaving seats for the two pilots and the Lowes, there still remained a pile of baggage, along with Mary Barrows and Jean Boyd.

November 17, 1930 at Lulu Field, Vancouver, British Columbia. Fueling the Consolidated Fleetster, NC 750V, at the Aero Club before taking off for Alaska. The plane had already had the wheel pants removed in preparation for landing in mud and slush on the way north.

Mary Barrows Photo

November 17, 1930. Pilot Joe Barrows with his partners, Ted Lowe and Mrs. Lowe at Lulu Field in Vancouver, British Columbia prior to their departure for Alaska in the Consolidated Fleetster, NC 750V.

The two planes took off on Monday, November 10, 1930, leaving the two women and their baggage to travel north on the Canadian Pacific Steamship Company's *Princess Norah* to Skagway, where they could cross over White Pass on the narrow-gauge railroad to Whitehorse, and rejoin the aerial expedition. The planes reached Prince George, British Columbia at 2:00 P.M., then went on to Hazelton. Finding the field there too small, they were forced to return to Smithers, British Columbia. Delayed there for days by stormy weather, the pilots spent the time fitting skis to the aircraft. On Saturday, November 14, one of them barely escaped a mishap; it dragged a wing on a tree when a takeoff in deep snow was attempted. The airport was on a hillside, further complicating matters.

Paddy Burke was missing in the Laird region with two passengers, and it was decided to join in the search for the Junkers; it was not a great deal out of their way. Leaving Smithers, British Columbia on Saturday, November 22, 1930, the two pilots headed their planes for Atlin, by way of Telegraph Creek. They were at Telegraph Creek for some days because of bad weather. The field there was small for the heavily-loaded planes so they decided to move them to Sawmill Lake, about a mile away, where they could fly off the ice. Here they made further preparations to continue their participation in the search for Burke and his companions, while the Lowes remained in a hotel.

Harry Blunt, in the Fairchild 71, was first off the lake on Wednesday, November 26, 1930, when he suffered an engine failure, and disappeared over a sparsely wooded hill. Joe Barrows, in the Fleetster, gunned the motor to taxi the plane across the lake and reach the crash site on foot. It was not to be; his plane ran into a soft area and came to a halt and the Fleetster sank up to its wings into the water beneath. Joe suffered a thorough soaking in the icy water while trying to open the hatch above the pilot's seat, through which he escaped. He watched in dismay as the plane settled, with its wing and horizontal stabilizer resting on top of the ice.

The two planes of Pacific International Airways enroute to Alaska in November of 1930; Consolidated Fleetster, NC 750V and Fairchild 71, with Joe Barrows, pilot of the Fleetster and Harry Blunt, pilot of the Fairchild. The skis were put on at Smithers, British Columbia so this picture was taken either there or at Telegraph Creek.

The Fairchild was found on the other side of the hill, a complete loss. Harry Blunt lay tangled in the wreckage with two broken knees, a broken shoulder and a few broken ribs. He was carefully moved to the small infirmary at Telegraph Creek.

Deciding the water-soaked Fleetster could be salvaged, Joe Barrows obtained the help of Joe Morrison, a former army aviation mechanic living at Telegraph Creek. With other men, they chopped a path through the ice, and used dog teams to drag the plane ashore. Barrows was also in the infirmary for a time, badly crippled with inflammatory rheumatism from his ducking, and unable to walk or use his right hand. He got a dog team to take him to the lake site, lying on the sled while he directed the other men in the salvage work. With the plane finally out on the solid ice near the shore, canvas canopies composed of tents were draped over the wing and tail sections, completely enclosing the plane except for its mid-fuselage section. With a wood stove going at all times within the tented area, the plane was slowly dried. The engine was drained and dried out; the ignition system disassembled and baked until dried. The instruments and some other components were ruined by the water; the plane would have to be flown without them. Joe lay on the cockpit floor, working one-handed on the wiring, in the final stages of readying the plane for flight. He determined to fly it somehow.

Everett Wasson, a young Californian who had taken up Canadian citizenship, and who was flying a Fairchild FC-2W2, GC-ARM, for the Treadwell-Yukon Company, Limited, had found the missing Burke plane on Monday, November 24, 1930, two days before Barrows had gone through the ice. Communications had been very irregular in the region. Wasson later brought in the two survivors and the body of Paddy Burke.

In Whitehorse, Mary Barrows, apprised of the situation in Telegraph Creek by tele-

Wednesday, November 26, 1930, the Fleetster sinks through the ice of Sawmill Lake near Telegraph Creek, British Columbia when Joe Barrows tried to taxi across to aid Harry Blunt who had crashed on takeoff in the Fairchild.

Drawn from the waters of Sawmill Lake near Telegraph Creek, British Columbia the Consolidated Fleetster is being dried out under a canopy of canvas tents heated by a wood stove.

Consolidated Fleetster, NC 750V, drying out under a canopy of canvas tents on Sawmill Lake. The stripped fuselage of the Fairchild 71 in which Harry Blunt crashed lies nearby. The Fairchild was a total loss.

Pilot Harry Blunt, taught to fly in California by Joe Barrows, recovered from his injuries and continued to fly for Pacific International Airways in Anchorage the following year.

Kay Kennedy Collection

gram, waited. Jean Boyd, her vacation over, had gone home by rail and ship. Mary spent her time closely following the Burke search and reporting it faithfully to the Seattle Times. This was where it was happening, for searchers went out from Whitehorse, and the survivors were brought in there. She went to the airport in a tractor-drawn sled on Thursday, December 18, 1930, with a Sergeant of the Royal Canadian Mounted Police, to witness the arrival of Wasson's plane with the body of Captain E.J.A. Burke. Another sound filled the air and she looked up to see the Fleetster overhead. Joe Barrows was flying it in to Whitehorse one-handed, with Joe Morrison working the stabilizer and other mechanical adjustments necessary to fly the plane. Harry Blunt, wrapped in blankets, lay on the cabin floor. The cockpit was without instruments; the pilot was flying by sight and sound. Both pilots were sent at once to the hospital by a Whitehorse physician.

Harry Blunt left the hospital, to travel on the *Princess Norah* arriving in Vancouver, British Columbia on Saturday, January 3, 1931. He walked off the ship on crutches, and immediately left for Seattle, to fly on to California as a passenger. Joe Barrows took the Fleetster, NC 750V, still with Morrison's help, to Telegraph Creek on January 3, 1931, to bring in Mr. and Mrs. Edward A. Lowe, Jr. and the load from the demolished Fairchild. Mary returned by train and boat to Victoria and the children, while Joe continued the trip north with Morrison and the Lowes. There were shops in Fairbanks where the Fleetster could be reconditioned and made airworthy. Joe Barrows was in Fairbanks on Tuesday, January 13, 1931, with his passengers in the Fleetster; the Lowes and Morrison went from there to Anchorage by train.

Alaskan Airways received a call in Anchorage on Wednesday, November 12, 1930, requesting a plane to pick up an injured man, Thomas Schulze, at Illiamna. Mrs. Schulze had traveled for three days by boat to get to Seldovia where a message could be sent out. Schulze, a government school teacher at Illiamna village, had slipped in a rowboat and fallen onto the oarlocks, injuring himself. A small plane was needed to land on a little lake, one-half mile from the village.

In response to a wire from Nieminen, Joe Crosson left Fairbanks in the Stearman, NC 5415, making it into Anchorage in three hours and fifteen minutes. Taking the plane, accompanied by Doctor Walkowski, Nieminen started down the Inlet for the injured man that same afternoon. Unable to get through, with bad weather conditions, the pilot returned to Anchorage. The next morning, Thursday, November 13, the men tried again with the same result.

Cecil Higgins, mechanic for Alaskan Airways in Anchorage, had replaced the motor in their Waco Model 10, NC 780E, under trying conditions at Kashwitna Lake in November of 1930. He is shown here posing with the plane, which Joe Crosson had flown on the Eielson-Borland search earlier in the year.

Crosson and Nieminen left for Kashwitna on their return, to bring in the Waco 10, NC 780E, at the site. Cecil Higgins had been installing a new motor in the plane, which had been at the lake since September 17, 1930. Crosson dropped off his fellow pilot and returned to Anchorage late in the afternoon, making the round trip in one hour and twenty minutes of flying time.

Other than its engine failure, the Waco was undamaged. With the new engine installed and checked out, the pilot and mechanic climbed in and took off for their base on the morning of Friday, November 14. Fighting his way through snowstorms, Nieminen finally landed at Anchorage. It was still impossible to get to Illiamna for Thomas Schulze. Matt Nieminen tried again, taking the Stearman, NC 5415, out alone on the morning of Saturday, November 15. The pilot was successful, returning that evening with the gravely injured man. An operation was performed within an hour of the plane's arrival by Doctor J.H. Romig of the Government hospital, after which Schulze was expected to recover.

Joe Crosson took the Stearman back to Fairbanks the following day, Sunday, making it in four hours of flight time, to arrive there at 3:00 P.M. Bad weather at Healy had forced him to follow a roundabout route through the valleys, coming in by way of Nenana.

Frank Dorbandt left Anchorage in the Bellanca Pacemaker for McGrath and lower Kuskokwim River points on Monday, November 17. He was carrying Mrs. Dixie Hall and her son, Robert, for Bethel, as well as mail and express for all scheduled stops. The pilot reached Bethel late Tuesday, fighting poor weather on the way downriver from McGrath. He was back in Anchorage at noon on Friday, November 21, coming in from McGrath. Bringing in Mrs. J. Fromberg from the river town, he flew around in the pass for forty-five minutes before the snow flurries cleared enough to let him through. He reported that Matt Nieminen was at McGrath, awaiting favorable weather there, for a flight to Fairbanks with passengers. Matt had taken two trappers, Joe Anderson and Ben Ryste, to the Two Lakes country in the Fairchild 71, NC 9153, going by way of Merrill Pass and landing at Sleetmute on his way to Flat.

The Keystone Commuter, NC 539V, came in on the Monday, November 17, freight train, and mechanics were ready to set it up for flying.

924

Frank Dorbandt and Lon Cope brought this Bellanca CH-300 Pacemaker to Anchorage on November 6, 1930. The six-place plane, NC 259M, was the second plane for Pacific International Airways fleet to arrive. It was put into immediate use, with Frank Dorbandt as pilot.

Mary Barrows Photo

Dorbandt was off in the Bellanca, NC 259M, at noon of November 24, 1930, with one hundred pounds of mail, freight, periodicals and other supplies. Weather on the Anchorage side of the Alaska Range was not favorable but the other side of the range was reported to be better. Frank had flown over 2100 pounds of freight and mail to Kuskokwim River and other points in the past two weeks. A varied sampling showed a hindquarter of beef, turkeys, weinerwurst, chickens, a Ford cylinder head, groceries, bananas, tomatoes, oranges, lemons, two suits of clothes, two pair of shoes, two hog carcasses, stationery, newspapers and magazines—all had found their way onto the plane, to be delivered along the way.

Matt Nieminen landed in Fairbanks the afternoon of Friday, November 21, coming from Iditarod with passengers Arnold Kobler, Harvey A. LaZelle, Perry Poirer and Charles Salmi aboard. He took off from Weeks Field on Sunday, November 23, enroute to Anchorage by way of Flat and McGrath. He carried two passengers for the first point. The pilot was able to return to his Anchorage base the morning of Wednesday, November 26, 1930; he had been away since November 17, when he had taken Anderson and Ryste to Two Lakes, with their 1000 pound outfit. He brought four passengers across the range to the port city: Evald Gustafson and Peter Thibault from Iditarod, and Paul Fromberg and Leo Rodrigue from McGrath. Rodrigue was a partner in the Nixon Fork mine with Rudolf Mespelt.

Pacific International Airways, Incorporated, had decided to go ahead on construction of their hangar on the new Municipal Airport. Using Dahl & Wanstad as contractors, the work was well underway when, late on Monday, November 24, a scaffolding upon which several carpenters were at work collapsed under their weight. Tumbling to the ground, two of the men were injured—Adrian E. Moorhead, with fractured ribs and a bruised chest, and Herman Johnson with severe bruising of the legs—both required hospitalization. Minor cuts and bruises were the lot of the other workmen.

Using the Waco 10, NC 780E, Nieminen took Charles Lind and a capacity load of freight to Kusilof on the afternoon of Thursday, November 27, returning before dusk in clear weather. He was flying on skis now. The pilot took the open-cockpit plane to Kashwitna Lake to pick up an outfit for Elmer Simco and Dick Tousley, departing in the afternoon with the load for delivery at their camp sixteen miles from Clarence Lake. He made a search for an oldtimer, William Whitteridge, overdue from his upper Talkeetna River workings, before returning to Anchorage. He landed at Curry for fuel but was able to obtain only twenty gallons, so the pilot went to Talkeetna for a conference with Commissioner Nagley, taking on fifty gallons of gas there. Taking off at 11:00 A.M. Saturday, November 29, on the search, Matt could see tracks in the snow about the miner's cabin and fears for his safety were somewhat alleviated. There was no place to land nearby.

Dorbandt, the sole Pacific International Airways pilot in Anchorage, returned from Bethel late on Wednesday, November 26, giving up his intention of going on to Goodnews Bay because of high winds at Bethel. Coming in from Aniak to the Kuskokwim River community it had taken five minutes to cover the twenty miles, flying with the wind. The return flight took thirty minutes to cover the same distance. When Dorbandt landed at Bethel the wind velocity was greater than the landing speed of the Bellanca, necessitating his holding the plane on the ground in flying position with the engine running, until residents got hold of it and held it until he could get it roped down. The flight in from Flat to Akiak, by way of Crooked Creek, a distance of about 200 miles, had taken one hour, giving a ground speed of 200 miles per hour. He had picked up Miss Chenowith, school teacher at McGrath, taking her to Akiak for treatment of a wound in her shoulder caused by the accidental discharge of a twenty-two caliber rifle, thought to be unloaded. The minor wound was treated and she returned to McGrath in the plane.

In response to an emergency call from Seldovia, Dorbandt and Cope flew to Homer on Friday, November 28, landing on a small lake there about 3:00 P.M. The patient, William Sundsby, had to be brought across Kachemak Bay by boat to the Homer spit, then brought to the lake. The airmen stayed overnight as the boat did not arrive until after 4:00 P.M. The fliers reached Anchorage shortly before 1:00 P.M. the following day, bringing in the sick man and an additional passenger. Sundsby had suffered two strokes, but was conscious and his condition deemed not critical at the hospital. Dorbandt left at 2:00 P.M. with a trapper named Waddell and his outfit, headed for Ross Lake at the head of the Susitna valley.

The Keystone-Loening Commuter, Model K-84, NC 539V, powered with the Wright J6-9 of 300 horsepower, had four seats for passengers and a landing gear that was raised and lowered by the pilot from the cockpit, giving it capabilities for landing on water or land, as the pilot wished. It could also be fitted with skis for winter operation. Assembly of the amphibian was nearly complete but it was not to be flight tested until January 4, 1931.

Frank Dorbandt was out again in the Bellanca, reaching Bethel on Tuesday, December 2, 1930, and he expected to continue on to Goodnews Bay. He planned to be back in Anchorage on Thursday, December 4. The Fairchild 51, NC 5364, was coming out of the shop after an extensive rebuild by Fred Bowman, following the crackup of October 2, 1930, at the old Municipal Airport. Dorbandt was planning to test fly it before the year was out.

Alaskan Airways announced they would name their planes in the near future. The Fairchild 71, NC 9153, was expected to become *Denali*, since it had flown over Mount McKinley.

Matt Nieminen was away in the Fairchild 71 on Monday, December 8, 1930, landing at Two Lakes enroute, arriving at Iditarod in the afternoon. Held there by poor weather until 11:30 A.M. Thursday, December 11, the pilot took off for McGrath, carrying Carl Lottsfeldt, superintendent of the Alaska Road Commission, and Fred Lusher, an old time prospector, as passengers. The flight was expected to take an hour, and Matt fueled the plane with three hours fuel before departure. Flying the regular route up Otter Creek and over to Moore Creek proved

926

Bob Hall, Moose Pass

Keystone-Loening Commuter, NC 539V, of Alaskan Airways, Incorporated, at Seward, Alaska.

impossible, and the pilot gave it up after twenty minutes. Following the Iditarod-Ophir winter trail, the pilot flew for another forty minutes before encountering fog that forced him to retrace his path to within twenty miles of Iditarod. Zig-zagging from one creek bottom to another, the pilot finally spotted an opening in the clouds, climbing to 4000 feet to top the layer. Flying northeast for twenty minutes and finding the undercast endless, Matt turned back, finding a hole through which he descended to within one hundred feet of the surface. Searching from one creek to another, frustrated by fog at every turn, the pilot finally ended up in a valley which broadened somewhat. He flew until a cabin was sighted, landing on his skis at 1:30 P.M. in the foothills on a hogback about one and one-half miles from the cabin.

The three men took the eight-pound pack of emergency rations, a 250-3000 caliber rifle and an axe from the plane, and began searching for the cabin. Matt broke trail, using a pair of skis he carried in the plane. Eventually they crossed a snowed-in blazed trail, turning left on it, only to retrace their tracks to follow the trail in the opposite direction. Finding the cabin about a half mile further on, a rude structure eleven by nine feet wide and five feet high that contained two bunks, a Yukon stove, kerosene lamp and some food, the men set up housekeeping. The trapline shelter cabin later proved to be on the Dishna River, about twenty miles above its confluence with the Innoko River. Sheltered and fed, the men spent the night in relative

927

comfort, Lottsfeldt going downriver at 7:30 A.M. the following morning in search of someone with a dog team to carry out word of their plight. Matt went back to the Fairchild 71 to tie it down and prepare it to receive the needed gasoline when it should arrive. Matt and Fred also kept signal fires going during the day, but of little use in the fog.

The following day, Saturday, December 13, was clear and, with a good smoke signal going, the pilot went back to the plane to sweep the snow from it so it could be more easily seen from the air. When within a quarter mile of the Fairchild, Matt saw another Fairchild 71 approaching the smoke signal at the cabin, circling for fifteen minutes before its pilot, Ed Young, spotted the plane and landed. Accompanied by Milton Rice, the Fairbanks pilot was soon at work helping Nieminen refuel his plane with the forty gallons he could spare. After about forty-five minutes Dorbandt flew over in the Bellanca, circling to see if anything was needed. Matt waved him on.

Matt returned to the cabin to leave the owner a note, explaining the use of it, as well as leaving the balance of the emergency supplies for the trapper. Returning to the plane he found Dorbandt, accompanied by miner Charles Ulsh and dredgeman Jack P. Taylor, had returned; he had misunderstood signals and thought gasoline was needed. He brought forty gallons.

The skis of Matt's plane had frozen fast to the snow over the three days and the help of all was needed to break them free. All three planes took off and arrived at Takotna in less than a half hour. S.E. Robbins, Alaskan Airways pilot from Fairbanks, was there to join the search.

Frank Dorbandt picked up Carl Lottsfeldt on Sunday, December 14, 1930, at a cabin some ten miles below the forced landing site and took him to Takotna. The Alaska Road Commission superintendent had selected a long clear space and snowshoed out in large letter, "Land Here."

The custom of Alaskan pilots in joining to hunt for one of their own, regardless of company affiliation, had been well demonstrated. The efficient manner in which the incident had been handled, and the happy conclusion to it was a good demonstration of airmen, as well as others, effectively and harmoniously working together toward a common end.

Matt was back in Anchorage by December 18, 1930. Frank Dorbandt came in to Weeks Field at Fairbanks, landing at 1:20 P.M. of December 24, with a sick person from Nulato. He remained over Christmas, leaving the city for Anchorage on the morning of Friday, December 26, 1930. He was carrying three passengers for the coast: Charles Milot of Nome, Mickey Goldstein and Lyman DeStaffany, fur buyers of Juneau and Seattle, respectively.

At the end of 1930, Alaskan Airways, Incorporated, had in Anchorage a Fairchild 71, NC 9153; an open-cockpit Waco Model 10, NC 780E; and the new Keystone-Loening Commuter K-84, NC 539V. The open-cockpit Travel Air 4000, C-193, had been taken to Fairbanks some time before. The other company, Pacific International Airways, Incorporated, had the Bellanca Pacemaker, NC 259M, and the Fairchild 51, NC 5364, to begin the new year. Joe Barrows and Harry Blunt were still in Whitehorse with the Consolidated Fleetster, NC 750V, *Polaris*, and expected at Anchorage in January.

NOTE: For details on P.I.A. and the Burke search, see Mary M. Worthylake's book, *Up in the Air*.

Pacific International Airways' Consolidated Fleetster, NC 750V, **Polaris,** *photographed in Canada on the way to Anchorage, was still in Whitehorse at the end of 1930. The Fairchild 71, lost at Sawmill Lake, stands behind the Fleetster in this photo.*

TRAVEL BY AIR

With

Alaskan Airways, Inc.

(Founded by Carl Ben Eielson)

OPERATING IN ALASKA, WESTERN CANADA AND EASTERN SIBERIA

Bases and Offices:

ANCHORAGE—   FAIRBANKS—   NOME—

JOE CROSSON, Chief Pilot   ARTHUR W. JOHNSON, General Manager

Headquarters:— FAIRBANKS, ALASKA

George King collection

Crosson Collection

930

Alaskan Airways, Incorporated

Eielson-Borland Relief
Expedition
Service Airlines

Fairbanks 1930

58

W ORK HAD BEEN RUSHED ON THE THREE Fairchild 71s of the Eielson-Borland Relief Expedition, using the former Wien hangar at Weeks Field; the other Alaskan Airways, Incorporated, hangars had been burned in the accidental fire of December 22, 1929.

All was in readiness on Thursday, January 2, 1930, as two of the Fairchild 71 planes prepared to depart for Nulato, on their way to the *Nanuk*. T.M. "Pat" Reid was off first in the Canadian registered CF-AJK, circling above the field while pilot Gifford Swartman and mechanic Sam Macauley prepared to depart in the second plane, NC 190H. Hurrying to get away with a cold engine, the heavily-loaded plane ran the full length of the field before struggling into the air at 11:00 A.M., while the crowd that had gathered watched the takeoff. The flight turned to disaster as the plane failed to gain altitude. The Fairchild veered off to the left toward a small ravine, its landing gear clipped through the brush, and it settled to the ground about fifty feet from the end of the field, turning completely around with the left wing

▲ *Spring, 1930. Alaskan Airways, Incorporated,*
was advertising increased services for their commercial
business following the Eielson-Borland search.

◄ *Fairchild 71 with Alaskan Airways employees,*
Left to Right: Robbie Robbins, General Manager
Arthur W. Johnson, and Chief Pilot Joe Crosson.

Fairbanks, Alaska, January 2, 1930. Fairchild 71, NC 190H, is ready to depart for Nulato on the way to the Nanuk. The plane crashed on takeoff with Gifford Swartman and Sam Macauley aboard. Pat Reid stands closest with his back to the camera.

Courtesy of Eleanor Stoy Reed

canted skyward. The crowd, rushing to the scene, found the two airmen practically uninjured; Swartman suffered only an apparently minor injury to his side where the fuselage gave inward. The plane was another matter. The right wing, upon which the Fairchild had pivoted, was a crumpled mass, and sections of the fuselage were twisted. The $18,000 plane was a loss, except for the nine-cylinder Pratt & Whitney engine of 420 horsepower, which represented about one-half the value of the plane. The wreck was left where it was until an insurance adjuster could inspect it. Meanwhile they needed a replacement as soon as possible, and a Fairchild was rushed north.

Pat Reid observed the catastrophe from the air and immediately landed. When the turmoil over the crash had subsided, Major Deckard and Captain Oaks announced the accident would occasion only a short delay as the third Fairchild was also ready, with a departure now planned for Friday morning, using the two planes remaining. James T. Hutchison, Alaskan Airways mechanic, accompanied Pat Reid to North Cape as a mechanic and welder, taking the necessary equipment with him. He was needed to repair the broken landing gear of the Alaskan Airways Stearman C-2B flown by Gillam. Matt Nieminen, who had arrived in Fairbanks on Monday afternoon, December 30, 1929, in the open-cockpit Travel Air 4000, C-193, was to fly the other Fairchild 71, NC 153H; his knowledge of the country and its peculiarities were invaluable.

The two planes were away from Weeks Field at 9:00 A.M. Saturday, January 4, 1930, passing over Tolovana at 9:30 and over Hot Springs at 9:47. They were making a ground speed of 130 miles per hour with a good tailwind. In the plane with Matt Nieminen were Major Deckard and Sam Macauley, while Bill Hughes and Jim Hutchinson rode with Reid. Matt, knowing the country, was in the lead, with Pat Reid close behind, although Reid had taken off first with Matt following fifteen minutes later. The two Fairchild 71s had an approximate gross load of 5400 pounds each. Snow was falling at Nome, with poor weather over the Seward Peninsula in general. Pilot Gifford Swartman and mechanic C.F.K. "Kel" Mews remained at Fairbanks for the time being. Captain Oaks, his work completed, returned to his home in Toronto on the next boat. (He was in Juneau on Monday, January 27, planning on leaving the following day on the *Princess Mary).* The two Fairchilds passed over Ruby at 11:00 A.M., making good time.

January 2, 1930. Fair-
child 71, NC 190H,
shortly after crash land-
ing near Weeks Field.

Courtesy of Jesse Rust

January 2, 1930. With
Pat Reid circling above
in the first Fairchild 71
to depart Weeks Field,
pilot Gifford Swartman
and mechanic Sam
Macauley crash landed
shortly after takeoff in
the second one, NC
190H. The pair suffered
only minor hurt but the
plane would never fly
again. Wrapped in
canvas, it awaits the
inspection of an
insurance adjuster.

Courtesy of Eleanor Stoy Reed

Fred Moller, held for some days at Tolovana by extremely cold weather, returned to Fairbanks on Sunday, January 5, 1930. He had intended to go to Nulato to bring in Corporal Van de Water of the U.S. Signal Corps, troubled by an infection of his right hand, but rapid improvement had removed the need for treatment. On returning from Teller on December 21, 1929, Harvey Barnhill had resigned as a pilot for Alaskan Airways, Incorporated, and departed for the States on the last boat, accompanied by his wife and daughter.

The two Fairchilds, hoping to complete a nonstop flight from Fairbanks to Nome on January 4, had reached a point five miles east of Norton Sound. Flying in heavy snow, Nieminen lost sight of the other plane and elected to return to Nulato, where he landed safely. Reid, in Fairchild CF-AJK, was unreported.

Bad weather kept Nieminen on the ground at Nulato through the following day. Frank Dorbandt made a flight from Nome to Unalakleet on Sunday morning but saw no signs of the missing Fairchild. In Fairbanks, Captain Oaks was preparing to send a search plane from there, in the event no word was received from Pat Reid. The red cabin Swallow, C 3542, was being readied for the flight; its motor was in somewhat better condition than that of the Travel Air 4000. The "red devil" also had a greater load capability.

In preparation, test flights were made on the plane the morning of Monday, January 6, with Swartman at the controls, and mechanic Mews also along. They held the plane in readiness at Fairbanks until other planes to the westward had completed a search. Matt Nieminen flew west out of Nulato on Monday, in an attempt to find Reid, but was forced back to his starting point by fog along the coast. Conditions on Tuesday were even worse, with snow and fog all along the route. Dog teams, sent out from Unalakleet expecting to reach the Bonanza roadhouse on Thursday, January 9, were to search the Ungalik River valley in the Nulato hills.

A tremendous windstorm swept through the Tanana valley on Wednesday, January 8, with winds reported in Fairbanks as high as forty miles per hour. Harold Woodward, mechanic for Alaskan Airways and student aviator, had his plane, the old Bennett-Rodebaugh Waco 9, No. 1, lifted aloft by the wind and carried up to a height of thirty feet. The plane, which had been standing unattended on Weeks Field, sailed over the hangar and was carried one hundred feet into a slough behind the building, where it was almost completely wrecked on landing. The motor had been removed from the plane for overhaul, lightening it considerably. The upper wing panels were ruined but repairs to the lower panels might be possible. The fuselage suffered some damage but the landing gear was all right; the plane had landed on its back. The wind, extending from the Seward Peninsula, had done a great deal of damage about Fairbanks during its two-hour blow.

Matt Nieminen, held at Nulato for several days, got away at 10:30 A.M. on January 10, 1930, to fly a route along the Yukon River to Unalakleet, turning northwest to continue toward Nome. The pilot considered this the best possibility as to the path Pat Reid might have followed when last seen. Matt was expected to return to Nulato to gas. Before any further word came from the Alaskan Airways pilot, a message was received by Alf Lomen on the afternoon of Saturday, January 11, that Pat Reid, Bill Hughes and Jim Hutchison had been forced down by

CF-AJK after forced landing in a creek bottom at the head of the Ungalik River on January 4, 1930. The men are making repairs to the right wing tip. Fortunately Pat Reid had repair materials and two mechanics with him.

934

Canadian pilot Pat Reid, with mechanics Bill Hughes and Jim Hutchison, was forced to land in a narrow creek bottom at the head of the Ungalik River about fifty miles from Unalakleet on January 4, 1930. Considerable damage was done to the right wing tip. Swinging the wing back to a better position, the men began emergency repairs to CF-AJK, and the plane got away on January 11.

T.M. "Pat" Reid Photo

weather at the Ungalik River, and were all right. One of the dog teams previously sent out from Unalakleet had returned with the message.

Reid had been forced by heavy weather to land in a narrow creek bottom about noon, January 4, 1930, at the headwaters of the Ungalik River, fifty miles from Unalakleet. The right wing tip was damaged in striking a rock during the landing. Putting up a lean-to, the party "siwashed"for five days while the two mechanics rebuilt the wing tip and adjacent ribs, using wood from a packing box in the plane as well as from the nearby spruce trees. Reid was fortunate in having the skilled aircraft mechanics along, as well as glue, fabric, dope and other materials the men were taking to the *Nanuk* to complete the repairs on the Stearman. They were able to swing the folding wing of the Fairchild 71 to the rear which placed the work area at a convenient level.

With the temporary repair completed, and with improving weather, Reid took off in the narrow valley on Saturday, January 11, to land at Unalakleet, only fifty miles away. Another storm moved in, with rain and wind from the sea stripping all of the snow from the shore. With the help of the Eskimo residents, the plane was dragged a long distance to an ice-covered slough, where a takeoff could be made. The Canadian pilot, with companions Bill Hughes and Jim Hutchison, arrived at Nome in their Fairchild 71, CF-AJK, on Wednesday, January 15. Permanent repairs to the right wing tip were made there in the next four days.

Matt Nieminen, flying the Fairchild 71, NC 153H, arrived in Nome from Nulato on Sunday, January 12, bringing Major Deckard and Sam Macauley. Nieminen and Deckard had made three attempts from Nulato to find Reid by plane, forced back each time by storms.

Alfred J. Lomen, manager of the Eielson-Borland search for The Aviation Corporation, called for pilots Frank Dorbandt and Ed Young to come to Nome for a conference. With Pat Reid and Matt Nieminen on the scene; they could get their collective ideas together for future efforts, and also share information. Frank Dorbandt had taken the Stinson SB-1, NC 877, as far as Unalakleet on Sunday, January 5, on a futile search for Reid's Fairchild, then still missing. Returning to Nome, he landed at Solomon—to be stormbound there for several days.

Frank came in to Nome about 1:30 P.M. on Wednesday, January 8, 1930. He was away for Teller at 2:00 P.M. the following day, with Clark Bassett and Vic Ross.

In Fairbanks, Canadian pilot Gifford Swartman had been readying the red cabin Swallow for flight, in case it should be needed in Nome. He test flew the biplane on Monday afternoon, January 13, 1930, and went up in the plane again the following afternoon. He was away for Nome at 9:30 A.M. Wednesday, January 15, accompanied by Canadian mechanic C.F.K. Mews. Sergeant William Glasgow of the U.S. Signal Corps accompanied the airmen as far as Nulato. With the increase in communications through there, Corporal Van de Water, with his infected hand, was not able to handle it and an operator was needed. With a load of about 800 pounds aboard, including equipment for the relief expedition that had just arrived by train, the "red devil" made good time, arriving at Nulato at 1:00 P.M. After a short fuel stop, Swartman took off again and arrived in Nome at 3:30 P.M. that same day. Ed Young, who had been hauling gas and oil from Nome to Teller, had come in. All the pilots who were to participate in the relief expedition, except for Crosson and Gillam, who were on the scene at the *Nanuk*, were now in the Seward Peninsula city to confer with Lomen.

There was also a need to get Alaskan Airways commercial services, practically suspended since November, reorganized and running again in both Anchorage and Fairbanks. Matt Nieminen and Alonzo Cope, taking Major Deckard whose work was completed with the arrival of the relief expedition equipment and men in Nome (now placed under Lomen's management), departed in the New Standard biplane, NC 174H, on the morning of Wednesday, January 15, 1930. Arriving at Nulato, the pilot waited for the moon to rise and flew on to Fairbanks in excellent visibility. After a few hours' sleep, the two airmen got away from Weeks Field at 9:15 A.M., arriving in Anchorage early in the afternoon on Thursday, January 16, 1930. They would immediately begin rounding up the trappers who had been taken to various locations during the early winter. (see Anchorage—1930, Chapter 57).

Frank Dorbandt came in from Teller about 11:00 A.M. Wednesday, January 15, in the Stinson Standard, NC 877, bringing his wife and Vic Ross with him, Ross flying the New Standard, NC 9190. Dorbandt was off for Fairbanks in the plane on Thursday morning, January 16, accompanied by his wife, Vida, and carrying mail. Stopping over at Ruby, Frank arrived in Fairbanks on Saturday, January 18, to resume the neglected commercial flying out of there for Alaskan Airways, Incorporated. Dorbandt flew to Fort Yukon on Sunday, January 19, 1930, with mining man Jack Weiline, returning from there with D.W. Flanigan, fur buyer from Anchorage.

Gifford Swartman arrived back on Weeks Field the same day, carrying L.E. Porsild, Canadian government reindeer man, and Mrs. Porsild. The pilot planned to return to Nome the next day but his side, strained in the wreck of the first Fairchild 71, was giving him trouble. He needed to take some rest. Swartman had returned to Nome from Deering at noon on Friday, January 17, taking off on his flight to Fairbanks in the red Swallow the following morning. (see Nome—1930, Chapter 59).

Percy Hubbard and Ralph Wien had the Hines-Hubbard (Service Airlines) J-5 Swallow biplane, C 2774, nearly finished on Saturday, January 11. With a few final touches on the motor, it was ready for a ground run-in of several hours. They planned to fly it soon, with Ralph Wien as the pilot.

Ralph flew to Ruby in the plane on Sunday, January 19, with Alex "Shorty" Gragen and Tom Lockhead. While the pilot was following the Yukon River, two natives sighted the plane and phoned ahead to Ruby for assistance. They had come across Fairbanks oldtimer Bob Kelly in a tent, helpless with a broken leg, and without food or fire. The leg had broken suddenly while Kelly was scooping up snow in a pan. He dragged himself the one hundred feet to his tent and, placing his dog alongside the leg for warmth, wrapped the two of them in a blanket. He lay there for two days until the natives happened by. The two men took him sixty miles to the Yukon River. Marking out a landing field on the ice, they waited until Ralph landed the Swallow to pick up Kelly and take him to the hospital. When the pilot landed at Fairbanks at 1:55 P.M. on Monday, January 20, the patient was immediately transferred.

Ralph was away again the next day for McGrath, carrying Deputy U.S. Marshal Joe Hubbard and his wife. Ralph made a flight from McGrath to Takotna and return with two passengers before coming in to Fairbanks. The next day, Friday, January 24, 1930, the pilot left at 8:55 A.M. for Fort Hamlin, above Rampart on the Yukon River, where he picked up the critically-ill Mrs. Drayton, from three miles above there. He brought the woman in to the government hospital at Tanana, along with her husband, before coming on to Fairbanks to land at Weeks Field about 4:00 P.M. the same day.

Swartman departed Nome in the red Swallow biplane on Tuesday, January 21, 1930. With a fuel stop at Nulato, he arrived at his destination about 3:45 P.M., carrying only a large shipment of mail. The pilot flew locally out of Nome before returning to Fairbanks the coming weekend.

Frank Dorbandt, in the Stinson B-1, NC 877, was off the morning of Wednesday, January 22, carrying mail and freight for Kuskokwim and Iditarod points, as well as T.A. Parsons, superintendent for the Northern Commercial Company, a passenger for McGrath. The pilot returned to Weeks Field late the following afternoon from Flat, with passengers Alex C. Matheson and George Adams. The mission built at Nenana suffered a fire on the day they flew over the area and Dorbandt and his passenger reported they could see the flames from the blazing structure. Frank was away again in the forenoon of Friday, January 24, for the Koyukuk and Kobuk country, carrying a load of freight for Bettles. From there he went on to Shungnak, on the Kobuk River, to pick up a passenger.

Dorbandt landed back on Weeks Field early on the afternoon of Monday, January 27. When he had arrived at Shungnak he found his passenger for Fairbanks had been picked up by Bill Graham, Northern Air Transport, Incorporated, pilot, and flown to Kotzebue. With a strong tailwind, Dorbandt had flown the course from Livengood to Fairbanks in eighteen minutes, at 199.80 miles per hour. His average rate from Bettles was 198.30. It was fortunate he was not flying the opposite direction in the strong winds. Graham came in the same day in the Stinson Junior, NC 475H, No. 1, from Nome, with two passengers: A.V. Cordovado of Deering, and W.H. Suksdorf of Nome. He soon returned to Nome.

With Alfred Lomen appointed as manager of relief operations on the Alaska side, and Joe Crosson in charge for The Aviation Corporation (AVCO) on the Siberian side, and with the husky Fairchild 71s on the scene in Nome, it was hoped the search for the missing airmen could move swiftly forward. Continuing storm on the Siberian coast and the darkness of midwinter pinned Crosson to the vicinity of the *Nanuk*. It was possible to fly when the weather was clear in the winter twilight of the day hours. But for some time there were no such favorable conditions; gales and snow were the norm. On January 1, 1930 (Siberian Time), Crosson had taken the open-cockpit Waco 10, NC 780E, aloft for twenty minutes on a test flight. The pilot did not get up again for over two weeks.

Harold Gillam's Stearman, NC 5415, damaged in a forced landing at the *Nanuk* on December 31, 1929, was being successfully repaired with help from the Russian steamer *Stavropol's* engineers. The vessel was still frozen in not far from North Cape. They were able to repair the landing gear without using Jim Hutchison, his welder or gas tanks, coming with

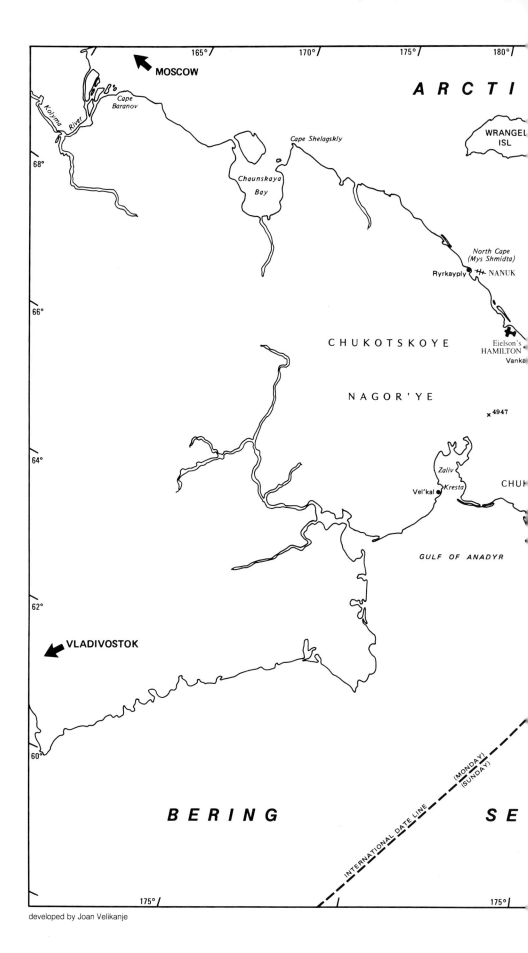

developed by Joan Velikanje

938

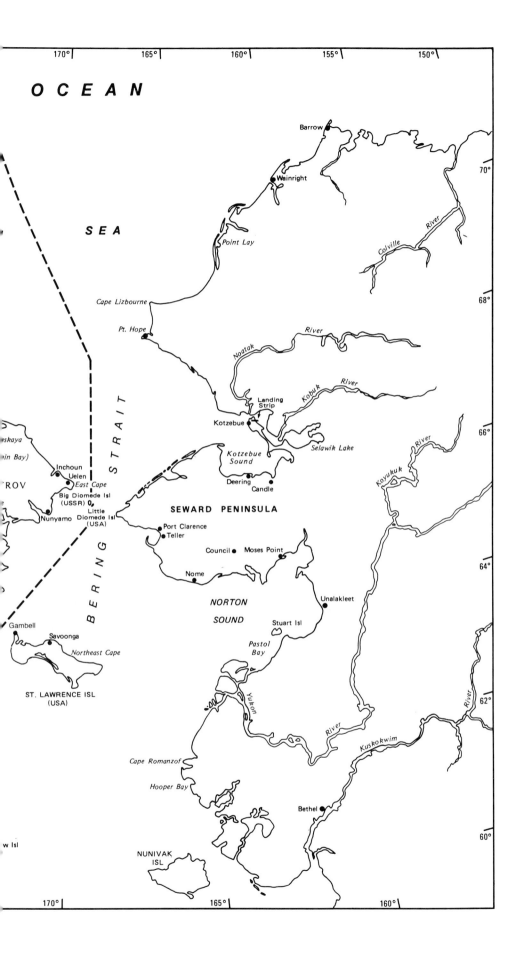

The three-masted schooner, **Nanuk,** *with a fortune in furs aboard, frozen fast in the ice for the winter near North Cape, Siberia. Planes of Alaskan Airways, Incorporated were able to move some of the furs to market, but it cost the lives of Carl Ben Eielson and Earl Borland.*

the Fairchilds. The Stearman was ready on January 20, and everyone on the cape watched, as the young pilot went aloft, winging the ship about the sky, once more free of the bonds of earth. The test was successful; even the skis and landing gear held up. Gillam was again ready to join Joe Crosson in his search.

A Russian-born United States citizen, and supercargo of the *Nanuk,* Tzaret Berdieff, had returned with the ship's dog team from a week's search, with reports that Eielson's plane had been seen over one reindeer camp and heard over another, about twenty-five miles west of the first camp to the south from North Cape, along the foothills. January 18 was the date upon which the first rays of sunshine would dissipate the almost total darkness then enveloping the

Crewmen aboard the **Stavropol**. *The man on the right is Doctor U.U. Kreszanev, who cared for the remains of the lost airmen. He was a member of the scientific party aboard the* **Stavropol**.

arctic regions. Crosson got away on January 17, 1930, on a flight to the deer camps back of the coast. He flew for two hours and fifteen minutes that day, making three landings without result. On his return he took Marion Swenson aloft for a view of the rising sun, still hidden beyond the curve of the earth from those on the surface. The girl was thrilled; it was her first sight of the source of light since the middle of November.

With permanent repairs to the wing tip of Reed's Fairchild 71, CF-AJK (NC 154H) completed on January 18, the two planes were now ready to move on to Teller to join the search. Piloted by Ed Young and Pat Reid, with mechanics Hughes and Macauley, they were off the Nome field at 9:45 A.M. Tuesday, January 21, 1930, landing at Teller at 10:30 A.M. They were held here for some days by continuing bad weather.

Following the various reports was extremely difficult; a number of times and dates were involved. Nome time was one hour less than Fairbanks time, with Siberian time one hour less than Nome. In addition, there was the International Date Line. Generally following the one hundred eightieth Meridian of Longitude, it zigzags between land masses to pass between Little Diomede and Big Diomede in Bering Strait, before turning northwest off the coast of Siberia. Pilots flying between Teller and the Siberian coast crossed this line, in effect flying into tomorrow. It was one day later at the *Nanuk* than it was at Teller, and one hour earlier. When it was ten o'clock on Tuesday in Nome or Teller, it was nine o'clock on Wednesday at the *Nanuk*.

Snow and wind held Crosson at the *Nanuk* from January 21 (Siberian date) but, with the

Canadian pilot T.M. "Pat" Reid with his Fairchild 71, CF-AJK, in frosty cold weather. The Canadian registration on the plane was officially transferred to American registration NC 154H in January of 1930 but not re-lettered on the plane until its return to Fairbanks.

first welcome rays of the sun shining over North Cape, January 26 dawned a fine, clear day. Crosson and Gillam were warming up their engines early, taking off the snow-covered ice at 9:30 A.M. to fly to Serdtse-Kamen, checking rumors that Eielson and Borland were heard flying east on that fateful day. Bundled in their open cockpits, the two pilots flew on down the coast for almost an hour; Gillam flew one or two miles inland, with Crosson paralleling his track some three or four miles farther in. Crosson sighted a glint of the sun's reflection and a peculiar shadow on the sameness of the snowy surface, and swung the Waco 10 over in that direction. It was a shadow cast by the low sun from the uptilted wing of the lost Hamilton, sticking up from the snow. Seeing his fellow pilot circling, Harold Gillam turned and came over, to see the completely-wrecked Hamilton buried in the snow drifts. Gillam, reporting the incident in March 1930, stated: "Joe was flying about six miles inshore and I about two. After one hour, I saw Joe start down in a spiral. Flying over, I found that Joe had recognized the left wing of the Hamilton and was looking for a place to land. We landed about 500 yards from the wreck".

Picking a smooth area on the snow-covered surface, Crosson landed, with Gillam close behind. They were on the tundra some ten miles in from the coast about ninety miles southeast of the *Nanuk*, in an area previously covered by the planes, and where the dog teams had passed. Had it not been for the shadow from the newly-rising sun, the snow-covered wreckage of the Hamilton, NC 10002, might have been again passed by.

Standing near the battered remains of the plane, the two airmen stared glumly at the wreckage. It was obvious to them that Eielson and Borland had been instantly killed, although there were no visible remains of the two men. The plane, headed southeast, had struck a slight knoll on a small island, in what appeared to them to be a marshy lagoon, striking at full speed while in a right bank. The right wing and landing gear were demolished, while the left wing canted up at about a forty-five degree angle, and was intact. The motor had torn away just forward of the cabin bulkhead, to be cast one hundred feet ahead of the rest of the plane; the tail and rear portion of the fuselage of the all-metal Hamilton had broken off just aft of the baggage compartment. The cargo of food and case gas was intact; the case of eggs only slightly

After landing at the wreck of the Eielson-Borland Hamilton and finding no signs of life about, Joe Crosson stands near the wing, his parka on the snow in front, before taking off and returning to the Nanuk to report "The search is over; we found the plane!"

Harold Gillam and Joe Crosson, flying about two miles apart, found the Hamilton wreck on January 26, 1930 (Siberian Date). Gillam stands before the wreck, Joe's parka on the snow before him.

damaged. When Crosson reached for the cabin door, it opened freely, a slab of bacon falling out onto the snow. Later on, when the motor was dug out, the aluminum alloy propeller was discovered to be wrapped about the 525 horsepower Hornet, showing that considerable power was being applied at time of impact; the throttle was also found bent over ahead of the full open position, substantiating the fact. The altimeter indicated 1000 feet of altitude, while the point of impact was about fifty feet above sea level. This may have been a factor in the accident. The clock was stopped at 3:30 P.M. The Hamilton had departed Teller at 10:45 A.M. November 9, 1929.

Crosson and Gillam dug about the wrecked plane for an hour but had no liking for the task. Taking a piece of the corrugated aluminum, Joe tied it in his front cockpit, along with the case of frozen eggs and some bacon from the Hamilton. The two airmen took off on their return flight to North Cape. Joe landed the Waco 10 near the ship, with Gillam following a minute later. It was just after noon—12:20 P.M.—and the pilots had been in the air an hour and forty minutes. Crosson quietly reported: "The search is over; we found the plane." His logbook sums up this important flight in a like manner: "Started Cape Serdtse. After about an hour out sighted Eielson Hamilton, landed, returned North Cape."

Radio operator Bob Gleason took off his skis and cranked up the *Nanuk*'s radio, notifying the operator at Teller and, by relayed messages to Barrow and other stations, of the finding of the lost plane. While the sad news was a shock to everyone, it took the pressure off

Pat Reid reached the **Nanuk** *at North Cape on January 28, 1930, in CF-AJK. While a more complete rebuild of the damaged wing tip had been done in Nome, the repair job still shows where the fabric had been coated with clear dope but not painted in color.*

The Fairchild 71s arrive at North Cape, Siberia in 1930, landing near the **Nanuk.**

944

North Cape, Siberia. Fairchild 71 circles the Nanuk *before landing on skis near the three-masted sailing schooner.*

Alaskan Eskimo men at Teller, Alaska in early 1930.

Alaskan Airways, Incorporated, Waco 10, NC 780E, parked on the ice near the Nanuk. *Flown by Joe Crosson.*

Early 1930. American planes at the* Nanuk *off North Cape, Siberia.

all those involved with the search efforts. They still had a task to perform in seeing the bodies of the two airmen were returned, as well as seeing that the contract with the Swenson Fur & Trading Company was fulfilled, including replacing the aviation gas borrowed from the Russians at North Cape.

The day following the finding of the Hamilton wreck, both Crosson and Gillam returned to the site. Taking Demetri Miroshnishenko, the Gostorg (Russian trading organization) representative at North Cape, and a sailor from the *Nanuk* named Williams, as well as two of the natives, the Waco and the Stearman were away early in the day, flying in good weather. Supercargo Tzaret Berdieff and Jimmy Crooks, from the *Nanuk*, had already left at 3:00 A.M. for the scene by dogsled. The pilots stayed for two hours while the men dug out the engine and some other areas, finding nothing of importance. The snow was very deep and hard-packed by the wind, making the work difficult. The two airmen returned to the *Nanuk*, Joe Crosson landing on the way in when they spotted the two dog teams. He gave them more explicit directions to aid them in reaching the Hamilton before taking off again in the Waco.

A few miles from the wreck scene was the cabin of a Russian trapper by the name of Petushkov. He had worked his traplines all winter, up and down the coast, without seeing the remains of the Hamilton, most likely because of the continuing darkness of winter. The diggers used the cabin occasionally to dry their fur clothing. On January 28, Crosson and Gillam went again to the wreck site, carrying more food and supplies for the searchers. They returned to the *Nanuk* the same day, after two hours in the air on the round trip.

946

◀ *The two Russian Junkers
F-13 planes were having a tough
time in Siberia. Brought to Pro-
vidence Bay by the icebreaker*
Litke *on November 23, 1929,
they arrived at North Cape on
January 29, 1930. This is a
Russian photo.*

▼ *Russian Junkers
F-13 buried in snow on
the Siberian coast.
Another Russian photo.*

Fog banks in the Ber-
ing Strait which had
practically, closed
off the air route to
Asia for the past two
and one-half months,
lifted to permit pas-
sage of the two Fair-
child 71s to the Si-
berian side. Ed
Young and Pat Reid,
with their two me-
chanics, Hughes and Macauley, were off Teller, Alaska at 9:30 A.M. Monday, January 27, 1930,
reaching the *Nanuk* five hours later (Tuesday, January 28 in Siberia). From the schooner, Bob
Gleason and Marion Swenson, along with others, watched Crosson and Gillam come in from the
wreck. Demetri Miroshnishenko also climbed out of the Waco, NC 780E, as he had work to do at
North Cape. Shortly before 2:00 P.M. the observers saw the Fairchild 71s headed for the ship. Ed
Young was first to land, at 2:15 P.M., in NC 153H, with Reid following shortly in NC 154H
(there hadn't been time to paint out CF-AJK when the plane was returned from Canadian
registration to its original United States registration number).

In Fairbanks, the Travel Air 4000, C-193, previously brought in from Anchorage by
Nieminen for overhaul, was ready to fly. Needing a break-in period on the motor, Frank
Dorbandt, resident Alaskan Airways pilot, took the open-cockpit plane to Wiseman to pick up
Captain E.G. Rowden, of the Detroit Gold Mining Company. Leaving in the morning from
Weeks Field on Wednesday, January 29, 1930, the pilot was back with his passenger before
3:00 P.M. The next day Rowden boarded the train for the south.

Ralph Wien, flying the Service Airlines Swallow biplane, C 2774, was away the morning
of Thursday, January 30, carrying Mrs. Georgia Hagen and Miss Josie Sheehan for McGrath;

The rugged headland of North Cape outlines Russian and American planes near the Nanuk.

A Russian Photo in the Crosson Collection

he stopped at Berry's Landing on the return flight to Fairbanks, to pick up nine live mink.

In Siberia, gasoline for the planes was a big problem. They must repay that which was borrowed from the Russians, as well as supply their own planes on the contract haul of furs and personnel from Siberia. There were eighteen cases in the Hamilton cargo; only a very few cans had sprung open in the crash. Ed Young had hauled with the Fairchild between Nome and Teller prior to departure from the Grantley Harbor community; Northern Air Transport, Incorporated, continued to haul some additional gas and oil out to Teller from Nome. Ed Young and Pat Reid brought as much case gas as they could in the Fairchilds on their first trip across the strait to the *Nanuk*, with more to be flown over later. The freight capabilities of the Fairchild 71s would be a great asset to the work ahead.

The day following Reid's arrival at the ship on January 28, Crosson flew the Canadian pilot to the scene of the wreck, again using the Waco. Gillam also went in the Stearman. The planes took in two Russians, food, sleeping bags and other supplies. The round trip was made in one hour and forty-five minutes of flying time. Storm and blowing snow had prevented searchers at the scene from working the four previous days.

The two Russian planes, Junkers F-13s, brought by the icebreaker *Litke* to Providence Bay on November 23, 1929, appeared at North Cape without any advance notice of their arrival on the afternoon of Thursday, January 29, 1930 (Siberian date). In Vladivostok, they had received a telegram from Moscow on November 7, authorizing them to aid in the Eielson search. The two planes arrived in Petropavlovsk, Kamchatka the twenty-second of November. On January 26 they left for East Cape. Undoubtedly they had experienced a difficult time at Providence Bay; they had been put ashore there from the *Litke* soon after its arrival. The first of the all-metal planes to arrive landed on its skis at the southwest curve of the bay at North Cape, coming in downwind with considerable speed. Landing about halfway from the shore, the pilot steered for the stern of the schooner on drifted, hard-packed snow. The first part of the run went all right, for the Junkers had not reached the drifts. When the pilot entered the rough area he was in for a surprise. Bounding a dozen feet in the air with each drift, the metal plane, clanking and bobbing over the surface with considerable speed, finally came to a halt when the right landing gear strut collapsed, with the wing tip tilting onto the surface of the snow.

The second pilot to land made a turn over the *Nanuk* and swung in to the wind. He zoomed past the bow of the ship, spectators running for cover as he passed over the four parked planes while only a dozen feet in the air. Not knowing his intentions, the watchers were apprehensive, but he put on power and climbed out, circling to come in a second time. Landing rather hot, about three-quarters of the way down the marked landing strip, the plane overran it into rough snowdrifts, to come to a halt just before the sandspit, without any damage to the plane. Parking near the other planes, the heavily-clad airmen climbed out of the open cockpit. A spare landing gear strut was brought from the cabin of the second F-13 to land, and the damaged Junkers was soon as good as ever. The two planes carried Soviet registration numbers CCCP-177 and CCCP-182; the first one flown by Mavriki T. Slepnyov and flight mechanic Fabio Fahrig, while the second one was flown by pilot Victor L. Galishev. The planes brought in a Soviet G.P.U. policeman with a police dog, who immediately went to the *Stavropol*. The two planes carried no fuel other than that in their tanks. The F-13s had closed cabins but the pilot and flight mechanic sat in an open cockpit up front behind a windscreen. The planes were powered with the 310 horsepower Junkers L-5 motor, a liquid-cooled inline powerplant of German design, as was the airplane itself. There were now six planes with airmen of three nations at the *Nanuk*.

North Cape, Siberia, in 1930. Representatives of three nations drawn together in an International search for the lost airmen. Left to Right: Mavriki T. Slepnyov, Russian pilot; Victor L. Galishev, Russian pilot; Joe Crosson, Alaskan pilot; Marion Swenson of the Nanuk; a Russian flight mechanic; another Russian flight mechanic; Ed Young, Alaskan pilot; Bill Hughes, Canadian mechanic; Harold Gillam, Alaskan pilot. The Waco Model 10, NC 780E, flown by Crosson, is in the background.

Courtesy of Bob Gleason

Crosson took Slepnyov to the search scene in the Waco 10 on January 30, 1930. The pilot used the Alaskan technique in landing on the short strip, coming in just over the stall speed for a short landing, to the Russian pilot's amazement and interest. Their pilots had always been taught to land with excess speed to maintain good control, which resulted in a much longer landing run.

The Soviet airman had been placed in charge by his government of the efforts to recover the bodies of the American airmen. The wreckage was scattered over several hundred square feet. While Borland's flying helmet, gloves and mittens had been found, no sign of the bodies was evident yet. He had probably removed these articles of clothing in the warm cabin of the plane before the accident. Harold Gillam had, on January 29, flown over two additional men from the Russian steamer, *Stavropol*, to assist in the digging going on, bringing two others back who were insufficiently clothed for the work. A storm kept the airmen on the

February, 1930. The tail section of the wrecked Hamilton lies on the snow at the wreck site, its registration number visible on the upper part of the plane's rudder. Many of the parts were widely scattered by the force of the impact.

George King Collection; Courtesy of Sheldon Museum

◄ *In late January, Russian workers at the wreck site were living under the most primitive conditions in tents such as the one dug into the snowbank to the left of these men.*

Crosson Collection

▼ *February, 1930. Russian searchers, under the direction of Mavriki Slepnyov, dug trenches through the hard-packed snow in every direction, search-ing for the bodies of the missing American airmen. Most of the men were from the Russian steamer* Stavropol, *also frozen in near North Cape for the winter.*

Crosson Collection

ground for the next few days. It also made the work of the searchers more difficult, for the trenches which the men were digging to a depth of five or six feet through the hard-packed snow and radiating from the wreck were filled by the wind and had to be redug when the storm passed. Living in tents at the scene made it hard enough. It stormed on February 2, 3, and 4.

Slepnyov received telegraphed instructions to fly to the wreck site and take charge of rescue operations. He wired back that he did not believe it possible to land the Junkers at the scene without cracking up. The reply ordered him to land regardless of conditions. On February 5, 1930, Slepnyov, taking three additional men with him, flew the Junkers CCCP-177 to the wreck site, Joe Crosson and Ed Young going ahead to pick the best landing place for the larger plane. The Russian pilot landed successfully and parked the large plane alongside the search area. Using snow blocks, the men built a shelter under the right wing to serve as a center for the activities going on at the scene. Joe Crosson returned to North Cape in the Waco 10 that same day, bringing Mavriki Slepnyov back; his plane remained at the site. Five dog teams had also left North Cape for the wreck site on the same day with supplies and five extra men. The Russian pilot, using Olaf Swenson as interpreter, questioned each pilot for his feelings about the cause of the accident for his official report to his government. The consensus was that the pilot had flown into rising ground in the near-darkness in bad visibility, and without adequate flight instruments to guide him in the white environment, while searching for a landing spot. Concluding the meeting with his condolences, the Russian airmen invited the other pilots to the *Stavropol* for dinner. They were easily encouraged into staying aboard for the night after the dinner; they had walked three miles over rough ice from the beach to the steamer. It was storming again.

Coming from Fairbanks in the Stinson Standard, NC 877, Frank Dorbandt arrived in Nome with a small quantity of local mail and a full freight shipment about 4:00 P.M. on Saturday, February 1, 1930. Canadian pilot Gifford Swartman accompanied him; he expected to fly a plane back to Fairbanks soon. Dorbandt had a rough time getting through, flying in fog

On February 5, 1930, Slepnyov flew his Junkers F-13 to the site of the Hamilton wreck and the men built a snow shelter under the right wing for the searchers who were living under the most primitive conditions in the bitter cold.

The Russian steamer **Stavropol** *in her very exposed wintering spot off North Cape, Siberia in 1930.*

much of the time from Nulato on. He landed at Golovin, getting a good weather report for the Nome area, and came on in. Swartman had previously left Nome in the red cabin Swallow, C 3542, on Thursday, January 30, for Fairbanks; taking mail, his mechanic, Mews, and mining engineer C.E. Alexander. Mews left Fairbanks for his home in Canada on Sunday, February 9, 1930.

Bill Graham, pilot for Northern Air Transport, Incorporated, had also arrived in Nome on January 30, coming from Fairbanks and Nulato in the Stinson Junior, NC 475H, stopping enroute at Unalakleet to bring in a native boy for hospital treatment for his frozen hands. Graham had left Fairbanks late on Wednesday afternoon. The pilot was off Nome again at 9:00 A.M. of Friday, January 31, for Fairbanks, carrying about 150 pounds of mail and two passengers: O.D. Cochran, Nome attorney, and J.H. Johnson, mining man from Deering. The Northern Air Transport pilot landed the Stinson Junior on Weeks Field that same afternoon.

Ole Eielson, the sixty-six year-old father of Ben Eielson, was on his way to Fairbanks. Boarding a train at Fargo, North Dakota, on January 29, he was met by Earl Borland's father, W.E. Borland, in Seattle. He sailed from there on the *Northwestern* on February 5, 1930. Traveling with Ole Eielson on the ship was the new general manager for Alaskan Airways, Incorporated, appointed by The Aviation Corporation under a three-year contract to succeed Ben Eielson when confirmation of the crash had been received in New York. Arthur W. Johnson had previously taught high school in Nome for two or three years, and was a friend of the Lomens. Graduating from the University of Minnesota, he had been trained as a pilot at Kelly Field in World War I, then serving as a flight instructor there and attaining the rank of captain. Since the Armistice he had been in business with his brothers at Jamestown, North Dakota, operating a firm selling tractors and other farm machinery. Johnson had kept up his aviation skills with annual training in the Air Corps Reserve. He had also managed the Jamestown flying field since its establishment four years before. Now he was operating a far-flung air service in Alaska, but doing little flying himself. Johnson's wife and three children were with him.

Frank Dorbandt left Nome in the Alaskan Airways, Incorporated, Stinson SB-1, NC 877, on Wednesday, February 5, 1930, for Fairbanks. He was carrying Grant R. Jackson, president of the Miners & Merchants Bank, and Mrs. Jackson, who were on their way Outside. It was Mrs. Jackson's first trip to Fairbanks; she had previously journeyed to the States by ship out of Nome. Stopping overnight in Ruby, the pilot arrived at Weeks Field on the afternoon of the following day. Dorbandt had been unable to wire ahead from Ruby; the operator was away at a newly-reported gold strike near there. Dorbandt had tried to leave Nome a day earlier but was forced to turn back at Bluff by fog and bad weather.

On the Siberian side, stormy weather had prevailed, with the searchers only able to work two days in the first week of February. Harold Gillam went to the wreck and back on Saturday, February 8 (Siberian date), bringing in Williams and a native named Ogpu. He reported no bodies found as yet. At 10:00 A.M. February 8, 1930, Pat Reid had taken off with mechanic Bill Hughes in Fairchild CF-AJK for Teller. He was carrying as passengers Olaf Swenson and his daughter Marion, as well as Captain Milovzorov of the *Stavropol* who was recovering from a serious bout with pneumonia. He would require better medical treatment than he could get aboard his ship. The Canadian pilot landed at Teller in a little over four hours of flying time. With stormy weather reported, they did not go on to Nome that day.

Joe Crosson left North Cape on Tuesday, February 10, 1930 (Siberian date and time) to fly to the wreck site, but was forced to turn back with engine trouble when ten minutes out. He tried again the following day but was forced back to the *Nanuk* by fog, a second time, flying for fifteen minutes in the Waco 10, NC 780E. The following day, Thursday, February 12, he went to the wreck and back, returning with two Chukchis, taking the usual hour and forty-five minutes of flying time. Crosson reported the searchers hard at work: they had found Eielson's helmet and part of the cockpit. They had cleared all the snow from around engine and cockpit, and were digging in the direction toward where the plane first struck the ground.

The Soviet Junkers, CCCP-182, departed North Cape for Saint Lawrence Bay on Saturday morning, February 8, with two sick men, a third man, and a small child aboard. All had been aboard the *Stavropol* when frozen in. One of the purposes of the two Junkers flying to North Cape originally, had been to remove the excess people from the Soviet vessel.

Pat Reid arrived in Nome with his three passengers at 11:45 A.M. Monday, February 10 (Nome date and time). Olaf Swenson was soon closeted with Alfred Lomen regarding the fast removal of his valuable fur cargo and extra personnel. Inquiries to the Department of State and Territorial officials about the use of the Russian planes to help in the removal resulted in approval of their coming in to Nome, should they be needed. Swenson and his daughter awaited a plane for Fairbanks, and accompanied Milovzorov to a Seattle clinic. From there, Swenson moved to obtain another trading vessel to replace the *Elisif*. (He was to secure the *Karise* later in the year). Pat Reid was awaiting better weather before leaving with a load of case gas for North Cape.

In Fairbanks, word was received that Joe Dunn, son of Mr. and Mrs. John Dunn of the

*February 7, 1930. Seattle schoolgirl Marion Swenson with her father, Olaf Swenson, at Teller, Alaska after flying in from the **Nanuk** with Pat Reid in CF-AJK. Swenson, ship-owner and former trader, once had the only Russian trading permit on the Siberian coast held by an American. He also spoke Russian and Chukchi. Now, in the winter of 1929-30, Swenson had a contract with the Soviets to bring in supplies and take out furs to the American markets.*

Lomen Brothers Photo

city, had made his first solo flight in Tacoma. Joe had gone Outside during the winter, to take up aviation. Another Fairbanks boy, Bill Lavery, was Outside taking flying lessons at the Curtiss-Wright Flying School in San Mateo, California. Not quite sixteen years old, he was one of the youngest flight students in the country. Within five years he would have his own air service in Fairbanks. In Boston, Father George H. Woodley of Anchorage was now finishing a flying course in a two-place Fleet training plane he had purchased from Colonial Flying Service. He was planning on having a Transport Pilot License on his return. An avid hunter in Alaska, his interest in aviation had been triggered by his brother, Arthur G. Woodley, a cadet at the army flying school at Kelly Field.

The fourth Fairchild 71 sent to Alaska had now arrived in Fairbanks, after it was transferred from the *Alameda* at Seward, Alaska, to the railway cars of the Alaska Railroad on Saturday, February 1, 1930; Major Deckard had boarded the same ship on his way Outside. The plane had been in passenger service for Universal Air Lines between Fort Worth and Tulsa, Oklahoma. It was dismantled at Tulsa and shipped by rail to Seattle. Taken up by Alaskan Airways, Incorporated, pilot Frank Dorbandt on the morning of Wednesday, February 12, the Fairchild 71, NC 9153, was put through a series of flight tests: the first by the pilot alone, and the third with passengers. The nine-cylinder Pratt & Whitney Wasp motor of 420 horsepower ran smoothly. Dorbandt took Mrs. H.E. Seneff and her niece, Miss Laura Gibson, to their home in Tanana. Deckard, a Captain in the U.S. Army Air Corps Reserve, was production manager for Fairchild Airplane Manufacturing Corporation, a subsidiary of The Aviation Corporation. This business connection with Fairchild had enabled AVCO to rapidly assemble the equipment and men for the Eielson-Borland Relief Expedition.

Pat Reid and mechanic Bill Hughes departed Nome for Serdtse-Kamen the morning of Wednesday, February 12, 1930. Carrying eighteen cases of gas in Fairchild 71, CF-AJK, they

February 10, 1930. T.M. "Pat" Reid, Canadian pilot, with Marion Swenson, the seventeen-year-old daughter of Olaf Swenson, owner of the Nanuk; *photographed upon their arrival in Nome, coming from the* Nanuk *and Teller, Alaska.*

Lomen Brothers Photo

▼ *February 10, 1930. T.M. "Pat" Reid, Canadian pilot, arrives in Nome with passengers from the* Nanuk. *Left to right: Bill Hughes, Canadian mechanic, Olaf Swenson, "Pat" Reid, Marion Swenson (daughter), and Captain Paul Milovzorov of the* Stavropol.

Lomen Bros. photo

Crosson Collection

Pat Reid's *Fairchild 71, CF-AJK, at the Hamilton wreck site. In the crash landing, the right ski stand had broken off and a ski was jammed through the cabin window (second from rear). Neither the pilot nor his cargo of gasoline suffered damage.*

The Nanuk's dog team, salvaged from the Elisif, was a great help to the ship's crew in getting about the coast from North Cape after the schooner froze in for the winter. The Chukchi sled had a bentwood hoop about half way down its length for the driver to maintain control. The team is hauling chunks of old sea ice, leached free of salt, to the Nanuk for drinking water.

Bob Gleason Photo

956

planned to unload at the cape and return to Teller the same day. Other planes would shuttle the gas to North Cape. Weather forced the plane back to Teller. Reid went out again from Teller on February 16, making it as far as Serdtse-Kamen, where he spent the night in a native yarang (skin hut) at Tapien. Caching his load, he returned to Teller the following day.

On February 21, 1930, he was off in CF-AJK by himself, with eighteen cases of gasoline in the cabin, two five-gallon cans to the case. Flying in good weather, except for a small area of fog near Kolyuchin Bay, which he flew over, he came to Amguema River and the site of the Hamilton wreck. North Cape and the *Nanuk* were farther up the coast. He could see Slepnyov's Junkers F-13 and Gillam's Stearman C-2B. Noticing a plume of smoke and thinking it a signal to land, the pilot put the heavily-loaded Fairchild down close to the Russian plane. It was a catastrophe. Sliding along the rough surface, the Fairchild struck a ridge of hard-packed snow, breaking a ski. The plane skidded around sideways, wiping off the landing gear and ending up with a ski jammed through one of the right cabin windows. Reid, in the plane alone, was uninjured except for his feelings. The side load on the plane, in wheeling about, had prevented the load from coming forward on to him. The cans of gas in the boxes were intact. However, considerable damage to the aircraft had resulted, the aluminum alloy propeller blades curled and the gear torn off. Once again Jim Hutchison and his welding tanks must travel north.

Canadian pilot Gifford Swartman, arriving in Nome as a passenger with Frank Dorbandt on February 1, got away from the Seward Peninsula city for Fairbanks in the New

Northern Air Transport, Incorporated, Stinson No. 1 the first plane acquired by Vic Ross rests on skis at Fairbanks, Alaska.

▲ *February, 1930. The wing of the Hamilton Metalplane, NC 10002, has been laid down from its uptilted position by the searchers at the wreck site in Siberia.*

▶ *February, 1930. Russians cluster about their stove under the wing of the Junkers F-13 in the snow shelter. All the gasoline in the wing tanks of the plane was eventually used as fuel for the stove. A handy teakettle in the foreground provided hot water for the ever-present stimulant.*

Standard biplane, NC 9190, on Saturday, February 15, 1930. He carried a cargo of mail and one passenger, Ben Mozee, the general reindeer superintendent for Alaska. The pilot arrived at Weeks Field on Sunday, February 16, returning to his home in Canada. Swartman departed Seward on the *Yukon* on Sunday, March 2, 1930.

Northern Air Transport, Incorporated, pilot Bill Graham arrived in Nome from Fairbanks on Friday, February 14. Flying the Stinson Junior, NC 475H, four-place monoplane, he brought in three sacks of first class mail and a quantity of miscellaneous freight. Graham had also picked up a native at Unalakleet; he was suffering the effects of freezing and was brought to Nome for medical attention.

Since there was no radio communication between the searchers at the wreck site and the *Nanuk*, Joe Crosson tried to send a plane between the two points every few days when the weather permitted. Harold Gillam, in the Stearman, NC 5415, took Berdieff, who had become an excellent dogmusher, and the two went down on Monday, February 17, 1930 (Siberian date and time) to learn that the body of Earl Borland had been found four days before their arrival, about one hundred feet from the plane's cabin and, in deep snow, only four feet from the engine of the wrecked Hamilton. The body was placed in a tent and the nineteen men at the site under Commander Mavriki Slepnyov continued their search for the body of Ben Eielson. Harold Gillam returned to *Nanuk* where an announcement was sent out on the radio of the discovery on Thursday, February 13, 1930.

Gillam took the Stearman, fueled with low-proof gasoline as they were now entirely out of aviation gas at the *Nanuk*, to the scene of the wreck again on Thursday, February 20, to learn that Ben Eielson's body had been found on February 18, on a slight knoll about 200 feet from the wrecked cabin of the plane and about 150 feet from that of Borland. A Soviet worker, T. Yacobsen had made the discovery. Both airmen had died instantly on impact. Only a light blanket of snow covered the remains of the pilot while those of the flight mechanic were found under five feet of hard-packed drifts. The wind had apparently blown away much of the snow that had covered Eielson.

The bodies of the two airmen were to be brought to the *Nanuk* in the Russian Junkers, CCCP-177, flown by Mavriki Slepnyov. Used as a shelter, all of the fuel in the plane's tanks had been consumed for heating and cooking. Since the Russians had left enough aviation fuel at North Cape to make the return trip to Saint Lawrence Bay, the pilot requested Gillam to fly him to the cape in the Stearman and return him to the Junkers the following day with enough fuel to fly the plane in to the *Nanuk*. This Gillam did, but was unsuccessful in trying to start the Fairchild 71 in the bitter cold weather on the following day, February 21, and gave it up. The men had wanted to use the Fairchild, which still had aviation fuel in its tanks, feeling it would perform better in the forty-below-zero weather than the Stearman, which was filled with low-proof gas.

The following day, February 22, they were successful in starting the engine but it cut out so badly they shut it down. Harold Gillam took Slepnyov and his gasoline to the Hamilton wreck site that same day, February 22 (Siberian date), and they were there when Pat Reid, seeing the smoke from a wood fire, mistook it for a signal to land and the Fairchild 71, CF-AJK, came sliding in to camp with its cargo of case gas. The landing gear was washed out and the propeller curled but Reid was unhurt. Gillam brought Reid in to the *Nanuk*, along with the news of the finding of the body of Ben Eielson. Eielson's father, waiting in Fairbanks, was given the sad news.

Knocking down the snow shelter under the wing of the Junkers, the Russian plane was moved to a level spot and the two bodies carefully placed in the cabin. Commander Slepnyov took off for North Cape on Saturday, February 22, 1930, to park again near the *Nanuk*. The bodies were removed to Demetri Miroshnishenko's sheet metal-covered building (the only building at North Cape) where they were thawed and placed in the traditional reclining position, and allowed to freeze again. A watch composed of one Russian and one American was posted at the building which was decorated with American and Russian flags.

In Fairbanks, Alaskan Airways pilot Frank Dorbandt was flying the new Fairchild 71, NC 9153. He took Deputy U.S. Marshal Fred B. Parker to Fort Yukon on Monday, February 17, to bring in a native who was judged insane. The man would be sent to Morningside Sanitarium in Portland, Oregon; the Territory had no such facilities. Dorbandt left the following day, Tuesday, with Jack Miller and Bill McConn, for Ruby. The two stampeders were headed for the Beaver strike. The pilot went on from Ruby to Nome. Dorbandt arrived there at

▶ *February, 1930. Russian plane commander Mavriki Slepnyov stands in a relaxed mood before a red and cream-painted Fairchild 71.*

▼ *February, 1930. The only building at North Cape, Siberia was this wood and sheet metal office and home of Demetri Miroshnishenko, Russian trade representative stationed here. Left to Right: Joe Crosson, Herb Larison, and Demetri.*

960

3:15 P.M. on the same day as his departure from Fairbanks, after four and a half hours in the air.

Dorbandt was off the next day on his return flight in the Fairchild, taking Olaf Swenson and his daughter Marion, Captain P.G. Milovzorov, and George Ashenfelter of Golovin. The plane arrived in Fairbanks late Wednesday afternoon; the three passengers departed on the southbound train the next morning, Thursday, February 20, 1930. The ailing Ashenfelter entered St. Josephs Hospital for treatment immediately upon his arrival at Weeks Field. Dorbandt was away for the Kuskokwim and Iditarod districts on Thursday, carrying Mrs. Frank Guskey and infant for McGrath, and Tony Lindstrom for Flat. He returned to Fairbanks from McGrath at 12:30 P.M. on Friday, February 21, making the flight in three hours and fifty minutes. It was twenty degrees above zero at 3000 feet during the flight, a virtual heat wave for that time of year. Anton Lindstrom of Flat had come in to attend a special hearing of the district court wherein he was given his final citizenship papers under a special congressional act relative to World War veterans.

Ralph Wien, flying the Service Airlines Swallow biplane, C 2774, came in from

February 26, 1930. The bodies of Eielson and Borland, their faces exposed, lie on Chukchi sleds covered with American flags sewn by Siberian women from red and blue muslin and white canvas. The two sleds were drawn between two loosely-formed lines composed of Americans and Canadians on one side, and Russians and natives on the other during the transfer ceremony.

Courtesy of Donald E. Young

February 26, 1930. With the three masts of the Nanuk looming above the Fairchild 71, NC 153H, flown by Ed Young, the bodies of Eielson and Borland are placed in the plane after the ceremony of transfer from the Russians to the Americans. Captain Weeding of the Nanuk stands closest to the camera.

Crosson Collection

Courtesy of Bob Gleason

Mavriki Slepnyov, bundled in heavy arctic clothing, at the brief transfer ceremony in which the bodies of Ben Eielson and Earl Borland were placed in the care of the Americans at North Cape. Left to Right: a Russian flight mechanic, Slepnyov, a Russian from the Stavropol and the First Mate of the Russian vessel who took over when Captain Milovzorov left.

962

Tolovana on Tuesday, February 18, where, on Monday, he had been forced to land by strong winds and rough air while returning to Fairbanks from Ruby. He made a flight on Wednesday with a passenger, getting within seven miles of his destination at Livengood, when he was forced to return by wind and turbulence. Ralph completed the flight on Friday, February 21, 1930.

February, 1930 at the **Nanuk.** *Left to Right: Pat Reid, Ed Young, Harold Gillam and Joe Crosson.*

The ceremony of the transfer of the bodies of the two Americans from the Russians took place at North Cape on Wednesday morning, February 26, 1930. Doctor U.U. Kreszanev, from the *Stavropol*, had cared for the remains of the two airmen. Taken from the hut, the bodies were placed on two Siberian dog sleds, wrapped in American flags sewn by the Siberian women out of red and blue muslin and white ship's canvas. With the men's faces exposed, the two sleds were drawn between two loosely-formed lines composed of Americans and Canadians on one side, and Russians and natives on the other.

Commander Slepnyov, representing the Soviet government, formally turned over the bodies to the custody of the American pilots for transportation to Alaska. G.E. "Ed" Young received the bodies on behalf of the Americans and they were then placed in his Fairchild 71, NC 153H, and the windows covered. The plane waited for the first break in the weather to take off for Teller and Nome.

Frank Dorbandt, Alaskan Airways pilot based in Fairbanks, departed there the morning of Saturday, February 22, 1930, in the new Fairchild 71, NC 9153, landing at Ruby with four passengers: Sylvester Howell, Ed Odegaard, Felix Boucher and Bill Kelly, who were traveling to the new gold strike at Poorman, where there was no landing field. He went on to Nome, arriving there on Sunday, February 23, 1930. An hour later he was off for Ruby again, carrying Dan Aldrich, prospector from Nome enroute to the strike; and bringing John Glass from Ruby to Fairbanks, landing Weeks Field on Monday.

Ralph Wien, who had been flying the Swallow biplane for Service Airlines while owners Percy Hubbard and Art Hines ran their Service Garage, was served with a restraining order on Monday, February 24, from Judge Cecil H. Clegg's court, to prevent him from engaging in competition in the airplane business with Alaskan Airways, Incorporated. As a shareholder and officer of Wien Alaska Airways, Incorporated, at the time of the sale of the firm to Alaskan Airways, Ralph was affected by a clause in the sales contract preventing the Wiens from competing with Alaskan Airways for a period of three years following the sale—as pilot, mechanic, or in a managerial capacity—although they could work for the larger firm, which they did for a time. The action was appealed, to be heard later in a San Francisco court.

Frank Dorbandt was away from Weeks Field on the forenoon of Tuesday, February 25, 1930, carrying two more stampeders for the strike at Poorman. Albin "Dutch Kid" Martin and John Desorte were dropped at Ruby, and the pilot returned the same day to Fairbanks. Fred Moller, Alaskan Airways mechanic and sometimes aviator, had recently overhauled the motor of his beloved Waco 9, *Anna*. He made a flight to Circle Hot Springs on Monday, February 24, taking Captain C.D. O'Flanagan as a passenger. Freddie returned that same afternoon, reporting about thirty persons at the springs.

H.W. "Harvey" Barnhill, who had left the employ of Alaskan Airways early in 1930, returned to Fairbanks on Monday, March 2, 1930. He began flying the Swallow biplane, C 2774, for Service Airlines. Barnhill had been in California with his wife and baby. Mrs. Barnhill, in poor health, had two operations while Outside. The pilot was out the afternoon of Monday, March 3, testing the Swallow in preparation for a resumption of flying by the company.

T.M. "Pat" Reid and Harold Gillam were already laying plans to salvage Reid's Fairchild 71, CF-AJK, from the wreck site of the Hamilton. Leaving *Nanuk* in the Stearman C-2B, NC 5415, on Wednesday, February 26, 1930 (Siberian time), they arrived at Teller at 4:45 P.M. Tuesday, February 25; they had crossed the International Date Line. Gillam had landed at the wreck site and put in fifty-five gallons of gas from Reid's wrecked plane, landing again at Tapien, on the coast where Reid had earlier established a gas cache. Bucking headwinds, he thought it advisable to add another ten gallons here.

Joe Crosson and Ed Young were the only two remaining Alaskan Airways pilots at the trading schooner. Bad weather kept them on the ground for several more days. Reid and Gillam arrived in Nome about 12:30 P.M. March 3, 1930, in the Stearman. Taking Alfred J. Lomen, Gillam returned to Teller to meet the expected arrival of the Fairchild 71, NC 153H, and the Russian Junkers, CCCP-177. The other Junkers, CCCP-182, flown by Galishev, departed *Nanuk* at 9:30 A.M. March 2, for Saint Lawrence Bay, carrying two women, a baby and a six-year-old child, and a man. All of the *Stavropol*'s passengers, except for six men and one woman, had now left by plane or dog team. The rest soon departed, leaving a crew of thirty-five on the steamer.

Off Nome at 2:30 P.M., the Stearman arrived in Teller at 3:30 P.M. The Fairchild 71, bearing the bodies of Carl Ben Eielson and Earl Borland arrived at Teller later in the day. Ed Young, the pilot, was accompanied by his flight mechanic, Sam Macauley, and Joe Crosson,

964

who had left his Waco 10, NC 780E, at the *Nanuk*; there was no fuel to bring it in. The funeral plane was away from North Cape at 10:45 A.M., arriving at Teller at 3:50 P.M. (Nome time). The Junkers, flown by Mavriki Slepnyov and Fabio Fahrig, was close behind; they left the ship at 11:05 A.M. and reached Teller at 4:30 P.M. They carried only baggage. The Russian and United States governments had given permission for the plane to accompany the bodies to Fairbanks as a token of respect on the part of the Russians. Stormy weather held the planes at Teller for some days. Reid's flight mechanic, Bill Hughes, had been in Teller ever since the day Pat Reid replaced him with extra fuel and flew across to crash land at the Hamilton wreck site on February 21, 1930. He was now reunited with his fellow airmen.

The first plane away from Teller was Harold Gillam, in the Stearman C-2B. Taking flight mechanic Bill Hughes and Nome businessman Alfred Lomen in the front cockpit, the pilot was off the ice at 1:00 P.M. Wednesday, March 5, 1930. The young flier, after a stormy flight, landed in Nome at 1:45 P.M. Weather kept the other two planes in Teller until the following day.

The pilots were warming up their planes at 7:00 A.M. Ed Young, with the funeral plane, NC 153H, with flight mechanic Macauley and pilot Joe Crosson, took off at 8:10 A.M., closely followed by Slepnyov and Fahrig in CCCP-177. Upon arrival over Nome, at 9:00 A.M., they continued to circle, observing the field which now had many windrows of hard-packed snow from the recent blow. While the crowd at the airfield watched, the planes finally turned for Ruby, convinced a landing would not be a good idea. The two planes arrived at Ruby at 3:00 P.M. Harold Gillam with Bill Hughes, who had come in to Nome the previous day, took off in the Stearman from the local field at 8:45 A.M., to beat the other two planes to Ruby, landing at 2:45 P.M. The planes had experienced strong headwinds while in the air for five hours. The pilots wired ahead from Teller to have the telephone wires that crossed the river at Ruby removed, so the pilots could land on the ice on the Yukon River. The aircraft were heavily loaded. The three planes remained there until the next day; the weather was unfavorable from Tanana to Fairbanks.

March 7, 1930. The Fairchild 71 bearing the bodies of the two airmen taxis in at Weeks Field with the Junkers F-13 following.

March 7, 1930. Slepnyov and Fahrig arrive in the Junkers F-13, CCCP-177, following the Fairchild 71, NC 153H, bearing the bodies of Ben Eielson and Earl Borland.

Russian Junkers F-13 before Alaskan Airways hangar on Weeks Field in Fairbanks in March of 1930. Slepnyov and Fahrig had accompanied the Eielson-Borland funeral plane from Siberia as a gesture of respect.

The Fairchild 71, the Junkers F-13 and the Stearman C-2B were away from Ruby on Friday, March 7, 1930; the funeral plane off at 8:15 A.M. with the two escort planes following in the above order at five-minute intervals. A large crowd waited in silence at Weeks Field for over an hour before the planes, flying in formation, appeared in the sky, the Fairchild 71, bearing the bodies of the two airmen, in the center. The Fairchild forged ahead on nearing the city, the others falling in behind in single file while they circled once before landing about 1:20 P.M. The Fairchild 71, NC 153H, taxied to the hangar and was drawn inside and the doors closed before the bodies were removed, still wrapped in the American flags. In the Fairchild, piloted by Ed Young, were Joe Crosson and Sam Macauley; the Stearman carried pilot Harold Gillam, Pat Reid and mechanic Bill Hughes. Commander Slepnyov, with mechanic Fabio Fahrig crewed the Junkers, as before. Neither of the Russians spoke much English but there were local residents on hand who could converse with them.

H.W. "Harvey" Barnhill was soon at work in his new position as pilot for Service Airlines. He hopped off shortly before noon on Thursday, March 6, 1930, for Tanana, where

966

*Alaskan Airways, Incorporated, Stearman C-2B, NC
5415, at Weeks Field. Harold Gillam flew this plane in
Siberia at the* **Nanuk.** *It was returned to Fairbanks in
the spring of 1930.*

two passengers awaited passage to Fairbanks. He had flown to Hot Springs the previous day
from Weeks Field with passenger C.L. Christensen. Frank Dorbandt, flying through thick
weather from Fish Lake to Fairbanks on Thursday, March 6, had arrived in Fairbanks from
Holy Cross, bringing Father Concanon, coming from there to enter the local hospital. Frank
had taken the Fairchild 71, NC 9153.

Bill Graham left Nome at 8:30 A.M. Thursday, March 6, in the four-place Stinson
Junior SM-2AA, No. 1, NC 475H, for Fairbanks. Taking Vic Ross, stockholder William A.
Oliver, and passenger Boris Magids of Deering, the pilot landed at Weeks Field in Fairbanks
the afternoon of Saturday, March 8, 1930. A new six-place Stinson Detroiter SM-1F, NC
404M, powered with a Wright J6-9 motor of 300 horsepower, plane No. 2 of the company, had
been shipped up on the *Yukon*. Arriving on the last train from Seward, it was awaiting the
airmen in Fairbanks. Soon after their arrival, the plane was transported to Weeks Field for
assembly. Frank Dorbandt took Boris Magids from Fairbanks to Seward to catch the *Northwestern* for the States. (see Anchorage—1930, Chapter 57). Vic Ross, flying the company
Stinson, NC 475H, left Fairbanks to return to Nome. W.R. "Bill" Graham remained for
several days, leaving with the new plane on the morning of Thursday, March 13, 1930, taking
about 200 pounds of mail and some express. He would pick up passengers on the way. Bill
Oliver was to take a later plane. Graham had made two test flights in the Stinson the previous
afternoon.

Memorial services for Carl Ben Eielson and Earl Borland were held in Fairbanks at the

Moose Auditorium the afternoon of Wednesday, March 12, conducted by the American Legion Post No. 11 and Pioneers of Alaska, Igloo No. 4. Pall bearers for Eielson were pilots Crosson, Young, Gillam, Slepnyov, Nieminen and Reid; and for Borland they were mechanics Basham, Hutchison, Moore, Fahrig, Larison and Higgins. Following the services, the caskets were escorted to Legion Hall, where they were to remain until the train taking them Outside departed in the morning. On Wednesday afternoon following the services, the American, Canadian and Russian aviators of the Eielson-Borland Relief Expedition were presented to the students and faculty of the Alaska College, with President Bunnell introducing the speakers. Doctor Frank de la Vergne, speaking for the United States, welcomed the visitors and offered heartfelt thanks for their help in the search. Commander Slepnyov, speaking in Russian with Mr. Nickoloff as interpreter, responded for the Russians. Fabio Fahrig, Slepnyov's mechanic, spoke of the airplane service carried on by his government along 3,000 miles of the Lena River in Siberia, where three planes make the round trips twice each week. Speaking in German, Fahrig's remarks were interpreted by Otto William Geist, of the college. Pat Reid spoke for the Canadians.

Doctor de la Vergne told of visiting the home of a friend in St. Petersburg, Russia, over twenty-five years ago, where he met a small boy, the son of his friend. Both were pleasantly surprised to find out that Fabio Fahrig was that same small boy.

Alaskan Airways, Incorporated lineup on Weeks Field in Fairbanks in the spring of 1930 after the return of the Eielson-Borland Relief Expedition. Left to Right: Fairchild 71, NC 9153; Fairchild 71, NC 153H; Stinson Standard SB-1, NC 877; Cabin Swallow, C 3542; New Standard D-25, NC 9190; New Standard D-25, NC 174H; Stearman C-2B, NC 5415; and Freddie Moller's Waco 9, C 2776, **Anna.**

Anchorage Historical & Fine Arts Museum

Weeks Field, March 1930.
Left to Right: Fabio Fahrig,
USSR; Mavriki Slepnyov,
USSR; Ole Eielson, Ben's
father; Joe Crosson, USA;
Pat Reid, Canada.

George King Collection

Crosson Collection

▲ *Mavriki Slepnyov, Russian pilot, was also photographed by*
CANN STUDIO in March, 1930.

▼ *Fabio Fahrig, Russian flight mechanic.*
Taken by CANN STUDIO in Fairbanks as a
gesture of good will to the visiting Russians
in March of 1930.

Crosson Collection

The funeral train, a double-header, left Fairbanks as four planes, flown by Crosson, Gillam, Young and Nieminen, circled overhead, and followed the train down the valley for a distance. Ole Eielson waved farewell from the rear platform of the last car. Also aboard the private car were Mrs. Borland and her two children, William and Earl, Jr. Her mother, Mrs. Adolph Wehner, went as far as Healy. Slepnyov, Fahrig, Reid, Macauley and Hughes were aboard the train: the Canadians on their way home and the Russian airmen to travel as far as Seattle, returning later to Fairbanks for their plane.

There were further services planned along the way, and the body of Earl Borland was interred at Acacia Memorial Park in Seattle, where his parents lived. The group met the airman's widow and her two children for the first time. Eielson's casket left Seattle by a Great Northern Railway train, riding in a private Pullman car, *Fort Union*, which was Amundsen's when he traveled east after his 1926 polar flight that ended at Teller. Accompanying the casket east were the airman's father, Ole Eielson, the North Dakota Honor Guard, the Canadian airmen and Olaf Swenson. Eielson's body was to be interred at Hatton, North Dakota, to be buried beside his mother. A brief stop was made at Wenatchee, Washington, where Eielson's sister, Adeline, was a school teacher.

There was no vacation for the pilots who had returned from Siberia. Three of the Alaskan Airways planes departed Weeks Field on the morning of Monday, March 17, 1930, for different sections of the country. Joe Crosson, flying the Fairchild 71, NC 153H, was away

March 1930. Alaskan Airways fleet on skis, lined up at Weeks Field following the Eielson-Borland search. The pair on the right are Mavriki Slepnyov's Junkers F-13, CCCP-177, which accompanied the funeral plane to Fairbanks from North Cape, Siberia, and the open-cockpit Swallow, C 1713. In the left rank are the Fairchild 71, NC 9153; Fairchild 71, NC 153H; Stinson Standard SB-1, NC 877, No. 7; cabin Swallow, C 3542, No. 4; New Standard D-25, NC 9190, No. 2; New Standard D-25, NC 174H; Stearman C-2B, NC 5415, No. 9; and Freddie Moller's Waco Model 9, OXX-6, C 2776, **Anna.**

for the Iditarod with Mrs. Anna Morris as a passenger, landing at McGrath before continuing on to Iditarod, and returning to McGrath the same day. He was five hours in the air. The pilot returned to Fairbanks the following day, making it nonstop from McGrath in two hours and forty minutes. Coming in at 10:30 A.M., he put in another four hours and fifteen minutes of flying in the Stinson Standard, NC 877, with a trip to Fort Yukon, Beaver and return to Fairbanks with a capacity load of freight.

Ed Young also went out on Monday, March 17, to Livengood, flying in the Stinson Standard, NC 877. He was returning Mr. and Mrs. T.H. Hudson to their home in the mining community. The following day, flying the Fairchild 71, NC 9153, he was away for Ruby and Tanana, taking Dean Ernest N. Patty of the Alaska College to the first stop. Dean Patty, interested in mining, planned to investigate a mineral proposition there. Young's second passenger, Deputy Marshal Fred B. Parker, was flying to Tanana to take into custody two prisoners and an insane person. The pilot returned to Fairbanks with the party the same day.

Matt Nieminen, accompanied by his wife, also left Fairbanks in the New Standard, NC 174H, on March 17. He was not so successful. Upon reaching Windy Pass, on the way to Anchorage, the pilot ran into a windstorm that had been blowing for two days. Unable to see the ground in the drifting snow and smoking hills, he returned to Fairbanks. At 11:00 A.M. the next morning, Matt and his wife left again, arriving at Anchorage without difficulty, in the afternoon, to resume his commercial flying there for Alaskan Airways, Incorporated.

Harvey Barnhill, flying the Service Airlines open-cockpit Swallow biplane, C 2774, also took off on Monday, March 17, 1930, for Fort Yukon and Circle Hot Springs. Taking a load of freight for Fort Yukon, he picked up two passengers at the springs on his return flight. Percy Hubbard, partner in Service Airlines and a student pilot, had made his first solo flight on Saturday, March 15, in the Swallow. He was thrilled with the experience.

March 12, 1930. American, Russian and Canadian aviators are presented to the faculty and students of the Alaska College. Peter Nickoloff, Fairbanks businessman, on the far right, served as interpreter for Slepnyov while Otto Geist, far left in the back, interpreted for Fabio Fahrig, who spoke in German.

Crosson Collection

Crosson Collection

Spring of 1930. New Standard D-25 on skis at Weeks Field. Alaskan Airways had installed a contoured reserve gas tank on the upper wing to extend the range of the five-place aircraft.

Harold Gillam, further seasoned by his flying experience on the Eielson-Borland search, was not long in going ahead with his plans for an air service in the Copper River valley. Leaving Weeks Field at noon on Tuesday, March 18, 1930, in the open-cockpit Swallow biplane. *Arctic Prospector*, which he had purchased from Arctic Prospecting & Development Company in September 1928, and in which he had made his first cross-country flight on February 2, 1929, the young pilot headed for Chitina, where he planned to base the new company. The lakes in the area could serve as a landing field for the balance of the winter. In the spring the community intended to develop an airstrip on a flat table-land some distance out

Pilot Harold Gillam of Alaskan Airways Stearman C-2B, NC 5415, No. 9. Gillam left Fairbanks on March 18, 1930 to start his own air service in the Copper River valley.

of town. River bars were to be used for landing spots in the outlying districts. It was a mountainous territory, known to have difficult weather. Gillam's aerial interest in this region had been developed during his stay at McCarthy in October, 1929, when he flew there with Bennett to pick up an injured miner at Chisana. He had also worked in earlier years, along with Cecil Higgins, as a heavy equipment operator at McCarthy. Gillam's Swallow was powered by an air-cooled 110 horsepower Warner Scarab radial engine. The pilot had ordered a second Swallow biplane, powered with a 225 horsepower Wright Whirlwind. The new plane awaited his arrival in Valdez, where it was assembled.

Young Bill Lavery, a student at the Curtiss-Wright Flying School at San Mateo, California, soloed on Wednesday, March 19, 1930, after seven hours and twenty minutes of dual instruction. Britton Rey, head of transportation for the flying school and a first cousin of the embryo pilot, announced his achievement in a wire to the elder Lavery in Fairbanks. The student had just turned sixteen on March 16.

Alaskan Airways pilot Ed Young was away for Fort Yukon and Circle in the Fairchild 71, NC 153H, on the morning of Friday, March 21. Taking Harry Horton, Fort Yukon merchant and trader, who was returning home from a vacation trip Outside, in addition to Richard Heyser and Miss Elsie Rasmussen for Circle, the pilot was off Weeks Field. Heyser was making repairs to the U.S. Signal Corps equipment. Joe Crosson left the same morning in the Stinson SB-1, NC877, on a flight to Livengood, taking Tolovana mining operator R. Hudson. On his return he brought in C.H. Laboyteaux, U.S. Commissioner at Livengood, with a total flying time of one hour and thirty minutes enroute.

Service Airlines pilot Harvey Barnhill took the company's Swallow, C 2774, off Weeks Field shortly before 1:00 A.M. Monday, March 24, 1930, carrying Mrs. Georgia Hagen and Miss Josie Sheehan for Flat. The air service had four students enrolled in a flying course at Fairbanks: Emil Jacobsen, L.P. Christensen, Frank Panting and Frank Mapleton. The owners were also piling up solo hours, for Percy Hubbard, on Saturday and Sunday, made round-trip flights to Nenana, landing on each trip after circling for some time. He now had five hours and twenty minutes solo time. His partner, Art Hines, soloed for the first time on Sunday, March 23, 1930. Barnhill brought in Virginia Howard from Ophir on his return to Fairbanks. He doubled as a flight instructor.

Northern Air Transport, Incorporated, pilot W.R. "Bill" Graham came in from the Seward Peninsula on Saturday, March 23, bringing Mrs. Marie Frantzen and her young son, John, from Nome to Fairbanks; they were enroute to the States. Bill was away again the morning of Monday, March 24, taking William A. Oliver, a business associate in the company, who had been in Fairbanks since the assembly of the new plane. Bill Graham was flying the six-place Stinson Detroiter SM-1F, NC 404M, No. 2. Vic Ross was flying the other company Stinson out of Nome. Graham also carried Jack H. Johnson, Nome district miner, who was returning from a trip to the States.

Spring of 1930. Left to Right: Chief Pilot Joe E. Crosson of Alaskan Airways, Incorporated; Pilot Ed Young; Chief Mechanic Bill Basham; James K. Crowdy, engineer of New York-Alaska (gold dredging) Company; and Charles A. Thompson, operations manager for Alaskan Airways.

Crosson Collection

With the backlog of flying out of Fairbanks taken care of, Alaskan Airways, Incorporated, turned its attention to finishing up at North Cape, Siberia. The damaged Fairchild 71,

CF-AJK (NC 154H), was still at the Hamilton wreck site, and was to be repaired and flown out. The Waco 10, NC 780E, was at the *Nanuk*, needing only fuel in order to fly it back to Alaska. Gasoline, borrowed from the Russians must be replaced, flying it from Teller along with other supplies for the *Nanuk*; and finally, the remainder of the cargo of furs at North Cape had to be brought into Fairbanks for shipment Outside. Joe Crosson and Ed Young, flying the two Fairchild 71s, NC 9153 and NC 153H, respectively, were away from Fairbanks on the morning of Sunday, March 23, 1930. General Manager Arthur W. Johnson accompanied the airmen; he went as far as Nome to make an inspection of the Seward Peninsula area served by his company. Two Alaskan Airways mechanics, Herbert Larison and Cecil Higgins, also went; Larison was flying to North Cape to accomplish repairs on the damaged Fairchild, as well as any other mechanician duties that should arise. Repair parts, tools and materials to do the salvage job were aboard the planes.

Landing at Ruby to refuel, Crosson and Young continued on, running into heavy fog about seventy-five miles from Nome, and were eventually forced to land at Fish River on Golovin Bay, where the party spent the night in a prospector's cabin. They had been in the air for six hours. A passenger, Dan Aldrich, had also boarded at Ruby. Taking off the following day, Monday, the two Fairchilds arrived at Nome after an hour's flight. In addition to the company material, capacity loads of mail and express from Fairbanks were brought to Nome.

Crosson and Young began the task of hauling gasoline on Tuesday, March 25, making two round trips from Nome to Teller with maximum loads, then going out to Teller with a third load to spend the night there after three hours and forty-five minutes in the air. The following day they came in to Nome and returned to Teller with a fourth load.

The Russian Junkers F-13, CCCP-182, was at Saint Lawrence Bay without fuel. Both Crosson and Young flew over to Siberia from Teller on Thursday, March 27, 1930, taking 380 gallons of case gas to Lavrentiya village on Saint Lawrence Bay, thus relieving the shortage. They returned to Teller the same day, flying three hours and twenty-five minutes on the round trip. Wind and fog held them on the ground at the Grantley Harbor community the following days.

Back in Fairbanks, Harvey Barnhill was again flying for Alaskan Airways, Incorporated, in the absence of Crosson and Young. He came in to Fairbanks on Wednesday, March 26, in the New Standard biplane, NC 9190, No. 2, after making a trip to Ruby, carrying Prosecuting Attorney E.B. Collins and Doctor J.A. Sutherland. The pilot went to Livengood and return the next day, taking a passenger, Moore, and a capacity load of freight for the mining community at Brooks. That afternoon he made a flight to Circle Hot Springs for Service Airlines in their J-5 Swallow, C 2774, taking John Locke out and returning with Captain O'Flanagan.

Frank Dorbandt, flying the Alaskan Airways Stinson Standard, NC 877, was away for McGrath and Bethel, flying a court party composed of Judge Cecil H. Clegg and Court Stenographer Louise Parcher to the lower Kuskokwim community for a session of court called for 2:00 P.M. Friday, March 28, 1930. After the court business in McGrath was taken care of, Dorbandt prepared to take the party on to Bethel on Friday, but suffered a mishap. Nosing up in a snowbank on takeoff, a bent propeller and other minor damages delayed the Stinson Standard's flight. Alaskan Airways manager Charles L. Thompson was endeavoring to locate Harvey Barnhill, who had left for the Iditarod on the same Friday morning. He planned on returning to Fairbanks the same afternoon by way of Ruby, with Dean Ernest N. Patty as a passenger. Barnhill was back as expected. Taking repair parts for Dorbandt's Stinson Standard, as well as mechanician Jim Hutchison, the pilot was away from Weeks Field in the New

Standard D-25, NC 9190, at 5:30 A.M. Sunday, March 30. Forced back to Fairbanks by storms in the Minchumina area, Barnhill went out a second time at 3:30 P.M. the same day, making it to McGrath that night. Leaving the mechanic and spare parts with Dorbandt, he took off early in the morning for Bethel with the court party, arriving there at 10:00 A.M. Leaving them to conduct the court business, Barnhill left an hour and a half later for Iditarod, where he overnighted. The pilot came through to Fairbanks on Wednesday, April 2, 1930, bringing a load of furs. Dorbandt and Jim Hutchison came in from McGrath that same afternoon with the repaired Stinson Standard, NC 877.

Stinson Standard SB-1, NC 877, powered with the Wright Whirlwind J5-CA of 220 horsepower. Acquired by Alaskan Airways when they purchased Bennett-Rodebaugh Company, the plane performed well for the firm.

Fred Moller was running a box ad in the local newspaper, advertising his newly-formed Fairbanks Air Express "passengers and freight transported to any part of Alaska" He was off in his Waco 9, C 2776, *Anna*, for the lower Yukon, at 11:30 A.M. Thursday, March 27, carrying Mrs. Jean Grey to Ruby. He returned from there, with a passenger, late in the afternoon of Friday, April 4, to crack his plane up on landing at Weeks Field. Neither party was injured but the plane was badly wrecked; his new endeavor was out of business.

Harvey Barnhill, flying Service Airlines Swallow, C 2774, was away for Ruby on Thursday, April 3, carrying Irving Reed, deputy mineral surveyor for the Territory, and George Albert Felch, a recent arrival from Spokane, who was interested in experiencing a gold stampede. Reed intended to inspect the Poorman placer field. The pilot also made several other flights in the region before returning.

Crosson and Young, holding at Teller since March 28 for a break in the weather, were again ready to cross the Bering Strait to reach the *Nanuk*. On March 31, Crosson tried to reach Nome, but a snowstorm forced him back to Teller. On April 1, starting late in the day because of fog, the pilot was able to reach the Seward Peninsula city after a thirty-minute flight. He returned the following day, Wednesday, April 2, finding it very windy at Teller. It was clear over the Bering Strait and he had hopes for the morrow.

April 3, 1930. Left to Right: Pilot Ed Young, mechanic Herb Larison and pilot Joe Crosson depart for the **Nanuk** *with a load of Red Crown Aviation Gasoline and repair parts for CF-AJK, including two sacked propeller blades to replace the bent ones. Cecil Higgins, mechanic, also came in the two Fairchild 71s as far as Teller.*

Crosson Collection

The airmen were ready on Thursday, April 3, taking off at noon in the two Fairchilds, accompanied by their mechanic, Herb Larison. Along with a load of case gas, they had provisions for the *Nanuk* and the repair materials for the damaged Fairchild. Encountering strong headwinds and fair visibility, Crosson made it through to land near the *Nanuk* after six hours and fifteen minutes of flying time. Ed Young was not so fortunate; he landed fifty miles short of the schooner to put gasoline from his load into the tanks before coming on to the *Nanuk*. Six men: Captain Weeding, Chief Engineer Bill Bissner, Radio Operator and Assistant Engineer Bob Gleason, Supercargo Tzaret Berdieff (who would later join the *Karise* at Cape Vankarem) and two seamen were remaining on the ship, awaiting the day she would break free of the ice.

Leaving Herb Larison and the repair materials, which included one ski stand for the damaged Fairchild, CF-AJK (NC-154H), at the *Nanuk*, the men loaded the two Fairchilds to capacity with the sacked bales of furs. The mechanic would go by dog team, if necessary, to the site of the wrecked Fairchild to do the repair work on it.

Soon after the *Nanuk* was frozen in, Olaf Swenson had set his daughter Marion, and Bob Gleason, to work making smaller sacks to ship the furs in the airplanes. Swenson cut the first patterns from tough cotton drill cloth he had brought along. The sacks were about eighteen

977

April, 1930. Fair-child 71, NC 9153, being unloaded at the Nanuk. Left to Right: Herb Larison, Joe Crosson, Demetri Miroshnishenko, Ed Young.

inches wide each way and thirty-six inches long. *Nanuk* had a hand-crank, table model sewing machine (which had also been used to make drill-cloth snow parkas) and this was set on the table in the saloon, with Marion and Bob on the settee: he turned the crank while she sewed. It gave the two young people an opportunity to become better acquainted. The furs had been received at the Russian outposts in very large sacks and the smaller rectangular sacks were needed to compress the furs tightly, getting the maximum amount into the plane's cabin. The furs were mostly arctic fox.

The following morning, Friday, April 4, 1930 (Nome date and time), Crosson in NC 9153 and Young in NC 153H as before, departed the ship to fly from North Cape to Teller to Nome in good weather and a strong tailwind, making the flight in five hours and forty-five minutes. They had landed on the Siberian coast at Gapin to gas up from a cache. The fur shipment, valued at $100,000, was processed at the Nome post office, to continue in the planes to Fairbanks the next day at mail rates. At the time of the Hamilton wreck in November of 1929, the bottom had fallen out of the fur market. In the ensuing four months it had once again risen to normal levels, and the market was good. Soon the rest of the fur was brought in, except for a small quantity of less valuable furs that remained on the ship.

The two Fairchilds arrived in Fairbanks on Saturday, April 5, after a five hour and forty-five minute flight from Nome, bringing General Manager Arthur Johnson with them. Cecil Higgins had remained in Nome for the present. The pilots reported greatly improved conditions on the route to Siberia, with long sun-filled hours for flying, in contrast to the grueling conditions experienced during the previous winter. They crossed the Bering Strait at 8000 feet, with many open leads and fast-moving ice below, and found good landing spots beyond that. At Saint Lawrence Bay there was a model village. The large log buildings were of recent construction and geometrically spaced in a new townsite that had been laid out by engineers.

Chukchis grouped about the dog sled with two repaired skis and one ski stand with its rubber shock absorber, prior to leaving the Nanuk *with mechanic Herb Larison for the Fairchild 71, CF-AJK at the Hamilton wreck site.*

Chukchi dog teams arrive at the Nanuk *with large bags of furs, mostly fox, to be placed in the vessel's hold.*

Northern Air Transport pilot Bill Graham had arrived in Fairbanks from Nome on Thursday, April 3, 1930, after dropping four passengers at Nenana to catch the southbound train. He was away in the Stinson Detroiter, NC 404M, the morning of Friday, April 4, taking

Grant Jackson to his home. Jackson had been to the States on business. The four hour and thirty-seven minute flight to Nome in continuous sunshine was a record. Frank Dorbandt was away the same day at 9:00 A.M. for Sleetmute, following receipt of a wire requesting a plane; a critically ill man must be rushed to the hospital at Fairbanks. Frank left the employ of Alaskan Airways, Incorporated, soon after, passing through Anchorage by train on Friday, April 11, 1930. He returned to the port city later in the year, as a pilot and shareholder in Pacific International Airways. (see Anchorage—1930, Chapter 57).

Commander Mavriki T. Slepnyov and his mechanic, Fabio B. Fahrig, returned to Fairbanks by train the night of Sunday, April 6, 1930. They had accompanied the bodies of Eielson and Borland to Seattle, and now the two airmen were returning to ship their Junkers F-13, CCCP-177, back to Russia by boat and rail, rather than fly it across to Siberia. While the plane was being dismantled by Alaskan Airways mechanics, to be placed on two flatcars of the Alaska Railroad, the community did its best to show its appreciation for the assistance given by the Russian airmen during the search. While in Fairbanks, the two had been unable to spend any of their money for food, lodging or clothing. They had been completely outfitted with new suits and accessories by the merchants, after arriving in the arctic clothing they had worn in Siberia. At a dinner hosted by the two Russian airmen at the Model Cafe on the evening of Wednesday, April 9, G.E. "Ed" Young and his wife, Mamie, Harvey Barnhill, Joe Crosson and Lillian Osborne were present, along with civic and educational leaders in the community. Peter Nickoloff and Otto Geist again served as interpreters.

Commander Slepnyov reported that all the passengers on the *Stavropol* had been safely transported out; the many sled dogs used in the rescue work returned to Saint Lawrence Bay. V.L. Galishev and his mechanic were reported to have arrived at the *Nanuk* at 2:15 P.M. Sunday, April 6 (Fairbanks time) to complete the final details of transportation for the Russians. The *Stavropol* was now down to its regular crew of thirty-five men.

The Russian pilot expressed his appreciation of the hospitality extended by the people of Fairbanks during the visit and presented a personal medal, which he had himself received previously from his government, to the three American pilots with whom he had worked: Crosson, Young and Gillam. The medal was mounted on a silver plaque for the presentation, inscribed with the words, "To brothers and friends from Slepnev (sic)." At the top, the names of the three American pilots were engraved. Doctor Frank de la Vergne, Mayor of Fairbanks, read two letters of appreciation which were being sent to M.I. Kalinan, President of the Central Committee in Moscow, and S.S. Kamenev, President of the Arctic Commission, also in Moscow, expressing the people of Fairbanks' appreciation for the cooperation and assistance rendered in the task of recovering and bringing back from Siberia the bodies of the American airmen. The following day the two Russian airmen again visited the Alaska College for lunch, attending an assembly at 1:00 P.M. to say goodbye to the students and staff. Slepnyov and Fahrig left Fairbanks that same day, Thursday, April 10, aboard the train that carried their plane to Seward. Placed aboard the steamer *Yukon*, for Seattle, it would be shipped from there to Japan, cross Japan by rail, and be put aboard a Russian steamer at Matsura.

Joe Crosson and Ed Young had gone right to work on their return from Nome on April 5, 1930. Joe was off for the lower Kuskokwim in Fairchild 71, NC 153H, on Monday, April 7, flying from Fairbanks to Iditarod and Bethel in six hours and thirty minutes of air time. He was back the next day, flying from Bethel to McGrath and landing at Weeks Field after a four hour and fifty minute flight.

On Friday, April 11, 1930, the day following the departure of the Russian airmen,

Alaskan Airways, Incorporated, Fairchild 71 on skis.

Crosson was again off, in the Fairchild 71, NC 9153, going to Iditarod, McGrath and back to Weeks Field. He carried as passengers Mr. and Mrs. William Duffy and Robert Thorsen. Ed Young had made a trip to Circle Hot Springs the previous day, bringing in Mr. and Mrs. McGowan. Harvey Barnhill, Service Airlines pilot, took off the morning of Friday, April 10, in the Swallow, C 2774, with a load of freight for Takotna and McGrath. He intended to make a flight to Cripple while there, with two passengers, and also go to Iditarod with two passengers, before returning to Fairbanks.

Service Airlines, operating a flying school in addition to its charter business, announced the acquisition of a second plane on Friday, April 11. The orange and green Swallow TP, C 688H, with a liquid-cooled OX-5 motor of ninety horsepower, had recently been received from the factory. Purchased by Percy Hubbard and Art Hines, it was being set up at the field. Two of the students of the flying school, Frank Mapleton and Frank Panting, soloed on the evening of Thursday, April 10, 1930, in the red and blue Swallow, C 2774.

The federal government was taking more interest in Alaska flying, announcing on April 11 that Wylie Wright, aeronautical inspector attached to the Department of Commerce had been assigned to duty in Alaska. The inspector had been in charge of the Portland, Oregon district, and would soon be coming north to make inspections in the Territory. He would examine pilots and mechanics and inspect flying equipment.

Joe Crosson, flying Fairchild 71, NC 9153, left for Anchorage at 10:30 A.M. Saturday, April 12, taking general manager Arthur W. Johnson. The pilot picked up his mother, Mrs. E. Crosson, as well as two new Alaskan Airways pilots, Grant N. Elliott and Sanis E. Robbins, who had arrived from the south on the steamer *Yukon*. The company had need of the pilots, for the dredgemen and mining men were coming north and there was more to do on the Siberian side. Manager Johnson wanted to inspect the Anchorage base of the company. Crosson returned to Weeks Field that same evening. (see Anchorage—1930, Chapter 57).

Warning sign posted at Weeks Field to warn of hazards associated with aviation. The public was not yet accustomed to many things related to flying.

Donald E. Young Collection

Don Adler had passed his student pilot physical examination with Doctor Frank de la Vergne and joined the ranks of the student pilots at the Service Airlines flying school, taking his first lesson with instructor Harvey Barnhill on the afternoon of Sunday, April 13, 1930, in the Swallow, C 2774. Barnhill had arrived at Weeks Field Saturday evening, bringing Miss Ruth Secor, teacher from Takotna; as well as Clara Reich and Anton Lindstrom of Ophir. Pilots Ed Young and Joe Crosson, delayed on Friday by bad weather reports from the lower Yukon, got away for Nome and Candle at 9:30 A.M. Sunday, April 13, 1930. Carrying J.K. Crowdy and other members of the New York-Alaska Company (NYAC) who planned on gold dredging at Candle that season, Young arrived Nome five hours later. He landed twenty minutes after Bill Graham, who had left Fairbanks on Saturday, but was forced down enroute by poor weather conditions.

Joe Crosson, flying the Fairchild 71, NC 9153, made the round trip from Weeks Field to Candle in the same day, landing at home base at 8:30 P.M. after nine hours and twenty minutes in the air. Pilots Grant Elliott and S.E. Robbins had been out test flying the New Standard D-25 biplane, NC 9190, on Sunday afternoon, getting familiar with the ship. Navy-trained Elliott had been flying for Alaska-Washington Airways out of Seattle, spending

Arthur W. Johnson, General Manager of Alaskan Airways, Incorporated, was a former military pilot but did not fly for Alaskan Airways. Following the death of Ben Eielson, he was sent up by The Aviation Corporation (AVCO) to take over management of the company in Alaska. Photo in April, 1930 with the Fairchild 71, NC 9153.

Crosson Collection

Chief Pilot Joe Essler Crosson of Alaskan Airways, Incorporated, in April of 1930 with the Fairchild 71, NC 9153.

Crosson Collection

the past two months on the Seattle-Wenatchee-Yakima run using Stinson and Lockheed Vega planes on wheels. He had a Transport Pilot License. Robbins, army-trained at March Field, had served as chief pilot and operations manager for T.C. Ryan Flying School in San Diego prior to coming to Alaska. He also had Transport Pilots License, Number 4694, as well as other aviation certificates and ratings.

The two new pilots, flying the New Standard, went to Fort Yukon and Beaver on Tuesday, April 15, 1930, leaving Weeks Field at 1:00 P.M. They were accompanying Joe Crosson, who took the Fairchild 71, NC 9153, loaded with freight. They returned at 6:30 P.M. the same day, having been three hours and thirty minutes in the air. Ed Young had arrived on Weeks Field from Candle at 7:00 P.M. Monday evening.

Harvey Barnhill was out test hopping the new Swallow TP (training plane), C 688H, of Service Airlines on Tuesday morning. The colorful orange and green biplane, to be used for training students, had dual controls, gasoline shutoffs, switches, choke and stabilizer trim controls in both cockpits. A factory-designed safety feature, a pull device running from the

◄ *Sanis E. "Robbie" Robbins arrived in Fairbanks April 12, 1930 to fly for Alaskan Airways, Incorporated. Photo taken the same month with Fairchild 71, NC 9153.*

▲ *Pilot-mechanic Tom Gerard of Alaskan Airways, Incorporated, taken in April of 1930. While Tom often flew for Bennett-Rodebaugh Company in 1929, he flew mostly short flights for Alaskan Airways, later working in the shop. He left Fairbanks in the summer of 1930 to open a garage business in Bellevue, Washington.*

◄ *Grant Elliott arrived in Fairbanks April 12, 1930 to fly for Alaskan Airways, Incorporated. He was soon stationed in Nome for the company. Photo taken in Fairbanks in April, 1930 with the Fairchild 71, NC 9153.*

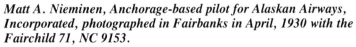

Matt A. Nieminen, Anchorage-based pilot for Alaskan Airways, Incorporated, photographed in Fairbanks in April, 1930 with the Fairchild 71, NC 9153.

George E. "Ed" Young, Fairbanks-based pilot with Alaskan Airways, Incorporated, photographed in April, 1930 with the Fairchild 71, NC 9153.

student cockpit to the instructor's, would allow the instructor to disconnect the student controls immediately should the situation ever occur wherein a student "froze" on the controls. Service Airlines was seriously working toward a Department of Commerce certificated flying school in Fairbanks.

Ed Young, flying a Fairchild 71 with five passengers, accompanied by Grant Elliott in the New Standard D-25, NC 9190, with a capacity load of freight, was away from Weeks Field at 10:00 A.M. Wednesday, April 16, 1930, for Iditarod. They planned to stop at Flat outbound, returning by way of McGrath and Takotna. The passengers for Iditarod were Andrew Thorsen, Richard Thorsen, Ben Dahl, freighter Donna LaChance, and for Takotna, Christian Erickson. Vance McDonald made the return flight from McGrath. The two planes were back with their passenger on Thursday. Young went out that same afternoon with two passengers for Hot Springs. Joe Crosson was also up on Wednesday, flight testing the Alaskan Airways Stinson Standard SB-1, NC 877, for thirty minutes.

Crosson, flying the Fairchild 71, NC 9153, was away in the morning of Thursday, April 17, 1930, for Ruby, to pick up Irving Reed, Territorial mining engineer, and three other

New Standard D-25, NC 9190, No. 2 of Alaskan Airways, Incorporated in flight. The plane was powered with a Wright J-5 Whirlwind motor of 225 horsepower. It is on a flight over snow-covered hills from Fairbanks to Iditarod at 7000 feet.

passengers. Reed, who had spent several days at the site of the recent strike made in the Poorman district, came in to Ruby by dog team to catch the plane. The Alaskan Airways pilot returned to Fairbanks with his passengers the same day, spending a total of five hours and twenty minutes in the air. The company had just been awarded Territorial mail subsidy between Fairbanks and Seward Peninsula and Yukon River points during the spring breakup when surface travel was virtually impossible. Alaskan Airways was the only one submitting a bid. The subsidy involved three mail trips over the route, scheduled for April 16, April 30 and May 14. Rates for passengers over the route would not exceed one dollar per passenger mile, with express shipments to be carried at .002 cents per pound per passenger mile, as approved by the Territorial Board of Road Commissioners.

Joe Crosson made a flight to a lake on Dennison Creek in the Fairchild 71, NC 9153, on Friday, April 18, 1930, along with Ed Young and "Robbie" Robbins in two additional planes. Young, carrying four prospectors into the Fortymile and Tanana headwaters: Abe L. McCord, G.A. Buhmann, Albert Bell and Charles Phillips, left at 9:30 A.M. with the other two pilots hauling their outfit of approximately a ton. Landing on a small lake at the site, after spending three hours in the air, they found the snow so soft they were unable to taxi in it on wheels. A freeze during the night allowed them to get away for Fairbanks the following morning in their empty planes. The return flight on Saturday took two hours and forty minutes of air time.

It was announced by Parks Air College in East St. Louis, Missouri, that Benjamin S. McFarland of Fairbanks had been awarded a Limited Commercial Pilot License following completion of a course which included fifty hours of flight instruction and two hundred hours of theoretical and practical ground work. McFarland signed up for advance work toward an Air Transport Pilot License. Oliver L. Parks, a former marine, was head of the government certificated school for training leading to qualification for all types of aviation certificates.

Alaskan Airways, Incorporated, with the spring breakup coming on, was worried about the deteriorating condition of landing spots on the Siberian side. There was still work to complete on their contract. Joe Crosson, flying the Fairchild, NC 9153, was off for the Seward Peninsula on Monday, April 21, 1930, in a race to beat the breakup. Feeling he would be unable to get off Weeks Field on skis with the load he wanted to take, the cargo was shipped to Nenana by train, where he planned to load the plane and take off the river ice. He was still there at noon the next day; rain during the day and snow falling through the night hindered his plans. Ed Young was also there, enroute to Ruby.

Crosson, with his two fellow airmen, S.E. Robbins and James T. Hutchison, finally got away on the ice in front of Nenana the forenoon of Thursday, April 24. Robbins was to bring back the damaged Fairchild at the Hamilton wreck site but, failing that, he would fly back the Waco 10, NC 780E, which was still at the *Nanuk*. Herb Larison had returned to the *Nanuk* after a ten-day stay at the wreck to report the need of a welder and his tanks, in order to complete the repair job on CF-AJK. A number of fittings on the plane had been found to be broken and welding was needed. Hence, Jim Hutchison had been included in the party. Larison had completed all the other repair work on the damaged plane. The planes would be loaded with furs on the return flight as there was still about 10,000 pounds of marten, fox and ermine pelts at the *Nanuk*. The remaining, less valuable furs, such as arctic ground squirrel, wolf, seal, and others remained on the vessel. Crosson gassed at Ruby, going on through to Nome and Teller, landing the evening of the same day with an air time of six hours and fifteen minutes.

Drifted in snow, the Fairchild 71, CF-AJK, lay at the Hamilton wreck site since February 21, 1930, when Pat Reid had landed the heavily-loaded plane with eighteen cases of gas in the cabin, and the landing gear gave way.

Crosson Collection

Crosson left Teller early in the morning of Friday, April 25, for Candle, but was forced to Nome by fog. He took off from there for Teller at 11:00 A.M., to hold there for favorable flying weather before crossing to Siberia. The pilot had been in the air six hours and fifteen minutes during the day, making three landings. The following day, Saturday, April 26, 1930, Crosson, Robbins and Hutchison were away from Teller in Fairchild 71, NC 9153, landing four hours and thirty

Herb Larison dug a hole under the snow-covered Fairchild and rebuilt the gear under it. With the propeller replaced and other repairs made, the plane was taxied up out of the hole. Joe Crosson flew it to the **Nanuk** *on April 27, 1930.*

minutes later at the wreck site of Eielson's Hamilton. Jim Hutchison repaired the landing gear fittings that needed welding on CF-AJK and Crosson took the plane off the next day for the fifty-minute flight to the *Nanuk* at North Cape. Robbins followed in NC 9153, the other plane. The landing surface at the trading schooner was rough from the snow's drifting. Besides the Alaskan Airways Waco 10, V.L. Galishev's Russian Junkers F-13, CCCP-182, was also there. Weather conditions on the Siberian Coast had been such that the plane had been held at North Cape since its arrival on April 6, 1930. The Russian pilot and his mechanic left the next day, carrying the last two members of the scientific expedition from the *Stavropol*. The *Nanuk* later wired, on May 6 (Siberian date) of the arrival of a dog team from Saint Lawrence Bay, that reported the safe arrival of the Russian plane at that point. The two scientists were to fly on to Vladivostok and then travel overland to Moscow.

April 28, 1930. Two Siberian natives (Chukchi) observe Alaskan Airways mechanics Herb Larison and Jim Hutchison (in welders' goggles) repair the tail ski from CF-AJK on the deck aboard **Nanuk.**

988

First Week of May, 1930. Alaskan Airways mechanic James T. "Hutch" Hutchison at the stern of the Nanuk. He had welded the damaged landing gear fittings on Fairchild CF-AJK at the Hamilton wreck site on April 26, to complete the repairs so that the plane could be brought in to Nanuk the following day.

Pilots Robbie Robbins and Joe Crosson at the Nanuk off North Cape, Siberia, the first week of May, 1930. They departed in the two Fairchild 71s on May 6, with forty sacks of valuable furs.

◀ *First week of May, 1930. Robbie Robbins stands on the ice at the bow of the three-masted sailing ship Nanuk. He had accompanied Joe Crosson on his returned to complete the contract with Swenson Fur & Trading Company in Siberia.*

April 28, 1930. In the after cabin of the Nanuk. *Left to Right: S.E. Robbins, Joe Crosson, Herb Larison and Captain R.H. Weeding of the* Nanuk.

Fur bales, sledged from the Nanuk *to be loaded on the Fairchild 71. Left to Right: Captain Weeding, seaman James Hearn, two Chukchis and mechanic Herb Larison.*

Fog once again held the American airmen at the *Nanuk.* It was comfortable on the ship with only five men aboard: the engineer, the captain, radio operator and two sailors. All the others had gone to the grounded wreck of the *Elisif* at Cape Billings to salvage material and such cargo as remained. On Tuesday, May 6, (Nome date) the two pilots and their mechanics

Joe Crosson at Teller, Alaska in the spring of 1930, winding up trips to Siberia delivering gas and returning with furs in the Fairchild 71.

Crosson Collection

left North Cape, Crosson again flying CF-AJK (NC 154H) and Robbins flying NC 9153. They were off at 8:00 A.M. loaded with forty sacks of valuable furs, landing on their skis at Teller at 2:00 P.M. It would be impossible to use wheels for some time. The four hour and forty minute flight was made without difficulty but, when an attempt was made to reach Nome, the pilots returned an hour and a half later, balked by a heavy snowstorm. The following day, Wednesday, May 7, the two Fairchilds were off, and arrived in Nome at about 3:00 P.M. to unload: the furs to be processed at the Nome post office to be forwarded to Fairbanks via mail plane. They were away at 6:00 P.M. that same day, returning to Teller, taking the Alaskan Airways mechanics, Hutchison, Larison and Cecil Higgins along.

Joe Crosson, flying Fairchild 71, NC 9153, accompanied by Robbie Robbins to fly the Waco 10 back from North Cape, left Teller on Thursday, May 8 for North Cape, making the flight in an even five hours. They landed at 2:00 P.M. to remain overnight on the *Nanuk*. The pilots did not get away until 12:30 P.M. May 10 (Siberian date and time), Crosson flying NC 9153 and Robbins in the Waco 10 with mechanic Herb Larison, who had returned to the *Nanuk* with them. The two planes landed on skis at Teller after a five hour and five-minute flight. They were carrying twenty-six bags of valuable furs. Some spare parts and equipment were left on the ship, to be unloaded at Nome when it finally worked free of the ice. A long lead, extending from North Cape almost to East Cape, was already open. July or August should see the ship free. All the Alaskan Airways flying equipment was out of Siberia except for the remnants of the Hamilton, which would remain there forever. Crosson wired Manager Arthur Johnson that he considered it inadvisable to make any further flights to Siberia at the present time. Wheels were needed for landing at Fairbanks, yet the north was covered in deep snow. Crosson had brought wheels with him for the Fairchild 71, but the Stinson Standard wheels were to be brought out from Fairbanks to put on the Waco 10. While Weeks Field was clear of snow, the Nome Municipal Airport had two to four feet of snow on it. To facilitate matters, Alf Lomen had arranged for it to be deeply furrowed to a depth of two feet, using a Hammon Consolidated Gold Fields road machine behind a Best "60" tracklayer tractor, then spraying the snow with oil to draw the sun's rays. Plans were made to land the ski planes on the ice at Golovin, relaying the cargo up to the high summer field which was clear of snow, for the flight on wheels to Fairbanks. The traffic for Nome was reversed, to be relayed in from Golovin by ski plane off the ice.

Crosson and Robbins brought the two Fairchild 71s and the twenty-six bags of fur in from Teller on Sunday, May 11, 1930, bringing mechanics Herb Larison, Jim Hutchison and Cecil Higgins in with them on the forty-minute flight. Joe Crosson went out that same day to Golovin to inspect the situation, to see if it would be possible to change from skis to wheels there for the flight to Fairbanks. He continued on to Teller before returning to Nome, flying three hours and fifteen minutes in NC 154H, making four landings. He had taken Robbins to Teller to bring in the Waco 10 to Nome. He went out Monday, May 12, the following day, to Hastings Creek, ten miles east of Nome, to inspect it for a ski-wheel change site. The pilot found this location satisfactory for the purpose and, taking Cecil Higgins, Jim Hutchison and a passenger for Fairbanks, R.T. Fulton of the Lomen Reindeer Corporation, the two pilots flew the Waco 10, NC 780E, and the Fairchild 71, NC 154H (CF-AJK) to Hastings Creek where the mechanics put on the wheels. Late that afternoon the two planes were off for Ruby, where they gassed and went on to Fairbanks. Landing on wheels at Weeks Field, at 2:00 A.M. Tuesday, May 13, 1930, with their passenger and sixteen sacks of furs from the *Nanuk*, the tired airmen

May 12, 1930 at Hastings Creek, ten miles east of Nome, with Fairchild 71, CF-AJK (NC 154H) for a ski to wheel change before going on to Fairbanks. Left to Right: Jack Warren, Jim Hutchison and Cecil Higgins with husky pup in his arms. Joe Crosson was flying the Fairchild.

went home to get some rest. They had been in the air for seven hours and thirty minutes. Mechanic Herb Larison had remained at Nome with the Fairchild 71, NC 9153. Bringing in the remaining sacks of fur waited until the Nome field was ready for a wheel operation. Northern Air Transport, Incorporated, pilot Bill Graham had made a successful trip to Fairbanks in the company's Stinson Detroiter, NC 404M, leaving Nome at 10:30 A.M. Wednesday, May 7, for Golovin, where he changed to wheels. He left there the afternoon of the following day, arriving in Fairbanks at 7:00 P.M. that evening, carrying Cliff Allyn and 900 pounds of furs from the Nome district.

The aviation business in Fairbanks had continued while the last two Siberian flights were being made. With Joe Crosson, Robbie Robbins and Jim Hutchison enroute from Nenana to Teller, Alaska, on Thursday, April 25, 1930, Alaskan Airways pilot Ed Young returned to Nenana from a round trip to Ruby, bringing in two passengers. The next morning the flier was off for Circle Hot Springs, Fort Yukon and Circle, taking Casper Ellingen to the Springs and Doctor Bart La Rue, dentist, to Fort Yukon and Circle. Doctor La Rue had arrived in the Interior from Ketchikan a few days before. The pilot planned on picking up Richard Heyser, U.S. Signal Corps operator, at Circle. Weeks Field was still too soft for planes, other than lightly-loaded ones. Grant Elliott picked Heyser up at Nenana, as well as two passengers who had come in from Ruby. Arnold Kobler and Harvey LaZelle, engineers for the Riley Investment Company, and another passenger for Medfra, were taken from Fairbanks to Nenana by Elliott. The three planned to leave from there with Young in the morning. An addition to the Alaskan Airways, Incorporated, hangar at Weeks Field was being built. The sixteen by twenty-four foot addition, provided separated space for passengers, pilots and an office. The building was on skids so that when a new hangar was constructed to replace the one destroyed by fire the previous winter, it could be readily moved.

Pilot Ed Young was away from Nenana again on Monday, April 28, for McGrath, carrying Captain George Green and a cook to work on Green's river boat. Young brought two passengers from McGrath and two from Ruby. Grant Elliott left Weeks Field on Tuesday, to ferry the two passengers from McGrath to Fairbanks. Elliott planned on flying to Flat on his

Fairchild 71s of Alaskan Airways, Incorporated are nested together for easy storage in the hangar in Fairbanks. By removal of four bolts, the wings could be folded back over the horizontal stabilizer giving an overall width to the plane of only twelve feet. In some cases it also placed the wings in a more workable position for the mechanic.

return, taking George Adams, businessman who had arrived from the States on Sunday, to his home in the community. On his return from there, the pilot was forced to land at Takotna when he encountered a snowstorm, and was still there on May 5; the field was so soft he could not get off. The next day it snowed. Weeks Field was now dry enough for daily use but required dragging to smooth down the ruts made during the thaw. Field conditions during spring break-up caused no end of trouble for the aviation business, the ones further north drying up long after the more southerly fields were ready for use. Ice on the lakes and rivers, normally used for winter landings, was now unsafe. In Fairbanks, officials waited for word from Ruby as to when the field there might be dry enough to bring in Mrs. Ben Mozee to the local hospital. Seriously ill at Kokrines, it was hoped she might be moved to Ruby to meet the plane. Taking the Stearman C-2B, NC 5415, Ed Young was off in the forenoon of Wednesday, May 7, 1930, for Ruby, to bring in Mrs. Mozee. Grant Elliott had been able to get off from Takotna the afternoon of May 6, after snow had ceased falling, landing on Weeks Field that same afternoon. Taking no passengers, he found it was all he could do to get off the muddy field at his departure point with the empty plane.

Bill Lavery returned to Fairbanks the first week in May from San Mateo, California, where he had been attending the Curtiss-Wright Flying School for some months. He had acquired about fifteen hours of solo time before leaving for his home in Fairbanks, where he intended to continue his aviation career.

Grant Elliott made three flights from Weeks Field to Livengood the afternoon of Friday, May 9, 1930. Taking a load of mail on the first flight, he returned to carry Mr. and Mrs. Michael Beegler as passengers on the second trip. On the third, he carried one passenger and a load of freight.

A.A. Bennett, well-known Alaskan aviator, returned to Fairbanks for a visit on Monday, May 12, 1930. Bennett had arrived in Seattle from Los Angeles about a month before, flying a seven-place cabin Zenith Z-6, built at the Zenith plant in Los Angeles. Along with Mrs. Bennett, he carried Sterling Price, the president of the Zenith company, Mrs. Price and Bennett's son. The flight to Seattle had taken twelve hours and fifteen minutes with two fuel stops enroute. The Bennetts left on Wednesday, April 16, to return to Los Angeles, with A.H. McDonald, a young Fairbanks businessman also making the trip in the plane from Seattle. The Prices had departed for Corvallis, Oregon to visit their son Gerald who was attending Oregon State College in that city. When Bennett came north again for a visit, he spoke of starting a flying service in Juneau with Zeniths on floats but it never came off. Evidently he could not interest capital investors. He did, however, on September 15, 1930, acquire a Zenith Z-6A No. 3, NC 392V, powered by a 420 horsepower Wasp C, which he operated in the northwestern states as Bennett Air Transport. Bennett left Fairbanks on Thursday, May 15, 1930, by the morning train for Anchorage, and a boat for Juneau and Seattle, where his wife was waiting.

Alaskan Airways, Incorporated, had submitted a bid through the Alaska Road Commission to the war department to carry government employees traveling on official business on the company's routes. The bid was accepted in mid-May of 1930 for the balance of the year. Services affected by the contract were the Department of Agriculture, the Forest Service, the Geological Survey and General Land Office, the Bureau of Education, the Bureau of Biological Survey, the governor of the Territory and the Alaska Road Commission. It was a solid piece of business for the aviation service. Alaskan Airways was now one of the main operating units of The Aviation Corporation (AVCO). Structural changes placed the Alaskan company operations under the direction of American Airways, Incorporated. More than sixty subsi-

994

diaries in the aviation field were included in AVCO's holdings. The operating air services were now grouped into five; Alaskan Airways, Incorporated, Colonial Airways Corporation, Universal Aviation Corporation, Southern Air Transport and Cuban Flying Service. James F. Hamilton, former president of New York State Railways, Incorporated, took the position of president of The Aviation Corporation.

Pilot Bill Graham, of Northern Air Transport, Incorporated, landed the Stinson Detroiter, NC 404M, on Weeks Field late in the afternoon of Tuesday, May 20, 1930, carrying Barney Olander, mining man from American Creek, along with a load of mail. Coming through Golovin, where the pilot changed his skis for wheels, he did not expect to have to reverse this on his return flight to Nome as the landing field on Bessie road was almost clear of snow on the east-west strip. The north-south still had some snow on it but it was melting rapidly. The break-up season was a tough time for the pilots, going from place to place and back again, either on wheels or skis. One landing field would be bare of snow and the next one covered with soft snow. Even dog teams found it difficult to make trips at that time of year owing to overflows and soft conditions on the trail.

Bill Graham was delayed in Fairbanks until Saturday, May 24, 1930, leaving Weeks Field in the morning with five passengers: Doctor and Mrs. E.A. Cushing who were bound for Golovin, John Froskland for Unalakleet, C.M. Allyn who was now manager of Northern Air Transport, Incorporated, for Nome, and Senator H.T. Tripp of Juneau. Graham's wife had reached Portland, Oregon, on May 20, coming from Bainbridge, Georgia, on her way to join her husband in Nome. Graham arrived at the Bessie road Municipal Airport at 7:00 p.m. Saturday, the same day of his departure from Fairbanks.

Major Wylie Wright, inspector for the aeronautical branch of the Department of Commerce, was in Fairbanks by mid-May, 1930, to explain regulations affecting commercial aviation in Alaska and elsewhere, and to give examinations for mechanic and pilot certificates under the air commerce act of 1926. All aircraft, whether licensed or unlicensed, must display registration numbers on both sides of the rudder, the lower side of the left wing and the top side of the upper right wing, plus an identification card displayed in the cockpit. Licensed aircraft were to have a letter or letters preceding these numbers: the Roman letters S for government planes, and C or NC for all commercial operating aircraft. Further, all licensed aircraft were to be periodically inspected by an aeronautics branch inspector to see that the ship was properly maintained in an airworthy condition. The plane must be given a line inspection by a licensed mechanic within twenty-four hours preceding flight and periodically, a minute and thorough inspection must be performed on it.

Anyone piloting a licensed aircraft must be a licensed airman. There were several types of pilot licenses: the Student Pilot License for the purpose of receiving instruction only under the supervision of an instructor who must be a licensed transport pilot, the Limited Commercial License which permitted the pilot to carry freight for hire, and the Transport Pilot License, which was the highest and permitted the pilot to carry persons or property for hire at any distance and to instruct students. Passenger-carrying grades of licenses were issued for six months and pilots were semi-annually given thorough physical examinations by a licensed medical examiner and, at the discretion of the aeronautics branch, they could be required to take additional flight tests. Passenger-carrying grades of pilots were not permitted to carry passengers in types of aircraft in which they had not been rated. Wylie Wright was busy for some days, getting everyone up to date under the regulations, including Joe Crosson.

Joe was aloft in the Fairchild 71, NC 153H, for forty-five minutes on May 16, 1930, making three landings and receiving a rating on his license for the type of aircraft he had been flying for some months. He was up again the same day in the New Standard D-25, NC 9190, for thirty minutes, for the same purpose. Aircraft mechanics also had to be licensed. Alaska's aviation industry was coming under tighter supervision for increased safety to the traveling public.

Crosson took the New Standard, NC 9190, to Fort Yukon and return on May 20, in the air for three hours and fifteen minutes. He went up the same day for a twenty-five minute flight over Fairbanks in Fairchild 71, NC 153H, going later in the day to the Eighteenmile roadhouse in the New Standard, a flight of thirty-five minutes without landing elsewhere. Following its return from Siberia, the Waco Model 10, NC 780E, was being completely overhauled in the shop to be taken to Anchorage and put on floats, and flown out of that base.

Alaskan Airways pilot Grant Elliott was off on Thursday, May 22, 1930, for Fort Yukon and Circle Hot Springs, with mail and freight. Leaving there, he encountered a storm area and returned to Fort Yukon, coming in the next day. The pilots were not flying much, waiting for muddy fields to dry in the north. Wiseman wired to the effect the field there had dried sufficiently and Joe Crosson was away in the New Standard D-25, NC 9190, on Saturday, May 24, making the flight there and return in four hours and forty-five minutes. Robbie Robbins, flying the Stearman C-2B, NC 5415, with Arthur W. Johnson in the front seat, accompanied him. Crosson brought in Bud Carpenter, Koyukuk mining man, and his sister, Clara, a Wiseman school teacher.

The Russian pilot, Slepnyov, had written his Fairbanks interpreter, businessman Harry Avakoff, from Honolulu, advising that he and Fahrig were leaving there, enroute to Japan by steamship, then leaving there to proceed to Moscow.

One Fairchild 71, NC 9153, still on skis, remained in Nome from the cleanup of the *Nanuk* contract. Taking a set of wheels for the plane from Fairbanks, Joe Crosson was off in Fairchild 71, NC 154H, from Weeks Field at 1:00 A.M. Tuesday, May 27, 1930. Robbie Robbins and Manager Arthur W. Johnson accompanied the pilot on the nonstop flight to Nome, arriving there at 4:45 A.M. (Nome time). Herb Larison, the Alaskan Airways, Incorporated, mechanic there, had the other Fairchild ready; the wheels were quickly installed. Loading the balance of the Siberian furs in the two Fairchilds, they took off at 3:30 P.M. Crosson returned shortly to have Larison correct a problem in the oil feed to the Pratt & Whitney Wasp engine, taking off a few minutes later on his interrupted journey to Fairbanks. Manager Johnson and Herb Larison remained behind until another trip. Flying nonstop again, Robbins landed Weeks Field at 9:15 P.M. and Crosson shortly after 10:00 P.M. Joe had been in the air eleven hours and twenty minutes, Robbins slightly longer. The 2000 white fox pelts, valued conservatively at $120,000, were removed from the planes. Another 500 pelts remained at Nome. Alaskan Airways pilot Grant Elliott was off on a round-trip flight to Livengood on Thursday, May 29, while the other two pilots rested from the arduous flight. Taking William Moore over, plus mail and freight, he returned with passenger Nick Mandich. Chief Pilot Joe Crosson was up for a forty-five minute flyover in NC 154H on May 30, Decoration Day. He went out the following day, Saturday, May 31, 1930, in the same plane, to bring in the balance of the furs at Nome. Accompanied by Alvin Polet, Alaska College student, and carrying a quantity of mail from Fairbanks, the pilot landed at Nome at 1:45 P.M. that same day, flying nonstop in four hours and forty-five minutes.

Taking off for Fairbanks Sunday afternoon, June 1, 1930, with the balance of the *Nanuk*'s white fox furs, plus a sack of first class mail, the pilot landed Weeks Field after a five hour and fifty minute flight. Manager Johnson and mechanic Herb Larison also came in with him.

Nome, Alaska in May, 1930. Left to Right: Robbie Robbins; Thomas A. Ross, Coast Guard commander in Nome; and Joe Crosson.

Bill Graham, Northern Air Transport pilot, had landed on Weeks Field the evening of Friday, May 30, in the Stinson Detroiter, NC 404M, after a flight from Nome. He had left there at 12:30 P.M. with William B. Miller of the Biological Survey, and 400 pounds of his equipment, and had landed at McGrath where Miller left the plane. Taking off from there at 4:50 P.M., he was in Fairbanks two hours and forty-five minutes later.

Harold Gillam, now operating Gillam Airways in the Copper River valley, came in to Fairbanks in his Whirlwind J6-7 Swallow, NC 430N, flying nonstop from Valdez. Landing at 2:15 P.M. on Friday, May 30, 1930; he had come in for inspection of the newly-assembled plane by Wylie R. Wright. Grant Elliott, flying the New Standard, NC 9190, took off for McGrath, Takotna and Flat at noon on Saturday, May 31. Bill Strandberg, Alaska College student, was his passenger for McGrath, going to join his father, Dave Strandberg, who was mining in the Kuskokwim. The pilot was looking forward to returning to see his fiancée, Miss Barbara Nudd, who was sailing on the *Yukon* from Seattle that same day. They were to be married on her arrival. S.E. Robbins was scheduled for a flight to Livengood at 3:00 P.M. to return Nick Mandich to the mining community. Grant Elliott landed back on Weeks Field Sunday, June 1, at 6:00 P.M., bringing mail.

Robbie Robbins left at noon on Sunday for Nulato, to await the arrival of the river steamer *General Jacobs*, upon which Father Delon was traveling from Holy Cross to Nulato.

The pilot brought the priest in to Fairbanks. Robbie had just completed a flight to Livengood, bringing in Pat Carrol and John Struck. The latter had been badly bruised and cut about the head when a cable broke, and entered the hospital for treatment. Robbins returned to Weeks Field on Monday, June 2, bringing in Father Delon, who took the train for the States on Wednesday.

Percy Hubbard, co-owner with Art Hines of Service Motor Company and Service Airlines, made his first long flight when he landed at McGrath on the evening of Monday, June 2, with his brother Russell and his brother-in-law, Ernie Gunther, in the front cockpit. Russell was joining his parents for the summer at the river town, while Gunther intended to return with the pilot. The elder Hubbard was deputy U.S. marshal at McGrath.

Joe Crosson, who had come in from Nome to land on Weeks Field at 10:30 P.M. on Sunday, June 1, 1930, got only three hours rest before he was away again, this time in the New Standard, NC 9190, to pick up his friend, Joe Quigley, at Moose Creek in the Kantishna. The hard-rock miner had been seriously injured in his Red Top Mine in a cave-in on May 21, sustaining what later proved to be a left leg fractured near the thigh and a badly bruised shoulder. The spunky miner had freed himself and crawled home. His wife, Fannie Quigley, had returned an hour later and summoned neighbors, who splinted the broken leg while all tried to make Joe comfortable. He was in a great deal of pain. One of the men, Bill Taylor, went overland to the railroad to summon aid, starting on May 30. When the telephone call came in, the pilot was away an hour and a half later in the open-cockpit plane, accompanied by Doctor Rex F. Swartz. Quigley was carried four miles from his home to the plane, which Crosson had landed on a bar in Moose Creek, the closest available spot. The splint had to be removed to allow the leg to fit in the cockpit of the plane, where he and the doctor sat, making it a painful process for the patient. The plane was off for Fairbanks, to land at Weeks Field with a round trip air time of three hours and fifty minutes. Joe Quigley was transported to St. Josephs Hospital where he was made comfortable. It appeared he would be there for the next three months. Joe Crosson went home to get some more sleep.

Preparing to refuel the Northern Air Transport Stinson on Weeks Field in Fairbanks.

Vic Ross Photo

June 7, 1930. Alaskan Airways pilot Grant Elliott and Miss Barbara Nudd were married in Fairbanks on the day of her arrival from Seattle. The airport gang had prepared a chariot for the pair by mounting an old rudder from the Stinson Standard, NC 877, on the rear of a Model T Ford. With Department of Commerce Inspector Wylie R. Wright at the wheel, and pilot Harold Gillam and mechanic Jim Hutchison in the rear seat, a trial run has just been completed.

Crosson Collection

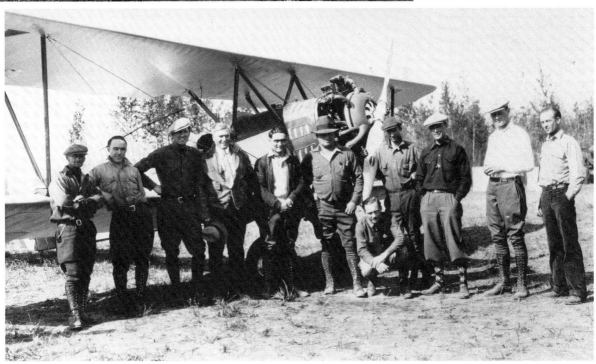

Crosson Collection

June, 1930. The airport gang assemble for a photo at Weeks Field, Fairbanks. Left to Right: Fred Moller, mechanic and sometimes pilot; Ed Moore, mechanic; Joe Crosson, pilot; unidentified man; Harold Gillam, pilot; Bill Basham, chief mechanic at Alaskan Airways; Wylie Wright, Department of Commerce aeronautical inspector (kneeling); Percy Hubbard, pilot; Sanis E. Robbins, pilot; Grant Elliott, pilot; Art Hines, pilot and partner of Hubbard in Service Airlines.

Robbie Robbins took the newly-overhauled Waco 10, NC 780E, to Anchorage on the morning of June 3, 1930, taking Lyle F. Hebert, commercial traveler, who had been awaiting passage at Tanana to the port city. Pontoons for the ship were awaiting its arrival and were quickly installed. Operated out of Anchorage, the biplane was the only water-based plane on Alaskan Airways' current fleet. Robbins returned to Fairbanks on Saturday, June 7, with the New Standard, NC 174H, taking with him his wife and Miss Barbara Nudd of Seattle. Miss Nudd became the bride of Alaskan Airways pilot Grant Elliott that same day, in a midnight ceremony at the Presbyterian church.

Percy Hubbard, visiting in McGrath with his parents, departed for Anchorage in the Service Airlines Swallow, C 2774, at 6:25 P.M. Friday, June 6, 1930, again accompanied by Ernie Gunther. Running into a heavy fog in the mountains, the young pilot became lost, finally going up to 12,000 feet and flying about in the mountain peaks for a couple of hours before finding his way back to McGrath at 11:00 P.M. In landing on the small, muddy field on his second try, the plane ran about eight feet before one wheel and

Percy Hubbard Photo

Percy Hubbard photo

▲ *Percy Hubbard, accompanied by Ernie Gunther, turned over on landing at the McGrath Airfield on June 6, 1930, after returning from an attempted flight to Anchorage. While the pair were uninjured, the Service Airlines Swallow biplane, C 2774, was a total loss except for the Wright Whirlwind J-5 motor.*

▶ *Russell Hubbard, Percy's brother, assists in dismantling the wrecked Swallow biplane, C 2774, at the McGrath airfield in June, 1930.*

Percy Hubbard in the cockpit of Service Airlines Swallow TP, C 688H, on Weeks Field. The new orange and green biplane was received from the factory in early April of 1930. It was powered by an OX- 5 liquid-cooled motor of ninety horsepower, and was intended to be used in training Fairbanks student pilots.

axle sank deep in the mud so that the lower wing on one side touched the ground, spinning the Swallow around and throwing it over onto its back. The pair unfastened their safety belts and crawled out uninjured.

The plane was another matter. In addition to other damage, the lower wing panels were broken on either side of the fuselage. The J-5 radial motor was undamaged and was removed and crated for shipment to Fairbanks. It arrived there almost a year later, going by way of Seattle and back to Fairbanks with freight charges of almost $500. Percy dismantled the rest of the plane and left it at McGrath. Some pieces undoubtedly found their way onto other aircraft later on. Percy Hubbard and Ernie Gunther were picked up and taken to Anchorage by Matt Nieminen on Sunday. The pair returned to Fairbanks by train on Thursday, June 12. Service Airlines fleet was now down to the OX-5 Swallow TP, C 688H.

Chief Pilot Joe Crosson of Alaskan Airways, Incorporated, departed Fairbanks for Anchorage in a Fairchild 71, NC 153H, with Arthur W. Johnson, Carl J. Lomen and chief mechanic Bill Basham as passengers. Away from Weeks Field at 11:15 P.M. Monday, June 9, the pilot flew nonstop to the port city in two hours and thirty-five minutes (see Anchorage—1930, Chapter 57). Intending to return the following day, Crosson was delayed by bad weather until Sunday, June 15, 1930. With passengers Mrs. Harry F. Morton, wife of the Anchorage attorney, Arthur W. Johnson, Carl Lomen and Bill Basham, the plane arrived at Weeks Field at 2:30 P.M., after four hours and ten minutes in the air. Crosson had intended to return by way of the Kuskokwim but, encountering a storm over Rainy Pass, the pilot elected to fly north to

Fairbanks over the railroad route. Grant Elliott had flown a round trip to Livengood on Friday night, June 14, taking Frank Nash, Alaska Road Commission superintendent, Peter Kaisen of the Museum of Natural History, and Sam Godfrey, manager of the Nome Creek Dredging Company, on the trip out. Pilots Vic Ross and Bill Graham, along with mechanic George Laiblin, came in to undergo examinations as to their airmen qualifications with Inspector Wylie Wright.

Two Alaskan Airways planes, Fairchild 71, NC 153H, flown by Joe Crosson, and the New Standard, NC 9190, flown by Grant Elliott, were off Weeks Field between two heavy showers on the afternoon of Monday, June 16, 1930. Crosson carried Mr. and Mrs. Carl J. Lomen, Mrs. G.J. Lomen and C.J. McGregor, assistant meteorologist who, with L. Lundberg, was establishing a United States Weather Bureau station in Nome. Herb Larison, Alaskan Airways mechanic, rode with Grant Elliott. The pair were to be stationed at Nome for the time being. The two planes arrived at the Bessie road Municipal Airport after a four hour and forty minute flight, nonstop. Crosson did some local flying in the New Standard in the next few days before returning to Fairbanks on Friday, June 20, 1930, in the Fairchild 71, NC 153H, taking six hours and ten minutes to make the nonstop flight.

S.E. Robbins had made two round trips to Livengood on Tuesday, June 17, bringing in Frank Nash and Sam Godfrey on the first trip, and Peter Kaisen on the second, to Fairbanks. It was reported that the aviation field at Tanana, now 300 feet wide and 1000 feet long, was in first class condition.

Alaskan Airways, Incorporated, was now advertising Midnight Sun flights, starting on Thursday night, June 19, 1930; flights left the airport at 11:30 P.M. to climb to more than 8000 feet in the air to see the sun at exactly midnight. They were charging ten dollars per passenger, with a minimum of five passengers to make the flight. Another tourist attraction would be the flights over the scenic wonders of Mount McKinley National Park. In a search for select routes and landing fields, S.E. Robbins left on the afternoon of Thursday, June 19, with General Manager Arthur W. Johnson and his young son on a scouting expedition. The Mount McKinley Tourist & Transportation Company was the first park concessionaire to be granted the privilege of operating planes in a national park, and had entered into an agreement with Alaskan Airways. It was planned to establish an airport at the base of Mount Eielson (formerly Copper Mountain) from which visitors were to be flown over the park. Robert E. Sheldon was manager of the transportation concession in the park. Several years previously, Joe Crosson had taken a few tourists aloft, in July, 1927, flying above the curve of the earth to see the magnificence of the sun on the northern horizon at midnight.

Crosson took his first Fairbanks flight of 1930 to see the midnight sun on Saturday, June 21, 1930, going to an altitude of 10,500 feet in the Fairchild 71, NC 153H, flying for forty minutes. He repeated the flight on the following Monday, going up to 9000 feet and flying for fifty minutes. On June 24, the pilot made a flight to Moose Creek, using the New Standard D-25, NC 9190, which was better suited to landing on a gravel bar on the creek. Flying for an hour and fifty minutes, the pilot remained overnight, returning the following day, Thursday, by way of Savage River, in the park; then going in to Weeks Field, he flew the same one hour and fifty minutes, after making a landing at Savage River.

Crosson made three midnight sun flights on June 26, 27, and 28, flying for forty-five minutes on each day in NC 153H and climbing to 9000, 8500 and 10,300 feet, respectively, to get the sun in view in all its glory. The flights were popular with the tourists as well as with Fairbanks residents. The pilot flew to Fort Yukon and return on Monday, June 30, 1930, in the New Standard, NC 9190, making the round trip with an air time of three hours and thirty-five minutes. He went up on another midnight sun flight that same evening, to 10,000 feet in Fairchild 71, NC 153H, taking the usual forty-five minutes.

Crosson flew from Fairbanks to Chicken Creek and Eagle on Tuesday, July 1, in the New Standard, taking two hours and forty-five minutes in the air. Remaining overnight, he came back the next day via Circle Hot Springs, Fort Yukon and in to Fairbanks, flying for four hours and twenty-five minutes. The chief pilot took two Territorial officials, Robert J. Sommers and Cash Cole, to Livengood and return in the New Standard, NC 9190, on Saturday, July 5, with an air time of one hour and thirty-five minutes. The men had gone to inspect the Livengood airfield. Crosson also made a short hop around the field on his return.

S.E. Robbins was also away on Saturday, in the Stearman C-2B, NC 5415, taking Doctor J.A. Sutherland to Fort Yukon and return, where he conferred with Doctor Grafton Burke about a patient at the Hudson Stuck Memorial Hospital. The pilot left again at 10:00 P.M. that evening in the Fairchild, taking Charles L. Thompson to Ruby where they picked up Mr. and Mrs. Dennis Coyle and daughter, returning during the night. Mrs. Coyle was in for medical attention.

Joe Crosson officially inaugurated the tourist airplane service in Mount McKinley National Park on Monday evening, July 7, 1930. Flying the Fairchild 71, NC 153H, the pilot departed at 7:00 P.M. with George A. Parks, governor of Alaska; Robert J. Sommers, Territorial highway engineer; Cash Cole, Territorial auditor; Arthur W. Johnson, general manager of Alaskan Airways, Incorporated; and Robert E. Sheldon, general manager of the Mount McKinley Tourist & Transportation Company, as passengers on the tour. Flying at 9000 feet, the pilot entered the park through Savage River canyon, to the Savage River campground, then turned southeast to follow the trail through Sable Pass and Polychrome Pass to Mount Eielson. Turning to Muldrow glacier, the pilot crossed it about ten miles above the moraine, then turned straight for McKinley. Both McKinley and Foraker were in view, with glacier and knife-like

Crosson Collection

Joe Crosson, flying a Fairchild 71, passes over Mount McKinley in the national park.

ridges revealed in clear detail in the strong light. Turning back to fly straight down the glacier, the party could see Wonder Lake, Lake Minchumina and the headwaters of the Kuskokwim River spread before them. Flying over the site selected for the new tourist hotel, Crosson returned, to land at the Savage River camp to spend the night; he had been in the air for three hours and forty-five minutes. His passengers were thrilled. In addition to the marvelous scenery, the party had sighted large numbers of the Dall sheep and one grizzly bear. The group left for Fairbanks at 10:30 A.M. the following morning, flying for fifty minutes on a direct course. Good progress was being made on the road into the park. The pilot was aloft in the same plane the following day, with tourists, on a fifty minute flight to view the midnight sun.

July 10, 1930. Joe Crosson, flying the Fairchild 71, NC 153H, flew his second scenic trip over the wonders of Mount McKinley National Park with a tourist party from the States. Left to Right: Pilot Joe Crosson; Mrs. G.A. Schmidt of Denver, Colorado; Mrs. Edward H. Smith of Cedar Rapids, Iowa; Thomas L. King and his father Lloyd L. King of Los Angeles; Mr. G.A. Schmidt of Denver; Sutherland Cook of Cedar Rapids, Iowa. The new service was to become increasingly popular with visitors. Construction of a road into the Park was underway.

Crosson left Weeks Field in NC 153H at 1:00 A.M. Thursday, July 10, 1930, for a second tourist trip through the park. Making the flight were Lloyd L. King, a Ford dealer at Huntington Park near Los Angeles; his son, Tom; Mr. and Mrs. G.A. Schmidt (both over seventy years of age); Ella Cook Smith and Sutherland Cook. The pilot returned at 4:25 A.M., after three hours and twenty-five minutes on the flight.

On Friday, July 11, 1930, Joe Crosson, accompanied by Alaskan Airways pilot S.E. Robbins, was away for McGrath in the Fairchild 71, NC 153H. Landing on a bar across from the river town, the pilots inspected the work going on at the McGrath airfield. Using a Best "Sixty" crawler tractor, road commission crews under Milton Rice were lengthening the field by 300 feet, and then increasing it another 400 feet, allowing the largest planes to use the strip. Picking up their two passengers for Fairbanks, Carl Shuttler and Fritz Tuttle, they returned that same evening to land at Weeks Field at 7:30 P.M., after a total of five hours and twenty minutes in the air.

On July 17, 1930, Joe Crosson was off in the New Standard biplane, NC 174H, on a flight from Fairbanks to McGrath, Iditarod, McGrath and return to Weeks Field. He flew a long day, spending nine hours and thirty-five minutes in the air. The pilot was away again, flying the Fairchild, NC 153H, in the forenoon of Monday, July 21, on a tourist trip around Mount McKinley. He was back that same day after a three hour and thirty minute flight. Going the same day to Moore Creek in the New Standard D-25, NC 174H, Crosson flew two hours and ten minutes before landing there to overnight. He came in the following day in two hours and fifteen minutes, going from Moore Creek to Savage River and Fairbanks.

Alaskan Airways pilot Robbie Robbins had gone to Tanana Crossing the evening of Saturday, July 19, in the New Standard D-25, taking Reverend E.A. McIntosh. The pilot was off Weeks Field on the forenoon of Tuesday, July 22, for Wiseman, stopping at Fort Yukon on the way to pick up Mrs. Ulen and child, who were returning to their home in Wiseman. Robbins also carried a supply of fresh fruit for the residents of the mining community. He planned on bringing Tom Morden to Fairbanks on his return from the Koyukuk.

Robbins was away again on the morning of Friday, July 25, 1930, in the New Standard, NC 174H, going to McGrath with William Gerweis and Pat Naghel of the Seelye government survey party. Crosson left at the same time in the Stearman C-2B, NC 5415, taking Surveyor Charles P. Seelye to the same point. He dropped Arthur W. Johnson at Savage River in Mount McKinley National Park on the way. Crosson went on to Flat and Holy Cross, to pick up H.W. Terhune, executive officer of the Alaska Game Commission, to take him to Unalakleet. The pilot put in six hours and five minutes in the air that day.

Leaving Holy Cross the next morning, Saturday, July 26, Crosson dropped his passenger at Unalakleet and cut back to the Yukon River to gas at Ruby before going on to Fairbanks; six hours and forty-five minutes in the Stearman for that day. The pilot was up the next day for twenty-five minutes in the Fairchild, NC 153H, on a local flight, going aloft again on Wednesday, July 30, flight testing the Stearman, NC 5415, for twenty minutes. Later that day he readied the New Standard D-25, NC 174H, for a flight to Takotna on an emergency call, but the weather held the pilot in Fairbanks until the following day. Departing with Doctor Rex F. Swartz the morning of Thursday, July 31, 1930, the pilot reached Takotna four hours later, where Mrs. Carl Lottsfeldt was caring for Chester V. Brink. The man had been severely injured when he was struck by a broken planer blade, the steel burying itself in Brink's right thigh, cutting into the bone. Weak from loss of blood, the man was treated and left in the care of the nurse; Doctor Swartz felt the wound would heal, while the flight in to Fairbanks might be too much for the wounded man. Crosson and the doctor returned to Fairbanks the afternoon of Friday, August 1, 1930, by way of McGrath, spending four hours and ten minutes in the air.

After about a year on the ground, Sam O. White's Golden Eagle monoplane, NC 569K, was taken aloft by pilot Ralph Wien on Thursday evening of July 31, 1930. The wooden propeller originally sent with the plane was unsuitable, severely damaging the LeBlond 7-D ninety horsepower engine. Now repaired and fitted with a new steel propeller, the ship performed satisfactorily. Sam White made his first solo flight in the plane on Tuesday evening, August 5, following some instruction from Ralph Wien.

Joe Crosson was up in the Alaskan Airways, Incorporated, Fairchild 71, NC 153H, for forty-five minutes on Saturday, August 2. He took the Stearman, NC 5415, to Nenana and return on Sunday, August 3, 1930, flying it in one hour and twenty minutes. In addition to the one passenger for the rail community, he carried lovely Miss Lillian Osborne. Joe and Lillian were quietly married there by Mrs. C.C. Heid, the commissioner at Nenana. The pair returned to Fairbanks, she to her office job at the Fairbanks Exploration Company and Joe to the business of flying.

The pilot was away from Weeks Field again on the morning of Monday, August 4, taking Dan T. Kennedy to the Mount Hayes district to inspect a field that had been picked by Kennedy, at the base of the mountain. Joe landed the New Standard, NC 174H, at the site before returning to Weeks Field. He had been three hours in the air.

Robbie Robbins was also away on Monday from Weeks Field for Fort Yukon, with a stop enroute at Circle Hot Springs to drop off Charles L. Thompson, Alaskan Airways traffic manager, who was on a leave of absence and intended to spend three or four weeks at the springs. At Fort Yukon Robbins picked up Frank E. Gannett, publisher of a chain of newspapers in the East. Gannett intended to fly to Mount McKinley Park and to Nome, then return to Whitehorse by air.

Joe Crosson with two passengers in the front cockpit of the three-place plane.

Crosson Collection

Joe Crosson took the Stearman, NC 5415, to Shungnak, Alatna and back to Fairbanks on August 5, landing at each point. He was up in the Fairchild 71, NC 154H, for thirty-five minutes the next day, flight testing the machine, following an extensive rebuild.

Bad weather on the Seward Peninsula had persisted for some time, preventing Alaskan Airways from making a flight to Nome. On Thursday, August 7, 1930, conditions had improved, with light fog reported at Golovin and Nome, but with indications for improvement later in the day. Joe Crosson, flying the Fairchild 71, NC 154H, was away in the forenoon, carrying Ernest Walker Sawyer, of the Department of the Interior; Major L.E. Atkins, of the Alaska Road Commission; and H.D. Stull, who was returning to his home in Deering after a trip to the States. Sawyer and Atkins would travel to various Seward Peninsula points from Nome with Alaskan Airways pilot Grant Elliott, presently stationed there. Crosson made the flight in five hours and twenty-five minutes, nonstop, coming back to Fairbanks the following day in five hours and ten minutes with John Lichtenberg as a passenger. Pilot Bill Graham, of Northern Air Transport, Incorporated, had finally gotten away for his home base in the Stinson monoplane on August 7, having been delayed in Fairbanks since July 25 by unfavorable weather on the Seward Peninsula. He carried a full load of mail.

Pilot S.E. Robbins, with Manager Arthur W. Johnson and chief mechanic Bill Basham, left for Mount McKinley Park on the afternoon of Friday, August 8, 1930, to make some tourist flights out of there. He was flying the newly-rebuilt Fairchild 71, NC 154H, the former Canadian registered CF-AJK used on the Eielson-Borland search.

Joe Crosson went out for a full day in the New Standard D-25, NC 174H, on the afternoon of Saturday, August 9, taking Bart C. Buckley to the north, and bringing in Irving McKenny Reed on his return. He put in eight hours and fifteen minutes in the air that day, flying to Beaver and Little Squaw, back to Beaver and returning to Little Squaw, then to Beaver and Fairbanks.

Joe Crosson was in need of a vacation. He had returned from the Eielson-Borland search to throw himself into the task of getting the commercial operations of Alaskan Airways running smoothly, using the Fairchilds and additional pilots hired by the company. The chief pilot had flown a great deal himself and, with the return of Ed Young from an Outside vacation with his family, was now able to get away. Lillian, a Cordova girl who had attended Alaska College for two years, was still working at her job with Fairbanks Exploration Company. In mid-August the newlyweds, accompanied by Joe's mother who had been visiting in Fairbanks

August, 1930. Lillian and Joe Crosson pose before a Great Lakes "Sport", 1-T-1A, at the Ryan factory in San Diego while on a slightly-delayed honeymoon. Married in Nenana, Alaska on August 3, they got away from Fairbanks in mid-August.

since last April, were driven over the Richardson Highway by Clark Bassett to Chitina, to board the train for Cordova. Here they caught a steamer for Seattle. Flying south from there to Los Angeles, in the cabin of a thirty-two place plane, a Fokker F-32, the pair continued on to San Diego. Here they stayed for some time, visiting Joe's relatives, as well as making a trip to Agua Caliente, a Mexican resort. Returning to Los Angeles, Joe had a precautionary appendectomy performed. He had occasionally been troubled by the ailment and did not want to suffer a severe attack at some remote spot in the north.

Meanwhile, back in Fairbanks, Bill Graham came in from Nome in the Northern Air Transport Stinson SM-1F, NC 404M, skirting storm areas to land at Weeks Field on the afternoon of August 21, 1930, with five passengers from the Seward Peninsula city: J.D. Harlan, manager of Hammon Consolidated Gold Fields; Doctor L.M. Waugh of the U.S. Public Health Service; C.W. Franklin, salesman; H.E. Seneff, special officer for prevention of liquor traffic among natives; and Leo W. Breuer, Territorial commissioner of education.

Robbie Robbins was away on Monday, August 25, on a sightseeing flight across the Arctic Circle, with Senators John B. Kendrick of Wyoming and John Thomas of Idaho, as well as Charles Sisson, assistant attorney-general of the United States. From Fairbanks, the pilot followed the general direction of the Steese Highway so his passengers could view the operations and ditch of the Fairbanks Exploration Company. He then swung over Circle Hot Springs and Circle, before continuing across the Arctic Circle to Fort Yukon. Joe Ulmer accompanied the party to point out and explain details along the way. Robbins landed back at Weeks Field at 1:30 P.M.; on his return he flew over the Preacher River country to the head of the Beaver, then crossing over to Chatanika.

Pilot Ed Young, back from a stateside vacation, and S.E. Robbins were off in two Alaskan Airways planes on the afternoon of Monday, August 25, for Wiseman. Carrying four passengers outbound: Lewis Carpenter, Koyukuk mining man, and his sister, a school teacher at Wiseman; Bob Marshall, a scientist traveling for a thirteen-month stay in the northern district (author of *Arctic Village* in 1933); and Al Retzlaf, who would be with him for the next few weeks, as well as a large amount of freight; the pilots were back at Weeks Field later in the day. Ed Young made an additional flight to Livengood the same day, taking Ole Niemi and Mrs. Bentley Falls outbound, and bringing in Blanche Cascaden and Miss Joy on his return. Ed Young made a valiant effort on the morning of Wednesday, August 27, to reach Iditarod and bring in Dave Strandberg's fourteen-year-old son, Odin, whose hand had been badly injured in a sheave block at the mine. Flying in low visibility and storm, the Fairbanks pilot reached a point about halfway between Lake Minchumina and Iditarod before he was forced back to Nenana. Matt Nieminen, flying from Anchorage, was finally able to get through and brought Strandberg and his son into Anchorage on August 28. (see Anchorage—1930, Chapter 57).

S.E. Robbins came in on Friday, August 29, 1930, from a stay of several days at Mount McKinley National Park. He had flown the Fairchild 71, accompanied by his manager, Arthur W. Johnson, into the Savage River camp on the same day the senatorial party had departed for the Park by surface means. While there, the pilot flew Senators Thomas and Kendrick, and Mr. Sisson, over the Muldrow Glacier on a sightseeing tour. Robbins brought Arthur W. Johnson and Charles P. Sisson back to Fairbanks on the fifty-five minute flight. The next day the pilot made a round–trip flight to Livengood, taking Luther C. Hess and C.H. Laboyteaux outbound.

Alaskan Airways pilot Ed Young flew the New Standard D-25, NC 174H, to Chicken on Friday, August 29, 1930, but was prevented by a strong crosswind on the field from leaving. He got away the next morning, fighting poor visibility all the way, through pelting rains and much low cloud cover, to cross the mountains with Hannah Johnson, resident of Jack Wade Creek, brought in to the hospital for treatment of paralysis.

Matt Nieminen, Alaskan Airways pilot based in Anchorage, came in to Fairbanks on Thursday, September 4, to pick up Charles P. Sisson, assistant attorney-general of the United States. Flying the Fairchild 71, NC 9153, the pilot was away at 3:05 P.M. of the same day, carrying Sisson, Manager Arthur W. Johnson and mechanic Cecil Higgins to the port city. George Mumford, the pilot's brother-in-law and cashier of the Bank of Alaska who had arrived in Fairbanks on the plane, remained in Fairbanks. Matt had been in the air for two hours and twenty minutes, northbound, taking an additional hour for the return, landing at Anchorage at 6:25 P.M.

Fairbanks pilot S.E. Robbins flew a Fairchild 71 to Anchorage on Saturday, September 6, 1930, to return Charles P. Sisson and Arthur W. Johnson to Fairbanks. Leaving the same day, the pilot reached a point some thirty miles beyond Curry before being forced back by storm conditions, and landed once more at Anchorage. The party departed a second time on Monday, September 8, and landed at Weeks Field shortly after noon. They had been joined in Anchorage by Brother George J. Feltes, SJ, a Jesuit missionary pilot who was bringing a diesel-powered Bellanca monoplane to Alaska to be used in the work of the church. The plane,

July 1930. Roosevelt Field, Long Island, New York. Blessing of the Catholic Missions Bellanca Pacemaker, **Marquette Missionary.** *Left to Right: Victor Ridder of Marquette League of New York, donors of the plane; Father William Flynn, their chaplain; Bishop Crimont, S.J., Bishop of Alaska; Judge Talley, President of Marquette League; Brother George J. Feltes, S.J., pilot of the plane; George Pickenpack, Bellanca factory pilot who flew as co-pilot to the west coast with Feltes.*

Oregon Province Archives

July 1930. Bellanca Pace-maker, Model CH-300 Special, NC 862N, at Roosevelt Field, Long Island, New York. Left to Right: George Pickenpack, Bellanca factory pilot who would accompany Feltes on his flight to the west coast; and Brother George J. Feltes, S.J., the first Jesuit pilot in the history of the 400-year-old order, who would be the pilot of the Marquette Missionary.

July 1930. Detroit, Michigan. The **Marquett Mission-ary,** *Bellanca CH-300 Special, NC 862N, on the airfield. The Packard Motor Car Company had supplied the nine-cylinder diesel DR-980 engine of 225 horsepower from its aircraft engine factory in Detroit. Left to Right: E.J. McKeon, Packard official; Brother George J. Feltes, S.J., pilot of the plane; Father Philip Delon, S.J., Superior-general of Northern Alaska Missions; Walter Cade, Packard chief mechanic and Father Walter Fitz-gerald, S.J., Rector of Seattle College.*

Detroit, Michigan. July 1930. The Packard diesel engine DR-980 with Standard steel propeller (ground adjustable) developed 225 horsepower at 1950 revolutions per minute, and weighed 510 pounds. It burned .40 pounds per horsepower hour of low-cost diesel fuel in cruise. The plane, christened the **Marquette Missionary,** *had been donated by the Marquette League of New York, the engine by the Packard Motor Car Company, and a year's supply of fuel, especially designed for cold-weather operation, by The Texas Company (Texaco).*

shipped from Seattle to Seward, arrived in Fairbanks on the passenger train on Sunday, September 7, 1930.

Brother Feltes first became interested in flying in his home state, California. He began training under Captain W.H. Royle in July of 1929 at the airport at Alameda, California, where the airman operated the Royle Flying School. Soloing on August 5, 1929, after eight hours of dual instruction, the embryo pilot continued his course to receive a Private Pilot License on August 28, 1929. About this time the Curtiss-Wright Flying School purchased the school from Royle, and Feltes continued his training with Curtiss-Wright, taking acrobatic flying (now called aerobatic) from Roy Hunt. The thirty-two-year-old student received a Limited Commercial Pilot License following the additional flight training.

Father Philip Delon, superior-general of northern Alaska missions, could use an airplane in his work on the Yukon and northwestern coast. He could make a circuit of the thirty-two missions by plane in two weeks, whereas several months were previously needed when boats and dog teams were used. Delon had chartered a plane on some of his visits and was pleased with the results. In Brother George Feltes the Jesuits had a pilot of their own, the first in the history of the 400-year-old order.

The Marquette League of New York, a Catholic service organization, offered to furnish a plane to the church. Feltes arrived in New York in January of 1930, to begin the process of selecting a suitable aircraft. He had studied the various makes and types of machines available and had flown several of them with their demonstration pilots, and now he settled on the Bellanca Pacemaker, powered with a diesel motor; both plane and motor were new to Alaska although the plane itself had a remarkable record in the States. Father Philip Delon had come in from Holy Cross, leaving Fairbanks on June 4, 1930, to join Brother Feltes in New York.

The orange-red monoplane with black striping was christened *Marquette Missionary*. It was moved from the Bellanca Aircraft Corporation plant at New Castle, Delaware to Roosevelt Field, Long Island, New York, to be flown from there to the west coast for shipment to Alaska. Insurance requirements called for the plane to be flown coast-to-coast by an airman with an Air Transport Pilot License, which Brother George Feltes did not yet have, so he served as pilot with the Bellanca factory pilot, George Pickenpack. Father Philip I. Delon and Walter H. Kade, Packard's chief mechanic from Detroit, made up the rest of the party. Taking off from Roosevelt Field on July 19, 1930, for Buffalo, New York, the *Marquette Missionary* began a leisurely trek westward. Among other places, a stop was made at Des Moines, Iowa, so Brother Feltes could visit a cousin, V. Kiliner, and his mother's other relatives.

There was a great interest on the part of aviation people across the country in the plane and its novel engine. Catholic church members also gathered at every stop to view the *Marquette Missionary* and meet Father Delon and Brother George Feltes. The Bellanca CH-300 Special, NC 862N, arrived at Grand Central Air Terminal near Glendale, California on July 30, 1930, on its way to Seattle, Spokane and Yakima. Brother Feltes was now flying the plane with Father Delon accompanying him. The pilot still had a Limited Commercial License, but would acquire Air Transport Pilot License No. 9389 at Mines Field near Los Angeles the following year. The plane was flown to San Fransisco next, arriving there on Thursday, July 31, 1930, where the party remained for about two weeks.

Feltes, again on his way north, landed the Bellanca at Portland, Oregon on Monday, August 18, creating the usual stir of interest among aviation people and the church community. Landing at Tacoma on the way, the *Marquette Missionary* arrived in Seattle on August 23, 1930. Here the wings and tail surfaces were removed from the plane and crated by Washington Aircraft & Transport Corporation for shipment on the steamer *Aleutian* to Seward, Alaska. The fuselage, complete with motor, was deck-loaded on the same ship. Father Delon and Brother Feltes, with their aircraft, passed through Juneau on Tuesday, September 2, still uncertain as to whether the plane would be assembled at Valdez and flown inland to Fairbanks, or be shipped from Seward on the Alaska Railroad. Apparently they had decided on the latter for Feltes arrived in Anchorage on Saturday, September 6, 1930 from the port of Seward, with the *Marquette Missionary* traveling on a flat car included in the day's passenger train for Fairbanks. He resumed his journey on Monday, flying up with Robbie Robbins in the Alaskan Airways Fairchild 71.

Unloading the orange-red with black striping Bellanca Pacemaker CH-300 Special, NC 862N, with its Packard DR-980 diesel motor of 225 horsepower, began at the railroad yard in Fairbanks on the morning of Tuesday, September 9, 1930. The plane was hauled to Weeks Field for assembly and testing.

The nine-cylinder radial, air-cooled engine had no carburetor, magneto or spark plugs, and had only one valve for each cylinder. It did have a separate fuel pump for each cylinder, making it an operating unit independent of the other eight. The heating oil it used for fuel posed little fire hazard as, unless properly atomized or used through a wick, it would not catch fire from an open flame. The four-cycle engine sucked only air into the cylinder on the down

Fall of 1930. Alaskan Airways pilot S.E. Robbins on Little Squaw airfield, looking south, with the Stearman C-2B, NC 5415, and a passenger.

stroke, compressing it greatly on the up stroke to a temperature of approximately 1000 degrees Fahrenheit. Just before the piston reached top dead center, a measured amount of fuel oil was injected by the individual pump into the cylinder, and ignited spontaneously by the heated, compressed air. Power from the rapid burning and expansion of the air was transmitted to the crankshaft and its propeller through the connecting rod as in a conventional gasoline engine. The gasses from the burning were exhausted through the same valve on the next up stroke of the piston. The engine weighed 510 pounds, somewhat more weight per horsepower than a gasoline engine. It was more prone to vibration due to the higher compression necessary to its operation. It was also less flexible than a gasoline engine through its various ranges of power. When throttled back to idle, the engine ran on only three of its nine cylinders, by design. In applying power from idle, there was some delay between throttling up and getting the increased power from the engine; an aspect familiar to fanjet engine pilots of today.

Warren Packard, heir to the Packard fortune, was killed in a crash on August 26, 1929, in Detroit, when the plane's motor stalled and his aircraft went into the river.

Enjoying excellent fuel economy and burning a very cheap fuel compared to gasoline, the engine also generated a very pronounced odor, familiar to current auto diesel drivers.

Ed Young took Joe Quigley, Kantishna miner, to his home on Tuesday, September 10, 1930, using the Stearman C-2B. He found the landing field, a gravel bar on Moose Creek, covered with high water and, unable to land, returned to Fairbanks.

Charles P. Sisson, delayed in Fairbanks for some time, was finally off for Nome on Sunday, September 14, 1930. Pilot S.E. Robbins, flying the Fairchild 71, also took Manager Arthur W. Johnson and Alaskan Airways mechanic Clark Bassett, who had been stationed at

Fairbanks all summer, but was now returning to duty at Nome. Robbins landed the party in Nome late that afternoon.

Ed Young, flying the New Standard biplane, left for Nome the same day, going by way of Takotna and Flat. He carried Mrs. Miller for Takotna and Henry C. Crook for Flat. Young intended to leave the New Standard D-25 at Nome and return with Robbins but, balked by unfavorable weather, returned from Iditarod in the New Standard to land Weeks Field at 2:00 P.M. on Thursday. He brought in an Iditarod youth who was to attend high school in Fairbanks.

Tom Gerard, former Fairbanks flier and mechanic, with his wife, the former Rose Haag, was now living in Bellevue, Washington where he intended to enter the garage business.

Vic Ross, Northern Air Transport pilot, landed a company Stinson on Weeks Field Monday afternoon, September 15, completing a flight from Nome. He brought Alvin Polet, son of Nome merchant Anton Polet, who was returning to continue his studies at the Alaska College.

Freddie Moller flew a school teacher, Miss Wilcox, to Alatna in mid-September to find a veteran prospector, Joe Mathews of the Wild River country north of Bettles, in serious condition in the village; there had been no way to summon an airplane and the man could not travel overland. Moller had to wait several days because of the weather; he finally took off with the patient but a storm forced him to return. Another start was made the next day, and Moller flew all the way to Tanana in a snowstorm. Refueling there, the pilot headed for Fairbanks but, flying in a fog hanging low over the whole country, turned back when in the vicinity of Hot Springs. Leaving the ill man in the care of Doctor Kaufman at the government hospital at Tanana, Fred Moller came in alone when the weather had cleared somewhat. Mathews died in the Tanana hospital in mid-October.

*September 18, 1930. The **Marquette Missionary**, NC 862N, at its intended base at Holy Cross, Alaska. Brother George J. Feltes, S.J. as pilot with Ralph Wien accompanying him as assistant pilot.*

The mission plane, *Marquette Missionary*, Bellanca CH-300, NC 862N, departed Weeks Field for Holy Cross on Thursday, September 18, 1930, with Ralph Wien as copilot, Brother George J. Feltes, SJ as pilot, and Father Philip Delon as a passenger. While Brother Feltes was familiar with the diesel-powered plane, he was new to Alaska and Ralph Wien had been hired as an additional pilot until Feltes could become familiar with the country and Alaska-style flying. Ralph Wien, under an injunction which prevented him from flying in competition with Alaskan Airways, Incorporated, for a period of three years following the sale of Wien Alaska Airways, could fly for the church since it was a private aircraft, not used in general commerce. Ralph had appealed the court decision to the United States Circuit Court of Appeals but the decision had been upheld in San Francisco on July 29, 1930. It prevented the thirty-two-year-old pilot from continuing in the employ of Service Airlines as a pilot, but he continued to work in the Service Garage as a mechanic.

After circling the mission about a mile away, the *Marquette Missionary* landed at Holy Cross at 4:15 P.M. on the same day as the departure from Weeks Field. Plans were to base the plane here.

Ralph Wien, Feltes and Delon remained at Holy Cross for a few days, going on to Nome with the Bellanca Pacemaker to land there on the afternoon of Wednesday, September 24. Here the churchmen attended the Sunday rites while the citizens carefully inspected the brightly-painted flying pulpit. Resident aviators and mechanics were especially interested in the diesel engine.

The same three left Nome on Monday, September 29, with snow flurries reported to the north. Landing at Pilgrim Springs, on the left bank of the Pilgrim River, the same day, a visit to the Catholic mission kept the party there until Wednesday, October 1, 1930, at which time the plane returned to Nome.

The Fairchild 71, flown by Robbins, that had arrived in Nome on September 14, left there on Friday, September 19, 1930, to return to Fairbanks but, encountering low visibility at Golovin, was forced to return to Nome. Carrying Charles P. Sisson and four other passengers, pilot Robbins got away again at 10:30 A.M. the next day. With good weather along the route, he reached Fairbanks that afternoon. On Sunday, September 21, Ed Young made a round-trip flight to Wiseman, carrying freight out and one passenger on his return. Grant Elliott hopped off for Ruby the same day. He picked up Ike P. Taylor there and took him to Flat, planning on bringing in Captain George Green, master of the Kuskokwim River steamer *Tana,* from McGrath to Fairbanks on his return flight. G.E. "Ed" Young was off Weeks Field at 12:20 P.M. on his second attempt to return Joe Quigley to his home in the Kantishna. Quigley had recovered from injuries suffered early in the summer in a mine cave in. Robbie Robbins also made a flight to Wiseman on Tuesday, returning with passenger Al Retzlaf. Elliott flew in to Weeks Field on Thursday afternoon, September 25, 1930. He brought in Captain Green from McGrath, and had also carried Ike Taylor from Ruby to Iditarod and McGrath and in to Fairbanks.

Robbins went out to Livengood on Friday, September 26, with a load of freight, bringing in Mr. Hudson on the return trip. Ed Young was away the same day for Van Curler's bar on the upper Chena River to pick up Mrs. J.H. Sullivan. Sullivan had hiked in, arriving on Wednesday night, reporting snow in the hills to be five and six inches in depth and up to his knees where it had drifted.

In Hatton, North Dakota, in mid-September, residents were awaiting the arrival of the largest souvenir of its most famous son. The single-engined Fokker *Alaskan* was to be presented to Ole Eielson, Carl Ben Eielson's father. Without a wing, which had been used on the trimotored Fokker by Wilkins in 1927, the plane had been stored in Seattle for the last three years.

The *Alaskan* was so large, even without a wing, that it was eventually stored by the State Historical Society in Bismarck, North Dakota. At the time of this writing there was an intent to move it to Bonanzaville, near Fargo, North Dakota, where a group had long-term plans to restore the plane to flying condition. They had secured the original design from Holland to use in constructing a wing for it. However, it has, in 1988, been placed in storage in Hatton, North Dakota.

The trimotored Fokker, fitted with its original wing once again, became the *City of San Francisco* and was sold to become an entry in the ill-fated Dole Race from San Francisco to Hawaii in 1928. It wasn't prepared in time and did not participate; later it was sold to Charles Kingsford-Smith who christened it the *Southern Cross*, flying to world-wide fame and an eventual resting place in a special glass-enclosed building in Canberra, Australia at the Commonwealth Museum.

Service Airlines, currently owning a Swallow TP with an OX-5 motor, had ordered an Eaglerock biplane with a Wright Whirlwind J-5 powerplant. With the plane enroute from Seattle, Percy Hubbard's company began the construction of a hangar on Weeks Field in late September, to house the two planes. Located just south of the old Bennett-Rodebaugh Company hangars, burned the previous winter, contractor Charles Schiek expected to have the building ready for occupancy in two weeks.

Alaskan Airways pilot Grant Elliott was off on Friday, September 26, carrying Assistant U.S. Attorney E.B. Collins and Doctor J.A. Sutherland, serving as Department of Justice physician. After holding an inquest and two autopsies, one at Ruby and one at Tanana, the two men returned to Weeks Field with the pilot, landing at 1:20 P.M. on Monday, September 29, 1930. Northern Air Transport pilot Vic Ross came in from Nome on Wednesday, October 1, carrying Mrs. Paul Potter and W.C. Bell as passengers. Pilot Ross left for his Nome base on Friday, October 3. Other planes leaving that same day were three of the Alaskan Airways fleet. Pilot S.E. Robbins was away for Nome, to pick up Arthur W. Johnson. He was taking out mechanics J.T. Hutchison and Gordon Springbett, to make repairs to the company's New Standard biplane damaged recently at Golovin. Ed Young hopped off for McGrath, taking Peter Michels and Fritz Tuttle. Grant Elliott was away for Tanana, taking E.B. Collins and Deputy U.S. Marshal James Hagen, and to Ruby with Deputy U.S. Marshal Fred B. Parker. A prisoner was brought in from each of the two stops.

Ed Young, in the Fairchild 71, came in from McGrath about 6:00 P.M. on Friday, having made the round trip in one day. He was away again for Livengood the following day, bringing in Carl Olander. Grant Elliott was back on Saturday afternoon, carrying Deputy Parker and the two prisoners. Robbie Robbins, headed for Nome, was holding at Nulato because of fog and snow on the route.

The *Marquette Missionary*, Bellanca CH-300 Special, NC 862N, was in Kotzebue, Alaska on Sunday, October 12, 1930, when tragedy struck.

Preparing for a flight to Deering with Father Walsh in the diesel-powered plane, Brother Feltes had warmed the engine for forty minutes before Ralph Wien made a test flight in the ship, after awaiting on the ground to allow two small snow flurries to pass through. About four inches of snow covered the strip but the wheel-equipped plane rose easily out of it. The pilot soon landed and reported the plane to be operating normally when Feltes stepped to the window on the pilot's side to inquire. A short local flight would be made to show Father Walsh, a non-Jesuit stationed at Kotzebue, how the plane performed. Father Walsh and Father

Delon seated themselves in the center of the cabin of the Bellanca, while Brother Feltes remained behind to lighten the load; with the snow on the field and no surface wind the plane could get off easier.

Ralph Wien made a good takeoff, flying a wide circle of about a mile, then running into a snow flurry. He idled the engine and circled back to the field but found himself rather high for a landing on the 750-foot field. Applying power to the engine he pulled up and, turning to the right, he flew back about a mile to lower his glide angle. Just prior to the turn toward the landing strip, he throttled back on the engine to about one-half power, and made a rather steep left turn. It seemed to the observers on the ground that the nose of the Bellanca was somewhat high in the turn and the plane stalled, or approached a stall, with the nose dropping, as the plane fell out of control in a tight spiral from an estimated 400 feet of altitude. After about one full turn of the spiral the pilot pointed the plane's nose straight down to regain speed, and increased power on the engine again. But the Bellanca was already about fifty feet from the ground without enough altitude for a successful pull out. The plane struck the ground head-on with a speed of perhaps a hundred miles an hour, remaining so, with the tail sticking straight up into the air, the motor driven about a foot or so into the frozen tundra at a location one-half of a mile east of the post office.

The people at the airport all ran to the scene, Brother Feltes arriving at the wreck first, but it was evident there was no hope of any of the three occupants surviving. The motor and structure forward of the main cabin were crushed, with the remainder of the plane undamaged. The fabric had not a wrinkle and the controls worked freely. The broken bodies of the three occupants were all forward, with everything inside the cabin and baggage compartment piled on top, the motor driven into the frozen tundra. The plane had struck the ground at 3:45 P.M. Sunday, October 12, 1930 (Nome time).

The bodies were quickly removed and pronounced dead by the coroner, Commissioner J.W. Southward, who was present in the crowd. Transported to the village, the remains were prepared for burial by George Mock, who at one time had worked with an undertaker, and Miss Carlson, a nurse. Carpenters working on a new school building built coffins. The remains of the *Marquette Missionary* were moved away from the strip behind the buildings. A coroner's jury impanelled at Kotzebue to inquire into the cause of the deaths held adverse weather conditions to be responsible.

Bill Graham Photo

Marquette Missionary, *the Bellanca CH-300, NC 862N, of the Catholic missions, stands parked before a mission building at Kotzebue, about one hour before the fatal crash on Sunday, October 12, 1930. The Packard DR-980 diesel engine is covered with a canvas engine cover against the weather.*

Bellanca CH-300 Special, NC 862N, the **Marquette Missionary,** *crashed at Kotzebue, Alaska on Sunday, October 12, 1930. The pilot, Ralph Wien, and his two passengers, Father Philip Delon and Father Walsh, Kotzebue priest, did not survive.*

Oregon Province Archives

Ralph Wien's body would be flown to Fairbanks, to be transported to the family plot in Cook, Minnesota. His wife, Julia, had collapsed upon hearing of the crash and had been taken to Saint Josephs Hospital. Her two small sons, Jimmy, four, and Bobby, two, were being cared for by friends. Because of her illness, the Fairbanks funeral was not held until Wednesday, October 29, with the family leaving with the casket by train the following day for Seattle and Minnesota, as pilot Joe Crosson circled overhead.

Sam White had wired the sad news to Noel Wien who was still Outside, but who was then preparing to return to Alaska. Robbie Robbins was in Nome with the Fairchild 71. Taking Manager Arthur W. Johnson and R.S. Pollister as passengers, the pilot departed Nome the morning of Tuesday, October 14, for Kotzebue and Fairbanks. The funeral plane arrived on Weeks Field at 7:45 P.M. that same evening, landing after dark with the aid of flares set out by the mechanics. The 425-mile flight had taken longer than usual with headwinds blowing forty miles an hour or more, whipping dust from the sandbars along the rivers in great clouds.

The body of Father William F. Walsh, a thirty-year-old priest who had recently arrived in Kotzebue from San Francisco, was to be sent to Oakland for burial. That of Father Philip I. Delon, head of the Jesuit missions in Alaska and a fourteen-year veteran of Jesuit service in the Territory, would be buried in Spokane, where he had studied and taught at Gonzaga University. A vessel standing offshore of Kotzebue awaited the bodies of the two priests. The ice was moving in and the boat could not remain long. Loading the two coffins into a small boat, the Kotzebue residents fought their way through the shore ice and, after a struggle, were able to load them aboard. Taken in to Nome, the coffins were put aboard the *S.S. Victoria,* the last vessel to sail from Nome that season for the trip Outside. The ship sailed on Saturday, October 25, 1930, with 200 passengers, including Brother Feltes who had come in by plane.

NOTE: There is a possibility the diesel engine of the *Marquette Missionary* may have lagged or stalled when the pilot reapplied the power, thus contributing to the wing stalling, or approaching a stall, on the Bellanca. No one will ever know for sure.

1018

Great credence must be lent to the detailed report of Brother Feltes, made soon after the accident. He was the most knowledgeable person present in the aviation field, with an intimate knowledge of the aircraft and its diesel engine; he had put a considerable number of hours in the aircraft and had been trained on it at the factory. He also observed the event from start to finish. His confidence in the Packard DR-980 engine remained, for he again brought a Bellanca Pacemaker with the same model of engine to Alaska the following year.

Inherently a German design, the Packard Diesel was soon to be dropped from use by the aviation industry because it lacked flexibility, dependability and had other undesirable characteristics that overcame its good points. Although a commercial failure, the design led to the diesel aircraft engines developed in Germany by Junkers, and used during World War II. The British at the end of the war developed the *Nomad*, a combination of a turbo-compressor diesel with a jet-augmented exhaust, driving two contra-rotating propellers. Too close to the jet age, the design was soon by-passed.

The **Marquette Missionary,** *NC 862N, lies behind church buildings at Kotzebue after being moved from site of the fatal crash that occurred on Sunday, October 12, 1930 when Ralph Wien was flying the plane.*

Oregon Province Archives

The Service Airlines new hangar on Weeks Field was nearing completion when the company's new Alexander Eaglerock biplane, NC 209Y, arrived in Fairbanks on Wednesday, October 15, 1930, purchased through Meals Eaglerock Sales Company of Valdez. Powered with a Wright Whirlwind J-5 motor of 220 horsepower, it was designed to cruise at 115 miles per hour with a 600-mile radius. Landing speed was thirty-five miles per hour. Percy Hubbard had requested special oversized wheels, equipped with brakes, fitted on the ship. Weighing only about 1,700 pounds empty, there was room for two passengers in addition to the pilot. The Service Airlines hangar, on its concrete foundation, could accommodate two planes, with a shop in the rear into which the nose of a plane could be worked on in cold

*Fairbanks, Alaska in 1930. Lineup of Northern Air Transport,
Incorporated and Service Airlines planes. Left to Right: Stinson
Detroiter SM-1F, NC 404M, NAT No. 2; Stinson Junior SM-2AA,
NC 475H, NAT No. 1; Eaglerock NC 209Y of Service Airlines;
OX-5 Swallow TP, C 688H, of Service Airlines. Alaskan Airways
hangar on left, Service Airlines hangar on right.*

Vic Ross Photo

Art Hines, partner with Percy Hubbard in Service Airlines and Service Motor Company, standing with the new Alexander Eaglerock, NC 209Y. Purchased through Meals Eaglerock Sales Company of Valdez, the plane arrived in Fairbanks on October 15, 1930. It was powered with a Wright Whirlwind J-5 motor of 220 horsepower. The photo is taken at Summit Lake.

Percy Hubbard Photo

weather when not practical to heat the entire hangar. Winter was on the way and the air company would be ready.

Bill Graham, chief pilot for Northern Air Transport, Incorporated, of Nome arrived on Weeks Field at 11:30 A.M. Thursday, October 16, 1930. Flying his Stinson monoplane No. 2, NC 404M, the pilot brought in Andy Nerland and Louis Husdale, employees of the Hammon Consolidated Gold Fields. He had also carried H.E. Seneff, liquor control agent, from Nome to Tanana. Graham had enjoyed good weather during the flight, stopping overnight at Ruby. The pilot had come in to Nome the previous Sunday, bringing an insane Eskimo to put aboard the *Victoria* for the States. (see Nome—1930, Chapter 59).

With clear weather in the Interior for the last few days, Alaskan Airways pilots were busy. Ed Young and Grant Elliott both made flights to Livengood on Thursday, October 16, bringing back Georgia Lee, Tom Verdi and Erik Nelson. The following day, Friday, Ed Young was off in the forenoon for Takotna and McGrath, to pick up two passengers. Grant Elliott went again to Livengood, taking a load of freight. The pilot was away in the forenoon on Saturday, returning to his base at Nome. He carried William Wagner, a civil service radio electrician attached to the United States Signal Corps, who was going to Nome to install a new radio tube transmitter at the Nome station. Expecting to spend about thirty days in Nome on the job, he then planned to go to Anchorage to make a similar installation. Ed Young was coming in from the Kuskokwim, expected Saturday afternoon.

Alaskan Airways, Incorporated, manager Arthur Johnson announced expansion plans on October 18, 1930. A Keystone Commuter amphibian, NC 539V, was shipped from the Keystone Aircraft Corporation plant at Bristol, Pennsylvania on October 14, and on October 7 a New Standard biplane was shipped from the New Jersey factory, both consigned to Anchorage, giving the base three planes. There was a possibility of bringing the New Standard on to Fairbanks, leaving the Fairchild 71, NC 9153, at the Anchorage base instead. Plans included assigning a second pilot to Anchorage, and a second one to the Nome base, to assist Grant Elliott in cleaning up the fall business on the Seward Peninsula. Independent offices for Alaskan Airways had been established in Nome by Manager Johnson on his recent visit there, with Dan Crowley in charge. Dan had accepted the position as manager of Alaskan Airways in Nome the previous fall, after serving for the past ten years as field manager for the Lomen Commercial Company. Crowley had been a resident of Nome since 1900. Work was being started on a hangar in Nome, a sixty by forty-five foot lumber and corrugated iron building with space to accommodate three planes. Nose hangars were to be built at one end so the motors could be worked on in the heated shop during cold weather.

In the coming spring Johnson expected to have a system in Fairbanks using a combination of land and water capability on some flying equipment for the summer months in order to give better service. The New Standard on the way to Anchorage was similar to the D-25s now at Fairbanks. One of the two currently being used had a canopy or lid that could be placed over the four-passenger front cockpit, or removed as necessary.

Joe and Lillian Crosson arrived back in Fairbanks on Friday, October 18, 1930, after a two-month honeymoon and vacation in the States. Following a stay in San Diego, the Crossons had traveled by train to St. Paul, where they visited with Andy Hufford, mechanic on the Wilkins 1926 Detroit Arctic Expedition. Hufford was now chief mechanic for Northwest Airways.

Again by train, the Crossons turned west to Hatton, North Dakota to make a promised visit with Ole Eielson at the home town of Carl Ben Eielson. Pat Reid and Sam Macauley came down from Winnipeg, and all were guests at a big banquet and reception. The Crossons later traveled the 250 miles by auto to visit Winnipeg. Traveling west again by rail, they saw Orval Porter in Spokane, now married and located there. The Crossons then visited Ben's sister, Adeline, in Wenatchee, Washington, before continuing on to Seattle. Arriving at the port city on Thursday, October 9, 1930, the couple departed on the steamer *Northwestern* for Cordova on the following day.

Harold Gillam flew his Swallow, NC 430N, over from Valdez on Thursday, October 16, to meet the Crossons at Cordova. He departed Mile 17 airport, with the couple aboard, at 10:55 A.M. on Friday. Passing over Chitina at 12:10 P.M., Gillam landed the Swallow at Copper Center shortly afterward, to remain overnight. Gillam continued on with his passengers to Fairbanks, landing on Weeks Field in mid-afternoon on Saturday. The flight from the coast had been made in four hours. In the two months the Crossons had been gone, they had flown only once, as passengers from Seattle to Los Angeles on the way south. Making their home on Fourth Avenue near Cowles Street, Joe Crosson was to resume his position as chief pilot for Alaskan Airways, Incorporated.

Ed Young was away from Weeks Field the morning of Tuesday, October 21, in the Fairchild 71; the plane loaded to capacity with mail, as well as one passenger, Carl Zetterlund. He dropped the man at Circle Hot Springs, along with mail for that point and for Circle. The field there would not accommodate the larger plane and the mail was taken over by John Palm in his auto. The pilot went on to Beaver and Fort Yukon with the balance of the mail. Pilot Young had come in from the Kuskokwim to Fairbanks on Saturday, October 18, 1930, bringing Archie Higgins, dredgeman, and William Lodge.

Joe Crosson was also up on Tuesday, October 21, in Stearman, NC 5415, flying for twenty minutes and making three landings at Weeks Field to get into the feel of flying again. He was off in the open-cockpit plane the next day on a round trip to Livengood, carrying mail. Matt Nieminen had come in from Anchorage in Fairchild 71, NC 9153, on October 21, then left for his home base on the following day, Wednesday.

Joe Crosson, again flying the Stearman, was away for Livengood on the afternoon of Friday, October 24, 1930, carrying Alaska Road Commission Superintendent Frank Nash. The superintendent was to inspect the airfield there and arrange for putting men to work enlarging the strip, making it possible for larger freight loads to be hauled in. Takeoffs and landings were virtually impossible on the current field when a crosswind blew, restricting its useage. Crosson made the round trip in the usual hour and one-half. Alaskan Airways, Incorporated, had been in the practice of carrying $10,000 of insurance on each passenger carried in their planes. It had now been raised to $25,000 per seat at no cost to the passenger. This insurance was a standard practice by the large carriers in the States, and a direct result of Alaskan Airways being part of The Aviation Corporation.

Bill Graham, Northern Air Transport pilot from Nome, landed his Stinson monoplane No. 2 on Weeks Field about 2:00 P.M. Tuesday, October 28, 1930, after fighting a heavy snowstorm all the way from Ruby, following the rivers. Winter was on the way. He had left Nome on the previous day and flown to Ruby, where he overnighted. He brought James K. Crowdy, manager, Ralph T. Hirsch and N.F. Lott, all of the New York-Alaska (gold dredging) Company. The pilot left for Nome on Wednesday, October 29, taking Russell G. Maynard, publisher of the *Nome Nugget*, as a passenger.

Joe Crosson made a short flight in the Stearman, NC 5415, on the morning of Thursday, October 30, slowly circling above the train bearing the body of fellow-airman Ralph Wien and his family as it left the Fairbanks station. He went to Livengood and back the same day in the plane, totaling one hour and fifty minutes for the day. Crosson left on a longer trip in the Stearman the following day, Friday, going to Ruby and return, with an air time of five hours and twenty minutes. S.E. Robbins was off Friday, October 31, 1930, for Ruby, Flat, Holy Cross and Nome, in a heavily-loaded Fairchild 71. Robbins was taking Johnny Glass, a native recently released from the federal jail after serving out a sentence on a drunk and disorderly charge, to his home in Ruby. An eleven-year-old native boy who had been under

Fairchild 71, NC 153H, on the river ice in front of Beaver, Alaska.

treatment at St. Josephs Hospital was being taken to the Catholic mission at Holy Cross. The weather enroute was good, with the exception of Solomon.

Alaskan Airways, Incorporated, was surveying their operations with the intent of setting up regular schedules on their routes, rather than making trips as the need arose. They planned to open with an initial flight on the Fairbanks-Nome route on Monday, November 17, with planes leaving thereafter on every second Monday. Stops enroute were planned for Tanana, Ruby, Nulato and Unalakleet. The Fairchild 71s were the planes to be used on the flights. When the Alaska Railroad train service ran on a ten-day basis in the winter, Manager Johnson planned to increase the number of scheduled flights to three monthly, with the flight leaving the day following the arrival of the train. On Monday, November 24, the company planned to inaugurate regular service to Circle Hot Springs, Circle, Fort Yukon and Beaver, also flying to those points on alternate Mondays. Gold dust was to be carried at regular express rates where the owner or consignee assumed the responsibility. Previously, double express rates were charged. A displacement rate would be offered on furs, in place of the double express rate. A schedule was also being set up from Anchorage into the Iditarod and Kuskokwim districts.

Freddie Moller returned to Weeks Field in his Waco 9 biplane, C 2776, *Anna*, having taken a load of freight to the Wild River country, six miles northeast of Bettles, for prospector Gus Wagner. He had been gone a week, bringing in Joe Smith from Bettles to Nenana, the passenger catching the southbound train enroute to the States.

To aid Matt Nieminen in ferrying passengers from the Iditarod and Kuskokwim to Anchorage, Joe Crosson left Fairbanks at 11:30 A.M. Friday, November 7, in the Fairchild 71, NC 153H. Flying from Weeks Field to McGrath to Flat, and back to McGrath the first day, he spent four hours and forty minutes in the air. On Sunday, November 9, the pilot flew from McGrath to Flat, back to McGrath, and on in to Anchorage, taking the plane out again to Medfra to spend the night. He had put in six hours and five minutes in the air. Crosson left Medfra the next morning, November 10, going to McGrath, Flat, and back to McGrath before coming in to Fairbanks, flying for four hours and forty minutes. He brought in Mr. Mespelt from Medfra, Mr. and Mrs. George Adams from Flat, and Fritz Tuttle from McGrath. Pilot S.E. Robbins came in almost simultaneously from Shungnak, with C.E. Alexander, Mr. LaRue and William James. The miners and dredgemen were moving in from the creeks as winter set in.

Alaskan Airways, Incorporated, received a shipment of four Irving parachutes of a type approved by the Department of Commerce, and used by the mail carriers in the States. Made of the highest quality Canton silk, the chutes were not intended for normal use by Alaskan Airways but were intended to meet the requirement of the U.S. Postal Service, in that mail contract pilots were required to wear parachutes when it was necessary to make trips in hazardous weather conditions. The airways intended to be prepared in the event they were awarded mail contracts.

Lomen Reindeer Corporation was having difficulty in driving a reindeer herd from the west coast of Alaska to the MacKenzie River for delivery to the Canadian government. Starting out from the Kotzebue Sound country, they were now at the Hunt River, a tributary of the Kobuk. With glare ice on the river, the deer had refused to cross for the last three weeks. Andy Bahr and his herders had tried every stratagem, even roughening the ice by chopping, and carrying snow on to it. Robbie Robbins, using a Fairchild 71, had already flown one load of supplies to them. After returning to the Kobuk, he had brought three passengers from Shungnak to Fairbanks, arriving there on November 10, 1930, leaving his mechanic, J.T. Hutchison, at Shungnak. Robbins was to make another four or five trips to ferry supplies across to the Noatak for the reindeer drive.

In response to a wire from Matt Nieminen in Anchorage, Joe Crosson left Weeks Field for the port city on Wednesday, November 12, taking the Stearman C-2B, NC 5415. He arrived in Anchorage three hours and fifteen minutes later. While there, he flew to Kashwitna to drop Matt Nieminen at the Waco 10, NC 780E, which had been under repair for some time, and now the pilot could bring it in to Anchorage. (see Anchorage—1930, Chapter 57). Crosson returned with the Stearman, flying it back to Fairbanks on Sunday, November 16, a four-hour flight by a roundabout route through the valleys, caused by bad weather at Healy. Joe flew a round trip to Livengood in the plane the next day.

Robbie Robbins was away from Weeks Field at 10:30 A.M. on Monday, November 17, 1930, for Kotzebue via the Kobuk. Doctor R. Edward Smith, who had been in charge of the Bureau of Educations' Yukon River hospital boat, and was taken severely ill the previous winter, had been confined to St. Josephs Hospital for several weeks. Now recovered, he and Mrs. Smith were returning to his winter station at Kotzebue with the pilot. Robbins also planned to stop at Shungnak to pick up Dan Crowley, manager of the Nome office of Alaskan Airways, and mechanic Jim Hutchison. The pilot intended to resume the ferrying of supplies from the Kobuk to the Noatak for the reindeer drive, after dropping his passengers at Kotzebue. They could connect there with Grant Elliott for Nome.

Joe Crosson's visit with Orval Porter in Spokane in October resulted in the former Wilkins mechanic accepting a position with Alaskan Airways in Fairbanks. Mrs. Porter arrived there by train on Monday, November 17, 1930. Orval arrived soon after; he had spent the last few weeks in Anchorage doing some work there for the company, which included setting up the Keystone Commuter.

The first scheduled flight of Alaskan Airways between Fairbanks and Nome, was away the forenoon of Tuesday, November 18, with Joe Crosson at the controls of the Fairchild 71, NC 153H. Four passengers: A.M. Hartford of the Fairbanks Exploration Company; Thomas Gaffney, Democratic candidate for auditor in the recent election; and Albert Aukon and Billy Komakhuk, reindeer field foremen for the Bureau of Biological Survey, were aboard the plane, the latter two leaving the plane at Golovin. Filling the balance of the load with mail, Crosson flew to Tanana and Ruby that day, taking three hours and ten minutes. He was off Ruby on November 20, flying to Nulato, Golovin and Nome in four hours and twenty-five minutes of air time. He had been delayed at Ruby and Golovin by weather. Crosson left Nome the following day, November 21, flying the Fairchild to Unalakleet and Ruby with J.H. Anderson and A.N. Nylen as passengers in three hours and forty-five minutes. He completed the flight the next day, bringing his passengers in to Weeks Field in two hours and twenty minutes of air time.

Ed Young, Alaskan Airways pilot, had made a round-trip flight to Fort Yukon and return, landing back on Weeks Field early in the afternoon of Friday, November 21. He carried mail and freight out, and returned with one passenger, Joe Droch. Matt Nieminen, Anchorage pilot for the company, came in to Weeks Field that same afternoon in the Fairchild 71, NC 9153, from Flat, bringing four passengers. He was away again on Sunday, November 23, 1930, enroute to his Anchorage headquarters via Flat and McGrath.

Young, leaving for Nome on the same day, with W.B. Miller of the Biological Survey as a passenger, was forced back by bad weather. He set out again the following day.

Robbie Robbins landed about noon on Monday, November 24, from Shungnak. He had brought Jim Hutchison and Dan Crowley to Fairbanks.

Flying the Fairchild 71, NC 154H, Alaskan Airways chief pilot Joe Crosson, was off Weeks Field at 9:45 A.M. Tuesday, November 25, 1930, bound for Wiseman. Deputy Marshal Fred B. Parker accompanied him. They were picking up Mrs. Jesse Allan, who had been judged insane and committed to Morningside Sanitarium in Portland, Oregon. Unable to make it to Wiseman, Crosson landed at Livengood and returned to Weeks Field after flying four hours and ten minutes. Sanis E. Robbins (Robbie) made a flight to Tanana, leaving at 9:15 A.M. Wednesday, November 26, and arriving back on Weeks Field at 12:45 P.M. after spending an hour in Tanana. Deputy Marshal Parker, making the flight, picked up Julius Henry, native, who had been committed to Morningside. The man was to be sent out the following week.

Ed Young flew in from Nome on Wednesday afternoon in a Fairchild 71, bringing three passengers: J.D. Harlan, resident manager of Hammon Consolidated Gold Fields; George Hellerich, a Hammon engineer; and radio electrician Wagner of the Signal Corps. Young had stopped overnight at Golovin, after leaving Nome early Tuesday afternoon.

Fred Moller also returned on Wednesday in his OXX-6 Waco 9, C 2776, following an extended trip to the Kobuk country. Moller had taken Bill Dugan, a prospector and miner from Fairbanks, to Long Beach in the mining district, arriving there on November 14, 1930. In attempting to take off on Sunday, November 16, the propeller on the Waco 9 struck a two-foot pole, shearing eighteen inches off the end of one blade and shattering the rest. Moller took the remnants to Dahl Creek where a Mr. Lloyd had a set of tools. The splintered section was trimmed and repaired, and a piece of spruce was fashioned in place of the broken section. Banding the two parts together with a homemade welding outfit completed the job, and the reconstructed propeller served for the balance of the flight. Freddie was good at fixing things but when it came to airplanes, he was good at breaking them.

Freddie Moller got away on Sunday, November 23, following the Reed River to Gull Pass, along the upper Noatak, rising terrain forcing him up to 6000 feet. He then flew down the Alatna River to Alatna village, where he made a landing. It was fifty below zero here on the ground when Freddie departed for Fairbanks on Wednesday, November 26. With a temperature inversion, it was only twenty below zero at 200 feet and only two below at 1000 feet. When the pilot crossed the Yukon, flying still higher, the thermometer lashed to his wing strut registered twelve above zero, Fahrenheit.

By the end of November Alaskan Airways was advertising special rates to Circle Hot Springs. It was the season for the hard-working miners and others with crippling ailments to soak in the hot baths at the resort. Four or more passengers in a group could fly from Fairbanks for fifty dollars per passenger each way, in cabin heated planes.

Robbie Robbins started off the month of December for Alaskan Airways, flying the company's New Standard biplane to bring in Commissioner Laboyteaux and mining man C.W. Hudson from Livengood. Dan Crowley, manager for Alaskan Airways, Incorporated, in Nome, had been in Fairbanks for several days conferring with General Manager Arthur W. Johnson and was now ready to return home. He left at 9:00 A.M. Tuesday, December 2, 1930, with Joe Crosson at the controls of the Fairchild 71, NC 153H. The pilot also carried his wife, Lillian, and Stinson factory mechanic Gale L. Alexander as passengers. Alexander was to repair a badly-damaged Northern Air Transport Stinson.

Stormy weather caused the pilot to call a halt at Ruby after two hours and fifteen minutes of flight. He remained there over Wednesday and Thursday, leaving on Friday to reach Golovin after stopping briefly at Unalakleet. He had been in the air enroute for three hours and thirty minutes. The party reached Nome at 10:30 A.M. Saturday, December 6, after overnighting at Golovin. Dropping his passengers, along with a large consignment of freight and express, Crosson returned to Golovin that same day, flying one hour and forty-five minutes on the round trip, to overnight there again. Lillian Crosson had remained at Grant and Barbara Elliott's place in Nome. The pilot put in two more hours of flying time in the Fairchild, flying from Golovin, Teller and again into Nome. He was helping Grant Elliott catch up on the business on the Seward Peninsula. Crosson continued to fly trips out of Nome for the next week. There was a great deal of freight to move, as well as passengers. One of the Northern Air Transport Stinsons, No. 2, was out of service and being repaired, and the other had engine problems.

On Tuesday, December 16, Crosson took off Nome, intending to go to Fairbanks. He got away from Koyuk the following day but weather forced him back. Later in the day he flew to Dime and returned to Koyuk. The ice went out and they were all stranded in the village, staying at Big Sam's roadhouse until the wind changed and the pilot could get away with his passengers. Crosson departed Koyuk in the Fairchild 71, NC 153H, on Friday, December 19, 1930, flying to Unalakleet and Nulato to overnight. He was now on the way to Fairbanks with Lillian Crosson, Charles Milot of the Lomen Corporation, H.L. Stull of Deering and Lewis Stull, the mining man's son. Lewis had an epileptic-like seizure in the plane which was extremely disturbing. The pilot was away from Nulato the next day, Saturday, making it to Ruby in one hour and fifteen minutes of flying, to remain overnight again. Crosson took the plane and passengers on to Fairbanks on Sunday, December 21, 1930, landing at Weeks Field after a three hour and ten minute flight. Lewis Stull, who had been ill, died less than twenty-four hours after his arrival.

When Joe Crosson departed for Nome on December 2, it left Ed Young and Robbie Robbins to handle the flying business out of Fairbanks. Young got away that same day, at 11:00 A.M. for Circle Hot Springs. He carried Lockie McLain as a passenger for that point, with Alaskan Airways office employee Dan McDonald making the round trip with the pilot. Robbins was off Weeks Field at 9:00 A.M. Friday, December 5, headed for Tanana and Ruby, with a stop scheduled at Manley Hot Springs on his return. He had one passenger, A.J. Burke, for Ruby. Robbins landed at Weeks Field at 3:00 P.M. that same afternoon, bringing in Vic Ross from Hot Springs (now Manley Hot Springs). The Northern Air Transport pilot had left his Stinson No. 1, NC 475H, there. The 225 horsepower Wright J-5 motor was disabled. Robbins went out again in the New Standard D-25 on Monday, December 8, 1930, taking C.W. Hudson to his home in Livengood.

In December, Alaskan Airways, Incorporated, in Fairbanks, was designated by the Department of Commerce, under the Civil Aeronautics Acts of 1926, as an approved repair station for the repair of aircraft; it had the repair equipment, shop facilities, personnel and manufacturers' repair data to make repairs to licensed aircraft. This was important to the company's maintenance program as well as to other repair customers.

Northern Air Transport, Incorporated, received their third Stinson, NC 495Y, on the train arriving on Sunday, December 7. Vic Ross was in Fairbanks to receive it and was preparing to assemble the Stinson Junior No. 3, a four-passenger cabin plane. It was powered with a 210 horsepower Lycoming motor, the first power plant of this type in the north.

Taking mail and express for Flat, McGrath and for Bethel, Alaskan Airways pilot G.E. "Ed" Young was off Weeks Field in the forenoon of Thursday, December 11, 1930. He expected to fly first to Flat, dropping the Bethel cargo for another plane to relay, and picking up businessman Harry Donelley for Fairbanks. The pilot went from Flat to McGrath to overnight there.

Matt Nieminen, Alaskan Airways pilot from Anchorage, was missing on December 11 in the Iditarod country. The company sent S.E. Robbins and Jim Hutchison, in the Stearman, NC 5415, out from Fairbanks on Sunday, December 14, 1930, to aid in the search, but Ed Young, already in the Kuskokwim flying a Fairchild 71, located Nieminen on the Dishna River before Robbins had time to join in the search. (see Anchorage—1930, Chapter 57). Accompanied by Milton Rice, Young landed on a snow-covered flat studded with small brush, and transferred forty gallons of fuel from his plane to Nieminen's Fairchild. Frank Dorbandt of Pacific International Airways of Anchorage came in with more fuel. All the planes took off safely and Young landed at Takotna where S.E. Robbins awaited them. The affair had ended well. The planes suffered minor damage to the belly fabric from the small brush. Ed Young and Robbie Robbins, flying together, left on the morning of Wednesday, December 17, 1930, landing at Weeks Field shortly after 3:00 P.M. the same day. Mrs. Kennedy and Mrs. Christiansen were passengers from Flat to Nenana, and Harry Donelley and Milton Rice came to Fairbanks.

Robbie Robbins was off in the Fairchild 71 the morning of Friday, December 19, for Circle Hot Springs and way points. He carried Assistant U.S. Attorney E.B. Collins and Mrs. Clarence E. Burglin, who were going to conduct an investigation into a murder at Fort Yukon, and Miss Clara H. Dickenson, a nurse who arrived from the States the day before and who was going to Fort Yukon also, to serve in that capacity. Robbins was back on Weeks Field on Sunday, December 21, bringing in Collins, Mrs. Burglin and John Alexander, an Indian prisoner. Joe Crosson had also arrived from Ruby.

Noel Wien, accompanied by his brother Sig, landed on Weeks Field, Fairbanks, from the States, on December 21, 1930. He had been away from Alaska for more than a year. His Stinson Junior SM-2AB, NC 490H, with a Wright Whirlwind J-5 motor, carried a logo of a modernistic pilot wing with Wien, Nome, Alaska, lettered in the shield. The Wien brothers were met in Fairbanks by Ada and baby Merrill, who had come by train and boat.

Vic Ross Photo

NOEL WIEN
PHOTO

Hatton, North Dakota, on December 8, 1930. Noel and Sig Wien were ferrying their orange and black Stinson Junior SM-2AB, NC 490H, from Virginia, Minnesota to Fairbanks when they stopped here to visit with Ben Eielson's father. Sig, making his first trip to Alaska, stands with Ole Eielson in the foreground. Ada and Merrill, the baby, were traveling by train and ship.

Back in Alaska after an absence of over a year, Noel Wien, who had left Fairbanks by train on September 19, 1929, landed on Weeks Field from the States at 11:50 A.M. Sunday, December 21, 1930. Flying his Stinson Junior SM-2AB, NC 490H, powered by a 220 horsepower Wright J-5, the former Alaskan pilot was accompanied by his brother Sigurd. Noel had arrived by auto in Detroit, Michigan on October 31, 1929, to take possession of the orange and black plane, staying with the Eddie Stinsons while it was being prepared. Noel, accompanied by Ada, flew the Stinson to Minnesota in easy stages. Their son, Merrill, was born on April 4, 1930. Noel decided to return to Alaska and take a job with Alaskan Airways. He drove Ada and the baby to Minneapolis on October 12, 1930, to put them on the train for Seattle. It was here that he heard of Ralph's death at Kotzebue; his sister phoned from Cook to read him a wire from Sam White in Fairbanks.

In silence the party returned to Cook to await the arrival of Ralph's family and the casket, which left Fairbanks on October 30, 1930. The funeral was held on November 14, with the remains of the thirty-two year-old aviator buried in the family plot at Cook, Minnesota.

The Stinson Junior, now at Virginia, Minnesota, the most convenient airfield to the family home at Cook, was prepared for the flight north. Again driving Ada and the baby to Minneapolis, where they were put on the train for Seattle to take a steamer to Alaska, Noel returned to Cook and the airplane. The Stinson was ready for the flight west, with a modernistic logo on the side of the fuselage of a pilot's wing with Wien, Nome, Alaska lettered in the shield, and Virginia, Minnesota to Nome, Alaska emblazoned above it in painted letters. Accompanied by his twenty-seven year-old brother Sig, the flier was off in the first week of December, 1930.

Stopping at Hatton, North Dakota on Monday, December 8, to visit Ole Eielson, Ben's father, the Wien brothers continued on to fly a northwesterly course across Saskatchewan and Alberta to Prince George, British Columbia. They arrived there on Friday, December 12. Ada and young Merrill had departed Seattle on the steamer *Yukon* on Wednesday, December 10. The Stinson Junior, NC 490H, landed at Telegraph Creek on Thursday, December 18, the pilot holding for better weather. Ada had arrived in Fairbanks by train on that same day. Noel flew from Atlin to Dawson on Saturday, stopping at Whitehorse only long enough to refuel. The 275-mile flight from Dawson to Fairbanks, in clear weather, was completed in three hours and five minutes.

Met in Fairbanks by his wife and son, Noel hurried his preparations to continue on to Nome, wanting to reach there in time to spend Christmas holidays with Mrs. Wien's parents, the Arthurs. The family, along with Sig, hopped off in the Stinson from Weeks Field at 10:00 A.M. Monday, December 22, 1930, making it to Ruby in two hours and ten minutes, continuing on to Nulato. They arrived in Nome at noon on the day before Christmas, December 24, after a stopover at Nulato.

Greeted by family and friends, the Wiens enjoyed the holiday season. Eight-month-old Merrill, who had slept most of the way on the flight to Nome, soon had a new mode of transportation, for his grandfather, William Arthurs, had an Eskimo make a small basket sled of hickory on runners of the same material, an Alaskan baby buggy that Ada could push about on the snow.

Ed Young, Fairbanks pilot for Alaskan Airways, arrived in Nome on Wednesday, December 24, 1930, with a huge load of mail and Christmas packages which the post office immediately sorted out. A second flight was necessary to remove the backlog in Fairbanks. Frank Dorbandt, Pacific International Airways pilot in Anchorage, came in to Weeks Field in Fairbanks, landing at 1:20 P.M., December 24, bringing in three passengers for the coast. On his way from Ruby he also picked up a sick person at Nulato. Spending Christmas here, he left for Anchorage with his three passengers: Lomen official Charles Milot of Nome, Mickey Goldstein and Lyman DeStaffany, fur buyers of Juneau and Seattle, respectively, on the morning of Friday, December 26, 1930.

Chief Pilot Joseph Essler Crosson was off Weeks Field the forenoon of Friday, December 26, for Chicken and Dawson. Flying the Fairchild 71, NC 154H, and carrying John Smacker, former dredgemaster for the Fairbanks Exploration Company, he completed the flight in three hours and twenty-five minutes. Remaining overnight at Dawson, the pilot left the following day, returning by way of Eagle to Fairbanks, taking three hours of air time. He brought in Miss Jean Dempster from Eagle.

S.E. Robbins had also gotten away from Weeks Field on Friday in the New Standard biplane for Chicken Creek, carrying Ted Tronstad and William Noel. He was back in Fairbanks on Saturday afternoon with Mrs. Mitchell, from Chicken Creek, as a passenger.

Art Hines and Percy Hubbard, Service Airlines pilots, landed their Eaglerock biplane, NC 209Y, on Weeks Field after dark on Friday afternoon, December 26, 1930, on their return from McGrath. They had flown to the upper Kuskokwim community on December 24, to spend the holiday with Percy's parents. The pair had good weather on the flight out, but found it rather heavy going in places on their return flight.

Vic Ross, Northern Air Transport pilot, was off for his home base in Nome on the morning of Monday, December 29, 1930. Carrying Doctor Rex F. Swartz as a passenger, Vic was making the flight in the newly-assembled Stinson Junior No. 3, NC 495Y. He had test flown the monoplane at Weeks Field the previous week. The plane was powered with the new 210 horsepower Lycoming.

Joe Crosson was off again on his last flight for the year, on Tuesday, December 30, 1930, in the Fairchild 71, NC 154H, going to Wiseman and return. He carried a large load of holiday mail and a passenger, Mrs. F.V. Ulen, wife of the U.S. Signal Corps operator at the mining community, who had recently returned from a trip to the States. Crosson made the round trip in four hours.

Carl Benjamin Eielson, photographed upon his arrival back in Alaska in July of 1929, bringing eastern capital which put the struggling aviation industry in the Territory on a solid footing. Today's network of aviation services is a fitting memorial to this early Alaskan pilot.

Vic Ross Photo

1034

Alaskan Airways, Incorporated

Eielson-Borland Relief
Expedition
Northern Air Transport,
Incorporated

Nome 1930

W ITH THE BEGINNING OF THE NEW YEAR in Nome, the Seward Peninsula communities were being served out of there by Northern Air Transport, Incorporated, with their one airplane, the Stinson Junior, NC 475H, flown by Bill Graham. Trips were occasionally being made by Alaskan Airways pilots but the company was concentrating on the search for their two missing airmen, Carl Ben Eielson and Earl Borland, with their two New Standard biplanes, NC 9190 and NC 174H and the Stinson SB-1, NC 877, at Teller most of the time. Joe Crosson and Harold Gillam were at the *Nanuk* in Siberia, with the Waco 10, NC 780E, and the Stearman C-2B, NC 5415. The three Fairchild 71s of the relief expedition were expected in from Fairbanks any day; the Bessie road Municipal Field had been plowed and leveled with tractors in expectation of their arrival. (Bessie road originally led to a large gold dredge of that name).

To further complicate things, word had been received on Saturday, December 28, that the Stinson Junior SM-2AA, NC 475H, flown by pilot Bill Graham for Northern Air Transport, with a heavy load aboard, had damaged its landing gear on takeoff at Deering. Repair supplies were needed from Nome to put the plane back in service.

Frank Dorbandt, flying the Stinson SB-1, NC 877, came in to Nome about 1:30 P.M. Wednesday, January 8, 1930. He had been stormbound at Solomon for almost a week. He was off for Teller at 2:00 P.M. the following day, taking his mechanic, Clark Bassett, as well as Vic Ross of Northern Air Transport. Ross planned on taking the New Standard D-25, now at Teller,

Northern Air Transport No. 2, NC 404M, at Nome.
William Cameron at left and Vic Ross at right.

Two Fairchild 71s of Alaskan Airways flying in formation. The cream and red planes were a pretty sight against the snow-covered mountains in the background.

bringing it in to Nome for the purpose of taking a load of freight to Elephant Point, plus carrying repair parts for the Northern Air Transport Stinson, still at Deering with a broken landing gear.

Matt Nieminen, carrying Major Deckard and Sam Macauley, arrived in Nome on Sunday, January 12, 1930, with the first Fairchild 71, NC 153H, of the Eielson-Borland Relief Expedition. The Canadian pilot, Pat Reid, arrived in the Fairchild 71, CF-AJK, on Wednesday, January 15. He was carrying mechanics Bill Hughes and Jim Hutchison, who had repaired the plane when it was damaged in an unscheduled landing at the headwaters of the Ungalik River. Both crews had suffered considerable delay and discomfort on the trip. (see Fairbanks—1930, Chapter 58).

Ed Young, who had recently brought in the New Standard, NC 174H, from Teller, began flying cargoes of gasoline and engine lubricating oil from Nome to Teller in the Fairchild 71, NC 153H, while more permanent repairs were being made to the damaged wing of CF-AJK at Nome.

Canadian pilot Gifford Swartman, with his mechanic C.T.K. Mews, had left Fairbanks in the Alaskan Airways red cabin Swallow. He arrived in Nome at 3:30 P.M. Wednesday, January 15, 1930. Swartman took off the following day for Deering, carrying repair parts for the damaged Stinson Junior, NC 475H. He also took William A. Oliver and a welding outfit to make permanent repairs to the Northern Air Transport plane. Swartman returned to Nome at noon on Friday.

Matt Nieminen was needed in Anchorage. Taking his mechanic, Alonzo Cope, and Major Deckard whose work was completed with the arrival of the relief expedition men and equipment in Nome, the pilot departed for Fairbanks in the New Standard, NC 174H, the morning of Wednesday, January 15, 1930. Frank Dorbandt had come in from Teller on this

▲ *Eielson-Borland relief plane, NC 153H, on the Nome field.*

▼ *Stinson Standard SB-1, NC 877, and Canadian Fairchild 71, CF-AJK at Nome, Alaska, in 1930.*

1037

*The arrival of a plane in an arctic village brought
young and old scurrying to the site to share in the
excitement. This group of Eskimos is meeting Northern
Air Transport Stinson No. 1 and its pilot.*

Vic Ross Photo

1039

same day, flying the Stinson Standard, NC 877, and bringing his wife, Vida, and Vic Ross with him. Ross flew in the other New Standard, NC 9190, from Teller. Frank and his wife left for Fairbanks the next afternoon in the Stinson biplane, carrying a load of mail.

On Saturday, January 18, Swartman, still flying the cabin Swallow, left for Fairbanks. Along with his mechanic, Mews, the pilot brought L.E. Porsild, Canadian government reindeer man, and Mrs. Porsild in to Weeks Field on Sunday.

The structural repairs to the wing of CF-AJK were completed on January 18, with the aid of a respected Nome carpenter, August Homberger. With mechanics Hutchison, Hughes and Macauley also working on the plane, it promised to soon be good as new.

Gifford Swartman returned to Nome in the red cabin Swallow, C 3542, at 3:45 P.M. Tuesday, January 21, 1930. Carrying only a cargo of mail and company material, the Canadian pilot had flown through from Fairbanks in one day. He expected to fly locally out of Nome for the rest of the week.

Bill Graham was back in business for Northern Air Transport, Incorporated. With the Stinson Junior, NC 475H, now repaired, he left Deering for Elephant Point on Sunday, January 19. He could have departed Deering earlier but the wind had blown all the snow from the airfield, and he must await a fresh snowfall for his skis. From Elephant Point the pilot went on to Kotzebue. He got away from there the next day, Monday, for Shungnak, expecting to be back in Kotzebue that afternoon. Bill Oliver was still at Deering. Graham left Kotzebue at 10:00 A.M. Tuesday morning, January 21, for Fairbanks, carrying two passengers, but was forced by snowstorms to hold at Deering. On January 24, he tried again to make it to Ruby but was forced back to Unalakleet. He got away on January 26, stopping to spend the night in Tanana, and landed in Fairbanks on Monday, January 27, 1930, with his two passengers: W.H. Suksdorf of Nome, and A.V. Cordovado of Deering.

The two Fairchild 71 planes, CF-AJK and NC 153H, of the Eielson-Borland Relief Expedition, took off from Nome at 9:45 A.M. Tuesday, January 21, landing at Teller at 10:30 A.M. Piloted by Ed Young and Pat Reid, with mechanics Hughes and Macauley, they were to be held there for some days by bad weather before going on to North Cape, Siberia. Both planes finally got away on January 27, to land at the *Nanuk* five hours later. (see Fairbanks—1930, Chapter 58), Pilot Vic Ross, of Northern Air Transport, Incorporated, was hauling gas and supplies from Nome to Teller for the expedition in the New Standard D-25, NC 9190, No. 2. He came in from Teller at 2:30 P.M. Thursday, January 23, after spending the night there.

It was on January 26 (January 25, Nome date) that Crosson and Gillam discovered the wrecked Hamilton and brought the sad news to the *Nanuk* to be radioed to others who waited. (see Fairbanks—1930, Chapter 58).

Frank Dorbandt arrived in Nome in the Stinson SB-1, NC 877, at 4:00 P.M. Saturday, February 1, 1930. Carrying a small amount of mail and considerable freight for local merchants, he also brought Gifford Swartman, who planned to fly another plane back to Fairbanks.

Swartman, held in Nome by weather, finally got away in the red cabin Swallow. He returned to Nome on the afternoon of Wednesday, January 29, from Kotzebue, bringing in C.E. Alexander from there. Carrying mining engineer Alexander, flight mechanic Mews and some mail, he was away the next morning for Fairbanks.

Vic Ross, still flying the New Standard, NC 9190, took Ralph Lomen, manager of the relief expedition at Nome, to Teller on Sunday, January 26, returning with his passenger shortly after noon on Monday. Ross took the plane to Shishmaref with freight on Wednesday, leaving at 9:00 A.M. and returning at 2:15 P.M. The pilot made two round trips from Nome to

Teller in the biplane with freight and supplies the next day. He brought in one passenger, Laurie Mattila, from Teller. Bill Graham, coming from Fairbanks in the Stinson Junior, NC 475H, arrived from Nulato the same day. He had stopped enroute at Unalakleet, to pick up a native boy with frozen hands for the Nome hospital.

Graham, in the Stinson monoplane, left at 9:00 A.M. Friday, January 31, 1930, for Fairbanks, carrying O.D. Cochran, Nome attorney, as a passenger. He flew to Candle first to pick up an additional passenger for Fairbanks, a mining man by the name of J.H. Johnson. Graham also had about 150 pounds of mail aboard. The pilot landed on Weeks Field that same afternoon at 3:30 P.M.

Grant Jackson, president of the Miners and Merchants Bank in Nome, left there for a trip Outside on Wednesday, February 5, 1930, flying with Frank Dorbandt in the Stinson SB-1, NC 877. Spending the night at Ruby, the pilot landed on Weeks Field the next day. Fairbanks was new to Mrs. Jackson; she had previously traveled from Nome by ship.

Pat Reid and his mechanic, Bill Hughes, were coming in from the *Nanuk*. Flying the Fairchild 71, CF-AJK, the pilot carried Olaf Swenson and his daughter Marion, as well as Captain Paul Milovzorov of the *Stavropol*, who needed medical attention. The Canadian pilot landed at Teller on February 7, coming on to Nome to arrive there at 11:45 A.M. Monday, February 10, 1930. Lomen was handy with his camera to record the group on film before conferring with Reid on the situation at North Cape regarding fast removal of the valuable cargo of furs and the extra personnel. The Canadian pilot would return in the Fairchild with a load of case gas while his passengers awaited transportation to Fairbanks in other planes. Reid reported the searchers at the Hamilton wreck site were still digging; the bodies of Eielson and Borland had not yet been discovered. Mavriki Slepnyov, with three men, had landed his Junkers F-13, CCCP-177, at the site, to take charge of the work there for the Soviet government. A snow house erected under the wing soon provided a better shelter for the workmen. A civil engineer from the *Stavropol* accompanied the Soviet pilot. He began charting the wreck site and the bits and pieces of the Hamilton as they were discovered, also laying out orderly paths for the diggers to follow in trenching through the hard-packed snow. It was hoped this would be more productive than a haphazard searching about.

The stockholders of Northern Air Transport announced the purchase of a second plane for the company: a Stinson Detroiter SM-1F, NC 404M. The six-place cabin monoplane was then being constructed at the Wayne, Michigan shops of the Stinson Aircraft Corporation. It was powered with a Wright J6-9 radial engine of 300 horsepower. The plane was shipped to Fairbanks to be assembled there and flown to Nome by Bill Graham. It was No. 2 for the Nome company. Vic Ross was still being held at Kotzebue by weather on February 10, 1930.

Pat Reid and mechanic Bill Hughes departed Nome for Serdtse-Kamen, on the Siberian side, the morning of Wednesday, February 12, 1930, carrying eighteen cases of gasoline in the cabin of the Fairchild 71, CF-AJK. They planned to unload at the cape and return to Teller, weather permitting. Weather did force the pilot back to Teller but he went out again on February 16, successfully caching the gas at the cape. (see Fairbanks—1930, Chapter 58). On his next trip from Teller on February 21, again with a full load of airplane fuel, he landed at the Hamilton wreck site and wiped the gear off CF-AJK. The plane was to remain there until May, 1930, when it was flown out by Joe Crosson.

Bill Graham was still in Fairbanks, with temperatures of fifty-five degrees below zero there on Wednesday, February 12. He landed on Thursday at Unalakleet, enroute home. Flying the four-place Stinson Junior, NC 475H, the pilot came in to Nome on Friday, February 14, with three sacks of mail and miscellaneous freight. He also took aboard a native at Unalakleet who was suffering from frostbite, bringing him to Nome for medical attention.

Bill Graham, in the Northern Air Transport Stinson, NC 475H, was away from Nome early Tuesday afternoon, February 18, for Golovin, taking Chief Deputy Cliff Allyn and his wife, and J.H. Hart. Graham returned about 3:30 p.m. with George Ashenfelter of Golovin, who was going Outside for medical treatment. The pilot took off in a short time to return to Golovin, taking L.E.Robinson as a passenger.

Frank Dorbandt came in from Fairbanks at 3:15 p.m. the same day, making the flight in four and a half hours with one stop at Ruby. After picking up Olaf Swenson and his daughter, and Captain Milovzorov, the pilot was away in the Fairchild 71, NC 9153, the next morning, also taking George Ashenfelter. The party arrived in Fairbanks late in the afternoon of Wednesday, February 19, 1930; his three passengers from the *Nanuk* caught the train the following morning for Seward, and a boat for Outside. Ashenfelter, who was ill, entered St. Josephs Hospital in Fairbanks immediately upon his arrival.

Carl Ben Eielson's body was found on Tuesday, February 18, ending the search for the two; the searchers had discovered Earl Borland's on Thursday, February 13. The bodies were brought to the *Nanuk* in the Russian Junkers, CCCP-177. (see Fairbanks—1930, Chapter 58). Bill Graham of Northern Air Transport arrived back in Nome on Sunday morning, February 23, 1930.

Frank Dorbandt, Alaskan Airways pilot from Fairbanks, arrived in Nome from Ruby on Sunday, February 23, in the Fairchild 71, NC 9153. An hour later he was away again for Ruby, carrying Dan Aldrich, a prospector from Nome who was enroute to the strike at Poorman. Bill Graham had arrived at his base the same morning, shortly after Dorbandt arrived, coming from Unalakleet with Mrs. Cliff Allyn and Mrs. Fred Webster and her daughter. The pair was coming to Nome for medical treatment. Graham was away again that afternoon for Unalakleet, returning late in the day with Deputy Marshal Cliff Allyn and two prisoners from upriver, plus J.H. Hart, as passengers. The pilot went out again on Monday afternoon, taking Father Post and a daughter of Fred Bourdon's to Pilgrim Hot Springs. Graham returned to Nome at 3:30 p.m. Vic Ross, the other Northern Air Transport pilot, went out in the Stinson Junior, NC 475H, on Tuesday, February 25, going to Shishmaref with freight and mail. On his return flight he brought in George Goshaw, fox farmer from there.

Airmen at the *Nanuk* were preparing to bring in the bodies of their two former comrades but bad weather was holding the planes at the schooner. (see Fairbanks—1930, Chapter 58) Nome was making plans for memorial services on their arrival, with all citizens requested to meet at the offices of the Nome Lighterage and Commercial Company, to march out to the planes where a tribute would be paid to the memory of the two fliers. One long blast of the city siren was to be given as a signal to assemble.

Pat Reid and Harold Gillam arrived in Nome about 12:30 p.m. March 3, 1930, coming from Teller. Taking Alfred J. Lomen, Gillam returned to Teller in the Stearman, to meet the expected arrival of the Fairchild 71, NC 153H, and the Russian Junkers, CCCP-177. The Stearman arrived at the Grantley Harbor community at 3:30 p.m., the Fairchild 71 from North Cape, bearing the bodies of Carl Ben Eielson and Earl Borland arriving later in the day. The Junkers F-13, flown by Commander Slepnyov and flight mechanic Fahrig, was close behind, landing at 4:40 p.m. (see Fairbanks—1930, Chapter 58). Stormy weather held the planes at Teller for some days.

Gillam, in the Stearman, got away first, on Wednesday, March 5, 1930, landing in Nome at 1:45 p.m. after a stormy flight. He brought in Canadian mechanic Bill Hughes and Alfred Lomen in the front cockpit. Weather kept the other two planes at Teller until the following day.

Ed Young, with flight mechanic Macauley and Joe Crosson riding with him in the funeral plane, took off at 8:10 A.M. Thursday, March 6, 1930, with the Junkers F-13, CCCP-177, flown by Mavriki Slepnyov and Fabio Fahrig, close behind. The two planes arrived over Nome at 9:00 A.M. The pilots continued to circle while observing the field, which now had many windrows of hard-packed snow from a recent blow. The planes turned for Ruby, convinced a landing would not be a good idea, and the assembled crowd watched from below. Harold Gillam, accompanied by Bill Hughes, took off in the smaller Stearman C-2B, and was awaiting the planes when they landed at Ruby. The three planes remained over, going on to Fairbanks the following day. (see Fairbanks—1930, Chapter 58).

Northern Air Transport pilot Bill Graham had taken off in the Stinson Junior on the afternoon of Monday, March 3, for Deering, Candle, Elephant Point and Kotzebue with a cargo of mail and freight. He was also returning a native prisoner to Kotzebue after he had served out his time in the federal jail. Graham was back in Nome on Tuesday afternoon from Deering, carrying mechanic George Laiblin and Boris Magids, the latter enroute to the States, summoned to Miami, Florida, where his brother, Sam, had passed away. Vic Ross took off at 8:30 A.M. Thursday, March 6, in the Stinson Junior, NC 475H, for Fairbanks. He was carrying Magids, pilot Bill Graham and company manager William A. Oliver. The latter pair were to begin assembly of the new six-place Stinson, NC 404M, that had arrived in Fairbanks. Held at Tanana by weather, Ross arrived on Weeks Field the afternoon of Saturday, March 8, 1930, where the new plane awaited.

Vic Ross soon departed for Nome in the Stinson Junior, No. 1. He was at Unalakleet on Thursday, March 13, and arrived in Nome about 4:00 P.M. Saturday, March 15, with Mrs. Ada Evans and a native woman as passengers from St. Michael, and L.E.Robinson from Unalakleet. Bill Graham had gotten away from Fairbanks in the new Northern Air Transport Stinson Detroiter SM-1F, NC 404M, on the morning of Thursday, March 13, 1930. He was off Fortuna Ledge for Nome about 3:00 P.M. on Saturday. The pilot came in to his home base about noon on Monday, March 17, from Unalakleet, with Eric Johnson as a passenger from Fortuna Ledge and Mrs. Pete Knutson from Unalakleet, plus about 225 pounds of first class mail from Fairbanks and Outside. He took off again at 1:45 P.M. for Taylor and Elephant Point, carrying Charles Nelson, the Lorraine brothers and Henry Wells as passengers for the first point of landing. He planned to return the next morning with Dan E. Crowley and wife from Unalakleet, making intermediate stops.

Vic Ross went out on Friday, March 21, taking off from Nome at 9:30 A.M. with Frank Miller for Teller, and Mr. and Mrs. Bill Cameron as round-trip passengers. He was back in Nome at 11:30 A.M. Bill Graham, in the Stinson No. 2, was off the same morning for Taylor, Deering, Candle and Elephant Point. Along with the mail and a cargo of freight, he carried Billy Sinhold as a passenger for Taylor Creek in the Kougarok section. Vic Ross took off shortly after noon of the same day in the Stinson No. 1, NC 475H, for Black River, a tributary of Norton Sound located south of St. Michael. He carried as passengers Frank Kern and a native woman by the name of Mary Kamkoff. Ross returned Saturday afternoon, having made the flight to St. Michael and Black River and back to St. Michael. He brought no passengers in. Bill Graham made another round-trip flight in the six-place Stinson, NC 404M, to Taylor Creek where he had dropped Sinhold, going on Saturday, March 22, 1930, and returning shortly before noon. Servicing the plane, he took off at noon for Fairbanks with mail and Mrs. Marie L. Frantzen and son John as passengers, who were going to Seattle. He arrived in Fairbanks with his passengers on Saturday, March 23, 1930.

Vic Ross, flying the Northern Air Transport Stinson, No. 1, left Nome on Sunday

Northern Air Transport Stinson No. 1 on the ice of
Grantley Harbor before the village of Teller, Alaska.

morning, March 23, 1930, with mail and freight for Kotzebue, Candle and Elephant Point. He came in to Nome about 2:30 P.M. Tuesday, March 25, bringing Dan Crowley and his wife as passengers from Elephant Point. Bill Graham had left Fairbanks in the Stinson No. 2, NC 404M, on the morning of Monday, March 24, taking Bill Oliver and miner J.H.Johnson as passengers. The latter was enroute to Deering. Graham overnighted in Unalakleet, and landed at 1:00 P.M. Tuesday in Nome. Graham was busy that afternoon overhauling his engine.

Alaskan Airways, Incorporated, must return to Siberia and continue the work that had begun prior to the loss of the Hamilton. The Waco 10, NC 780E, at the *Nanuk* must be returned, as well as the Fairchild 71, CF-AJK, still lying among the snows at the Hamilton wreck site. Further, the gasoline borrowed from the Russians during the search must be replaced and the balance of the furs from the trading schooner brought to market.

Joe Crosson and Ed Young, flying the two Fairchilds, NC 9153 and NC 153H, respectively, were off Weeks Field on the morning of Sunday, March 23, 1930. Manager Arthur Johnson, and mechanics Herb Larison and Cecil Higgins were also along. Miner Dan Aldrich was picked up at Ruby and brought to Nome. The men had spent the night in a prospector's cabin at Fish River on Golovin Bay, seventy-five miles out on the route, due to heavy fog. Taking off from there the following day, Monday, the two planes landed in Nome after an hour's flight. They carried capacity loads of express and mail, as well as repair parts and equipment for the damaged Fairchild CF-AJK (NC 154H). (see Fairbanks—1930, Chapter 58).

On Tuesday, the two planes were carrying full loads of case gas to Teller, making two round trips each before going out with a third load to spend the night there. The following day they came in to Nome, returning to Teller with a fourth load.

Vic Ross was away in Stinson No. 1 from Nome on the morning of Thursday, March 27, 1930, going to White Mountain. Pilot Bill Graham, in Stinson No. 2, took off also for Deering, Elephant Point and Kotzebue with mail, and passenger J.H. Johnson for Deering. Ross was back in Nome on Friday morning about 10:00 A.M. He carried, as passengers, Mr. Neely of the Bureau of Education school at White Mountain, and a native named Abraham Lincoln. Mr. Neely's daughter accompanied her father.

Crosson and Young, holding at Teller for a break in the weather since March 28, were again ready to cross the Bering Strait to reach the *Nanuk*. On March 31, 1930, Crosson tried to reach Nome, but was forced back to Teller by a snowstorm. On April 1, the pilot was able to reach the Seward Peninsula city, coming in at 4:45 P.M. He returned to Teller the following day.

Bill Graham, flying the Northern Air Transport, Incorporated, Stinson Detroiter, NC 404M, returned to Nome from White Mountain and the north on Tuesday, April 1, 1930. He had been held at White Mountain for several days by fog. The pilot carried Mrs. Tom Roust as a passenger from Candle. Tom had been bitten by the flying bug; Mrs. Roust purchased the old Standard J-1, Hisso-powered biplane that Noel Wien had brought to Nome, and which was now the property of Alaskan Airways, Incorporated. Roust hoped to reassemble the plane, which was in storage, and have it flown to Candle where he could reconstruct the fuselage and wings at his leisure.

Bill Graham departed Nome for Fairbanks in the Stinson Detroiter, NC 404M, on the morning of Wednesday, April 2, 1930. He was carrying four passengers for Nenana: J.H.Hart, Leo Seidenverg, and Mr. and Mrs. John Froskland from Shaktoolik, as well as mail for the interior city. He returned from Fairbanks about 1:45 P.M. Friday, April 4, with banker Grant R. Jackson as a passenger, plus mail and a quantity of freight. The trip from Fairbanks to Nome had been made nonstop in the record time of four hours and thirty-seven minutes, cutting eight minutes off any previous flight.

Vic Ross, flying Stinson No. 1, NC 475H, was away for Dime on the morning of Wednesday, April 2, with Mrs. Arthur Johnson and two children, and for Unalakleet with Mrs. Fred Webster and her boy. He was back the same day, to go out again on Thursday morning for St. Michael and Fortuna Ledge, with Mrs. Ada Evans and Eric Johnson as passengers. He went again to St. Michael on Friday, April 4, 1930, returning witnesses for the government to their homes.

Alaskan Airways pilots Joe Crosson and Ed Young, flying the two Fairchild 71s, NC 9153 and NC 153H, with their mechanic, Herb Larison, got away from Teller at noon on Thursday, April 3, for the *Nanuk*, arriving there that same day with heavy loads of case gas, supplies for the ship, and repair materials for CF-AJK. Leaving Larison at the ship to make repairs on the damaged Fairchild at the Hamilton wreck site, the two pilots came in to Nome on Friday with heavy loads of baled furs. (see Fairbanks—1930, Chapter 58). The two planes, carrying the valuable furs, went on to Fairbanks the next day, leaving mechanic Cecil Higgins in Nome but taking Manager Arthur Johnson in with them. Along with other business for Alaskan Airways, Incorporated, in the Nome area, Johnson had discussed plans for the construction of a winter and summer hangar for their planes at the airfield, to serve as a terminal for their Seward Peninsula business.

Pilot Bill Graham, flying the Stinson, NC 404M, departed on the morning of Monday, April 7, 1930, for Fairbanks. He was carrying Mrs. Vic Ross, enroute to Seldovia to visit her relatives. The pilot also carried a quantity of furs. The plane arrived on Weeks Field the same day.

Vic Ross, taking the smaller Stinson, NC 475H, was away in the afternoon for Candle, Elephant Point and Kotzebue. Mrs. Tom Roust was a returning passenger to her home in Candle. Mail and a quantity of freight made up the balance of the load. He returned as far as Golovin that day, holding there for better weather before coming in. Ross had taken three native boys from Elephant Point to Golovin. The pilot landed in Nome at 10:00 A.M. on Wednesday, bringing Tom Roust in from Candle. Roust got busy overhauling the old Standard J-1. He had been interested in airplanes for several years and wanted to use the machine to get enough flying time to obtain a license. In the meantime he must take an early plane to St. Michael to put the motorship *Donaldson* in condition for the opening of navigation.

Bill Graham, in the Stinson Detroiter, NC 404M, No. 2, arrived from Fairbanks about 2:00 P.M. Sunday, April 13, 1930, carrying mail and passengers: Mr. and Mrs. Bud Harper, Cal Sears and Ralph T. Hirsch, a mining engineer with the new company taking over the Keewalik Mining Company, bound for Candle. Alaskan Airways pilot Ed Young arrived at 2:30 P.M. that same day, carrying J.K.Crowdy, manager of the New York-Alaska (gold dredging) Corporation (NYAC), which was taking over the Keewalik company on a twenty-year lease. He carried other members of the firm also: F.A. McDougall, Frank Lott, and Chris Asmussen. Joe Crosson, flying the Fairchild 71, NC 9153, departed Weeks Field with Young, but had flown direct to Candle, returning to Fairbanks the same day. Young left Nome for Candle about 10:30 A.M. on Monday.

Bill Graham took Ralph Hirsch to Candle, leaving Nome at 10:00 A.M. Monday, April 14, 1930. He went on to Kotzebue to deliver a second passenger, Julius Silverman, from Nome. Graham went on to Fairbanks with mail and furs from there, as well as three passengers: Jack Hooper, Harry Strong and Mrs. W.H. Lehmann, wife of the radio operator at Kotzebue. The pilot was weather-bound at Weeks Field for a few days on his arrival there.

Tom Roust was hard at work getting the old Standard J-1 biplane back together and the motor tuned up. Noel Wien had used the plane in June of 1927 when first starting up in business in the Nome district. Roust got some help from local mechanics. He and his friends pushed the plane on to the Bessie road airfield on Friday, April 18, 1930. With the Hispano-Suiza motor running, Tom climbed into the open cockpit and prepared to taxi about the field on the skis he had built and installed. The Hisso was running well and the would-be pilot was soon

The Northern Air Transport Stinsons were to become a familiar sight at the villages of the Seward Peninsula in 1930 as pilots Bill Graham and Vic Ross covered their territory. Here cans of aviation gasoline have been brought down from the trader's store to refuel Stinson No. 1.

maneuvering about on the landing field. Enthusiastically applying a little too much power, Roust found himself off the snow and in the air before he realized it. His only flying had been on planes enroute, while traveling between Nome and Candle, when the pilots had let him take the controls.

There was nothing for him to do but carry on. He circled the plane around back of town and came in to the field from the Bering Sea side. Throttling back and gliding down to the landing field, everything went well until touch down; he got a bit rattled on his throttle control. The plane touched down and bounded into the air for a short distance, losing momentum and turning over on one wing and its nose, to throw the pilot out onto the snow as it came to a sliding halt. Tom leaped up, uninjured but for a fractured nose, shouting triumphantly, "I can fly, I can fly!" He immediately began making plans for repairing the plane, which was not substantially damaged.

Vic Ross returned to Nome from Shishmaref the evening of Friday, April 19, 1930, where he had dropped off passenger George Goshaw and the mail. Pilot Bill Graham, flying Stinson No. 2 of Northern Air Transport, Incorporated, had left Fairbanks the same morning. He arrived in Nome at 1:30 P.M. Saturday, coming by way of Akiak, with J.D. Harlan and Ben Mozee as passengers.

Both Northern Air Transport planes were held for a time at Nome by continuing bad weather. Vic Ross, flying the Stinson No. 1, NC 475H, was finally away on Tuesday morning, April 22, 1930, carrying James K. Crowdy and a native man for Candle. The pilot went on to Kotzebue before returning to Nome. Bill Graham, in Stinson No. 2, was also off on Tuesday morning, flying to Taylor Creek in the Kougarok section. He was carrying as passengers Nick Niccon, a cook, and miner Jim Moullos who were enroute to Dick Creek; and George Thompson for Taylor Creek. Graham was back about 1:00 P.M. after a successful flight. He was away again the same afternoon for Wales, carrying George Waldhelm and family. Unable to land, the pilot returned to Nome about 6:00 P.M.

Graham was away the next morning, Wednesday, April 23, 1930, for Council, carrying Henry Gumm and Fred Mebes, plus some freight which included a quantity of fresh meat. He was back in Nome about 3:30 P.M.

Vic Ross, flying the Stinson Junior, No. 1, as usual, came in shortly before noon on Thursday, April 24, 1930, from Candle, carrying mail and a shipment of furs. He was off again that same afternoon for St. Michael, taking Tom Roust, who was going there to work on overhauling the motorship *Donaldson*. Graham went out the same morning, successfully landing the Waldhelm family at Wales. He departed again, carrying L.E. Robinson of the Bureau of Education to Shishmaref. Joe Crosson, flying the Fairchild 71, NC 9153, came in from Nenana, where he had put on his load, on Thursday afternoon. With him were mechanic Jim Hutchison and a new pilot for Alaskan Airways, Sanis E. "Robbie" Robbins. They were on their way to Siberia to salvage the Canadian Fairchild, CF-AJK, from the Hamilton wreck site, or failing that, bring in the Waco 10, NC 780E, still at the *Nanuk*. (see Fairbanks—1930, Chapter 58). Crosson went on to Teller the same day of his arrival in Nome. The following morning he attempted to fly from there to Candle but fog forced his return to land at Nome. He returned to Teller, departing Nome at 11:00 A.M. Friday, April 25, 1930. He intended to go to Siberia from there. Vic Ross, flying the Stinson No. 1, was also off from Nome on Friday afternoon for Elephant Point, with Dan E. Crowley as a passenger. The pilot expected to fly to the Hunt River where the reindeer drive to northern Canada was in progress. Bill Graham was in Teller, expecting to go to the *Nanuk* with the Stinson No. 2 to bring in a load of furs for Alaskan Airways. Held by fog, the trip was finally given up. Graham, with his mechanic, William Oliver, returned to Nome on Wednesday, April 30, 1930. The pair went back to Teller on Thursday, but learning the weather at the *Nanuk* was still poor, left there for a flight to Candle, Deering, Elephant Point and Kotzebue. They returned to Nome at 5:50 P.M. on Friday, May 2, 1930. Along with their other stops they had flown a trip from Elephant Point to

Hunt River for the Lomen Reindeer Corporation, taking Dan Crowley to survey the situation with the herd, now at that point, as well as flying into the Colville River section to pick out a route for the 3000-animal herd to follow. The herd was to remain in the Hunt River section during the fawning season. An attempt was being made to thaw the snow on the Nome Municipal Airport on Bessie road by plowing it up with crawler tractors and spraying the snow with crude oil to attract the heat of the sun.

Bill Graham hopped off Sunday, May 4, 1930, for Candle and Deering, with John Skain and Teddy Breen as passengers for the first stop, but dense fog prevented a landing and the Stinson six-place plane returned to Nome. Graham had been intending to make a flight to Fairbanks for some time but poor landing conditions had delayed him. It was near impossible to take off from Nome on wheels because of the soft snow in the area, while Fairbanks was free of snow. This was a common problem during breakup. The pilot made a trip to Golovin to see if it was possible to make a change from skis to wheels at that point. Graham left Nome in the Stinson Detroiter No. 2, NC 404M, about 10:30 A.M. Wednesday, May 7, 1930, for Golovin, White Mountain and Council, accompanied by Cliff Allyn who was going through to Fairbanks, and another passenger for Council. The pilot took the wheels for the plane to Golovin, where Allyn remained to get things ready for the changeover. Graham went on to Council with his other passenger, stopping at White Mountain to pick up Jimmy Dexter. The boy had suffered a broken arm and the pilot took him to the hospital at Nome before returning to Golovin. The flight to Fairbanks was important to many. The Northern Air Transport plane was expected to carry $50,000 worth of furs to market from Seward Peninsula points, as well as a large consignment of first class letter mail enroute to the States. Included in this mail were large orders from merchants in and around Nome for supplies to be sent into the districts from the States aboard the first vessels sailing from Seattle on the opening of navigation. Graham got away from Golovin at 1:00 P.M. Thursday, May 8, 1930, after changing to summer landing gear. The pilot, carrying Cliff Allyn and 900 pounds of furs, plus the mail, arrived on Weeks Field at 7:00 P.M. that same evening.

Joe Crosson, flying the salvaged Fairchild 71, CF-AJK (NC 154H) and Robbins, flying Fairchild 71, NC 9153, with their mechanics, Larison and Hutchison, got away from the *Nanuk* in Siberia at 8:00 A.M. Tuesday, May 6, (Nome date). They landed at Teller on skis at 2:00 P.M. carrying forty sacks of valuable furs. The following day, Wednesday, the two planes arrived in Nome at 3:00 P.M. to unload the furs for processing at the Nome post office and to be forwarded to Fairbanks via mail plane. The pilots were away again at 6:00 P.M. that same day, returning to Teller, taking Alaskan Airways mechanics Hutchison, Larison and Higgins along. (see Fairbanks—1930, Chapter 58).

Crosson and Robbins were back in Nome with twenty-six bags of furs from the *Nanuk*, and their three mechanics in the two Fairchilds on Sunday, May 11, 1930. They had picked up Higgins in Teller. Crosson took Robbins to Teller again that same day; he flew the Waco 10, NC 780E, from there to Nome. The pilot had crossed the strait with Crosson on Thursday, May 8; bringing the Waco in to Teller on May 9, 1930, after remaining overnight on the *Nanuk*.

The two pilots landed at Golovin to inspect the location for a possible skis-to-wheels change. Leaving there, Crosson dropped Robbins at Teller and went on in to Nome. He went out on Monday, May 12, to Hastings Creek, some ten miles east of Nome, to inspect the site for a ski-wheel change, finding it satisfactory. Taking mechanics Cecil Higgins and Jim Hutchison, and a passenger for Fairbanks, R.T. Fulton of the Lomen Reindeer Corporation, the two pilots flew the Waco 10, NC 780E, and the Fairchild 71, CF-AJK (NC 154H) to Hastings Creek where the mechanics put on the wheels. Late that afternoon the planes were off

Teller, Alaska. Two Fairchild 71s, CF-AJK and NC 9153 following their flight from the Nanuk on May 6, 1930. Joe Crosson flew in CF-AJK while Robbie Robbins, walking toward the camera, flew in NC 153H. The two pilots went on to Nome the following day.

for Ruby, where they gassed and went on to Fairbanks. Landing on wheels at Weeks Field, at 2:00 P.M. Tuesday, May 13, 1930, with their sixteen sacks of furs from the *Nanuk* and their passenger, the four tired airmen went home to get some rest. Herb Larison had remained at Nome with the Fairchild 71, NC 9153.

Pilot Vic Ross, flying the Stinson Junior, No. 1, arrived back in Nome at 9:30 P.M. Saturday, May 10, 1930, coming from Elephant Point. He carried as passengers, Dan Crowley, R.T. "Bob" Fulton and Doctor L.E. Benson, all of whom were connected with the Lomen Reindeer Corporation activities in the north. Doctor Benson, with the reindeer drive at Hunt River, was ailing and was being brought to Nome to be placed in the Maynard-Columbus Hospital, while he awaited plane transportation to the Outside. He suffered from frosted lungs incurred on a trip to the Kobuk during the past winter. Ross was busy having his engine overhauled the next day.

Bill Graham was in Fairbanks awaiting the arrival of the incoming train with mail and three passengers from the Outside. He arrived at Golovin about 3:30 P.M. Tuesday, May 13, 1930, landing on the high summer field which was now clear of snow. Passengers, mail and freight were transferred down to the Golovin Bay ice, where the wheels were changed to skis for the balance of the trip. Graham, carrying passengers from the States; Boris Magids, Mrs. Sam Magids and Jack Hammer, arrived in Nome about 7:00 P.M. on Wednesday. He also brought about 200 pounds of mail. The pilot took his three passengers on to Kotzebue the following day. On his return from there he picked up J.K. Crowdy, Deputy Marshal George Wagner and a native prisoner as passengers from Candle. Vic Ross had taken off Thursday morning for Igloo with Ben Mozee as a passenger. He returned at 10:00 A.M. and was off at

1052

2:00 P.M. with a load of freight for Elephant Point and Candle, but was forced by fog to return to Nome; he landed at 6:00 P.M.

Bill Graham, in the Northern Air Transport plane No. 2, was away at 9:30 A.M. Friday, May 15, 1930, enroute to Fairbanks via Golovin and Unalakleet. Carrying Barney Rolando as a passenger for the States, and Miss Mabel LeRoy, a nurse returning to Unalakleet, a change to wheels was made at Golovin, where he picked up an additional passenger for Fairbanks. The pilot also carried mail. Graham was still stormbound at Golovin on Monday.

Nome was rapidly moving into the summer season with W.J. "Billy" Rowe, the transfer man, busy with teams and road graders cutting down the snowbanks on the streets so that wagons could be put to use instead of sleds. The fire department changed from the winter chemical sled to the summer chemical wagon on May 16, 1930. In a few days water was pumped into the empty fire mains and the drain valve closed. The Municipal landing field on Bessie road was practically free of snow on the east-west strip. The north-south landing strip still had considerable snow on it but would be free of it in a few days with the melting temperatures. At this time of the year, considered the break-up season, it was difficult getting from place to place with one landing field clear of snow and the next one covered with soft snow. Then too, mud was a problem until the fields dried out.

Bill Graham was away from Golovin about 11:00 A.M. Tuesday, May 20, 1930, carrying Barney Rolando and a second passenger for Fairbanks. He landed the Stinson Detroiter, NC 404M, on Weeks Field late in the afternoon that same day.

Vic Ross, who was holding at Nome, changed his skis for wheels on the summer field on Sunday, May 18. He was off for Golovin on Tuesday morning, going on to Unalakleet where he picked up the young son of Fred Webster, bringing him in to the Nome hospital for treatment of appendicitis. The pilot landed at the Bessie road airport about 2:30 P.M. He was away the same evening for Candle, carrying J.K. Crowdy and a load of freight. Crowdy was in charge of the NYAC activities there. Ross planned to be back the same day. However, it was snowing at most places on the Seward Peninsula.

Northern Air Transport pilot Bill Graham returned to Nome from Fairbanks at 7:00 P.M. Saturday, May 24, 1930, having left Weeks Field in the Stinson No. 2 the same morning with five passengers, mail and express. He landed at Unalakleet to drop John Froskland off before going on to Golovin to offload Doctor and Mrs. E.A. Cushing of the Biological Survey. The plane arrived in Nome with Senator H.T. Tripp of Juneau, and Cliff Allyn, the latter having made the round trip to the interior city. Cliff was now manager of Northern Air Transport Incorporated, for Nome. W.R. "Bill" Graham's wife had reached Portland, Oregon on May 20, coming from Bainbridge, Georgia on her way to join her husband in Nome. The pilot expected to return to Fairbanks but delayed some days to allow the Bessie road airport to dry up a bit more. It was in poor condition from the break-up.

Vic Ross was off Nome on Monday morning in Stinson No. 1 for White Mountain, bringing a sick woman into the hospital. Her husband accompanied her. Shortly after noon he was away again for Candle with a load of freight, coming back the same day. The pilot was away again, on wheels, for Keewalik on Tuesday, taking Deputy Marshal George Wagner and a load of freight, returning about 3:30 P.M. that afternoon.

Joe Crosson arrived at Nome in the Fairchild 71, NC 154H, at 4:45 A.M. Tuesday, May 27, 1930, from Fairbanks, having left there at 1:00 A.M. He carried General Manager Arthur W. Johnson of Alaskan Airways, Incorporated, and Robbie Robbins. Included in the load was a set of wheels for the Fairchild 71, NC 9153, still on skis at the Nome Municipal field. At 3:30 P.M. the two Fairchilds made a successful takeoff from a poor field, carrying almost all the balance of the Siberian furs that were previously brought to Nome from the *Nanuk*. Crosson returned to the field shortly after takeoff to have an oil feed problem adjusted on the Pratt & Whitney Wasp engine. He was away again shortly, to follow after Robbins. Manager Johnson and mechanic Herb Larison remained in Nome until another trip. The two pilots arrived on Weeks Field late that evening after an arduous day.

Vic Ross hopped off for Keewalik and Kotzebue in Stinson No. 1 on the morning of Wednesday, May 28, 1930. He dropped a passenger at Keewalik and took Frank Fellows on to Kotzebue. He left there for Nome the next morning but was forced to return on account of bad weather. The pilot did return to Nome on Friday afternoon and reported the waters of the Keewalik River so high it was impossible to land at Candle. He went back to Deering and picked up Boris Magids and Mrs. Bess Magids (sister-in-law) and took them on to Kotzebue; finding a better landing there on wheels than at Nome. The next day he had taken off from Kotzebue for Candle with Richard Sundquist but, finding it impossible to land, finally dropped

Pilot Vic Ross of Northern Air Transport, Incorporated, was issued Transport Pilot's License No. 14809 on July 16, 1930 in Fairbanks by Aeronautical Inspector Wylie Wright. Good for one year, it was subsequently endorsed for renewal by the same inspector.

Courtesy of Sylvia Ross

1054

Pilot Vic Ross of Northern Air Transport, Incorporated, in Nome was issued his Airplane and Engine Mechanic's License and Identification Card on July 16, 1930 in Fairbanks. Wiley Wright, Aeronautical Inspector for the Department of Commerce was in Alaska that summer, examining all airmen and aircraft. He issued License No. 9375 to the former master mechanic of the Alaska Road Commission.

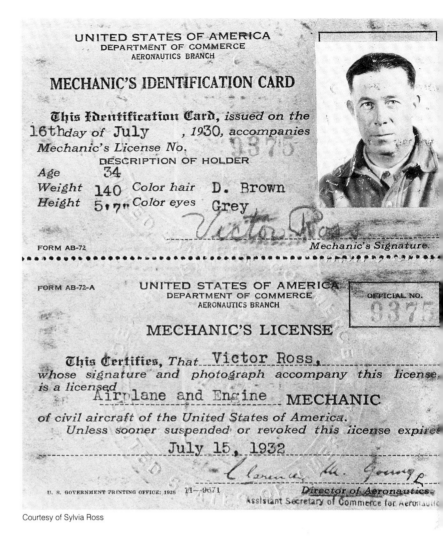

Courtesy of Sylvia Ross

his passenger at Keewalik. Taking off again on his return trip to Nome, he was forced back by fog, later coming through to Nome.

Recent rains and warm weather were hastening the break-up with ice moving out of the Snake River at Nome. Ice movement in the Bering Sea in front of the city was observed, with an open lead showing about a half mile offshore, although the shore ice was still fast. The first boat of the season, the *Silver Wave* of the Arctic Transport Company, reached Nome at 12:30 P.M. Saturday, May 31, 1930, bringing a cargo of freight including fresh fruit and produce, which Nomeites had been long without. The *Arthur J. Baldwin* had also sailed from Seattle on Friday.

Alaskan Airways pilot Joe Crosson arrived back in Nome from Fairbanks at 1:45 P.M. on Saturday, May 31, bringing Alaska College student Alvin Polet home for the summer. Crosson was away in the Fairchild 71, NC 154H, on Sunday afternoon, June 1, 1930, taking Manager Johnson, mechanic Herb Larison, a sack of first class mail and the balance of the white fox furs with him. He landed the plane on Weeks Field after a five hour and fifty minute flight. Bill Graham, in the Stinson No. 2 had gotten away from Nome on Friday, May 30, 1930, for Fairbanks, via McGrath. He carried U.S. mail, a quantity of express, and W.B. Miller of the Biological Survey as a passenger for McGrath. Taking off from the river town at 4:50 P.M., he was on Weeks Field two hours and forty-five minutes later.

Nome, Alaska 1930. Stinson Detroiter, NC 475H, of Northern Air Transport, Incorporated. this four-place Model SM-2AA was powered with a J6-5 of 165 horsepower. It was the first plane to be put into service by the Nome company. Mechanic George Laiblin in front. In August of 1930 Ross replaced the engine with a seven-cylinder Wright of 225 horsepower.

Vic Ross Photo

Some of the Nome hunters were beginning to utilize planes for their outings. Banker Grant R. Jackson and Jack Dowd hopped off for Solomon River with pilot Vic Ross in the Stinson No. 1 for a day's shooting for ducks and geese on Sunday, June 1, 1930. They were back that evening. Ross left for Golovin at 3:50 P.M. Monday, June 2, with Alfred Lomen and Charles H. Milot as round-trip passengers. He was back on Tuesday about 1:00 P.M. with the two men. The pilot was away again on Wednesday, June 4, for Shelton, carrying miner Harvey Grant and a native as passengers. He returned, to go out again to Shelton and Taylor, with

Duffy O'Connor and the U.S. mail. Bill Graham was still at Fairbanks with the Stinson No. 2. All three mammoth electric-powered gold dredges of the Hammon Consolidated Gold Fields were now going full blast about three miles back of Nome. The company had about 200 men working, with more to be added.

Vic Ross, forced to return to Nome Saturday evening, June 7, went out again on Sunday with Senator Tripp and mechanic George Laiblin for Fairbanks. Both Ross and Laiblin were to undergo examinations as to their qualifications while at Fairbanks by Department of Commerce Inspector Wylie Wright. Bill Graham was already there and would also be examined. Graham arrived back at Nome in Stinson No. 2, NC 404M, on the afternoon of Sunday, June 8, 1930, bringing Mrs. Victor Ross and a Miss Sammons, who was taking a steamer from Nome to the States. The pilot also brought mail and express.

Word that the *S.S. Victoria* was only thirty miles out from Nome on her first trip of the navigation season north sent Bill Graham aloft in the Stinson No. 2, to greet the ship. The plane was off at noon on Saturday, June 14, with three passengers aboard. As well as greeting the vessel it was a clever means of advertising to the inbound passengers that air service to

Northern Air Transport at Nome, Alaska. Stinson No. 2 at left and Stinson No. 3, NC 495Y, with its 210 horsepower Lycoming motor, at the right.

Vic Ross Photo

1058

outlying points was available at Nome. Graham went out about fifty miles over fog and low-lying clouds, not picking up the ship until on his return track. The pilot zoomed around her several times to show the plane off.

Tom Roust returned to Nome on Friday, June 13, 1930, on the motorship *Silver Wave*. He had been overhauling the *Donaldson* at St. Michael and reported the work finished and the craft launched. Roust turned to his true love, the Standard J-1 he had acquired from Alaskan Airways the previous winter. Replacing the skis with wheels was his current chore.

Vic Ross was away in the Stinson No. 1 of Northern Air Transport on Sunday morning, June 15, 1930, with a passenger for Candle, plus carrying mail and express both ways. Bill Graham, in Stinson No. 2, took off for Deering and Kotzebue the same afternoon, carrying Messrs. Burns, Anderson and Jerry Coffin for Deering. On his return flight he brought in Doctor and Mrs. White from Kotzebue, and H.L. Stull and John DeBuhr from Deering, plus mail and express. Doctor White and his wife planned to sail on the *Victoria*. Ross hopped off Monday morning, June 16, 1930, for Council, with Mr. and Mrs. Clyde Glass as passengers, plus a quantity of mail and express. In landing on a river bar, the plane suffered damage to its landing gear.

Pilot Joe Crosson of Alaskan Airways arrived in Nome Monday evening, to land at the Bessie road Municipal field after a five hour and forty minute flight nonstop in the Fairchild 71, NC 153H. He was accompanied by a new pilot with the company, Grant Elliott, flying the New Standard, NC 9190. Crosson carried Mr. and Mrs. Carl J. Lomen, Mrs. G.J. Lomen and C.J. McGregor, assistant meteorologist to be stationed in Nome with L. Lundberg to establish a United States Weather Bureau station there. Lundberg, coming from Washington, D.C., had arrived on the *Victoria* to take charge of the new station. Mechanic Herb Larison came in with Grant Elliott in the New Standard.

On Wednesday, June 18, 1930, Joe Crosson, accompanied by Grant Elliott, flew the New Standard, NC 9190, from Nome to Teller and Pilgrim Hot Springs and return, with two hours and forty minutes in the air. Bill Graham was still detained at Golovin, and Vic Ross at Council by bad weather. Crosson had taken Mr. and Mrs. J.I. Anderson to Teller to relieve Mr. and Mrs. Jack Warren who had been managing the Lomen Commercial Company store at Teller. The Warrens were going Outside because of Jack's failing health.

Bill Graham, in the Stinson Detroiter, NC 404M, flew to Golovin on Thursday, June 19, 1930, taking Joe Crosson, E.F. Bauer and Harry Strong as passengers. The pilots and Mr. Bauer selected a new landing site near the village, soon to be placed in commission so that planes could land and take off regardless of the direction of the wind. Crosson had already been out that day, going to Council in the morning with two passengers in the New Standard, NC 9190.

Crosson, having familiarized Grant Elliott with the Seward Peninsula operation of Alaskan Airways, Incorporated, departed Nome for Fairbanks on Friday, June 20, 1930, flying the Fairchild 71, NC 153H, and making the flight in six hours and ten minutes. The company had some midnight sun flights scheduled and Crosson wanted to fly them.

Tom Roust was aloft again in the repaired Standard J-1 for his first takeoff on wheels on Saturday, June 28, 1930. In returning to the Municipal Airport on Bessie road, he undershot the landing field about 150 feet, landing on the tundra close to the road. Very little damage resulted from the mishap and he soon had the plane ready for another go at it. However, it was not to be, for a group of drunken miners started up the Hisso in the small hours of Sunday morning, intending to take a joy ride. Roust was awakened with the news that his plane was a total wreck on the tundra, a short distance off the field, and the marshal's office was investigating the affair.

Vic Ross and mechanic William A. Oliver, of Northern Air Transport, Incorporated, returned to Nome on Wednesday, July 2, from Council. The pilot had met with an accident in landing at the village on June 16 under poor spring conditions. The Stinson Junior, No. 1, was out of commission. Bill Graham was away for Fairbanks at 10:15 A.M. Wednesday, July 2, in the Stinson Detroiter, No. 2. He carried J.D. Harlan, manager of Hammon Consolidated Gold Fields, and a Mrs. Guthmuller who had arrived on the steamer *Victoria* to meet her daughter. The girl had already left Nome via the Yukon River boats and the mother was taking the plane to join her in Anchorage. The pilot was back in Nome at 1:30 A.M. Monday, July 14, with express, 147 pounds of mail, and J.D. Harlan as a passenger. Graham went out to Golovin early that same afternoon, returning with Joe Dexter as a passenger. He was off again late in the afternoon for Kotzebue, with mail, express, and E.E. Patterson and daughter as passengers. Patterson would inspect some of his trading posts in that vicinity.

Alaskan Airways pilot Grant Elliott and his wife, the former Barbara Nudd, and a passenger, L.J. Palmer, arrived in Nome about 4:00 A.M. on Monday, July 14, 1930. Coming from Fairbanks in the New Standard, NC 174H, the pilot was to be stationed in Nome for the company. The couple moved into a three-room apartment.

Bill Graham was off late on Tuesday, for Golovin, with trader Joe Dexter as a passenger, proceeding from there to Candle. He returned in the six-place Stinson from there about 4:30 P.M. Wednesday, with Jim Crowdy, Charles Randall, C.V. Olson and postal inspector Swenson as passengers. Grant Elliott, local pilot for Alaskan Airways, took off about 12:00 P.M. Wednesday, for Teller, returning in the New Standard about 3:30 P.M. with J.H. Anderson and Jack Warren as passengers. The pilot had another flight to Elephant Point and Candle, with Tom Roust, Carl Lomen, L.J. Palmer and Dan Crowley as passengers, plus some mail. He landed Crowley and Roust at Candle as the field at Elephant Point was dotted with mud puddles. The two passengers left by small boat for Elephant Point. The pilot returned from Candle and Kotzebue about 7:00 P.M. Thursday, July 17, bringing Carl Lomen and L.J. Palmer of the United States Biological Survey. The Swenson Fur & Trading Company vessel *Nanuk*, which had been frozen in all winter at North Cape, arrived in Nome the morning of Thursday, July 17, sailing for Seattle at 5:00 P.M. the same day. Julius Silverman boarded the vessel for the trip south.

Bill Graham, flying Northern Air Transport, Incorporated, No. 2, NC 404M, made a flight to Candle and return on the evening of Wednesday, July 23, 1930. He went again to the same place the morning of the following day, taking J.K. Crowdy as a passenger, as well as mail and express. Pilot Grant Elliott of Alaskan Airways had returned from Teller to Nome early Wednesday evening.

Graham was preparing for a flight to Fairbanks. He was away at 6:30 P.M. Friday, July 25, with Auditor Patriquin of the Hammon company, plus a heavy load of first class mail. The pilot arrived on Weeks Field at 12:15 A.M. on Saturday in the Stinson No. 2. Cliff Allyn, the Nome manager for the company was expecting the plane back on Monday.

Samuel Anaruk, Bureau of Education teacher and Eskimo from Little Diomede Island, came in to Nome on August 2, 1930, on the motorship *Good Hope*. He reported hearing airplanes flying over the island the previous fall, crossing from Alaska to Siberia. In each case he let the native children out of school to watch, as most of them had never seen a plane before. They were greatly excited. After the early part of November there were no more planes until about January, when they began to hear them again. The teacher did not know what the planes were going back and forth for but realized there must be some trouble somewhere. He decided to lay out a field on the ice for the planes to land on, in case it was necessary. Sam Anaruk

Canadian Fairchild 71, CF-AJK near the Nome radio tower in 1930. Added to Alaskan Airways fleet, the plane would bear United States registration number NC 154H.

Tom Martin Collection

made two triangles of wood, painting them red and placing one on the left, the other on the right side of the level ice field; fastening a black cloth flag at the top of a long pole he planted it in the ice at the north end of his field. Although no planes landed, they could have in case of necessity, for a smooth area of about 1500 feet in length had been prepared for them. The teacher learned about the deaths of Eielson and Borland, and the reason for the planes, when the Coast Guard cutter *Northland* arrived at the island in the latter part of June. There were 137 people wintering on the island, without communication. (Twenty-five years later one of Sam's seven children, "Axel" Anaruk, became an aircraft mechanic for Pacific Northern Airlines in Anchorage.)

Bill Graham, flying the Northern Air Transport No. 2, arrived back in Nome from Fairbanks late on Thursday afternoon, August 7, 1930. Joe Crosson, flying the Alaskan Airways Fairchild 71, NC 154H, also arrived in Nome late Thursday afternoon. He had made the five hour and twenty-five minute flight from Fairbanks nonstop. Crosson was carrying Ernest Walker Sawyer of the Department of the Interior, Major L.E. Atkins of the Alaska Road Commission, and H.L. Stull, who was returning to his home in Deering after a trip Outside. Sawyer and Atkins intended to travel to various Seward Peninsula points from Nome with Alaskan Airways pilot Grant Elliott, presently stationed there. Crosson was away the next afternoon for Fairbanks, carrying merchant John Lichtenberg as a passenger. He completed the flight in five hours and ten minutes nonstop.

Grant Elliott, flying the New Standard, NC 9190, was away from Nome the morning of Friday, August 8, 1930, for Akiak on the Kuskokwim River. He was accompanied by his mechanic, Herbert M. Larison, and completed the flight in one day, to Akiak and back to Moses Point. He came in to Nome from there on Sunday. The pilot then flew back to Golovin and brought in W.B. Miller, Miss Ruth Reet and L.J. Palmer to Nome. Miller had made the trip with Elliott from Akiak.

Bill Graham, in the Stinson No. 2, NC 404M, flew from Nome to Golovin on Saturday, August 9, 1930, taking Ernest W. Sawyer and Major Atkins as passengers, returning the same evening alone. Grant Elliott went out in the New Standard that same afternoon at

2:00 P.M., picking up the two men at Golovin. He dropped Major Atkins off at Solomon, returning to Nome about 4:00 P.M. with Sawyer.

On Sunday, August 10, Bill Graham left in the Stinson No. 2 for Deering, Candle and Kotzebue, with passengers H.L. Stull for Deering, and Mrs. Walter Dowd for Kotzebue. While the pilot was there, Mrs. Magids chartered Graham to scout around Kotzebue Sound for the Magids' lighterage tug, which was waiting out a storm. Graham located the tug, finding it in no distress. He returned to Nome that same day.

The arrival of the *S.S. Baldwin* in the Nome roadstead on August 10 brought new equipment and supplies for Northern Air Transport, Incorporated. Included in the shipment was a set of newly-developed airwheels for each of the company's Stinsons. The four-place Stinson SM-2AA, NC 475H, had been undergoing repairs and refurbishing; also a new 225 horsepower engine was installed in place of the original 165 horsepower Wright R-540. The low-pressure (six pounds) airwheels resembled a great doughnut with a small hub and axle. They absorbed much more of the shock experienced in landing and taking off, as well as providing a wider tread on soft ground or snow. Compared to the more narrow, high-pressure tires, the airwheels were a distinct advantage in an Alaskan operation. The two pilots, Graham and Ross, were enthusiastic after test hopping the planes on Wednesday, August 13, with the new wheels installed. There was little increased drag in the air, and landings and takeoffs were smoother.

On Friday morning, August 15, 1930, all three of the Nome-based planes were away from the Bessie road Municipal Airport. Vic Ross had left in Stinson No. 1 for northern points, taking Ernest W. Sawyer, Interior Department inspector who was making an official investigation of the reindeer situation, and Major Atkins of the Alaska Road Commission, making a tour of the developmental projects being worked on by Alaska Road Commission. Ross arrived at Kotzebue on August 15 at 9:00 P.M. with Atkins and Sawyer as passengers. His new engine was working fine and the added power was a blessing over the old engine. He expected to leave Kotzebue for Elephant Point, Keewalik, Deering and Nome on Sunday, August 18, 1930.

Bill Graham, off in the Stinson Detroiter No. 2, was taking Ross Kinney to Council to investigate the possibilities of a landing field there. The pilot also took Commissioner of Education Leo W. Breuer, who was in the region inspecting Territorial schools. Graham was back the same evening with both passengers.

Grant Elliott, flying the Alaskan Airways New Standard, NC 9190, was away for Fairbanks taking L.J. Palmer of the Biological Survey, and Lieutenant Palmer of the Signal Corps. Meeting company pilot Robbie Robbins at Ruby, they transferred their respective loads and returned to their separate bases. Elliott was back in Nome late on Friday, the same day.

Bill Graham, in Stinson No. 2, made a flight to the north on Monday morning, August 18, 1930, taking as passengers Leo W. Breuer and Grant Jackson, the latter flying to Deering. On Tuesday, August 19, 1930, both Northern Air Transport planes were at Keewalik, awaiting more favorable weather to return to Nome. Grant Elliott was holding in Nome, waiting for better weather before flying to Pilgrim Hot Springs to inspect their landing field. Graham returned to Nome from Candle at 2:30 P.M. Wednesday, August 20, bringing back Breuer, Grant Jackson and Ross J. Kinney as passengers. Vic Ross had gone to Unalakleet with Sawyer and Atkins, having been storm-bound at Keewalik. He was waiting at Unalakleet for Anchorage-based pilot Matt Nieminen of Alaskan Airways to pick his two passengers up and take them to Anchorage. Nieminen was storm-bound at Kaltag. (see Anchorage—1930, Chapter 57). The weather all over the area had been stormy and was giving all the pilots a troublesome time.

Bill Graham, in the Stinson Detroiter No. 2, got away in the morning of Thursday, August 21, for Fairbanks. He carried five passengers from Nome: J.D. Harlan, Doctor L.M. Waugh of the U.S. Public Health Service, C.W. Franklin, salesman, H.E. Seneff, special officer for prevention of liquor traffic among natives, and Leo W. Breuer, Territorial commissioner of education. Circling around storm areas, the pilot landed at Weeks Field that same afternoon. Graham was back in Nome about 8:00 P.M. Sunday, August 24, 1930.

Grant Elliott, Alaskan Airways pilot, made a round trip to Pilgrim Hot Springs on Thursday, August 21, with E.F. Bauer of the Alaska Road Commission, to inspect the landing field there. In addition to Bauer, the pilot brought Mrs. George F. Maynard as a passenger to Nome. Vic Ross had returned from Unalakleet that same day; his two passengers there had been picked up by Nieminen. Grant Elliott, in the New Standard, NC 9190, of Alaskan Airways, made a flight to Solomon on Sunday, August 24, 1930, returning with Miss Emily Ivanoff as a passenger. The pilot was planning a flight to Kotzebue as soon as the weather permitted.

Bill Graham flew the Northern Air Transport Stinson No. 2 to Shishmaref on Monday, September 1, 1930, taking Mr. and Mrs. Anton Polet as round-trippers. He went out again on Tuesday afternoon to Pilgrim Hot Springs, with Mr. and Mrs. Grant Jackson, and Doctor and Mrs. O'Hara as passengers. Alaskan Airways pilot Grant Elliott took off on a round trip for Teller on Wednesday afternoon, September 3, 1930, with mail and passengers, also taking mechanic Herb Larison and Mrs. Elliott. Both Northern Air Transport Stinsons came in to their base at Nome from Pilgrim Hot Springs, with passengers, on the same day.

Word came in from Candle that an exploding blow torch in Robinson & Greenberg's store had caused a fire that burned several buildings in the town on August 29, 1930. Besides the store, Roust's roadhouse, Person store and the U.S. marshal's house and some small cabins were burned. With a high southwest wind blowing, the flames that first came through the side of Robinson & Greenberg's store had traveled to the marshal's house at the end of the block in fifteen minutes. Fairbanks was suffering a flood.

Vic Ross was off in the Stinson Junior, NC 475H, No. 1, on Thursday morning, September 4, for Deering and other northern points, carrying as passengers Miss Madelaine Calkins and A.F. Wright on the round trip. Grant Elliott left in the New Standard biplane, NC 9190, for Egavik, carrying as passengers Alfred J. Lomen and Hans Samuelson, plus his mechanic, Herb Larison. While taking off from the Golovin field on Friday, September 5, Elliott met with an unfortunate upset. The pilot had some difficulty in getting off and the plane turned over at the edge of the field, breaking the propeller and part of the landing gear. Elliott and Alf Lomen escaped without injury but mechanic Larison cracked a couple of ribs and Hans Samuelson lost three front teeth. With the exception of Samuelson, the men arrived in Nome on the motorship *Donaldson* on Saturday morning, September 6, 1930.

Alaskan Airways pilot S.E. Robbins, flying a Fairchild 71, departed Weeks Field for Nome on Sunday, September 14, 1930. Carrying Charles P. Sisson, assistant attorney-general for the United States, as well as Manager Arthur W. Johnson and mechanic Clark Bassett, the pilot landed on the Nome Municipal Airport on Bessie road late the same day. Vic Ross had departed for Fairbanks in the Stinson Junior No. 1 on Sunday morning, landing at Ruby for gas. Carrying Alvin Polet, who was returning to the Alaska College for his second year as a student, the Northern Air Transport pilot arrived on Weeks Field on Monday afternoon, September 15, 1930.

The Fairchild 71, flown by Robbie Robbins departed Nome on Friday, September 19, to return to Fairbanks but, encountering low visibility at Golovin, was forced to return to Nome.

Robbins got away at 10:30 A.M. the following day, carrying Charles P. Sisson and four other passengers. Flying in good weather, he landed the Fairchild 71 on Weeks Field that afternoon.

Captain A.P. Jochimsen, ice pilot, now in command of the *Karise*, a third Swenson Fur & Trading Company vessel, had radioed from Cape Serdtse-Kamen on the Siberian coast for a plane to pick him up. Jochimsen was seriously ill and needed to be hospitalized at Nome. The nearest float-equipped plane was at Anchorage: the Fairchild 51, NC 5364, of Pacific International Airways. Frank Dorbandt and mechanic Lon Cope arrived in Nome at 10:00 A.M. on Sunday, September 21, 1930; he had left Anchorage on Saturday. (see Anchorage—1930, Chapter 57). Fueling up, the two airmen were off again for Teller, going from there across the Bering Strait to Cape Serdtse-Kamen where they landed the float plane in an area of slushy water near the *Karise*. Crewmen in a small boat had kept the landing area free of ice.

After delivering a case of fresh fruit to the crew of the vessel and refueling the Fairchild 51, they placed the sick man aboard; Dorbandt and Cope took off immediately, to land at Teller on the American side at 6:00 P.M. Sunday and spend the night there. The United States Coast Guard cutter *Northland* had stood by in Bering Strait for their crossing.

The Fairchild left Teller early the next morning, Monday, September 22, 1930, arriving in Nome at 8:30 A.M. Captain Jochimsen, suffering from kidney trouble and unable to speak, was taken to Maynard-Columbus Hospital. Dorbandt wired the *Karise* concerning ice condition to aid the vessel in their navigation through the ice in the approaching winter conditions. Dorbandt, still in Nome on September 24, received a call to pick up a sick man at Holy Cross on his way to Anchorage. Dorbandt and Cope reached Holy Cross on Wednesday, September 24, to find Matt Nieminen had picked up the patient a short time before. Cope and Dorbandt went on to Anchorage, arriving there on the evening of Thursday, July 26, 1930. (see Anchorage—1930, Chapter 57).

Northern Transport pilot Bill Graham was away from Nome in Stinson No. 2 on Monday morning, September 22, to bring back to Nome two passengers from Kotzebue for the steamer *Victoria* which was outbound from Nome. He came in Tuesday evening, with Mr. and Mrs. D.H. King and meteorologist C.J. McGregor, all coming from Kotzebue. McGregor was returning from a trip to Point Barrow. Vic Ross was getting ready for a trip to Fairbanks, planned for Saturday. The pilot left Nome on Friday morning in Stinson No. 1, taking Mrs. Charlotte Potter, whose husband had worked in the engineering department of Hammon Consolidated Gold Fields prior to his departure for Peru. He had died there and his wife was hurrying Outside to meet the boat at New York that was bringing her husband's body back to the States. Ross was delayed enroute, forced back to McGrath by snowstorms. He arrived in Fairbanks on Wednesday, October 1, 1930.

Arthur W. Johnson had been in Nome for the past three weeks for the purpose of expanding Alaskan Airways operations in the region. Two planes were to be based at Nome: a New Standard biplane with an enclosed cabin, NC 174H, holding four passengers, and a seven-place Fairchild 71 cabin plane with a 425 horsepower Wasp engine. A large shop equipped with modern machinery had recently been completed in Fairbanks where major repairs to all equipment could be made, with the Nome planes making periodic trips to the Weeks Field base for inspection and overhaul. Clark Bassett, licensed mechanic who had spent the summer at the Fairbanks base to become more familiar in the company's repair and service methods, had recently returned to Nome to relieve Herb Larison of his duties. Larison had returned to Fairbanks.

The Catholic mission's Bellanca CH-300 Special, NC 862N, arrived in Nome on the afternoon of Wednesday, September 24, 1930, coming from Holy Cross. Flown by Brother

George J. Feltes SJ, with Ralph Wien as copilot and Father Philip Delon as a passenger, the *Marquette Missionary* with its Packard DR-980 diesel engine drew a lot of attention from local church and aviation people, as well as the other residents. (see Fairbanks—1930, Chapter 58). The three men left Nome on Monday, September 29, with snow flurries reported to the north. Landing at Pilgrim Hot Springs on the left bank of the Pilgrim River, a visit to the mission kept the party there until Wednesday, October 1, 1930, at which time the plane returned to Nome.

Northern Air Transport pilot Bill Graham, flying the Stinson No. 2, was away from Nome on Tuesday, September 29, for Deering, Candle and Kotzebue with a quantity of fresh fruit for the northern camps, mail and three passengers: Mrs. R.B. Julian for Elephant Point, Arthur Wright for Deering and Chief Deputy A.O. Brown for Kotzebue. Wright and Brown also returned with the pilot. Graham returned to Nome on Wednesday, reporting he had landed and taken off in four inches of snow at Kotzebue, and had found the balloon tires performed well in the snow. He also brought jeweler Jerry Coffin and two others from Deering, as well as his two round-trippers. Coffin was catching the *Victoria* for the States.

Northern Air Transport pilot Vic Ross departed Weeks Field for Nome in the Stinson Junior, NC 475H, on Friday, October 3, 1930. Pilot Robbins, of Alaskan Airways, was also away for Nome, carrying company mechanics J.T. Hutchison and Gordon Springbett, who were going to make repairs to the company's New Standard biplane, damaged on takeoff at Golovin on September 5, 1930. Forced back, to hold at Nulato for some days by snowstorms on the route, the pilot finally made it through to Nome. Vic Ross was holding at Unalakleet for the same reason. Bill Graham left Nome on Saturday afternoon for Golovin with Mrs. Fagerstrom and her child. He returned the same day with two passengers.

The U.S. marshal's office in Nome chartered the Northern Air Transport, Incorporated, Stinson Detroiter, NC 404M, for a flight to Point Barrow to pick up an insane Eskimo for transport south on the *Victoria*, the last steamer for Seattle of the season. Loading the plane with fresh meat, fruit and watermelons for the northern community, pilot Bill Graham was off for Kotzebue on Thursday afternoon, October 9, 1930. Deputy Marshal Cremer and company manager Cliff Allyn accompanied the airman, taking several issues of the *Nome Nugget* to deliver at the remote community as well as mail. Graham planned on stopping at Kotzebue, Point Hope, Wainwright and Point Lay. The flight left Kotzebue on October 10, spending the night at Point Hope. They landed at Point Barrow on a sandspit between the government buildings and the village at 1:45 P.M. of the following day.

On Sunday, October 12, 1930, the pilot made the entire 615 miles to Nome, with a short stop at Kotzebue where Graham took a snapshot of the *Marquette Missionary* parked before the mission building. The insane native made no trouble for his two guards; he seemed to enjoy the trip immensely. Varied weather conditions were encountered going both ways, the pilot flying in sunshine for periods, then running into long stretches of fog and snow. There was practically no visibility for 350 miles of the distance going up, and for 250 miles on the return. Barrow had about six inches of snow with deep drifts. Salt water in the lagoon was frozen to a depth of four inches, with fresh water frozen much deeper. However, the Arctic Ocean and Bering Sea were completely free of ice as far as the pilot could see from the plane.

Vic Ross was still holding at Unalakleet on October 11. Robbins, holding at Nulato, made an attempt to reach Nome the same day, but was forced back to land at Nulato again. It was a bad time on the Fairbanks-Nome route.

The *Marquette Missionary*, Bellanca CH-300 Special, NC 862N, was in Kotzebue on Sunday, October 12, when tragedy struck. The wheel-equipped, diesel-powered plane was preparing for a flight to Deering with Father Walsh when Ralph Wien went aloft with Fathers

Lineup of Northern Air Transport, Incorporated, and Service Airlines planes on Weeks Field, Fairbanks, Alaska. Left to Right: NAT Stinson No. 2, NC 404M; NAT Stinson No. 1, NC 475H; Service Airlines Eaglerock, NC 209Y; Service Airlines OX-5 Swallow TP, NC 688H.

Delon and Walsh on a short demonstration flight. Brother Feltes, waiting on the ground, observed the plane as it made an approach to the landing strip, going around to circle back for a second landing approach. It seemed to the observers on the ground that the nose of the plane was rather high in the steep turn, the plane stalling or approaching a stall, as the Bellanca fell out of control in a tight spiral from an estimated altitude of 400 feet. With the nose pointed straight down and power on the engine again, the plane struck the ground head-on, killing the pilot and his two passengers. (see Fairbanks—1930, Chapter 58, for details).

Bill Graham, chief pilot for Northern Air Transport, Incorporated, took off on Monday morning, October 12, 1930, for Kotzebue, taking Father Post of Nome over. He planned to return the same day, stopping at Deering. Vic Ross had finally completed the flight from Fairbanks with mail, coming in to Nome on Sunday, October 11; he had been on the way since October 3. Robbins, in the Alaskan Airways Fairchild 71, who had also made it in to Nome, hopped off for Kotzebue on Tuesday morning, October 14, taking Manager Johnson and Ray Pollister with him. Enroute to Fairbanks, the pilot picked up the body of Ralph Wien at Kotzebue. The funeral plane arrived on Weeks Field at 7:45 P.M. that same evening, landing after dark with the aid of flares set out by the mechanics. Pollister had left the trading schooner *Karise* at Nome, believing that by coming to Fairbanks by plane and taking the train to Seward, he could reach Seattle far ahead of the schooner. Bad weather had held him in Nome for twenty days and the *Karise* arrived in Seattle on the same day as Pollister landed there. The *Karise* had been 120 miles up the Kolyma River, which is located 500 miles northwest of North Cape (now Mys Shmidta, or Cape Smith) for Siberian furs, during the summer shipping season. The *Karise* also picked up the merchandise salvaged from the wrecked *Elisif*, delivering it to Siberian destinations. Twice she had been trapped in the ice pack but southerly blows had come up, opening the ice for her to proceed south.

Vic Ross flew to Teller on Friday, October 17, 1930, returning in the evening with Nome attorney James Frawley and Tom Peterson. He went out the next afternoon for Teller, carrying mail and bringing in as passengers Mrs. M. Mathews and George McAdams. That same morning he had gone to Pilgrim Hot Springs with Sister Louise, continuing on to Candle before returning to Nome.

Bill Graham, in the Stinson Junior No. 2, had gone to Fairbanks, arriving there at 11:30 A.M. Thursday, October 16, 1930. The pilot brought in to Weeks Field as passengers, Andy Nerland and L. Husdale, employees of the Hammon Consolidated Gold Fields, as well as H.E. Seneff, liquor control agent, whom he had dropped at Tanana. Flying in good weather, the pilot had overnighted at Ruby. Graham returned to Nome from Fairbanks on Friday, October 17, setting a new record for the flight of four hours and five minutes, and breaking his previous record by fifteen minutes. The Stinson was a speedy plane. He carried only express as Alaskan Airways had picked up the Nome mail at the post office twenty minutes before Graham's arrival there. The Northern Air Transport pilot took off from Nome on Saturday morning, October 18, 1930, for Deering and Kotzebue. It was Alaska Day, celebrating the transfer of the Territory from Russia to the United States in a ceremony at Sitka on October 18, 1867. The pilot carried A. Cordovado for the first stop.

Grant Elliott was away from Fairbanks in the forenoon of Saturday, October 18, returning to his base at Nome. He carried William Wagner, who was going to Nome to install a new radio-tube transmitter at the Nome station. The Alaskan Airways, Incorporated, pilot was now based in Nome, as before.

Alaskan Airways announced on October 18, 1930, the appointment of Dan Crowley as their manager in Nome, with independent offices. Dan had accepted the position the previous fall, having served for the past ten years as field manager for the Lomen Commercial Company. Crowley had been a resident of Nome since 1900. Work was being started on a hangar in Nome, a sixty by forty-five foot lumber and corrugated iron building with space for three planes. Nose hangars were to be built at one end so the motors could be worked on in the heated shop during cold weather. Pilot Grant Elliott and mechanic Clark Bassett made up the balance of the staff.

Bill Graham departed Nome on Monday, October 27, 1930, for Fairbanks, flying the Northern Air Transport Stinson Junior, NC 404M, as usual. Overnighting at Ruby, he went on the next day to land at Weeks Field about 2:00 P.M. Tuesday, following the rivers through a heavy snowstorm. He brought in James K. Crowdy, manager, Ralph Hirsch and N.F. Lott, all of New York-Alaska (gold-dredging) Company. The pilot left for Nome on Wednesday, October 29, 1930, taking Russell G. Maynard as a passenger. On Saturday, November 1, while taking off the Nome Municipal field in a no-wind condition, Graham failed to lift free of the ground when reaching the end of the strip. The Northern Air Transport six-place Stinson No. 2, NC 404M, heavily-loaded with Marshal Jones, District Attorney Hart and a prisoner named Gus Cremidas, bellied in on the tundra at the end of the field, with no injuries to the occupants of the plane. Graham had to take the passengers over Sunday morning in the four-place Stinson No. 1.

Grant Elliott returned to Nome on Saturday, November 1, after taking James Frawley to make connections with Anchorage pilot Matt Nieminen of Alaskan Airways, who flew the attorney to Seward to make connections with a steamer for the States. S.E. "Robbie" Robbins arrived at Nome on Saturday, November 1, 1930, in a Fairchild 71; he had left Weeks Field the previous day for Ruby, Holy Cross and Nome. He had overnighted at Holy Cross where he had dropped an eleven-year-old native boy for the Catholic mission. Robbins was also carrying Johnny Glass, a native recently released from the federal jail after serving out a sentence on a drunk and disorderly charge, to his home in Ruby. The pilot brought a small quantity of letter mail in to Nome. Robbins, in the Fairchild, was away again on Thursday, November 6, for Elephant Point and the Hunt River, where the Lomen Reindeer Corporation drive was stalled, the animals refusing to cross on the glare ice. Robbins carried Dan Crowley, Alaskan Airways local manager, and Sam Segoak, a native traveling to join the drive at the Hunt River. The pilot also had his mechanic, Jim Hutchison, with him. Pilots never liked to travel without a flight mechanic; aside from the sometimes necessary mechanical repairs that arose, handling a large aircraft on the ground by the pilot where no other help was available could be a problem. It was intended to use the aircraft to transport two and a half tons of supplies from the headwaters of the Kobuk River, through Howard Pass into the Colville River section where there was to be a new reindeer camp.

Grant Elliott took the Alaskan Airways New Standard biplane to Teller on Friday, November 7, carrying Ole and Mrs. Stenfeld as passengers. The pilot also carried mail and express, returning to Nome at 1:00 P.M. Elliott was scheduled to fly to Unalakleet on Monday with three passengers, and to shuttle over to St. Michael to bring two passengers to Unalakleet. Crosson, now returned to Fairbanks from a vacation Outside, picked up the five, taking them to Fairbanks. Elliott flew back to Nome, picking up five passengers enroute and delivering them to their several destinations. Mail, express and freight were also carried.

Both Northern Air Transport, Incorporated, and Alaskan Airways, Incorporated, announced their intent to maintain a regular schedule between Nome and Fairbanks over the winter: once every ten days for the first company and every second Monday for the larger firm.

Damages to the Stinson No. 2, which Bill Graham had bellied in off the Nome Municipal Airport on November 1, 1930, were more extensive than first thought; the tail end of the fuselage was damaged and out of alignment. A factory-trained, expert mechanic was needed to make repairs. Officials had wired the Stinson factory for such a person, plus equipment to do the job. They also placed an order for a second Stinson Junior, similar to No. 1 but with an improved motor, the Lycoming 210 horsepower engine that was serving so well in the States.

The first scheduled flight of Alaskan Airways between Fairbanks and Nome departed Weeks Field on Tuesday, November 18, 1930, with Joe Crosson at the controls of the Fairchild 71, NC 153H. Four passengers: A.M. Hartford of the Fairbanks Exploration Company, Thomas Gaffney, Democratic candidate for auditor in the recent election, and Albert Aukon and Billy Komakhuk, field foremen for the Bureau of Biological Survey, were aboard; the latter two left the flight at Golovin. Crosson was off Ruby on November 20, flying to Nulato, Golovin and Nome. Delayed at Ruby and Golovin by weather, he arrived at the Bessie road Municipal field on the same day. Crosson left Nome on Friday, November 21, with J.H. Anderson, A.N. Nylen and carpenter-mechanic Gordon Springbett. The pilot overnighted at Ruby, coming in to Weeks Field the next day. The first dog team mail of the season also left Nome on Friday morning, November 21, 1930, with Pete Curran, Jr. at the handlebars of the basket sled. He carried a capacity load of mail bound for the Outside, as well as for intermediate points. The airplane had not yet eliminated this companion service in Alaska.

Vic Ross was off Nome in the Northern Air Transport Stinson Junior, No. 1, on Saturday morning, November 22, 1930, bound for the Buckland district, carrying Ben Mozee and Superintendent Morelander, of the Bureau of Education. Mozee returned with the pilot.

Mail for Deering was dropped as they passed over the village. The pilot was back with Mozee on Tuesday, November 25, 1930.

The planes were now able to land on the Bering Sea ice, rather than having to go down to the Nome River or the Municipal Airport at Nome. Three planes had landed on the ice in the past week, only one hundred feet from their company offices. The ice was good up and down the coast. With only about an inch of snow over the smooth surface, the ice made an excellent landing field; it was the only time since Russ Merrill and mechanic Lon Cope had landed their Travel Air 4000, C-193, before Nome on April 4, 1927, that the ice had frozen in smoothly and could be used by planes. Alaskan Airways now had their nose hangar set up on the beach in front of their office and Northern Air Transport was considering moving theirs down. Nome passengers would have curb service if the ice remained stable throughout the winter.

Ed Young was away from Fairbanks for Nome on Sunday, November 23, with W.B. Miller of the Biological Survey as a passenger. Forced back by weather, he set out again the following day, overnighting at Nulato. Taking off from there at 9:00 A.M. Tuesday, November 25, he arrived in Nome the same day. Grant Elliott had made a flight on Sunday, November 23, to Igloo, Teller and Wales, with Albert Schmidt and L.E. Rynning as passengers. Unable to land at Wales, they picked up Tommy Petersen and brought him in to Nome. The pilot went out again on Tuesday morning on a return trip to Igloo with Petersen, also taking Rynning and Schmidt to Teller. On Wednesday, flying the cabin New Standard, which had been repaired, Elliott was off at 9:05 A.M. Wednesday, November 26, 1930, for Golovin and Unalakleet. He was back on the ice in front of Nome at 1:00 P.M., carrying Tony Nicholas and Pete Olsen as passengers from Unalakleet.

Alaskan Airways pilot Ed Young was away from Nome on Tuesday afternoon, November 25, for Fairbanks, carrying J.D. Harlan, George Hellerich and radioman Wagner of the Signal Corps. Stopping overnight at Golovin, the pilot arrived at Weeks Field on Wednesday afternoon with the Fairchild 71. Northern Air Transport pilot Vic Ross, flying the Stinson Junior No. 1, was away from Nome for Fairbanks at 9:45 A.M. Wednesday, November 26, 1930. He was delayed in Nome some hours to exchange his wheels for skis before departure.

Grant Elliott made a round trip to Council, bringing Mr. and Mrs. H.M. Hansen and a native girl to Nome on Saturday, November 29. Vic Ross was on the field at Manley Hot Springs with motor trouble, on his way to Fairbanks. Robbins brought the pilot in to Weeks Field on December 5; his 225 horsepower Wright engine in the Stinson was disabled.

Alaskan Airways pilot Joe Crosson, flying the Fairchild 71, NC 153H, departed Weeks Field at 9:00 A.M. Tuesday, December 2, 1930, for Nome. The pilot was carrying Dan Crowley, Nome manager for the company, Gale L. Alexander. a Stinson factory foreman from Wayne, Michigan who had arrived in Fairbanks by train the previous Sunday, and who was traveling to Nome to repair the damage to Northern Air Transport's Stinson Detroiter No. 2, and Crosson's wife, Lillian. Stormy weather halted the flight at Ruby. Remaining there over Wednesday and Thursday, the pilot left on Friday, reaching Golovin after stopping at Nulato and briefly at Unalakleet. The party reached Nome at 10:30 A.M. Saturday, December 6, 1930. Crosson was doing some local flying out of Nome. He returned to Golovin that same day, flying from there to Teller and back to Nome on Sunday.

Northern Air Transport manager Cliff Allyn was soon closeted with Stinson mechanic Alexander, seeing to repairing the Stinson Detroiter, NC 404M. With it out of service and Stinson No. 1 at Manley Hot Springs with a bad motor, the company was temporarily out of equipment. By Saturday, December 13, the repaired plane was almost ready to fly; one or two minor adjustments remained, as well as doping the new fabric on the fuselage. The entire tail surfaces of the plane had been repaired. The company hoped to have the plane in the air the first of the week.

The new four-place Stinson, NC 495Y, ordered by Northern Air Transport, Incorporated, arrived in Fairbanks by train on Sunday, December 7, 1930. Vic Ross was there to receive it and was preparing to assemble the Stinson No. 3. The plane was powered with a 210 horsepower Lycoming engine, the first powerplant of this type in the north.

Joe Crosson, flying the Alaskan Airways Fairchild 71, NC 153H, took off early on Friday, December 12, for Candle, with mail, freight and a passenger by the name of Mr. Pistaris. Stormy weather at Candle forced the pilot to land at Keewalik, held there by poor visibility and snowstorms. He did not get away until Sunday, flying to Deering before coming in to Nome.

Alaskan Airways pilot Grant Elliott was taxiing the company's New Standard cabin plane, NC 174H, out on Friday afternoon, December 12. Suddenly, the new shore ice in front of the town, that served as a landing site, gave way beneath the plane; the motor sank into the sea water and the tail tilted up. The ice, three inches thick where the plane taxied, evidently had a weakness at that particular spot. There were no passengers in the biplane and the pilot scrambled out uninjured. He had intended to move the New Standard to the Nome River ice to pick up a load of freight and passengers for northern points. The plane was pulled out of the

December 12, 1930. Grant Elliott sank through thin sea ice at Nome, Alaska while taxiing out near shore. The pilots had started using the ice in front of town for a landing field. The plane was hauled out and the motor overhauled due to its salt water immersion. It was Alaskan Airways New Standard cabin plane, NC 174H, converted from open cockpit with the installation of a factory-built canopy over the passenger area. The pilot sat behind in an open cockpit.

Sylvia Ross Photo

water late that day. The motor, immersed in sea water, needed a careful overhaul before it could be put in service again.

Alaskan Airways pilot Joe Crosson departed Nome for Fairbanks on Tuesday, December 16, in the Fairchild 71, NC 153H. He had his wife, Lillian, aboard, Charles Milot of the Lomen Corporation, H.L. Stull of Deering and Lewis Stull, the man's son. Bad weather forced the pilot to land at Koyuk village at the mouth of the Koyuk River, near the head of Norton Bay. The party stayed at Big Sam's roadhouse but there was no means of notifying Nome of their delay. The ice moved out, leaving only a large cake for an airport. Leaving his passengers in the village, Joe took the Fairchild off the bit of ice the next day, alone and empty, landing back on the space again. He took off a second time, going to Dime and returning to Koyuk, where he landed.

Crosson was finally able to get away with his passengers on Friday, December 19, 1930, landing at Unalakleet and reaching Nulato with a flying time of two hours and fifteen minutes for the day. The pilot was away the following day, continuing to Ruby where he again spent the night. Crosson took the plane and passengers on to Fairbanks on Sunday, December 21, 1930, landing on Weeks Field after a three hour and ten minute flight. Lewis Stull, who had suffered an epileptic-like seizure during the flight from Nome, was taken to the hospital but died less than twenty-four hours after their arrival.

The Northern Air Transport, Incorporated, Stinson Detroiter No. 2, NC 404M, was test hopped in Nome on Friday, December 21, 1930, and pronounced fit for service. Pilot Bill Graham was planning a flight to northern points soon. Alaskan Airways' New Standard biplane, NC 174H, was soon ready to fly again, following its unfortunate dip in the Bering Sea.

Noel Wien had returned to Alaska, after an absence of over a year. Flying his Stinson Junior SM-2AB, NC 490H, the pilot had landed on Weeks Field on Sunday, December 21, 1930. Accompanied by his brother, Sigurd, Noel had flown the plane up from Virginia, Minnesota. His wife, Ada, and their young son, Merrill, met the brothers in Fairbanks, having traveled by train, boat and train. (see Fairbanks—1930, Chapter 58).

Hurrying to reach Nome in time to spend the Christmas holiday with Mrs. Wien's parents, the Arthurs, the family and Sig Wien were off Weeks Field on Monday, December 22, 1930, making it to Ruby in two hours and ten minutes, then continuing on to Nulato. They all arrived in Nome at noon on the day before Christmas, December 24, after overnighting at Nulato. The orange and black Stinson was a beauty.

Alaskan Airways pilot Ed Young also arrived in Nome from Fairbanks on Wednesday, December 24, 1930, with a huge load of mail and Christmas packages, which the post office immediately sorted out.

Vic Ross, Northern Air Transport pilot, was off Weeks Field for his home base in Nome on the morning of Monday, December 29, 1930. Carrying Doctor Rex F. Swartz as a passenger, Vic was making the flight in the newly-assembled Stinson Junior No. 3, NC 495Y. He had test flown the monoplane at Weeks Field during the previous week. When the Stinson No. 1 at Manley Hot Springs was repaired, the company would have three good Stinsons in Nome to serve the community. Alaskan Airways based the cabin New Standard biplane at Nome, and scheduled the Fairchild 71s in from Fairbanks every two weeks. The planes also flew to Seward Peninsula points when at Nome.

Epilogue

AT THE END OF 1930 THE AIRPLANE WAS well established in the transportation system in Alaska. Aided by the Territory, which vigorously pursued its program of building airports wherever they were needed and the local communities could join with them in sharing the cost, the use of the airplane had expanded along natural routes to the far corners of Alaska. These paths down rivers, along the coasts and across mountain ranges were to develop into scheduled routes in the not-too-far future.

Governmental agencies were finding the airplane a useful tool in accomplishing their many projects—a great timesaver. The fishing and mining industries had become heavy users of the aerial services, and would continue to do so. Tourists, merchandise brokers and salesmen, fur buyers and business people of all types were avid users. Interspersed among these were the general citizenry, their daily movement by air kept the aviation services going throughout the year when many of the specialized customers were out-of-season. A bonus to the citizens was the rapidity and ease with which the sick and injured could be transported to a hospital for medical attention. The willingness of the Territory's airmen to make every effort to answer such a call, with the assistance of those on the ground, resulted in the saving of many lives. The tradition would continue.

While the Territory did subsidize some routes at certain times of the year, the Federal government had not budged as yet on establishing air mail in Alaska as a regular Contract Air Mail Service. Until such time, financing and expansion was difficult. The Federal government did however, by the end of 1930, establish a few weather forecast centers in Alaska, namely Juneau, Fairbanks and Nome. Communication services were also being improved, a necessity for a successful aviation system.

The 1930 census listed the population totals for Alaskan and certain Canadian cities as follows:

Ketchikan	3796
Wrangell	916
Petersburg	1249
Juneau (Capital)	4037
Sitka	1053
Skagway	492
Cordova	979
Valdez	441
Seward	832
Anchorage	2276
Nenana	291
Fairbanks	2099
Nome	1213
Hyder	254
Hazelton, British Columbia	500
Atlin, British Columbia	500
Whitehorse, Yukon Territory	541
Dawson, Yukon Territory	819

This population swelled tremendously each summer with seasonal workers and visitors. The Air Commerce Bulletin of September, 1930 listed for Alaska the following:

Licensed planes	11
Unlicensed planes	5
Air Transport pilots	5
Limited Commercial pilots	3
Private pilots	6
Licensed mechanics	15

Reviewing the growth and the happenings of the aviation industry in these early years has been a joy, and I would like to share it with all of you. Perhaps I can take you further in subsequent volumes.

THE AUTHOR

Bibliography

Allen, Richard Sanders, *Revolution in the Sky*, those fabulous Lockheeds, the pilots who flew them. The Stephen Greene Press 1964 (a revised edition is forthcoming).

Amundsen, Roald and Ellsworth, Lincoln, *First Crossing of the Polar Sea*. Doubleday, Doran & Company, Incorporated 1928

Brower, Charles D., *Fifty Years Below Zero*. Grosset & Dunlap 1942

Clarke, Basil, *Polar Flight*, Ian Allan, Ltd. London 1964

Cloe, John H., *Top Cover for America*. The Air Force in Alaska 1920-1983. Pictorial Histories Publishing Company. Missoula, Montana 1984

Crichton, Clarke, Jr., *Frozen-in*, the Adventures of the *Nanuk*'s cabin boy North of Siberia. G.P. Putnam's Sons 1930

Ellis, Frank H., *Canada's Flying Heritage*. University of Toronto Press 1954

Ellis, Robert E., *What—no Landing Field?* (booklet) Chilkat Press, Haines, Alaska 1969

Gleason, Robert J., *Icebound in the Siberian Arctic*. A story of the last cruise of the fur schooner *Nanuk* and the international search for famous arctic pilot Carl Ben Eielson. Alaska Northwest Publishing Company. Edmonds, Washington 1977

Glines, C.V. (edited by), *Polar Aviation* Franklin Watts, Inc. 1964

Gorst, Wilbur H., *Vern C. Gorst, Pioneer and Granddad of United Airlines*. Gorst Publications. Coos Bay, Oregon 1979

Grierson, John, *Challenge to the Poles*. High-lights of Arctic and Antarctic aviation. G.T. Foulis & Co. Ltd. London 1964

Jupter, Joseph P. *U.S. Civil Aircraft* (in 9 volumes). Aero Publishers, Inc. 1962-1981

Harkey, Ira, *Pioneer Bush Pilot*. The story of Noel Wien. University of Washington Press 1974

Kennedy, Kay J., *The Wien Brothers Story*. (booklet) Published by Wien Air Alaska 1967

Loening, Grover, *Amphibian*. The Story of the Loening Biplane. New York Graphic Society Ltd. 1973

Lombard, Laurence M., *Flight to Alaska—1930.* Author-published by Dow Jones Books 1966

Mills, Stephen E. and Phillips, James W., *Sourdough Sky.* Alaska's Interior bush pilots. Superior Publishing Company 1969

Nobile, Umberto, *My Polar Flights,* an account of the voyages of the airships *Italia* and *Norge.* G.P. Putnam's Sons 1961

Orth, Donald J., *Dictionary of Alaska Place Names.* U.S. Government Printing Office. Washington 1967

Place, Marian, *New York to Nome.* Story of the 1920 Alaska Flying Expedition (Black Wolf Squadron). Macmillan & Company 1972

Potter, Jean, *The Flying North.* The Macmillan Company 1947

Ricker, Elizabeth M., *Seppala, Alaska Dog Driver.* Little, Brown and Company 1931

Rossman, Earl, *Black Sunlight, a Log of the Arctic.* Oxford University Press 1926

Satterfield, Archie, *Alaska Bush Pilots in the Float Country.* Superior Publishing Company 1969

Swenson, Olaf, *Northwest of the World.* Forty years trading and hunting in northern Siberia. Dodd, Mead & Company 1944

Toland, John, *The Great Dirigibles,* their triumphs and disasters. Dover Publications, Inc. 1957

Wambheim, H.G., *Ben,* the life story of Col. Carl Ben Eielson (booklet). Hatton, North Dakota 1930

Worthylake, Mary M., *Up in the Air.* An aviator's wife's story of early days of commercial aviation, from 1924 to 1938, including in Alaska. Woodburn, Oregon 1977

The microfilmed files of the Alaska newspapers for this period as supplied to the author-researcher by the Alaska Historical Library, State of Alaska, in Juneau.

The microfilmed files of the Seattle newspapers for this period as supplied by the City of Seattle Library.

Ships' logs in the National Archives. Naval photographs in the visual section of same.

Records from the office of Naval Aviation History and Archives in the Washington Navy Yard, Washington, D.C.

Records and photographs from the Depository Services Section of the United States Air Force in Arlington, Virginia.

Photos and other material from the University of Alaska, Alaska and Polar Regions Department at Fairbanks, Alaska.

Photos and other material generously loaned by families and individuals as noted by credit lines with each photo. My heartfelt thanks to all, for they made this confluence of Alaska's aviation history possible.

Index

Alaska Guides Association, Incorporated, 636, 638, 639, 876.

Alaska Road Commission Superintendent Frank Nash, 1023.

Alaska Road Commission was publishing a book on airport facilities-1930, 868.

Alaska Railroad steamer *Alice,* 712.

Alaskan Aerial Survey Detachment-1929, 586, 601.
Loening OL-8As, 590.
Navy photographers, 585.
USS Gannet AVP-8 and covered barge YF-88, 593.

Alaskan Aerial Survey Expedition of 1926, 585.

Alaskan Airways, Incorporated, took over Anchorage Air Transport on 8/20/29, 641, 712, 764.

Alaskan Airways, Incorporated took over Bennett-Rodebaugh Company on 8/2/29, 639.

Alaskan Airways, Incorporated, took over Wien Alaska Airways on 8/1/29, 710.

Alaskan Airways, Incorporated-1929:
Eielson arrives in Anchorage on 7/20/29 to form the new company, 638, 647.
Eielson arrives in Fairbanks to expand the new company there, 708.
crew of six mechanics at Fairbanks, 713.
with a total of ten airplanes, 713.
activities in 1929, 716, 719, 721, 731, 735, 741, 749, 762, 763, 764.
Siberian contract announced with Swenson Fur & Trading Company on 10/26/29, 769.
Clark Bassett, company mechanic from Nome, 728.
Pilot Ed Young from Fairbanks, 710.
was painting its fleet all one color with a company number on each plane, 715.

Alaskan Airways, Incorporated-1930:
Pilot Matt Nieminen, 884.
activities in 1930, 892, 897.
plans for a new hangar on the Municipal Airport (later Merrill Field), 898, 910.
activities in 1930, 923, 926, 964, 970, 974, 986.
Crosson, Robbins and Hutchison to *Nanuk,* 987.
hangar at Weeks Field was being built, 993.
the flying equipment was out of Siberia, 991, 994.
activities in 1930 out of Fairbanks, 1000, 1002, 1005, 1007, 1015, 1022, 1024, 1025, 1028, 1031.
activities in 1930 at Nome and in Siberia, 1035, 1046, 1047, 1055, 1059, 1063, 1064, 1067, 1068, 1069, 1071.

Alaska-Washington Airways, Incorporated-1929:
Pilot Robert E. Ellis, 559.
Lockheed Vega *Juneau,* NC 432E, 567.
Lockheed Vega *Ketchikan,* NC 657E, 572, 576.
Lockheed Vega *Sitka,* NC 200E, 574.

activities in 1929, 550, 555, 564, 567, 569, 573, 582.
floating hangar, 571, 577.

Alaska-Washington Airways, Consolidated (holding company) in 1930, 781, 782.

Alaska-Washington Airways of Puget Sound, 784.

Alaska-Washington Airways-1930:
colorful brochures, 783.
floating hangar, 828, 838, 865.
Lockheed Vega *Ketchikan,* NC 657E, 800.
Lockheed Vega *Skagway,* NC 103W, near Juneau, 825.
Lockheed Vega *Taku,* NC 102W, in Juneau, 825.
Lockheed Vega *Ketchikan,* NC 657E, arrived at Victoria, British Columbia, 821.
activities in 1930, 781, 784, 799, 803, 805, 812, 813, 821, 825, 826, 834, 837, 839, 842, 845, 855, 864, 869, 872, 873.

Alex Crone, Vancouver, British Columbia air engineer-1930, 855.

Alexander Bancroft Holden, general operations manager, 570, 583, 915.

Alexander Eaglerock biplane, NC 209Y, 1019, 1022, 1031.

Alexander Eaglerock, C 6316, *Spirit of Valdez* (No. 2)-1930, 880, 882, 883, 884, 886, 888. In 1929, 623, 624.

Alfred J. Lomen, manager of Nome Lighterage Company and Lomen Reindeer Corporation, 685, 735, 758, 777, 964, 1042, 1057, 1063.

Allan E. Horning, son of Anchorage residents Mr. & Mrs. H.S. Horning, 646.

Allen E. Hasselborg, guide-1930, 812.

Alonzo "Lon" Cope, chief mechanic for Anchorage Air Transport in 1929, 635, 638, 641, 647.

Alonzo "Lon" Cope, mechanic for Alaskan Airways in 1929, 643, 712, 735, 742, 776. In 1930, 892, 893, 894.

Alonzo "Lon" Cope bring up a Fairchild 51 from the States in August of 1930, 805, 843, 853, 855, 876, 899, 900, 904, 905.

Alonzo "Lon" Cope and Frank Dorbandt bring up a Bellanca Pacemaker, NC 259M, in October 1930 for Pacific International Airways, 854.

Alonzo "Lon" Cope as partner and chief mechanic in 1930 for Pacific International Airways, 906, 907, 908, 913, 1064.

Alvin Polet, son of Nome merchant Anton Polet, an Alaska College student, 714, 764, 996, 1014, 1055, 1063.

American Airways, Incorporated (later American Airlines), 709, 994.

American Legion pays last respects to Carl Ben Eielson-1930, 895.

American plane flown from Whitehorse to Seattle in 1930 by Clayton Scott, F-71, NC 377M, 840.

American, Russian and Canadian aviators presented to the faculty and students of Alaska College in 1930, 972.

Amtorg Trading Corporation of New York, Russian agency for doing business with United States firms, 669, 676.

Anan Creek, where bears fished the tumbling waters, 804.

Anchorage Air Transport, Incorporated, 632, 634, 638, 641.

Anchorage Municipal Airport, 637.

Anchorage Woman's Club in 1930 sponsoring a memorial to Russ Merrill, 907.

Andrew "Andy" Bahr, reindeer foreman for Lomen, 761, 766, 1025.

Andy Hufford, mechanic on Wilkins 1926 Detroit Arctic Expedition, 1023.

Andy Simons, field manager for Alaska Guides, Incorporated, 638, 913.

Anscel E. Eckmann, pilot for Alaska-Washington Airways:
  1929: 544, 546, 549, 550, 551, 555, 558, 559, 560, 564, 566, 569, 570, 572, 578, 581, 601.
  1930: 787, 799, 812, 815, 818, 819, 821, 823, 828, 835, 839, 851.
  named Chief of Operations for A-WA to succeed Commander W.E. Wynn, 840.

Antarctic experiences with Sir Hubert Wilkins, 702.

anti-collision lights were installed-Fairbanks 1929, 719.

Anton Lindstrom of Flat, 961.

Anton Polet, Nome merchant, 1063.

ANT-4, named for its designer, Andrei Nikolaevich Tupolev, 1929, 669, 673, 679.

Anyone piloting a licensed aircraft must be a licensed airman, 995.

approved repair station for the repair of aircraft, Fairbanks 1930, 1028.

Archie Higgins, dredgeman, 1023.

Arctic Ocean, broken ice, 736.

Arctic Prospecting & Development Company, 686, 699, 731, 972.

Arctic Prospector, Swallow biplane, 880, 972.

Ardell Dayton, mechanic, 551, 574, 578.

Arthur F. "Art" Hines, partner in Service Motor Company, 732, 879, 964, 974, 981, 998.
  also partner in Service Airlines in 1930, 1022, 1031.

Arthur G. Woodley, cadet at the army flying school at Kelly Field, 954.

Arthur W. Johnson, general manager of Alaskan Airways - 1930, 898, 903, 952, 974, 981, 983, 1008, 1018, 1027, 1053, 1063.

Atlin, British Columbia, 569, 658.

Attorney Harry F. Morton - 1930, 884, 906, 908, 913.

Attu, Alaska, 670.

August H. Buschmann, canneryman, 547, 565, 570.

August Homburger, carpenter at Nome, 764.

Avery Black (Eckmann's partner), 559.

Aviation Corporation of America (AVCO), a holding company registered in Delaware, 639, 647 (rescue team), 734, 994.

Aviation School, Incorporated, 559.

Barbara Nudd of Seattle arrived Fairbanks 6/7/30 to wed pilot Grant Elliott, 884, 902, 997, 999, 1000, 1060.

Barbara Wing, wife of A-WA pilot J. Clark Wing, 807, 809, 845, 851.

Barnes-Gorst hangar on Lake Union, 546.

B.B. Mozee, general superintendent for reindeer in Alaska for Bureau of Education, 632, 957.

beaching wheels placed under the floats to roll the planes up the sloping ramp, 828.

Beaver, Alaska, 1024.

Bellanca Pacemaker CH-300, NC 259M, of P.I.A.-1930, 854, 855, 915, 916, 925.

Bellanca Pacemaker CH-300 Special, NC 862N, *Marquette Missionary,* 1009, 1010, 1012, 1017, 1018, 1064.

Bellanca factory pilot, George Pickenpack, 1012.

Bellanca Pacemaker which had been flown up from Vancouver, B.C. to salvage Burke's Junkers,-1930, 863.

Ben Eielson (Carl Benjamin), general manager of Alaskan Airways, 1929, 564, 633, 638, 641, 643, 647, 702, 704, 708, 709, 714, 716, 717, 722, 724, 728 (Eielson missing), 747, 749, 762, 764, 769, 770, 771, 777 (Relief Expedition), 891, 893, 894, 895, 959, 961, 962, 963, 965, 967, 970, 1035, 1036, 1037, 1040, 1042.

Benjamin S. McFarland of Fairbanks, 986.

Bennett-Rodebaugh Company - 1929:
  hangars on Weeks Field 681, 683.
  Stinson Standard SB-1, NC 877, and photo party on April 7, 1929, 696, 697.
  activities in 1929, 706, 708, 709.
  entered Seward Peninsula business 7/20/29, 761.
  acquired by Alaskan Airways on 7/29/29, 712, 762.
  activities in 1929, 748, 755, 760.
  former hangars of B-R Co. burned on Weeks Field in 1930, 1016.

Bering Strait, 1046.

Berryman's Kotzebue Fur & Trading Company, 764.

B.F. "Frank" Heintzleman, assistant district forester, 564, 592, 601, 834.

Graham departed Seattle with it on 4/17/29, 556, 562.

Loening arrived in Juneau April 18, 1929 and hopped passengers there, leaving for Seattle on April 23, 563.

Scott and Graham left in Loening *Alaskan* from Seattle on 5/1/29 on its second flight to Alaska and arrived in Cordova on May 7, the first plane to that city, 608, 610.

Loening departed Cordova for Seattle on 6/3/29 after a month's successful operation out of there, including a trip to Anchorage and Lake Tustumena on the Kenai, 568, 636.

Scott went east to fly a second Loening, NC 9158, to Seattle for Gorst Air Transport, 619, 620.

1930

Scott and flight mechanic Frank Wadman left Seattle for Alaska on 5/19/30 in Boeing B-lE, NC 115E, to Ketchikan, and chartered fishing parties, etc. out of there for a time, 787, 788, 789, 792.

Scott and flight mechanic John Selby departed Ketchikan in Boeing B-lE, NC 115E, on 7/3/30 for Cordova, 837, 869, 886.

Scott and Selby departed Cordova for Ketchikan 7/10/30. They were forced down in Icy Bay with engine problems and were picked up later by Bob Ellis of A-WA and returned to Cordova, 867, 872, 874.

Scott and Myrtle Smith returned to Juneau by ship. They would ferry a Fairchild 71, NC 377M, from Whitehorse to Seattle. John Selby would fly to Juneau with Bob Ellis and take a mechanics job with Pioneer Airways in Ketchikan. The remains of the Boeing B-lE were later salvaged by a canneryman from Ketchikan named Iverson, 838, 840, 875.

Gostorg (Russian government trade organization in Siberia), 719.

Governor George Alexander Parks, of the Territory of Alaska, 326, 476, 477, 513, 544, 548, 563, 567, 591, 601, 608, 793, 826, 904, 1003.

Graf Zeppelin:
announced as coming to Fairbanks on polar flight, a plot of land secured for a port and mast, 8/20/29, 713.

plans for a port readied for estimated arrival of 9/10/29, 715.

concrete being poured for mast and anchors 10/24/29 as delays mount, 717, 720.

project cancelled 12/23/29 by sponsor, the Aero-Arctic Society, 742.

Grant N. Elliott, pilot for Alaskan Airways - 1930:
arrived Fairbanks 4/12/30 to fly out of there for A.A., 984, 985, 994, 997, 999, 1000.

married to Barbara Nudd upon her arrival Fairbanks 6/7/30, 902, 999, 1000.

now stationed in Nome as pilot for A.A., 1006, 1016, 1028, 1059.

arrived Nome 7/14/30 with Barbara Elliott, officially based there now, 1060, 1061, 1062, 1067, 1070.

sank through thin sea ice at Nome in cabin New Standard NC 174H, on 12/13/30 but salvaged the plane, 1070.

Grant Pearson, student flier from McKinley Park, 705.

Grant R. Jackson, president of Miners and Merchants Bank in Nome, 401, 515, 685, 706, 758, 953, 980, 1041.

Grantley Harbor, before the village of Teller, 727, 1044.

Gulf of Alaska flight to Cordova, 610.

Gus Gelles, secretary-treasurer of Alaska Guides, Incorporated, and Charles A. Davis, stock foreman for the company, 638.

H.A. "Doc" Oaks, Canadian pilot from Montreal, 647, 734.

Haakon B. Friele, fish packer, 72, 419, 446, 447, 569, 637, 803, 834, 838, 869, 875.

Hamilton Metalplane H-45, NC 10002:
acquired by Wien Alaska Airways in late 1928, 515, 517 (Volume One).

flown by Wien Alaska Airways in 1929 until sold to Alaskan Airways on 8/1/29, 654, 682, 683, 684, 701, 710, 751, 752, 759, 770.

installation of Pratt & Whitney Hornet of 525 horsepower in mid-August of 1929, 710, 712.

Eielson departed Fairbanks and arrived in Nome 10/29/29 to fly to North Cape, Siberia on first trip to *Nanuk,* 722, 725.

Eielson and Borland depart Teller 11/9/29 for North Cape, never to return. Crosson and Gillam discovered the wrecked Hamilton Metalplane on 1/26/30, 749, 728, 957, 959, 1041, 1047.

hangar on Tongass Highway at the hydroport, 853.

Harold Woodward, student pilot, 705, 710.

Harry L. Blunt, Pacific International Airways pilot, 821, 855, 856 (crashed in F-71 at Sawmill Lake), 915, 916, 919, 923, 928.

Harry T. Davidson, Wien Alaska Airways pilot, 687, 694, 698, 708.

H. W. "Harvey" Barnhill, pilot:
joined staff of Alaskan Airways as a pilot in Fairbanks, 643, 714.

on search for Russ Merrill - 1929, 646, 647.

flying for Alaskan Airways out of Fairbanks in 1930, 898, 903, 918, 923, 924.

picked up new pilots, Grant Elliott and Sanis E. Robbins in Anchorage on 4/12/30, 981, 983.

at Teller and the *Nanuk* with Robbins, bringing in the balance of the furs and the two remaining airplanes, Fairchild CF-AJK and the Waco 10, 991, 992, 1046, 1047, 1053.

flying out of Fairbanks for Alaskan Airways for balance of 1930, 1059, 1061, 1068, 1069, 1071.

officially inaugurated tourist airplane service in Mount McKinley National Park on 7/7/30, 1003, 1004, 1005.

took his first Fairbanks flight of 1930 to view the midnight sun; it became a favorite tourist attraction, 1002.

Joe Dunn student pilot and son of Mr. & Mrs. John Dunn, 953.

Joe Morrison a former army aviation mechanic living at Telegraph Creek, 921, 923.

Joe Quigley miner in Kantishna on Moose Creek 728, 998, 1013, 1015.

Joe Walsh, guide from Mayo on Burke search, 856, 858-862.

John Blum, a former Cordova boy and owner of Northwest Air Service in Seattle, 550, 560, 574, 803, 886.

John Selby, mechanic - 1930:
  with Clayton Scott of Gorst Air Transport, 798, 799, 803, 805, 806, 809, 837.
  with Pioneer Airways in Ketchikan, 838, 850, 867, 871, 872, 875.

John Stewart, assistant flight mechanic for A-WA in 1930, 832.

John W. Gilbert, 845.

John W. Troy, owner and publisher of the *Daily Alaska Empire,* 815, 852.

Joseph H. Meherin, commercial traveler and early rider, 707, 759, 853.

Joseph L. Carman, Jr., president of Alaska-Washington Airways, and owner of Aviation School, Incorporated, 548, 557, 567, 583, 799, 826, 835, 836.

Judge Cecil H. Clegg, 697, 974.

Judge G.J. Lomen, 764, 1059.

"Jump" Goodwin, mechanic for A-WA in Seattle, 812.

Junkers F-13, CCCP-177, flown by Russian pilot Mavriki Slepnyov at North Cape, Siberia in early 1930, 898, 900, 947, 951, 959, 965, 966, 980, 1041, 1042, 1043.

Junkers F-13, CCCP-182, flown by Russian pilot V.L. Galishev at North Cape, Siberia in early 1930, 953, 964, 974, 988.

Junkers L-5 motor, a liquid-cooled inline powerplant of German design, 949.

Junkers F-13, CF-AMX, belonging to Air Land Manufacturing Company of Vancouver, British Columbia, flown by E.J.A. "Paddy" Burke in 1930, 791, 817, 820, 829, 830, 832, 846, 853, 861, 862, 864, 916.

Junkers W-34, fitted with a Pratt & Whitney Wasp motor of 420 horsepower. Lufthansa Airlines left Berlin on 11/18/29 for a flight to Moscow with George King, 729.

Junkers Corporation of America, at Roosevelt Field, 716.

Karise, a third Swenson Fur & Trading Company vessel on the Siberian coast, 912, 953, 1064.

Kashwitna Lake, a Waco engine change in winter of 1930, 911, 1025.

Keewalik Mining Company, 1047.

Kennecott Mining Company, 607, 880, 886.

Kennicott, Alaska, 607.

Ketchikan air facility, 547.

Ketchikan, Alaska, 781.

Ketchikan hydroport, 789, 794, 820, 830.

Keystone Loening Air Yacht C-2-C, *Alaskan,* NC 9728, flown by Clayton Scott and Gordon Graham to Cordova in 1929, 542, 544, 546, 561, 568, 607, 608, 609, 799.

Keystone Loening Commuter K-84 amphibian, NC 539V, of Alaskan Airways arrived Anchorage by train on 10/14/30 for assembly, 915, 918, 924, 927, 928, 1022.

Kintz Boat Basin in Seattle, 571.

Klawock Lake on Prince of Wales Island, 796.

Kolyuchin Bay, 100 miles beyond East Cape Siberia, 753, 757, 778.

Kostrometinoffs of Sitka, 564.

Kotzebue, Alaska, 1016, 1025.

Koyuk village, at the mouth of Koyuk River, 1028, 1071.

Kvichak Station in Bristol Bay, 834.

Laird district of British Columbia, 831, 846, 853, 916.

Lake Dorothy in Southeastern Alaska, discovered in 1929, 579, 580, 601, 602.

Lake Hasselborg on Admiralty Island, an 8.5-mile-long body of water, 575, 576, 577, 601, 812, 833, 840, 852.

Lake Manzanita, 793.

Lake Minchumina, 683.

Lake Spenard at Anchorage, 876.

Lake Union in Seattle, Washington, 571.

Lake Washington in Seattle, Washington, 673.

Land of Soviets, Russian ANT-4 (Strana Sovetov):
  flies Moscow to New York in 1929, 669, 670, 672, 673, 674, 677, 679.

brought Waco 9, C 2775, in from Nome to Fairbanks on 7/23/29, 708, 712, 761.

soloed Earl Borland 9/23/29, 717.

flight instructions to Percy Hubbard, 732, 733.

Ralph and his father, J.B. Wien, 762.

Ralph Wien, pilot - 1930:

flying Service Airlines Swallow, C 2774, to McGrath 1/30/30, 947, and other flights for them, 961, 964.

served with restraining order to prevent flying in competition to Alaskan Airways under terms of purchase agreement of Wien Alaska Airways, (2/24/30), 964.

soloed Sam White 8/5/30, 1005.

departed Weeks Field with Brother George Feltes on 9/18/30 for Holy Cross in *Marquette Missionary* diesel Bellanca, 1015, 1064.

crash of *Marquette Missionary* in Kotzebue on 10/12/30 resulting in death of Ralph and his two passengers, 1016, 1018, 1019, 1024.

Ray S. Pollister, vice-president of Swenson Fur & Trading Company, 688, 714, 753, 764, 1018, 1064.

R.A. Zeller, superintendent of Tongass National Forest, 592, 602.

Reflection Lake on Revillagigedo Island, 792, 796, 803, 804, 805.

reindeer drive from Alaska to the McKenzie River in northern Canada in 1930, 1025, 1050.

reindeer drive stalled at the Hunt River, the animals refusing to cross on the glare ice, 1052, 1068.

remains of Roy J. Davis and Russ Merrill's Curtiss F flying boat, No. 475-U, 903.

Representatives of three nations drawn together in an International search, 949.

Reverend Marsden, pastor of the Presbyterian Church, in the Tsimshian village of Metlakatla, 822.

Rex Beach stories, *The Iron Trail*, 802, 872, *The Silver Horde*, 793, 801, 802.

R.H. Sargent, topographic engineer of the Department of Agriculture, 586, 592, 593, 596, 600.

R.H. Stock, construction superintendent for Wright Construction, 787, 795, 826.

Richard Heyser, U.S. Signal Corps operator, 973, 993.

Richardson Highway over Thompson Pass, 639, 885.

Richard F. "Dick" Gleason, A-WA pilot in Seattle, 548, 567.

R.1. Van der Byl, Canadian pilot from Vancouver, 856, 862.

RKO Studios, 793, 799, 801, 804.

Roald Amundsen's private Pullman car in 1926, *Fort Union,* 970.

Robert E. "Bob" Ellis, pilot and navigator - 1929:

as navigator on A-AW first nonstop flight from Seattle to Juneau on 4/15/29 in Lockheed Vega *Juneau,* NC 432E, flown by Anscel C. Eckmann with flight mechanic Jack Halloran, 546, 547, 551, 555, 559, 560.

Ellis leaves Juneau 4/30/29 with Eckmann, picking up Mrs. Kostrometinoff in Sitka to carry her to a hospital in Seattle, 564.

Ellis arrives in Juneau with Floyd Keadle and mechanic Ardell Dayton on 7/31/29 in the Vega *Juneau.* Leaving there for Ketchikan and Seattle on 8/1/29, they reached their destination that evening, which ended Ellis' flying in Alaska for that year, 578.

Robert E. "Bob" Ellis, pilot - 1930:

Pilot Ellis and flight mechanic Frank Hatcher left Seattle on 4/25/30 in the Vega *Taku,* NC 102W, for Ketchikan and Juneau. His bride, Margaret, was in the cabin, 786.

further operations in Southeastern Alaska that summer, 804, 813, 825, 832, 833, 840, 844, 845, 853.

flights to Cordova, and on to Nakeen in Bristol Bay, 869, 874, 875.

located and picked up Clayton Scott and John Selby on 7/13/30 after their forced landing in Icy Bay in the Gorst Air Transport Boeing B-lE, NC 115E, returning them to Cordova, 875.

Robert E. Sheldon, general manager of Mount McKinley Tourist & Transportation Company, 1003.

Robert J. Gleason served as radio operator aboard *Nanuk,* 719, 732, 744, 944, 947.

Robert J. Sommers, of the Territorial Road Commission, 547, 551, 608, 826, 843, 869, 908, 947, 1003.

Robin "Pat" Renehan, A-WA pilot -1930, 800, 801, 803, 805, 807, 817, 836, 838, 839, 842, 845, 851, 855.

Route of the Gipsy Moth, 137M, on Lombard and Blodgett's flight to Alaska, 811.

Roy C. Lyle, prohibition director of the 20th District, which included Washington, Oregon and Alaska, 755, 759.

Roy J. Davis, 629.

Roy F. Jones, general manager of Pioneer Airways in Ketchikan, 542, 794, 795, 797, 802, 804, 805, 807, 809, 813, 823, 834, 849, 853.

R.R. Payne of Vancouver, B.C., production manager of New England Fish company, 833, 839, 869.

Ruby, Alaska, 757.

Rudolph "Rudy" Gaier, of Stony River, 635, 637, 643 (assistant mechanic), 645, 646, 647.

Russian Junkers F-13s, 900, 948.

Russian searchers, 950.

Russian icebreaker *Litke,* 734, 948.

Russian Junkers W-33, a single-engined plane on floats, 719, 769.

Russian airmen, Krassinski, Valvitca and Leongard in W-33, 719.

Russian official inspects the ship's papers, 692.

Russian plane, *Land of Soviets,* URSS-300, 678.

Russian steamer at North Cape, *Stavropol,* 719, 734, 952.

Russ Merrill, pilot for Anchorage Air Transport, Incorporated:

1929 - 613, 629, 632, 634, 638 (sole AAT pilot as Dorbandt had left), 756.

Russ and his wife, Thyra, take vacation trip to Seward by train, boat to Valdez, auto over the Richardson Highway to Fairbanks arriving there 8/10/29, then a round trip to Circle before returning, 639, 711.

Anchorage Air Transport sold to Alaskan Airways at a general meeting the evening of 8/19/29, Russ will stay on as pilot, 641, 712.

Russ Merrill, pilot for Alaskan Airways, Incorporated, in Anchorage - 1929:

took off Cook Inlet on 9/16/29 in the Travel Air 6000, C-194, No. 1, with a piece of mining machinery for NYAK. Was never seen again, 642, 716.

after much searching two pieces from the plane were found, a piece of the fabric and a banking level, proving the plane had gone down in the Inlet, 645, 646, 917.

sailing vessel *M.S. Elisif* (proper name in Norwegian), 688.

Saint Lawrence Bay, 978, 980, 988.

salvage party from Vancouver, British Columbia - 1930, 863.

Sam Clerf, prospector-rancher from Washington State, 817, 847, 855.

Sam Macauley, Canadian mechanic, 747, 947, 964, 1023, 1036, 1043.

Sam 0. White, gamewarden, 703, 886, 1018.

his Golden Eagle monoplane, NC 569K, 714, 886, 1005.

made his first solo flight in the plane, 1005.

Samuel Anaruk, Bureau of Education teacher and Eskimo from Little Diomede Island, 1060.

Sanis E. "Robbie" Robbins, pilot for Alaskan Airways - 1930, 884, 898, 901, 928, 984, 987, 989, 991, 997, 1000, 1002, 1008, 1009, 1013, 1016, 1024, 1025, 1027, 1029, 1031, 1050, 1063.

Sawmill Lake, near Telegraph Creek, B.C., 920, 922.

schedule advertising the fares and flights of Alaska-Washington Airways, 785.

schedule of the Eastern Washington Route, 782.

Scott and Selby, after their five-hour fight to save the *Nugget,* 873.

Seattle flying Service, a flight operation and aircraft repair service in Seattle, Washington, 541, 544, 608.

Seattle, Washington, 564.

Semyon Shestakov, aircraft commander and pilot, age 31, 669, 670, 672, 677, 730.

Sergeant Leopold, of the Royal Canadian Mounted Police, 862.

Service Airlines - 1930, 879, 886, 894, 964, 966, 971, 974, 981, 982, 998, 1015.

Swallow biplane, C 2774, 947, 961, 1000.

Swallow TP trainer, C 688H, 1001.

new hangar on Weeks Field - 1930, 1019.

seven-plane floating hangar to serve as Alaska-Washington Airways base in Seattle - 1930, 815.

Seversen & Bailey trading post at Portage, on Lake Illiamna, 637, 893, 906.

Seward, Alaska residents gather on beach in 1929 to greet *Land of Soviets,* 671.

Shepard Point packing plant, 618.

Siberian Eskimos at North Cape, 691, 743.

Sierra, the last boat of the season out of Nome, 724.

Sigurd "Sig" Wien, 1030, 1071.

Silver Wave, of the Arctic Transport Company (Lomen's), 1055.

Sitka, Alaska - 1929, 561, 563, 574, 672, 827.

Skagway airport - 1930, 827.

Skagway, Alaska - 1929, 580, 595.

Skeels, a new ski-wheel combination developed by Lon Cope, 634, 635.

Soviet registration numbers on Junkers F-13s, CCCP-177 and CCCP-182, 949.

Soviet worker, T. Yacobsen, had made the discovery, 959.

S.S. Victoria was only thirty miles out of Nome on her first trip north of the navigation season, 1058.

S.S. Yukon, 645.

Standard J-1 biplane, 1046, 1047, 1059.

Stanley Adams, in the J.R. Heckman & Company store in Ketchikan, 788, 789, 790, 792.

Starr Calvert, president of Peril Strait Packing Company, 794, 798.

Stavropol, small Russian steamer at North Cape, Siberia in 1929-1930, 734, 747, 949, 951, 964, 980, 988.

Stearman C-2B, NC 5415 - 1929:

Noel Wien flew to Walker Lake on 2/3/29 to inspect damaged Stearman with a view to purchasing it from Arctic Prospecting & Development Company, 686, 751.

repair and retrieval of Stearman C-2B, 699, 701, 703.

damaged in forced landing when Ralph Wien on way to Wiseman on 5/10/29, 710.

ownership transferred to Alaskan Airways on 8/1/29 with the acquisition of Wien Alaska Airways, 710.

young Harold Gillam left Fairbanks on 12/9/29 in the Stearman biplane, now powered with the J4-B motor, to join the search for Eielson and Borland in Siberia, 735, 736, 776.

Gillam crossed Bering Strait in the Stearman after leaving Teller on 12/19/29, to make it to *Nanuk* on the following day, 738, 739, 778.

engine failure on takeoff at the *Nanuk* on 12/31/29 resulted in damage to the Stearman in a forced landing, 743.

Stearman C-2B, NC 5415 - 1930:

Gillam flies to Hamilton wreck site in Siberia in February, 1930 in the repaired Stearman, 959.

Reid and Gillam arrive Nome in C-2B on 3/30/30, flying back to Teller to meet the funeral F-71 with the bodies of Eielson and Borland, 964.

Gillam arrived back in Fairbanks with the Stearman, NC 5415, on March 6, 1930, along with the Fairchild 71 and the Junkers CCCP-177, 966, 967.

Joe Crosson, accompanied by Lillian Osborne, flew the Stearman to Nenana on 8/3/30, where they were quietly married by the commissioner

back from a two-month vacation in the States, Crosson flew the Stearman again on 10/21/30, 1025.

Robbins and "Hutch" Hutchinson fly to Dishna River on 12/14/30 to hunt for the overdue Matt Nieminen, 1029.

Steve Selig, 790, 816.

Stinson Detroiter No. 2, C 5262, No. 8, (Wilkins to Wien to Alaskan Airways No. 8) 645, 694, 708, 720, 724, 730, 735, 751, 761, 763, 767, 769, 770, 777.

Stinson Standard SB-1, NC 877 (Tom Gerard to Bennett-Rodebaugh to Alaskan Airways No. 7), 641, 681, 683, 696, 701, 707, 729, 759, 764, 776, 777.

1930 - 951, 974, 976, 1035, 1037.

Stinson Junior SM-2AA, NC 475H, No. 1 of Northern Air Transport, Incorporated, - 1929, 767, 771, 775.

1930 - 952, 957, 967, 1028, 1035, 1040, 1041, 1043, 1046, 1056, 1060, 1062, 1063.

Stinson Detroiter SM-lF, NC 404M, No. 2 of Northern Air Transport, Incorporated, - 1930, 967, 974, 995, 1020, 1022, 1041, 1043, 1051, 1067, 1069, 1071.

Stinson Junior with 210 horsepower Lycoming, NC 495Y, No. 3 of Northern Air Transport, Incorporated, - 1930, 1028, 1032, 1070, 1071.

Stinson Junior, SM-2AB, NC 490H, with 220 horsepower Wright J-5 (Noel Wien brought it up in 1930 and sold it to Alaskan Airways in 1931), 1029, 1030, 1071.

Stinson SM-8A *Northbird,* NC 991W, of Pioneer Airways - 1930, 807 (second Stinson of P.A. arrives in Ketchikan the first week of August, 1930, flown up by Jim Dodson), 807, 808, 813 (arrived Juneau 9/2/30), 814, 815 (swamped at City float in Ketchikan on 9/19/30), 846, 853 (back in service).

Stinson SM-8A, *Sea Pigeon,* NC 935W, of Pioneer Airways - 1930, 795 (Loren McHenry overshot at Reflection Lake on 6/29/30), 796, 803, 804 (salvage of *Sea Pigeon* from Reflection Lake, 805 (flew into Ketchikan 8/1/30), 809, 846 (rebuilt *Sea Pigeon* arrives from Seattle 9/19/30), 813, 816, 852 (*Sea Pigeon* upside down in water at Juneau on 9/24/30), 817, 823, 834, 846, 849, 850.

Stinson factory mechanic Gale L. Alexander, 1027, 1068, 1069.

suddenly, the new shore ice in front of the town of Nome that served as a landing site, gave way beneath the New Standard, NC 174H, 1070.

Swallow biplane, C 2774, of Hubbard and Hines' Service Airlines:

1929 - installed Wright Whirlwind J-5 motor of 225 horsepower and Hubbard was instructing in the open-cockpit plane, 732,733.

1930:

Ralph Wien, who had been flying the Swallow for Service Airlines, ceases on 2/24/30, 964.

Harvey Barnhill, who returned to Alaska and Fairbanks on 3/2/30 began flying the Swallow for Service Airlines, 964, 966, 971 (Hubbard soloes 3/15/30), 974 (Hines soloed 3/23/30), 976, 981 (Frank Mapleton and Frank Panting soloed 4/10/30), 982, 998 (Hubbard to McGrath on first cross-country), 1000 (Hubbard starts for Anchorage on 6/6/30, returns to McGrath in heavy weather and Swallow 2774 damaged beyond repair in landing.

Swallow biplane, *Arctic Prospector,* purchased by Gillam from Arctic Prospecting & Development Company in September, 1928 with OX-5 engine. Put in Warner Scarab 110 on 9/25/28:

1929:

Gillam makes first cross-country on 2/2/29, 686.

noses over Swallow on 4/24/29, 700.

flight testing with new Warner Scarab 110 motor, 731.

flying Swallow 12/27/29. Also received Swallow agency for Alaska, 733.

1930:

Gillam leaves Fairbanks in Swallow on 3/18/30 for Chitina to start his own business. He had returned from the Eielson Borland search a seasoned pilot, 879, 972.

Gillam and Meals in McCarthy on 6/17/30 getting *Arctic Prospector* ready to take it to McCarthy for Department of Commerce relicense of plane and pilot. They were successful, 884.

Swallow biplane, C 1713, of Bennett-Rodebaugh Company which they had received about November, 1926, installing a Wright Whirlwind J4-A purchased from Wilkins. Swallow passed to Alaskan Airways in acquisition of B-R Company on 7/29/29:

1929:

photo of B-R fleet before their hangar in early 1929, 683.

Swallow nosed over at Livengood on 4/29/29, 701.

1930:

Alaskan Airways fleet of planes lined up on Weeks Field after the Eielson- Borland search shows the Swallow, C 1713, at front right, 970.

Swallow (cabin) C 3542, No. 4, of Bennett-Rodebaugh Company, arrived in Fairbanks 9/14/27 with Wright Whirlwind J-4 motor. Transferred to Alaskan Airways in acquisition of B-R on 7/29/29.

1929:

Bennett goes to Chicken with mechanic to repair Swallow, C 3542, damaged by pilot landing there on 11/5/28, 699.

Bennett and Tom Gerard on 5/1/29 to bring in the now-repaired Swallow, C 3542, 702.

Swallow, C 3542, saved from disastrous hangar fire of 12/22/29, 741.

1930:

Canadian pilot Swartman left Fairbanks with Canadian mechanic C.F.K. "Kel" Mews in red cabin Swallow, C 3542, on 1/15/30 for Nome to aid in Eielson-Borland Expedition, 936.

Swartman and Mews left Nome in the Swallow on 1/3/30 to return to Fairbanks, 952.

Swallow TP (training plane), C 688H, powered with OX-5 motor, for Service Airlines:

Swallow offloaded at Seward late in February of 1930 and traveled by rail to Fairbanks for assembly there, 879, 981.

Harvey Barnhill test flew 4/15/30, 983.

Photo of Swallow C 688H on Weeks Field, 1001.

Service Airlines, down to the one Swallow, orders an Eaglerock and begins construction of a hangar on Weeks Field, 1016.

Swallow biplane, NC 430N, with J6-7 of 225 horse-power consigned to Charles Harold Gillam is off-loaded in Valdez in late February of 1930 for assembly there, 879.

Test flight by Gillam on 3/28/30. Departed for Chitina and McCarthy on 4/1/30. 880.

Gillam flew NC 430N to Fairbanks on 5/30/30 to get Department of Commerce inspection on the newly-assembled plane, 883, 997.

Flying the Copper River Valley and White River district in 1930, 869, 876, 881, 882, 883, 884, 885, 886.

Gillam flew NC 430N to Cordova on 10/16/30 to pick up Crossons and take them to Fairbanks, 1023.

Swenson Fur & Trading Company, 688, 719, 769, 1064.

Swenson- Herskovits, 687, 752.

Taku River district in Southeastern Alaska, 571, 572, 580.

Tanana airfield, 1002.

Taylor & Drury Post on Teslin Lake, 657.

Telegraph Creek, British Columbia, 841, 920, 921.

Teller, Alaska, 1929: 735, 740, 770, 773, 774.

1930: 947, 965, 987, 991, 1046, 1047, 1051, 1052, 1064.

Territorial air mail subsidy, 705, 758, 986.

Territorial Game Warden Samuel 0. White, 714.

Territorial Health Commissioner Harry Carlos DeVighne, 567.

Thayer Lake, with *Taku*, NC 102W, 835.

The Aviation Corporation (AVCO), registered in Delaware, 709, 914.

T.H. Cressy, Canadian air engineer, 856.

Thomas A. Ross, USCG commander in Nome, 997.

Thomas Johnson, A-WA mechanic, 809, 816, 817, 853.

Thomas "Courageous Tom" Peterson , Teller merchant and manager of Teller Lighterage Company, 685, 758.

Thutade Lake, some 300 miles northeast of Hazelton, B.C., 856.

Thyra Merrill widow of former Anchorage pilot Russ Merrill, 639, 643, 644, 904.

Thyra's boys Bob and Dick Merrill, 643.

T. M. "Pat" Reid, Canadian pilot, 747, 947, 953, 954, 955, 963, 964, 968, 1023, 1036, 1041, 1042.

Tom Berryman, of Kotzebue Fur & Trading Company, 764, 766.

wind J-5 of 225 horsepower for Waco 10. Test flown by Noel Wien and Ed Young on 9/1/29, 713, 714.

Bennett and Gillam to McCarthy in Waco 10 on October 3, 1929 to pick up injured miner at Chisana, 717.

Crosson and Gillam cross Bering Strait in Waco 10 and Stearman C-2B to go to North Cape and the *Nanuk,* 736, 774.

1930:

Crosson and Gillam find wrecked Hamilton, 945.

Waco left at *Nanuk* when funeral planes leave, 965.

Departed Nenana 4/24/30 to return to *Nanuk* to retrieve Waco, Fairchild 71 and complete balance of related business, 974, 1046, 1050, 987.

Robbins, flying Waco 10, left North Cape for Teller on 5/10/30 (Siberian date), back at Weeks Field 5/13/30, 991, 992, 1050.

Waco 10, NC 780E, overhauled in Fairbanks and taken to Anchorage by Robbins on 6/3/30 to be put on floats there to give the base water capability, Floats installed 6/3/30, 902, 996, 1000.

Matt Nieminen, the Anchorage pilot for Alaskan Airways, is forced down on Kashwitna Lake on 9/17/30 in the Waco, which requires an engine change, 910, 911, 924, Higgins changing engine in November, 1930, the plane had been at the lake since September 17, 1925.

Crosson took Nieminen to Kashwitna Lake on November 14 and Matt and Higgins took off in the Waco 10 that same day to land at Anchorage, 923.

WAMCATS system of communication by U.S. Signal Corps, 688.

Warner Scarab 110 horsepower, air-cooled motor, 654, 731, 880, 973.

Washington Aircraft & Transport Corporation in Seattle, 794, 1012.

Walker Lake, 686, 699, 700, 701.

Warren "Ace" Dodson, Jim's son, 813.

Waterfall cannery, on Prince of Wales Island, some 200 miles south of Sitka, 673, 674.

W.E. Boeing of Boeing Aircraft Company, 842.

Weeks Field in Fairbanks, 664, 742, 877, 883, 969, 1030.

W.E. Wynn, general operations manager for Alaska-Washington Airways, 785, 826.

Wells Ervin, 631.

Western Canada Airways, Limited, 807.

W.H. "Barney" Barnhill was returning to Alaska, 894.

Whitehorse, Yukon Territory, December 10, 1930. The rescued and the rescuers stand near the hangar, 860.

Whitehorse, Yukon Territory, Everett Wasson, twenty-four-year-old flier who had come to Canada from San Diego, California two years before, 855.

Whitehorse, Yukon Territory, 830, 831, 854, 856, 858.

Wien Alaska Airways Incorporated, 1929 (sold to Alaskan Airways, Incorporated, on 8/1/29:

Flying out of Fairbanks to Nome, etc., 681, 683, 700, 713, 751.

Ralph Wien, flying for Service Airlines, receives restraining order on 2/24/30 against competing with A.A. under purchase agreement, 964.

Noel Wien and Calvin "Doc" Cripe leave Nome on 3/7/29 for Siberia and the *Elisif,* 688, 690.

Purchase Stearman C-2B and Ralph takes Earl Borland to Walker Lake on 4/16/29 to do repairs to the damaged plane, 699.

Wien Alaska Airways awarded Territorial mail subsidy contract between Fairbanks and Nome on 5/16/29 and Noel and Ada are married in Nome on 5/19/29, 758.

Dorbandt joins Wien as Nome-based pilot, arriving 7/23/29, 638, 761.

Wien Alaska Airways hangar on Weeks Field before sale of air service to Alaskan Airways, 711, 747.

Wien Alaska Airways sold to Alaskan Airways on 8/1/29, 639, 681.

Noel Wien family departs Fairbanks by train for Outside on 9/19/29, 715.

Wilbur Irving, circulation manager of the Cordova Times - 1929, 613, 618, 876.

Wilkins-Hearst Antarctic Expedition, 716, 717.

Willard S. Gamble, Parker Cramer's companion on flight, 633, 653, 655, 657, 699, 757.

William A. Oliver, shareholder in Northern Air Transport, and a mining operator, 751, 769, 886, 967, 974, 1036, 1043, 1050, 1060.

William Allen Egan never lost interest in aviation and its people, 886.

Billy Egan of Valdez, 881, 882.

William Arthurs, postmaster at Nome - 1930, 752.

William Cameron, 1035, 1043.

William F. Walsh, a thirty-year-old priest at Kotzebue in 1930, 1018.

William Gill, Anchorage student pilot in Seattle, 631, 693.

William "Bill" Strong, 788, 792, 829, 832.

William Sulzer, former governor of New York and head of Chisana Mines, Incorporated, 880.

wireless (see radio), 573, 610, 615, 719, 911.

W.J. "Billy" Rowe, the transfer man and freighter in Nome, 1053.

work was being started on a hangar in Nome, 1023, 1067.

W.A. Joerss, German pilot from Vancouver, B.C., 847, 856, 862.

W.R. "Bill" Graham, pilot for Northern Air Transport:

1929: 742, 748, 768, 769, 771, 775.

1930: 952, 957, 967, 974, 979, 982, 993, 995, 997, 1002, 1007, 1008, 1022, 1024, 1035, 1040, 1041, 1046, 1047, 1050, 1052, 1053, 1058, 1061, 1062, 1064.

Women's National Aeronautical Association, 851.

wreck site of Eielson's Hamilton Metalplane, 957, 988.

Wright Whirlwind J-5 motor of 225 horsepower, 886, 892, 897, 1019, 1028, 1069.

Wright Whirlwind J5-CA motor of 225 horsepower, 976.

Wright Whirlwind J6-9 motor of 300 horsepower, 905, 915, 1041.

Yakutat, Alaska, 619, 799, 833, 837, 838, 871.

yarang (skin hut), 957.

Zenith 6 cabin plane of Bennett-Rodebaugh Company arrived in Fairbanks November 1, 1928, test flown by Ed Young 11/3/28.

Passed to Alaskan Airways in acquisition of B-R on 7/29/29.

1929: 686, 693, 701, 706, 708, 727, 730, 741, 759.

1930: Bennett's proposal of a Zenith on floats, 884.

Bennett's Zenith Z-6A, No. 3, NC 392V, powered by a Pratt & Whitney Wasp C of 420 horsepower, which he operated in the northwestern states as Bennett Air Transport, 888, 994.